William Faulkner

Translated by **Miriam Watchorn**
With the collaboration of **Roger Little**

Foreword by **Philip Weinstein**

André Bleikasten

William
Faulkner

A Life through Novels

INDIANA UNIVERSITY PRESS Bloomington and Indianapolis

This book is a publication of

Indiana University Press
Office of Scholarly Publishing
Herman B Wells Library 350
1320 East 10th Street
Bloomington, Indiana 47405 USA

iupress.indiana.edu

The paper used in this publication meets the minimum requirements of
the American National Standard for Information Sciences—Permanence
of Paper for Printed Library Materials, ANSI Z39.48–1992.

Cataloging information is available from the Library of Congress.

ISBN 978-0-253-02284-4 (cloth)
ISBN 978-0-253-02332-2 (ebook)

Manufactured in the United States of America

1 2 3 4 5   22 21 20 19 18 17

CONTENTS

4 The First Flowering   127

5 Midway   199

6 From *Pylon* to *Go Down, Moses*   244

7 The Dark Years   324

FOREWORD

THE GREAT NINETEENTH-CENTURY French romantic Chateaubriand titled his last work *Mémoires d'outre tombe.* In English this is rendered as *Memoirs from Beyond the Grave*, but the title's deeper resonance suggests memories clarified, sifted, accessed by way of some ultimate light. André Bleikasten's *William Faulkner: A Life through Novels* recalls Chateaubriand's work in a couple of ways. It is appearing in English seven years after Bleikasten's death. More pertinently, it bears (page after page) the overwhelming impress of Bleikasten's authority. Over the course of his thirty-five years of publication devoted to Faulkner, Bleikasten, though French, became the most distinguished interpreter of America's greatest twentieth-century novelist. His *William Faulkner: une vie en romans*—which was handsomely recognized by the Académie française when it first appeared in France (2007)—is Bleikasten's magnum opus.

The word "overwhelming" is not an adjective normally bestowed on commentary on fiction. With respect to Faulkner, we are likely to find it only in a few of his critics, and it turns out that these are mainly French. Malraux, Camus, and especially Sartre were the philosophical thinkers who recognized—as early as the 1930s—the extraordinary provocations wrought into Faulkner's art. They saw in him not a Southern writer, and even less a race writer, but rather a metaphysical novelist, a supremely *modern* writer.

Faulkner's American critics (from George Marion O'Donnell in the 1930s through Cleanth Brooks in the 1960s) were mainly concerned with interpreting him as a regional figure. Not until John Irwin's *Doubling and Incest / Repetition and Revenge* (1976) and John Matthews's *The Play of Faulkner's Language* (1982) did Faulkner's investment in the philosophical conundrums of his century begin to receive the attention they deserved.

Irwin stressed Nietzsche and Freud as Faulkner's imaginative precursors. Matthews identified Derrida's problematic of language as an enabling lens for grasping the stakes of Faulkner's experiments with narrative. In Nietzsche, Freud, and Derrida we see the literary turn toward critical theory that flourished in America throughout the 1970s and 1980s. But Bleikasten was there ten years earlier. To do justice to the thinking he draws on, we must add the names of Blanchot, Barthes, Lacan, and Foucault (the French component), as well as those of Jakobson and Chomsky (the poetics of language), Hegel (the drama of consciousness), and Bakhtin (the dialogic tensions that keep Faulkner's prose fiercely self-embattled). This is not to speak of the relevant body of criticism devoted by American academics to Faulkner; for decades he was wholly familiar with its output as well.

My verb above is "draw on." It is impossible to peg Bleikasten as an exponent of any of the critical and philosophical voices he learned from as he produced his own. Indeed, one of his most memorable critical performances occurred at the Faulkner and Yoknapatawpha Conference held in August 2000 in Oxford, Mississippi. The weather at that time of year tends to vary from very hot to intolerably hot. Bleikasten gave his talk—"Faulkner in the Singular"—on perhaps the hottest day of the conference (I was there when he spoke). But the greater heat that day radiated, arguably, from the challenged band of critics in that audience: a sample of Faulkner's ablest commentators, for the most part an angry crew. With customary fearlessness, Bleikasten had called into question their predictable devotion to currents of thought imported from European (mainly French) quarters. Bleikasten was not opposed to these currents of thought; he knew them upside down. The key texts of psychoanalysis, linguistics, poetics, and sociology were all familiar to him. He (probably the only one in that room) had read them in their original language—in his formative years in the 1950s and 1960s—and they deeply informed his thought. But they did not foretell where his thought was headed. They did not testify to a Foucauldian or Lacanian or Derridean reading of Faulkner whose lines of development were predictable in advance. Bleikasten found it deplorable to attach Faulkner's remarkable texts (in wholesale manner) to bodies of thought that, however seductive, were foreign to Faulkner's own deployment of language. His entire career was devoted to "Faulkner in the Singular"—a Faulkner whose resonance, richly illuminated by the largest range of modern thinkers, was finally a resonance all its own.

Bleikasten was born in Strasbourg, France, in 1933, and he was quick to say that Alsatian history had marked him for life (even as northern Mississippi's history had marked Faulkner for life). The young Bleikasten grew up at home in both French and German; English was his third language, a latecomer. (But what English he was capable of writing!) As an Alsatian, he experienced World War II from dizzyingly close up: one uncle was murdered by the Nazis; another was decorated by them. One of Bleikasten's salient memories dates from 1945, when (as a grateful twelve-year-old) he watched the GIs liberating Strasbourg, passing out chocolate and chewing gum as they walked the streets. Bleikasten's love affair with Faulkner's work does not grow directly out of this affection for the Yanks. It would take another seventeen years before he signed on to his *doctorat d'État* on Faulkner. But his undeviating admiration of American courage and spirit probably dates from America's leadership role in World War II as well as from its generous international politics in the decade that followed.

Bleikasten was from the beginning a brilliant student, drawn especially to the humanities. Soon his research interests were devoted to literature written in English, with a focus on British fiction. In fact, he was set to write a dissertation on the novels of D. H. Lawrence, a preference that sheds a certain light on Bleikasten's cast of mind. In Lawrence's work he would have found passion (similar in some ways to the passion he found in Faulkner). No less, he would have found a mind-set rooted deeply in country rhythms, committed to unearthing men and women's deepest motives. Lawrence's work centered on psychic struggle; his characters labor to free themselves. When on receiving the Nobel Prize in 1949 Faulkner described his abiding concern as "the human heart in conflict with itself," he could have been speaking about Lawrence. In one of Bleikasten's many irreplaceable essays, he compared the "temperature" of writers, noting that while Joyce and Mann were "cool," Faulkner was "hot." "Hot" in the sense that Faulkner grasps his people in life-or-death situations. "Hot" as well, perhaps, in Faulkner's capacity to enter wholly into the mind-set (and heart-set) of his characters. Not to argue on their behalf, but (as a writer) to *become* them. Lawrence, too, was "hot."

We will never know what Bleikasten might have written on Lawrence. Instead, a fateful event—Faulkner's death in July 1962—changed Bleikasten's professional trajectory. Dead, Faulkner had become, finally, a permissible object of the French university system's research agenda. (One was not allowed to write the big thesis—the *doctorat d'État*—on a living author.) Along with Michel Gresset and François Pitavy, Bleikasten was accepted in his bid to write on Faulkner. It would take him almost ten years to complete the magisterial "Parcours de Faulkner" (weighing in at almost one thousand pages), and in this decade he would become—and remain—fast friends with Gresset and Pitavy. The three of them would become known as "the French troika"; their work on Faulkner in the 1970s is luminous in both its reach and its grasp. During that decade only Irwin's book, mentioned above, deploys a conceptual framework of kindred sophistication.

Bold as his criticism was, Bleikasten's work was no less remarkably economical. As it turned out, inside the prodigal "Parcours de Faulkner" nestled the bulk of Bleikasten's output for the next two decades. Devoted to four of Faulkner's early masterpieces—*The Sound and the Fury, As I Lay Dying, Sanctuary,* and *Light in August*—"Parcours" opened up each text as it had never been opened before. There was, first of all, Bleikasten's unwavering focus on the minutiae of textual behavior. (No detail in these novels is too small to catch his attention and reveal meanings one had not suspected.) At the same time, Bleikasten's conceptual frame—always in play but never signaling in advance the path of his argument—allowed these stunning novels to reveal their widest implications. Four sub-books, each devoted to one of the Faulkner novels he was scrutinizing, come together in "Parcours." It is no surprise that, given their quality, two of them were swiftly translated into English in the 1970s. In this way Bleikasten found his audience of American scholars (many of them "innocent" of French). By then he was launched. For the next fifteen years he would both extend his grasp of Faulkner's world and refine the insights he had birthed in "Parcours." Then, in the late 1980s, he reengaged "Parcours," translating/transforming it into English as *The Ink of Melancholy: Faulkner's Novels from* The Sound and the Fury *to* Light in August (1991). Although I had read both of the earlier sub-books when they appeared, I was unprepared for the comprehensive brilliance of *The Ink of Melancholy*. It is not only the best book we have on the early Faulkner; it is also a book after which one could go to one's grave with professional pride: one would have acquitted one's duties handsomely.

But Bleikasten, far from played out, was just hitting his stride. A voracious reader and thinker, he not only produced essay after essay (all compelling, some matchless) on Faulkner in the 1990s, as well as books on Flannery O'Conner and Philip Roth. He also contributed countless articles and reviews (on the widest range of topics) to the French journal *Quinzaine littéraire.* Throughout this period, no less, he contemplated undertaking—post-retirement—a history of the Western novel from Cervantes to the current day. The Faustian scope of such a project probably dooms it to failure, but in Bleikasten's hands what a "magnificent failure" it might have been! The quoted phrase is of course Faulkner's reference to his dearest novel, *The Sound and the Fury.* Faulkner early—and Bleikasten late—were roused most by the most daunting challenges. As it turned out, Faulkner was to have the last word: by eliciting once more Bleikasten's critical energies. As Bleikasten put it in an interview with Géraldine Chouart, Faulkner (though long dead) was still not ready to let him be. An editor in charge of a little-known press had urged Bleikasten to write a biography of Faulkner. Bleikasten reasonably declined this proposition more than once—there were already too many biographies of Faulkner out there—but the editor was tenacious. Despite himself, Bleikasten started to become interested. He said yes. Synthesizing what he had come to know about Faulkner over the years, this big book (four years in the writing, a lifetime in the making) appeared in 2007. It was published by a modest press, and it garnered for him no advance. But *William Faulkner: une vie en romans* was too impressive to remain unknown. Within a year the Académie française bestowed on it their prize for the best literary biography of its year. Nine years later it is finally seeing the light in English.

The length of *William Faulkner: A Life through Novels* may recall Joseph Blotner's fifteen-hundred-page two-volume biography of Faulkner (published in 1974). No comparison could be less just. Irreplaceable as Blotner's work is, with respect to the day-by-day and year-by-year doings of its subject, that biography is notably modest when it comes to saying what Faulkner *means*: why we should read him, what we will find there. Modesty was never one of Bleikasten's traits, and his magnum opus does not suffer from it. Instead, this final work supplies what we have lacked for the past four decades: a reading of both Faulkner's life and his work that is equal to the task. I do not forget that from Cleanth Brooks, fifty years ago, through my own brief endeavor five years ago, Faulkner has been the subject of some eight to ten critical and literary biographies. Some of them—Joel Williamson's especially—have opened up the historical context of Faulkner's life more tellingly than Bleikasten does, but none of them can match Bleikasten's capacity to say, again and again, exactly how Faulkner's work *works*. It is as though Bleikasten has (through the labor of decades) descended into the imaginative labyrinth of the master. He reports, eloquently, on what he sees there.

We would not have this book, save for the tenacious devotion of Aimée Bleikasten to the final work of her deceased husband. She has labored hard to secure its translation and to locate, in Indiana University Press, its appropriate home. (This is the press that brought out Bleikasten's earlier work in English.) Now that it is appearing, who are its prospective readers? Anyone who loves Faulkner is likely to care for this book, though professional Faulknerians will not find in it the contemporary references that may seem to signal the future of Faulkner studies. Bleikasten had passed the point of investment in such a future; what he wanted was to register his deepest mark, now. He wanted to distill, in one book, all that he knew about his favorite writer's life and work—and to do so in plain words. Lay readers will engage this book with pleasure. All they need is a measure of interest in Faulkner's work in order to respond to its author's insights. "*Mon coeur mis à nu*" ("my heart nakedly exposed"): so Baudelaire described the inner life of his poetry. Bleikasten attends tirelessly to the unfolding of Faulkner's imaginative forms; he reveals them to us "*mis à nu*." You don't have to take my word for this claim. Rather, you might sample the following four passages (each focused on one of Faulkner's early masterpieces):

> In Benjy's world, there are only *effects*. Everything happens, anywhere and anyhow, nothing is explained and what happens always happens like the sudden tear of a lightning bolt. Strictly speaking, Benjy's distress is not even suffering (suffering takes time, occupies time and requires a suffering subject); it is only pain, a naked pain that passes through him, shoots through him (*dolere*). He screams with pain but does not even know that he has burned himself. Punctuated with screams, groans, tears and silences, his monologue does not register cause, distance, or time lag. (on *The Sound and the Fury*)

Everything in *Sanctuary* seems to be overseen by a single *eye*, bulging with horror and repulsed with disgust. There is no multiple viewpoint, such as one finds in *The Sound and the Fury* and *As I Lay Dying*. This does not mean that the narration is not twisted, not full of ellipses, detours and delays. The most violent scenes are elided: Temple's rape with a corncob is never directly described, nor are the murders of Tommy and Red, Goodwin's lynching or Popeye's hanging. The action is always ahead or behind, ahead *and* behind. Everything is already *missing in action*. Nothing is lived or named upon its occurrence, it is only apprehended after the fact. Disaster is always flagged and anticipation is always in a rearview mirror. As soon as she arrives at the Old Frenchman's homestead, Temple lives in horrified anticipation of her rape. Time tenses up and contracts, gives no respite, allows no distancing. Nothing happens that has not already happened. (on *Sanctuary*)

For each Bundren, there is a death to be lived through, a dead woman to kill. (on *As I Lay Dying*)

He [Joe Christmas] is never the same color, he is always the other race. (on *Light in August*)

If you can resist the intelligence, wit, and verve of these passages, then this book may not be for you. But if these passages speak to you—as promise, if not already as premise—then you may find *William Faulkner: A Life through Novels* a veritable Open Sesame of insights. In it Bleikasten speaks from beyond the tomb.

Philip Weinstein

TESTIMONY AND ACKNOWLEDGMENTS

AS ANDRÉ BLEIKASTEN'S WIFE, I was by his side over many years of work and would like to bear witness to the genesis of this book, his last: *William Faulkner: une vie en romans*, published in Paris by Editions Aden in September 2007, which has now been translated into English under the title *William Faulkner: A Life through Novels*. As André himself acknowledged in an interview with Géraldine Chouart and Anne Crémieux on January 5, 2006, "randomness and chance" often played an essential role in his life and in the development of his academic career.

Fate determined that William Faulkner was to die on July 6, 1962, after being unseated by a horse one last time. In France at the time, a doctoral dissertation could only be written about an author who was already dead, a sort of signing off of his or her work. André, then very interested in the American novel, naturally proposed to write his thesis on this American novelist, whose novel-writing style, fictional audacity, and dizzying complexity he deeply appreciated. This was the start of his long companionship with William Faulkner, which was to last all his life.

To prepare his dissertation, titled "Parcours de Faulkner," André Bleikasten was awarded a Harkness Fellowship in 1967, which enabled us to spend four months in Charlottesville, Virginia, where Faulkner had lived and where many of his manuscripts were kept. After that, in 1969–1970, he received a grant from the ACLS (American Council of Learned Societies) to spend a full year in the same university town. We made the trip on the magnificent liner *Le France*, marveling at Bartholdi's Statue of Liberty as we entered New York at four in the morning. During this second stay at Jefferson University in Charlottesville, we discovered two other French researchers preparing a thesis on Faulkner—Michel Gresset from Paris and François Pitavy from Dijon—who were also living there with their families.

We became fast friends. The conversation never waned, with Faulkner the main topic.

André was surprised to receive a letter from Indiana University Press (IUP) asking him if he would be interested in publishing the translation of his study of *As I Lay Dying*, edited in France by Colin in 1970, in a book on William Faulkner that also included a contribution by Pitavy on *Light in August* and a preface by Gresset. It was thus through IUP that André was given access to American and English readers. The first book, *As I Lay Dying*, was published in Bloomington in 1973, in a translation by our English friend Roger Little in collaboration with the author. After this came *The Most Splendid Failure: Faulkner's "The Sound and the Fury"* in 1976, and, in 1990, the translation of his doctoral thesis, "Parcours de Faulkner," under the wonderful title *The Ink of Melancholy: Faulkner's Novels from* The Sound and the Fury *to* Light in August, both published by IUP. With IUP again, he published *The French Face of Faulkner* in 1995, in collaboration with his friend Michel Gresset. André translated these latter books himself with welcome assistance from his English-speaking friends and colleagues. As he said later in the 2006 interview, without these publications, "nobody in the United States would have read me."

For the French version of this critical biography, *William Faulkner: A Life through Novels*, "randomness and chance" were again at work. André spoke of it with humor and detachment at the end of the 2006 interview:

> Fortunately—or unfortunately—I have never managed to get away from Faulkner. I had no plans to write a Faulkner biography. There are five already, why write a sixth? But in 2004, I received an unexpected phone call: a publisher I didn't know and who remains relatively unknown, asked me to write a life of Faulkner. I at first refused. He insisted, harried me gently for months until I finally gave in. I don't regret it for a moment. I immersed myself and it's now been two years since I started working on this biography. I hope to finish it before the end of the year and trust that it will be different from the others. The commentary on the work will in any event take up as much room as the historical facts. When the life is the work . . .

I am very moved writing these few lines, because it brings back to mind the ups and downs of library research, reading and editing the initial drafts, then editing and rereading the printed proofs and correcting errors. We had many a long conversation, at home and during our walks, on Faulkner's life, his characters' complicated relationships, and on the fantastical situations they put themselves in. We also spoke about Jean Arp, because I was preparing an academic conference on his art and poetry, which took place in late January 2009, when André was already very ill.

So many memories jostle in my mind. I started to become familiar with Faulkner after reading André's early studies of him. I also followed my husband as he traveled around the United States on Faulkner's trail between 1967 and 1987 to Charlottesville, Virginia; to Columbia, South Carolina, where James B. Meriwether had invited him to come as a visiting research professor and where we met Noel Polk and his family; to Tulsa, Oklahoma, again as visiting research professor, this time at the invitation of James G. Watson; to Memphis and Philadelphia, where Philip and Penny Weinstein showed us the sights and where André gave lectures; then to Boston University, where we stayed several months and were welcomed so warmly by John T. Matthews and his wife and where I finished my own doctoral dissertation on Jean Arp. We also often went to the major gatherings on Faulkner in Oxford, Mississippi, where André's lectures were obviously much appreciated.

The French version of the Faulkner biography was published in September 2007 and André was delighted at its favorable reception. In the fall of 2008 he was awarded, in quick succession, the Prix de la Recherche from the Société des Anglicistes de l'Enseignement Supérieur (SAES) and the Association Française d'Etudes Américaines (AFEA); the Prix France-Amériques; and, in late November, the prestigious Prix de la Biographie Littéraire from the Académie française, which he received in the Institut de France before a gala evening held by the permanent secretary, Madame Hélène Carrère d'Encausse, in honor of the award winners.

André was happy to receive these accolades, but he was even happier on these occasions to meet all of his colleagues and friends from all over Europe and even the United States. At that time he was already very ill and died the following year, on February 15. I still miss him every day.

The idea of translating André's final testimonial to William Faulkner had been broached before he died. We did not discuss it much, because I was worried that the task would daunt him when I could see he was becoming weaker and weaker by the day. I knew, however, that it was his most cherished wish. Thus, from 2010 the idea of translating the biography began to take hold. The publisher of the French version was unable to help. Fortunately, André had retained translation rights. I therefore had a free hand to publish this translation myself.

The problem now was to find someone motivated enough to take on the translation and carry it through to the end—an awesome task, given that it totals over seven hundred pages. Aware of André's high standards when it came to translating his texts in English, having read his correspondence with Indiana University Press on previous translations, I knew that I could not embark lightly on this adventure. I discussed the matter with our friends and André's colleagues. Eventually, it was through Roger Little, our long-standing English friend, who for many years had been Professor of French at Trinity College, Dublin, that a solution was found. As I mentioned above, he had already collaborated on the translation of André's study of *As I Lay Dying*. However, Roger was unable to undertake this long-term task on top of his many other activities. He therefore recommended a colleague from Dublin City University who was familiar with the work of William Faulkner and wished to engage in an eminently literary translation—Miriam Watchorn had the will and the courage to take on the task. It was decided to complete the translation chapter by chapter and that Miriam would discuss any delicate questions arising with Roger Little, who also reviewed and edited each chapter before Miriam sent me the final version. Throughout this work, Roger Little was a trusted and well-heeded advisor. I would like to thank him for his exemplary patience.

As the book deals with William Faulkner's life and work, it contains many passages from autobiographical texts, Faulkner's letters, statements by his friends, and extracts from his novels. André had cited these from existing French translations, often translated or retranslated by himself. They thus had to be found in their original version in order to include them in the translation.

Fortunately, André had explained to me how the books by and on Faulkner were arranged on his bookshelves, and, seeing the work involved in researching books in academic and public libraries to properly cite the quotations, I quickly decided to do this work myself using André's library. It would have been difficult for the translator to undertake this research. However, André's bookshelves did not contain all the texts. For these, I was helped by André's friends, particularly a close American friend, Noel Polk, a professor at the University of Mississippi and an expert on Faulkner who had, with Joseph Blotner, finalized the Library of America edition of Faulkner's work. This edition was very useful to both me and Miriam in identifying quotations from Faulkner's novels. Noel Polk was extremely helpful, especially for the first chapters, which deal with the history of the southern United States. Sadly, Noel died in 2012 and hence will not have the pleasure of seeing his generous collaboration honored here. Another very helpful collaborator was Aurélie Guillain, professor of American Literature at the University of Toulouse, who had been André's doctoral student for her dissertation on William Faulkner. Despite many other calls on her time, she regularly helped me find quotations I had been unable to find in my husband's abundant Faulkner collection and also read through the translation. I would like to express my heartfelt gratitude for her priceless contribution.

This translation, of which Miriam Watchorn is the main author, with the regular and very precious collaboration of Roger Little, is the work of a highly motivated and resolute team, because there were many difficulties along the way and at times courage flagged. But we all held out until we arrived at this definitive version, which I hope will find a readership in English-speaking countries. And let's wager that even André Bleikasten would not be too unhappy with the final outcome.

It took four years, after much editing, to arrive at a final manuscript, which was sent on April 14, 2015, to Robert J. Sloan, editor in chief at Indiana University Press in Bloomington. Robert immediately expressed his interest in André's last book, having retained an excellent impression of *The Ink of Melancholy*, published in 1990 by the press. When he retired in late June 2015, he handed over André's Faulkner biography to Raina Polivka, who was also very interested in the book, made the initial arrangements for publication, and sent me a publishing agreement. I would like to express my heartfelt thanks to both of them, to their team, and to Darja Malcolm-Clarke, for allowing the publication of this great book, a book that is the result of many years André Bleikasten devoted to William Faulkner. To me, André is present and alive in this book, alongside Faulkner, whose life and work are as one and whose dizzying complexity never ceases to fascinate.

I am keenly aware that this book would never have seen the light of day without the support and advice of many academics and friends. I am particularly indebted to André's American friends and colleagues. I have already spoken of Noel Polk. I would like now to make particular mention of Philip Weinstein, a very close friend of André's, who from the start encouraged me to embark on this translation and who is himself a major expert on William Faulkner (in 2010, he published an important biographical essay titled *Becoming Faulkner,* which he dedicated to André) and has written the foreword to this translation. More than anyone, Philip knows the high esteem with which André was held among Faulkner experts in Europe and the United States.

Now I must make do with all of those wonderful memories of a past now gone and be thankful that this book brings André back to life. I would like to end by thanking my family and friends for the care and support they have given and continue to give me. My thoughts turn in particular to my friends, English scholars Claudine Thomas, Pierre Boulay, and Albert Hamm, who agreed to translate letters and texts into English; and to René Fugler, an old friend of André, who reviewed the manuscript many times at my request. Thanks also go to our close friends Brigitte and Paul-Henri Bourrelier, Claude Coulomb, Danielle Bruckmuller, and Anne and Dominique Foata, who were of great comfort to me after André's death. André's sister, Anne-Lise, and my family gave me much moral support during that difficult time and followed the preparation of this, André's last book, with great attention.

At the end of the 2006 interview, André spoke from the heart: "I sincerely regret not having spent a few entire years in the United States, really lived there and taught there." During our frequent visits, we were always happy in the United States and I would happily have lived there with him.

In the last weeks of his life, as he came around from a surgical procedure, he saw me and thought he was at home, even though we were in the hospital. When I tried to set him right, he straight away replied: "Wherever you are, that's my home!" Whenever we were in America, that was our home. In a way, America became our second homeland.

Aimée Bleikasten

Publisher's note: Aimée Bleikasten passed away September 21, 2016, shortly before the publication of this book. IU Press would like to thank Roger Little and Miriam Watchorn for overseeing the book's final preparations in her stead.

INTRODUCTION

THERE IS A FAULKNER ENIGMA. In 1948, in his preface to *Moustiques*, the French translation of *Mosquitoes*, Raymond Queneau noted that "of all the American writers, Faulkner is the one who seems the most mysterious."[1] While Sartre, no less intrigued by the man behind the writer, concluded his essay "Sartoris" as follows: "We need to know him."[2]

More than forty years after Faulkner's death, seven hundred of his letters are available, along with all of his published interviews, testimonials from his family, his friends, his neighbors, and all those who were close to him, plus half a dozen biographies. Over the years this has been supplemented by a raft of unpublished material, both poetry and prose, most of which dates from the author's youth. However, it is not at all certain that Sartre's prayer has been answered. While we are now more aware of the contours of Faulkner's life and work, we are still in the dark about how a minor anachronistic poet from the Deep South became one of the greatest novelists of the twentieth century.

One response would be simple astonishment, without seeking to find out more. After all, if he has done little or nothing but write, if the adventure of writing was his only great passion, is the life of a writer, as a person, really worth telling? In what way could this life have any interest apart from his work? And besides, what life? By tradition, the biographer refrains from any recourse to fiction, concentrating instead on the facts—that is, on what in a life has appeared, been seen, heard, recorded, archived, on what has been irrefutably attested. There can be no biography without testimony. Third parties always seem to creep in between the biographer and his subject. These are the people who provide more or less reliable information on what an individual has said or done that the biographer uses to compose his narrative. However, this mediation is also a screen; unless the subject kept a diary, we will never know him in the enclosure of his solitude, out of sight, at times when he was there only to himself.

In other words, what is perhaps the most lively part of a life is out of our reach. As Paul Valéry noted in *Mauvaises Pensées*: "We write about the life of a man, his work, his deeds, what he said and what was said about him. But the most real part of this life eludes us. A dream he had, a singular sensation, a minor ache, a surprise, a glance, treasured or haunting pictures, a song going around his head, moments of absence—all of this is much more *him* than what we can know."[3]

Of the journey of a man who once lived and has ceased to live, we can follow only the traces that he left behind, in his public acts and in the memory of those who knew him. But the life of a writer, even the most banal, the most unassuming, leaves other traces. The traces preserved in archives and memories are supplemented by the legible and more or less enduring trace of the writer's work; and fiction, even where it is far removed from a confession, is almost always in a way an *auto-bio-graphy*.

For novelists the life lived goes hand in hand with the life written, and the latter is not simply the transcription of the former. Writing novels as Faulkner did does not entail turning away from life, but rather living it differently, accessing another life in and through writing. Faulkner (who could doubt it?) lived *The Sound and the Fury*, just as Melville lived *Moby-Dick*. This is not the case for every writer, but for those martyred saints of the modern novel—Flaubert, Melville, Conrad, James, Proust, Joyce, Kafka, and Faulkner—life was indistinguishable from the act of writing.

This does not mean that all distinctions should be erased and that the life of a novelist should be confused with his fiction. But the fiction, through a thousand tricks and detours, can be traced back to the life, the one crisscrossing the other and telling an obscure kind of truth.

This truth is necessarily fragmented, the truth of a life that writes like a counter-life, like an anti-fate. This is the truth of an existence that is at once re-apprehended, crossed out, reinvented, and avenged by the powers of fiction. The most stringent form and most secretive purpose of literature is not to represent life but rather to investigate its mysteries and mitigate its shortcomings. As Fernando Pessoa noted: "As with all art, literature is proof that life is not enough."[4] For Faulkner, life on its own was not enough. Hence, the astonishing and mystifying play of masks from the end of adolescence to later in life and right up to the end: Faulkner the wounded, limping wartime pilot; Faulkner the hobo; Faulkner the dandy; Faulkner the gentleman farmer of Mississippi; Faulkner the gentleman rider of Virginia.

In his work as a writer, a "professional liar" (as he defined himself in *Mosquitoes*), Faulkner was hardly any less two-faced or duplicitous than any other, but everything changed when writing took hold of his life and his life became implicated, without restraint or reservation, in his fiction. Therefore, his biography is primarily what he himself constructed with his words in his books. Rewriting it—after the fact, from a distance, in the third person, as a biographer—would ideally involve telling the tale of a path stubbornly forged, word for word, sentence by sentence, book by book. As Proust noted, we learn more about Flaubert by examining his use of verbs than by scrutinizing his poor life. Nabokov agreed: "The best part of a writer's biography is not the record of his adventures but the story of his style."[5] Ultimately, the only thing that matters is the adventure of writing, the journey made, the project realized—in short, the work: "To me the author is not important, it's the work," said Faulkner in a 1955 interview in Japan. "To me, the story, the poem, is much more important than who wrote it" (*LG*, 136–37). The story of a writer, if he truly is a writer, is the story of his life *in* his work.

A life both mislaid and saved, lost and regained. Faulkner would have liked to disappear from his books—or into his books?—and be no more than the name of their author:

> It is my ambition to be, as a private individual, abolished and voided from history, leaving it markless, no refuse save the printed books; I wish I had had enough sense to see ahead thirty years ago and, like some of the Elizabethans, not signed them. It is my aim, and every effort bent, that the sum and history of my life, which in the same sentence is my obit and epitaph too, shall be them both: He made books and he died. (*SL*, 285)

However, he may not have been wholly sincere in his paradoxical "ambition" to efface himself. In any event, when these lines were sent to Malcolm Cowley in 1949, it was already too late, the damage had already been done. Faulkner had not only written and signed two books of poems, over a dozen novels, and two short story collections; by the time he reached his fifties, he already had a public image, in Europe and the United States, and the beginning of a legend surrounded him, which he himself had actively helped forge. And at the end of that same year, in Stockholm, the members of the Swedish Academy were preparing to award him the Nobel Prize in Literature. Faulkner died famous and covered in honors, the photo of the silver-haired gentleman farmer in a worn tweed jacket was in all the newspapers, and he, who railed against and feared biographers, became their prey upon his death.

His troubled private life was now an open secret. It was already known that he was an alcoholic (through neurosis and family tradition) and that alcohol had finished him off. We now know that World War I had ended before he could take part, before he had even learned to fly a plane, and that his war wounds were pure invention. We also know that his marriage to Estelle Oldham was a disaster from the start and that over the years he consoled himself as much as he could with ever younger mistresses. The Faulkner enigma still stands, however; it has never ceased to fascinate, and without wishing to solve it, one may try to approach it.

We know little about Shakespeare and yet we manage very well without such knowledge. But we still want to know *who* wrote *Hamlet*; we still want to know *who* wrote *The Sound and the Fury,* even if it means coming away disappointed, as often happens when we find out more about a confused or mediocre life. The difficulty, whether we are dealing with Faulkner or Hemingway, Proust or Joyce, Céline or Aragon, is to contemplate strength and frailty simultaneously, the radiant grandeur of the writer and the weaknesses of the man. Faulkner asked himself the question and his answer was clear-cut: "I think that a writer is a perfect case of split personality. That he is one thing when he is writer and he is something else while he is a denizen of the world" (*FU*, 268). Already in *Mosquitoes,* his second novel, he had one of his characters say: "A book is the writer's secret life, the dark twin of a man: you can't reconcile them" (*N1*, 461). And in 1953, in a letter to his girlfriend Joan Williams, he marveled at the tenacity of the relationship between his work and "the country man whom you know as Bill Faulkner" (*SL*, 348). Proust, in *Contre Sainte-Beuve,* said as much when he declared that "a book is the product of another *me* than that which we manifest in our habits, in society, in our vices."[6]

Proust's phrase caught on. Almost unanimously it was held as self-evident throughout the twentieth century. At a time when all schools of thought, or almost all, denounced the self as a delusion and placed the subject on trial, and when the vanguard of literature theorists dismissed the "author" in favor of a clean-shaven "scribe," literary biography obviously fell out of favor. This trend was reversed in France from the end of the 1970s on: the decoupling of writer and work is no longer self-evident, and biographical curiosity seems to have regained its legitimacy.

Not that Proust was wrong and Sainte-Beuve right. The distinction between the manifest self and the hidden self is not without relevance, but these are not separate entities; between the two there are crossing points and gateways, just as there are between the life and the work. The fact that Faulkner was born into a middle-class American family at the very end of the nineteenth century and that he spent most of his life in that *mezzogiorno* that is the southern United States is not unimportant to anyone who wishes to understand him better. His identity as a writer is not an unworldly essence. Attempting to comprehend what is most comprehensible in this identity is not moving away from it; trying to understand Faulkner as both a visible and a public figure in his environment and time does not mean turning away from him.

The Deep South explains Faulkner up to a point—his ways of thinking, of speaking, of feeling, and of living—and some of these idiosyncrasies find their way into his novels. This does not mean that the South explains the writer, his work even less so. Faulkner's books can be discussed, commented, analyzed, interpreted at will; the life of their author does not deliver any key to them. However, the work itself does shed an oblique light on the life underneath the fiction and on the man underneath the writer. It shows them while hiding them, hides them while showing them, traces and retraces the outline without deciphering it. Faulkner's novels are not autobiographical novels in the usual sense of the term, but what is written in them is indeed his life and what is missing from his life, and he applied himself so deeply to the task that he seems to have forgotten himself and lost himself in it. Even when he was not writing, he sometimes gave his entourage the impression that he was floating between two worlds and two identities, that he was both himself and another at the same time, that he was living in both the real and an imaginary world. His brother John remarked that he had never known anyone who identified more than Bill with what he was writing. He noted that at times it was difficult to say who was who, one no longer knew if Bill was still himself or the character in the story. And yet one knew that the two were the same, that they were inseparable (*MBB*, 275).

Faulkner wrote Malcolm Cowley in November 1944: "I am telling the same story over and over, which is myself and the world" (*SL*, 185). There can be no writing without the ambiguities of reflection and the vagaries of the double. Writing always means writing oneself and attempting to read oneself through writing: telling a story is telling one's *own* story, one's own life, and doing so first to oneself, which, for Faulkner, also applies to the novelist's characters: "Every time any character gets into a book, no matter how minor, he's actually telling his biography—that's all anyone ever does—he tells his own biography, talking about himself, in a thousand different terms, but himself. Quentin was still trying to get God to tell him why in *Absalom, Absalom!*, as he was in *The Sound and the Fury*" (*FU*, 275).

Like Quentin, Faulkner was "telling his own biography," and Quentin was one of his fictional doubles that enabled him to do so "in a thousand different terms." Just as Balzac is more or less Louis Lambert, Rastignac, and Rubempré; Proust more or less Swann, Saint-Loup, or Bergotte; Joyce more or less Stephen Dedalus and Leopold Bloom; Faulkner is more or less Horace Benbow, Quentin Compson, and Gavin Stevens. A novelist of Faulkner's caliber cannot be restricted to a single identity; his life was not just *one* life, nor even a double life. A novelist would not be a novelist unless he had multiple lives, would not be himself unless he was other than himself and knew how to be in the plural form. And with Faulkner this plural is not simply made up of obvious doubles such as Horace Benbow, Quentin Compson, Gavin Stevens, Harry Wilbourne, and the reporter in *Pylon*. The novelist is, to varying degrees, all of his characters at once. Each represents a virtual identity, a self in waiting: Quentin was him, to be sure, but so were Jason, Christmas, Sutpen, Ike, Lucas, Harry, and Flem, and also Caddy, Addie, Temple, Lena, Joanna, Judith, Charlotte, and Eula—right down to the last of the last inhabitants of Yoknapatawpha, down to Benjy the idiot, Popeye the psychopathic killer, and Darl the madman.

Self and non-self, a self other than myself, at the uncertain crossroads of all my possible selves. With the same gesture, I declare myself and hide myself. With the same stroke, I write myself and erase myself. These are the endless paradoxes of fiction.

Faulkner is now read throughout the world. A universal writer, he is one of the twentieth-century writers with the closest ties to the geography, history, and culture of a region. Faulkner was born, lived, and died in a rather deprived rural area, whereas most of his European counterparts—Proust, Joyce, Mann, Kafka, Döblin, Musil, Broch, Gadda, Céline, and Nabokov—were city dwellers. During his lifetime the novel had its pastoral seasons, but since Lesage and Marivaux, Defoe and Fielding, most of the novelists who counted were urban novelists. It was in Paris and Vienna, the two nerve centers of Western culture between the start of the twentieth century and the Great War, that modern literature, painting, and music were born. At that time the eyes of cultured America were on old Europe. In the 1920s Francis Scott Fitzgerald, Ernest Hemingway, and other young Americans in conflict with the country of their birth moved to Paris, London, the Côte d'Azur, or Tuscany, just as Henry James, Edith Wharton, Gertrude Stein, Ezra Pound, and T. S. Eliot had done before them, just as Richard Wright and Henry Miller would do later.

Faulkner, like most Southern writers of his generation, preferred the solitude and discomfort of internal exile. In 1925 he spent six months touring around Europe before returning home to Oxford, Mississippi. It was here, in his "little lost almost illiterate town" (*SL*, 319), among his own, despite them and against them, that he would do most of his writing. He was initially labeled a rural, regionalist writer in the United States, but this, of course, was wholly incorrect. Classifying Faulkner as merely a Southern novelist would be as incongruous as calling Flaubert a Norman writer, Thomas Hardy a Dorset novelist, or Kafka the chronicler of Prague. "I'm inclined to think that my material, the South, is not very important to me," he told Malcolm Cowley. "I just happen to know it, and don't have time in one life to learn another one and write at the same time" (*FCF*, 14–15).

The subject matter of the novelist is always contingent. What is important is what he draws from it, the manner in which he appropriates it, works it, and imposes his designs on it, the manner in which the randomness of facts is obliterated in the necessity of the oeuvre. The fact remains that no text can be reduced to itself. The fact remains that Faulkner belonged to a region and inherited a history. The South was his place, his family, and he was attached to it by all the fibers of his being. As he himself noted in his draft introduction to a new edition of *The Sound and the Fury* in 1933, writing on the South, for him as for all Southerners, was and could only be a way of writing about oneself: "Because it is himself that the Southerner is writing about, not about his environment: who has, figuratively speaking, taken the artist in him in one hand and his milieu in the other and thrust the one into the other like a clawing and spitting cat into a croker sack. And he writes."[7]

Faulkner, a Southern writer, wrote from that original violence that was both inside and outside him, undertaking to describe it and portray it, endeavoring to make sense of it and doubtless to keep it at a distance as well, to keep it at bay, free himself of it. While as a novelist he was motivated by various things, one of his chief motivations was the desire to understand his heritage, seeking an answer to the questions Shreve McCannon asks Quentin Compson in *Absalom, Absalom!*: "*Tell about the South. What's it like there. What do they do there. Why do they live there. Why do they live at all*" (N3, 145; italics in original). This questioning was the product of a passionate and ambivalent relationship, epitomized by the conversation between Shreve and Quentin at the end of the novel:

> "Now I want you to tell me just one thing more. Why do you hate the South?"
>
>   "I dont hate it," Quentin said quickly, at once, immediately; "I dont hate it," he said. *I dont hate it* he thought, panting in the cold air, the iron New England dark: *I dont. I dont! I dont hate it! I dont hate it!* (N3, 311)

Another example, almost echoing the final lines of *Absalom, Absalom!*, can be found in "Mississippi," a fine semiautobiographical essay published in 1954, which ends with these words: "Loving all of it even while he had to hate some of it because he knows now that you dont love because: you love despite; not for the virtues but despite the faults" (*ESPL*, 42–43).

Faulkner did not deny his roots. Viscerally attached to his community; heir to its legacy of suffering, pride, humiliation and shame; haunted by its ghosts and legends, he could not conceive either his life or his work outside the land of his birth. His loyalty to tradition was sometimes suffocating; his tribal allegiances at times blinded him. He did not, however, eulogize rootedness; he was no nostalgic poster boy for the lost South. His novels play with Southern mythology without taking it on board; they do not celebrate any lost paradise and do not call for restoration. His work is first and foremost the trace of a wandering, the chronicle of a quest without map or compass. His is both a work of memory and imagination and a work of reflection, where reflection does not predate writing but takes place within it and is co-extant with it. In his novels Faulkner reinvents the South, its history and legends, but in reinventing them, he *rethinks* them, without prejudice, concession, or indulgence; he seeks a truth that is always fleeing, fleeting, and that can be approached only through the uncertain paths of fiction.

Others undertook this quest at the same time. In the 1920s, in the aftermath of World War I, after decades of lethargy and isolation, the South was beginning to wake up and enter the new century. This gave rise to an upsurge in new voices, the wonderful adventure of the Southern Renaissance, a blossoming of talent that the South had never seen before and that was to last through the 1950s.

This renaissance was more artistic than intellectual. Novelists, short story writers, and poets were the shining lights of this renaissance. There was no renewal in historical thinking, and political thought was distressingly impoverished. What sets Faulkner apart from his Southern contemporaries and places him above them is that in his greatest books, the fictional imagination soars above all nostalgia and becomes instead an implacable questioning of the South. To assess Faulkner's singular daring, just compare his work to the Agrarians, those Southern intellectuals of the 1920s and '30s who, far from submitting the old order to critical examination, became its most ardent defenders. In 1930 a dozen of them—writers such as John Crowe Ransom, John Gould Fletcher, Donald Davidson, Allen Tate, Stark Young, and Robert Penn Warren; historians such as Frank Lawrence Owsley—published a manifesto titled *I'll Take My Stand: The South and the Agrarian Tradition*. In the throes of the Great Depression, these intellectuals unhesitatingly proclaimed themselves retrograde. "It is out of fashion these days to look backward rather than forward," states Ransom. "About the only American given to it is some unreconstructed Southerner, who persists in his regard for a certain terrain, a certain history, and a certain inherited way of living."[8] Claiming to be followers of Thomas Jefferson, these avowed reactionaries believed that they could hold up the traditional values of the rural South—Protestantism, patriarchy, community, attachment to the earth—against the chaos and deprivation of the capitalist, industrial North. To make the old slave-owning South a model society required a great deal of nerve and blindness. Crowe Ransom had plenty of both, defining, without batting an eyelid, the Old South as a "kindly society," where relations between social orders were "friendly" and where slavery was "humane."[9]

For Ransom and his friends, returning to the land of their ancestors, to a subsistence economy, to sound peasant virtues, and to the tried and tested values of the gentry was the only route to salvation. Faulkner was their contemporary; he was, like them, a Southerner, and this pastoral mythology was not entirely foreign to his sensibilities. But Faulkner the novelist was no fool. He knew that "the South [was] dead, killed by the Civil War,"[10] that only its specter remained, and that the South could be born anew only if it managed to rid itself of its phantoms. Almost his entire work is haunted by the still scorching memory of the total disaster of the South's defeat. In his novels this dead, still dying South, this ever dying, ever surviving South, weighs like a succubus on all destinies. It continues to haunt the living and stops them from living, but Faulkner has no intention of reversing the course of time and returning to it.

Faulkner's work as a writer was a work not only *of* memory but also *on* memory, a calling into question that could be done only in solitude and that he strove to keep questioning for a long time (almost through *Intruder in the Dust*). The Agrarians had simple and peremptory answers because they evaded the real questions. They invented a bucolic South of convenience and advocated an outdated ideology founded on amnesia. Faulkner knew that his heritage had no final will and testament.

NOTES

1. Raymond Queneau, preface to *Moustiques*, Editions de Minuit, collection "Points," 1.

2. Jean-Paul Sartre, "Sartoris," *Situations I* (Paris: Gallimard, 1947), 13.

3. Paul Valéry, *Œuvres II*, ed. Jean Hytier (Paris: Gallimard, Pléiade, 1960), 886.

4. Fernando Pessoa quoted by Antonio Tabucchi in *Une malle pleine de gens* (Paris: Bourgois, 1992), 31.

5. Nabokov, *Strong Opinions* (1973; New York: McGraw-Hill, 1981), 154–55.

6. Proust, *Contre Sainte-Beuve* (Paris: Gallimard, Idées, NRF, 1954), 157.

7. William Faulkner, Introduction to *The Sound and the Fury*, *Mississippi Quarterly* 26 (Summer 1973): 410–15.

8. John Crowe Ransom, quoted in *I'll Take My Stand: The South and the Agrarian Tradition by Twelve Southerners* (New York: Harper & Row, 1962), 1.

9. Ibid., 14.

10. William Faulkner, Introduction to *The Sound and the Fury*, *Mississippi Quarterly* 26 (Summer 1973): 410–15.

ABBREVIATIONS

MOST OF THE WILLIAM FAULKNER quotes are indicated in the complete edition, *William Faulkner, Novels*, ed. by Joseph Blotner and Noel Polk, New York: Library of America, 1994–2006. The references are indicated in the text by the letter *N* (Novels) followed by the volume number (1 to 5) and page number. For example, for volume 5, published in 1999: (*N5*, 563) The five volumes are detailed below with the letter *N* in the alphabetical list of abbreviations.

ALG   Meta Carpenter Wilde and Orin Borsten, *A Loving Gentleman* (New York: Simon & Schuster, 1976).

B   Joseph Blotner, *Faulkner: A Biography*, 2 vols. (New York: Random House, 1974).

B1   Joseph Blotner, *Faulkner: A Biography*, 1 vol. (New York: Random House, 1984).

CNC   Ben Wasson, *Count No 'Count* (Jackson: University Press of Mississippi, 1983).

CS   *Collected Stories* (New York: Random House, 1977).

DGS   Louis Brodsky, *The De Gaulle Story: A Comprehensive Guide to the Brodsky Collection*, vol. 3 (Jackson: University Press of Mississippi, 1984).

ESPL   *Essays, Speeches & Public Letters* (New York: Random House, 1966).

ELM   *Elmer, Mississippi Quarterly* 36, no. 3, Mississippi State University (Summer 1983): 337–447.

EPP   *William Faulkner: Early Prose and Poetry*, ed. Carvel Collins (Boston: Little, Brown, 1962).

FA   *Father Abraham*, ed. James B. Meriwether (New York: Random House, 1944).

FCF   William Cowley, *The Faulkner-Cowley File: Letters and Memories, 1944–1962* (New York: Viking Press, 1966).

FOM   Murry C. Falkner, *The Falkners of Mississippi* (Baton Rouge: Louisiana State University Press, 1967).

FU   *Faulkner in the University*, ed. Frederick L. Gwynn and Joseph Blotner (Charlottesville: University of Virginia Press, 1959).

KG   *Knight's Gambit* (New York: Random House, 1949).

LG   *Lion in the Garden: Interviews with William Faulkner, 1926–1962*, ed. James B. Meriwether and Michael Millgate (New York: Random House, 1968).

LMF   *Thinking of Home: William Faulkner's Letters to His Mother and Father, 1918–1925*, ed. James G. Watson (New York: W. W. Norton, 1992).

LP   A. I. Bezzerides, *William Faulkner: A Life on Paper* (Jackson: University Press of Mississippi, 1980).

M   *Mosquitoes* (New York: Liveright, 1955).

Ma   *The Marionettes*, ed. with an introduction by Noel Polk (Charlottesville: University Press of Virginia, 1977).

MBB   John Faulkner, *My Brother Bill: An Affectionate Reminiscence* (New York: Trident Press, 1963).

MD   *Mayday* (London: University of Notre Dame Press, 1976).

MF/GB   *The Marble Faun and the Green Bough* (New York: Random House, 1965).

N1   *William Faulkner*, ed. Joseph Blotner and Noel Polk (New York: Library of America, 1985–2006). Vol. 1 (2006). *Novels 1926–1929: Soldiers' Pay, Mosquitoes, Flags in the Dust, The Sound and the Fury.*

N2   *Faulkner*, Vol. 2 (1985). *Novels 1930–1935: As I Lay Dying, Sanctuary, Light in August, Pylon.*

N3   *Faulkner*, Vol. 3 (1990). *Novels 1936–1940: Absalom, Absalom!, The Unvanquished, If I Forget Thee, Jerusalem [The Wild Palms], The Hamlet.*

N4   *Faulkner*, Vol. 4 (1994). *Novels 1942–1954: Go Down, Moses, Intruder in the Dust, Requiem for a Nun, A Fable.*

N5   *Faulkner*, Vol. 5 (1999). *Novels 1957–1962: The Town, The Mansion, The Reivers.*

NOS   *New Orleans Sketches*, ed. Carvel Collins (New York: Random House, 1968).

RN   *Requiem for a Nun* (New York: Random House, 1951).

SL   *Selected Letters of William Faulkner*, ed. Joseph Blotner (New York: Random House, 1977).

US   *Uncollected Stories*, ed. Joseph Blotner (New York: Random House, 1979).

WFO   James W. Webb and A. Wigfall Green, *William Faulkner of Oxford* (Baton Rouge: Louisiana State University Press, 1965).

William
Faulkner

1
FA(U)LKNER, MISSISSIPPI

A LITTLE HISTORY, A LITTLE GEOGRAPHY

"Faulkner, Mississippi" is the title given by Edouard Glissant to his handsome meditation on William Faulkner's work. "Faulkner" is the name of a man, a name that became the hallmark of a great writer. "Mississippi" is the name of a territory, taken from the name of a great river. The two go hand in hand. For those who are not from there, have never been there, have never lived there, Mississippi exists only because of a handful of prestigious names associated with it. The Magnolia State would hold little interest for us if Oxford had not been the birthplace of a novelist of great stature, if Tupelo had not been the native town of one of the creators of rock 'n' roll, and Clarksville had not been the home of the Delta Blues.

Made of ink and paper, Faulkner's Mississippi is a fictional landscape held together solely by the unifying force of words and that knows no time other than the condensed or dispersed time of his stories. Faulkner often spoke of his "apocryphal county" (*SL*, 232), thereby signaling both the marginal and fictional status of his universe.[1] However, apocryphal texts exist only by opposition and analogy to canonical texts. Although Faulkner's Mississippi is imaginary, it is nevertheless modeled on the geographical and historical land. Mississippi, in the southeastern United States, is a place that can be visited, with landscapes that can be contemplated and photographed. With its small towns, villages, and hamlets; its plains and hills; its fields of cotton and corn; its woods, rivers, and swamps, the state of Mississippi is located on the western border of the "Old South," south of Tennessee, west of Alabama, and east of Arkansas and Louisiana. Mississippi is first and foremost the Delta—or the "Black Counties"—an almond-shaped, exceptionally fertile floodplain that extends to the east of the river between Memphis and the mouth of the Yazoo River in Vicksburg, home of the richest plantations prior to the Civil War. But Mississippi also includes Piney Woods south of the Delta, red clay hills to the northeast, the tail end of the Appalachians, coastal plains, and cypress swamps—a land with less fertile earth, long populated in the main by owners of small farms and by fishermen and hunters with not a patch of land between them.

Historians of the South agree that over the last 150 years, the state of Mississippi has been the most closely wedded to the idea of the Confederacy. However, its history is shorter and less rich than that of the other "Old South" states. It started with a single episode in the settlement of the West. In 1817, when Mississippi joined the Union, two-thirds of its territory was still part of that shifting area of settled and unsettled land known as the frontier. It was inhabited by Choctaws and Chickasaws (population between twenty thousand and thirty thousand). For many years they resisted Spanish and French attempts to subjugate them, but they had traded with Europeans as far back as the eighteenth century. By the start of the nineteenth century, they appeared to have converted to the Western market economy and even owned plantations and slaves. However, from 1830 on they were dispossessed of their lands in treaties that favored white pioneers and speculators and forced to move elsewhere. The years that followed saw an influx of sons of planters from Virginia, North and South Carolina, Tennessee, and Alabama as well as poor farmers and city dwellers hoping to acquire cheap land and make a fast buck. Many of them brought their black slaves with them, attracted by the cotton, the cultivation of which was continually expanding westward and the price of which was continually rising.

At that time the territory that would come to form the state of Mississippi was both the Far West and the Deep South. It was a frontier land, with a population of mostly young and male migrants and a mobile, scarcely organized society. Few Mississippians were natives of Mississippi. Most came from neighboring states, and many were ready to move on and try their luck elsewhere. The population was also widely dispersed, with isolated farms at the center of landholdings and a handful of hamlets at crossroads, where farmers came to pick up supplies at the general store. Some may have had a forge, a small wooden church, and perhaps a tavern. People lived at a distance from one another. The family, often extended, was the only core of durable social relations. The only communities that were forming at this time were religious communities, all Protestant—Methodist, Presbyterian, or Baptist—and these would make a key contribution to the culture of the South. However, beyond the communities a society was being built; a highly hierarchical class system was being set up with, at the top, a rich, sometimes very rich, minority and, at the bottom, black slaves and a minority of poor, sometimes very poor, whites. Up to 1861 between the two there was a majority of plain folk, independent farmers or yeomen, followed in time by the middle classes—businessmen, lawyers, doctors, teachers, and public servants—living in small, growing towns such as Oxford, the seat of Lafayette County.

The owning and ruling class were the planters. With few exceptions their social origins were barely different from those of the poor whites, and although keen, their class consciousness owed nothing to tradition. In fact, they were generally entrepreneurs who had made their fortune from cotton, and some of them were recent immigrants from Europe. Even though they put on the airs of Virginian gentlemen, they were not descended from them, nor were they their heirs in any sense of the word. Nonetheless, the rich of the South were among the richest in the country. In 1860 the twelve most prosperous counties were beneath the Mason-Dixon Line, and the highest per capita income was in Adams County, Mississippi. However, for many years life remained harsh for everyone in the state. Before they built their handsome colonial mansions, even the richest often lived in modest log cabins. Joseph Ingraham, a Yankee visitor, noted at the time that "many of the wealthiest planters are lodged wretchedly, a splendid sideboard not infrequently concealing a white-washed beam—a gorgeous Brussels carpet laid over a rough-planked floor."[2] The frontier was characterized by its contrasts of ruggedness and riches.

In the 1830s, apart from a number of counties along the river, the Mississippi economy was not yet entirely devoted to the production and sale of cotton. Everything would change over the next decade. King Cotton became an almost absolute monarch, "omnipotent and omnipresent" (N4, 625), and its reign would last many long years. However, in 1836 there was an initial alert when, in order to end the excesses of speculation and curb inflation, President Andrew Jackson issued a circular requiring that all future real estate transactions be in cash. In 1837 panic was unleashed in the United States as banks suspended payments. In 1839 the price of cotton fell and the real estate market collapsed, immediately prompting many to leave for Arkansas, Louisiana, and Texas. However, toward the end of the 1840s prices started to rise again, yields improved, and the cotton trade recovered, ushering in an era of progress and prosperity for white Mississippi that would endure right up to the Civil War.

The cotton trade was based on the plantation system, which was inextricably linked to slavery. To maximize profitability, the planters needed labor that was abundant, submissive, and cheap. This led to the arrival in Mississippi of over one hundred thousand African slaves from the 1830s onward. Only the largest planters had substantial numbers of slaves, but almost half of all Southern families owned at least two or three slaves. In Mississippi before the Civil War, slaves accounted for more than half of the population, the highest percentage after South Carolina. The southeastern states had the harshest living and working conditions, the cruelest punishments inflicted for disrespect or indiscipline, and the lowest life expectancy. The state of Mississippi had a sinister reputation: the blacks called it "Goddamn Mississippi."

This "peculiar institution," as slavery was called at the time, was part of the very foundation of the economic, social, and political order of the South. As soon as the abolitionist Yankee North started to contest slavery, its justification drove all political discourse. The slavery issue was also increasingly poisoning relations between the Southern states and the rest of the Union. Southern sectionalism emerged at the end of the 1840s and continued to grow. By the end of the 1850s it had become a collective hysteria. Anyone expressing any doubt about the legitimacy of slavery became suspected of plotting with the abolitionists. The separatist fire-eaters had soon silenced the moderates attached to the Union. Those who thought differently were publicly denounced and armed militia were deployed to intimidate and punish them. All dissidence now equated to treachery. There was no further public debate, no further dissent. The issue was no longer whether Mississippi was going to leave the Union but when.

Abraham Lincoln was elected president of the United States on November 6, 1860. On December 20, South Carolina seceded, followed on

January 9, 1861, by Mississippi. In Oxford bells were rung and cannons fired to celebrate the event. A month later the Constitution of the Confederate States of America was voted in. April saw the start of a long war. The Mississippians did not yet know what a heavy price they were to pay. Lafayette County raised fourteen companies and enlisted more than two thousand men, fired by patriotic fervor and the euphoria of war. Then in the spring of 1862, after the carnage of the Battle of Shiloh, the first convoys of wounded soldiers and cartloads of corpses began to arrive home. The war was no longer something fresh and joyous. In September 1862 northern Mississippi was invaded by Ulysses S. Grant's army, and in December the city of Oxford was occupied. The white civil population went to ground, fled, or, sometimes, collaborated with the occupier. Blacks abandoned their masters or rose up against them. Daily life became increasingly difficult as the war took its toll with requisitioning, vandalism, pillaging, and penury. Nothing was as it had been and nobody knew what tomorrow would be like. Doubt started to seep in, people became increasingly demoralized, and there were more and more desertions. Dissident voices were eventually heard denouncing a war where "the poor man was fighting for the rich man's negroes."[3]

In August 1864, on the orders of General Andrew Jackson Smith, Oxford was sacked and burned down by Union troops. Nobody believed in a Confederate victory anymore. Between August 1864 and the capitulation of the Confederates at Appomattox in April 1865, the civil population of Mississippi struggled to survive. There were no further significant military engagements in the region and there was little left to pillage. The barns and haylofts were empty, the fields destroyed, the towns in ruins. After the Confederate defeat, Mississippians counted their cripples and their dead; over a third of the young men enlisted in the Confederate Army had died on the battlefield, while another third returned home minus a limb.

～

Although slavery was officially abolished in 1863, this did not mean freedom for the four million black slaves. Soon back on track, thanks to the equivocations of Lincoln's successor, President Andrew Johnson, the Southern whites resolved to restore their supremacy. In his inaugural address in 1865, Governor Benjamin G. Humphreys of Mississippi declared unambiguously that "our government is and always will be a government of white men." In 1865, while the South was still under military occupation, Mississippi legislators took the lead, adopting a range of laws restricting black rights— prohibiting them from working without a contract, from hiring or leasing farms, and from vagrancy. The entire prewar criminal legislation remained in force except that corporal punishment, which formerly had been inflicted on slaves by their masters, was now ordered by the courts. Meanwhile, the planters were violently opposed to the literacy and education of emancipated slaves; their schools were burned down, and their white teachers, most of them from the North, were reviled, harassed, assaulted, beaten, and sometimes killed.

Promptly following Mississippi's example, the other Southern states in turn voted for "black codes" rendering the "freed" slaves second-class citizens at the mercy of whites. But in 1866 the Radical Republicans won the congressional elections. A year later they decided to divide the South into five military districts and set up rules for the establishment of new governments. In 1868 the Fourteenth Amendment restated that the American nation was made up of free citizens who were equal before the law. In 1870 the Fifteenth Amendment confirmed that all citizens were entitled to vote, regardless of race. Republicans came south to mobilize their future black voters and form associations of white opponents to Democrats. In July 1866 electoral lists began to be drawn up throughout the state. According to a final check published in September 1867, Lafayette County had 2,413 registered voters—1,464 whites and 949 blacks. Two months later the blacks of Lafayette County voted for the first time. Despite the abstention of half of the electorate, the Republicans won with a comfortable majority.

This was the start of Reconstruction, a period long execrated by white Southerners and their historians as a time of "federal tyranny," "military despotism," and "black domination," and, regrettably, Faulkner saw fit to repeat this story in his novels *The Unvanquished* and *Requiem for a Nun*. In fact, in Mississippi after the Civil War, when blacks were finally allowed to take part in politics, their elected representatives adopted a low profile. In the first legislature under the new constitution, they were very much in the minority (making up just two-sevenths of the House and with even less representation in the Senate[4]) and occupied mostly lowly positions. What is more, the first two governors during the Reconstruction, James L. Alcorn, a scalawag, and Adelbert Ames, an alleged carpetbagger, were honest, capable men.[5] The Radicals of Mississippi voted in new laws; created a much better education system than anything that had been in place previously; and renovated and built public buildings, hospitals, and asylums for the disabled. It is a fact not sufficiently appreciated that Mississippi was the best-governed Southern state after the war. However, the whites would not accept that their taxes were being used to fund black schools. Opposition to the Radicals hardened; the Democrats called for white solidarity, courted "loyal" blacks, and intimidated others, going as far as to reserve open graves for those who dragged their feet. This strategy paid off. In 1868 the electorate of Lafayette County voted overwhelmingly against the adoption of the state's new constitution.

Conservative Democrats, as they were now known, had an armed wing, the Ku Klux Klan, a clandestine paramilitary group organized and led by the former Confederate general Nathan Bedford Forrest. The first targets of this shadowy army were white and black Republican leaders and their aim was to sow terror. Congress eventually voted in the laws to ratify the Fourteenth and Fifteenth Amendments and end the violence, and Grant's administration took energetic measures to disband the Ku Klux Klan. However, the first public Klansmen trial in Oxford, in June 1871, took a farcical turn. The unruly and notorious lawyer Lucius Quintus Cincinnatus Lamar—elected two years later to the House of Representatives of Mississippi and later US Secretary of the Interior and Justice of the Supreme Court, whose names Faulkner later gave to McCaslin's ancestor in *Go Down, Moses*—floored a police officer with a punch and, to the frenetic applause of both the public and the defendants, defied the court to arrest him.

No holds were now barred to bring an end to Reconstruction. During the 1875 electoral campaign, a Mississippi newspaper clearly nailed its colors to the mast: "All other means having been exhausted to abate the horrible condition of things, the thieves and robbers, and scoundrels, white and black, deserve death and ought to be killed [. . .]. Carry the election peaceably if we can, forcibly if we must."[6] Militia were organized with the dual purpose of sabotaging the Republican campaign and terrorizing the black population. At Republican election meetings, armed agitators slipped into the crowd to cause trouble, and the ensuing scuffles often ended in fatalities. On Election Day the blacks remained holed up in their cabins or hid in the swamp, while those few who dared go to the polls were shot at. Rifle clubs scoured the countryside shooting anyone defending democratic, antiracist values and sometimes slaughtering entire families. Crimes were now being committed in broad daylight and with faces uncovered.

In 1875 the Radicals lost the elections. In 1877 the last federal troops withdrew and the "natural leaders"—that is, the old white elite—regained control. However, in Mississippi the Delta planters were no longer the sole masters. The ruling class now included more and more businessmen and lawyers converted to industrial and financial capitalism, who considered themselves the Redeemers of the South. Although their ideological references and interests did not coincide precisely with those of the large planters, they were, like them, opposed to Republicans.

The Republicans had lost and would not return to power for a long time. The end of the 1870s marks the beginning of the Democrats' absolute dominance; up to 1992 all Mississippi governors were Democrats. For decades their electoral success was assured through recourse to intimidation and blackmail, through economic sanctions taken against the recalcitrant, and, where necessary, ballot box stuffing and vote buying. This was the start of "gun politics," using the type of summary justice set out in what is known as the Mississippi Plan. While there had been no major financial scandal under the Republicans, embezzlement and fraud became endemic under their Democrat successors. At the constitutional convention of 1890, Judge J. B. Chrisman described the political mores of his state over the last fifteen years: "It is no secret that there has not been a full vote and a fair count in Mississippi since 1875. [. . .] In other words, we have been stuffing ballot boxes, committing perjury, and here and there in the state carrying the elections by fraud and violence."[7]

At the same convention, jointly organized by the Delta planters and the hill farmers (133 white delegates, 1 black delegate), the state constitution was amended to prevent blacks from exercising their right to vote. Again, Mississippi set the example, followed by all the Southern states between 1895 and 1908. In 1892 the percentage of blacks allowed to vote in Lafayette County stood at 11 percent. At the start of the twentieth century it had fallen to between 1 and 4 percent. The Jim Crow laws were enacted and extended from year to year, with no reaction from the federal government.[8] Interracial marriages were formally prohibited in the new Mississippi constitution of 1890. Segregation was imposed on boats, trains, taxis, trams, and buses and was de rigueur in restaurants, schools, hospitals, and other public places, including washrooms. At the same time, what had been up to that point de facto segregation was now enforced by law, and violence perpetrated on blacks by whites worsened and became commonplace. It was arguably at its worst in the South between the end of Reconstruction and World War I. Blacks were intimidated and humiliated on a daily basis, and lynchings were widespread (averaging three a week in the 1890s). Often preceded by lengthy torture and mutilation, these horrific events most often took place in broad daylight, sensational shows performed in front of large crowds that included women and children, and nobody thought to take offense. The local press reported on these "shows" with obscene complacency. Nobody raised a single voice to denounce these barbaric practices, least of all the Baptist pastors.

This openly racist legislation suited the whites, but above all it served the interests of rich landowners, bankers, and businessmen. The sharecropping system that took hold after the Civil War discreetly reestablished slavery under a different name; landowners divided their land into lots and leased them out to farmers who undertook to cultivate them and give the owner a share of the crop. Without their own resources the new sharecroppers were at the mercy of the landowners, who provided them with tools, seed, animals for plowing, and enough to live on until the next crop was shared out, while awarding themselves usurious interest rates on everything that had been advanced and securing a share of the crop for themselves. The rare farmers who remained independent got deeper and deeper into debt, found it increasingly difficult to pay their bills, lived more on credit, and were often forced to mortgage and then sell off their land, becoming sharecroppers in their turn. Up until the end of the nineteenth century, cultivating someone else's fields and paying rent to the owner was almost unthinkable for a white farmer. By 1910 over half the white farmers in Lafayette County had lost their independence. Now all that set them apart from black farmers was the color of their skin.

For the first time, whites and blacks were directly competing on the labor market and were equally powerless to change its rules. They no longer were able even to choose their crop. Now, more than ever, cotton was king. Encouraged by their creditors to grow more and more, farmers became increasingly dependent on price fluctuations. Their conditions continued to worsen and their discontent rose. In Lafayette County more farmers were cultivating land that did not belong to them, land that was eroded and exhausted by over-farming. By the turn of the century, Mississippi was in a very sorry state indeed. It was no longer a good place to live, and, to make things worse, the state was affected by deadly epidemics of yellow fever at the end of the 1870s and again at the end of the 1890s. Many white families left Mississippi for Texas, while blacks went to Chicago or Detroit to look for work, hoping to finally escape from the unbearable conditions they had been forced to live under since the end of Reconstruction.

The political expression of all this frustration and resentment dates back to 1876, with the revolt of the rednecks, whose agrarian and ultra-racist populism would dominate Southern politics for over two decades. In 1903 they gained the upper hand in Mississippi; thanks to a new law that replaced party conventions with primary elections, James Kimble Vardaman—the "Great White Chief," who always dressed in white and traveled only on an eight-wheeled log wagon drawn by white oxen—was elected governor. After an arduous campaign, he won the 1911 Senate elections with an overwhelming majority, defeating Leroy Percy, one of the last representatives of the Delta aristocracy. In 1911 Vardaman's acolyte Theodore G. Bilbo, a Baptist preacher, became lieutenant governor. In 1916 Bilbo was in turn elected governor and then reelected in 1928. Like Vardaman, he ended his political career as a senator for Mississippi in Washington. Accomplished demagogues, despised by the upper classes but adulated by the mass of poor whites, Vardaman and Bilbo dominated political life in Mississippi for decades. Like Ben Tillman in South Carolina and Tom Watson in Georgia, they were apparently on the side of the poor whites. They denounced the rich and powerful, played country folk against town people, but, above all, stoked racial hatred by fulminating against blacks. Vardaman publicly declared that the black man was "a lazy, lying, lustful animal, which no amount of training can transform into a tolerable citizen." He approved of lynchings and even went so far as to coldly envisage the "final solution." "We would be justified," he said, "in slaughtering every Ethiop on the earth to preserve unsullied the honor of one Caucasian home."[9] Eighteen blacks were lynched in Mississippi in 1903, the year Vardaman was elected governor, and sixty-four more would die before the end of his term in 1908. Bilbo's racism was just as resolute. A fierce defender of "the purity of Anglo-Saxon, Celtic and Teutonic blood," he also approved of lynching and to the end of his life fought for segregation and against blacks' right to vote.

It must be admitted that these populists were behind a number of social and economic reforms. Vardaman fought against industrial monopolies, imposed tariffs on railroad companies, built roads, introduced public health measures, and brought about some improvements to the school system. Black schools, however, had no place in this system. The reformism of Vardaman and Bilbo promised progress and social justice only to whites. The economic order remained otherwise unchanged. Mississippi remained the state with the lowest average income per capita, $126 per head of population in 1900, compared to over $500 in the rest of the South and over $1,000 in the United States as a whole. The reign of the rednecks was long, however, and longer in Mississippi than anywhere else. It ended with their electoral defeat in 1925, but after World War II, Bilbo was still there and continued to represent Mississippi in the US Senate.

This is how Henry L. Mencken, the famous Baltimore writer, described the state of Mississippi in 1931:

> It has few natural resources, and suffers from a bad climate and a backward population. It produces only a fourth as many candidates for "Who's Who in America," relative to its population, as Massachusetts. It has no efficient police, as its lynching record shows, and its government is in the hands of office-seekers of low character. It is also deficient in decent hospitals, colleges, newspapers and libraries. [. . .] In the midst of its hordes of barbaric peasants there is some native stock of excellent blood. But the young men of this stock, finding few opportunities at home, have to go elsewhere. Altogether, it seems to be without a serious rival to the lamentable preeminence of the Worst American State.[10]

This was no exaggeration. Thirty years later or earlier, much the same thing could have been said. It cannot be denied that throughout William Faulkner's life, Mississippi remained both the poorest and the most backward state in the United States and carried out the most lynchings of all the Southern states. Blacks were still subjugated by whites and the tradition of lynching continued in Lafayette County as elsewhere. A black man named Nelse Patton was hanged in Oxford on September 8, 1908 (Faulkner recalled this incident in "Dry September" and *Light in August*), while another was burned alive and then skinned on May 22, 1917, in front of a jubilant crowd. As in the previous century, few white Mississippians believed lynching was a criminal act, and many saw it as a necessary evil, even boasting of its prophylactic powers. On July 1, 1919, the editorial of the *Clarion Ledger*, a daily newspaper in Jackson, was very clear on the matter: "There is a cure for lynchings in the South and that cure lies within the hands of the negroes themselves—remove the cause and the lynchings will stop of themselves, but so long as busy-bodies . . . preach social equality to the negro, drastic measures will be taken to impress upon him that this is a white man's country to be ruled by white men as white men see fit."[11]

Economically, Mississippi continued to lag behind. Fifty years after the Civil War, most of the population, white as well as black, still lived in poverty, and the great crash of 1929 was even more devastating here than elsewhere. The price of cotton fell disastrously. By 1930 fifty-nine banks had closed their doors and another fifty-six closed in 1931. In 1932 the state economy was bankrupt and its wealth in ruins. Thousands of small white and black farmers were plunged into poverty, often losing their work, their house, and their land in one fell swoop. In a single day in April 1932, one-quarter of all Mississippi land was sold at auction to pay off unpaid taxes. This desolation can be seen in photographs of emaciated farmers on the threshold of their cabins or on the side of the road. These photographs were taken by great reporters—most of them sent by the FSA (Federal Security Administration) set up by Roosevelt—such as Arthur Rothstein, Ben Shahn, Dorothea Lange, Russell Lee, and especially Walker Evans, who came to work in Mississippi before joining James Agee in Alabama to share with him the poverty-stricken life of three sharecropper families in Hale County, an experience that was to form the basis of an acclaimed poetic reportage called *Let Us Now Praise Famous Men* (1941).

Mississippi, which remained unaffected by most of the policies implemented under the New Deal, continued to stagnate. At the end of the 1930s, the WPA (Work Projects Administration) guide of Mississippi described Lafayette County as "an agricultural formerly prosperous area whose existence is now threatened by erosion and a single-crop economy." The small town of Mississippi like Oxford had grown and modernized, but the countryside still offered the same scenes of devastation and dilapidation: red ravines sculpted by erosion, rudimentary log cabins, abandoned colonial houses, weed-infested fields, and badly maintained roads, dusty or muddy depending on the season. After World War I the South started to emerge from its torpor and catch up with the rest of the country. World War II saw a measure of prosperity begin to return. However, it was not until the 1970s that the South finally caught up in economic terms.

It was also at this time, over a hundred years since their official emancipation, that Southern blacks finally became full-fledged citizens. War had not done much to improve their situation. At the start of the 1960s, 86 percent of them still lived below the poverty threshold and migrating north remained their only route to salvation. Between 1955 and 1960, 60 percent of blacks arriving in Chicago to find work were from the South, three-quarters of them from Mississippi. For blacks, continuing to live in the South meant both resigning themselves to poverty and accepting being treated as third-class citizens. Nothing protected them from the arbitrary violence that threatened to blow up, unpunished, at any moment. And in Mississippi it was often worse than elsewhere. Although there had been fewer lynchings since the end of the redneck era, there were twenty-eight during the 1920s and over a dozen in the 1930s.[12] More discreet racist killings resurfaced with renewed vigor in the 1950s and 1960s, when blacks started to actively campaign for their rights.

At the start of the 1960s, barely 5 percent of Mississippi blacks were registered to vote (in the neighboring state of Georgia, almost 40 percent of blacks were registered), and there were none at all registered in some counties. Segregation had not loosened its grip. As far back as 1946, however, the President's Committee on Civil Rights, appointed by Harry S. Truman, had proposed measures to improve the access of minorities to employment, public transport, and the voting booths and to ensure fairer administration of justice. In a message to Congress, Truman urged it to implement the measures recommended by the commission. Southern members of Congress immediately reproached him for these "excesses" and, breaking with the Democratic Party, fielded their own candidates at the presidential election in November 1948. In Mississippi, as in Alabama, South Carolina, and Louisiana, these candidates won an overwhelming majority (87 percent).

Once again Mississippi was at the forefront of racist action, as it had been in 1875 when dealing the final blow to Reconstruction and in 1890 when it deprived blacks of their civil rights. A third Mississippi Plan led to the setting up of White Citizens' Councils in June 1954, which were determined to ward off the evils of a second Reconstruction and maintain segregation at all costs. On May 17, in its ruling on the *Brown v. Board of Education* case, the US Supreme Court broke with the doctrine of "separate but equal," which it had upheld since 1896, and prohibited segregation in schools. A year later the Court announced that federal judges would be required to apply the law. It soon became apparent that they would do so. So once again the white South took fright, particularly those in the Deep South, which had a larger black population. A resistance movement was immediately formed to prevent the "unwarranted exercise of power by the Court" as stated in the Southern Manifesto, which was signed by a majority of Southern deputies in March 1956. White Southerners used delaying tactics and violence to delay or even inhibit the implementation of the new laws. In response to the Supreme Court rulings, the Mississippi state legislature voted in laws aimed at blocking integration and set up a commission to break the civil rights movement.

Faulkner died before President Kennedy sent federal troops into Oxford in 1962 to end the riots provoked by James Meredith's application to register at the University of Mississippi. The author's death also came before the 1964 Freedom Summer campaign, which ended in one thousand arrests, thirty-five firearm incidents, thirty attacks on buildings, thirty-five churches set on fire, eighty beatings, and at least six deaths. Medgar Evers, president of the NAACP Mississippi State Conference, was killed in June 1963, and in 1966 Vernon Dahmer, a civil rights activist, was killed in Hattiesburg. All of these crimes were largely approved by white Southern society, the criminals were rarely apprehended, and on the rare occasion when they came to trial, the all-white jury hastened to acquit. In the case of the three activists killed by the Ku Klux Klan in 1964, made famous by Alan Parker's 1988 film, *Mississippi Burning*, only seven of the accused were given prison sentences. Since then, many years after the events, proceedings have been reopened. In 1994 Byron de la Beckwith was tried for the third time for the murder of Evers and sentenced to life imprisonment. In 1998 Sam Bowers was charged for the fifth time for the murder of Dahmer and also sentenced to life imprisonment. Finally, Edgar Ray Killen, the ex-organizer of the Ku Klux Klan and the presumed instigator of the triple murder in 1964, was sentenced in June 2005 to sixty years in prison but released two months later after payment of a six-hundred-thousand-dollar bond.[13]

However, after the bloodshed of the 1960s, Mississippi, as elsewhere in the South, did change, albeit more slowly than the other Southern states and only under outside pressure. Since 1965, blacks have played an increasing role in politics, and Mississippi is now the state with the second-highest number of blacks in elected positions. Serious efforts have been made to reduce social inequality. According to recent surveys, there are now more poor blacks in Wisconsin and Illinois than in Mississippi. Nevertheless, income per capita among whites remains double that of blacks. Two-thirds of all prisoners in Mississippi are black, even though blacks now account for just 36 percent of the population.

The history of Mississippi is one of a long resistance to History. While it is true that Mississippi was affected by the turbulence of the twentieth century and that it was not spared by change, fundamentally its economic, political, and social organization from the mid-nineteenth century to the end of the 1960s was dominated by the same forces and the same interests. For almost half a century, Mississippi society was divided and torn apart by its contradictions: a single-minded, one-party "closed society" and a pseudo-democratic, almost totalitarian, society where anyone who diverged in any way from orthodoxy ran serious risks.[14] This orthodoxy was based on the dogma that whites were biologically superior to blacks and on the certainty that it was absolutely essential to avoid any mixing of the races, to maintain blacks in a state of inferiority and therefore to uphold the status quo at all costs. "If we start off with the self-evident proposition," remarked Ross Barnett, governor of Mississippi from 1960 to 1964, "that the whites and colored are different, we will not experience any difficulty in reaching the conclusion that they are not and never can be equal."[15] Also, inequality was all the more unquestionable because its theological foundation lay in a fiercely archaic and fundamentalist form of Protestantism, which saw the slightest attempt at reform as the work of Satan.

The preservation of this South was to be ensured through immutable laws and institutions and guaranteed forever through the indomitable sovereignty of each of the states of the Union. This led to dyed-in-the-wool conservatism in the management of public affairs and a suffocating conformity in intellectual and cultural life. There was no opportunity for public debate or for a free press; up until the 1960s, reactionary rags such as the *Daily News* and the *Clarion Ledger* systematically censured information on burning crosses, racist murders, and torched black churches. Free thinking was suspect, and the slightest challenge to the dominant ideology, the slightest criticism of its ravages was seen as an attack on the established order.

It is also true that education was rarely a priority in Mississippi, which had no public school system before 1870 and where the schools, both white and black, were for many years the worst in the country. Mississippi was regressive in all areas of civil life, rejecting out of hand anything that had a hint of modernity or progress. Obscurantism was de rigueur. In the eighteenth century the secular spirit of the Enlightenment had started to win over the elites in Virginia and both Carolinas. Nothing of the sort happened in Mississippi, which for a long time remained the lawless land of the Wild West, with a tradition "closer to Dodge City than to Williamstown" as Walker Percy so cruelly described it.[16] Always recalcitrant, always lagging behind, Mississippi is one of five states that in the 1920s voted in laws prohibiting the theory of evolution from being taught in its schools. It was the last state to abolish prohibition and the last to ratify the Thirteenth Amendment.

What possible significance could literature have in these conditions? The literary South never measured up to the North. Since Edgar Allan Poe, from Richmond, Virginia, it had produced no major figure. Only a handful of women, such as Kate Chopin and Ellen Glasgow, salvaged its honor. At the start of the twentieth century, Henry James likened the South to an invalid in a wheelchair, defining it as a "great melancholy void."[17] In 1917 Mencken described it as a cultural desert in his essay "The Sahara of the Bozart." In the South where the young Faulkner grew up, people still believed that writing poetry or novels was not really a man's work. Thus, at the beginning of the twentieth century, writers were quite rare and not very well regarded. Mencken was right: "Down there a poet is now almost as rare as an oboe-player, a dry-point etcher or a metaphysician. It is indeed amazing to contemplate so vast a vacuity."[18] Art did not count in the tradition of the South. It was not one of the values of its culture and never had been.

Faulkner knew this better than anyone. In 1946 he wrote to Malcolm Cowley:

> Re. literature (songs too) in the South 1861–65. It was probably produced but not recorded. The South was too busy, but the main reason was probably a lack of tradition for inventing or recording. The gentlefolk hardly would. For all their equipment for leisure (slavery, unearned wealth) their lives were curiously completely physical, violent, despite their physical laziness. When they were not doing anything—not hunting or superintending farming or riding 10 and 20 miles to visit, they really did nothing: they slept or talked. They talked too much, I think. Oratory was the first art; Confederate generals would hold up attacks while they made speeches to their troops. Apart from that, "art" was really womanly business. It was a polite painting of china by gentlewomen. (SL, 216)

Faulkner's second draft of his introduction to a new edition of *The Sound and the Fury* in 1933 began with this abrupt statement: "Art is no part of southern life."[19] However, it went on to say:

> Yet this art, which has no place in southern life, is almost the sum total of the Southern artist. It is his breath, blood, flesh, all. Not so much that it is forced back upon him or that he is forced bodily into it by the circumstance; forced to choose, lady and tiger fashion, between being an artist and being a man. He does it deliberately; he wishes it so. This has always been true of him and of him alone. Only Southerners have taken horsewhips and pistols to editors about the treatment or maltreatment of their manuscript. This—the actual pistols— was in the old days, of course, we no longer succumb to the impulse. But it is still there, still within us.[20]

In Southern society in the early twentieth century, art was not important; for Southern artists it was everything, and they gambled their life on it. Writing, for them, meant going their own way. Writing was answering an internal demand in the woefulness—but also sometimes the proud exaltation—of extreme solitude and exposing oneself to the disapproval of all.

In the eyes of this society, anyone claiming to be an artist was suspected of both lacking virility and wishing to stand out by betraying their Southern identity. Faulkner himself put it in the following terms in a letter to his mistress Joan Williams on March 9, 1950: "You can see now how it is almost impossible for a middle class southerner to be anything else but a middle class southerner; how you have to fight your family for every inch of art you ever gain and at the very time when the whole tribe of them are hanging like so many buzzards over every penny you earn by it."[21] Being an artist, a writer, freely in Mississippi at the start and even in the middle of the twentieth century remained an act of defiance. It required much courage and stubbornness, which Faulkner had in droves.

THREE FATHERS, TWO MOTHERS

In the beginning is the story of a man who was nothing and who wanted to become somebody, the story of a poor man who wanted to become rich and succeeded in doing so—in short, the kind of success story so well loved in America. This man was William Clark Falkner (hereafter W. C. Falkner). His great-grandson always mentioned him in the biographical information solicited by his editors. He sent this note to the publisher of *The Marble Faun* in September 1924:

> Born in Mississippi in 1897. Great-grandson of Col. W. C. Faulkner [sic], C.S.A., author of "The White Rose of Memphis," "Rapid Ramblings in Europe," etc. Boyhood and youth were spent in Mississippi, since then has been (1) undergraduate (2) house painter (3) tramp, day laborer, dishwasher in various New England cities (4) Clerk in Lord and Taylor's book shop in New York City (5) bank and postal clerk. Served during the war in the British Royal Air Force. A member of Sigma Alpha Epsilon Fraternity. Present temporary address, Oxford, Miss. "The Marble Faun" was written in the spring of 1919. (*SL*, 7)

And he wrote this to Malcolm Cowley in December 1945:

> The name is "Falkner." My great-grandfather, whose name I bear, was a considerable figure in his time and provincial milieu. He was prototype of John Sartoris: raised, organized, paid the expenses of and commanded the 2nd Mississippi Infantry, 1861–62, etc. Was a part of Stonewall Jackson's left at 1st

Manassas that afternoon; we have a citation in James Longstreet's longhand
as his corps commander after 2nd Manassas. He built the first railroad in our
country, wrote a few books, made grand European tour of his time, died in a
duel and the county raised a marble effigy which still stands in Tippah County.
The place of our origin shows on larger maps: a hamlet named Falkner just
below Tennessee line on his railroad." (SL, 211–12)

In this December 1945 letter to Cowley, Faulkner, always ready to tell tall
tales, took a few liberties with the truth, but for once he was telling the truth
about his great-grandfather.

His ancestors had left Scotland for the New World in the eighteenth
century. According to family legend, the first Falkners to arrive in America
disembarked at Charleston, South Carolina, sometime before the War of
Independence. They were two brothers, the elder of whom settled in Hay-
wood County, North Carolina, close to the Tennessee border. One of his
sons, Joseph, married Caroline Ward, from Carolina. They had three sons,
the eldest of whom, William Clark, the great-grandfather of the novelist,
was born in Knox County, Tennessee, on July 6, 1825. Around 1840, after a
childhood spent in St. Genevieve, a small town in Missouri on the banks of
the Mississippi, William Clark, at the age of just fifteen, left his family for
unknown reasons and walked to Ripley, a small town in Tippah County, in
northeastern Mississippi, in search of an aunt who was married to a certain
John Wesley Thompson. On his arrival he learned that the aunt's husband
had been accused of murder and was in Pontotoc prison, almost forty miles
away. Thompson, who defended himself, was acquitted and embarked on a
career as a lawyer. He was like a second father to the young Falkner.

In Ripley, W. C. Falkner began to learn about the law, earned his living
working in the county prison, and soon developed a keen sense for business. When a killer condemned to death by hanging told him his life story,
he wrote it up in his own style and made a thousand dollars selling twenty-
five hundred copies on the day of the execution. Falkner proved adept at
seizing opportunities, at making a quick buck one way or another, at earning more and more money, and at building a fortune.

The Mexican-American War broke out in 1846. In October, at the age
of twenty-one, Falkner joined Jefferson Davis's First Mississippi Volunteer
Regiment. However, in April 1847 he disappeared inexplicably and against
orders. A few days later he was found stretched out on the ground with a

crushed foot and three fingers missing. Was it an ambush or an affair of honor? This question remains unanswered. After recovering from his injuries, Falkner married Holland Pearce, a rich heiress from Tennessee, on July 9, 1847. He settled in Ripley, was called to the bar, and was taken on by his uncle John's law firm. Because his wife's dowry included a number of slaves, he bought some plots of land to set himself up as a planter. In September 1848 Holland gave him a son, John Wesley Thompson Falkner, the writer's future grandfather. Just one year later, his wife died of tuberculosis. His widowhood did not last long. In 1851 he married Elizabeth (Lizzie) Vance. Their first child was born in 1853, followed by seven more. It has come to light in recent years that he also fathered a number of children with slaves. Like many Southern planters (and like Thomas Sutpen in *Absalom, Absalom!* and Carothers McCaslin in *Go Down, Moses*), he had a number of black mistresses; one of them, Emeline, whose skin was almost white, gave him at least one daughter, if not two. W. C. Falkner's statue can be visited in the Ripley cemetery today, as can the grave of "Mrs. Emeline Lacy Falkner."

All went well for W. C. Falkner in the 1850s. By the end of the decade, according to his own estimates, his property assets were worth ten thousand dollars and his movable assets forty thousand. Then the Civil War broke out. A secessionist from the outset, and later an advocate of "white supremacy," Falkner raised his own company, the Magnolia Rifles, and then joined the regular units of the Mississippi. He was elected colonel of an infantry regiment and fought—bravely, according to several witnesses—in the Battle of First Manassas. The high command commended him for his exceptional bravery. But his regiment, which had paid a heavy price for his temerity, forsook him, choosing instead to elect a commander who was more careful with men's lives. This led Falkner to raise another regiment in June 1862, this time a cavalry regiment called the First Mississippi Partisan Rangers. They operated alongside the regular army and specialized in raids, horse stealing, destroying bridges, and sabotaging railways (Faulkner's novel *The Unvanquished* was inspired by this regiment). According to legend, Falkner rode with General Nathan Bedford Forrest during the last years of the war. In fact, frustrated in his military ambitions despite his prowess, he resigned from the Confederate Army in 1863, took up residence in Pontotac, and immediately started a career in contraband, as a blockade runner. At the time, cotton was worth $2.50 per pound, so there was potential for huge profits. With the money earned in illegal cotton trading, Falkner bought essential goods, such as salt, or medication, such as quinine, and sold them in Mississippi at exorbitant black market rates.

After the war, far from being ruined, he promptly took up the challenge of reconstruction and became, in the space of a few years, one of the richest and most influential men in Tippah County. He resumed his activities as a lawyer and businessman and invested in both movable and immovable assets. In 1872 he entered into a deal with the state to acquire a holding in the Ripley Railroad Company, which was to build twenty-five miles of railroad from Ripley to Middletown, Tennessee. In 1886 he envisaged extending the line southward to New Albany and Pontotoc. To take control of the company, which was now called Ship Island, Ripley, and Kentucky Railroad Company, he bought out his partner, Richard Jackson Thurmond. Work started immediately, but construction costs were high. To reduce them, Falkner, without compunction, hired a hundred convicts from the state at the very reasonable rate of fifty dollars per year per head. The line was inaugurated in triumph in 1888 and was dotted with stops named after him.

Now all that was missing was a political career. In the mid-1850s Falkner had joined a nationalist nativist party founded in New York in 1850 called Order of the Star-Spangled Banner, better known as the Know-Nothing Party, but joined the Democrats after being beaten in 1855 by his uncle John. Years later, in the fall of 1889, he stood for the party at the state elections. On November 5 he was voted in with a comfortable majority. However, victory was short-lived. Later that afternoon, as he left his office and walked toward the Ripley main square, Richard J. Thurmond suddenly appeared and shot him with a .44-caliber pistol. Falkner collapsed, blood pouring from his mouth. It is said that before losing consciousness, he turned to his killer and asked: "Why did you do that, Dick?" After many hours of agony, he died during the night on November 6, 1889.

Such murders were common currency in the Mississippi of the time, and even in the genteel small town of Oxford there was nothing exceptional in such an incident. Violence was an inheritance from the days of the frontier. Its primary victims were blacks, but it also affected whites, men of punctilious virility, ready to settle their disputes with weapons. W. C. Falkner was one such man. Violence ran through his life like a red thread. According to rumor, when he set out for Mississippi as a young man, he had been in a fight with his brother and had left him for dead. In Ripley the first violent incident took place in the spring of 1849, when a man named Robert Hindman attempted to join the Knights of Temperance, a secret society to which Falkner belonged. Falkner opposed his application, or at least that is what people thought. Hindman took him violently to task. He shot Falkner three times at point-blank range, but each time his revolver jammed. Falkner finally drew his knife and stabbed Hindman several times, mortally wounding him. At the trial he pleaded legitimate defense and was acquitted. Later, Erasmus Morris, a friend of Hindman, picked a quarrel with him about a farm tenancy and, once again, shots were fired. Falkner killed his adversary, but this time the prosecuting attorney was the younger brother of the man he had killed in 1849. Even so, he was again acquitted. As he left the courthouse, Hindman's father shot at him but also missed. Magnanimous, Falkner picked up the bullet and let him go. Twice accused of murder, he was acquitted both times.

There was no scandal about these acquittals. Nonetheless, it is true that Falkner was a hothead and always ready to fight. His violent death was the almost inevitable culmination of a ruthless vendetta. Ever since he had ousted Thurmond from the railroad company, the two men had been at daggers drawn and often provoked each other. Falkner publicly declared that Thurmond had made a fortune on the backs of widows and orphans while Thurmond called Falkner a murderer. On November 1, 1886, three years before their final confrontation, they were both charged with "swearing and blasphemy" and ordered to pay a fine. Another time, Falkner stood before Thurmond, his thumbs in his waistcoat armholes, and said: "Well, Dick, here I am. What do you want from me?" Thurmond floored him with a punch, but Falkner stood up again and continued to taunt him. Falkner knew that Thurmond wanted him dead. Fifteen days before his murder, he said as much to a friend. He also told him that he had killed enough men and that he no longer carried a gun. On the same day, he wrote his will.

A man of violence, the law, and letters, W. C. Falkner left nobody indifferent. By turn admired, loved, envied, and detested, he was assuredly a highly colorful figure—not a great man, arguably, but a devil of a man, larger than life. A photograph of him taken around 1889 portrays a man with a piercing gaze under brushy eyebrows; long, curly silver hair; and white moustache and goatee, wearing a silk cravat. All he needs is a felt hat like

Buffalo Bill and a pair of pistols under his greatcoat to make him look like a bandit or an outlaw like in the Westerns. William C. Falkner was a man of the South and of the Wild West. He started out, as he readily admitted, "young, barefoot and penniless," and of the good people of Ripley in the first half of the nineteenth century, none had climbed higher than him. He was a self-made man, a parvenu, a nouveau riche, one of those ambitious "new men" like Thomas Sutpen in *Absalom, Absalom!* who started with nothing and built their fortune through energy, audacity, and perseverance and without too many scruples.

It is therefore wrong to state, as it often has been, that William Falkner "belonged to an old aristocratic family ruined by the Civil War." It takes three or four generations for a commoner to rise above his roots, and William was in fact the first aristocrat of his family. While Herman Melville, the grandson of a major who had taken part in the Boston Tea Party of 1773 and of a general of the War of Independence, could legitimately pride himself on his genealogical tree, the same could not be said of Faulkner. There was nothing to justify any aristocratic pretensions, either on the paternal side of the Falkners or on the maternal Butler side. Both families undoubtedly commanded respect within their community, but they were middle-class businesspeople of the kind that emerged in Mississippi from the mid-nineteenth century. They were, therefore, small-town folk rather than country squires.

Members of this altogether ungentlemanly upper class had their own lifestyle and their own ways of thinking and acting, their own references and values. They were not uncultured brutes, and the urge to write was felt in the family as far back as William C. Falkner, who wrote in his spare time. At the age of twenty-six, he self-published a long narrative poem inspired by the Mexican-American War, "The Siege of Monterrey," and his first novel, *The Spanish Heroine* (1851). Fifteen years later he published a play, *The Lost Diamond* (1867). But his greatest success was *The White Rose of Memphis*, initially published as a magazine serial in 1881. This colorful, five-hundred-page novel was reprinted twenty-four times and remained in print throughout his lifetime.

Like his great-grandson later on, W. C. Falkner wanted to leave his mark on the collective memory. Not only did he have a three-story "Italianate villa" built in 1885, as kitsch as can be, but he had also had his own

Carrara marble tombstone sent from Italy, comprising a four-meter-high plinth and a statue over two meters high. No doubt he would have liked his statue to stand in Ripley's main square, but the authorities decided instead to place it in the town cemetery. Faulkner would later take inspiration from this statue in his novel *Sartoris* when describing the statue of Colonel John Sartoris: "He stood on a stone pedestal, in his frock coat and bareheaded, one leg slightly advanced and one hand resting lightly on the stone pylon beside him. His head was lifted a little in that gesture of haughty pride which repeated itself generation after generation with a fateful fidelity, his back to the world and his carven eyes gazing out across the valley where his railroad ran, and the blue changeless hills beyond, and beyond that" (*N1*, 870). Thus elevated as a statue, the "Old Colonel" was also monumentalized in the family's memory. For the Falkners, W. C. Falkner soon became the *Urvater*, the original father, the founding member of the tribe. The celebration of his exploits brought them together, year after year, in the same rituals presided over by the unvanquished aunts later immortalized by the novelist, and for the survivors of the Partisan Rangers, the family organized meetings to commemorate their leader's exploits. Although he never met his great-grandfather, William Faulkner himself felt his influence even more. For him the Old Colonel was almost a presence. He told a journalist who came to interview him in 1952: "People at Ripley talk of him as if he were still alive, up in the hills some place, and might come in at any time. It's a strange thing; there are lots of people who knew him well, and yet no two of them remember him alike or describe him the same way. [...] There's nothing left in the old place, the house is gone and the plantation boundaries, nothing left of his work but a statue. But he rode through that country like a living force" (*FCF*, 81).[22]

It is no accident that in his autobiographical notes, Faulkner said nothing about his own father, referring exclusively to his paternal great-grandfather. Through his legendary transfiguration, the Old Colonel had become for him, from adolescence, what his own, rather dull progenitor had not been and could never have been: a Father in capital letters, idealized as a founding father, entrenched in the mute transcendence of immortal death and at the same time a prestigious role model to be copied. Unable to equal his wartime exploits, Faulkner wanted to surpass him at least as a writer, as if literature, which for his ancestor had been nothing but a lucrative diversion, could become for him the pursuit of the heroic quest by other means.

It will come as no surprise to learn that William Clark Falkner was soon included in the work of his great-grandson. He appears in the early work *Flags in the Dust*; in the form of Colonel John Sartoris, a Civil War hero, a great soldier, and grand builder; and reappears a little later, under the same name, as a major character in *The Unvanquished*. Less directly, he inspired the grandfather idolized by Gail Hightower in *Light in August* and especially Thomas Sutpen and Lucius Quintus Carothers McCaslin, the formidable ghostly masters in *Absalom, Absalom!* and *Go Down, Moses*. In addition, most of Faulkner's novels deal with the often tragic issues of filiation.

———

Faulkner's paternal grandfather, John Wesley Thompson Falkner, was born in 1848, the only child of William Clark Falkner and Holland Pearce. Between the death of Holland and his remarriage, the Old Colonel left the child in the care of his uncle, Judge John Wesley Thompson, and aunt Justianna, a childless couple who raised John as their own.

Named after his uncle, John Wesley Thompson Falkner was initially known in the county as Captain Falkner, and then as the Young Colonel—a purely honorary title, inherited from his father, the Old Colonel, even though he had never been in the army. He studied law at the University of Mississippi, was called to the bar in 1869, and the same year married Sallie McAlpine Murry, the elder daughter of John Young Murry, a respected doctor in Ripley. They had a son, Murry Cuthbert in 1870, followed two years later by a daughter, Mary Holland, and in 1882 by a second son, John Wesley Thompson Falkner Jr. (J.W.T. Jr.).

The Young Colonel joined his uncle's law practice and soon gained a highly favorable reputation as a lawyer. In 1885, at the age of thirty-seven, he left Ripley and set up as a lawyer in Oxford, which, as the seat of the federal court of Mississippi and of the state university, was central to political life in northern Mississippi and offered better career opportunities than Ripley. The eloquence of his arguments was admired by all. If you want to kill somebody, they said in Oxford, do it on a Saturday night, call Johnnie the next day, and he'll get you off.

What's more, like his father before him, the Young Colonel also had a good head for business and succeeded in almost anything he turned his hand to. He had a stake in a number of local businesses, including a cotton oil mill, a transport company, a hardware store, and the new Oxford Opera House, where, as Murry C. Falkner relates (*FOM*, 49–53), his grandchildren would later watch minstrel shows and the first silent movies. In 1910 he cofounded the First National Bank of Oxford—a rival to the Bank of Oxford—running it for ten years. A man of progress, more concerned with public service than his father had been and always brimming with projects, he threw himself headlong into his municipal responsibilities and played a major role in the modernization and sanitation of Oxford, which, thanks to him, obtained better water services, a more modern sewage system, paved roads, and many other improvements to daily life.

His political career started as brilliantly as had his career as a lawyer and businessman. The voters of Lafayette County elected him to the state legislature in 1891 and to the state Senate in 1895. Under Grover Cleveland he was appointed assistant US district attorney and served for many years as administrator of the University of Mississippi. However, to everyone's surprise and despite the support of the *Oxford Eagle*, he was trounced at the Senate elections of 1903 by a populist candidate named G. R. Hightower and never again stood for any elected position other than those that were strictly local. Politics continued to interest him, however, and around 1910 he grew close to James Vardaman, supporting his candidacy, taking part in his electoral campaigns, and even chairing the Vardaman Club in Oxford. He also joined forces with a close associate of Vardaman and Bilbo, Lee Russell, a country boy from the hills on the make with a promising political career, who was elected lieutenant governor in 1915 and governor in 1919. Whether sincere or opportunistic, the Young Colonel derived no benefit from this alignment with redneck populism. In 1911, when Vardaman was elected to the Mississippi Senate and Bilbo was elected lieutenant governor, John Wesley Thompson, despite a vigorous campaign to be elected county prosecutor, did not win. He immediately applied, successfully this time, for the post of secretary of the Mississippi Senate.

The Falkners did not keep a low profile. Just like his father, the Young Colonel was proud of his success and showed off his wealth. Where William C. Falkner had his Italianate villa in Ripley, at the end of the 1890s, John Wesley Thompson Falkner built what became known by the family as the Big Place, just below the main square on the corner of South Lamar Street and University Avenue in Oxford, a three-story building topped with

domes in the most ornate Victorian style. His clothes were just as osten-
tatious. Always extremely well turned out in white linen or black alpaca,
with a panama hat, a solid gold watch chain across his waistcoat, a walking
stick with a golden knob in his hand, or strapped up in his handsome Free-
mason's uniform, the Young Colonel cut a fine figure. And, like his father,
he was a loudmouth, a smoker of big cigars, and a heavy drinker who went
on such legendary benders that his wife eventually had him committed to
a drying-out clinic in Memphis. One anecdote speaks volumes about this
character: One day when he was drinking and carousing around Oxford's
main square with companions as drunk as he was, he stood up in his Buick
convertible and flung a brick through the window of a bank. Later, when
asked why he had done it, he answered: "It was *my* Buick, *my* brick, and *my*
bank!"

Some found his bluster amusing, but others found it annoying. Nevertheless, in his small town John Wesley Thompson was well-respected. He
was not so lucky in his private life. In December 1906, Sallie died of cancer.
He never recovered from this loss; one day Faulkner's brother John found
their grandfather lost in his memories, writing Sallie's name in the air with
his walking stick (*MBB*, 73). In 1912, however, he married again, to a formidable young widow who was only interested in his money and whom he
divorced less than a year later, with a payoff worth thousands of dollars. As
he aged, he became increasingly irascible and solitary. He became so deaf
that sometimes he put his ear trumpet between his teeth to sense the sound
vibrations. He continued to run his businesses, but in the last years of his
life his energy faded and his prestige declined. In 1920 his partners in the
bank asked him to resign as president. He imposed conditions on his departure but lost control of the bank. Out of spite, he took all of his money out
of the bank and, according to family legend, put it in two tin buckets before
lodging it with the rival bank.

John Wesley Thompson Falkner had run his course. On the morning of
March 1, 1922, at the age of sixty-three, he died in his bed of a heart attack.
His death marks the end of the heroic phase of the family story. William
Faulkner was twenty-five years old.

The Young Colonel was not a legendary figure like his father, the Old
Colonel, but for the young Faulkner this rowdy, eccentric grandfather was
arguably as important as his great-grandfather, who had died eight years

before his birth. Between the two of them there was not only much affection but real affinity as well. Billy—as he was then called—often went to the Big Place to listen to his grandfather's stories about the Civil War; to hear him talk of the role played by the Old Colonel in that war; and to play with his great-grandfather's walking stick, gold watch, and, an even more precious relic: the pipe that had fallen from his mouth and broken when he was shot down by Richard J. Thurmond. The Old Colonel would never have become for Faulkner the Father crowned in death by the majesty of a capital letter if his grandfather had not told him all about his adventures.

William Clark Falkner was the mythical founder of the line and, as noted by Murry C. Falkner in his memories (see *FOM*, 6), the young Faulkner identified with him and modeled himself on him. John Wesley Thompson, although not a hero of the Civil War, was a worthy son of his father and was his natural successor as patriarch of the clan. He played a decisive role in Faulkner's life and had the paternal authority that was lacking in Faulkner's own father. Faulkner also inherited a number of his traits and manners, such as his courteous manner with ladies, his taste for elegance, and his love of uniforms.

———

Murry Cuthbert, elder son of John Wesley Thompson Falkner and father of William Faulkner, was born on August 17, 1870. He was five foot eleven, blue-eyed and square-jawed, had the long aquiline Faulkner nose, hands like paddles, and later in life developed an impressive paunch. However, this solidly built man inherited none of the intelligence or energy of his father or grandfather. In his youth he languished in the University of Mississippi for barely two years and left without graduating. Murry loved the open air and large open spaces, and his dream at the time was to go and live somewhere in Texas on a ranch, as a cowboy. Instead, however, he started working for the railroad company founded by his grandfather. In 1888 he was shoveling coal and wearing the peaked cap and cuffed gloves of a mechanic. Within two years he was chief conductor. His headquarters were in a hamlet of scarcely five hundred souls called Pontotoc. In 1898 his father appointed him company auditor and treasurer. Murry did not see his future elsewhere. Meanwhile, his father had started to invest in real estate and the telephone, and in May 1902, without consulting his eldest son or anyone else, he decided to sell off the thriving Gulf & Chicago Railroad Company for just seventy-five thousand dollars. Murry, dismayed at losing his job, initially thought of borrowing the money to buy out the company. Although his father urged him to leave Ripley and settle in Oxford, Murry wanted to try his chances in Texas and finally realize his old dream of becoming a rancher. However, his wife, Maud, was firmly opposed to the idea and, as always, the father had his way. In September that year the family left Ripley, the Old Colonel's town, and set up home in the Young Colonel's house in Oxford, where Murry had grown up.

In Oxford, Murry first worked as an earthworks overseer, then bought a livery stable from O. I. Grady and ran a transport company on behalf of his father. Finally, from 1905 he ran the Oxford Oil Company. His duties at the stables left him ample leisure time. He had black employees to look after the horses, white coachmen to ferry customers, and in winter he always had old friends sitting around the stove in his office telling hunting and fishing stories while passing around a jug of whiskey. However, with the arrival of the automobile and the railroad, the fortunes of his livery stables declined. Increasingly embittered and withdrawn, Murry started to drink. He sometimes left the house to call on friends and arrived home drunk early the next morning. At times he disappeared from Oxford for days at a time without explanation. His professional failures were arguably not only down to bad timing. Buying a store that sold lighting and heating oil just when Oxford was starting to convert to electricity was not necessarily a bad idea, but Murry was not an enterprising entrepreneur and the company was badly run. It was later sold off at a loss.

In 1912 the comfortable house on South Street was also sold. Some of the income from this sale was likely put toward the purchase of the hardware store on Oxford's main square. Yet again, this new enterprise failed and Murry was forced to sell the smaller house he had bought on North Street. At first the family stayed in the Big Place, later moving to an ugly little yellow-painted house, nicknamed "the birdcage." In late 1919 they moved to an old three-story red-brick house on campus. Thanks to his father's contacts, Murry eventually found work as assistant secretary in the administration department of the University of Mississippi, which provided him with an annual income of fifteen hundred dollars. He fulfilled his duties impeccably and was promoted to secretary and business manager of the university. But in 1930, after twelve years there, he was fired when he refused to hand over a sixth of his salary to Governor Bilbo's electoral machine. Murry was then sixty and had little time left. As his health declined, doctors forbade him to drink and imposed a draconian diet. To entertain himself he spent his time reading dime novels or pasting photos of horses and dogs cut out of magazines onto the blank pages of old railroad registers. From time to time he spent long hours pacing in the gallery of the house, "almost like a demented person." His final years were miserable, and his heart finally gave out one August morning in 1932. "He just gave up," said Faulkner. "He got tired of living" (quoted in *B1*, 308).

Murry's life was a failure, but his misfortunes do not incite pity. Murry was not larger than life; he was insignificant, although this did not prevent him from being a domestic tyrant in the patriarchal tradition of the South. He demanded that lunch be served at noon sharp and left the house if there was any delay. During meals, which he presided over like a tyrant, he imposed silence on his sons until such time as, having wiped his mouth one last time, he placed his napkin in its silver ring and rose from the table. Communication was not his forte. He didn't open up easily, said little, and was quick to anger. Although he cut a sorry figure compared to his father and grandfather, he had inherited one of their character traits. Like them, he was hotheaded and trigger-happy, and, like theirs, his life at times resembled a Western, a melodrama, or a farce. For example, one day in 1891, to avenge the honor of a woman he was courting, he picked a quarrel with Elias Walker, a Pontotoc grocer, and knocked him senseless. That evening he went to the drugstore to buy some headache powders and Walker shot him in the back, leaving a hole "as big as a fist." As Murry lay on the ground, Walker aimed his pistol at him. According to witnesses, Murry said to him: "Don't shoot me anymore. You've already killed me." To this sublime melodramatic plea Walker is said to have replied, "I want to be damned sure," and shot him right in the face. One of the bullets lodged at the back of his throat. He was brought back to his house more dead than alive. When his father learned what had happened, he ran to avenge his son, cornered Walker in a hardware store, grabbed him by the lapels, lifted him with one hand, and with the other shoved the revolver into his ribs. He pulled the trigger six times, in vain. Walker managed to struggle free and pull out his own gun, wounding the Young Colonel in the hand. Cared for by his mother,

Murry, who was believed to be near death, eventually vomited up the bullet, made a full recovery, and went back to his job at the railroad company. This incident did not mean he had lost his taste for fighting. Barely six months after his arrival in Oxford, there was a violent altercation with a police officer that ended with the latter being stabbed and thrown through a store window, just like in a Western. Murry kept alive the family tradition of spectacular violence inaugurated by his grandfather. And, like his father, his grandfather, and later his son, he became a prodigious drinker over the years.

Otherwise, there was absolutely nothing remarkable about the man. He had simple tastes. His only passions were hunting, horses, dogs, and the railroad—open-air, manly pursuits.

His elder son was not like him at all. Even physically, they were the complete opposite of each other: one was big and burly, the other a skinny, scrawny thing. There was a chasm of incomprehension between this uncultivated father and his writer son. Murry did not see anything of himself in Billy and understood nothing of his aspirations. Billy's desire to become a writer was beyond Murry's comprehension. That he was able to earn money from writing baffled the father. When Faulkner signed his first contract in Hollywood, his father could not believe that he was being paid five hundred dollars a week for "mere scribbling" and asked him if the check was legal (*B1*, 303). And while he was at it, he thought Billy would do better to write Westerns, like those he liked to read himself (*MBB*, 171). While his wife loved Shakespeare, Dickens, and Conrad, his own literary taste did not extend further than James Fenimore Cooper, Zane Grey, and James Oliver Curwood. This uncouth man did not read even one of his eldest son's books. This did not hinder him from hating them; he even tried to prevent the publication of *Sanctuary* and, once the novel had been published, strongly advised a student he met on the campus of the University of Mississippi against reading it.

His sons remembered Murry as a rough, rugged man whose "capacity for affection was limited" (*FOM*, 12). However, he was not a wholly absent father. He liked to entertain his sons in his stable and bring them into the woods. He taught them how to ride, hunt, and fish and told them stories of wolves and panthers. Faulkner readily acknowledged that his taste for hunting and his love of horses came from his father. He later told Cowley that he had partly grown up in his father's stables: "Being the eldest of four boys, I escaped my mother's influence pretty easy, since my father thought it was fine for me to apprentice to the business. I imagine I would have been in the livery stable yet if it hadn't been for the motor car" (*SL*, 212). As always, Faulkner was exaggerating, but it is true that for two years, from 1908 to 1909, he spent a lot of time in his father's stables and that on Saturdays he sometimes went to cash bills on his behalf in the area around Oxford. However, from adolescence he started to distance himself from him. Fundamentally, Murry and his eldest son had nothing in common and nothing to say to each other.

Of Faulkner's three fathers, Murry was the least important. When asked, "Sir, in *Sartoris* you sort of skipped over one generation of the Sartoris family between the old Bayard and the young Bayard. Is there any reason for that?" Faulkner responded, "From '70 on to 1912–14, nothing happened to the Americans to speak of" (*FU*, 251). Why 1870? Perhaps because 1870 was the year when Murry was born. It is as if for Faulkner there had been a hiatus not only between the son and the father but between two generations, as if the lineage had been broken.

In the fall of 1896, while visiting Oxford, Murry met a young woman named Maud Butler at his sister's house. A few weeks later, on the last Sunday of October, without telling anyone, Maud and Murry got married.

Maud, the daughter of Charles Edward Butler, was well-born. The Butlers were one of the oldest and most respected families in the county. They had arrived in Mississippi early in the 1830s, settling there even before the Native Americans were driven out. Charles George Butler, Lafayette County's first sheriff and surveyor, traced out the blueprint of the town that was to become its capital. Having acquired 120 acres in the heart of the future town of Oxford, he built a hotel, the Oxford Inn, which became emblematic of the Butlers' prosperity until the fateful day during the Civil War when General Smith's Union troops set it on fire. After the war his widow sold off most of the property. In 1868 Charlie Edward Butler, the youngest of her three sons, married Lelia Dean Swift, originally from Arkansas. In the beginning he was not very successful in business and was even compelled to borrow money to support his family properly. However, in 1876 he was elected town marshal, becoming a tax inspector at the same time. From that time on, the Butler family lived comfortably. It seemed that nothing could endanger its position in Oxford. However, an initial setback occurred on August 5, 1883, when Charlie Butler, in the course of his duties as a police officer, killed Sam Thompson, the disreputable chief editor of the *Oxford Eagle*, after arresting him for being drunk in public. The trial took place in 1884 and Charlie was acquitted. During the 1880s his municipal duties increased considerably. He was reelected town marshal in 1884 and 1886, but a year later an event occurred that was to change everything. Close to Christmas in 1887, Charlie disappeared forever, taking with him the town's money and, according to rumor, "a beautiful octoroon."

Lelia, his wife, was thirty-eight, his son Sherwood eighteen, and Maud sixteen. The father's desertion was not without ramifications, and Lelia and Maud both found it hard to grieve, although the scandal did not affect them adversely. Friends helped them to pay off the debts Charlie had left behind, and the town agreed to reduce their property tax. Despite this, they were forced to sell their house in 1888. To survive, Lelia did all kinds of work. In September 1889 Maud entered the Industrial Institute and College for the Education of White Girls of Mississippi in Columbus but left after a year without graduating, probably due to lack of money and because she had decided to take care of her mother. Maud never pursued any further education. However, she was an independent, intelligent, and determined young woman who had not given up all of her aspirations. She believed in the power of education and culture. She loved the fine arts but not music, a trait shared by her eldest son.

After Maud's death, her family found hundreds of landscapes and portraits she had painted over the years. Like her mother, she knew how to draw and enjoyed painting. Like her mother, she was an austere and fervent Baptist. And like her mother, she was a woman of character, proud and sensitive, reserved and energetic, whose straight talking disconcerted the people close to her and whose toughness sometimes made her appear arrogant.

Maud was assertive and knew how to impose her will on her family. She was the queen, the sovereign, the uncontested matriarch. She was just a tiny slip of a woman, so small that she had to have shoes specially made to fit her. She was barely five feet tall, slim, and good-looking, with delicate features and beautiful brown, almost black eyes that dominated her face.

One might wonder why she was so eager to marry. Murry and Maud married before they knew each other well—in fact, they practically eloped. Despite this, the argument that their attraction was love at first sight is wholly improbable. Miss Maud, as she was known, and Murry had nothing in common. They soon realized this and the lively, agile woman found it increasingly difficult to put up with her oafish husband. She began to despise him and later hated him all the more since he was also a drunkard. But Maud's personality was too strong to put up with him without reacting. His heavy drinking horrified her as much as it did his mother, and she periodically forced him to undergo treatment for alcoholism at the Keeley Institute, near Memphis, where for the same reasons Sallie had previously dragged the Young Colonel. Over the years these treatments became something of a holiday for the family while at the same time a ritual of penitence and atonement for Murry. Maud and all of her sons accompanied her husband each time, as if by taking the children to witness their father's decline, she wanted to increase his humiliation. Maud was not a woman who forgave easily. Even during the final years, when Murry was already ill, she did her utmost to make his life miserable—for example, hiding his phonograph records or sliding them under the cushion of his favorite chair. Her aversion to him never let up and she never passed up an opportunity to speak badly of him. She took a malicious delight in pointing out that Jason, one of the Compson brothers in *The Sound and the Fury*, and one of Faulkner's most odious characters, was inspired by Murry: "He talks just like my husband did. My husband had a hardware store uptown at one time. His way of talking was just like Jason's, same words and same style" (*B1*, 217). On her deathbed Maud asked her eldest son:

> "Will I have to see your father there?"
> "No," he said, "not if you don't want to."
> "That's good," she said. "I never did like him." (679)

As much as she was a frustrated wife, she was a fulfilled mother. The love she refused her husband Maud lavished on her four sons, albeit without showing it too much, almost without expressing it. It is difficult to imagine her bending over Billy in his bed to give him a good-night kiss. Maud Faulkner was not overprotective in the mold of Proust's mother. She loved all of her sons, and doubtless the firstborn—whom she called Billy to the end—more than the others, and her sons were all deeply attached to her, but the mother-child relationship was not physically close; it even seemed to exclude tenderness. Maud neither knew how nor wanted to show her affection. It was a matter of propriety and dignity. Good manners, for her, meant not pouring out one's feelings, not showing any feelings, shouldering all the responsibility, and suffering in silence. As the years went by, the more her husband discredited himself through his incompetence and drunkenness, the more hardened Maud became in her stoicism: *Don't Complain, Don't Explain* was the motto written in red letters on a sign on the kitchen wall in her house. To withstand, endure, and keep quiet was a lesson Faulkner learned well.

Maud embodied reserve, rigor, even rigidity. But let there be no misapprehension: this detachment was a mere façade. Maud was not demonstrative, she was not like a Mediterranean or Jewish mother, but in her own harsh, Protestant way she was nevertheless a very possessive mother, who held formidable sway over her four sons. Even after they were grown up and married, the sons continued to feel her influence, and in her eyes none of her daughters-in-law were good enough. She hated them all. When Johncy, her third son, came to pay his respects to her, his wife had to wait outside in the car. Estelle, Billy's wife, fared no better. Maud found her "flighty—a sort of butterfly,"[23] and wasted no time in letting her know she wanted nothing to do with her.

In some ways Billy was the most dependent of her sons, the one who took longest to cut the umbilical cord. At almost thirty he still expected her to do everything, still expected her to cater to his every whim. On April 7, 1925, he wrote her from New Orleans: "Moms, dear heart, I just opened the parcel tonight. Sheets and tooth paste—enough for anyone. That's all I need" (*LMF*, 197). Maud was still the nurturing mother; it was she who ensured that he lacked for nothing, who bought him his soap and toothpaste, sent him underwear and socks, and supplied him with cakes and cookies.

Faulkner would love other women, but Maud would remain his first love right up to the end. His attachment to her was unfailing. Even at thirty-two, after his marriage to Estelle, he visited her every day and had coffee with her, and when he was away from Oxford he never failed to write her. It was he who was with her as she lay dying. All his life, William Faulkner was a good son—affectionate, deferential, and attentive—and in return Maud was passionately devoted to her firstborn son, her favorite, her chosen one, the one she called "the light of my life." It is unlikely that she understood the writer or approved of his daring. She was offended by *Soldiers' Pay*, his first novel, and it is not clear whether she ever read *Sanctuary*. However, when Murry fulminated about the horrible novel written by his eldest son, she told him: "Let him alone [. . .]. He writes what he has to" (*B*, 687). Maud was pious, but she was no prude, or at least not always. The day after her death at eighty-eight, piles of books and reviews were found in her bedroom. On her bedside locker there was a copy of *Lady Chatterley's Lover*.

Without his mother's love, Billy Falkner would never have become William Faulkner. When he started writing, she was his first reader. He dedicated his first book to her, and the title of his second poetry collection, *The Marble Faun*, is like an echo of her name, Maud Faulkner. Her trust in him, her belief in him and in his vocation were unwavering. She had always known that he was brilliant, and at difficult times when everyone, even his closest relatives, abandoned or condemned him, at times when his failures might have shaken his faith in himself, she was by his side, giving him the strength to carry on.

(Afterthought: this man adored by his mother is the same novelist who puts the following words into the mouth of one of his heroes: "If I could say Mother. Mother" (*N1*, 949), and of another: "I cannot love my mother because I have no mother" (*N2*, 61). Mothers never love enough, it would seem.)

———

William Faulkner's other mother was black. Her official name was Caroline Barr, but Billy and his brothers called her Mammy Callie. We know that she was born in North Carolina, but the date remains uncertain: in 1840 according to the date on her gravestone, in 1844 according to the 1870 census. According to her, she was sixteen when she was emancipated, at which time she took the name of her former owner, Colonel Barr. She started as a servant to John Wesley Thompson Falkner and then worked for Billy's parents from 1902 after they moved to Oxford. Years later, when Billy, Estelle, and Estelle's children moved to Rowan Oak, Faulkner's primitive Greek Revival home, she moved into a small cabin behind their house.

Mammy Callie remained with the Faulkner family for almost forty years. Her status was highly ambiguous, like that of the "house niggers" under slavery. Like the Latin *gentes*, the old families of the South incorporated relations of bondage. Mammy Callie was a member of the Faulkner tribe. Although she did not share a table with her masters, she had a rocking chair beside the fireplace, where she sat and rocked in the evening, a wad of chewing tobacco under her lower lip, always clothed in a starched dress, a white apron, an immaculate kerchief, and her little buttoned boots. Physically, she did not look at all like the traditional "mammy"; she had nothing in common with the buxom nurturing mother of Southern legend. Like Miss Maud, she was small and slight, weighing barely 110 pounds, but as William's first brother, Jack, noted in his memoirs, "Like our Mother she was [. . .] big in will power and a sense of right and wrong" (*FOM*, 13). There was much affection between her and the little Falkners: according to John, they all loved Mammy; she was their shepherdess (*MBB*, 48). They also respected the authority delegated to her by Miss Maud, which she always exercised with discernment. As Jack said: "It was understood that, while Mother always had the last say, we were never to disobey Mammy Callie. And we never did—at least, not for long" (*FOM*, 13). All accounts agree that the place occupied by Mammy Callie within this white family was not simply that of a mere servant, and for the Falkner brothers she was indeed a second mother.

According to the writer's daughter, nobody was more important to the young Billy than Mammy Callie.[24] She was important as a maternal figure, providing the young Faulkner with the warm tenderness that Miss Maud was unable to give, and was also a valuable source of stories for the budding writer. Billy and his brothers used to listen to her for hours on end, recounting ghost stories and her memories of the time of slavery, the Civil War, Reconstruction, and the Ku Klux Klan. We know that she was the model—or at least one of the models—for Callie Nelson in *Soldiers' Pay*, Dilsey Gibson in *The Sound and the Fury*, Molly Beauchamp in *Go Down, Moses*, and Aunt Callie in *The Reivers*.

Mammy Callie died on the evening of January 31, 1940, at the age of one hundred or thereabouts. On February 4, as she had wished, Faulkner delivered her funeral oration, his eyes full of tears. The *Commercial Appeal*, a daily Memphis newspaper, published the oration (although we cannot be sure that the transcription is accurate). After the oration, at Faulkner's request, a choir sang "Swing Low, Sweet Chariot," Mammy's favorite hymn. Her headstone in the Oxford cemetery reads: "MAMMY Her white children bless her."

On February 7, 1940, Faulkner sent the full text of his oration to his editor Robert Haas:

> Caroline has known me all my life. It was my privilege to see her out of hers. After my father's death, to Mammy I came to represent the head of that family to which she had given a half century of fidelity and devotion. But the relationship between us never became that of master and servant. She still remained one of my earliest recollections, not only as a person, but as a fount of authority over my conduct and security for my physical welfare, and of active and constant affection and love. She was an active and constant precept for decent behavior. From her I learned to tell the truth, to refrain from waste, to be considerate of the weak and respectful to age. I saw fidelity to a family which was not hers, devotion and love for people she had not borne.
>
> She was born in bondage and with a dark skin and most of her early maturity was passed in a dark and tragic time for the land of her birth. She went through vicissitudes which she had not caused; she assumed cares and griefs which were not even her cares and griefs. [. . .] She was born and lived and served, and died and now is mourned; if there is a heaven, she has gone there. (*SL*, 118–19)

This text was not published until 1965 (see *ESPL*, 151–52). In the meantime, Faulkner used it to compose his dedication to her in *Go Down, Moses*:

To MAMMY
CAROLINE BARR
Mississippi
(1840–1940)
Who was born in slavery and who gave
to my family a fidelity without stint
or calculation of recompense and
to my childhood an immea-
surable devotion and
love

The portrait of Mammy Callie painted by Faulkner conforms to the notion of the mammy already seen in *Uncle Tom's Cabin* and after the Civil War in many Southern novels, from *Red Rock* (1898) by Thomas Nelson Page all the way to *Gone with the Wind* (1936). The canonized mammy of tradition was the perfect mother: nurturing, faithful, devoted, loving, with a wide smile and large breasts, both carnally powerful and completely desexualized. We now know that Mammy Callie had five husbands and many children. We know that at even up to the age of sixty, she still sometimes ran away; that from time to time she left without warning, heading for Tennessee or Arkansas with her latest lover; and that often many weeks would pass before she returned. John Falkner and Murry C. Falkner furtively refer to these escapades in their memoirs. William said nothing at all about them; the mammies in his fiction are all paragons of virtue.

CHILDHOOD

Each childhood is unique, each childhood multiple. William Cuthbert Faulkner had more than one birth, identified with more than one family, and invented more than one genealogy. In the spring of 1930, he instructed his friend Ben Wasson: "Tell them I was born of an alligator and a nigger slave at the Geneva peace conference two years ago" (SL, 48). According to the birth register, he was born on September 25, 1897, on Jefferson Street, New Albany, Union County, Mississippi, the first of four sons of Murry Cuthbert Falkner and Maud Butler.

It is not clear whether Faulkner, like Rousseau, thought of his birth as the first of his misfortunes, but his entry into the world was not auspicious. Billy was a tiny, sickly baby, prone to colic. He cried for nights on end, and night after night his mother rocked him in her arms to soothe him. Perhaps the colic was behind the somewhat neurotic relationship that Faulkner later had with nutrition and mastication, as evidenced in the words of Meta Carpenter: "People," said Bill, "should eat in the privacy of their rooms" (ALG, 35). The newborn's first contact with the world was not ideal, and the mother-child symbiosis would be seriously disrupted. Like all children, Billy would have preferred to remain an only child and have his mother all to himself. For a small child, a mother is not for sharing. But by the time he was two, his mother was no longer his alone; she no longer belonged solely to him, and he had to share her affections with Murry Charles Jr. ("Jack"), his first brother, an anorexic infant who monopolized the entire house for months on end. Billy became ill. Again, in October 1901, one month after the birth of John ("Johncy")—the day before his fourth birthday—both Billy and Jack contracted scarlet fever and almost died.

The Falkner family's move in September 1902 from Ripley to Oxford, where the Young Colonel lived, was another upheaval. However, apart from

Murry, nobody in the family was sorry to leave godforsaken Ripley, and as far as we know, Faulkner's childhood was a happy one. As one of his brothers tells it, for the little Falkners the arrival of Maud and her sons in Oxford on September 24, the day before Billy's fifth birthday, was a source of wonderment and the start of a grand adventure:

> We arrived at Oxford after dark and were met at the station by our grandfather and grandmother Falkner with some of their servants to aid in getting us to Grandfather's house, where we were to stay until Father arrived with the family furniture. We descended from the coach, and Bill and I were speechless with wonder; never had we seen so many people, so many horses and carriages, and so much movement everywhere. And the lights—arc lights! (B, 96)

A few days after their arrival, the Falkners settled into a comfortable house on Second South Street, where the family of John Wesley Thompson Falkner had lived for over a dozen years before recently moving to the Big Place.

At the time, Oxford had a population of two thousand, much more than Albany or Ripley. With its central square, courthouse, post office, stores, banks, and small restaurants, it offered all the amenities of a small town at the turn of the century. On Saturday the streets were lively, as farmers came to make purchases and sell their produce, and horses and mules were bought and sold. However, the small town was not an enclosed space; the fields and woods were very close by. Billy's childhood was that of a country boy, out in the open air among the hills and rivers like Tom Sawyer, like a Winslow Homer illustration. Since Miss Maud had decided that her sons would not go to school until the age of eight, Billy and his brothers spent their time playing marbles, hide-and-seek, and leapfrog; flying kites; riding their ponies; or watching the fruit trains from Louisiana lumbering noisily through Oxford at sunrise. Mammy Callie often took them for walks in the woods, where she taught them the names of the birds they saw. In the springtime they climbed trees, stealing eggs to add to their collection. Their little world was populated with animals: dogs, mules, cows, and horses, but also raccoons, wild cats, opossums, hares, squirrels, foxes, stags, and bears. Just under ten miles northeast of Oxford, where the Tippah River meets the Tallahatchie, the Falkners owned a large cabin called the Club House, where Billy and his brothers went to shoot squirrels and hunt opossums. They also fished for catfish in the muddy waters of Davidson's Creek. From the age of seven, Billy accompanied his father and grandfather to hunters' encampments out in the wilderness. A year later Murry began to teach him how to hunt and gave him an air gun. At ten he was given a .22 long rifle and at twelve a real hunting rifle.

Faulkner grew up with his brothers in a society that was still patriarchal, where male identity was unambiguous and defined according to a lofty code of manliness. However, his childhood did not lack female presence. There was his mother, of course, but also his grandmother, Alabama ("Aunt Bama"), his paternal great-aunt to whom he retained a lifelong attachment, and in lieu of a sister, his cousin Sallie Murry, the daughter of his aunt Mary Holland Wilkins, a tomboy who accompanied the little Falkners on their escapades and shared their games. Jack and John, Faulkner's two brothers, later mentioned the affection that bound them to her. "Throughout our childhood Sallie Murry and Bill and John and I could not have been any closer had we been sister and brothers," says Jack (*FOM*, 7). According to John, it was as if all four belonged to the same family (*MBB*, 70). Later, talking about Caddy Compson in *The Sound and the Fury*, Faulkner recalls that he had never had a sister and implies that it was to make up for this absence that he invented "my beautiful and tragic little girl."[25] There is good reason to think that the rebellious Sallie was one of the models for this character.

Billy was no child prodigy. He was a child among children, although not quite the same as the others. Not content with merely playing games of his age, he changed the rules or invented new ones. Neighboring children sometimes joined the little Falkners to help them build miniature villages. One of them remembers: "We built walks, streets, churches, and stores. Both William and his Grandmother were good at improvisation and at using materials to hand . . . William was the leader in these little projects. He had his Grandmother's artistic talents for making things, and his imagination was obvious even then" (*B*, 96). Billy was the boss; it was he who took the initiative and gave orders. His brothers trusted him and he readily took advantage of this authority, leading them up the garden path or utterly bewildering them. When Johncy was three, Billy asked him: "How can I be older than you when your birthday is the day before mine?" (87). But not all the stories were harmless. One day, from the top of the second-floor gallery of an uncle's office, the little horror sprayed passersby with his water pistol.

He had a fondness for nasty practical jokes and took advantage of his brothers' credulity to play mean tricks on them. One cold, frosty day, he talked them into putting their tongues on an iron rail used for attaching horses, knowing full well that they would get stuck. Another time, he staged a fake Christmas for his little brother John and convinced him that Father Christmas was coming, going as far as hanging up Christmas stockings and filling them with knick-knacks bought with his pocket money. He also convinced John that he would be able to fly with wings made of corn husks and encouraged him to jump from a third-floor window, at the risk of killing himself. Even at this early stage, he was a demon of perversity and mystification.

Miss Maud let her sons play their games, but she also unfailingly attended to their instruction and education. She taught them to read before they went to school, imparting her taste for reading and her love for literature, from primers and Brothers Grimm fairy tales to her own favorite writers. Thus Billy read Shakespeare, Fenimore Cooper, Balzac, Dickens, Conrad, and Victor Hugo. In later life he also recalled his grandfather's library, where he discovered Scott, Dumas, and *Quo Vadis*, the historical novel popular at the time that had won its author, the Polish writer Henryk Sienkiewicz, the Nobel Prize in Literature in 1905 (see *ESPL*, 226–27). But his early reading was not confined to novels. Billy was also an avid reader of *American Boy*, a magazine with modern pretensions, which often discussed steam engines and flying machines and which may have been the origin of his passion for aviation.

In September 1905, at age eight, Billy started attending the local school, and for the first two years all went well. He was a quiet, studious student and was moved up a class. As often happens with small boys, he was in love with his teacher, Miss Annie Chandler. But he had little interest in school and would happily have done without it. In one of his interviews at the University of Virginia, he said he had never liked going to school and had stopped going as soon as he was old enough to play truant without getting caught.[26]

For Billy the paradise of childhood was already fading. He first experienced loss and bereavement at about the age of ten, when both grandmothers died within six months of each other. Both of these two remarkable women were important figures to their grandson. The matriarch Sallie

McAlpine Murry Falkner, the Young Colonel's first wife, was very keen on history, particularly the Civil War. She founded a reading club and wrote poems, one of which was published in the *Oxford Eagle* under the initials S.M.F. Faulkner's maternal grandmother, Lelia Swift Butler, whom Billy and his brothers called Damuddy, was an intelligent woman with a frustrated vocation. In 1890 she had won a scholarship to study sculpture in Rome but gave it up to raise her daughter. When she came to stay with Maud and her grandchildren in Oxford in 1904, she had not lost her taste for the fine arts, spending hours in front of her easel, making dolls, and sculpting figurines out of soap and butter. For Billy she made a policeman eight inches tall, dressed in a blue uniform in the style of the nineteenth century, with a bell-shaped cap and shiny brass buttons. Billy called him Patrick O'Leary, made him his first character, and played with him in the attic on rainy days. It was also Damuddy who sometimes brought him to Sunday service at the First Baptist Church and made him read the Bible.

In late 1906, four days before Christmas, Sallie Murry Falkner died after suffering for long months from stomach cancer. The children, initially kept away, were allowed into the parlor of the Big Place to hear the pastor administer the last rites, and later they were admitted to the funeral cortege. At dusk on June 1, 1907, Damuddy, for whom Billy had a deep affection, also died of cancer, in the Falkner house, where she had stayed throughout her illness.

After these two deaths, another family event took place that was traumatic for Billy: the birth on August 15, 1907, of Dean Swift, the fourth son, named after his paternal grandmother who had just died. A happy Murry called him his birthday gift to his friends. Billy had greeted the arrival of his first two brothers by becoming sick, and although this time he did not take ill, he nevertheless seems to have seen the event as an act of betrayal and abandonment. Little Dean had a scalp disease, and Maud and Mammy Callie were kept busy for months preparing ointments and making silk bonnets—so busy, in fact, that his older brothers were left to their own devices or in the care of their grandfather.

After the birth of Dean, Billy's behavior changed. The ten-year-old withdrew, fell silent, became gloomy, and shut himself off. He became a distracted student, his grades slipped, and he became a dunce. One of his classmates would later remember him as a little chap who spent hours on the school playground watching rather than playing.[27] He was less and less diligent in his schoolwork. He played truant from time to time, and even when he deigned to attend class, his mind was elsewhere, indifferent to what was happening around him. He spent his time reading, writing, and drawing. Within the family he was considered to have inherited the artistic gifts of his maternal grandmother. He was already good at drawing, covering the margins of his books with sketches and making ink drawings for his school's yearbook. He loved books and stories from an early age. He loved listening to the hunting and fishing stories told by the men of Oxford in his father's stables, the reminiscences of Civil War veterans meeting on the main square near the courthouse, the anecdotes related by his paternal grandfather, and the stories of long ago that Mammy Callie told him. He soon became a captivating storyteller himself, keeping his brothers, cousins, and pals spellbound with fantastic tales of his own invention, and soon came to understand and exploit the market value of a story. In the winter of 1910, instead of bringing in the coal himself, he persuaded one of his friends, who was stronger than him, to do the job by telling him a story of his own devising, ending each day's installment on a note of suspense to keep him wanting to hear more. Already he was taking liberties with the truth; already he was blurring the boundary between fact and fiction. His cousin Sallie recalled that "when Billy told you something, you never knew if it was the truth or just something he'd made up."[28] Inspired by the wartime prestige and literary success of the ancestor whose name he bore, he already had a keen sense of his vocation. As early as age nine, when his teacher asked him what he wanted to do when he grew up, he invariably answered: "I want to be a writer like my great-grand-daddy."

In 1910, the year Billy turned thirteen, his mother noticed that he had developed poor posture and that his shoulders were slightly stooped. She decided to make him wear a corset, which could only have exacerbated his sense of being different. Although intended to straighten his back, the corset restricted his freedom of movement, thus limiting his sporting activities and putting him at a remove from friendship with boys of his own age. But Billy wore the corset without protest and seems even to have borne it as a sort of mortification. After two years it was removed and he was able to go back to playing baseball, rugby, and tennis.

Was he, as has been implied by most biographers, "traumatized" by these two years of wearing the corset? Nothing shows that he was affected on a lasting basis. All we know is that until the end of his days he had his own particular way of holding himself. However, this haughty and yet pathetic carriage, which surprised those meeting him for the first time as much as his small stature, may also have had something to do with his Southern identity. His mistress Meta Carpenter remembered him "walking like elderly Southern gentlemen I remembered from childhood—the lower torso thrust forward, the upper part of him leaning backward, so that he was slanted in motion, so that he was almost tilted" (*ALG*, 16–17).

In 1912 Murry's livery stables were flagging. Murry was drinking. The atmosphere in the family was gloomy. It was at this time that another family began to draw the attention of the young Falkners, particularly Billy. It was the Oldhams, who had moved to a large house on South Lamar Street in 1903, four hundred yards from the Young Colonel's house. The Oldhams were one of the grandest families in town. After studying law at the University of Mississippi, Lemuel Earl Oldham was appointed a circuit court judge and later a judge of the federal court of Mississippi. His beautiful wife, Lida, née Allen, counted among her ancestors the legendary Sam Houston, who was not only the first governor of Texas but also a general in the Civil War, an Episcopalian bishop, and a member of Congress. Republican in a South that was still overwhelmingly Democratic, the Oldhams were not really popular in Oxford, but this was of little consequence to them. They lived very comfortably, boasted an impressive ancestry, and in any case held themselves to be superior to their neighbors and fellow citizens, including the Falkners. This was more than class consciousness—it was caste arrogance. However, this did not prevent them from entertaining, which they loved to do. Of course, their house was not open to all; only people from the same world were invited. The Oldhams threw parties at Halloween and on Christmas morning, when the traditional eggnog was served. Receptions at the Oldhams were worldly affairs, and their house was one of those, rare in Oxford, where room was made for culture and where people were interested in art and music. There were two grand pianos in the parlor; Lida was an excellent pianist and often played duets with her daughters. There was also a tennis court behind the house, and between games a maid would come and serve lemonade. The Oldhams lived in grand style and did not hide it. In Oxford they were considered very grand indeed.

For the adolescent Faulkner, they became like a second family—a happy family, or at least one that he perceived as happy, and therefore very different from his own. This family was, to him, like a delayed version of Freud's *Familienroman*, the individual myth that children invent to overcome the disappointment created by their real family. In the Oldhams, Billy found, or believed he had found, what he could not find in his own family: a relaxed atmosphere, a refined lifestyle, and a shared taste for the arts. He was often at their house, ate with them, kissed the mother's hand, and sometimes acted as chauffeur for the father.

And then there was Estelle, pretty little Estelle, the eldest daughter, whom Billy got to know in the Big Place when she came to play dolls with his cousin Sallie. Estelle was precocious, already showing her femininity, already playing the lady. She loved lace and ribbons and was already being noticed for her mannerisms. She was a flirt and was already exercising her charms on boys. It has been said that she cast a spell on little Billy at the early age of seven, when her family had just settled in Oxford, and that one day, seeing the three brothers pass by her window, she said to Magnolia, her nurse: "See that little boy? I'm going to marry him when I grow up" (B1, 16). Estelle and Billy were attracted to each other because they were alike. They had the same love of reading; the same propensity for daydreaming; probably the same desire to stand out, to be noticed, and, if possible, admired; and the same expectation that their destiny would be out of the ordinary. They soon fell in love. Later, Estelle recalled that they met every day in the meadows and fields, watching clouds and interpreting their shapes. They were already making plans and saw themselves as married, living happily in the country as chicken farmers.[29]

THE ATTITUDES OF ADOLESCENCE

Adolescence is a troubled time, a search for identity. Faulkner's adolescence did not start well. In contrast to the Oldhams, his family had fewer resources and were finding it increasingly difficult to keep up appearances. Now almost seventeen, Billy was becoming increasingly withdrawn. He gave up sports, read everything he could lay his hands on, wandered through the hills, watched people, and listened in on their conversations. His solitary ramblings took him at times to western Mississippi, where he met the River

People who fed him chocolate cake and possum pie. He also toured the Gulf of Mexico, Memphis, the Delta, and New Orleans (*LP*, 49–50).

Billy wanted to live his life, even though he didn't know where he was going. He certainly had no intention of pursuing the ready-made path of a professional career. Although worried, his mother held her faith in him. His father was not happy, but Billy paid little heed to his reproaches. While not outwardly disrespectful of Murry, he held him in low esteem and, cruelly, never failed to display this when the opportunity arose. One day his father was in a good mood and offered him a big cigar. Billy thanked him politely, broke the cigar in two, stuffed his father's pipe with half of the cigar, and lit it. His father watched him without saying a word, then turned and walked away. As Faulkner later joked: "He never gave me another" (*B1*, 52).

Even though he did not get along with his father, he never abandoned his family. However, adolescence changed his view of it and he began to feel suffocated. In his last year of school, he met Phil Stone, the youngest son of "General" James Stone, a lawyer and banker just like his own grandfather. Four years older than Faulkner, Stone was studying law at Yale. A classics graduate, he was a lover of literature. Having heard that Billy wrote poetry, he was eager to meet him. The young men became friends and saw each other often between 1914 and 1916. Each time Stone returned from Yale, he found Faulkner on the veranda of the white-columned Stone mansion, where they talked literature or politics while drinking iced tea served by a black servant. The Stone house had a huge library with rare books such as the first edition of Swinburne's *Laus Veneris* given to L.Q.C. Lamar, the previous owner of the house, by Jefferson Davis.

Without making a great fuss of his poems, Stone quickly sensed Faulkner's genius. "Anybody could have seen that he had a real talent,"[30] he later stated.

But it was not enough for Stone to acknowledge this; he soon took on the role of mentor and started to play Pygmalion. He subsequently overestimated his role in the formation of the writer, and his childishness and bad faith with regard to Faulkner's work after the awarding of the Nobel Prize in Literature suggests that he did not really understand it. Stone never forgave his friend for having so speedily extricated himself from his influence and was clearly jealous of his success. Nevertheless, during these years he was a major influence on the young Faulkner: "There was no one but me with whom William Faulkner could discuss his literary plans and hopes and his technical trials and aspirations. [. . .] Day after day for years—and his most formative years at that—he had drilled into him the obvious truths that the world owed no man anything; that true greatness was in creating great things and not in pretending them; that the only road to literary success was by sure, patient, hard intelligent work."[31] In 1916 things had not yet reached this stage. Billy was facing even more failure at school. This time even John Wesley Thompson Falkner, his grandfather, was worried. To give his grandson a taste of work, he took him on in January as a bookkeeper at his bank. Billy agreed willingly enough to spend a few hours at the bank every day, although nobody ever saw him actually doing any work there. He probably spent the time reading, writing, and working his way through his grandfather's liquor cabinet—he was already drinking more than was reasonable. Later, he joked about this time in his life: "Quit school after five years in seventh grade. Got job in Grandfather's bank and learned medicinal value of his liquor. Grandfather thought janitor did it. Hard on janitor" (*SL*, 47). This was the beginning of what soon turned into chronic alcoholism. At hunting parties Bill drank corn mash moonshine made in the pine forests. At eighteen he spent entire nights in the company of Charlie Crouch, the town drunk. Miss Maud was appalled and disapproving to see her son coming home after his nighttime excursions, appearing at breakfast disheveled and reeking of alcohol. Although he was rarely seen drunk, everyone noticed that he was drinking heavily. In the South at that time, drinking was still considered to be an affirmation of manliness. Like his slim moustache, the young Faulkner's alcoholism was a way of showing anyone who may not have already noticed that he was now a man.

It may also have been a way of forgetting his small stature. Although his father was well-built and at least two of his brothers—John and Jack— were tall and broad-shouldered, Faulkner took after his short mother (like Reverend Shegog in *The Sound and the Fury*, Popeye in *Sanctuary*, Rosa Coldfield in *Absalom, Absalom!*, and Flem and Mink in *The Hamlet*) and for a long time suffered from the fact that he measured just five feet four. How could he prevent people from looking down on him? This question tormented him so much that he asked one of his Clarksdale friends if she knew of a way of growing taller, and when she asked why he was so eager to gain a couple of inches, he answered: "I think it would be a pretty good life for a while."[32] In the early 1930s, when one of his brothers complimented him on his recent success as a novelist, he explicitly linked this to his size: "Well," the writer answered, "as big as you are, you can march anywhere you want, but when you're little you have to push" (B, 658). Later, to Meta Carpenter, whom he loved and who loved him, he said: "I'm short and not much to look at" (ALG, 80).

His short stature is not enough to explain either the man or his work. Nevertheless, Faulkner was painfully self-conscious about it and had a significant inferiority and insecurity complex, particularly in his love affairs. He tried everything to make other people forget about it, and it was arguably one of the reasons for his two great passions, aviation and riding. Riding a horse and flying high are two ways of becoming taller and more elevated, of gaining height.

In a 1958 interview at the University of Virginia, when asked why Sherwood Anderson had introduced so many tall characters in *Winesburg, Ohio*, he answered as follows:

> It could be that that was his first book, the first writing he did, and probably more of his own subconscious wishes appeared in that than would have appeared if he had got in the habit of writing and discharging that younger. He was getting along toward forty years old when he wrote that book. He was a short man that probably all his boyhood had wished he were bigger so he could fight better, defend himself. It could be that that is the reason, though it may be that he simply admired tall people whatever the reason that some people admire tall people. But it's just possible it was because he himself was short— when he was sitting behind a table like this he looked like a big man, but when he stood up he wasn't. And I think that he maybe would have liked to have been more imposing-looking, that at that time he didn't realize that probably it's not how high a man is, it's what in his face that makes him imposing-looking. (FU, 259–60)

In speaking about Anderson, Faulkner was speaking about himself. Being different from others worried him, but at the same time he felt the need to accentuate his difference, to make it even more visible and more provocative in the way he dressed. As far back as age ten, he had sought to differentiate himself by sporting a boater. In 1916, when he started to work for his grandfather, elegance seems to have become a major preoccupation. On working days he could be seen every morning dressed to the nines and walking in a very dignified manner toward his grandfather's bank, in the shade of elm and holm oak trees. Although relatively poorly paid, he opened an account in a men's store in Memphis and bought luxury shoes and seventeen-dollar suits that he then had altered by his mother so that they would fit him better. Also, while most Oxford students rented their evening suits for grand occasions, Faulkner bought a sumptuous "Styleplus" suit for twenty-five dollars. An extraordinary photograph taken in 1918 shows him at twenty-one, posing as a young dandy in a dark, tailored suit, light-checked waistcoat, white shirt with a high starched collar, and broad-striped silk tie, his hair impeccably combed and parted down the middle, leaning slightly on a walking stick, his head bowed as if in thought.[33] His outfits changed, however. A year later, at the start of the university year, his future friend Ben Wasson encountered a "small slight fellow" on campus, "wearing a pair of baggy, gray flannel trousers, a rather shabby tweed jacket and heavy, brown brogans."[34] It didn't matter whether he dressed as a dandy or as a bohemian; the important thing was not to go unnoticed.

Faulkner could no longer imagine his life without Estelle Oldham. He wanted to marry her. But as far as Estelle's parents were concerned, that was out of the question. Before she could even think of marriage, their eldest daughter had to complete her education. In the fall of 1913, Estelle left Oxford for Mary Baldwin College, a bastion of Presbyterianism in Staunton, Virginia. This first separation, together with the severe atmosphere of the institution, weighed on Estelle. In 1915 she returned to Oxford and persuaded her parents to let her enroll as an unregistered student at the University of Mississippi, where she took courses in English, philosophy, and psychology. It was the beginning of the happiest time of her life. She was slim, delicate, almost frail, but also "as pretty as a little partridge" (to use Jack Falkner's description). Nobody could withstand her charm; all were seduced by her chatter and gracious manners and impressed by her stylish, extravagant grooming. An alluring, manipulative tease, this pint-size Southern belle already knew how to handle herself with boys, how to flatter them and turn their heads while giving them nothing. According to Ben Wasson, who knew her well: "She was always thoroughly absorbed in whatever a man was saying to her. One would have thought, watching her as she listened to a man, that he was the most fascinating and brilliant creature in the world" (*CNC*, 77).

Emily Whitehurst Stone, Phil Stone's wife, remembered that "the boys were just crazy about Estelle. She just looked like skin and bones, a walking skeleton, but she had whatever it takes" (*LP*, 44). She soon became the darling of the University of Mississippi, or "Ole Miss." Estelle attended all the society parties and balls at Gordon Hall, where black Memphis musicians came to play, such as the renowned trumpet player W. C. Handy, "father of the blues" and the (disputed) author of "St. Louis Blues," "Memphis Blues," "Yellow Dog Blues," and "Beale Street Blues." As the fashion for the tango and the Charleston did not arrive until the madcap 1920s, people danced the waltz, the foxtrot, and the one-step on these occasions. Bill also came to these balls but more as an observer than a participant. A poor dancer (earning him the nickname of "leaping toad"), he sometimes asked Estelle to leave the person she was dancing with to dance with him. The rest of the time, he watched from the sidelines, saying nothing.

For the Oldhams it was understood that Estelle would marry a young man from their own world, wealthy if possible. Cornell Franklin, an ambitious businessman, good-looking, and from a good family, seemed to them to fit the bill perfectly. But Estelle was not in love with him any more than she was with her other beaus, and without rejecting him outright, she let her reservations be known. When her mother asked her why she was not wearing the magnificent engagement ring Cornell gave her, she responded that she had lost it, while in fact she had hidden it at the back of a drawer. She told Bill that she was ready to run away with him, but the elopement did not happen. Estelle did not really have the strength to withstand her parents. The day before the wedding, she allegedly cried all night. Nonetheless, she spurned Bill and married Cornell in accordance with her parents' wishes. The wedding was celebrated in the First Presbyterian Church of Oxford on April 18, 1918. It was a splendid affair, making the headline of the *Oxford Eagle*. The bridesmaids were dressed in pink georgette; Cornell, all in white, was resplendent, with gilded braiding and a ceremonial sword hanging from his black leather belt. Estelle wore a sumptuous dress of white satin brocade, with a train and needlepoint lace trimming, and a cone of orange blossoms on her veil.

Faulkner did not come to the wedding; in fact, he left Oxford to avoid having to attend. However, in a letter sent to his mother on April 21, he asked in a postscript to be told "about Estelle's wedding" (*LMF*, 52).

In August 1914 World War I broke out. Three years later the United States entered the war. For the time being, the prestige of action seems to have appealed to the young Faulkner more than literary glory. As he said himself in his foreword to *The Faulkner Reader*, published in 1954: "because I hadn't thought of writing books then. The future didn't extend that far. This was 1915 and 1916; I had seen an aeroplane and my mind was filled with names: Ball, and Immelman and Boelcke, and Guynemer and Bishop, and I was waiting, biding, until I would be old enough or free enough or anyway could get to France and become glorious and beribboned too" (*ESPL*, 180).

At twenty Bill had dreams but as yet no plans. The ideal for him would have been a heroic life, brief and glorious, ending in a "glorious death" like the young hothead Achilles in Homer's Greece. In "Carcassonne," his fine prose poem written in 1925 or 1926, his double, the cavalryman poet, proclaims his desire to accomplish something "bold and tragic and austere," picturing himself "on a buckskin pony with eyes like blue electricity and a mane like tangled fire, galloping up the hill and right off into the high heaven of the world" (*CS*, 895). When Faulkner wrote this lyrical text, he was no longer a young man, but he still remembered the dream of weightlessness, ascent, and apotheosis of the young man he had been.

For the young Faulkner, as for other young Americans in search of heroism, the United States' entry into the war in April 1917 was an unexpected opportunity to achieve the desire for a dazzling destiny and a sublime death. His first thought was to enlist in the army (at the time, the air force was still attached to the signal corps), but he was not yet twenty and feared that he would be thought too small and too frail. Later he said that before going to the recruitment center, he had stuffed himself with bananas and drunk as much water as possible to achieve the required weight, but, as with almost everything he told subsequently about his military "experience," this was pure fabrication. In fact, it has not even been proven that he attempted to enlist in 1917—there is no official record of this.

In early April 1918, at the invitation of his friend Phil Stone, Faulkner left Oxford for New Haven, Connecticut. Stone put him up in his apartment at 120 York Street and found him a job as a bookkeeper in an arms factory, the Winchester Repeating Arms Company. "I don't think he is going to be homesick," Stone wrote his mother. "I have introduced him around to all of my friends and acquaintances, some of them rather brilliant people, and they seem to like him very much. He is a fine, intelligent little fellow and I think that he is going to do a lot some day; I certainly am glad that I got him away from Oxford for he was just going to seed there."[35] In New Haven, Faulkner spent time in the Brick Row Book Shop on 104 High Street, where he met Stephen Vincent Benét, still a very young poet, and Robert Hillyer, an older poet who had been in the war.

He had not given up on his plan to enlist in the army and now tried to find a place in the prestigious Canadian Royal Air Force (formerly the Royal Flying Corps). In early June he contacted the British consul in New York. On June 7, 1918, he wrote to his parents from New Haven:

> It's the chance I've been waiting for now. Everything will be my way, I can almost have my pick of anything, I'll be in at the wind up of the show. The chances of advancement in the English army are very good; I'll perhaps be a major at the end of a year's service. I have thought about it constantly. This chance will not last [. . .]. I shall probably have to enlist in the line and take my chances of promotion, which I'd rather do than get in the U.S. Army [. . .]. It's rather hard to explain in a letter just how I feel, but you both know that already, how badly I've always desired to go. At the rate I am living now, I'll never be able to make anything of myself, but with this business I will be fixed up after the war is over. (*LMF*, 63–64)

On June 14 he presented himself at the RAF's New York recruitment office, passing himself off as English, with false papers that stated that he had been born in London and was living there and fake letters from an imaginary pastor declaring that he was indeed a gentleman. The next day he resigned from the Winchester company to return home to Oxford, where he spent a few days before leaving for New York in early July. He was then sent to Toronto to be officially inducted. Having passed all of his tests, he was accepted as a "cadet for pilot." Like the other recruits, he was given a uniform, a gray woolen greatcoat, and a cap with a white band identifying him as a student pilot. He initially spent three weeks at the Jesse Ketchum School, learning the rudiments of military discipline. Then on July 26, having become a member of the cadet squadron, he was transferred to Long Branch camp, northwest of Toronto, on the banks of Lake Ontario, where he received ground training for five months and learned about telegraphy, topography, navigation, and aerodynamics. On September 20 he entered the military aeronautical school at Wycliffe College, which at the time was part of the University of Toronto.

There was no question of raw recruits taking flying lessons before completing basic training, and the armistice was signed before these lessons even started. But for Faulkner that didn't matter. The young cadet was not inclined to bow before the caprices of history. Moreover, throughout his time in Canada, his inventiveness became even more fertile than before. He passed himself off as eight months younger and increasingly identified himself as a young English gentleman. He told others he was an Anglican, claimed to have been born in Finchley in the county of Middlesex, referred to his acquaintances in the English aristocracy and to hunting parties, and passed himself off as a graduate of Yale. His English accent was impeccable.

In his weekly letters to his mother and other family members, his lies were just as self-assured. As early as August, he reported on his flights, and on November 24, 1918, a fortnight after the armistice and shortly before he was demobilized, he complained to his parents: "I am rather disappointed in the Royal Flying Corps, that is, in the way they have treated us, however. I have got my four hours solo to show for it, but they wont give us pilot's certificates even. Nothing but discharges as second airmen. It's a shame. Even the chaps who have their commissions and are almost through flying are being discharged the same way" (*LMF*, 135).

When his brother Murry asked him if he had had any flight incidents, he replied:

Yes, I did, as a matter of fact. The war quit on us before we could do anything about it. The same day they lined up the whole class, thanked us warmly for whatever it was they figured we had done to deserve it, and announced that we would be discharged the next day, which meant that we had the afternoon to celebrate the Armistice and some airplanes to use in doing it. I took up a rotary-motored Spad with a crock of bourbon in the cockpit, gave diligent attention to both, and executed some reasonably adroit chandelles, an Immelman or two, and part of what could easily have turned out to be a nearly perfect loop. (*FOM*, 90–91)

On November 11, 1918, a week after his ground training, the armistice was signed, and in December Faulkner was demobilized and sent home. The war ended before he had had time to learn to fly an airplane and die a hero's death in the skies above France. His brother Jack, who had enlisted at the age of nineteen in the marines, had seen action on the French front, been gassed in Champagne, and received shrapnel wounds in the right knee and in the head in the Forest of Argonne. It was not until late December that the family learned he was still alive and would be due home soon. While Jack actually went to war and very nearly never came home, Bill had to invent his war.

Like Cadet Julian Lowe at the start of *Soldiers' Pay*, his first novel, and later like Percy Grimm in *Light in August* and David Levine in *A Fable*, the young Faulkner felt that "they had stopped the war on him" (*N1*, 3). Imagination, therefore, took over where the facts were lacking. In early December 1918, when Faulkner returned home, the family gathered on the platform of the Oxford railway station to witness a dashing young officer in RAF uniform alighting from the train. With his Expeditionary Corps cap, his Sam Browne belt, and the wings stitched onto his tunic, the outfit was complete. He had a slight limp and was leaning on a walking stick. What nobody knew at the time was that the lieutenant's uniform and braiding had been bought and that the limp was affected. In the weeks that followed, Faulkner persisted with the deception: he continued to strut about everywhere in uniform, saluted any real veterans he met on the street, and willingly let himself be photographed in his handsome lieutenant's uniform, in a variety of poses and with varying accessories (a cigarette dangling from the corner of his mouth, leather gloves, a cane, a pocket handkerchief inserted in his sleeve). He cultivated an elegant limp and never went anywhere without his walking stick in order to give the impression that he had been wounded in the leg during a flight. He even told anyone who cared to listen that he had had a metal plate implanted in his skull following another injury.

Claiming Jack's injuries for his own, perhaps without even realizing it, he lied to his parents, his brothers, his friends, and later his son-in-law, his mistresses, his editors, his colleagues in Hollywood, and his doctors, and he persisted in these lies for a very, very long time. In the fall of 1921, during his first visit to New York, and in 1925 in New Orleans, he continued to refer to his glittering service record in the RAF and to limp as a result of his feigned injury. In an issue of the New Orleans–based *Double Dealer* on which he collaborated, readers learned that he had been seriously injured. In early 1930, when *Forum* purchased "A Rose for Emily," his first short story to appear in a national magazine, he sent the chief editor a biographical notice that reads as follows: "War came. Liked British uniform. Got commission R.F.C., pilot. Crashed. Cost British gov't £ 2000. Was still pilot. Crashed. Cost British gov't £ 2000. Quit. Cost British gov't $ 84.30. King said, 'Well done'" (*SL*, 47).

Even in his most intimate relationships, Faulkner boasted of his wartime exploits. He had Meta Carpenter believe that his airplane had been shot down on a mission over France. She did not learn the truth until after his death. The legend was so widely believed that in 1945 Malcolm Cowley, presenting the writer in his anthology, repeated the tale of the wounded aviator. After consulting the 1942 edition of *Twentieth-Century Authors*, a usually trustworthy reference work, he wrote in his introduction that Faulkner had trained to be a pilot in Canada, that he had "served at the front in the Royal Air Force, and, after his plane was damaged in combat, had crashed behind the British lines" (*FCF*, 87). However, this time Faulkner, fearing that his imposture would be exposed and without telling all the truth, convinced Cowley to write only that "he was a member of the RAF in 1918" (92, 98).

Faulkner's war memories were false memories, his injuries purely imaginary. But as we know, imaginary injuries, invisible injuries can be real and can take as long, if not longer, to heal than others. The war haunted Faulkner to the extent that later, in his drunken ravings, he relived moments of anguish and terror during air combat that he could only have experienced in his imagination. Meta heard him scream: "They're going to get me! Oh, Lordy, oh, Jesus!" [. . .] "They are coming down at me! Don't let them! They're coming at me! No! No!" And when she asked him what was wrong, he answered: "The Jerries! Can't you see them? [. . .] Here they come again! They're after me! They're trying to shoot me out of the sky. The goddamm Jerries, they are out to kill me. Oh, merciful Jesus!" (*ALG*, 143).

It is unlikely that Faulkner was faking his dreams. His fake injuries were real traumas; his false memories begat real nightmares.

———

That said, he was a faker; he liked to cheat. But cheating does not just mean misleading; it also means rewriting history. Throughout his life, Faulkner applied himself to rewriting history, to hiding faults. He played tricks with the truth, skirted around it, and made up new truths. He lied in order to breathe easier.

The ennui of just being oneself can become unbearable. This is what makes some turn to writing novels. The novelist is someone who needs to elude himself, to go see elsewhere and perhaps not just in his dreams or when he is writing. He needs these imaginary worlds and his doubles not just to invent them but also to play with them and to put them into play, to put them on the stage and dramatize them, to find an audience for them. Faulkner loved to surprise and mystify those close to him, and, as Ben Wasson notes, he displayed from childhood "a rare ability to dramatize himself interestingly."[36] Loath to inhabit his banal civil identity, he invented other identities for himself. Later, after he became a novelist, he brought imaginary characters to life in his invented tales. For now, he acted out these roles and watched himself perform. He created innumerable masks. It is pointless to look for a face behind these masks, or if we do, the face must be apprehended as the total of these masks. In any event, to become somebody, one needs to start by pretending, by taking on and playing a role.

In 1919, at the age of twenty-one, Faulkner found himself back in Oxford with no qualifications, no resources, and no plans. Oxford started to weigh on him. He wanted to go and live elsewhere. But his mother was ill and wanted him to stay, at least until Jack came home. As with all demobilized soldiers, he was offered the opportunity to go to college. After a summer of indolence, drinking, and poker games, he eventually resigned himself and registered at Ole Miss for French, Spanish, and English literature on September 19, 1919. However, he was no more assiduous as a student than he had been as a pupil and did not take any exams. He also kept himself aloof, maintaining a haughty distance. According to a classmate, they "found him queer. He spoke to no one unless directly addressed. He mingled not at all with his classmates." Another student remembered a literature professor asking him, after reading a monologue from *Othello*: "Mr. Faulkner, what did Shakespeare have in mind when he put those words in the mouth of Othello?" "How should I know?" Faulkner replied. "That was nearly four hundred years ago, and I was not there" (*B*, 251). Extravagant, insolent, arrogant, a poser, and a show-off, Faulkner was not popular on campus and his first poems were mocked and pastiched. It was at this time that people started to called him Count No 'Count, a nickname that made fun of both his aristocratic airs and his chronic poverty and stuck with him long after he had left college.

In the summer of 1920, to make a little money he did odd jobs here and there, including a stint as a painter. At one stage he even used ropes so that he could paint the spire of a bell tower without assistance. However, he was also seen on the tennis courts and golf courses. He met up with friends and made new ones, and as soon as he had a few dollars in his pocket, he went up to Memphis with his friend Phil Stone to do the round of the speakeasies, gambling dens, and bordellos of Gayoso and Mulberry Street. There, he drank beer or bourbon and chatted with the girls, although he was never seen going upstairs. From time to time, he also went to Clarksdale, a blues town in the Delta. On these trips he made friends with some slightly shady characters, such as the flamboyant Reno DeVaux, a former professional gambler and owner of New Christal Gardens; Dot Wilcox, who owned a beauty salon; and Mary Sharon, an ample-bosomed brothel keeper, who later was the inspiration for Miss Reba in *Sanctuary*, *The Mansion*, and *The Reivers*. However, he had not yet left childhood behind. He loved to play with Dean, his youngest brother, and a neighbor's two sons, taking them to the nearby woods with their friends, teaching them how to handle a rifle and the rudiments of hunting, and thrilling them with his stories around the evening campfire.

In the fall of 1920 Faulkner reregistered at Ole Miss. Along with Ben Wasson and Lucy Somerville, he founded a drama club called the Marionettes and wrote a short play of the same title. However, at twenty-three he dropped out at the start of his second year at college, without any qualifications. Talking later about his time at Ole Miss, he confided in Cowley: "attended 1 year at University of Mississippi [. . .], studying European languages, still didn't like school and quit that. Rest of education undirected reading" (*SL*, 212). Undirected? Not quite. Encouraged by his mother, Faulkner had been an avid reader since childhood. He had read and reread not only the Bible, the Greek tragedies, and Shakespeare but also *Don Quixote* and the great classical and premodern novelists. He read and reread all of Fielding, Scott, Dickens, Dumas, Balzac, Flaubert, Melville, Henry James, Dostoyevsky, Conrad, and Proust. We also know that he had read a good deal of *Ulysses* in the early 1920s and that he had started out as a great lover of poetry, reading most of the great nineteenth- and early twentieth-century English and French poets, from Keats and Swinburne to T. S. Eliot and from Baudelaire to Mallarmé and Verlaine. Admittedly, this Francophile's French was atrocious, he did not have as much grounding in theology as Joyce, and his pictorial culture bore little comparison to that of Proust or Beckett. According to several accounts, he was indifferent to music (although most of the women he loved were music lovers and musicians) and readily expressed his preference for "the thunder and music of prose [which] take place in silence" (*LG*, 248).[37] But one should always take Faulkner's public declarations with a pinch of salt, as his work contains many musical references and music is present in several of his titles. "That Evening Sun," the title of a short story initially published as "That Evening Sun Go Down," comes from the song "St. Louis Blues" by W. C. Handy; "Go Down, Moses" is from a Negro spiritual sung by black slaves; "If I Forget Thee, Jerusalem" comes from a psalm; and "Requiem for a Nun," the title of which he was most proud, echoes the grand requiem masses composed by Mozart, Verdi, Berlioz, and Fauré.

Although he started out as a provincial self-educated man, Faulkner was nevertheless a writer of immense culture, who, although wary of the strident modernism of the militant avant-garde movements, was extremely attentive to all signs of modernity. To see him as an untrained genius is to do him a disservice. Faulkner was no Proust in clogs and dungarees.

But at the start of the 1920s he was still a nobody. With no stable employment and more broke than ever, he gave up the elegant outfits that had cost his parents so much. There would be no more dandy. There would be no question of paying out to maintain an elegant figure, at least in the short term. But Faulkner was never short of a role. His repertoire expanded to include that of a barefoot, hairy hobo. The young Faulkner now wore old torn pants, moth-eaten sweaters, and mismatching socks—sometimes even mismatched shoes. He no longer looked after his mustache, shaved less often, and let his hair grow.

The warrior, the dandy, and the hobo are all marginal figures outside the normal rules of conduct. For Faulkner these were provisional, borrowed identities. Through these three eccentric modes of opposing prevailing conventionality, he distanced himself and cultivated his singular difference. These three identities can be found in his novels, in characters who gamble their lives away because they can't or won't take responsibility.

However, Faulkner himself only partly yields to temptation; his identifications are playful rather than alienating. Pretending for fun, pulling the wool over people's eyes, means performing roles without investing in them, without taking the risk of forgetting oneself, of losing oneself. And Faulkner did not perform just for himself, alone in front of the mirror. There can be no role without a theater, no actor without an audience. Faulkner's antisocial nature needed an audience in order to be acknowledged and accepted as such, but this acknowledgment and acceptance canceled out the antisocial stance so that it became nothing but comedy. Later, after he became a famous writer, Faulkner continued to play with masks, his favorite being the grouchy bear.

In the meantime, Billy's eccentricities and alcoholism were starting to set people talking. The people of Oxford did not rate his chances very highly. Even those close to him were starting to become exasperated and turn away from him. His father's brother, John Wesley Thompson Falkner Jr., a judge and banker known for his harsh frankness, readily condemned him in public. "He's a Falkner," he said to a group of men gathered in front of the First National Bank, "and I hate to say it about my own nephew, but, hell, there's a black sheep in everybody's family and Billy's ours. Not worth a cent." (B1, 117–18). Would this young man of means turn out to be a good-for-nothing, just like his father, albeit differently?

In the fall of 1921, with forty dollars to his name, he took the train to New York City for the first time. The Mississippian novelist Stark Young, introduced to him by Phil Stone and who had urged him to make the trip, let Faulkner borrow his studio for a few days and found him a job in Manhattan, at the Doubleday bookshop at the corner of Thirty-Eighth Street and Fifth Avenue. At the time, the shop was run by a friend of Young's, Elizabeth Prall, the future Mrs. Sherwood Anderson.[38] Faulkner impressed the customers with his competence and charmed the female clientele (especially the older ladies) with his courteous manners, his English accent, and his very British elegance. He turned out to be an excellent salesman. After a few days he left Young's studio and moved into an unheated garret at 655 Lexington Avenue, near Central Park, subsequently moving to a more comfortable room at 35 Vandam Street in Greenwich Village, paying $3.50 a week in rent. During his free time, he set off to discover New York. In a letter to his mother, he described his first trip on the subway: "The experience showed me that we are not descended from monkeys, as some say, but from lice. I never saw anything like it. Great crowds of people cramming underground, and pretty soon here comes a train, and I swear I believe the things are going a mile a minute when they stop. Well, everybody crowds on, the guards bawling and shoving, then off again, at top speed. Its like being shot through a long piece of garden hose" (*LMF*, 157–58). A fervent admirer of painting, he visited the Metropolitan Museum of Art and saw "some priceless statues and paintings, some marvelous water colors by Cezanne and some of Americans" (159). He also spent long hours reading and writing poetry and fiction. His alcohol intake continued apace, and Young was amazed at the capacity of this slim young man of twenty-four to imbibe such quantities. The Bohemian atmosphere of Greenwich Village suited him, and he thought New York City both wonderful and unpleasant (159), but he didn't plan to stay—he wanted to go home. His first stay in New York lasted only a few weeks. He would return many times but never again lived there for any length of time.

On December 10, 1921, he was back in Oxford. This was the start of the most Chaplinesque episode of his life—Faulkner the postman. Stone had written him that the position of postmaster at the University of Mississippi was vacant and urged him to apply. Although he took the exam, his appointment was merely a formality, because his application was backed by his future father-in-law, the influential Lem Oldham, meaning that the other two candidates had no chance. Faulkner was immediately appointed acting postmaster and was made permanent in March 1922. His annual salary was fifteen hundred dollars, but he does not seem ever to have entertained the idea of seriously fulfilling his duties. He was incredibly casual in doing his job, even though his new duties were not particularly onerous. All he had to do was sort and deliver the mail and sell stamps at the counter. Faulkner left letters and packages to accumulate in his little office on campus—some were even found in the garbage—and paid little heed to his customers. He preferred to spend his time writing, composing poems and drafting reviews, or reading the *Atlantic Monthly*, the *New Republic*, the *Nation*, or the *Dial*, the magazines and reviews ordered by subscribers, drinking whiskey, or playing bridge with his friends. His absences, provocative manner, and negligence eventually brought him to the attention of the authorities. On September 2, 1924, Mark Webster, a postal inspector, sent him a three-page letter setting out the complaints of thirty-three users and listing his many shortcomings, accusing him of reading magazines and writing a book while on duty, of inviting friends to play cards or dominoes, of leaving the office to play golf, and of having no interest in delivering the mail. Faulkner was ordered to reply to these accusations within five days. The authenticity of this letter has not been established, and it is not entirely impossible that Phil Stone had a hand in writing it.[39] If Faulkner did respond, his letter has not survived. However, we do know that a few days later he told one of his fellow card players: "I reckon I'll be at the beck and call of folks with money all my life, but thank God I won't ever again have to be at the beck and call of every son of a bitch who's got two cents to buy a stamp" (B1, 118).

Officially "allowed to resign," he handed over the keys, the books, and thirteen hundred dollars in receipts to his successor on October 31, 1924. That same year, he also resigned as scoutmaster for the Oxford Boy Scout troop, a position that he had held for several months and had performed with zeal and talent, following a slanderous campaign by a preacher who thought him unfit for the job.

Faulkner was twenty-seven. His brothers John and Jack, although younger than him, were now both married and engaged in what is known as active life—one as an engineer, the other as an FBI agent. For him, nothing had really changed since his return from Canada in 1918; he was still single with no employment in sight and had no future prospects apart from the forthcoming publication of *The Marble Faun*, his first book of poetry. This latent, indecisive period went on and on; nothing was yet decided. Faulkner knew that he could not live indefinitely off his parents, but for the time being he did not appear to be worried—or if he did, he certainly did not let it show.

When a female friend reproached him for doing nothing with his life, he retorted: "All I want to do is write."[40] He wanted to devote his life to writing, and in the midst of all his uncertainty, he was certain that he had what it took to be a writer. In a 1924 letter he told Ben Wasson that he knew he had talent. Perhaps, as he himself may have believed, he had more than talent. In the same letter, he added—with a trace of humor so as not to appear too pretentious—that when his liver was working and he wasn't constipated, he thought there was genius in his writing.

NOTES

1. Taken from Medieval Latin, "apocrypha" traditionally refers to biblical and evangelical texts not recognized by the Church, but it has also taken on the secular meaning of "inauthentic."

2. Joseph Ingraham, quoted by James Oakes in *The Ruling Class: A History of American Slaveholders* (New York: Random House, 1983), 82.

3. Quoted by Don H. Doyle in *Faulkner's County: The Historical Roots of Yoknapatawpha* (Chapel Hill: University of North Carolina Press, 2001), 229.

4. See C. Vann Woodward, *The Burden of Southern History* (New York: Random House, 1960), 101.

5. According to the terminology of Southerners opposed to Reconstruction, "carpetbaggers" referred to adventurers who came down from the North to make their fortune in the South, while "scalawags" referred to Southern collaborators. A brilliant officer of the Northern army, promoted to general at twenty-nine, elected senator for Mississippi in 1870 after having been commander of the military district of Mississippi and Arkansas, Ames did not fit the stereotype.

6. Quoted by Kenneth M. Stampp in *The Era of Reconstruction, 1865–1877* (New York: Vintage Books, 1965), 201.

7. Judge J. B. Chrisman, quoted in ibid., 179.

8. The name Jim Crow comes from the song "Jump Jim Crow," written in 1828 by Thomas Dartmouth "Daddy" Rice, the first white to publicly appear in blackface. From 1837 "Jim Crow" referred to racial segregation.

9. Quoted by Albert D. Kirwan in *The Revolt of the Rednecks: Mississippi Politics, 1876–1925* (New York: Harper Torchbooks, 1965), 146.

10. Henry L. Mencken, "The Worst American State," *American Mercury* 24 (November 1931), 371.

11. Quoted by Neil R. McMillen in *Dark Journey: Black Mississippians in the Age of Jim Crow* (Urbana: University of Illinois Press, 1990), 237.

12. The last lynching took place in Oxford on September 18, 1935. The victim, Elwood Higginbotham, was one of the leaders of the local union of sharecroppers. See the documents reproduced in the appendix by Arthur F. Kinney in *Go Down, Moses: The Miscegenation of Time* (New York: Twayne, 1996), 140–48.

13. [Translator's note: Killen was found guilty of three counts of manslaughter on June 21, 2005, the forty-first anniversary of the crime. He appealed the verdict, but his sentence of three times twenty years in prison was upheld on January 12, 2007, by the Mississippi Supreme Court.]

14. See James W. Silver, *Mississippi: The Closed Society*, new exp. ed. (New York: Harcourt, Brace & World, 1966).

15. Quoted in ibid., 25.

16. Walker Percy, "Mississippi: The Fallen Paradise," *Harper's*, April 1965, 168.

17. Henry James, "Richmond" (1906), in *Collected Travel Writings* (New York: Library of America, 1993), 672.

18. H. L. Mencken, "The Sahara of the Bozart," in *Prejudices*, 2nd series (New York: Knopf, 1920), 136.

19. William Faulkner, "An Introduction to *The Sound and the Fury*," *Mississippi Quarterly* 26 (Summer 1973): 410.

20. Ibid., 411.

21. Letter from Faulkner to Joan Williams, March 9, 1950, Faulkner Collection, Alderman Library, University of Virginia, quoted by Jay Parini in *One Matchless Time: A Life of William Faulkner* (New York: Harper Collins, 2004), 319.

22. Reported by Robert Cantwell in "The Faulkners: Recollections of a Gifted Family," *Faulkner: Three Decades of Criticism*, ed. Frederic J. Hoffman and Olga W. Vickery (East Lansing: Michigan State University Press, 1960), 56.

23. Interview by Judith L. Sensibar with Jill Faulkner Summers, in *The Origins of Faulkner's Art* (Austin: University of Texas Press, 1984), 209.

24. Interview by Jay Parini with Jill Summers in 2003. See Parini, *One Matchless Time*, 19.

25. William Faulkner, "An Introduction to *The Sound and the Fury*," ed. James B. Meriwether, *Southern Review* 8 (N.S., 1972): 705–710.

26. Unpublished interview dated June 5, 1957.

27. John B. Cullen, *Old Times in the Faulkner Country* (Chapel Hill: University of North Carolina Press, 1961), 3–4.

28. Robert Coughlan, *The Private World of William Faulkner* (New York: Harper & Brothers, 1954), 43.

29. [Translator's note: see Joel Williamson, *William Faulkner and Southern History* (New York: Oxford University Press, 1993), 168.]

30. Quoted by Coughlan in *Private World of William Faulkner*, 48.

31. Phil Stone, "Faulkner: The Man and his Work," in James B. Meriwether, "Early Notices of Faulkner by Phil Stone and Louis Cochran," *Mississippi Quarterly* (Summer 1964): 162–63.

32. See Williamson, *William Faulkner and Southern History*, 214.

33. See James G. Watson, *William Faulkner: Self-Presentation and Performance* (Austin: University of Texas Press, 2000), 20.

34. Ben Wasson, "The Time Has Come," *Delta Democrat-Times* (Greenville, Mississippi), July 15, 1962. See also *CNC*, 25.

35. Quoted in *Thinking of Home: William Faulkner's Letters to His Mother and Father, 1918–1925*, ed. James G. Watson (New York: W. W. Norton, 1992).

36. Wasson, "Time Has Come."

37. In *A Loving Gentleman*, Meta Carpenter reports that Faulkner saw music as "white and opaque and distant" (*ALG*, 130).

38. See Stark Young, "New Year's Craw," *New Republic*, February 12, 1938, 283.

39. See Joan St. Crane, "Case No. 133733-C: The Inspector's Letter to Postmaster William Faulkner," *Mississippi Quarterly* (Summer 1989): 229–45.

40. Quoted by Williamson in *William Faulkner and Southern History*, 193.

2
APPRENTICESHIPS

PAN AND PIERROT: THE FIRST MASKS

There is a long list of writers who were also painters or illustrators and a slightly shorter list of writers whose first vocation seems to have been painting, with literature merely in second place. It is almost as if every success is offset by failure, as if the enterprise of writing could be only an acrobatic catch-up exercise. Does this mean that all writers are failed painters? Faulkner, in any case, is not, no more than D. H. Lawrence, Dos Passos, Nabokov, Günter Grass, or Claude Simon. But, like them, he knew how to draw and enjoyed it, and it may not be wholly fortuitous that he was drawing before he started to write or that his drawings were published before his writings. In 1911, at the age of fourteen, he submitted a drawing to a national magazine. This first drawing, in ink, was published—signed (without the *u*) "William Falkner"—in the 1916–1917 issue of *Ole Miss*, the annual newspaper of the University of Mississippi. The drawing portrays a spindly dancing couple: the man is seen almost face-on, bald, his face reduced to two lines for the eyes, and a tiny heart-shaped mouth, with gloved hands like talons and wearing a suit and pointy shoes; his partner, seen in profile, is wearing a frilly dress and, like him, is disproportionately thin (see *EPP*, 68). Two other drawings appeared in the same newspaper in 1917. One of these, under the title "Social Activities," shows three figures, also extremely elongated. It portrays two men in suits and a young woman in a transparent dress set against a vertical black and white chessboard. The other drawing portrays another couple with the caption "Red and Blue" written alongside in large capitals; the woman, expressionless, with a long neck and long legs, is more naked than clothed in her Empire bustier and bloomers, while the man is buttoned up to the neck in evening dress. This was the first in a series of sketches published through 1925. The influence of Aubrey Beardsley and art nouveau is evident, as is that of John Held, Ralph Barton, and other well-known cartoonists of the period. There is also a discreet hint of cubism, which was unveiled in America at the Armory Show in New York in 1913. Although there was nothing original in Faulkner's elegantly stylized drawings, they are far from mediocre. They reveal a style that is both fluid and firm, and the ingenious arrangements of straight lines and curves and skillful contrasts between black and white are appealing. Faulkner's drawings, like the illustrations in some of his early writings such as his play *The Marionettes* and the poetry collection *Mayday*, are undeniably those of a talented young draftsman.

However, by 1926 Faulkner had realized that his artistic vocation lay elsewhere. In "Bill," a poem written that year, he confessed: "His heart's whole dream was his, had he been wise, / With space and light to feed it through his eyes, / But with the gift of tongues he was accursed."[1]

Faulkner drew from early childhood. He wrote poems from adolescence. From 1916 to 1924 he wrote almost nothing else. Before becoming a novelist, he wanted to be a poet and saw himself as one. He persisted on this career path for nearly ten years and always regretted not having become one: "I've often thought that I wrote the novels because I found I couldn't write the poetry, that maybe I wanted to be a poet, maybe I think of myself as a poet, and I failed at that, I couldn't write poetry, so I did the next best thing" (*FU*, 4).

On August 6, 1919, "L'Apres-Midi d'un Faune," a poem in forty verses, was published in the *New Republic*. The title is taken from the pastoral poem by Stéphane Mallarmé, while the text of the poem is signed "William Faulkner." This is his first published poem and it also marks the first time that "Faulkner" is used instead of "Falkner." This was a poet naming and declaring himself. He was twenty-two years old.

In the following years, through 1925, many of his poems were published in student reviews. Between 1919 and 1921 a good dozen were published by the *Mississippian*, the University of Mississippi student paper. In these poems Faulkner disgorges his readings and reveals himself above all as an insatiable thief of words, phrases, tropes, and titles. Everything is borrowed.

His first poems are aggregates of reminiscences, mosaics of quotations. In other words, the intertexts are so laden with meaning that the text often struggles to detach itself. Faulkner's own poetic voice is barely audible. His poetry contains innumerable echoes, from A. E. Housman, William Butler Yeats, T. S. Eliot, and Conrad Aiken to the Romantics, the Pre-Raphaelites, the Decadents, and the Symbolists. Plagiarism and pastiche abound and at times the young poet goes so far as to bluff.

In the *Mississippian* of August 6, 1919, Faulkner published a slightly revised version of "L'Apres-Midi d'un Faune," already published in the *New Republic*, and Mallarmé resurfaces in "Naiad's Song." However, apart from their titles, these two poems have nothing in common with the French poet. Four poems published in the *Mississippian*—"Fantoches," "Clair de Lune," "Streets," and "A Clymene"—are more or less free, more or less successful adaptations of Verlaine's *Fêtes galantes* and *Romances sans paroles* or, more probably, of the translations of these poems by Arthur Symons, the poet and essayist who introduced the French Symbolists to the English-speaking world. In truth, these adaptations are more sloppy than creative. For example, in "Fantoches," "Scaramouche" takes a final *s* and "Pulcinella" loses its initial *l* (rendered awkwardly as Pucinella); Verlaine's "excellent Bolognese doctor" wears a kimono for the purposes of rhyme; and the poem ends, inexplicably, with the line "*la lune ne garde aucune rancune*," lifted from T. S. Eliot's "Rhapsody on a Windy Night," itself inspired by "Complainte de cette belle lune" by Jules Laforgue. Similarly, "Clair de Lune" and "A Clymene" diverge awkwardly from the poems they are modeled on, and while "Streets" is more successful, the nostalgic simplicity of Verlaine's final tercet could have been better rendered. Although the young Faulkner was alive to the sensual, dreamlike atmosphere of *Fêtes galantes*, he was unable to recreate it in his own poems. As with many English-speaking poets of his time, he was interested in French poetry, but his French was too mediocre for him to draw on. Therefore, his titles should be approached with caution. "L'Apres-Midi d'un Faune" owes little to Mallarmé but much to Robert Nichols, a long-forgotten imitator of the Pre-Raphaelites, and "Une Ballade des Femmes Perdues," one of the most delicate and successful of Faulkner's early poems, echoes "La Ballade des dames du temps jadis" but, apart from the epigraph, owes nothing to François Villon.

The influence of Algernon Charles Swinburne was far stronger, far more durable, and far more fecund. It is blatant in "Aubade," a poem probably written in 1916 that remains unpublished,[2] the model for which was *Before Dawn*. Similarly, in the poem "Sapphics," published on November 26, 1919, and later incorporated in the *Lilacs* volume, Faulkner paraphrases, condenses, and comments on Swinburne's poet of the same name, reusing the latter's metaphors and syntax but reducing the number of stanzas from twenty to just one. Another exercise in compression is "Hermaphroditus," a sonnet reprinted in the novel *Mosquitoes* and later in *A Green Bough*, which is ostensibly derived from a poem in four sonnets by Swinburne but in fact repeats only the first four verses and retains only one metaphor.

As Faulkner himself admitted in 1925, his early discovery of Swinburne was decisive at the initial stages of his brief poetic career:

> At the age of sixteen, I discovered Swinburne. Or rather, Swinburne discovered me, springing from some tortured undergrowth of my adolescence, [. . .] making me his slave. My mental life at that period was so completely and smoothly veneered with surface insincerity—obviously necessary to me at that time, to support intact my personal integrity—that I can not tell to this day exactly to what depth he stirred me, just how deeply the footprints of his passage are left in my mind. [. . .] Whatever it was that I found in Swinburne, it completely satisfied me and filled my inner life. (*EPP*, 114–15)

If the young Faulkner succumbed to the somewhat facile charms of this English cousin of Baudelaire, it is because what he found in him nourished and transported his adolescent dreams. Swinburne's poetry sings of blood, voluptuousness, and death, with its fiercely pagan Greece, its rich corrupting scents, and its bewitching musicality. His poetry is redolent of Romanticism, albeit a dying Romanticism, one that is darker, more frenetic, and more baneful than the poetry of Wordsworth, Keats, and Shelley. This was indeed a mark of Baudelaire's indirect influence. The callow young man from the provinces needed a good dose of spice, and in Swinburne he found everything he could possibly wish for. He didn't stop there, however. Swinburne was the poet of Faulkner's adolescence and he never quite stopped reading him. According to his daughter, he had a copy of Swinburne's poems beside his bed until the day he died. But from the earliest poems, other influences were at work.

While Faulkner's early poems are mere schoolboy exercises, this particular schoolboy was avid for learning and learned quickly. It is entirely possible that he already had a confused idea of what he would later write, because he soon assembled his poetry into poetic suites and even books, where they were set out and organized into themed series. He designed four of these books in the 1920s: *The Marble Faun* (1919–1924), *Lilacs* (January 1920), *Vision in Spring* (1921), and *Helen: A Courtship* (1926). A fifth book was published in 1933—*A Green Bough*—his second published book of poems.

Of these poetic suites, *The Marble Faun* is the best known, because it was published in 1925 by the Four Seas Company, a small publishing house in Boston that had already published Conrad Aiken and William Carlos Williams. In this volume Faulkner assembled poems written as early as 1919, which he reworked in 1923 and possibly again in 1924.

They are poems of youth, as noted by Phil Stone in the preface, and as such contain "the deficiencies of youth—diffuseness and overexuberance, impatient simile and metaphor" as well as immaturity. The poems do not, however, have the dazzle of youth. *The Marble Faun* is the work of a young poet who is no Keats or Rimbaud, but the meticulous care taken in composing this pastoral cycle of nineteen poems attests to the formal rigor later to be found in the skillful structure of most of Faulkner's novels.

In this long elegiac poem, the height of artifice is combined with the transparency of confession. The poet appears here in one of his earliest masks, taken from the pseudo-pagan antiquity of the Romantic poets, the Symbolists, and the Decadents in the 1890s. The faun represents the power of desire in all its animal savagery. The marble faun represents that same energy set in the inert coldness of stone. In contrast to Mallarmé, Faulkner's faun did not experience the fire of noon, even in dream. The unrepentant rapist and abductor of nymphs becomes no more than a voyeur shivering in the snow. Dionysian ardor is followed by morose ecstasy:

Why am I sad? I?
Why am I not content? The sky
Warms me and yet I cannot break
My marble bonds. That quick keen snake
Is free to come and go, while I
Am prisoner to dream and sigh
For things I know, yet cannot know,
'Twixt sky above and earth below.
The spreading earth calls to my feet
Of orchards bright with fruits to eat,

Of hills and streams on either hand;
Of sleep at night on moon-blanched sand:
The whole world breathes and calls to me
Who marble-bound must ever be.
(*MF/GB*, 12)

In *The Marble Faun* we hear the long, plaintive cry of a pensive prisoner. Immobile, captive, literally mired in its body of stone, its only breath is a sigh, it speaks only to whimper, and it sees only to become distressed at the distance separating it from the orchard nearby, whose fruit it cannot taste. This member of the living dead, exiled far from earthly seasons, is obviously a self-portrait. Beneath the mask of the tantalized faun can be glimpsed the torment of a dreamy, idle adolescence, impatient to finally race toward the adventure that is life. Both a trick and an avowal of modesty, the mask retains effusiveness in the stiffness of a fixed attitude. Solitary, in mourning for himself and for the world, Faulkner's faun Narcissus is looking for a place to gather up the broken pieces of the mirror and recapture his lost image. His immobility and silence convey the difficulties encountered by a writer who has not yet chosen to be one and who is asking himself what he will have to pay to become one.

We do not know if the poems in *The Lilacs* were written before or after those in *The Marble Faun*, but the typed version of this collection (partly destroyed in a fire at Phil Stone's house in 1942) is dated January 1, 1920. The collection is made up of thirteen poems, some of which had already been published in the *Mississippian*. The overall tone is elegiac, as *The Marble Faun* had been, but Faulkner shows himself to be even more eclectic in his choice of models and clearly more attentive to the possibilities offered by modernist poetry. In "The Lilacs," the first poem, from which the collection derives its name, late romanticism is allied with early modernism, the alliterative music of Swinburne is married to the stridency of Eliot. In this long poem—probably written just after the 1918 armistice, published in 1925 in the *Double Dealer*, and reprinted in a new version in 1933 at the start of *A Green Bough*—Faulkner plays with a number of stylistic registers, from the most mundane, contemporary prose to the traditional vocabulary of poetic discourse. "The Lilacs" is both a war poem—the lament of a wounded, mutilated airman destined to death in life—and a timidly erotic poem in the vein of Swinburne. Here Eros and Thanatos meet and are the same. As in "Nympholepsy," one of Faulkner's earliest prose pieces, death is a femme fatale: "I felt her arms and her cool breath. / The bullet struck me here, I think / In the left breast" (*MF/GB*, 8).

The figure of the wounded aviator haunted Faulkner throughout both his life and his work, appearing as early as *Soldiers' Pay*, his first novel. However, he found his first poetic roles in his reading, in the already faded fin-de-siècle literature. From the emblematic figure of the faun it is only one short step to Pierrot, the character from the commedia dell'arte, first resuscitated in the pantomimes of Gaspard Deburau, transformed by Gautier, Banville, Baudelaire, Mallarmé, Verlaine, Huysmans, Laforgue, Edmond Rostand, and Beardsley into the dreamy icon of the unhappy artist and later adopted as a poetic persona in turn by T. S. Eliot, Wallace Stevens, and Conrad Aiken.

Faulkner's Pierrot fits into this rich poetic lineage as early as *Vision in Spring*, the collection of poems he gave Estelle in 1921, probably revised in 1923 before being sent to the Four Seas Company in Boston and not published until 1984. Pierrot appears by name in the title of the third poem, called "The World and Pierrot: A Nocturne," and as with the poetic persona in *The Marble Faun*, he is represented as a sad and solitary dreamer. Uncertain of his identity and his destiny, he twists and turns in a lunar world of ice peaks and deserts. But Pierrot, in these poems, is also in love: he is both lover and husband. In "Marriage" (republished in *A Green Bough*), the most autobiographical poem in the collection, he watches, "laxly reclining," a woman seated at a piano, "her plastic shadow on the wall," the play of flames in the fireplace giving the impression that a hand is touching the keyboard, "playing a music of lustrous muted gold," until "his brain, stretched and tautened, suddenly cracks."[3] In *Vision in Spring* Faulkner's poetry is enhanced with new accents—more intimate, more urgent and new orientations are drawn. That said, his poetic writing remains uneven and derivative. T. S. Eliot is present throughout, and in "Love Song," the ninth poem, riven with rupture and repetition, provocative dislocation and dissonance, Faulkner unashamedly plagiarizes "The Love Song of J. Alfred Prufrock," which has, rightly or wrongly, been understood as pure parody. However, *Vision in Spring* is more than a patchwork of quotes. New voices surface here and Pierrot is less distant, less evanescent than the earlier faun, becoming almost a character in a novel or a play. Pierrot truly becomes a dramatic character in *The Marionettes*, a one-act fantasy in verse and prose written by Faulkner in December 1920, illustrated with ink drawings and

bound in six copies. He gave this piece the same name as the club he founded with Ben Wasson and Lucy Somerville.

This is how he sets the scene:

> The sky is a thin transparent blue, a very light blue merging into white with
> stars in regular order, and a full moon. At the back center is a marble colon-
> nade, small in distance, against a regular black band of trees; on either side of it
> is the slim graceful silhouette of a single poplar tree. Both wings are closed by
> sections of wall covered with roses, motionless on the left is a peacock silhou-
> etted against the moon. In the middle foreground are a pool and a fountain.
> (*Ma*, 45–46)

With its "regular" ordering of stars and trees, the perfect symmetry of
graceful poplars, the contrast between black and white, the marble colon-
nade, and the fountain and pool, it is difficult to imagine a more stylized set,
frozen in its geometry. We are in the artful, deliberate space of a formal garden—a classical garden in the French style, the antithesis of nature. It could
have been designed by Ellison, owner of *The Domain of Arnhein*, or drawn
by Aubrey Beardsley. Not to mention the moon, the roses, and the peacock.

And here in his white costume is Pierrot, the evanescent hero of the
play, initially drawn exactly as Beardsley would have done and then described in a caption accompanying the drawing:

> Pierrot is seated at right front in a fragile black chair beside a delicate table.
> His left arm is curved across the table top, his right arm hangs beside him, and
> his head rests upon his curved arm, face toward front. He appears to be in a
> drunken sleep, there are a bottle and an overturned wine glass upon the table, a
> mandolin and a woman's slipper lie at his feet. He does not change his position
> during the play. He is dressed in white and black. Flung across the chair back is
> a scarf of black and gold Chinese brocade. (*Ma*, 46)

The Pierrot in *The Marionettes* is not Pedrolino, the oafish young lover of
the Italian tradition, nor is he the nervous clown as imagined by Gautier,
Verlaine, and Laforgue. He also has a double from the start, as the play contains two Pierrots: the drunken "Pierrot" described at the start, who sleeps
and remains immobile throughout, and the "Shade of Pierrot," the charmer
with the mandolin who appears later. The artist's new double is therefore
himself given a double, a figure between stasis and movement, silence and
speech. This means that all the action of the play can therefore be interpret-

ed as the dream of an unmoving Pierrot, and in this respect he has a certain similarity to the petrified faun of the poems. Again we find ourselves in the solitary, frozen gardens of the unreal.

Marietta, the heroine of *The Marionettes*, has been rightly compared to Mallarmé's Hérodiade and Oscar Wilde's Salomé. Here again Faulkner is using a character that has already been mythologized—La Belle Dame sans Merci—whose shadowy powers fascinated so many poets, painters, and composers in the late nineteenth century. At the same time, Marietta is the first sketch of the young narcissistic virgin who will later be encountered in the writer's early novels. It should be noted that her role in the play is less sustained than that of Pierrot. Like the nymphs of poetry, she is an object of lechery, but unlike them, she also feels desire. She is another persona of the writer, a portrait of Narcissus in the form of Echo. The overly ordered garden, with its peacocks and stonework, its bouquets of roses and moonlight—all this familiar symbolism unfurls around Marietta, echoing her cold beauty. Enamored of her own reflection, she gazes at and admires herself in the water, like Mallarmé's Hérodiade gazes at herself in the mirror, "cold water by ennui frozen in [its] frame,"[4] and she dies, not because she has seduced and abandoned a lover, but because she has loved herself too much, because swapping her beauty for death was the only thing she could do. But death is not the enemy of beauty; beauty is beyond death. Upon her return, Marietta, gazing at her reflection, discovers that she has not changed and that she is as beautiful as ever. Her beauty is now the epitome of beauty, the splendor no longer of a living body but of an object of art. Marietta is compared to an "ivory tower" and a "little statue of ivory and silver" (*Ma*, 43), her hair is heavy with gold, her breasts become "ivory crusted jewels" (45), her hands "two links of a silver chain" or "little pieces of smooth silver" (105). These metaphors, in the tradition of the Song of Songs, wrap themselves so luxuriously around Marietta that they eventually smother her. Her literal death is by drowning, a death by water; her textual death is due to excessive rhetoric. At the end of the play, the young abandoned woman has become a hard, sparkling icon.

Distaste for organic material and a penchant for mineral metaphors were a constant theme in French poetry, from Gautier and Baudelaire to Mallarmé and the Parnassians. Precious stones, ivory, and silver are leitmotifs in Wilde's *Salomé*. Nothing in *The Marionettes* escapes the iconic and rhetorical code of the Symbolist tradition. The play recalls Wilde's ornate eroticism, even down to its images and metaphors. In fact, the road that will lead Marietta from angst-ridden awakening of desire to narcissistic death is traced with infinitely more subtlety in Faulkner's novels. However, in this outmoded staging, questions are beginning to take shape and obsessions to form. The play's first drawing summarizes these with almost allegorical simplicity. Pierrot is seen from behind, between two funereal candlesticks, with Marietta lying dead at his feet. All of Faulkner's work—his poetry, novels, and short stories, at least until *The Sound and the Fury*—is bound up with the three figures of Narcissus, Eros, and Thanatos.

Faulkner's early writings use masks and mirrors to poeticize the torment and confusion of an adolescence that seems never-ending. They all bear the mark of narcissism, an unhappy narcissism that cannot be reduced to the captivation of a subject with his own image. Far from losing themselves in ecstatic self-contemplation, the male characters onto whom Faulkner projects his desires have eyes only for the woman. Pierrot weeps for his lost loves or dreams of being an irresistible charmer, while the faun is distressed at being made of marble. The scene in both the poem cycles and *The Marionettes* is erotic and narcissistic, a leafy theater or a garden made glossy by moonlight, traversed by nymphs and naiads with silky skin and flowing locks, furtively inviting onlookers to look but forbidding them to touch.

(SELF)CRITICISM

In 1925, the year when he turned to prose, Faulkner carried out an initial assessment of the "pilgrimage" that led him to the flamboyant romanticism of Swinburne, Shakespeare, Keats, and Housman. In it he readily acknowledged that his love for poetry had begun as mere posturing and showing off and that his early poems were nothing but the naive outpourings of a provincial young man short of love and identity:

> I was not interested in verse for verse's sake then. I read and employed verse, firstly, for the purpose of furthering various philanderings in which I was engaged, secondly, to complete a youthful gesture I was then making, of being "different" in a small town. Later, my concupiscence waning, I turned inevitably to verse, finding therein an emotional counterpart far more satisfactory. (*EPP*, 115)

It is also revealing that in his prose reviews published between 1920 and 1925, Faulkner never ceases to question himself obliquely and is always ready to perceive his own moods and worries in others and to detect weaknesses in them that he knows are also his. Thus, in his review of the book of poetry by Mississippian William Alexander Percy, *In April Once*, Faulkner compares the author to "a little boy closing his eyes against the dark of modernity which threatens the bright simplicity and the colorful romantic pageantry of the middle ages with which his eyes are full" (*EPP*, 72). When he says, "Mister Percy—like alas! how many of us—suffered the misfortune of having been born out of his time" (71), he is confessing his own feelings of loss and exile.

These reviews, often polemical and sometimes insolent, tell at least as much about Faulkner as the writers purportedly being reviewed. In truth, apart from Conrad Aiken and Edna St. Vincent Millay, very few contemporary poets find favor with Faulkner. He pokes fun at Vachel Lindsay "with his tin pan and iron spoon" and at Alfred Kreymborg "with his lithographic water coloring" and reproaches Carl Sandburg for "his sentimental Chicago propaganda" (*EPP*, 75). In Millay, by contrast, he finds "a lusty tenuous simplicity" and "a strong wrist" (85). Aiken is the only one whose poetry he admires unreservedly, seeing in it "one rift of heaven blue" in "the fog generated by the mental puberty of contemporary American versifiers" (74).

Immaturity, lack of strength and vigor, and verbosity are also what Faulkner reproaches of Joseph Hergesheimer, a successful 1920s novelist: "No one since Poe has allowed himself to be enslaved by words as has Hergesheimer. What was, in Poe, however, a morbid but masculine emotional curiosity has degenerated with the age to a deliberate pandering to the emotions in Hergesheimer, like an attenuation of violins" (*EPP*, 101). Faulkner accuses Hergesheimer of wallowing in frosty preciousness. In his eyes, *Linda Condon*, an exquisite but futile book, is not a real novel:

> It is more like a lovely Byzantine frieze: a few unforgettable figures in silent arrested motion, forever beyond the reach of time and troubling the heart like music. His people are never actuated from within; they do not create life about them; they are like puppets assuming graceful but meaningless postures in answer to the author's compulsions, and holding these attitudes until he arranges their limbs again in other gestures as graceful and as meaningless. (101–102)

For the young Faulkner, Hergesheimer is "a strange case of sex crucifixion turned back on itself" (101), and at the end of his essay he compares him to "an emasculate priest surrounded by the puppets he has cared and clothed and painted—a terrific world without motion or meaning" (103).

References to sexuality abound in these essays. Faulkner was evidently intrigued by the psychosexual roots and impulses of literary creation, and his brief experience of writing had already taught him that narcissism and literature are intricately intertwined. "Writing people are all so pathetically torn between a desire to make a figure in the world and a morbid interest in their personal egos—the deadly fruit of the grafting of Sigmund Freud upon the dynamic chaos of a hodge-podge of nationalities" (*EPP*, 93).

Note here the reference to Freud, making a rare appearance in his writing, but Faulkner did not wait for the invention of psychoanalysis to discover that every artist, beginning with himself, desires "honour, power and the love of women."[5]

These reflections are meant to be general, but they border on the confessional. It seems in these essays as if Faulkner is criticizing himself through the intermediary of other writers. The criticisms of Hergesheimer could just as easily have been leveled at the young author of *The Marble Faun* and *The Marionettes*. The vain, charming little drama of *Linda Condon*, where the clamor of the outside world reaches us only as "as a far faint sound of rain" (*EPP*, 102), is barely distinguishable from the lunar world of Faulkner's Pierrot and of his marble faun. His condemnation of the static aestheticism of Hergesheimer is an oblique condemnation of his own immaturity, and it indirectly anticipates his later definition of what should be the true aim of every artist: "to arrest motion, which is life, by artificial means and hold it fixed so that 100 years later when a stranger looks at it, it moves again since it is life" (*LG*, 253). According to Faulkner, this ambitious aim was never more successfully achieved than by John Keats, whose odes contain "the spiritual beauty which the moderns strive vainly for with trickery, and yet beneath it one knows are entrails; masculinity" (*EPP*, 117).

Almost all of his essays suggest that what Faulkner calls for is the radiating vigor of a "healthy" "masculine" literature. It is somewhat surprising that at the outset of his writing career, he saw fit to invoke the antimodern, macho, and retrograde ideology he attacked in his later novels. However, this is not so surprising given that Faulkner, exasperated with his own aes-

theticism, was looking for new bearings, new paradigms, and that his celebration of Keats's masculinity was first and foremost an affirmation of his
newly found desire to rid his writing of this vapidity and to finally give it the
density and force it was lacking.

No less remarkable in these essays is Faulkner's manifest concern to see
a national literature capable of drawing on the as yet unexplored wealth of
the American experience and give its credentials to what he saw as the most
vigorous language of modern times. There was nothing new about this preoccupation; in the nineteenth century, Hawthorne, Melville, Emerson, and
Whitman had already expressed the same hopes and had devoted all their
talent to making this happen. Curiously, in 1922 Faulkner still believed that
"America has no drama or literature worth of name" (*EPP*, 87). But at the
same time, he disowned those who found "America aesthetically impossible" (94). He also believed firmly in the possibility of a national literature
and asserted that every writer needed to have deep cultural roots: "Art is
predominantly provincial; i.e., it comes directly from a certain age and a
certain locality" (86). Not that this meant he was ever drawn to a career as a
regional writer. The important thing for him was to discover that his knowledge and experience of the South were enough to nourish his creation:
"Sound art [. . .] does not depend on the quality or quantity of available
material: a man with real ability finds sufficient what he has to hand" (94).

IN NEW ORLEANS

Since 1919 Billy Falkner had called himself William Faulkner. He had not
really changed his name, as "Faulkner" is not a pseudonym like "Stendhal"
is for Beyle, "Twain" for Clemens, "Céline" for Destouches, or "Orwell" for
Blair. The switch from "Falkner" to "Faulkner" involves merely adding a
single, silent letter in the same way that Hawthorne had added a *w* to "Ha-
thorne" and Melville an *e* to "Melvill." The only remarkable thing about the
change is that Faulkner was reestablishing the way the family name had
been spelled before his great-grandfather removed a letter, as he states in
this letter to Cowley:

> My first recollection of the name was, no outsider seemed able to pronounce
> it from reading it, and when he did pronounce it, he always wrote the "u" into
> it. So it seemed to me that the whole outside world was trying to change it, and

usually did. Maybe when I began to write, even though I thought then I was writing for fun, I secretly was ambitious and did not want to ride on grandfather's coat-tails, and so accepted the "u," was glad of such an easy way to strike out for myself. (*FCF*, 66)

While retaining a semblance of belonging, of genealogy, the new spelling was also a way of marking a difference, a difference that is not heard, but read. This subtle scratching out of the father's name, a discreet revendication of his own name, free of lineage, was part and parcel of the Faulknerian enterprise and one that many of the novelist's characters emulated.

An account had been opened. At first, "William Faulkner" was a name with no guarantee (like an uncovered check), a signature and a promise that remained to be honored. In 1925 Faulkner had not yet honored this promise. He was no longer a young man—he was approaching thirty—but he was still living from day to day. As a writer he had not achieved anything remarkable, his career was in its infancy, and there was nothing yet to suggest the emergence of the novelist, although this was just around the corner. Faulkner was taking his time. Like Proust, he was a genius who matured slowly. But from now on, he wrote constantly. From now on, everything would happen very quickly. A writer, a great writer, was about to be born.

In early January 1925 Faulkner left Oxford for New Orleans, where he had already gone in the fall of the previous year to see Elizabeth Prall, whom he had met in New York four years earlier and who had in the meantime become Sherwood Anderson's third wife. This time he went to New Orleans intending to embark for Europe as soon as possible. On his arrival he initially checked into Hotel Lafayette with Phil Stone, and then, after the latter left, he was put up on the third floor of one of the Pontalba Buildings by Elizabeth Prall, who, during the first few weeks of this second sojourn, was his landlady, his bookkeeper, and his cook. Finally, on March 4 he moved into 624 Pirate's Alley. "I have a nice room," he wrote his mother. "There are two of us—Piper, a newspaper man, and I. We have two rooms, a court and a kitchen on the ground floor of a lovely paved alley facing the garden of St. Louis cathedral—the best spot in New Orleans in which to live" (*LMF*, 187). The painter and architect William Spratling, who at the time lived on the third floor of the same building and who soon became his friend, later remembered "a skinny little guy, three years older than I, and was not taken very seriously except by a few of us."[6] The bohemian cosmopolitan milieu of the French Quarter (also known as Vieux Carré), the Left Bank of this "Paris of the South," as New Orleans was known at the time, welcomed the young Faulkner with open arms, and he seems to have felt immediately at home. The six months spent in New Orleans were to prove decisive in his intellectual development. As soon as he arrived, he started associating with journalists such as John McClure and Roark Bradford, took up with writers and artists, and spent long evenings chatting and drinking with them in the city's cabarets, such as the one on Franklin Street, two steps from the canal, where the jazz clarinetist George "Georgia Boy" Boyd used to play. Through all of these meetings and conversations, Faulkner took part in the intellectual and artistic exuberance of the 1920s. A new world was opening up to him. He discovered the nascent science of anthropology and psychoanalysis alongside the newest, most experimental forms of modern poetry and fiction. He almost certainly read Joyce's *Ulysses* in 1924 and a little later the abridged version of James George Frazer's *The Golden Bough*, published in 1922.

It is less certain to what he extent he was familiar with the thinking of Freud. He later told Jean Stein: "Everyone talked about Freud when I lived in New Orleans, but I have never read him," mischievously adding: "Neither did Shakespeare. I doubt if Melville did either, and I'm sure Moby Dick didn't" (*LG*, 251). Faulkner always denied any debt to Freud, and when he was asked where he had learned "psychology," he answered that he had no idea: "Only what I have learned about it from listening to people that do know. What little of psychology I know the characters I have invented and playing poker have taught me. Freud, I'm not familiar with" (*FU*, 268). However, it is highly likely that he did read Freud, at least a little. In *Elmer*, his unfinished novel, the borrowings from Freudian symbology are evident. That said, Faulkner was not interested in ideas. Theoretical speculation and the abstractions of philosophy left him cold, and he had no taste for literary debate. It would be wrong to draw the conclusion that he was not familiar with the new thinking of his time. In his interviews in the 1950s, he acknowledged his debts, albeit often reluctantly, downplaying their significance. What he learned from psychoanalysis and anthropology probably came spontaneously, from random conversations rather than methodical reading. This didn't stop him from using these ideas to his advantage.

Of all the people he met at this time, Sherwood Anderson was no doubt the most significant. Faulkner and Anderson had already met during Faulkner's brief stay in New Orleans in the fall of 1924, as recounted by Faulkner in one of his interviews at the University of Virginia: "I had gone to call on [Elizabeth Prall], because I wasn't going to bust in on Mr. Anderson without an invitation from him, I didn't think that I would see him at all, that he would probably be in his study working, but it happened that he was in the room at the time, and we talked and we liked one another from the start" (*FU*, 230). When Anderson came back from a conference tour in early March 1925, the men quickly became firm friends. Over forty and already famous, Anderson was then working on *Dark Laughter* and the young Faulkner on his first novel, *Soldiers' Pay*. They both spent their mornings writing, strolling around town in the afternoon, while evenings found them "with a bottle" (*ESPL*, 9). Although twenty years separated them, the loquacious Anderson and the quiet Faulkner got along famously. The former liked to hold forth; the latter liked to listen or—generally after a few drinks—to talk nonsense. It was a win-win situation for both men, one where they even went so far as to dream up the "Al Jackson letters." Later, in "A Note on Sherwood Anderson," Faulkner told how they came to improvise this series of tall tales:

> One day during the months while we walked and talked in New Orleans—or Anderson talked and I listened—I found him sitting on a bench in Jackson Square, laughing with himself. I got the impression that he had been there like that for some time, just sitting alone on the bench laughing with himself [. . .]. He told me what it was at once: a dream: he had dreamed the night before that he was walking for miles along country roads, leading a horse which he was trying to swap for a night's sleep—not for a simple bed for the night, but for the sleep itself; and with me to listen now, went on from there, elaborating it, building it into a work of art. (*ESPL*, 3)

Faulkner and Anderson both started making up other stories and fantastic characters. They found these tall stories so funny that they decided to write them down in letters that they would exchange, "such as two temporarily separated members of an exploring-zoological expedition might" (*ESPL*, 7). Faulkner's first letter to Anderson told how Al Jackson, a descendant of President Andrew Jackson, raised sheep in a swamp, thinking about how "wool grew like anything else"; how his sheep gradually turned into aquatic creatures; and how Claude, his second son, spent so much time in the water that he turned into a shark (*US*, 475). In his response, Anderson referred to the character of Flu Balsam, a fish-herd, and Faulkner, in a second letter, described other members of the Jackson family, such as Herman Jackson, the inventor of a system to make pearl buttons out of fish scales, who died of convulsions after reading Walter Scott's complete works in twelve and a half days.

Because each was busy with other projects, their collaboration on the Al Jackson letters was short-lived. Anderson had started to write *Tar*, the story of his Midwest childhood. Faulkner was working on his second novel, mostly in the morning, astounding his friends with his energy and concentration. Anderson relates how he heard Faulkner's typewriter as he crossed the corridor, morning, noon, and often night: "He typed all the time."[7] William Spratling was equally impressed by Faulkner's impressive work ethic: "By the time I would be up, say at seven, Bill would already be out on the little balcony over the garden tapping on his portable, an invariable glass of alcohol-and-water at hand."[8] From Anderson, Faulkner got all the help and encouragement he needed. But it did not take him long to judge Anderson and to discover the limits of his talent, and, no more than Ernest Hemingway, Faulkner could not resist the temptation to mock Anderson's mannerisms and poke fun at the foibles of the man himself. In *Sherwood Anderson and Other Famous Creoles*, Spratling's 1926 self-published collection of caricatures—the same year as *Torrents of Spring*, Hemingway's longer and crueler parody—Faulkner imitated the style of his benefactor.[9] Anderson took it badly. On April 29 he wrote to his editor Horace Liveright about Faulkner's behavior toward him, complaining about Faulkner's ingratitude and saying that he no longer wished to write to him personally. Far from saying he was sorry, Faulkner made things worse in *Mosquitoes*, his second novel, where he used the Al Jackson letters to build a portrait of Anderson that was more mischievous than nasty, easily recognizable in the character of Dawson Fairchild.

Although not as ungrateful as Hemingway, Faulkner never denied his debt to Anderson. In 1925 he paid homage to him in the *Dallas Morning News* in a brief commentary on seven of his books (see *NOS*, 132–39). He repeated this homage in "A Note on Sherwood Anderson," an essay published in the *Atlantic* in June 1953 (*ESPL*, 3–10) and in a 1956 interview with

Jean Stein, asserting: "He was the father of my generation of American writers and the tradition of American writing which our successors will carry on. He has never received his proper evaluation. Dreiser is his older brother and Mark Twain the father of them both" (*LG*, 249–50). Faulkner all but publicly paid homage to Anderson in the speech he gave at the Nobel Prize award ceremony in Stockholm in 1950.

For years, Anderson refused to see Faulkner. However, the two eventually met again and reconciled at a cocktail party in New York in 1937. Faulkner relates in his 1953 essay: "There was that moment when he appeared taller, bigger than anything he ever wrote. Then I remembered *Winesburg, Ohio*, and *The Triumph of the Egg* and some of the pieces in *Horses and Men*, and I knew that I had seen, was looking at, a giant in an earth populated to a great—too great—extent by pygmies, even if he did make but the two or perhaps three gestures commensurate with gianthood" (*ESPL*, 10).

In the winter of 1925, at a party in Bill Spratling's apartment, Faulkner met a young sports reporter, James R. "Pete" Baird, and his twenty-one-year-old sister, Helen. In an (undated) letter written in the late thirties, Faulkner recalls an aggressive girl with a sulky jaw and yellow eyes, in a cotton dress, with suntanned legs sitting on Spratling's balcony "not thinking even a hell of a little bit of me," adding that perhaps she had "already decided not to."[10] It is true that Helen spared scarcely a thought for him, but he thought of her often and put these thoughts down in verse. At the time she was only twenty-one. She had come to New Orleans from Nashville, Tennessee, to learn how to sculpt. While not exactly beautiful, she was, according to one of her friends, "extremely attractive." Like Estelle, she was a petite brunette and an upper-class Southerner, but there the resemblance ends. Helen apparently had nothing of the Southern belle about her, and undoubtedly Faulkner would not have been so attracted to her if she had not been so different from the women he had met up until then, particularly if she had not been so different from Estelle. Where Estelle was mannered, Helen, in her paint-spotted smock, appeared free and natural. Her character, energy, vivaciousness, and acerbic charm came from childhood. She did not pose, had no regard for convention, no taste for show. Helen did not try to hide the large burn scar she had from a childhood accident, which Faulkner discovered the first time he saw her in a bathing suit. Everything about her seemed to say, *Accept me as I am or go on your way.*

Faulkner and Helen met several times in New Orleans in early 1925. In June, just before Faulkner left for Europe, they saw each other in Pascagoula, a seaside resort on the Gulf of Mexico near Mobile Bay. Faulkner read her his poems and told her stories; she scolded him about his drinking. They went walking on the beach, swam together, and went sailing, nothing more. Accounts of Helen's feelings toward Faulkner at the time differ. According to a letter Helen wrote to Carvel Collins, who planned to write a biography of Faulkner (which never materialized), Faulkner was an exceptional man to know—an unparalleled companion, the type found only in books. However, this letter dates from November 29, 1951, and there is no evidence that Helen had any deeper feelings for this exceptional companion. In 1925 the eccentric young man in white shirt and twill pants amused her but did not inspire any respect in her. One day she stood him up and kept him waiting on the doorstep for four hours. When she finally arrived, he told her it was nothing, that he had been working. Helen did not take him seriously, either as a man or as a writer. When *Soldiers' Pay* was published, she strongly advised one of her friends against reading it. Helen was his second big love and again it ended in failure, perhaps even more painful than the last time. Because it was unrequited, it could not even give rise to regrets. Faulkner started to court Helen, marshalling the aid of literature. He dedicated *Mayday* to her in January 1926: "to thee O wise and lovely this: a fumbling in darkness." In June he offered her fifteen sonnets, handwritten and hand-bound, titled *Helen: A Courtship*. In September he dedicated *Mosquitoes*, his second novel, to her. Each of his texts at the time was a type of madrigal or love letter. Faulkner was aware of this, putting these cynical words into the mouth of the novelist Fairchild in *Mosquitoes*: "I believe that every word a writing man writes is put down with the ultimate intention of impressing some woman that probably don't care anything at all for literature" (*M*, 250).

Helen was not in the slightest impressed. When Faulkner asked her to marry him, she turned him down flat, and, more conformist and bourgeois than she appeared, when the time came for her to choose a husband, she set her sights on Guy Campbell Lyman, a young lawyer from New Orleans with a promising career. They married in May 1927.

Nevertheless, Helen left an indelible mark on Faulkner's work. She was the model for Patricia Robyn in *Mosquitoes*. Many years later, in *If I Forget Thee, Jerusalem*, she reappears as Charlotte Rittenmeyer, also a sculptress, who also bears a burn scar. Faulkner also remembered her in a couple of short stories, such as "Doctor Martino." Although Helen inspired him, she was never his muse. As far as we know, she never showed any interest in the writer. She may eventually have read the fifteen sonnets he dedicated to her, but she never read *Mayday* or *Mosquitoes*, and it would not be surprising to discover that she never read any of his novels. They did, however, see each other again from time to time after she married Lyman. They met for the last time in October 1955 in Pascagoula, where Faulkner visited her with his last mistress, Jean Stein. Helen had meant a lot to him, but he meant so little to her that she had no scruples about selling the letters and manuscripts he had sent her.

THE SWITCH TO PROSE

During his stay in New Orleans in 1925, between January 4, when he arrived, and July 7, when he left for Europe, Faulkner published poems, essays, and a review. In Paris he wrote sketches for the *New Orleans Times-Picayune*, sonnets for Helen Baird, and started work on "Elmer." This was the year when his apprenticeship in narrative prose truly started. But he had already been writing stories for a long time. A first short story, "Landing in Luck," appeared in the November–December 1919 issue of the *Mississippian*, one year after the armistice. It is the short tale of the first flight of Cadet Thompson, a fictional story with autobiographical overtones, inspired by Faulkner's recent experience as a cadet in the RAF in Canada. This tale was the start of his career as a storyteller, a modest start, as the anecdote was too flimsy, the humor overly volatile to show evidence of the promise of true talent.

"The Hill," a short prose poem, appeared in the same magazine on March 10, 1922. In it, Faulkner sets out the rural backdrop of his novels for the first time and introduces his first character, the unnamed "tieless casual." It is obviously a story of youth, written in rather stilted language, but the novelist's future work is heralded with astonishing clarity. Faulkner's writing was moving away from the traditional pastoral, and the vagueness of his theatrical gardens was being replaced by a rural landscape with more definite contours. The description of the hamlet in the valley, seen from the top of a hill by a day laborer, is without a doubt the first sketch of what was later to become the novelist's mythical Jefferson. Moreover, the contrast between the hill and the valley is rich in symbolic resonance. While the valley and its sleeping hamlet evoke "joys and sorrows, hopes and despairs" (*EPP*, 91) of people eking out a living, the hill overlooking them is portrayed as a high place between heaven and earth, haunted by the lofty dream of a free, sovereign existence. It is also no coincidence that the scene takes place at sunset, which represented for Faulkner, as Michel Gresset has noted, "the moment when all revelations become possible."[11] In "The Hill" the dusk mediates what is to happen to the wandering day laborer. But what in fact happens to him? Not much, in truth: "For a moment he had almost grasped something alien to him, but it eluded him; and being unaware that there was anything which had tried to break down the barriers of his mind and communicate with him, he was unaware that he had been eluded" (91–92). Dusk offers the promise of revelation. For a brief moment, the laborer stands "on one horizon and stared across at the other, far above a world of endless toil and troubled slumber; untouched, untouchable" (92). Although it seems that all the conditions are reunited for a Joycean epiphany, the spirit remains captive and enchained, and not even the attempt to break them pierces to the light of consciousness. There is no illumination, other than the laborer discovering "the devastating unimportance of his destiny" (92). "The Hill" is the tale of an epiphany missed. Like the faun imprisoned in marble, the vagrant's contemplation is in vain. Like the faun, he is a sort of double of the other failed watcher, the artist determined to see the invisible.

"The Hill" could thus be read as an ironic parable of the ambitions, always disappointed, of all art, like Borges's definition of the esthetic phenomenon as "this imminence of a revelation which does not occur."[12] "The Hill" was followed three years later by "Nympholepsy."[13] Once again, a day laborer climbs a hill at sunset, slowly coming back down into the valley after nightfall. However, this time there is a hint of a story. The tension comes from the fugitive apparition of a female figure, at first merely glimpsed, then frenetically and vainly pursued by the laborer. While remaining out of reach, this "something" that he almost grasped in "The Hill," here materializes in the desirable body of a hunted woman. Faulkner again uses the theme of the mysterious "white woman," a nymph or naiad, which he had already made frequent use of in his poems. In "Nympholepsy" the silent confrontation of the self and the world related in "The Hill" becomes a meeting with the other sex. The stakes of the quest have changed, because instead of an austere, almost abstract drama of the impossibility of knowing, "Nympholepsy" portrays the nightmare of thwarted desire and the impossibility of pleasure. This time a god is watching from a distance, both indifferent and tyrannical, a god "whose compulsions he must answer long after the more comfortable beliefs had become out-worn as a garment used everyday" (*US*, 334). Who is this enigmatic god? The sinister Pan? The fact remains that the man is panic-stricken and believes his end is nigh: "You are going to die, he told his body, feeling that imminent Presence again about him [. . .]. For an arrested fragment of time he felt, through vision without intellect, the waiting dark water, the treacherous log, the tree trunks pulsing and breathing and the branches like an invocation to a dark and unseen god" (334). It is at this moment that everything turns upside down and the laborer falls into the stream:

> In his fall was death, and a bleak derisive laughter. He died time and again, but his body refused to die. Then the water took him.
>
> Then the water took him. But here was something more than water. The water ran darkly between his body and his overalls and shirt, he felt his hair lap backward wetly. But here beneath his hand a startled thigh slid like a snake, among dark bubbles he felt a swift leg; and, sinking, the point of a breast scraped his back. Amid the slow commotion of disturbed water he saw death like a woman shining and drowned and waiting, saw a flashing body tortured by water; and his lungs spewing water gulped wet air. (335)

Here is water again, the metaphor of female death and the femme fatale. Faulkner pursued this theme throughout his career. The death of Ophelia by drowning is the epitome of erotic death. Drowning had already featured in *The Marionettes* and *Mayday* and again in *The Sound and the Fury*. The dual text of "The Hill" and "Nympholepsy" marks a dual threshold—to the "world" of the novelist and to the space of a creative work.

This as yet embryonic fictional universe can be glimpsed in three other short stories Faulkner wrote before 1924 that remained unpublished for many years. These were "Moonlight," "Love," and "Adolescence." On the face of it, these stories are as banal as their titles. All three are stories of desire and love, and two feature an adolescent as the main protagonist. The unfinished story "Love," the most convoluted and melodramatic of the three stories, portrays a handsome, brave squadron leader, an ex-pilot unjustly suspected of never having flown (a knowing, ironic nod to the author himself), and bored young women drinking tea. The ex-pilot is part of the "lost generation," the young women are taken from T. S. Eliot's early poems and Faulkner's "The Lilacs," and the crafty, wise Indochinese servant of the squadron leader comes straight out of Kipling. "Moonlight" relates the defeat of two pimply, pretentious young men looking for sexual adventures. "Adolescence" is the most interesting of the three, and as its title indicates, it is another story about young people: a love affair between Juliet Bunden, a young woman who looks like a tomboy, and a little rascal named Lee Hollowell, who is ruined by a cruel, interfering grandmother. Many critics have noted the signs and signals of future novels in this story, noting, for example, that the love story of Juliet and Lee prefigures the moonlit love scene of Donald and Emmy in *Soldiers' Pay*, that Juliet is a preliminary sketch of Jo-Addie in *Elmer* and of Patricia Robyn in *Mosquitoes*, and, finally, that Mrs. Bunden, Juliet's mother, is the precursor to Addie Bundren, the heroine of *As I Lay Dying*, even down to her name.

Two series of prose pieces follow. The first, made up of eleven short vignettes, appeared in January and February in the *Double Dealer*, the avant-garde New Orleans review. The second, comprising sixteen longer texts than the first, appeared in the literary Sunday supplement of the *Times-Picayune* between February and September. In many respects these are poetic prose pieces or even prose poems. The vignettes in the *Double Dealer*, in particular, are brief lyrical monologues, whose plaintive tone and affected rhetoric are strongly reminiscent of Faulkner as fin de siècle poet. Here, however, the satyrs and nymphs of the earlier poetry are replaced by an urban fauna of cobblers, dock workers, beggars, sailors, smugglers, mobsters, and whores, characters taken from the daily spectacle of the street, whose soliloquies are intertwined in a nostalgic round of lost illusions. These are simple people of meager means, many of whom live on the margins. Their picturesque shadows have something in common with Anderson's grotesques in *Winesburg, Ohio*. They are also reminiscent of Stephen Crane, and the naturalist tradition is evident in the attraction for the underbelly of society.

With these pieces Faulkner took a decisive step toward fictional prose, and from then on he would move toward the flexible and internalized realism that the critics of the day as yet vaguely associated with the "impressionistic method" ascribed to writers as different as Flaubert, James, Conrad, Crane, Anderson, and Joyce. He was already experimenting with new techniques, playing with the possibilities of the narrative voice, blurring chronology, and varying registers and viewpoints. In the vignettes that appeared in the *Double Dealer*, the narrative is constantly in the first person, and the short internal monologues in some of the longer stories published in the *Times-Picayune*—"Home" or "Out of Nazareth," for example—give a timorous foretaste of the two Joycean novels, *The Sound and the Fury* and *As I Lay Dying*.

In learning to write prose, Faulkner repeated the same procedure he followed in his poetic endeavors. He started by shamelessly and almost systematically imitating his more innovative elders. Read today, these vignettes are obviously Faulkner's; readers already familiar with his work will recognize the terrain immediately. David, the young, innocent, and carefree vagrant from *Out of Nazareth*, for example, is a Christlike figure, and the pregnant woman with the quiet faith to whom he is compared prefigures Lena Grove in *Light in August*. The lyrical end to "Frankie and Johnny" (a short story that remained unpublished until 1978) portends both the happy pregnancy of Lena and the unhappy pregnancy of Dewey Dell in *As I Lay Dying*:

> Frankie lay in the kindly dark, lightly stroking her young belly, staring out upon a dark world like hundreds of other girls, thinking of their lovers and their babies. She felt as impersonal as the earth itself; she was a strip of fecund seeded ground lying under the moon and wind and stars of the four seasons, lying beneath grey and sunny weather since before time was measured; and that now was sleeping away a dark winter waiting for her own spring with all the pain and passion of its inescapable ends to a beauty which shall not pass from the earth. (*US*, 347)

Again in "The Kingdom of God," another sketch with a religious title, and one of the best in the series, a simpleton with eyes the color of cornflowers

starts screaming when the stem of the daffodil he is holding is broken—
Benjy Compson, the idiot in *The Sound and the Fury*, is not far off. Similarly,
in "The Liar"—one of the last texts to be published in the *Times-Picayune*
and one of the first to mention horses and the rural world—Ek is an early sketch of V. K. Ratliff, teller of fantastic tales in *The Hamlet*, while the
Starnes, a family of poor hillbillies, foreshadow the turbulent Snopes tribe.

All of these sketches contain a germ of the novels and short stories
to come, whether through a trait, a motif, or a character. But on top of all
these hints, what is also striking is the extraordinary facility with which the
young writer is practicing his scales. Faulkner learned from his predeces-
sors with staggering speed. Some of these stories are excellent. "Country
Mice" starts masterfully, the dialogue is keenly observed and hilarious, and
the tale is told with consummate skill. Similarly, in "The Liar," a delicious
story in the Southern tradition of oral storytelling and also a quietly ironic
fable on the relationships between fiction, lying, and truth, Faulkner's talent as a storyteller shines through.

But however promising, the student's sketchbook does not have the
same value as the later masterpieces. The stories are uneven and the suspicion remains that some of these texts were written without much conviction. Faulkner needed money, and as with the later short stories he wrote
for mass-circulation magazines, he sometimes obligingly gave readers what
they wanted. For example, "Episode," a story about an old couple down on
their luck, is overly sentimental; "Jealousy" brazenly exploits the tried and
trusted formulas of the melodrama; and "Yo Ho and Two Bottles of Rum"
is little more than an obvious pastiche of Conrad. Incontestably, Faulkner
had skill and a lot of drive, cunning, and verve, but Anderson's words of
warning to the young budding virtuoso were pertinent: "You've got too
much talent. You can do it too easy, in too many different ways. If you're not
careful, you'll never write anything" (*ESPL*, 7).

Mayday, dated February 27, 1926, was originally one of those booklets
that was handwritten, illustrated, and bound by Faulkner's hand that he
more often than not gifted to women he was hoping to seduce. Dedicated
to Helen Baird, the initial version of *Mayday* is a forty-eight-page volume of
prose that can be read as a fairy tale (this is how Faulkner referred to it in a
letter to his mother), an allegory, and a short coming-of-age story. Tenny-
son in his poetry and the Pre-Raphaelites in their paintings were inspired

by the Arthurian legend and the tradition of courtly and chivalresque novels to evoke a dreamlike Middle Ages. In contrast, the myth was mocked by Beardsley in his illustrations for *Le Morte d'Arthur* and by James Branch Cabell in *Jurgen* (1919), his most scandalous and best-known book. *Mayday* was also a satire and a parody, and its debt to *Jurgen* is obvious. Faulkner assiduously borrowed from Cabell's novel not only in the themes and motifs of his text and the mocking tone of his writing but also in terms of the vocabulary, layout, and illustrations used.

The *Mayday* illustrations comprise two black-and-white drawings and three lithe, unusual watercolors—"The vision in the chapel," "The return to earth," and "The final vision"—the only watercolors by Faulkner that have survived. Their stylized arabesques, very close to the formal processes of art nouveau, may seem outdated, but, just as with his early drawings and the illustrations in *Marionettes*, they nonetheless reveal indisputable talent and great delicacy in their color work.

Mayday is the story of a quest. A young knight, Sir Galwyn of Arthgyl, gives up on society and, escorted by two allegorical "little characters" named Pain and Hunger, sets out on a quest to find the ideal woman seen in a dream: "a face all young and red and white, and with long shining hair like a column of fair sunny water" that made him think of "young hyacinths in the spring, and honey and sunlight" (*MD*, 50). For seven days he travels through a magical forest "where enchantments were as thick as mayflowers" (53). Then he meets three princesses. The first is Yseult, betrothed to the king of Cornwall, a pretty flirt whom he surprises as she is emerging, naked, out of the water in which she has been bathing. She is not the least discommoded by his intrusion, but he is so unmoved by her charms that he flees at the first opportunity. Elsy, daughter of the king of Wales, does not move him either. She invites him to spend the night with her in a tent, but he hastens on. The third he only barely escapes from. This is Aelia, the daughter of Aelius, prince of the Merovingians, who bears him upward in her heavenly chariot drawn by nine white dolphins.

All of these meetings are disappointing. The three princesses seek only to please and to seduce. Galwyn admires and compliments their beauty but cannot bear their posturing or prattling. Each time, he becomes overcome with impatience, and wonderment soon turns to weariness: "It is sharper than swords to know that she who is fairer than music could not content me for even a day" (*MD*, 71). None of them are what he seeks, indeed no woman can be, because what he wants and hopes for is from another world, outside reality.

The quest ends on the banks of an enchanted river where Galwyn finds "one all young and white, and with long shining hair like a column of fair sunny water" (*MD*, 87). This is the woman he had seen in a dream before setting out. Here, finally, is the ideal woman he was seeking, but she cannot become his lifelong companion. He can join her only by drowning, because, as Saint Francis of Assisi tells him, she is in fact "Little Sister Death"—an allegorical figure borrowed from *Canticle of the Creatures*, whom Faulkner had already portrayed as a young girl with "a young body all shining" and "eyes the color of sleep" in *The Kid Learns*, a sketch published in 1925 in the *Times-Picayune*.

Mayday is little more than an amiable fantasy. However, as with all of the young Faulkner's texts, it prefigures in many ways the work to come. Echoes of *Mayday* can be heard in *The Sound and the Fury*, at the very start of Quentin Compson's monologue when, upon waking, he hears the tick-tock of his watch: "Like Father said down the long and lonely light rays you might see Jesus walking, like. And the good Saint Francis that said Little Sister Death, that never had a sister" (*N1*, 935).[14] The return of "Little Sister Death" in the novel makes Quentin Compson's imminent drowning in the Charles River a repetition of Galwyn's suicide for love. However, in the meantime, the allegorical "Little Sister" of the fable takes the name and face of Caddy, the sister with whom Quentin is incestuously in love.

Similarly in *Mayday*, as later in his early novels, maxims and aphorism abound. One example is this blasé definition of man, which could be describing old Compson in *The Sound and the Fury*: "To my notion man is a buzzing fly blundering through a strange world, seeking something he can neither name nor recognize and probably will not want" (*MD*, 71). Like *The Marble Faun* or *The Marionettes*, *Mayday* is a minor meditation on the paradoxes and wounds of desire, and this now outdated prose parody at times contains astonishingly modern reflections. Thus Galwyn notes, after meeting Yseult: "It occurs to me [. . .] that it is not the thing itself that man wants, so much as the wanting of it" (71). The desire for love means wanting an obscure object that is always evasive or lost and for which all objects, those that are real and can be possessed, can be only poor substitutes. For Faulkner that desire would never be anything else.

NOTES

1. Carvel Emerson Collins and William Faulkner, *Helen, a Courtship; and Mississippi Poems* (New Orleans: Tulane University Press, 1981), 112.

2. See Linton Reynolds Massey, *Man Collecting: The Works of William Faulkner*, an exhibition catalog compiled by Joan St. Crane and Anne E. H. Freudenberg, University Press of Virginia, 1975, 126.

3. William Faulkner, "Marriage," *Vision in Spring* (Austin: University of Texas Press, 1984), 68.

4. Stéphane Mallarmé, *Œuvres complètes*, ed. Henri Mondor and G. Jean-Aubry (Paris: Gallimard, Pléiade, 1945), 45.

5. Sigmund Freud, *A General Introduction to Psychoanalysis*, trans. James Strachey (1920; New York: Liveright, 1966), 328.

6. William Spratling, "Chronicle of a Friendship: William Faulkner in New Orleans," in William Spratling and William Faulkner, *Sherwood Anderson and Other Famous Creoles* (New Orleans: Pelican Bookshop Press, 1926), 11.

7. Sherwood Anderson, *We Moderns: Gotham Book Mart, 1920–1940* (New York, 1940), 29.

8. Spratling, "Chronicle of a Friendship," 35.

9. Spratling and Faulkner, *Sherwood Anderson*; Ernest Hemingway, *Torrents of Spring* (New York: Scribner's, 1926).

10. William Faulkner letter, undated, William B. Wisdom Collection, Tulane University Library, New Orleans.

11. Michael Gresset, *Faulkner ou la fascination: poétique du regard* (Paris: Klincksieck, 1982), 55.

12. *Labyrinths: Selected Stories and Other Writings*, ed. Donald A. Yates and James E. Irby (Harmondsworth: Penguin, 2000), 223.

13. This text was probably written at the beginning of Faulkner's stay in New Orleans, but this cannot be ascertained. The title comes from the Greek *nympholeptos*, meaning possessed by nymphs, in a state of rapture. Faulkner may have borrowed the term from Swinburne, George Moore, or Conrad Aiken.

14. Francis of Assisi also appears briefly in *The Wishing Tree*, the lovely children's story that Faulkner wrote for his adoptive daughter, Victoria Franklin, in 1927.

3
BIRTH OF A NOVELIST

THE FIRST NOVEL: *SOLDIERS' PAY*

On February 16, 1925, Faulkner wrote to his mother: "Right now I am 'thinking out' a novel. As soon as I get it all straight, I will begin work" (*LMF*, 184). This is the first written mention of what was to become his first published novel. He set to work right away, throwing himself into it. In the spring of 1925, in New Orleans, he was so taken up with writing his novel that he forgot to write to those who were nearest and dearest to him. Intrigued by his silence, Phil Stone telegraphed him: "WHATS THE MATTER DO YOU HAVE A MISTRESS?" Faulkner's reply was, "YES AND SHES 30000 WORDS LONG" (*B1*, 135).

Most of Faulkner's novels originate in the expansion of a short story or the assembling of several stories, already published or unpublished. The first, *Soldiers' Pay*, already illustrates this rule: an attentive reading of the handwritten manuscript and the first typed version, found in 1970, showed that behind the novel were two probably unfinished and unrelated short stories.[1] Moreover, in working on this book, Faulkner proceeded in a manner that thereafter became habitual. First of all, he wrote the story out by hand, with his small, tight, elegant handwriting, which was—as will be familiar to anyone who has tried to decipher it—barely legible, and then revised the manuscript, typing it up after that while making new corrections. He pushed himself to move on, scribbling a note to himself in the margins of the typescript: "Work." He followed this injunction tenaciously. "My novel is going splendidly," he wrote his mother in early April 1925. "I put in almost 8 hours a day on it—I work so much that the end of my 'typewriting' finger is like a boil all the time" (*LMF*, 195).

In the same letter, Faulkner reports that after reading a chapter, Sherwood Anderson promised to recommend the novel to his editor, Horace Liveright, contradicting what he later told Jean Stein in this regard in 1956 (see *LG*, 249–50). On May 12, in another letter to his mother, Faulkner announced that he had completed the manuscript:

> I finished my novel last night. I think I wrote almost 10000 words yesterday between 10:00 am and midnight—a record, if I did. 3000 is a fair day's work. I am kind of sorry, I never have enjoyed anything as much. I know Ill never have as much fun with the next one—which by the way I am all ready to go to work on—when I have had a short holiday. All necessary now is to correct it then have it neatly typed and send it to the publisher. (*LMF*, 208)

By the end of May he had sent the typescript to New York publisher Boni & Liveright. On October 16, 1925, at the end of his stay in Paris, a letter from the publisher informed him that his first novel had been accepted.

The initial title was *Mayday*, but the publisher decided instead to call it *Soldiers' Pay*. Overjoyed at the prospect of becoming a published author, Faulkner did not oppose this change and so the novel appeared under its new title on February 25, 1926.

Soldiers' Pay is, in many respects, a novel of the "lost generation." John Dos Passos in *Three Soldiers* (1921) and E. E. Cummings in *The Enormous Room* (1922) had been the first to publish in this genre, and nobody knew better how to capture the despair of that generation than Hemingway in *The Sun Also Rises*. Published the same year as Hemingway's first novel, *Soldiers' Pay*, Faulkner's first novel, is part of the same movement. However, by the mid-1920s the disenchantment of the postwar period was no more than a pose, and figures such as the sad young man, the demobilized soldier, or the Fitzgerald-style flapper had already become nothing more than stereotypes. *Soldiers' Pay* is a novel of and for its time. Traces of James Branch Cabell, Joseph Hergesheimer, and Aldous Huxley, successful 1920s writers, can be found in this book. Faulkner borrowed from the elegant libertinism of the first, the erudite languor of the second, and the teeming ideas of the third. T. S. Eliot, whose influence was already tangible in many of Faulk-

ner's poems, would also loom over many of his novels. Even Aubrey Beardsley, one of Faulkner's models for his illustrations, leaves traces here that
are legible if not strictly visible. Finally, the young novelist cites poems that
were to appear in 1933 in *A Green Bough*. He had not yet entirely given up
on the idea of being a poet.

A postwar novel, *Soldiers' Pay* starts with the lively retelling of the return of combatants, followed by a description of the small town of Charleston, Georgia, which is getting ready to welcome them home. There is no
central plot, but the novel revolves mainly around the long wake organized
for Lieutenant Donald Mahon, a young fighter pilot, maimed, disfigured,
almost dumb, and soon to be blind, who comes home from the war to die
among his own—one of those temporary survivors of the Great War who
resurface in *Flags in the Dust*. Faulkner also alludes to them in several short
stories, such as "Ad Astra," when on November 11, 1918, Armistice Day, a
captain asks his companions: "What will you do? What will any of us do?
All this generation which fought in the war is dead tonight. But we do not
yet know it" (CS, 421).

Like *As I Lay Dying* three years later, *Soldiers' Pay* is first and foremost
the story of a death. Plunged into a semi-comatose state, with no past, no
future, Mahon cannot come back to life but also cannot die as long as he
has not recovered his memory, even for an instant—that is, the awareness
of his identity in time: "And suddenly he found that he was passing from the
dark world in which he had lived for a time he could not remember, again
into a day that had long passed, that had already been spent by those who
lived and wept and died, and so remembering it, this day was his alone: the
one trophy he had reft from Time and Space. Per ardua ad astra" (N1, 234).

It is only when he remembers and finally recovers his day alone, his day
of glory and light, relives one last time in all its intensity his fatal meeting
with the enemy airplane, and can say to his father "That's how it happened"
(N1, 235), that he becomes himself again and deliverance becomes possible.
Now that the past has woken up and welded itself again to the present, Mahon has a future again, albeit a backward future, a future of death.

More icon than character, Mahon, the man living on borrowed time,
lost in the world without being part of it, is the first sketch of that animal—
incomplete and infirm, unconvinced of his own existence and almost de-
fenseless against reality, always already defeated, always dispossessed of

himself, and yet also recalcitrant, indomitable, invincible—that Faulkner tirelessly portrays in his novels.[2]

Through this character hovering between life and death, Faulkner begins an enduring questioning of time and memory, of awareness and identity. Mahon's pathetic fumbling in the dark as he lies dying is like the inverted emblem of the arduous task that Faulkner himself is about to undertake. For the novelist the search for identity is inconceivable outside time: anamnesis, the rediscovery of past knowledge, is required; the buried past needs to be brought to light and brought to life. The dying Mahon has to find at least a fragment, a shard, of this past to enter into *his* death. Faulkner's responsibility, apparently, is to make the return journey, not to die, like his hero, but to be finally born to writing, real writing, which bears absence and presence, which is death and life together. Descending to the most obscure, most secret parts of his memory, sinking down to the deepest time and place, where it ceases to be personal and melds into the memory of all, and then coming back up, exorcising it and recreating it through the magic of language—this is the primordial quest.

Mahon is the foreshadowing of this quest. In the novel he is a man dying among the living and an ironic reminder of the horrors of war in the middle of the futile busyness of a small Southern town. In this dual function he is the opposite of Januarius Jones, an obese satyr with "eyes, clear and yellow, obscene and old in sin as a goat's" (*N1*, 229), whose libidinous restlessness acts as a counterpoint to the long, slow death of the wounded warrior. The vulgar hedonism of Jones is the antithesis of Mahon's warlike romanticism, although the two are bound together by a secret affinity. Jones, in fact, is a flabby caricature of Mahon before the war: a young, spirited lover, "with the serenity of a wild thing, the passionate serene alertness of a faun" (63). The contrast between the two characters is also one of before and after, of a lost lust for life and an execrable present: the love between Mahon and Emmy was a serious, tender idyll, while the lechery of Jones is merely the libido of a buffoon.

Both a wake and a ballet of desire, *Soldiers' Pay* is something of a dance of death. That Mahon's funeral coincides with the moment when Emmy finally succumbs to the perverted onslaught of Jones is evidently not fortuitous. Such forced coincidences show that Faulkner still had much to learn about handling irony. The young novelist piles on the effects but does not yet know how to control them. In this first novel the portrayal of the comedy of the sexes remains juvenile in its studied cynicism, but, for the first time, desire and death are perceived as complicit forces: "Sex and death: the front door and the back door of the world. How indissolubly are they associated in us! In youth they lift us out of the flesh, in old age they reduce us again to the flesh; one to fatten us, the other to flay us, for the worm. When are sexual compulsions more readily answered than in war or famine or flood or fire?" (*N1*, 236). The complicity of Eros and Thanatos haunts Faulkner from his earliest writings, and it resurfaces in his first novel. But *Soldiers' Pay* barely touches and strokes a hesitant sexuality: "Touch and retreat no satiety" (156). Between sophisticated banter and vaudeville, the intrigues, escapades, and pursuits of this novel revolve around a trio of young women. One of them is Cecily Saunders, Mahon's stupid, pretty fiancée, a cousin of the nymphs and naiads of his early poems and of the narcissistic Marietta in *Marionettes*, with "her body created for all men to dream after. [. . .] Her body, which was no body, crumpling a dress that had been dreamed. Not for maternity, not even for love: a thing for the eyes and the mind" (*N1*, 179). The perverse yet vernal Cecily, girl-flower, girl-bird, girl-poplar—a character likely inspired by Estelle Oldham, Faulkner's first love—is the first of a cohort of young androgynous women in his fiction. She reappears in less stylized form in *Mosquitoes* as Patricia Robyn and in darker, more troubling form as Temple Drake in *Sanctuary*. In contrast to Cecily stands Emmy, the loyal nymph, simple and submissive, loving and nurturing—the first of his motherly figures, loved from an early age and unforgettable. The third woman, Margaret Powers, a neurotic war widow with black eyes and hair, a livid face, and a scarlet mouth "like a scar" (*N1*, 29), marries the dying warrior. Margaret Powers is a curious character, at once maternal nurse and angel of death, a tormented young widow and reincarnation of the turn-of-the-century femme fatale: "Beardsley [. . .] had drawn her so often dressed in peacock hues, white and slim and depraved among meretricious trees and impossible marble fountains" (22).

Strictly speaking, this first novel is not autobiographical as is so often the case with first novels, but all that we now know of Faulkner's youth points to the fictional transposition of a double failure that was still raw. In his dumb immobility, Donald Mahon is the warrior version of the marble faun and "Shade of Pierrot" in *Marionettes*. The fact that the young males in

Soldiers' Pay are spurned suitors is also no accident. Mahon is abandoned by Cecily, his frivolous fiancée, just as the young Faulkner was abandoned by Estelle; George Farr, Cecily's future husband, suffers the agonies of morbid jealousy; Joe Gilligan's romantic love for Margaret Powers is hopeless; and even Januarius Jones, the unflagging skirt chaser, remains perpetually unsatisfied.

On top of the sentimental failure comes the failure, no less stinging, of a heroic dream. The Great War was over before the young Faulkner was able to play his part. Before fiction echoed this cruel frustration, his embroidering of the truth was the first avowal and the first denial. In *Soldiers' Pay* fiction takes over the embroidering. The first 130 pages of the novel drafted by Faulkner had "cadet" Julian Lowe as protagonist, a boy of nineteen, gauche, naive, and inconsolable, just as the cadet Faulkner had been, at being deprived of his war. However, in the published version of the novel, Lowe—a character prefigured by the cadet Thompson in "Landing in Luck"—is no longer the central figure. He has entered into the orbit of another character, with whom he fully identifies, a character he would have liked to be and is sorry that he is not: "To have been him [. . .] Just to be him! Let him take this sound body of mine! Let him take it. To have got wings on my breast, to have wings; and to have got his scar, too, I would take death to-morrow" (*N1*, 33–34). This wounded hero, this warrior shot down, is Donald Mahon, another character prefigured in Faulkner's early writing, in particular "The Lilacs" and "An Armistice Day Poem," two of his earliest poems. Mahon is the epic double of Lowe. He is also another double of the novelist and is easily recognizable as such; there are plenty of physical similarities between Mahon at eighteen and Faulkner at the same age. When he looks at his photograph, Jones is struck by the "thin face with a delicate pointed chin and wild, soft eyes" (51). Like Faulkner on his return from Canada, Mahon wears the uniform of a British officer and has a copy of *A Shropshire Lad*, a collection of poetry by Alfred Edward Housman that the young Faulkner greatly admired and knew so well that he quoted verses to his friends (see *B1*, 49). From imposture to fiction, the wounded warrior becomes a character in a novel. Faulkner is starting to "lie truthfully." Just like Johnny Sartoris in *Flags in the Dust* some time later, Donald Mahon is the portrait of the *dreamed hero*, a representation of the ideal, inaccessible self. Julian Lowe, on the other hand, is the mocking portrait of the young dreamer, dazzled and fascinated by the prestige of heroic action that he can never live up to. *Soldiers' Pay* also has strong autobiographical overtones; the true birth of the novelist is yet to come. However, the traces are blurring; the mirrors are shaking.

Formally, *Soldiers' Pay* breaks with the conventions of realism and proudly flaunts its modernity. As early as the first section of the first chapter, which relates the return of the demobilized soldiers, the reader is surprised by the mischievous exuberance of a language that mixes military slang, fragments of bawdy songs, literary allusions, and lyrical flights of fancy. What follows is less virulently stylized, but throughout the novel Faulkner continues to experiment with rhetorical and narrative processes as he had already done in his New Orleans writings. The tale is not told chronologically and contains many fragmentations. Scenes and vignettes succeed one another in a pattern that seems to owe more to cinematic editing than to the traditional novel. Without notice, the story switches from one stylistic register to another and the narrative focus is extremely fluid. The viewpoint is most often that of the omniscient narrator, but Faulkner also makes use of free indirect speech and, less successfully, stream of consciousness. Margaret Powers invokes her husband who died in the war thus: "Dick. Dick. Dead, ugly Dick. Once you were alive and young and passionate and ugly, after a time you were dead, dear Dick: that flesh, that body, which I loved and did not love; your beautiful, young, ugly body, dear Dick, become now a seething of worms, like new milk. Dear Dick" (N1, 33).

Soldiers' Pay is a novel that is constantly moving; the narrative perspectives alternate, voices succeed each other, idioms and tones overlap. However, all this dispersion does not lead to disorder. On the contrary, Faulkner's first novel confirms the remarkable attention to composition that he had already shown in *The Marble Faun* and *Vision in Spring*. While it is true that the text is very fragmented, with its nine chapters divided into subsections that often are nothing more than brief dialogs, the novel's structure is nonetheless rigorously delineated, and Faulkner makes constant use of symmetry and parallels. The tale of Mahon's return in the second section of chapter 2 is paralleled by the tale of his death in the final section of chapter 8. The entire novel is organized around these two expected events, and the end matches the beginning: in the first chapter Joe Gilligan, on the train bringing the demobilized soldiers home, falls for Margaret Powers; in the final chapter another train carries off forever the young woman he loves.

As Faulkner was later to acknowledge, there was a good deal of play in this first novel, but this play was not in the least gratuitous. This book must be given its proper place in the writer's career: a link between the poetry and prose of youth and the novels to come.

———

In February 1926, on the publication of *Soldiers' Pay*, Faulkner was in New Orleans. Only twenty-five hundred copies of the first edition were printed, but by May over two thousand had been sold—quite encouraging for a first novel. The reviews appeared from April on and were overwhelmingly positive. The anonymous review published in the *New York Times* on April 11 praised the young novelist's "hard intelligence" and "consummate pity." The *Independent*'s critic hailed the book as "an extraordinary performance." In the *New Orleans Times-Picayune*, John McClure saw it as "the most noteworthy first novel of the year," and Donald Davidson, in the *Nashville Tennessean*, found it far superior to Dos Passos's *Three Soldiers*. Four years later, when *Soldiers' Pay* was published in the United Kingdom, Richard Hughes, the author of the extremely popular *A High Wind in Jamaica* (1929), in his preface to the British edition, and the novelist Arnold Bennett, in a review for the *Evening Standard* (June 26, 1930), both found much to praise.

However, the book received only negative reactions in Oxford. It did not scandalize the town to the same extent as *Sanctuary* would a few years later, but it was largely disliked, as were all of Faulkner's novels up to *Intruder in the Dust*. Phil Stone offered to donate a copy to the university library but this was turned down. Even within Faulkner's family, consternation reigned. Forewarned about the novel's shocking nature, his father did not even deign to open it. His aunt Mary Wilkins, née Holland—the one they called "Auntee"—wrote him to tell him the best he could do would be to leave the country. His mother, whom one would have thought might be more understanding, was of the same opinion: "There wasn't anything else for Billy to do after that came out—he couldn't stay here" (*B1*, 177).

AN AMERICAN IN PARIS

Since the nineteenth century, the European tour meant a return to the cradle of Western culture to every cultivated American. Faulkner also undertook this pilgrimage. At the end of June 1925, three weeks after his return to

Oxford, he went back to New Orleans to embark on the cargo ship *West Ivis*. His traveling budget was modest; in his pocket he had some of the money from his contributions to reviews, fifty dollars given him by the Young Colonel, and an advance of thirty dollars from the *Times-Picayune* for three new "sketches." He was accompanied by his friend Bill Spratling, and before leaving he reassured his mother that they would not be left to their own devices and that they wanted for nothing. On the eve of his departure, he wrote to her: "Bill and I have been given by kind friends a hundred of addresses of nice people in Europe who will feed us" (*LMF*, 213).

The *West Ivis* set sail on July 7, 1925. After a four-week crossing, Faulkner and Spratling disembarked in Genoa on August 2. They went to a somewhat louche cabaret with the first mate and chief engineer to change their money and were soon joined there by some girls. A round of beer was ordered and Spratling began to dance. When he reached "that stage where everything seemed irresistibly amusing," he threw a few coins under the table to see what his dancing partner, her pimp, and their companions would do. A row broke out. Arrested by the carabinieri, Spratling spent the night in the filthy Genoa jail, and the American consul and a city hall official had to be prevailed upon to secure his release the next day.[3]

Faulkner first visited Rapallo, in northern Italy, where Ezra Pound was composing his *Cantos*; Pavia, "a lovely place—quite old, little narrow streets, all cobbled, and only about two automobiles in town" (*SL*, 8); and Milan, where he was enchanted by the cathedral: "This Cathedral! Can you imagine stone lace? Or frozen music? All covered with gargoyles like dogs, and mitered cardinals and mailed knights and saints pierced with arrows and beautiful naked Greek figures that have no religious significance whatever" (9). He then spent "2 days at a grand village on an Alp above Stresa" (9), crossed the Simplon Pass in August, stopped off in Montreux, traveled through Switzerland, stopped in Geneva, and on August 11 took the train for Paris, arriving the next day. He first took a room in a small hotel in Montparnasse (full board at thirty francs a day) and then moved to a furnished room on the top floor of 26 de la rue Servandoni, near the Luxembourg Gardens, where, as he wrote his great-aunt Alabama, he spent most of his time: "I write there, and play with the children, help them sail their boats, etc. There is an old bent man who sails a toy boat on the pool, with the most beautiful rapt face you ever saw. When I am old enough to no longer have to make excuses for not working, I shall have a weathered derby hat like his and spend my days sailing a toy boat in the Luxembourg Gardens" (19).

At the time, the exchange rate was very favorable for American visitors. The young Faulkner was able to live on just two dollars a day. He let his beard grow: "Makes me look sort of distinguished, like someone you'd care to know" (SL, 18), and, in a letter to his great-aunt Bama he enclosed a small self-portrait in ink showing him with a beard. A photograph taken by his photographer friend William Odiorne shows him in profile, sitting in the Luxembourg Gardens, pensive, sporting a thick black beard, and wearing a rough tweed jacket and felt hat.[4] He bought a beret, perhaps to look more French or more artistic. He dressed like a bohemian but conscientiously visited the city sights and sent his mother often detailed reports of his days. Between August 6 and October 15, Miss Maud received no fewer than twenty-five letters and postcards, from which we can more or less piece together how her son spent his days. On Sunday, August 16, only three days after arriving in Paris, he took a riverboat to Suresnes, crossed the Bois de Boulogne, stopped off at the Arc de Triomphe, went down the Champs-Élysées to Place de la Concorde, had lunch in a bistro, took the metro to Bastille, and went to Père-Lachaise Cemetery to visit the grave of Oscar Wilde. That evening he wrote a long letter to his mother telling her all about his day. The letter ends with a description of the Cathedral of Notre-Dame that echoes the description of Milan Cathedral, sent a few days earlier, and that he recalled many years later in *A Fable* and *The Town*: "The cathedral of Notre-Dame is grand. Like the cathedral of Milan, it is all covered with cardinals mitered like Assyrian kings, and knights leaning on long swords and saints and angels, and beautiful naked Greek figures that have no religious significance what ever, and gargoyles—creatures with heads of goats and dogs, and claws and wings on men's bodies, all staring down in a jeering sardonic mirth" (SL, 12).

On his own or with friends, Faulkner strolled around the streets of Saint-Germain-des-Prés and the Latin Quarter, had a drink on the terrace of Les Deux Magots, wandered around under the chestnut trees in the Luxembourg Gardens, spent entire days in the Louvre admiring the great icons of Western art—the *Winged Victory*, the *Venus de Milo*, the *Mona Lisa*—and "the paintings of the more-or-less moderns, like Degas and Manet and

Chavannes" (*SL*, 13). He also went to see a futurist and vorticist exhibition, the private collections of Matisse and Picasso, and marveled at Cézanne's paintings. On September 2 he visited the International Exhibition of Modern Industrial and Decorative Arts, open since April, with a French sculptor. He found it interesting, "like reading a gorgeous fairy tale," but found there "nothing especially good." To his taste, for once stereotypical, it was "too colorful, too French" (17).

Like a good tourist, he also spent an evening at the Moulin Rouge. He wrote to his mother: "Anyone in America will tell you it is the last word in sin and iniquity. It is a music hall, where ladies come out clothed principally in lip stick. Lots of bare beef, but that is only secondary" (*SL*, 24). However, he was not just titillated by the nudity of the dancers. The vulgarity of the spectacle, to his eyes, did not mean there was no beauty in it: "Their songs and dances are set to real music—there was one with not a rag on except a coat of gold paint who danced to a ballad of Rimsky-Korsakoff's, a Persian thing; and two others, a man stained brown like a faun and a lady who had on at least twenty beads, I'll bet money, performed a short tone poem of the Scandinavian composer Sibelius. It was beautiful" (24).

At the time, Paris was the capital of emigration and the most cosmopolitan city in the world. It was also the rallying point of a fervently Francophile American bohemia. "America is my country and Paris is my home town," said Gertrude Stein.[5] In the first ten years of the new century, the American colony gravitated around her and her brother Leo. In the 1920s at least a third of what would later be called the Modernists set up home in Paris: young painters like Charles Demuth and Stuart Davis; avant-garde composers like Virgil Thompson and George Antheil; and writers like Ezra Pound, Scott Fitzgerald and Ernest Hemingway. All of these people frequented the cafés, restaurants, and bars of Montparnasse: Le Dôme; La Coupole; La Rotonde; Le Gypsy; Le Select, the first café open at night; Le Jockey, where jazz was playing well before *La Revue Nègre* in 1925; or the tiny Dingo Bar in rue Delambre, where Hemingway first met Fitzgerald. Another meeting place for ex-pats was Sylvia Beach's now legendary bookstore *Shakespeare & Company* at 12 rue de l'Odéon, whose regulars, already known or as yet unknown, were Antheil, Pound, Wilder, Anderson, Fitzgerald, Hemingway, Archibald MacLeish, Djuna Barnes, and James Joyce, already recognized by some as a literary giant and the first beneficiary of Sylvia Beach's extraordinary generosity.

Faulkner had heard of this Anglo-American Paris of the Roaring Twenties, later recalled by Hemingway in *A Movable Feast*, but his visit there was short. One day he bumped into Pound, and another day in a café near Place de l'Odéon he saw Joyce, the only writer he remembered seeing during his stay in Paris (see *FU*, 72). We also know that he spent a few evenings at the salon of Gertrude Stein at 27 rue de Fleurus, although he never mentioned it.

For Faulkner, as for any cultivated American, France was the country of writers and painters. But no doubt more than for some, it was for him a tragic country, still wounded by the Great War, the war that continued to haunt him, all the more so because he had not taken part but wished he had. In an admirable letter to his mother dated September 6, he mentions all the young soldiers who died in the war:

> And near the cathedrals, in the religious stores, any number of inscriptions to dead soldiers, and always at the bottom: "Pray for him." And so many many young men on the streets, bitter and gray-faced, on crutches or with empty sleeves and scarred faces. And now they must still fight, with a million young men already dead between Dunkirk and the Vosges, in Morocco. Poor France, so beautiful and unhappy and so damn cheerful. (*SL*, 12)

In late September he left Paris to visit the battlefields. On the twenty-first he left for Rennes; the next day he was in Rouen. From Rouen he went to Amiens, and from there to Compiègne and Pont-Sainte-Maxence. It was raining. Faulkner recalled that the 1918 German offensive had cost the lives of half a million men and described the countryside ravaged by war: "Trenches are gone, but still rolls of wire and shell cases and 'duds' piled along the hedge-rows, and an occasional tank rusting in a farm yard. Trees all with tops blown out of them, and cemeteries everywhere" (*SL*, 26). He returned to this topic on October 3: "It looks as if a cyclone had passed over the whole world at about 6 feet above the ground. Stubs of trees, and along the main road are piles of shell cases and unexploded shells and wire and bones that the farmers dig up. Poor France!" (28) On September 28 he arrived in Compiègne, near where the armistice was signed in the railway carriage at Rethondes. The next day he was on the road back to Paris, via Senlis and Chantilly. He would later recall this ten-day trip when writing *A Fable*.

In early October, Faulkner took the train for Dieppe and then took the ferry across the channel to spend a week in England. From Newhaven he traveled to London, where he was immediately struck by the fog, which was "not only greasy but [...] full of coal smoke" (*SL*, 29). Although he liked English food, he was not much taken by London. He found the city dirty, sad, and much too expensive for his wallet. Nevertheless, he visited Buckingham Palace, Westminster, the Tower of London, Piccadilly, St. Paul's Cathedral, Trafalgar Square, Mayfair, and "all those old coffee houses where Ben Jonson and Addison and Marlowe sat and talked" (29). But what he liked most of all was the lush green countryside of Kent: "Quietest most restful country under the sun. No wonder Joseph Conrad could write fine books here" (30).

He returned to Paris on October 16. A letter from Boni & Liveright was waiting for him, informing him that his first novel was to be published under the title *Soldiers' Pay*. The envelope also contained an advance of two hundred dollars. In late November he packed his bags and on December 9 he took the train for Cherbourg and bought a third-class ticket home on the S.S. *Republic*. On the nineteenth, a few days before Christmas, he landed in Hoboken, New Jersey. At the end of the month, after a brief stay in New York, he returned to Oxford with his beard and his pipe, more disheveled than ever.

In all, his trip, which was supposed to take a lot longer, had taken barely five months—hardly an odyssey. However, Faulkner made it a point of honor not to be a tourist like others, convincingly playing the somewhat conventional part of the traveling artist in the Romantic tradition. In his letters he speaks of his hatred for the vulgarity of American tourists. The postcard he sent to his mother from Domodossola, Italy, started with the words: "Full of Americans—terrible" (*SL*, 10). He disliked Switzerland all the more because for him it was a scaled-down version of America. He wrote Aunt Bama: "Switzerland is a big country club with a membership principally American. And I am quite disgusted with my own nationality in Europe. Imagine a stranger coming in your home, spitting on your floor and flinging you a dollar. That's the way they act" (19). Faulkner was one of those Americans who are ashamed of their compatriots when they come across them abroad. By contrast, he had plenty of admiration and affection for aristocrats, laborers, and country folk. In a letter dated September 10, 1925, he recounts a brief, idyllic stay in an Italian village:

[It is] a hamlet in the mountains above Maggiore, where I lived with the peasants, going out with them in the morning to cut grass, eating bread and cheese and drinking wine from a leather bottle at noon beneath a faded shrine with a poor little bunch of flowers in it, and then coming down the mountain at sunset, hearing the bells on the mule jingle and seeing half the world turning lilac with evening. Then to eat supper outdoors at a wooden table worn smooth by generations of elbows, to get mildly drunk and talk to those kind quiet happy people by signs. (19)

Like many American artists and writers of his generation, the young Faulkner was attracted to a way of being in France and Italy that was the complete opposite of the American way of life, a slower, more nonchalant pace, an indolent dolce vita: "No automobiles, and people enjoy themselves so calmly—no running about at all. It seems to be part of the day to do as little work as possible and have as much calm pleasure as you can" (*SL*, 9). He appreciated the gaiety, the conviviality, and the happiness of being together demonstrated by the French and Italians: "The Latin peoples do their holidays so jolly [. . .] laughing and talking and wishing each other well" (12). He also envied them their sexuality, more natural, more fulfilled than American Puritanism:

After having observed Americans in Europe I believe more than ever that sex with us has become a national disease. The way we get it into our politics and religion, where it does not belong anymore than digestion belongs there. All our paintings, our novels, our music, is concerned with it, sort of leering and winking and rubbing hands on it. But Latin people keep it where it belongs, in a secondary place. Their painting and music and literature has nothing to do with sex. Far more healthy than our way. (24)

At the time, these comparisons between European and American culture were common currency. In truth, Faulkner's musings on the psychology of peoples are not always cliché-free: "The French are polite but not really courteous; they are not kind-hearted [. . .] but they are heroic" (28); "every one [. . .] in France spends the evening sitting in cafes playing cards or listening to music" (*LMF*, 225).

He was charmed by Europe. He enjoyed discovering France and Italy and would return later with pleasure. In 1955 he told Cynthia Grenier:

"France and Italy are two of my favorite countries. I feel Paris is a kind of home for me. It's a part of everyone's cultural background. There's the liberty here to be an artist. It's in the air" (*LG*, 216). However, in contrast to Fitzgerald, Hemingway, and so many other of his compatriots of the lost generation, Faulkner did not settle down abroad.

In the biographical notice sent to his editor in September 1924, he wrote "Oxford, Mississippi" as his "temporary" address. Was he seriously thinking of leaving his hometown to go live and write elsewhere? It is highly unlikely. On October 17, 1925, a few weeks before leaving Paris to return home, he wrote to his father:

> I have just been thinking myself that I have been away from our blue hills and sage fields and things long enough. [. . .] I've seen people and different things, I've walked a lot in some fine country in France and England, but after all its not like mounting that northeast hill and seeing Woodson's ridge, or the pine hills on the Pontotoc road, or slogging through those bare fields back of the campus in drizzling rain. (*LMF*, 218–19)

Faulkner was eager to return to his native Ithaca, eager to see its fields and hills once more. As in 1918, the first time he ventured outside the South, he was homesick. On April 6 of that year, just two days after arrival in New Haven, Connecticut, he told his father that he was terribly homesick. And when he was in Toronto, on November 15, he wrote to his mother: "Won't it be good to get home! I dream about it every night, now" (130). Any time he lived anywhere but Rowan Oak, he became homesick. More evidence of this can be found in this letter he sent to Estelle from Hollywood on March 2, 1936: "Getting along fine [. . .] I wish I was at home, still in the kitchen with my family around me and my hand full of Old Maid cards" (*SL*, 94–95). Although it is true that he did quite a lot of wandering during his youth, the wanderer, as we know, was just one role among others, and he saw himself as violently sedentary (see *US*, 431). He was attached to a place although unable to find a footing, unable to be at home with himself. Speaking of himself in the third person in a letter to Malcolm Cowley dated 1945, he acknowledged that on his return to Oxford after the armistice of World War I, he did not feel at home: "At home again in Oxford, Mississippi, yet at the same time not at home" (*FCF*, 74). For this sedentary traveler, elsewhere was right here: the outside was on the inside, distance was close-up, disorientation was in the close at hand, and the strange was in the familiar. In later years he revisited Paris and Rome a number of times, discovered Greece, and happily toured the world on behalf of the State Department. From 1956 on he also divided his time between Oxford and Charlottesville. But Virginia was still the South. He continually distanced himself, moved away, but never too far and never for too long. Nothing illustrates better the singular relationship that Faulkner had with his native land than the lucid, mischievous letter he sent to James Southall Wilson on September 24, 1931: "You have seen a country wagon come into town, with a hound dog under the wagon. It stops on the Square and the folks get out, but that hound never gets very far from the wagon. He might be cajoled or scared out for a short distance, but first thing you know he has scuttled back under the wagon; maybe he growls at you a little. Well, that's me" (*SL*, 17).

In his youth Faulkner was not a great traveler. However, the few months he spent in Europe in 1925 left their mark on his work; remembered places and landscapes were recorded in the topography of his novels. On September 6 he wrote to his mother:

> I have just written such a beautiful thing that I am about to bust—2000 words about the Luxembourg gardens and death. It has a thin thread of plot, about a young woman, and it is poetry though written in prose form. I have worked on it for two whole days and every word is perfect. I havent slept hardly for two nights, thinking about it, comparing words, accepting them and rejecting them then changing again. But now it is perfect—a jewel. I am going to put it away for a week, then show it to someone for an opinion. So tomorrow I will wake up feeling rotten, I expect. Reaction. But its worth it, to have done a thing like this. (*SL*, 17)

The Luxembourg Gardens and death, death in the garden, a young girl called Temple—this is the final scene of *Sanctuary*.

INCOMPLETE PORTRAIT OF THE ARTIST AS AN ARTIST: *ELMER*

Just after his arrival in Paris, after sending Liveright the typescript of *Soldiers' Pay* and temporarily setting aside *Mosquitoes*, Faulkner launched himself in the composition of a new novel. On August 23, 1925, he told his mother that he was "in the middle of another novel, a grand one" (*SL*, 13). Faulkner had become more self-assured. At age twenty-eight he was more confident than ever in his future as a writer and increasingly proud of what he wrote. He found his text on the Luxembourg Gardens and death "perfect—a jewel," and his next novel would be "awfully good." On September 10, most likely referring to the text he had mentioned four days earlier in a letter to his mother, he wrote his aunt Bama that he had just finished "the most beautiful short story in the world. So beautiful that when I finished it I went to look at myself in a mirror. And I thought, Did that ugly ratty-looking face, that mixture of childishness and unreliability and sublime vanity, imagine that?" (20). Faulkner was amazed that he had written such beautiful stories. He marveled at them, as if they were beyond his capabilities, as if they had been written by someone else and all he had done was transcribe them. This wonderment, where pride mixes with humility, would recur thirty years later when, toward the end of his career, Faulkner professed himself amazed that he had written books such as *The Sound and the Fury* and *Absalom, Absalom!*, telling Joan Williams about the prodigious gift he had had.

At first his new novel seemed to write itself and he was very happy with it: "I think right now its awfully good—so clear in my mind that I can hardly write fast enough" (*SL*, 14). The writing of what was to become *Elmer* advanced without a hitch. On September 2, 1925, Faulkner wrote his mother: "I am working steadily on my novel" (16). Four days later he was already at "over 20,000 words" (17), and by the tenth he was at "about 27,500 words now. Perhaps more" (20). On September 22, in another letter to his mother, he described the book's hero and summarized the plot thus: "Elmer is quite a boy. He is tall and almost handsome and he wants to paint pictures. He gets everything a man could want—money, a European title, marries the girl he wants—and she gives away his paint box. So Elmer never gets to paint at all" (25). On October 15, on his return from England, he informed his mother that he had started work again on his novel, after which he makes no further mention in any letter. Faulkner gave up writing *Elmer*, because, as he later confessed, "it was funny, but not funny enough."[6]

—

Elmer was conceived as the portrait of the artist as an artist, or, more accurately, as the portrait of the writer who is not yet a writer as a painter who is not yet a painter. A Joycean bildungsroman, the story leads its hero from a solitary childhood and tormented adolescence to an early marriage. When the story begins, Elmer Hodge has been traveling on a cargo ship for twenty days (like Faulkner on the *West Ivis* in his first Atlantic crossing), which is approaching Sicily. On the bridge during the crossing, moved by the scenes and landscapes he sees flowing by, he is drawn into long, retrospective reveries. His most haunting, most nightmarish memory is the deepest: the "red horror" (*ELM*, 345) of the night his house burned down. Elmer, who was five at the time, had awoken "into a mad crimson world where things hurt his feet and one side of him seemed to curl bitterly, smelling heat and people, strange people" (345). What remains is the memory of faces glimpsed and scenes observed in the infernal light of the fire. Elmer remembers "his mother's face—but was this his mother, this stark un-human face? Where [was] that loving querulous busy creature whom he knew?" He sees his father, "lean-shanked in his short nightshirt trying to put on his trousers," and his sister, "fiercely erect as ever, watching the fire in a dark proud defiance" (345–46). A family is drawn that would resurface many times in Faulkner's future work: a mismatched couple, with a mother who is both strong and distant, "bitter-faced" and "strange" (347); an insubstantial, almost grotesque father who has no authority; and a single daughter, always a bit of a tomboy, surrounded by brothers.

The most astonishing and moving scenes in *Elmer* are the scenes of childhood, dominated by the troubling figure of the beloved sister, Jo-Addie, "with whom he slept, with whom he didn't mind being naked," whom he had worshipped "quietly because of her fierce integral pride, her disgust with her dull and cunning brothers" (*ELM*, 346, 348). Along with Juliette in "Adolescence" and Cecily in *Soldiers' Pay*, Jo is one of Faulkner's first young androgynous women: "her breast was nil," "her legs were thin and unformed," and her belly "flat as an athlete's on her little wary hips" (348, 351). Jo's gender is vague; with her coarse cloth trousers, she resembles "a small boy in his larger brother's short pants" (351). At the age of eleven Elmer slept naked with his sister, in the same bed, under the same sheets. Fondling, caressing, furtive touching—in these scenes of discreet nocturnal intimacy, Faulkner's writing brilliantly hints at the precarious paradise of childhood love: indistinct desires that are already forbidden, innocent desires that are already illicit: "He would have liked to go to his sister, to touch her, her flesh or even her dress. But he did not dare" (349). And again, "When she was asleep first he would touch her, just once, lightly" (352–53). Elmer's memories of his sister are ones of happy feelings: "To feel something, to hear and see all at the same time—it was too much, it was to be too happy" (352). The intimacy between little Elmer and Jo is like a prenatal bond rediscovered: "just to have Jo beside him in the close friendly darkness, the two of them like an island in a dark ocean" (353). Happiness rediscovered, happiness lost, the first sorrow: one night, without warning, Jo disappears. After her departure, as if to excuse herself for having abandoned him, she sends him "a snug cardboard box containing eight colored wax crayons" (355). Elmer can no longer sleep with his sister, but he can draw. Was this to be the birth of a vocation?

In any event, the question posed by *Elmer* is the question of how one becomes an artist and how one fails at becoming one. In the development of Elmer Hodge, as in that of Stephen Dedalus, art and sex are inseparable. However, in Faulkner's novel, sexuality occupies much more place than it does in *Portrait of the Artist as a Young Man*. *Elmer* retraces the psychosexual development of its hero from pre-puberty and the "the throes of puberty" (*ELM*, 378) to adulthood. His path is without any great surprises; initially attached to Jo, Elmer, at the end of childhood, falls in love with his schoolmistress, a rancid old maid for whom he has "a fine sexless passion" (365). He is then fascinated by idealized, aestheticized versions of himself—particularly a boy older than himself, "slender and beautiful as any god and as cruel" (366), whom he admires from afar until the day he is knocked down by him: "He knew for the first and the last time the god's touch: such an ecstasy that his very willingness to be overthrown made his fall the harder" (366–67). After this short homosexual phase, his first true heterosexual experience takes place in a barn with a plump young neighbor with a "full red mouth" that was "never quite closed" (374). At eighteen he seduces and impregnates Ethel, a girl who is "merely deliciously soft: a series of young raptures" (432), who eventually leaves him to marry another. Jilted and betrayed, he enlists in the army. Wounded by his own clumsy hand during a grenade-launching training exercise, he is determined to conquer the woman of his dreams. He believes this woman is Myrtle, the daughter of a Texas oilman, "a star, clean and young and unattainable for all of her [. . .] humanness" (359), whom he meets in Houston in 1921. With a limp caused by a war wound, he asks her to marry him in vain, then, as in a Henry James novel, the young woman leaves for Europe with her mother to complete her education. As he tells his mother in a letter dated September 22, 1925, Faulkner intended to have his young hero succumb to the charms of the

Old Continent and meet a femme fatale who would turn him away from his artistic vocation. As always with Faulkner, the female image of woman is split: all the women whom Elmer met—all carnal and fleshy, all described in the same mouthwatering terms, from the "soft rich curves" of Velma to the "distracting curved body" of Ethel (378, 436)—contrast with the cold, indifferent, and inaccessible woman of his fantasies: "a Dianalike girl with an impregnable integrity, a slimness virginal and impervious to time or circumstance. Darkhaired and small and proud, casting him bones fiercely as though he were a dog, coppers as if he were a beggar, looking the other way" (378, 435).

A recurring figure of the feminine in Faulkner's work is the narcissistic virgin, desirable and cruel, an ambiguous and more or less phallic version of the idealized woman—that is, both overrated and disembodied. If Faulkner/Elmer had painted her, she would have evoked Cranach's graceful nudes or Schiele's angular nudes more than the curves of Rubens and Renoir. Ideality is something Elmer seeks in both art and women. As a child he drew factory chimneys and armless people "sweeping upward in two simple lines from a pedestal-like base: lines that entranced him with clean juxtaposition, pure and meaningless as marble." Later, in puberty, he starts "trying to draw [men and women] and make them conform to that vague shape somewhere back in his mind, trying to reconcile what is, with what might be" (*ELM*, 378). The question here is how to overcome the antagonism of the prosaic actuality of the world and art in its exalting ideality. This question would resurface in *Mosquitoes*. Whatever the answer, here, almost comically, it is confirmed that in Faulkner's eyes aesthetic creation is born out of the turmoil of desire and is closely bound to Eros. Elmer's relationship to painting is almost fetishistic and the satisfaction he gains from it is almost masturbatory, as underlined in a rather clunky manner at the start of the novel in the description of the painter's gestures:

> To finger lasciviously smooth dull silver tubes virgin and yet at the same time pregnant, comfortably heavy to the palm—such an immaculate mating of bulk and weight that it were a shame to violate them, innocent clean brushes slender and bristled to all sizes and interesting chubby bottles of oil . . . Elmer hovered over them with a brooding maternity, taking up one at a time those fat portentous tubes in which was yet wombed his heart's desire, the world itself—thick-bodied and female and at the same time phallic: hermaphroditic. He closed his eyes the better to savour its feel. (345)

But the happiness of painting does not exhaust the passion of the painter. In "A Portrait of Elmer," the novella that draws from this unfinished
novel and was not published until 1979, Faulkner has his hero say: "I want
it to be hard. I want it to be cruel, taking something out of me each time. I
want never to be completely satisfied with any of them, so that I shall always
paint again" (US, 638). For Elmer painting is also the experience of having
something taken out of him and a chronicle of dissatisfaction. The desire to
create is never assuaged by the work. Even finished, the work is never complete, but its very incompletion ensures that it is continued. Faulkner restated this in interviews: the artist loyal to his vocation devotes himself to an
interminable task, and his successes are measured against the splendor of
his failures. However, as Faulkner announced to his mother, the character
of Elmer was not destined like Stephen Dedalus to persevere to the end of
his vocation, and if the novel had been finished, this dilettante would have
married a nice, pretty girl and put away his brushes.

Elmer is not just a book where painting is often mentioned; it is also a
text that is constantly *haunted* by painting. As with the Postimpressionist
painters, painting seems to have been for Faulkner all about colors. Of all
his novels, Elmer is by far the most "colorful." Both hated and feared and
irresistibly attractive, red is ablaze everywhere. It is the "red horror" of the
night when the family home burns down, the red of the crayon in the box
sent by Jo. Sexuality also constantly casts a red glow. The mouths of the
women Elmer desires are all red: Velma's "full red mouth"; Myrtle's tender,
red mouth; Ethel's fresh, red lips; and the scarlet mouth of an Italian prostitute. Finally, red is the royal color of painting: red "all red" (*ELM*, 363), the
painting of a French painting—a Fauvist perhaps? Vlaminck? Matisse?—
seen by Elmer in a Chicago art gallery, of which he retains only the almost
monochrome ardor and from which "he had learned that no color has any
value, any significance save in its relation to other colors seen or suggested
or imagined" (363).

In addition to red, *Elmer* has the white skin of women; the honey tone
of hair; the lemony yellow of Myrtle's dress; the yellow of an armchair, a
cane, or a lampshade; the green of the banks of the Mersey; the blue-gray
or khaki of uniforms; the navy blue of caps; and all other "colors of war"
(*ELM*, 363). There are colors—words of color, color in words—on almost
every page. *Elmer* is the mad dream of a polychrome novel.

Like *Soldiers' Pay* and *Mosquitoes*, what we have left of *Elmer* is the work of a young, ambitious novelist who manifestly has the resources to achieve. Yet if this novel remained unfinished, it is because its author did not yet know how to structure his tale coherently and knew that he didn't. *Elmer* nevertheless remains a text that holds its own, that reads from start to finish like a polished work. It is not yet Faulkner at his best, but it is Faulkner for sure, with finely worked, energetic, surprising prose that is almost always vigorous and often funny. And, more transparently than *Soldiers' Pay* or *Mosquitoes*, the novel is an autobiographical fiction. There are a number of analogies between Elmer's parents—a weak, rather ridiculous father and an embittered, tormented mother—and the writer's. The young Elmer is, like the young Faulkner, a solitary observer. Later, like Faulkner, he comes back from the war without having been to the front and walks with a cane, "interesting and limping" (*ELM*, 360). Like Faulkner again, he does the round of New York art galleries on his return from Canada. His first romantic experiences are reminiscent of Faulkner's relationship with Estelle Oldham at the start of the 1920s, and "Ethel" echoes "Estelle": Elmer is spurned, just as Faulkner was by his childhood friend. But in truth this goes beyond autobiography in that the story is written in the third person and the narrative voice has the detachment of irony.

From a formal viewpoint, *Elmer* is more daring than the "New Orleans Sketches" and *Soldiers' Pay*. The influence of Conrad is perceptible in the narrative strategy, particularly the more systematic and already skilful use of flashback, prefiguring the long flashbacks of *Light in August*. The debt to Joyce is patent in the symbolic orchestration of the story and the use of inner monologue, where the narrative order is subordinated not to chronology but to the puzzling logic of mental associations, a process reused with much more subtlety and force in *The Sound and the Fury* and *As I Lay Dying*. Thematically, Elmer intimates later developments: the motif of brother-sister incest, already tackled in *Mosquitoes* and taken up again in *Flags in the Dust*, *The Sound and the Fury*, *Sanctuary*, *Absalom, Absalom!*, and *The Hamlet*. Finally, Elmer's sister is the first of a long line of female characters, and her name is evocative of both Caddy Compson in *The Sound and the Fury* and Addie Bundren in *As I Lay Dying*.

Faulkner kept the typescript of *Elmer* and plundered it relentlessly over the next twelve years. Not only did he compress the text to make it into a novella, more sober and more caustic, but he also reused scenes and characters and incorporated entire passages in his later work. Thus, the pages of the first chapter of book 3, manifestly inspired by Flaubert's *Temptation of Saint Anthony*, which describes Elmer's drunken fantasies—the oriental procession, the six men and their torches, the heralds and their trumpets, the elephant carrying the decapitated head of a black woman—appear again almost word for word in the last chapter of *Mosquitoes* (see *M*, 303–306). Similarly, Elmer's Italian misadventure, inspired by Spratling's incarceration in Genoa, provided Faulkner with the main incidents in the short story "Divorce in Naples" (published in *These 13* in 1931). Faulkner was very quick to learn how to use leftovers.

A DIVERSION: *MOSQUITOES*

At the beginning of his stay in Paris, Faulkner wrote to his mother on August 23, 1925: "I have put the 'Mosquito' one aside. I dont think I am quite old enough to write it as it should be written—dont know quite enough about people" (*SL*, 13–14). Nonetheless, the first chapter of *Mosquitoes* was finished by the end of his stay in Europe. After his return he divided his time between Oxford, New Orleans, and Pascagoula. In February 1926 he returned to New Orleans, where he would share an apartment with Spratling at 632 St. Peter Street. In the spring he was in Oxford, but he spent the summer in Pascagoula, in the house owned by the Stones, and with other friends. It was there, near the end of the summer, that he finalized the typescript of almost five hundred pages of his second novel, which bears the inscription "Pascagoula, Miss / September 1, 1926" on the last page. A few days later he returned to Oxford to see his family and a few friends and, in particular, to have Phil Stone read through his text and have it typed up with all of its corrections by Stone's secretary, Sallie Simpson. After some final reworking, he sent the definitive version to Boni & Liveright, who agreed to publish it and sent him a preliminary payment. They took the liberty of deleting four passages deemed too risqué without informing the author, but he did not take exception to this when reading the proofs.[7] Dedicated "To Helen, Beautiful and Wise," *Mosquitoes* was published on April 30, 1927.

⁓

Faulkner seems to have had as low an opinion of *Mosquitoes* as most critics: "That one, if I could write that over, I probably wouldn't write it at all. I'm not ashamed of it, because that was the chips, the badly sawn planks that the carpenter produces while he's learning to be a first-rate carpenter, but it's not [. . .] an important book in my list" (*FU*, 262). According to the novelist himself, therefore, *Mosquitoes* was only a modest novel of apprenticeship. Faulkner plagiarizes himself abundantly, as he had already done in *Soldiers' Pay*, and he also borrows extensively from other authors. Like *Linda Condon*, the novel by Hergesheimer that he roundly criticized in the *Mississippian* in 1922, *Mosquitoes* portrays a sculptor who is fascinated and inspired by a beautiful young girl. Mr. Talliaferro, one of the main characters, owes much to J. Alfred Prufrock, T. S. Eliot's ridiculous hero, to whom Faulkner had already referred in some of his poems, and the indeterminate dream related (in italics) in the novel's epilogue (taken from *Elmer*) is strongly reminiscent of "Circe," episode fifteen of *Ulysses*. More than in Faulkner's first novel, *Mosquitoes* also contains Wildean epigrams and the imprint of Huxley's eloquent, ironic, and facetious *Crome Yellow* (1921), *Antic Hay* (1923), and *Those Barren Leaves* (1925). This time the characters are, as in Huxley's work, intellectuals, artists, writers, dilettantes, and a handful of parasites whom Mrs. Maurier, a rich widowed patron of the arts, brings together for a four-day cruise on Lake Pontchartrain. Like Huxley's country houses, *Nausikaa*, the yacht on which they are sailing, is just an expedient to justify interminable conversations. With *Mosquitoes*, Faulkner is venturing into terrain that is unfamiliar to him: the novel of ideas.

On the surface the structure of *Mosquitoes* is very simple. The characters are presented in a prologue of over forty pages. Next come four sections, each corresponding, as their title suggests ("The first day," "The second day," etc.), to one of the four days of the voyage. In the epilogue the characters scatter without anything of note having happened. Nothing happens, nothing can happen in this closed, closeted little world, nothing but preliminary flirtations and a short-lived elopement into the swamps. The characters are mostly borrowed from the artistic bohemia of the French Quarter of the mid-1920s and are identifiable, as in a roman à clef. We know that the character of the novelist Dawson Fairchild was a satirical portrait of Sherwood Anderson, who forgave Faulkner only with great difficulty. Mark Gordon, the sculptor, resembles Bill Spratling; Julius Kaufmann, "the Semitic Man," is based on Julius Weis Friend, one of the editors of the *Double Dealer*. After the "Sketches" *Mosquitoes* is the first literary trace of Faulkner's stay in New Orleans, and it contains the memory of the women he desired and loved: the voluptuous Jenny Steinbauer owes her name to Gertrude Stegbauer, a pretty young stenographer whom he courted unsuccessfully in Charleston in 1925; and Patricia Robyn, Mrs. Maurier's niece, is the first fictional version of Helen Baird, to whom the novel is dedicated.

Like *Soldiers' Pay*, *Mosquitoes* gives an account of hidden, unrequited, or corrupted desires, and questions the ambiguities and deadlocks of sexuality. Everything in this novel points to a crisis of differences. Sexual identity is not the only thing that becomes uncertain. Traditional roles are increasingly hazy or interchangeable: men become more feminine and women more masculine. The likeness of the twins Patricia and Josh Robyn is so strong that it blurs gender differences: "Just as there was something masculine about her jaw, so was there something feminine about his" (*M*, 46); the poet Eva Wiseman is lesbian while the poet Mark Frost appears to be asexual. Dorothy Jameson is a foolish virgin on the rebound. As for the effervescent Ernest Talliaferro, he confesses to Gordon, "The sex instinct [. . .] is quite strong in me" (9), but as early as page 30 we learn that, for him, desire "had long since become an unfulfilled habit requiring no longer any particular object at all" (26), and soon after, it is confirmed that this wholesale buyer of women's clothes is all talk and no trousers and is perhaps even impotent. The sexual misery is widespread, with one exception: Gordon, the highly virile red-bearded Gordon, with "a face like that of a heavy hawk" (12), enjoys making love, preferably with prostitutes. In one of the novel's last scenes, we see him "lift a woman from the shadow and raise her against the mad stars, smothering her squeal against his tall kiss" (339). But as Patricia had understood, rather than take the risk of loving a living woman, Gordon prefers to sculpt what he calls his "feminine ideal" (26), a young marble virgin, armless, legless, and headless: "Say, you haven't got any sweetheart, or anything, have you?" Patricia asks him. "No," he answers. "How did you know?" (270).

One of the poems quoted in *Mosquitoes* is "Hermaphroditus," taken from *Satyricon in Starlight,* a book of poetry by Eva Wiseman. Dawson Fairchild provides this commentary:

> It's a kind of dark perversion. Like a fire that don't need any fuel, that lives on its own heat. I mean, all modern verse is a kind of perversion. Like the day for healthy poetry is over and done with, that modern people were not born to write poetry any more. Other things, I grant. But not poetry. Kind of like men nowadays are not masculine and lusty enough to tamper with something that borders so close to the unnatural. A kind of sterile race: women too masculine to conceive, men too feminine to beget. (*M*, 252)

For this champion of a "healthy" and "masculine" poetry (as Faulkner was himself in his essays published from 1920 to 1925), modern poetry—the kind of poetry the young Faulkner tried to write—is in its "perversion" an appalling corruption of poetry. From Théophile Gautier to Baudelaire, from Baudelaire to Huysmans and Remy de Gourmont, from Swinburne to Burne-Jones and Beardsley, homosexuality and hermaphroditism haunted poets and painters alike, both in France and England. However, far from exalting the androgyne as the perfect double incarnating the artist's dream of beauty (as in Gautier's *Mademoiselle de Maupin*),[8] Fairchild sees in this confusion of the sexes only degeneracy, impotence, and sterility and is quick to denounce art in itself as a sickness. In his eyes, art is a "perversion" and always has been, although he admits that "a perversion that builds Chartres and invents Lear is a pretty good thing" (320).

In *Mosquitoes* there is much talk of sex, and it is mentioned in the very first sentence of the prologue, when poor Mr. Talliaferro feels obliged to confess to Gordon that the sex instinct is his "most dominating compulsion" (*M*, 9). People talk about sex in this novel; they talk about nothing else. All that is left of language is a rustling: "Talk, talk, talk: the utter and heartbreaking stupidity of words. It seemed endless, as though it might go on forever. Ideas, thoughts, became mere sounds to be bandied about until they are dead" (186). The word is both negation and substitute of the thing, speech is always the ultimate void and the filling of the void: "Well, it is a kind of sterility—Words," says Fairchild. "You begin to substitute words for things and deeds, like the withered cuckold husband that took the Decameron to bed with him every night, and pretty soon the thing or the deed becomes just a kind of shadow of a certain sound you make by shaping your mouth a certain way" (210). The sexual analogy is not accidental and the same comparison is found in *Elmer*, in *Flags in the Dust*, and in the introduction written by Faulkner in 1933 for a new edition of *The Sound and the Fury*. The book brought to bed replaces bodily desire, as the reading experience temporarily produces the illusion of desire. The same goes for the artist: writing serves as a stand-in for what the writer is lacking. Art is like an immense metaphor: literature, like sculpture, is the execution of a substitution.

The contradictory Fairchild does not, however, condemn language. No sooner does he denounce words as a vain travesty than he reaffirms their capacity, under certain conditions, assembled in a certain order, to produce something living: "I don't claim that words have life in themselves. But words brought into a happy conjunction produce something that lives, just as soil and climate and an acorn in proper conjunction will produce a tree" (*M*, 210).

Sterile words? Or fertile words? Through Fairchild's statements, Faulkner, for the first time, questions language, just as other writers had been doing for some time, on both sides of the Atlantic. From the mid-nineteenth century, Flaubert, in *Madame Bovary*, made his narrator say, "Language is a cracked kettle on which we beat out tunes for bears to dance to, while all the time we long to move the stars to pity."[9] Similarly, Hugo von Hofmannsthal denounced the bankruptcy of language in *The Lord Chandos Letter*. Again, in this text dating from 1895: "Words have been placed before things. [. . .] Ordinarily, it is not words that are in thrall to men but men who are in thrall to words. Words do not give themselves up, they unravel the thread of an entire life."[10]

However, no more than Flaubert or Hofmannsthal had done, Faulkner did not retreat into silence like Rimbaud. The point was not to abandon language but to reappropriate it and make it an instrument of research. The fact that Faulkner first tried poetry (which, since the Romantics, had been "the essential word"), that he initially wanted to be a poet, is of course no accident. But it was in writing his first novels that he started to explore the limits of language, to take the measure of its multiple constraints, and to sense as yet unsuspected possibilities. Not that he never tried to bend it and close it on itself by removing its referential and communicative functions. For this great molder of words, writing was not an intransitive verb.

The relationship of language to reality would remain at the heart of his thinking as a novelist, and this thinking was carried out both *in* and *by* his novels. It should also be noted that already in *Mosquitoes*, the question of literature was extended to the question of art. Writer features alongside sculptor and sees himself as an artist among artists. The question posed by Faulkner in this novel, as he had already started to do, in more naive and summary fashion in *Elmer*, is art, what it should be, its relation to the world and to the self of the artist. *Mosquitoes* does not propose any theory, but it seems clear that before embarking on his grand enterprise of novelist, Faulkner felt the need to take stock and outline, obliquely, without taking himself too seriously, his own aesthetic credo.

In *Mosquitoes* he clearly distances himself from the fin-de-siècle aestheticism of his earlier writing. The contrast between Mark Gordon's marble torso described at the start of the novel and the clay mask described at the end shows Faulkner moving toward a less idealistic conception of art and therefore one that is more concerned with the roughness of reality. The sculptor's first masterpiece is "the virginal breastless torso of a girl, headless, armless, legless, in marble temporarily caught and hushed yet passionate still for escape" (*M*, 11). The second sculpture is a mask of Mrs. Maurier. It is completely different:

> It was clay, yet damp, and from out its dull, dead grayness Mrs. Maurier looked at them. Her chins, harshly, and her flaccid jaw muscles with savage verisimilitude. Her eyes were caverns thumbed with two motions into the dead familiar astonishment of her face; and yet, behind them, somewhere within those empty sockets, behind all her familiar surprise, there was something else— something that exposed her face for the mask it was, and still more, a mask unaware. (322)

The very choice of material and model indicates the new direction taken. Instead of the cold purity of marble, Gordon prefers gray clay, and instead of sculpting the equivocal body of a young girl, he portrays a foolish old woman, looking for the mask behind the face, the face behind the mask, and discovering a mask-face that shows a glimpse of what it is intended to hide. The virginal torso was born of the desire to rescue art from life, while the portrait of the old woman shows a willingness to bring life back to art. This does not mean that Gordon contents himself with a flatly figurative art form; in its harsh stylization, the mask with its empty sockets evokes a figure by Giacometti or a portrait by Rouault. It is life not imitated but surprised and laid bare, the distressing revelation of human misery. However, the less formalist aesthetic to which *Mosquitoes* leads remains a project; it does not take effect in the text. Gordon the sculptor heralds the arrival of Faulkner the novelist but at the same time outdoes him: his portrait of Mrs. Maurier goes beyond caricature to grasp the truth of an individual; in the novel the character is little more than a grotesque cardboard mask.

Like Joyce in *Portrait of the Artist as a Young Man*, Faulkner, in his second novel, seeks to clarify his relationship with literature. There are a number of similarities between the two books: they are both attached to the tradition of Romantic idealism, taking some of their metaphors from Christianity, and the most often recurring artist figure appears each time as a proud and fierce falconer.[11] Moreover, the definitions of the aesthetic experience and creation proposed by Faulkner echo those of Joyce, whose "enchantment of the heart" is echoed by Faulkner's "Passion Week of the heart" (*M*, 307).[12] According to Romantic tradition, far from being opposed to life, art is itself part of life: in *Portrait*, Stephen's plan is to "recreate life out of life,"[13] and the moment of inspiration is defined as that privileged instant when "in the virgin womb of the imagination the word was made flesh";[14] in *Mosquitoes*, Fairchild assimilates artistic creation with procreation, and the "Semite" says, "Dante invented Beatrice, creating himself a maid that life had not had time to create" (*M*, 339). Nevertheless, for all that he perpetuates it, art is also a manner of transcending life, a victory over death: whereas Stephen dreams of creating "a living thing, new and soaring and beautiful, impalpable, imperishable,"[15] the torso sculpted by Gordon is described as "passionate and simple and eternal in the equivocal derisive darkness of the world" (11).

In contrast to the Joycean aesthetic, Faulkner's owes nothing to medieval scholasticism or Thomist theology, and his reflections on art, attributed to various characters, have little in common with the ambitious speculations of the arrogant Stephen. Also, for Faulkner, creation is less of an "ecstasy" than an "agony" and a "passion" (in both senses of the word). The truth of art, like life, is to be sought in suffering. As Gordon says at the end of the novel: "Only an idiot has no grief; only a fool would forget it. What else is there in this world sharp enough to stick to your guts?" (*M*, 329).

Another revealing difference is that while Joyce's *Portrait* is the chronicle of an education, the tale of the birth of Stephen/Joyce to literature, *Mosquitoes* has no central figure behind which a recognizable Faulkner is hidden. Faulkner's desire for autobiography appears to be more diffuse, less mobile, and more playful. Faulkner also starts to tell his story and he weaves this story into his work to the end. But as he tells his story, he forgets himself, gets lost, and reproduces himself in his fiction. As in *Soldiers' Pay*, *Mosquitoes* has many doubles. *Soldiers' Pay* was the portrait of the young Faulkner as a former combatant; *Mosquitoes* portrays him as both artist and aesthete. While Gordon, the accomplished artist, represents the ideal self, the dilettantes and prattlers around him are other versions of Faulkner, the failed poet.

Also noteworthy is the appearance in the middle of the novel of a strange individual named Faulkner. The pulpous Jenny tells her niece about meeting "a funny man. A little kind of black man." "A nigger?" asks the niece. "No. He was a white man," answers Jenny, "except he was awful sunburned and kind of shabby dressed—no necktie and hat. He said I had the best digestion he ever saw, and he said if the straps of my dress was to break I'd devastate the country. He said he was a liar by profession, and he made good money at it, enough to own a Ford as soon as he got it paid out. I think he was crazy. Not dangerous: just crazy" (*M*, 145). Jenny is hesitant about his name—"Walker or Foster or something"—but eventually remembers: "Oh, yes: I remember—Faulkner, that was it" (145). The novelist hides himself in the folds of his book, discreetly, just as painters portrayed (and hid) themselves in their paintings among saints, heroes, or kings. He makes a cameo appearance in his novel, like Hitchcock and Welles in their films, or like Max Beerbohm in *Zuleika Dobson*.

This furtive, facetious self-portrait was nevertheless *signed*, added to which is an oblique disavowal by the young novelist of his recent past as a poet. The poems in the novel attributed to Eva Wiseman are in fact three of his own poems, and they are the subject of discourteous remarks by Dawson Fairchild and Julius Kaufmann. *Mosquitoes* evidently contains its share of self-derision. Increasingly irritated by the complacent poses of aestheticism, Faulkner settles his score with himself even more so than with his friends and former journeymen, and he settles it swiftly, without delay or tenderness, ironically and humorously.

Compared to his later novels, *Mosquitoes* certainly has few merits. Despite its verbosity, its catchy turns of phrase, its obvious borrowings and outdated mannerisms, this second novel of apprenticeship is nevertheless a step in the right direction, and we can sense the impatient young novelist who knows that he will do much better. While the story is slight, its narrative treatment contains some surprises. Like *Soldiers' Pay*, *Mosquitoes* breaks with linear storytelling, tries out a number of techniques, at times successfully: the inner monologues in this second novel are indisputably more skilful and more convincing than in the first. For example, Mark Gordon's inner monologue in the prologue, where words appear chaotically thrown together, with no punctuation and almost no syntax, clearly herald Quentin Compson's monologue in *The Sound and the Fury*. Similarly, Mrs. Maurier's hypothetical biography, put together by Julius from hearsay, contains the seeds of Conradian conjecture that is later found in *Light in August* and even more so in *Absalom, Absalom!* Finally, the temptation of theater, to which Faulkner later succumbs in *Requiem for a Nun*, appears already in a number of conversations presented as dialogues from a play (see *M*, 237–38).

Mosquitoes retains a mischievous freshness and good-natured irony signaling that this novel is less dated than *Soldiers' Pay*. It is no surprise that French stylist Raymond Queneau wrote the preface to the French translation. Conrad Aiken called it "a distinctly unusual and amusing book," adding that it was "good enough to make one wish that it were better." In Faulkner's career this novel was but an amiable diversion, one last "cruise," one final detour before he came down to earth.

———

The publication of *Mosquitoes* attracted little attention, but, like *Soldiers' Pay*, Faulkner's second novel had its supporters. At least two reviews—in the *New York Herald Tribune* and the *New York Evening Post*—hailed the novel in glowing terms. The authors of these reviews were hardly newcomers: Lillian Hellman, who had already recommended the book in a reading note written for Horace Liveright, and the perceptive Conrad Aiken, who found it "delicious" and said that the name of Mr. Faulkner should be added to the short list of those from whom one could reasonably expect, in the years to come, a first-class novel.[16]

Meanwhile, Faulkner continued to write diligently. By late September 1926 he had returned to New Orleans, where he moved back into his friend Bill Spratling's top-floor apartment. Days began with a short walk in the French Market near the Mississippi River, where he went every morning for coffee and doughnuts. Afterward, he returned to his room to work until evening, when he met his friends in the French Quarter for long nocturnal libations.

Mosquitoes was hardly finished when Faulkner started working on two other novels. In the winter of 1926–1927, he worked on one of them, "Father Abraham," but after writing about twenty pages he set it aside, intending to return to it later. This was the beginning of the story of the sinister, astonishing Snopes tribe, who later provided the substance of several short stories and three novels. The other novel he began working on, titled *Flags in the Dust*, told the story of the Sartoris family, a great Southern family in decline. His friend Phil Stone described both of these undertakings as follows: "Both are southern in setting. One is something of a saga of an extensive family of typical 'poor white trash' and is said by those who have seen that part of the manuscript completed to be the funniest book anybody ever wrote. The other is the story of the aristocratic, chivalrous and ill-fated Sartoris family, one of whom was even too reckless for the daring Confederacy cavalry leader, Jeb Stuart."[17]

NOTES

1. See Margaret J. Yonce, "The Composition of *Soldiers' Pay*," *Mississippi Quarterly* (Summer 1980): 291–326. These documents are part of the Henry W. and Albert A. Berg Collection and belong to the New York Public Library.

2. For more on the Faulknerian man-child, see the study by Aurélie Guillain, *Faulkner: le roman de la détresse* (Rennes: Presses Universitaires de Rennes, 2003).

3. See Spratling and Faulkner, "Chronicle of a Friendship," 37, 38.

4. See Jack Cofield, *William Faulkner: The Cofield Collection* (Oxford, MS: Yoknapatawpha Press, 1978), 71.

5. Gertrude Stein quoted in "An American in France," in Philip Rhav, ed., *Discovery of Europe: The Story of American Experience in the Old World* (Boston: Houghton Mifflin, 1947), 571.

6. William Faulkner, interview with James B. Meriwether, March 12, 1958, in *Mississippi Quarterly* (Summer 1983): 340.

7. On the censored passages, see Minrose C. Gwin, *"Mosquitoes'* Missing Bite: The Four Deletions," *Faulkner Journal* (Autumn 1993–Spring 1994): 31–41. The article reproduces the four passages, including this reflection attributed to the novelist Fairchild: "There'd sure be a decline in population if a man were twins and had to stand around and watch himself making love."

8. Faulkner had a copy of Gautier's novel in his library, and we know that "I love three things: gold, marble and purple; splendor, solidity, color," the opening sentence of the "Wealthy Jew" character sketch published in 1925 (*NOS,* 3) and repeated verbatim in *Mosquitoes* (*M,* 306, 308), is lifted from *Mademoiselle de Maupin* (Paris: Gallimard, collection "Folio," 1973), 226.

9. Gustave Flaubert, *Madame Bovary,* translated by Lydia Davis (New York: Viking, 2010).

10. Hugo von Hofmannsthal, "Eine Monographie," in *Gesammelte Werke, Prosa I* (Frankfurt: Fischer Verlag, 1950), 265–67.

11. Associated by name with the legend of Icarus, Joyce's alter ego, Stephen Dedalus, mentions the flight of the falcon several times. In *Mosquitoes* there are repeated references to Gordon's falcon-like face. This bird of prey is already echoed in the novelist's name, as "Faulkner" is of course another spelling of "falconer."

12. James Joyce, *A Portrait of the Artist as a Young Man* (1916; Harmondsworth: Penguin Edition, 1992), 235.

13. Ibid., 186.

14. Ibid., 236.

15. Ibid., 184.

16. Review reprinted in Conrad Aiken, *A Reviewer's ABC,* ([New York]: Meridian Books, 1958), 199–200.

17. Text quoted by J. B. Meriwether in "Sartoris and Snopes: An Early Notice," *Library Chronicle of the University of Texas* 7 (Summer 1962): 36–37. See *N1,* xl.

4
THE FIRST FLOWERING

THE INVENTION OF YOKNAPATAWPHA:
FLAGS IN THE DUST

On February 18, 1927, Faulkner announced to Horace Liveright, the publisher of *Soldiers' Pay* and *Mosquitoes*, that he was "working now on two things at once: a novel, and a collection of short stories of my townpeople" (*SL*, 34). The novel was *Flags in the Dust*. He worked on through the spring and summer of 1927, euphorically it would appear, as in late July he told Liveright that "the new novel is coming fine" and that it was "much better than that other stuff" (*SL*, 37). As attested by the handwritten note at the bottom of the last page, the typescript was completed on September 29, four days after his thirtieth birthday. At almost six hundred pages, his third novel was much longer than the first two.

Faulkner appeared happy with the job done. On October 16 he wrote Liveright: "At last and certainly, as El Orens' sheik said, I have written THE book, of which those other things were but foals. I believe it is the damdest best book you'll look at this year, and any other publisher. It goes forward to you by mail Monday" (*SL*, 38).[1] A few weeks later, Liveright bluntly told him how disappointed he was:

> It is with sorrow in my heart that I write to tell you that three of us have read *Flags in the Dust* and don't believe that Boni and Liveright should publish it. [...] It is diffuse and non-integral [. . . and] lacks plot, dimension and projection. The story really doesn't get anywhere and has a thousand loose ends. If the book had plot and structure, we might suggest shortening and revisions but it is so diffuse that I don't think this would be any use. My chief objection is that you don't seem to have any story to tell and I contend that a novel should tell a story and tell it well. (*B*, 50)

Faulkner responded on November 30: "It's too bad you don't like *Flags in the Dust*." He nevertheless defended his third novel: "I'd like for you to fire it on back to me, as I shall try it on someone else. I still believe it is the book which will make my name for me as a writer" (*SL*, 39). Liveright's letter had not shaken Faulkner's conviction in his vocation as a writer, but he was no longer so sure that he could make a career out of it. He told Phil Stone at the time: "I think I not only never will make any money, I will never get recognition either."[2] His despondency and distress are also evident in a letter he sent to Liveright in February 1928: "I dont know what we'll do about it, as I have a belly full of writing, now, since you folks in the publishing business claim that a book like that last one I sent you is blah. I think now that I'll sell my typewriter and go to work—though God knows, it's sacrilege to waste that talent for idleness which I possess" (39). However, he did not give up on the ambition to publish his third novel and set to work at revising the manuscript. He wrote to Aunt Bama: "Every day or so I burn some of it up and rewrite it, and at present it is almost incoherent. So much so that I've got a little weary of it and I think I shall put it away for a while and forget about it" (40–41). However, in February 1928 he sent the typescript of the fifth version of the book to Ben Wasson, his old friend from Oxford, who was now living in New York, where he worked for a large literary agency, the American Play Company. Wasson agreed to help him find a publisher. After being turned down a number of times, Wasson managed to place the novel with Harcourt Brace & Company and even secured a three-hundred-dollar advance for Faulkner. The contract arrived on September 20, 1928. Alfred Harcourt wanted another title, however, and demanded that the text of the novel be substantially cut. He asked Wasson to edit the novel for fifty dollars. Wasson accepted the job but brought Faulkner to New York in the early fall to work with him. However, Faulkner had no wish to revise the text yet again. He had better things to do: he was on the point of finishing *The Sound and the Fury*. It was probably Wasson who oversaw most of the edits imposed by Harcourt, but it is unlikely that he did not consult the author. Indeed, according to Wasson himself, Faulkner did much of the rewriting.[3]

The text was heavily edited. The novel as it was initially published was significantly reduced and changed: characters were sacrificed, entire episodes disappeared, and the whole plot was now centered on the Sartoris clan, to the detriment of the Mitchells and the Benbows. There were fewer

Snopeses than in the initial version, with only Flem, Montgomery Ward, and Byron remaining, the last a troubling character whose role was considerably reduced. It is this new version, less dense but also less rich, of Faulkner's third novel, dedicated to Sherwood Anderson, that was published on January 31, 1929, with a print run of 1,998 copies, under the title *Sartoris*. The novel did not appear under its original title and in its original form until 1973.

In writing *Sartoris* Faulkner started to understand how he could play to his advantage his intimate knowledge of the South, the land, the men, and their turbulent history. *Sartoris/Flags in the Dust* marked an important discovery:

> With *Soldiers' Pay* I found out writing was fun. But I found out after that not only each book had to have a design but the whole output or sum of an artist's work had to have a design. With *Soldiers' Pay* and *Mosquitoes* I wrote for the sake of writing because it was fun. Beginning with *Sartoris* I discovered that my own little postage stamp of soil was worth writing about and that I would never live long enough to exhaust it, and by sublimating the actual into apocryphal I would have complete liberty to use whatever talent I might have to its absolute top. It opened up a gold mine of other peoples, so I created a cosmos of my own. (*LG*, 255)

In advising him to write about "that little patch up there in Mississippi where you started from" (*ESPL*, 8), Sherwood Anderson had shown him the way. With this novel, Faulkner finally came into his own and the desire to write became an ambition to create a body of work.

The first two novels had been inspired by his own very recent past. Some autobiographical elements remain in the third, but the novelist's imagination no longer contented itself with reshaping his personal experience; this time it took over his family's entire backstory. A new character appears in this novel that is strongly reminiscent of the "Old Colonel": Faulkner himself confided to Malcolm Cowley that his great-grandfather "was the prototype for John Sartoris" (*FCF*, 66). And thanks to Joseph Blotner's biography of Faulkner, we know that most of the other characters were probably modeled on family members or on citizens of Oxford he knew personally or had heard of.

Faulkner wrote the novel *Sartoris* at the age of just thirty, but already he had a nostalgic sense that the world he was living in was coming to an end. This prompted him to take the initiative, to ward off the threat of an imminent loss, the will to retain at least a trace:

> All that I really desired was a touchstone simply; a simple word or gesture, but having been these 2 years previously under the curse of words, having known twice before the agony of ink, nothing served but that I try by main strength to recreate between the cover of a book the world as I was already preparing to lose and regret, feeling, with the morbidity of the young, that I was not only on the verge of decrepitude, but that growing old was to be an experience peculiar to myself alone out of all the teeming world, and desiring, if not the capture of that world and the feeling of it as you'd preserve a kernel or a leaf to indicate the lost forest, at least to keep the evocative skeleton of the dessicated leaf.[4]

The purpose here is to recreate a lost world from its last remnants, as an archaeologist reconstructs the history of a long-lost civilization from a fragment of papyrus or shard of pottery. For Faulkner this was when memory, its afterglow and revival, started to cast a spell. *Flags in the Dust* is a treasure chest, like the one old Bayard opens in his attic in the third chapter of the novel's second section: "From the chest there rose a thin exhilarating odor of cedar, and something else: a scent drily and muskily nostalgic, as of old ashes, and his hands, well-shaped but not so large and a shade less capable than his father's, rested for a moment upon a brocade garment. The brocade was richly hushed and the fall of fine Mechlin was dustily yellow, pale and textureless as February sunlight" (*N1*, 613–14). Punctuated by long flashbacks, this voluptuously meticulous inventory continues over another two pages, with lace; swords; pistols; kepis; uniforms; yellowing, carefully bound papers; and, finally, the voluminous family Bible where Old Bayard records the date of the death of his son John. After this comes a meditation on time and the fate of the Sartoris family, which brings us to a turbulent episode in his childhood during the Civil War, ending with the memory of a skull glimpsed that is in fact his own face reflected in the water of a river. A skull is the only thing missing from this hoard of relics to make it a *vanitas*, such as might have been painted by Philippe de Champaigne in the seventeenth century.

Relics and ghosts abound in *Flags in the Dust*. A ghostly scene, a shadow theater, is superimposed on reality: "Behind these dun bulks and in all the corners of the room there waited, as actors stand within the wings beside the waiting stage, figures in crinoline and hooped muslin and silk; in stocks and flowing coats; in gray too, with crimson sashes and sabres in gallant sheathed repose;—Jeb Stuart himself perhaps, on his glittering garlanded bay or with his sunny hair falling upon fine broadcloth beneath the mistletoe and holly boughs of Baltimore in '58" (*N1*, 588).

Flags in the Dust is the first of Faulkner's novels to portray the paradoxical nature of Faulknerian *temporality*, the first to suggest that past and present do not occur consecutively but coexist and are contemporaneous. As Gavin Stevens says in *Requiem for a Nun*: "The past is never dead. It's not even past" (*N4*, 535). It is not certain whether Faulkner read Henri Bergson, but his conception of time is extremely close to that of the French philosopher; it similarly postulates the contemporaneous nature of the past and the present, their reciprocal enveloping or—in opposition to Bergson—their mutual negation. Just as the present implies a past and is only comprehended once it is over, the past also implies a present, echoes it without being negated or erased by it, retains its form as it passes and is always already there.

Flags in the Dust places us in a time of returns and revenances. The past breaks through the cracks of the present. The edges of time open up, and a multitude of ghosts readies itself to take over the stage. The first of these ghosts is "Colonel" John Sartoris, the founding ancestor. His son, Old Bayard, and old man Falls, who served under him, haunt the edges of both *Sartoris* and *Flags in the Dust*. This haunting is prestigious, fascinating, and crushing. The dead man, freed "of time and flesh," has "a far more palpable presence" (*N1*, 3) than the living. The scene of his apparition contains echoes of the paternal ghost in *Hamlet* except that the father remains invisible and silent and his son is old and deaf. There is no voice beyond the grave. However, this inaugural scene speaks volumes about the formidable power of ghost masters. We learn that everything happens "as though that other were so much more palpable than mere transiently articulated clay as to even penetrate into the uttermost citadel of silence in which his son lived" (543). After death, the father lives on through his son, inserts himself into the "uttermost" of his "citadel," and takes up residence there, a parasite that cannot be eradicated.

In Faulkner's work the dead refuse to cross to the other bank; they do not want to die. Instead of moving away and falling little by little into oblivion, they return unceasingly, reminding the living that they are still there. This means that the living do not take over from the dead and that their time is doomed to repetition: nobody escapes from the inevitability of recurrence; the past is enacted indefinitely on the stage of the present. In *Flags in the Dust* the action takes place between the spring of 1919 and that of 1920. The story takes place chronologically, following the cycle of the seasons, but it soon becomes clear that the time of memory is as important, if not more so, than the time of the action.

Flags in the Dust is Faulkner's first genealogical novel. The story encompasses four generations of the same family. In the present tense of the action, the first generation is represented by Virginia Sartoris Du Pre, sister of "Colonel" Sartoris; the second by her son, Old Bayard; the fourth by Young Bayard, the last of the line, born in 1893 and orphaned in 1901. The third generation, that of Young Bayard's parents, is absent, and the fact that they are of the same generation as the author's parents is no coincidence. With Faulkner, progenitor fathers rarely match up.

"Young Bayard" is the hero of the novel. Like Donald Mahon in *Soldiers' Pay*, he has come back from the war and, like him, he is a fatally wounded airman, although his wounds are not physical. Both men are lost, and for both a woman is the furtive incarnation of the illusory promise of healing—Margaret Powers for Donald, Narcissa Benbow for Bayard. But Bayard is mostly defined by the copycat rivalry binding him to his identical twin brother, Johnny, who has just died gloriously in the skies over France. The themes of twinhood and identity are disorienting. Johnny the hothead is a simple reincarnation of the first Bayard Sartoris, the Old Colonel's older brother, killed during a memorable raid during the Civil War, and it is no coincidence that he is given the same name as his great-grandfather. Here kinship becomes more complicated, as in other Faulkner novels (particularly in *The Sound and the Fury*), due to the recourse to homonymies, dual personalities, and inversions: *Flags in the Dust* tells the story of two pairs of brothers named John and Bayard, separated by several generations. The first Bayard is killed during the Civil War while his brother John survives it. John has a son named Bayard II, who is father to John II, who in turn has twin sons, John III and Bayard III. Both sons go to war (in 1914–1918), but this time it is John who dies and Bayard who comes home. With three Johns and four Bayards in four generations, the reader needs to be attentive.

Repetition, however, never means identical reproduction. While the recurring first names mark continuity, the persistence of the same heroic dream down through the generations does not save the Sartoris family from decline. Bayard III would like to die a hero as his brother did, but he cannot. Johnny's death is his, but it also means that his death has already taken place and has been stolen from him. What remains is the shame of having survived, compounded by the guilt of having wished for the death of a brother who left life with a panache Bayard knows he cannot emulate. This explains Bayard's wild despair, the suicidal fury that drives him to wish to become his double's double at the very moment when he chooses death. However, he lacks the kind of heroism this requires. The hero's death cannot be equaled. Bayard is eventually killed two years after John in a banal airplane accident. He leaves no trace other than the inscription of his name on a tombstone, beside his brother's empty grave, not far from the statue of the Old Colonel, an effigy on its plinth, head raised "in that gesture of haughty pride which repeated itself generation after generation with a fateful fidelity" (*N1*, 343). For the last Bayard there will be no statue or epitaph.

As with Donald Mahon, Bayard is a fictional double of the young Faulkner. Horace Benbow, the talkative lawyer who resurfaces again in *Sanctuary*, is another (although he also shares some traits with Ben Wasson and Phil Stone). The contrast between the two characters is marked, however: on one side a taciturn, tormented virility; on the other a doleful anxiety, bittersweet introspection, troubled dreaming, feverish words, and the posturing of an aesthete. But as both return from war, they have become strangers to their family and their community, and Bayard's fascination for his brother is mirrored in Horace's quasi-incestuous attraction to his sister. Both are extremely narcissistic figures antithetically embodying the young Faulkner's two great romantic temptations. A distant descendant of the dark handsome hero of the Gothic novel and Byron's fierce rebels, Bayard represents the failure of the heroic dream, the impossible desire to transcend the finite through the apotheosis of a glorious death. Horace, a belated, decadent version of the Southern gentleman, embodies the temptation to flee reality through the enchantment of imagination and the magic of art. The former is the pathetic portrait of a failed young hero; the latter, like the talentless painter in *Elmer* and the fake artists in *Mosquitoes*, is his ironic portrait of a failed poet.

The fates of Bayard and Horace both go astray, both lack grandeur. Compared to the Civil War, commemorated as a grand gesture that will never be equaled, World War I is shown to be a wasteful absurdity. The past, nevertheless, is not glorified at the expense of a mediocre present. More than a nostalgic celebration of Southern mythology, *Flags in the Dust* investigates its genesis, the as yet fumbling beginning of an archaeology that will be pursued more keenly and more severely in *Absalom, Absalom!* and *Go Down, Moses*. The most important thing, finally, is not history or myth, but the work of memory and oblivion, of condensation and displacement through which reality is turned into fiction after the fact. From the first pages, this mythmaking is shown in the story of the first Bayard's suicidal prowess, a story not only constantly repeated by Miss Jenny over the years but also transfigured through her repetition into pure legend:

> She had told the story many times since (at eighty she still told it, on occasions usually inopportune) and as she grew older the tale itself grew richer and richer, taking on a mellow splendor like wine; until what had been a hair-brained prank of two heedless and reckless boys wild with their own youth, was become a gallant and finely tragical focal-point to which the history of the race had been raised from out the old miasmic swamps of spiritual sloth by two angels valiantly fallen and strayed, altering the course of human events and purging the souls of men. (*N1*, 549)

What haunts the Sartorises is therefore nothing but a fine heroic tale that they themselves have created from their rememberings and forgettings and that resembles the work of the novelist himself. However, the epic legend of the Sartoris family has become a deadly magic; "Sartoris" eventually becomes just the password to a hereditary will to die: "For there is death in the sound of it, and a glamorous fatality, like silver pennons downrushing at sunset, or a dying fall of horns along the road to Roncevaux" (875).[5]

The writing of *Flags in the Dust* opens up for Faulkner a space that his writer's imagination would transform into a space and time, a cosmos all his own. In this third novel a deeper, wider memory than simple remembrance starts to unfold. The novelist's investigation extends to his family, the town, the county, and the South, both past and present, which encompasses them all.

When Faulkner was asked in what order his novels should be read, he sometimes recommended starting with the book then called *Sartoris*, the book that contained "the germ of my apocrypha" (*FU*, 285). This novel marks the first appearance of Jefferson, the seat of an imaginary county initially called "Yocona," then, from *As I Lay Dying* onward, "Yoknapa-tawpha," the ancient Native American name of the same river in Lafayette County, meaning "land divided."[6] Faulkner brings us on an exhaustive tour of this county as early as this novel. The scene is set; all Southern society is there: its customs and rituals, from the countryside to the small town, from whites to blacks, from the bigwigs and shopkeepers to the yeomen farmers of the mountains and the poor hillbillies. The only people missing from this census are the Native Americans.

Many of the minor and major characters who will return in later novels and short stories appear here for the first time. The Sartorises and their black servants make a reappearance in *The Unvanquished*; the Snopeses feature in a number of short stories and, many years later, in the trilogy that bears their name. And Horace Benbow and his sister, Narcissa, return in *Sanctuary*.

A hold-all, crossroads novel, *Flags in the Dust* marks the end of an apprenticeship. The novelist's ambition henceforth rivals that of Balzac in scale. Everything is there, within reach. This is Faulkner at the threshold of his life's work, and everything points to the fact that he already holds all the threads that will form its framework. However, nothing is as yet fully controlled and mastered, and in contrast to the first two novels, the third is more classical than modern in structure. With *Flags in the Dust* Faulkner discovers his "cosmos" but remains unsure about his own artistic resources. His writing still has some way to go, but it is now within reach. Faulkner is about to become Faulkner, and already his desire to write is a desire to create an oeuvre.

THE MOST SPLENDID FAILURE:
THE SOUND AND THE FURY

At the end of 1928 Faulkner turned thirty. To make a little money, he undertook small jobs, sold refreshments on the local golf course, repainted houses and barns, designed shop signs, and sometimes polished hunting horns. However, he remained dependent on his family and friends. Despite his modest incipient fame, he was still unable to make a living from writing. His first two novels did not sell well, the third was initially turned down by his publisher, and national magazines showed little eagerness to publish his short stories. In contrast to his three brothers, Faulkner seemed to have no future.

Nevertheless, a writer had been born. A novelist had reached the heart of his work. Nineteen twenty-eight marks the start of the most prolific and inventive period of his career. After *Flags in the Dust* more and more novels came, thick and fast. Between April and October 1928 Faulkner wrote *The Sound and the Fury*. Between January and May 1929 he wrote the first draft of *Sanctuary*. And as soon as he had corrected the proofs of *The Sound and the Fury*, he started on *As I Lay Dying*, which he completed in forty-seven days. After this novel was published, he returned to *Sanctuary* and rewrote it in full. After just a couple of weeks, the definitive version was published in February 1931. Six months later he started work on what was to become *Light in August* in 1932. Five novels—and what novels!—in just four years. During this time he also submitted almost forty short stories to the major national magazines, two-thirds of which were published. These were years of plenty, years of grace. From the outset, the audacity of his novels won him the respect of the happy few, although his genius as a novelist was still not recognized and praised as it deserved. The general public ignored him (and would continue to do so for a long time to come), print runs were small, and sales were poor. Nobody had yet realized that Faulkner, without any warning, had turned literature on its head.

—

In 1937, in conversation with Maurice-Edgar Coindreau, Faulkner related the genesis of *The Sound and the Fury* for the first time: "That novel began as a short story. I thought it would be interesting to imagine the thoughts of a group of children on the day of their grandmother's funeral, whose death had been kept from them, their curiosity before the agitation in the house, their efforts to penetrate the mystery, their assumptions and conclusions about what was happening."[7] He started work on the third story about the Compson family—after "That Evening Sun" and "A Justice," both published in 1931—in April 1928. The title, "Twilight," is underlined twice on the first page of the manuscript of the novel.

Children are confronted with the enigma of death, "their efforts to penetrate the mystery." It was an idea for a novel, probably inspired by a distant memory—the death of Damuddy in 1907—but it was not yet ready to be told. Faulkner did not really know what he was doing when he started writing what was to become *The Sound and the Fury*. Piqued at the lack of success of his first novels, he had decided to do without publisher and public and to free himself from any constraint in order to write what he liked: "One day it suddenly seemed as if a door had clapped silently and forever to between me and all publishers' addresses and booklists and I said to myself, Now I can write. Now I can just write."[8] "There is a story somewhere about an old Roman who kept at his bedside a Tyrrhenian vase which he loved and the rim of which he wore slowly away with kissing it."[9]

One door closes and all the windows open; everything becomes possible again. A writer finally gives himself permission to write, to write just for himself, to write only as he likes and for his own pleasure, and immediately the writing takes hold of him as it never had before. With *The Sound and the Fury*, everything begins; everything begins again. For Faulkner it was first of all the overwhelming experience of writing carried by its own urgency, with no ulterior motive and no idea where it was going: "When I began the book, I had no plan at all. I wasn't even writing a book."[10]

And yet *The Sound and the Fury* is where Faulkner first asserts his identity as a writer, when Falkner becomes Faulkner for evermore. While writing his first, blistering masterpiece, he experienced "the emotion definite and physical and yet nebulous to describe which the writing [. . .] gave me—the ecstasy, that eager and joyous faith and anticipation of surprise which the yet unmarred sheets beneath my hand held inviolate and unfailing—will not return."[11] Does this mean that *The Sound and the Fury* was written in the joyfulness of an unbroken state of grace? In the 1933 introduction previously mentioned, Faulkner points out that the novel was the only one of the seven he had written without making an effort, without tension, without afterward having the feeling of exhaustion, relief, or disgust. Other, later commentaries seem to contradict or at least qualify this assertion. During a 1957 interview, for example, he stated: "It was the one that I anguished the most over, that I worked the hardest at, that even when I knew I couldn't bring it off, I still worked at it" (*FU*, 61).

For Faulkner, working and reworking the text did not mean smoothing it out, but rather acknowledging its rough edges. It meant going to the end of his daring, a daring that extended beyond writing to the unexpected and often disconcerting arrangement of characters on the page. *The Sound and the Fury* is a syntax, a rhetoric, a text, but also a punctuation and a typography and, according to Faulkner, the first novel printed with different colored inks.[12] *The Sound and the Fury* was intended to be a text not only to be read but also to be looked at. Nothing was left to chance.

In this book a story is written rather than simply told. As indicated by the title of the novel, borrowed from the famous monologue in *Macbeth*, it is a confused story, "full of sound and fury." In all likelihood Faulkner himself had a confused idea of the story before writing it. In the beginning there was just a situation, condensed into an image: "It began with a mental picture. I didn't realize at the time it was symbolical. The picture was of a muddy seat of a little girl's drawers in a pear tree where she could see through a window where her grandmother's funeral was taking place and report what was happening to her brothers on the ground below" (*LG*, 245).

How to tell the story of an image? How to convert the image into words and unfold it? In short, how to draw a text out of it? Faulkner had barely started writing when the first difficulties arose:

> By the time I explained who they were and what they were doing and how her pants got muddy, I realized it would be impossible to get all of it into a short story and that it would have to be a book. [. . .] I had already begun to tell it through the eyes of the idiot child since I felt that it would be more effective as told by someone capable only of knowing what happened, but not why. I saw that I had not told the story that time. I tried to tell it again, the same story through the eyes of another brother. That was still not it. [. . .] I tried to gather the pieces together and fill in the gaps by making myself the spokesman. It was still not complete, not until 15 years after the book was published when I wrote as an appendix to another book the final effort to get the story told and off my mind, so that I myself could have some peace from it. It's the book I feel tenderest towards. I couldn't leave it alone, and I never could tell it right, though I tried hard and would like to try again, though I'd probably fail again. (*LG*, 245)

If we are to believe Faulkner's account of the genesis of *The Sound and the Fury*, the four sections making up the novel were all vain attempts to recount a story, and the novel itself was nothing other than the combination of these four failed accounts. Faulkner was right but he was also wrong: it would be doing an injustice to this book to reduce it to the sum of its failings.

The virtual "mental image" of the narrative, the generative image of the novel, was a sort of "original scene." It imposed itself on Faulkner like a secret to be deciphered. At the heart of the enigma is Caddy Compson, a miniature Eve perched on the forbidden tree of knowledge, whom Faulkner called "the beautiful one, [his] heart's darling" (*FU*, 6), and who was, more than any other female figure in his work, a girl of desire and of mourning. As the novelist himself notes at the end of his introduction: "I, who had three brothers and no sisters and was destined to lose my first daughter in infancy, began to write about a little girl" (*LG*, 159). Caddy was conjured up to fill a gap. The gamble was untenable, the desire thwarted: Faulkner's writing not only does not fill the gap; it stops trying to mask the insufficiencies of reality with the ploys of fictional illusion. Desire is represented throughout the text without ceasing to be desire.

Caddy is forever fleeing, forever disappearing. Here she is in her wedding dress, as seen, or rather glimpsed, by her brother Quentin. He catches merely a glimpse of her in a mirror, in memory she will be no more than the reflection of a reflection: "*Only she was running already when I heard it. In the mirror she was running before I knew what it was. That quick her train caught up over her arm she ran out of the mirror like a cloud, her veil swirling in long glints her heels brittle and fast clutching her dress onto her shoulder with the other hand, running out of the mirror*" (*N*1, 939). Caddy is the elusive Eurydice of the descent into hell that, for Faulkner, starts with this novel. A dead flame in an empty hearth, she sets the entire book alight with her extinguished fire.

Caddy is lost, disappeared, all the more desired and "alive" because she is lost, living only that false life, that shimmering image produced by memory, fantasy, or hallucination. Another way of (re)producing this image is through the novelist's imagination, within the confines of a book, "because of that ineluctable law that ensures one can only imagine what is absent."[13]

Caddy is no longer there but is also everywhere: in reflections, shadows, clouds, rain, fire, wind, running water, and in the heady scent of honeysuckle—a fluid, impalpable, evanescent figure in both space and time. It is she, the unforgettable missing person, who is invoked in turn by her three brothers, Benjy, Quentin, and Jason. Three voices are heard in strange monologues that cannot be framed or mediated and whose narrative vocation is uncertain. However, there is a story here, and it is, as in so many of Faulkner's stories, a dark family story. Through the three narrating brothers, the reader finds out, by trial and error, as if blindfolded, the relentless, pitiful fall of the house of Compson.

The first of these monologues, Benjy's, was designed as a prologue, an anticipatory draft telling, searching for the words to tell, the story of the fall, for the first time, urgently and chaotically. Benjy as imagined by Faulkner is a being "without thought or comprehension; shapeless, neuter, like something eyeless and voiceless which might have lived, existed merely because of its ability to suffer in the beginning of life" (*LG*, 160). Benjy has no words, he is *infans*. He has no words to say what is missing, he has no words to tell of his misfortune. But the words are there, on the page, lined up one after the other, replacing the missing words, and if Benjy says nothing to anyone, there is nevertheless a tale in what Faulkner has him say; there is enough material to make a story or stories. Benjy remembers nothing and remembers everything. He has no memory; he *is* his memory, a memory made up of blind fumblings and blinding recollections, outside any will, any intent. The past constantly invades Benjy's consciousness, although he does not recognize it as such, and his memory starts to function only when called on by a present feeling or situation—the biting cold, passing under a fence, the feel of a nail—that calls and recalls what was.

Benjy is the sum of his failings and miseries along with his poor words: he is "trying to say" (this expression appears in the scene with two schoolgirls and earns him a beating). His words are between silence and shout, but his impossible monologue already says almost all there is to say and know. What he says is said with a misleading simplicity and a shaky transparency that are not the same as legibility. This postponed legibility is apparent from the first paragraph of the novel:

> Through the fence, between the curling flower spaces, I could see them hitting. They were coming toward where the flag was and I went along the fence. Luster was hunting in the grass by the flower tree. They took the flag out, and they were hitting. Then they put the flag back and they went to the table, and he hit and the other hit. Then they went on, and I went along the fence. Luster came away from the flower tree and we went along the fence and they stopped and we stopped and I looked through the fence while Luster was hunting in the grass. (*N1*, 879)

This sounds like a story, a short, very simple story, but the reader is unable to connect these words to the circumstances in which they are intoned or to situate the represented objects in a context that would make them comprehensible. *The Sound and the Fury* begins without a beginning—not only in medias res but also into the middle of extreme confusion, in a space with no bearings and a time with no contours. Individuals engage in violent acts, come and go, and one of them, identified by name, is looking for "something." Someone is looking for something; someone is saying, or trying to say, something. But no one reading the start of the novel for the first time could guess that the narrator is a simpleton and that he is telling, in his own way, what he saw and heard one day, on the other side of a fence, on a golf course.

If we compare this abrupt opening with those of the three previous novels, it becomes clear that the rules of the game are now completely changed, that readers will have to tease these out as they read, and that this will not be easy. A figure, if not an identifiable subject, is drawn during the first monologue, although it is true that one would hesitate to call Benjy a speaker. While in the text of the novel what he tries to say is inevitably relayed through words, what he says is only what he would say if he could talk. This pre-vocal language as imagined by Faulkner still traces out the boundaries of his world, the pre-subjective, pre-verbal, pre-logical world of early childhood. For Benjy, everything comes under the heading of sensation, feeling, and suffering, everything is reduced to reflexes and tropisms, to confused sensations and to the raw intensity of pleasure and pain. It is not that he is deprived of all knowledge: this visitor of cemeteries "feels" his father's imminent death, and after the death he howls like Dan the dog. Similarly, he senses the awakening of Caddy's sexuality and pushes her toward the bathroom when she no longer smells "like trees." However, he has no consciousness, no power of reflection, no self-awareness. Benjy never talks of himself, except one time, in the scene with the mirror at the end of his monologue: "*I got undressed and I looked at myself, and I began to cry*" (*N1*, 933).

What Benjy discovers in the mirror, and what makes him cry, is the evidence of his castration. Paradoxically, he recognizes himself only in something that is missing, in the dispossession of his masculine identity. His mutilated body has become strange; even his pain is not his. When he burns himself, it is not he who cries out; it is not he who feels pain:

> I put my hand out to where the fire had been.
> "Catch him," Dilsey said. "Catch him back."
> My hand jerked back and I put it in my mouth and Dilsey caught me. I could still hear the clock between my voice. Dilsey reached back and hit Luster on the head. My voice was going loud every time.
> "Get that soda," Dilsey said. She took my hand out of my mouth. My voice went louder then and my hand tried to go back to my mouth, but Dilsey held it. My voice went loud. She sprinkled soda on my hand. (N1, 922)

In Benjy's world there are only *effects*. Everything happens, anywhere and anyhow, nothing is explained, and what happens always happens like the sudden tear of a lightning bolt. Strictly speaking, Benjy's distress is not even suffering (suffering takes time, occupies time, and requires a suffering subject); it is only pain, a naked pain that passes through him, shoots through him (*dolere*). He screams with pain but does not even know that he has burned himself. Punctuated with screams, groans, tears, and silences, his monologue does not register cause, distance, or time lag. He is assailed with the urgency of the immediate. From euphoria to apathy, he passes swiftly to pain and from pain to soothing. The things he loves include the red flames in the fireplace, flowers, cushion, and Caddy's lucky shoe. When these things "go away," he cries; when they come back, he calms down and falls silent. These comings and goings are reminiscent of the *fort/da* game described by Freud. The difference here is that instead of a small boy playing with a reel, Benjy neither initiates nor controls the game. His distress is due to absolute abandonment. Benjy loses everything all the time, because he does not know how to give anything up. This leads to the catastrophe that is the disappearance of the woman who means everything to him.

Words from a man with no words: Benjy's narrative is untenable. His brother Quentin's narrative is also untenable in its own manner. A title date again—June 2, 1910—is the very last day of Quentin's life, at Harvard, from the time he wakes to his final preparations for suicide. Again, no indication is given here of the time or place of the narrative, and, what's more, as a narrator, Quentin can only be dying or dead. Either he sees his past unfold before him at the "infinitesimal instant of death,"[14] or his voice comes from beyond the grave, speaking to us posthumously, like Addie in *As I Lay Dying*.

As we pass from the first monologue to the second, we leave the limbo of innocence and go straight into the morbid universe of sin. Benjy's desperate attempts to communicate are replaced by Quentin's feverish effusiveness. However, they are united through their wounded childhood. Both lacked a mother, to such an extent that it is impossible for either to say her name: "*if I'd just had a mother so I could say Mother Mother*" (N1, 1009). The same feeling of destitution materializes in this childhood memory: "When I was little there was a picture in one of our books, a dark place into which a single weak ray of light came slanting upon two faces lifted out of the shadow. [. . .] I'd have to turn back to it until the dungeon was Mother herself she and Father upward into weak light holding hands and us lost somewhere below even them without even a ray of light" (N1, 1010).

Instead of a mother, Quentin has a sister. As with Benjy, Caddy becomes the focus of Quentin's quest for love. However, this quest does not come without recrimination. From earliest childhood, ambivalence constantly marks his relationship with Caddy (manifested in the very first scene, near the stream, in the incident of the muddy drawers), and everything is acted out on a dual stage. Sexuality and death, indistinct hauntings for Benjy, fold in upon themselves in Quentin's case and turn against him in his twofold obsession with incest and suicide. Quentin loves Caddy as Roderick Usher, in Poe's tale, loves Madeline and as Narcissus loves his twin sister, Echo, in Pausanias's version of the myth: his female double. At the same time, he loves her with that exclusive love that a small boy has for his mother. He fantasizes about going beyond the point of no return, of committing incest, to avoid losing her or rather to repossess her. "*If it could just be a hell beyond that: the clean flame the two of us more than dead. Then you will have only me then only me then the two of us amid the pointing and the horror beyond the clean flame*" (N1, 966). In this way innocence will be regained by deviating from the most transgressive culpability and the "clean flame" required to punish the culprits. Quentin's hell is heaven upside down, a topsy-turvy paradise, childhood rediscovered, to which incest is the shortest path.

Fantasy constantly twists Quentin's narrative; its imploding obsession forces it off course and destroys all coherence. His consciousness is assailed by painful memories and he loses his stream of thought: "It was quiet, hardly anyone about *getting the odor of honeysuckle all mixed She would have told me not to let me sit there on the steps hearing her door twilight slamming hearing Benjy still crying Supper she would have to come down then getting honeysuckle all mixed up in it*" (N1, 976). At the end of the monologue, the absence of punctuation, syntactical breaks, and the uncertainties of his proclamations trigger a linguistic disarray: "I had forgotten the glass, but I could *hands can see cooling fingers invisible swan-throat where less than Moses rod the glass touch tentative not to drumming lean cool throat drumming cooling the metal the glass full overfull cooling the glass the fingers flushing sleep leaving the taste of dampened sleep in the long silence of the throat*" (1010). It is not that Quentin is incapable of fulfilling his function as narrator; he performs the task admirably when recording his final day. He cannot fulfill it without *failing*, he is incapable of delivering a sustained narrative, and the more he gets bogged down in his monologue, the less control he has over his language and the more his words become strangled "in the long silence of the throat." At this point there is nothing more than pulsation, breathlessness, and a trembling of the senses.

Like Benjy, but also unlike Benjy, Quentin fails to say what he has to say, and what he says *is said* more than said by him or rather *is resaid*, almost without him being aware of it, as if he is delirious. His narrative is nothing but a long, tortured litany, overshadowed by his impending death.

A hostage, like Benjy, to a childhood that cannot be overcome, Quentin fearfully tenses himself against the adult world. His nostalgia for lost innocence is the regressive dream of an asexual existence: "It's not not having them. It's never to have had them then I could say Oh That That's Chinese I don't know Chinese" (*N1*, 965). Sex is Chinese, Hebrew, a language he does not know and does not want to know. Quentin wants to hide from desire. He turns down any initiation, any apprenticeship; no one can help him become himself. His parents are no help to him. His mother—cold, whiny Mrs. Compson—was never there for him, or for Benjy or Caddy, and Mr. Compson, his father, to whom he talks at the end of his monologue, is more of a brother than a father to him: the wisdom of this garrulous old drunk is the wisdom of derision and death, distilled in cynical aphorisms, echoing his distress without providing any solution. Quentin is alone with his anguish and incapable of freeing himself, incapable of taking any action. Everything turns against him and sends him back into an impotent culpability. He wants to avenge Caddy's honor but cannot, because Dalton Ames and Herbert Head, his sister's seducers, are merely carrying out his own desire by proxy. For him there is no ego to assert, no other to confront. His subjectivity is not self-awareness, self-possession, or self-presence in a world that is present; it is outside him, out of reach. He has no means of taking possession of his subjectivity; there is no way for him to find himself.

Quentin talks about himself in the first and third persons and does not know what tense to conjugate: "I was I was not who was not was not who" (*N1*, 1007). He looks for his identity in vain. "*Non fui. Sum. Non sum*" (1010–1011): these Latin words occur at the end of his monologue, at the moment of the great internal breakdown preceding his suicide. They summarize his failure to reconcile being, nonbeing, and having been. Quentin then turns to the future, but this future is conjugated in the negative; it is only an absence of future, a promise of peace in oblivion: "And then I'll not be. The peacefullest words. Peacefullest words" (1010). If death robs us of time, Quentin's time is already borrowed, time for death or time in death.

When he wakes up on the morning of his suicide, when his awareness returns to himself and to time, the countdown has already started and his obsession with time immediately merges with anxiousness about his impending death. This is why he places his watch upside down on the dresser and then breaks it and pulls off the hands. This does not stop the watch ticking, however: "Only when the clock stops does time come to life," Mr. Compson tells him (*N1*, 942). But this is already saying too much: for Quentin the time of experience—"sensible time," as Claude Romano calls it[15]—is no better than the homogenous, measurable time of clocks and calendars. Time, for him, is mostly repetition, the endless return of the past to a present with no presence. Time is out of joint, dislocated, always behind or ahead of itself, where past and present coexist without ever being able to harmonize. There are no visitations, no "happy moments" as in Proust. There is no merging, nothing but an anguishing confusion. Time is not lost or rediscovered; time is not even transcended but rather suspended and collapsed, a *meantime*, time in a fault line in time. Repetition is loss in that what comes back always comes back lessened. For Quentin, each time the past resurfaces, it is as if to taunt the present and make it wince in the mirror of repetition. The events of his final day—his encounter with the little Italian girl, his arrest for allegedly molesting her, his fight with Gerald Bland—are both poignant summaries of his absurd situation and comical addenda to the story of a blighted life.

To the end, Quentin wanders like a sleepwalker in an indefinite space and time where everything comes undone and falls apart: "I seemed to be lying neither asleep nor awake looking down a long corridor of gray half-light where all stable things had become shadowy paradoxical all I had done shadows all I had felt suffered taking visible from antic and perverse mock-

ing without relevance inherent themselves with the denial of the significance they should have affirmed" (N1, 1007).

One could say, as Faulkner does, speaking both for himself and through
his characters, that the past is never dead, it is not even past, that time is a
present that carries in it all past and all future. One could also say, without
too much contradiction, as Saint Augustine did, that the past is no more,
the future is not yet, and that the present is simply the sliding boundary
between these two nothingnesses. And that therefore time is nothing. But
this nothing trumps everything. For Quentin it is the reductio ad absurdum of his desires, his hopes and even his sorrow, and it is the dual impossibility of being himself in time and of escaping alive outside time that leads
him to flee into the non-time of death.[16] However, at the very instant when
he is ready to leave it for good, the world is already far away from him; it is
no longer a world that is fully real for him; his separation from the living is
already almost consummated.

Quentin's suicide can be read as a protest against the tyranny of time.
But his death is no more heroic than his life. As heralded in the daydreams
of his last day, it is revealed as the last and most successful of his fevered fictions, allowing him in extremis to achieve the magical reconciliation of his
contradictory desires. His death is sacrificial, both expiatory and liberating.
To ensure that his body disappears forever, he takes care to weigh himself
down with two flatirons before throwing himself into the river. The water
will eat away the flesh, strip it down to the bone, and, in turn, the bones will
disappear under the sand: "And I will look down and see my murmuring
bones and the deep water like wind, like a roof of wind, and after a long
time they cannot distinguish even bones upon the lonely and inviolate
sand" (N1, 938). As his imagination roves beyond his death, Quentin spontaneously comes across the purifying water associated with the swims of
his childhood and adolescence. What does he expect from his suicide, the
ultimate purification rite? That the water will once and for all wash away
the sin of living, that it will deliver him from the flesh, and that it will release him from time forever. Only then will the fault be redeemed, the debt
repaid. As he approaches death, water holds out the promise of forgiveness,
oblivion, and peace. And yet it remains an *aqua femina*, the source from
which mermaids spring. For Quentin, death by water is also the accomplishment, through destruction, of the wish for the forbidden union with

his sister: incest is finally consummated and immediately expiated. White wedding, black wedding. All will finally become peaceful in the great maternal tranquility of the water. There will be a return to prenatal calm and, even better, to the calm before life begins. Regression to one and to zero, to all and to nothing.

The third section, "April Sixth, 1928," comes almost thirty years after Quentin's suicide. Another voice—vulgar, sardonic, peremptory (and sometimes, without realizing it, caustic and funny)—is heard: that of Jason, the third brother. After the "internal" monologue/polylogue, with its folds and its returns, its delays and its detours, comes a theatrical soliloquy, a voice-off, speaking out loud to no one in particular. Far from fading away, speech here is ostentatiously staged: "Once a bitch always a bitch, what I say. I says you're lucky if her playing out of school is all that worries you" (*N1*, 1015). From the very first sentence, an *inquit* signals the presence of a narrator, from the second the pronoun "you" puts the addressee in his place. Throughout his monologue, Jason calls on his putative audience to bear witness, punctuating his assertions with "I say" or "like I say" as if to seal the authority of the person speaking and to guarantee the validity of what he says through the vehemence of his utterances. But in fact this vehemence both masks and unmasks their impoverishment and madness. Jason wants to take over, to grab language (just as he grabs the two hundred dollars Caddy sends him every month for her daughter). His strident assertions of independence and furious protestations against the order of things resonate in the void, and he continually fails to master his words. In fact, everything escapes him: time, fortune, and even his niece, the unruly Miss Quentin, who eventually runs away with the money from the safe. No matter how much he fights and struggles, always on the lookout for a bargain or for mischief, this so-called self-proclaimed man of action is nothing but a troublemaker. And the more agitated he gets, the more he falls behind: "Just let me have twenty-four hours" (1080), he implores at the end of his monologue. But he will never be on time; he will never have the time to be on time.

It could be said that Jason is himself unfinished, unloved, worn down like his brother Quentin by a familial neurosis, but he is firstly a disappointed grandee who has come down in the world, a boy from a good family fallen on hard times, working in a hardware store, who believes himself to be the spokesperson for the outcasts of 1920s Southern society: ruined planters, toiling storekeepers, smallholders crushed by debt. Not that he feels any empathy, but his speech distills their rage and rancor perfectly. Jason looks down on those around him, distrusts everyone, and bears a grudge against the whole world, but it is no coincidence that the prime objects of his disdain are those inherited from the prejudices of his class, his gender, and his race. This oafish, paranoid white Southerner makes fun of intellectuals, holds the Yankees in contempt, fears the Jews, and despises the blacks. This old bachelor who frequents prostitutes is a militant misogynist who prides himself on knowing women. In truth he knows no one, which does not prevent him from having thoughts, although even these are not really his own. If one were to remove his skull, one would find in his brain merely a collection of commonplaces. Jason has an answer for everything and questions nothing. He has cut-and-dried, peremptory opinions, all formed from the basest stupidity. There is no reflection, no doubt, not one single original thought. The revolt of this mediocre loudmouth is the height of conformity, and his conformity is the height of self-ignorance.

Jason thinks he is cunning. In fact his cunning leads to his being trapped by his own malice. At the end of his final misfortune, his last humiliation, as revealed after his monologue, in one of the last scenes of the novel, he is nothing more than a poor puppet with broken strings, a victim in turn, barely less pitiable or less lost than Quentin or Benjy: "He sat there for some time. He heard a clock strike the half-hour, then people began to pass, in Sunday and Easter clothes. Some looked at him as they passed, at the man sitting quietly behind the wheel of a small car, with his invisible life ravelled out about him like a wornout sock" (*N1*, 1118).

Benjy, Quentin, and Jason, each in his own way, are *betrayed* by their monologues. They do not tell their story; their story is revealed without their realizing it. "April Eighth, 1928," the novel's final section, provides an ironic counterpoint to their closed monologues. After the stream of consciousness of three characters, the novel switches to an anonymous narrator who is outside the story. Released from all suspect intercessors, the reader can finally take a step back.

The story switches from inside to outside, as if after hearing voices in the dark we can now see and hear the speakers in broad daylight. This "big man" (*N1*, 1118), lumbering, hairless, and drooling, is this not Benjy? That man, "cold and shrewd, with close-thatched brown hair curled into two stubborn hooks, one on either side of his forehead like a bartender in caricature, and hazel eyes with black-ringed irises like marbles" (1092), is that not Jason?

The eyes take their revenge; everything becomes visible. But the scene is distressing. The section opens on the description of a cold, gray dawn, which evokes the end of the day more than the beginning and is reminiscent of the twilight in which Quentin was wandering. Here, on the threshold of her cabin, is Dilsey, the old black servant, with her "stiff black straw hat perched upon her turban"; her dress "in color regal and moribund"; and her shapeless, old woman's body, whose "skeleton rose, draped loosely in unpadded skin that tightened again upon a paunch almost dropsical" (N1, 1081). Combining the most cruelly accurate realism with a sort of baroque magnificence, the preliminary portrait of Dilsey exhibits all the scars of poverty, decrepitude, and death, but at the same time it aggrandizes her and transfigures her into a sovereign figure, a queen with no visible kingdom, both waned and unvanquished.

This final section is full of speculation and conjecture, irony and paradox. Everything is bathed in a new light, and it is no coincidence that more space is given to Dilsey and the black community than to the Compsons, or that it ends with a description of how black people celebrate Easter, culminating in Reverend Shegog's extraordinary sermon. There is another text here, a *holy* text, which is both disfigured and transfigured by the preacher's singular rhetoric, who speaks about the crucifixion and resurrection of Jesus Christ and the promise of redemption and who evokes the topicality of this past that lives on, that is still present, as Saint Bernard says, *hodie usque ad nos*, even to us today.

Other voices are also heard, first that of the preacher, which changes from a cold "white" voice into a burning "black" voice, followed by *the* voice for which he is now but a docile instrument: "With his body he seemed to feed the voice that, succubus like, has fleshed its teeth in him. And the congregation seemed to watch with its own eyes while the voice consumed him, until he was nothing and they were nothing and there was not even a voice but instead their hearts were speaking to one another in chanting measures beyond the need for words" (N1, 1104). The voice is initially carnal, incarnate, and then becomes a voice without body, the voice of nobody. An empty voice, without subject, a voice of myth, the only one capable of bringing the faithful together in the overwhelming reciprocity of hearts. The scene encompasses mirages of presence and of sharing, miracles of renaissance and of resurrection, a dream of words beyond any words. The black preacher here becomes the ideal double of the writer himself, at the dreamed-of moment when his authorial signature is reabsorbed into the nameless authority of the sovereign verb. Thus the novel secretly wends its way to the success of its failure, a success nonetheless constantly postponed, always just out of reach, for which writing amounts to testing the impossible.

There is no denouement, no resolution. Looping the loop, the end of the novel brings us back to its beginning, to Benjy and Luster, his black caregiver, this time with both seated in the surrey bringing them to the Jefferson cemetery. Once at the courthouse square, Luster, instead of taking the usual route and turning right, swings the horse to the left of the Confederate soldier statue. Benjy starts to bellow. Jason then reappears suddenly; resuscitated in all his fury, he takes the reins, whips the old mare, punches Luster, and reestablishes the order compromised by the latter's escapade.

After this last flash of violence with its final screams, the book ends on the image of a reassured Benjy: "The broken flower drooped over Ben's fist and his eyes were empty and blue and serene again as cornice and façade flowed smoothly once more from left to right, post and tree, window and doorway and signboard each in its ordered place" (*N1*, 1124). The end is riven with irony. The story ends with the restoration of a derisory order, just as the text ends with an arbitrary decision. The only thing fulfilled in this work is its nonfulfillment.

This was a predicted failure, forecast and necessary, failure as the inevitable fate of the work. Faulkner knew better than anyone that no words can express what the novelist wants to say and that no book can make up for the failings of language and exhaust the madness of writing. When the book was finished, Faulkner looked back over it and realized that it was still unfinished, that his story was still pending. No matter that he returned to it four times, the story closest to his heart remains untold and almost nothing of what he wanted to say is said.

But failure has its own beauty, defeat its own victory. When Faulkner was asked which of his books he considered his best, he answered: "The one that failed the most tragically and the most splendidly. That was *The Sound and the Fury*—the one that I worked at the longest, the hardest, that was to me the most passionate and moving idea, and made the most splendid failure" (*FU*, 77).

⁓

Herman Melville said: "He who has never failed cannot be great [. . .] Failure is the true test of greatness."[17] Samuel Beckett, on the subject of Bram Van Velde said: "To be an artist is to fail, as no other dare fail, failure is his world."[18]

Faulkner dared. However, the awareness that failure is unavoidable does not contradict the intimate certainty that *The Sound and the Fury* is a wholly unconventional book, written outside all tradition, an all-new novel, an unprecedented text, the like of which had never been written before. Ben Wasson tells us that Faulkner came to see him in New York one morning, in his room in Greenwich Village, throwing a large envelope stuffed full of paper on the bed and saying: "Read this one, Bud. It's a real son of a bitch." Before leaving, he added: "This one is the greatest I'll ever write. Just read it" (*CNC*, 89). In October 1928 he wrote to his great-aunt Alabama, telling her that he had just finished "the damndest book I ever read. I dont believe anyone will publish it for 10 years" (*SL*, 41). He was wrong on this point; he did not have to wait as long as he thought. Alfred Harcourt refused to publish his new novel, but in the meantime Harrison (Hal) Smith had left Harcourt to found his own publishing house with the English publisher Jonathan Cape. The new firm offered Faulkner a contract in February 1929, which Faulkner signed.

Producing the book posed a few problems to the publisher. Faulkner never typed up his manuscripts without going back over them and correcting them. He did the same with *The Sound and the Fury*, changing how the text was presented, increasing the number of passages in italics in the first monologue, reworking the novel's sections, and adopting freer, more daring punctuation. When he received the galleys in early July in Pascagoula, where he was on honeymoon with Estelle, Faulkner found that his friend Wasson had removed all the italics, inserted spaces to signal temporal breaks, and had even made some additions to the text. Furious, Faulkner protested. In a long letter, he explained the coherence to Wasson of his presentation choices and asked him to respect these: "I hope you will think better of this. Your reason above disproves itself. I purposely used italics for both actual scenes and remembered scenes for the reason, not to indicate the different dates of happenings, but merely to permit the reader to anticipate a thought-transparence, letting the recollection postulate its own date. Surely you see this" (*SL*, 17). Wasson did as Faulkner asked. On October 7, 1929, *The Sound and the Fury* was published as the writer wanted, with all of the editor's changes and additions removed.

Only Evelyn Scott, a poet and novelist from Tennessee who read the novel proofs, recognized its powerful originality from the start, and Jonathan Cape published a six-page opuscule by her in praise of the novel, which it distributed along with the book. In the *New York Herald Tribune*, Faulkner's friend Lyle Saxon was one of the rare critics to hail his genius and point out his singularity. He called it as merciless as anything that had come from Russia. He compared William Faulkner to James Joyce, Marcel Proust, Chekhov, and Dostoyevsky before concluding that this was futile, as Faulkner was unquestionably American. He went on to wonder what readers and other critics would make of the book, concluding that many would think Faulkner mad. While admittedly *The Sound and the Fury* was mad, monstrous, and terrible, the same applied to life as reflected in the novel. Saxon went on to say: "I believe simply and sincerely that this is a great book." Favorable reviews also appeared in the *New York Times* and the *Saturday Review of Literature*, but at the time, Ernest Hemingway and Thomas Wolfe were attracting much more interest than Faulkner. *A Farewell to Arms* and *Look Homeward, Angel*, published at the same time as *The Sound and the Fury*, attracted much more critical attention.

While Hemingway's novel quickly became a best seller, it was a year and a half before the admittedly modest first print run of 1,789 copies of *The Sound and the Fury* sold out. A second print run of 500 copies was made after *Sanctuary* was published in February 1931, and a third of 1,000 in November. Over ten years later, at the start of the 1940s, *The Sound and the Fury* was still on sale for $2.50 a copy.

THE MOST HORRIFIC STORY: *SANCTUARY*

Faulkner had barely finished *The Sound and the Fury* when he started work on another novel in the winter of 1928. He wrote the first draft between January and May 1929. On May 6, 1929, he signed a preliminary contract with the publisher Cape & Smith for "a novel" before he had even finished typing it up. As the handwritten date on the last page shows, the typescript was finished on May 25. Faulkner sent this to Harrison Smith. As he states in his famous preface to the 1932 edition, Smith, after reading it and getting three employees to read it, responded: "Good God, I can't publish this. We'd both be in jail" (N2, 1030). But one month after the publication of *As I Lay Dying*, the editor must have changed his mind, because on May 16, 1930, against all expectations, Faulkner received the galleys of *Sanctuary*.

The rest of the story is well known, told by Faulkner later, several times, in his own inimitable way: "And I read it and it was so badly written, it was too cheaply approached. The very impulse that caused me to write the book was so apparent, every word; and then I said I cannot let this go" (*LG*, 123). As Faulkner writes in his 1932 preface, there were only two things to do: "tear it up or rewrite it" (N2, 1030). Hesitating for a while, he at first contemplated giving up any hope of publishing it, but Smith, who had already invested money in the novel, would not hear of it. They eventually agreed on a compromise: both author and publisher would share any resetting costs beyond the normal cost of correcting proofs.

Faulkner set to work immediately: "So I tore the galleys down and rewrote the book" (N2, 1030). In less than a month he deleted almost all of the first six chapters of the first draft (which devoted much space to the conjugal misery of Horace Benbow and his equivocal relationship with his sister Narcissa), stuck the remaining pieces together, wrote up the connecting passages, and expanded on a number of scenes, such as Godwin's lynching. The entire text was profoundly changed. The publisher received the redrafted galleys toward mid-December 1930.

The collation of the five drafts of the text of *Sanctuary* leaves us in no doubt as to the seriousness with which Faulkner undertook its revision. He wanted to be judged on this entirely redrafted text, as was confirmed in a 1955 interview: "Remember, the one you read was the second version. At that time I had done the best I could with it. The one that you didn't see was the base and cheap one, which I went to what sacrifice I could in more money than I could afford, rather than to let it pass. The one you saw was one that I did everything possible to make it as honest and as moving and to have as much significance as I could put into it" (*LG*, 123–24). Faulkner rewrote *Sanctuary* "trying to make out of it something which would not shame *The Sound and the Fury* and *As I Lay Dying* too much," and he believed that he had, all in all, "made a fair job" (*N2*, 1030).

Nonetheless, *Sanctuary* was originally conceived as a money-making enterprise. The 1932 preface starts with an admission of venality: "This book was written three years ago. To me it was a cheap idea, because it was deliberately conceived to make money" (*N2*, 1029). This confession gave rise to much misunderstanding and initially confirmed the worst suspicions of Faulkner's detractors. Although it should not be taken literally, it is still a confession. It was both an admission and a provocation.

———

After the rigorously private *The Sound and the Fury*, a book of secrecy and solitude, came a public book, destined to answer the prayers of the hypothetical average reader. To win over such readers, their tastes needed to be flattered and their expectations met: "I took a little time out, and speculated what a person in Mississippi would believe to be current trends" (*N2*, 1030). This is how Faulkner came to invent "the most horrific tale" imaginable (1030).

Truth be told, it was not pure invention. In a New Orleans nightclub in the mid-1920s, a young woman had told him the true story of a rape committed with a strange object followed by her detention in a brothel. The seeds of *Sanctuary* were in this sordid story. Similarly, Popeye, the novel's psychopathic mobster, was modeled on a Memphis gangster with the same nickname: Neal Karens Pumphrey, a villainous Southerner who emulated Al Capone, Dutch Schultz, Leg Diamonds, and other Dillinger-type gangsters, who was the talk of the town and had already inspired a character of Faulkner's in "The Big Shot," a short story likely written in 1929.

Faulkner's imagination did the rest. He pulled it off brilliantly. *Sanctuary* owes more to the melodramatic motivations of the Gothic novel and to the tried-and-tested thriller than his previous novels. Beauty and the Beast, virgin and monster, innocence abandoned to a fate of vice and crime—it is this venomous fable already told two hundred years earlier in *Clarissa* and revisited in the eighteenth century in a more fantastical, obscene, and darker register by de Sade, Horace Walpole, and M. G. Lewis, a register that

Faulkner reinvents in his own way. The connection between *Sanctuary* and the whodunit is even more blatant. Published in the same year as *The Glass Key* and a year after *The Maltese Falcon*, Dashiell Hammett's two masterpieces, Faulkner's novel is obviously a hard-boiled, tough-guy novel, born out of the vogue for pulp magazines, to which Hammett, Raymond Chandler, James McCain, and Horace McCoy would give its credentials during the 1930s. It should also be noted that at the time when Faulkner was writing *Sanctuary*, organized crime was starting to inspire Hollywood directors. The vogue for gangster movies started in 1927 with Josef von Sternberg's superb *Underworld*. The year 1930 saw Mervyn Le Roy's *Little Caesar*, 1931 William Wellman's *The Public Enemy*, and 1932 Howard Hawks's famous *Scarface*. With the success of these films, organized crime achieved the status of folklore, and the silhouette of the gangster—battered fedora, gray mac, a cigarette in the corner of his mouth—entered popular mythology. Of all Faulkner's novels, *Sanctuary* is certainly the one that owes the most to the codes of popular literature and the iconography of mass culture, particularly the cinema and comic strip of the late 1920s. But although Faulkner appropriated characters and scenarios from popular fiction, he did so to corrupt and subject them to his own ends. As André Malraux judiciously notes in his preface to the French translation, *Sanctuary* is a detective novel without the detectives, and the discovery of the criminal is not the real story. The novel is certainly melodramatic in the calculated excesses of its plot construction. But the ugliness of vice does not serve here to act as a foil to the luster of virtue. In Faulkner's books no one is innocent.

Sanctuary drags melodrama into derision that is blazing and icy by turns, and its darkness is of another ilk than that of the *roman noir*. Faulkner transposes the asphalt jungle of the hard-boiled novel to the muggy heat of the still-rural South. True, the characters of Horace Benbow; Belle, his ferocious wife; and his sister, the ultra-narcissistic Narcissa, had already featured in *Flags in the Dust*. But the Benbows take up less space than in the novel's first draft, and most of the characters come from worlds other than the upper class of Mississippi. They include a psychopathic gangster, small-time crooks, bootleggers, a brothel madam and her girls, corrupt politicians, and shady judges. The action takes place in a clandestine distillery in the remote Mississippi countryside, a Memphis brothel and gambling joint, and a Jefferson courthouse. Everything that happens is either terrifying or revolting: murders, a rigged trial, a lynching, a hanging, and, to make matters worse, a rape by corncob.

Everything in *Sanctuary* seems to be overseen by a single eye, bulging with horror and repulsed with disgust. There is no multiple viewpoint, such as one finds in *The Sound and the Fury* and *As I Lay Dying*. This does not mean that the narration is not twisted, not full of ellipses, detours, and delays. The most violent scenes are elided: Temple's rape with a corncob is never directly described, nor are the murders of Tommy and Red, Goodwin's lynching, or Popeye's hanging. The action is always ahead or behind, ahead *and* behind. Everything is already *missing in action*. Nothing is lived or named upon its occurrence; it is only apprehended after the fact. Disaster is always flagged and anticipation is always in a rearview mirror. As soon as she arrives at the Old Frenchman homestead, Temple lives in horrified anticipation of her rape. Time tenses up and contracts, gives no respite, allows no distancing. Nothing happens that has not already happened. See how quickly Temple in her panic slips from future to present, from present to past:

> And she began to say Something is going to happen to me. She was saying it to the old man with the yellow clots for eyes. "Something is happening to me!" she screamed at him, sitting in his chair in the sunlight, his hands crossed on the top of the stick. "I told you it was!" she screamed, voiding the words like hot silent bubbles into the bright silence about them until he turned his head and the two phlegm-clots above her where she lay tossing and thrashing on the rough, sunny boards. "I told you! I told you all the time!" (N2, 250)

Or later, at the dance, just before Popeye kills Red, Temple, a widow before her time, desiring her dead lover:

> [Popeye] gave her the glass. She drank. When she set the glass down she realised that she was drunk. She believed that she had been drunk for some time. She thought that perhaps she had passed out and that it had already happened. She could hear herself saying I hope it has. I hope it has. Then she believed it had and she was overcome by a sense of bereavement and of physical desire. (343)

The past is yet to come, the future imperfect. Between imminence and remanence lie the inevitable and the irremediable.

Sanctuary employs all the modalities of Faulknerian temporality—its distortions, its discontinuities, its interferences, its speed surges, its slow moments, its dizzy spells. The paradoxical and uncontrollable time of panic, when the body loses awareness and its activity is reduced to reflexes passively recorded by consciousness. Thus this description of Temple, in the moments after the fatal car accident: "Still running her bones turned to water and she fell flat on her face, still running" (N2, 205). And Temple again, after being surprised by a hidden voyeur: "For an instant she stood and watched herself run out of her body, out of her own slipper. She watched her legs twinkle against the sand, through the flecks of sunlight, for several yards, then whirl and run back and snatch up the slipper and whirl and run again" (242).

This is the unsettled time of nightmares. Few other novels give the feeling of reliving a bad dream and leave, once the book is finished, the same taste of oblivion. A worrying strangeness, a worrying familiarity grabs hold of the reader from the very first scene. The book opens as follows: "From beyond the screen of bushes which surrounded the spring, Popeye watched the man drinking" (N2, 181). Popeye is there on the threshold of the book as if he had always been there, a voyeur lying in wait, immobile, dumb, silently spying on Horace Benbow as he kneels down to drink from a stream. Named in his first appearance, Popeye, as Jean-Jacques Mayoux has noted, is already fully present.[19] He has a heavy presence, as oppressive as a threat. A gnome suddenly emerging from the depths, in this novel Popeye is the hallucinating "symbol of evil" (*FU*, 88), and this character from a Gothic novel has no character trait that does not signify his malevolent essence: he has a wizened, puny body; a face with a "a queer, bloodless color as though seen by electric light" (N2, 181); he wears a tight black suit, a stiff hat; and his pants and shoes are muddy. Like all of Faulkner's monsters (for example, Flem Snopes), Popeye is a hybrid being, between nature and artifice, between the living and the inanimate, between human and inhuman, and the description of him over the course of the novel is a collage: rubber eyes, steel or aluminum arms, doll's hands, wax head. There is something of the automaton in him, something of the animal also. "Across his vest ran a platinum chain like a spider web" (182), and when he watches Temple having sex, he neighs like a horse.

For two hours Popeye and Horace crouch down face-to-face, looking at each other over the stream that separates them and mingles their reflections, where one has come to drink and the other only spits. Popeye holds Horace at his mercy; Horace, paralyzed, submits to his rule. In the almost unbearable tension of this silent confrontation, violence threatens, the reign of terror has already begun. In *Sanctuary* everyone lives constantly in suspicion and fear. We are in a paranoid world where the presence of the other is unfailingly sensed as intrusion or menace. *Homo homini lupus.* Wolf or dog, as in the mise-en-abyme telling of the tribulations of the brothel madam's poodles, which are sometimes aggressive and ready to bite, sometimes mad with terror (see *N2*, 286–87). The same nastiness is everywhere. It's a dog's world—either the monotony of the kennel or the terror of oblivion.

The action takes place in three "sanctuaries": the Old Frenchman place, an abandoned Mississippi plantation that has become a hideout for crooks; Memphis, city of prostitutes and the underworld, with its speakeasies and whorehouses; and the small town of Jefferson, with its jail and courthouse. Each of these territories is a confined, forbidden space. Going in from outside or out from the inside means exposing oneself to aggression or escaping its menace. Anyone who ventures outside his original environment loses the protection it provides. These three spaces are sanctuaries only by euphemism: they are the absolute opposite of holy places, or rather they are places that have remained holy only because they have been desecrated, and while they serve for a time as a refuge, the right of sanctuary is always flouted in the end.

The story of *Sanctuary* is a story of intrusions and expulsions in a world with no laws or rules. This lack of order is reflected first in the disorder of bodies, in the convulsions of hysteria and in the spasms of lust, in the abandonment of defeated flesh and in the rigidity of the corpse. Nausea in *Sanctuary* is the appalling discovery of the body in the weight of its inertia and the contingency of its being; it is also the fascinated horror before the obscene swarming of organic life that, almost from its generation, is already courting death, carrying it within itself as the inexorable law of its fate; finally, it is the revolt against everything in the body that frustrates our desire for identity and our will to control.

The story deals with not only the puritan obsession with fallible, culpable flesh that needs to be disciplined and punished but also the modern obsession with the lustful body, the sick body, the tortured body, the mutilated body, the corrupt body. It refers obliquely to painters such as Goya,

Géricault, Munch, Soutine, Schiele, Dix, and Bacon, and to writers such as de Sade, Hoffmann, Poe, Flaubert, Proust, Kafka, Céline, Beckett, Bataille, and Guyotat.

Bodies, in Faulkner's novels, are not sanctuaries. There is no point in looking to them for signs of interiority or transcendence. They contain no presence, no mystery, other than that of their reproduction and their extinction. What dignity could there be for such bags of skin riddled with holes? The bodies in this story don't know how to hold themselves up or to hold themselves back. Everything pushes them to reveal themselves shamelessly; everything pushes them to deliver their grubby secrets. Disgorging, bleeding, drooling, spitting, sweating—through all of this discharge and oozing, the skin endlessly exhibits its misery and heralds its future as carrion. In *Sanctuary* the language of bodies is reduced to a nauseous epiphany of sexuality and death best summarized as "that black stuff that ran out of Bovary's mouth" (*N2*, 184).[20]

"My Lord, sometimes I believe that we are all children, except children themselves" (*N2*, 373), cries Horace in a rare moment of lucidity. In *Sanctuary* no one is in the right place. No one is the right age either. The children are no longer children; the adults are not yet adults. There are no "grownups" in Faulkner.

Childhood innocence is a misleading fallacy. In Faulkner's works innocence is a flaw. It is not yet evil but it is a necessary condition for evil; it leads to it and foments it. Look at Virgil and Fonzo, the two young Snopes boys adrift in Miss Reba's brothel, and Uncle Bud, the bad-tempered little boy who gets drunk on beer during his tea party. These children are already about to be initiated into what the Madam calls "meanness" (*N2*, 353).

Ruby's child, with "its pinched face," its "gaunt, veined skull," and its "its lead-colored eyelids" (*N2*, 259), starts to die as soon as it comes to life, prefiguring both the "crucified" innocent and, insofar as its scrawny childhood resembles that of Popeye, emblematic of a gestating evil. Pap, the deaf, blind, gluttonous old man, lapses into a second childhood on the threshold of death—his senile grimace has the same innocence. Childhood is less dreadful for the child than for the adult who has not been able to put his childhood to death and in whom it persists like a tenacious poison, the most efficient accomplice to evil. *Sanctuary* draws us into an infernal nursery. Here the distress, anguish, and cruelty of early childhood resurface. From the first pages it becomes clear that tough guy Popeye is all bravado, a poor child frightened by almost anything. When after nightfall he moves away from the stream in the company of Horace, he chooses a longer path to avoid the dark woods. When an owl passes by, he panics: "The something, a shadow shaped with speed, stooped at them and on, leaving a rush of air upon their very faces, on a soundless feathering of taut wings, and Benbow felt Popeye's whole body spring against him and his hand clawing at his coat. 'It's just an owl,' Benbow said. 'It's nothing but an owl'" (183–84). The scene has its counterpoint in chapter 9, when Temple walks on "something" and clings to Ruby, who tries to reassure her, telling her, "It's just a rat" (236). The rat is to Temple what the owl is to Popeye: it is the same apparition of "something," the same terror, the same reflex to grab onto someone. Later, alone, with no one else around, Temple holds on to objects, pulls her coat around her, and clings feverishly to her bed covers, "her arms crossed, her hands clutching her shoulders" (229), her body immobilized.

Both characters' fear revives the terror of childhood. Popeye, the depraved runt, and Temple, the young narcissistic virgin, are alike in their incompleteness and immaturity. Twin figures caught up by evil, they undoubtedly form the most fearsome couple imagined by Faulkner.

Popeye and Temple reflect each other just as, in another manner, Horace reflects Popeye from the first scene of the novel. These are mirrored figures, couples and doubles. For Horace, at the stream, Popeye is at first literally a reflection, a liquid image, and in this blurred, broken image, Popeye's reflection is indistinguishable from his own. Popeye is the *other* Horace, *his* other, his dark, evil double who fascinates him and whom he can know only through lack of awareness. Horace is a neurotic middle-class intellectual; Popeye is a dangerous pervert. The former is talkative to the point of verbal diarrhea while the latter confines himself to injunctions and insults. But it is no coincidence that they both have a sick mother, and the aptly named Popeye, who comes to the brothel to watch Temple and Red having sex, is not so very different from Horace spying on Little Belle and her lovers in the Virginia creeper.

Both men are voyeurs. In fact, in *Sanctuary* all the men, from the idiot Tommy to Senator Clarence Snopes, are voyeurs, each of them a potential or impotent rapist. At the Old Frenchman place, everything starts with watching; everyone observes, keeps watch, and spies (the verb *to watch* is tirelessly repeated from scene to scene). Horace's erotic dreams are also always caused by something seen or half seen, something that is at least partly linked to the visible. The most revealing scene in this regard is the one with the two mirrors described by Horace in his first conversation with Ruby: "And then I saw her face in the mirror. There was a mirror behind her and another behind me, and she was watching herself in the one behind me, forgetting about the other one in which I could see her face, see her watching the back of my head with pure dissimulation" (N2, 189). Mirrors as keyholes. Horace spies on Little Belle, who spies on Horace, spying on him spying on her in a looped voyeurism.

What moves Horace to the point of vertigo, troubles him to the point of nausea, is not Little Belle herself, her woman's body, but the reflection of her face in a mirror and, even more, her photograph, whose magical power is such that it brings him to the brink of hallucination not once but twice.

Initially, Horace is not suspicious. A thin, sorry object, nothing but "dead cardboard" (N2, 294) at the discretion of whoever looks at it, the shiny photo of Little Belle at first seems nothing more than a relic or fetish. But each time Horace looks at it, its fixed absence becomes curiously animated. In his Memphis hotel room, after his conversation with Ruby about Temple, he sees it moving around "as if of its own accord," and the image is "blurred [. . .] like something familiar seen beneath disturbed through clear water" (294). Horace then sees "with a kind of quiet horror and despair [. . .] a face suddenly older in sin than he would ever be" (294).[21]

At the end of chapter 23, after listening to Temple's terrifying confession, Horace goes home, picks up a photo of Little Belle lying on the bedside table, holds it in his hands, and looks at it. The photo immediately bursts into life: "Communicated to the cardboard by some quality of the light or perhaps by some infinitesimal movement of his hands, his own breathing, the face appeared to breathe in his palms in a shallow bath of highlight, beneath the slow, smoke-like tongues of invisible honeysuckle" (N2, 333). Horace sees this as "invitation and voluptuous promise and secret affirmation" (333). Then, overcome by nausea, he runs to the bathroom and throws up. He "sees" her as he is vomiting:

> The shucks set up a terrific uproar beneath her thighs. Lying with her head lifted slightly, her chin depressed like a figure lifted down from a crucifix, she watched something black and furious go roaring out of her pale body. She was

bound naked on her back on a flat car moving at speed through a black tunnel, the blackness streaming in rigid threads overhead, a roar of iron wheels in her ears. The car shot bodily from the tunnel in a long upward slant, the darkness overhead now shredded with parallel attenuations of living fire, toward a crescendo like a held breath, an interval in which she would swing faintly and lazily in nothingness filled with pale, myriad points of light. Far beneath her she could hear the faint, furious uproar of the shucks. (333)

Amid the turmoil of this stupefying hallucination scene, Horace, the horrified witness to evil, sees himself in an active role. Temple's raped body, confused with Little Belle's desirable body, is also his body—fantasy-like, a bisexual body, the rapist raped[22]—plagued by nausea and the "black thing" that escapes from it and also comes from him: vomit, blood, sperm, whatever.

The black of nausea, the black of terror. This is the blackness of evil hidden in each of us, and the interplay of identification, of split and multiple personalities, ironically underlines its omnipresence. The crowd scenes in chapter 19 are revealing in this regard. On the railway platform, Horace watches "young men in collegiate clothes" (N2, 295). When the train arrives, "they pushed gaily forward, talking and laughing, shouldering aside older people with gay rudeness, clashing and slamming seats back and settling themselves" (296). All of the following scenes in the train—the cheating students, their bawdy jokes, their lack of regard for adults (296–97)—reveal the vulgarity and boorishness of these unleashed pups. In these group scenes, the indictment of "innocence" is conjugated in the plural: these braying young students are worth no more than their elders. Horace watches their female companions pass by "in a steady stream of little colored dresses, bare-armed, with close bright heads, with that identical cool, innocent, unabashed expression which he knew well in their eyes, above the savage identical paint upon their mouths" (298). The same faces, the same mouths, the same looks. For Horace these young girls are doubles of Temple and Little Belle, a mob of Temples, a mob of Little Belles. Similarly, he later discovers a growing mob of Popeyes between Lee Goodwin's trial and lynching. "I saw her," says one of the traveling salesmen. "She was some baby. Jeez. I wouldn't have used no cob" (383). We are not far from the students' bawdy jokes, the salacious, tipsy sadism of the traveling salesmen. Gangs of adolescents or groups of adults, a parading or angry crowd, it is always the same horde, the same pack of wolves or the same herd of sheep, more or less vile, depending on the occasion.

Beyond violence there is only deceit. Temple's rape is a sham coupling between a half virgin and a subhuman man, triggered by the desertion of an ersatz gentleman. Red's burial is a carnival funeral against a backdrop of canticles and jazz, a wake full of laughter and drink that ends in "a sudden pandemonium of chairs and screams" (N2, 351). Goodwin's trial is a parody of justice with bent judges, a perjurer, a false innocent, and a false culprit. The law is continually ridiculed; the law makes a mockery of the law. The trials of Goodwin and Popeye come one after the other and they are alike. In each one the die is cast; each time the defendant's lawyers arguments are futile. At the end of both trials the jury retires for exactly eight minutes and returns with the same verdict, condemning both men to death for a crime they did not commit. The irony is that Popeye, the actual guilty party in the first trial, is condemned in the second for a murder he did not commit.

It is Temple, the judge's daughter, who perjures herself to save her rapist and sends Goodwin to his death, and this perjury is all the more revolting in that it seems to have no motive. The injustice is doubly arbitrary, an injustice guaranteed by silence. At the end of the trial, the old judge bustles Temple out of the courthouse to stop her from saying any more. The important thing is to avoid any scandal. Narcissa Benbow cynically says to her brother: "I dont see that it makes any difference who did it. The question is, are you going to stay mixed up with it? When people already believe you and she are slipping into my house at night" (N2, 306). Justice is the last concern of those who are supposed to defend it. Eustace Graham, the clubfooted district attorney, betrays his charge's secret to get the information he needs from Narcissa to win the trial; Clarence Snopes, a Mississippi state senator, spends most of his time hanging around brothels and sells information to the highest bidder. There is no one to state and impose the law. All the fathers are ineffective. The only paternal figures are Pap, the deaf, dumb and blind old man at the Old Frenchman place, and Temple's father, whom she calls on in vain at moments of distress: "My father's a judge; my father's a judge" (214). As for Horace, his failure to ensure that justice is triumphant shows the impotence of idealism in the face of widespread corruption.

"You've got the law, justice, civilization," he says to Goodwin in prison (N2, 270). The following passage delivers a stinging refutation of his naive humanistic beliefs. The law does not protect the innocent; justice will not be done. But Faulkner's irony has more than one trick: the law is also invoked by those who generally deride it. "There ought to be a law": this thought runs like a refrain throughout the novel. Thus Clarence Snopes, in his anti-Semitic tirade, says: "The lowest, cheapest thing on this earth aint a nigger: it's a jew. We need laws against them. Drastic laws" (363). Popeye calls for a law against alcoholism: "I told him about letting them sit around all night, swilling that goddam stuff. There ought to be a law" (246). Horace also invokes the law, when he complains to Little Belle of troubling summer nights: "Night is hard on old people. [. . .] Summer nights are hard on them. Something should be done about it. A law" (386). The law Horace wants is a law against nature, against sex, against women, that would provide a guarantee against the disorder of life and protect him from himself. Popeye and Snopes want laws *against*, laws that prohibit or repress. But their call for law also betrays disarray and fear. The absence—or corruption—of laws signals the general bankruptcy of the Law as a principle of order. Lawlessness leads not just to corruption and injustice but also to chaos and death. In *Sanctuary* death is in charge, and Popeye, the little black man, is its most zealous agent, before in turn becoming its victim. His own death is no more important to him than those of others, and his hanging is in fact a form of suicide. Horace, however, after hearing Temple's confession, also calls for death: "Better for her if she were dead tonight [. . .]. For me, too. He thought of her, Popeye, the woman, the child, Goodwin, all put into a single chamber, bare, lethal, immediate and profound: a single blotting instant between the indignation and the surprise. And I too; thinking how that were the only solution. Removed, cauterized out of the old and tragic flank of the world" (331–32). For Horace, this desire for death, for extermination even, is linked to the horrified discovery of evil and oblivion: "Perhaps it is upon the instant that we realize, admit, that there is a logical pattern to evil, that we die, he thought, thinking of the expression he had once seen in the eyes of a dead child, and of other dead: the cooling indignation, the shocked despair fading, leaving two empty globes in which the motionless world lurked profoundly in miniature" (332). This "logical pattern to evil" actually has no discernible logic, and the pattern turns out to be nothing but the recurrence of the same motif. There is no order hidden beneath the disorder, no necessity underneath the random anarchy. Only one thing is certain: the world is running headlong toward its own destruction; the end is nigh.

As the novel moves toward its conclusion, there are more and more signs that the world is dying. The final movement is the slowing down of a soft, silent fall, an almost gentle subsiding into inertia. Death has the last word, literally. The conclusion is threefold: Popeye is seen lying in his prison cell, placidly counting down the days to his execution; after running away, Horace is back in Kinston, defeated and resigned, back pathetically in the sanctuary of home; and Temple and her father are in Paris, dead souls among the dead queens of a garden at dusk:

> In the pavilion a band in the horizon blue of the army played Massenet and Scriabin, and Berlioz like a thin coating of tortured Tchaikovsky on a slice of stale bread, while the twilight dissolved in wet gleams from the branches, onto the pavilion and the sombre toadstools of umbrellas. Rich and resonant the brasses crashed and died in the thick green twilight, rolling over them in rich sad waves. Temple yawned behind her hand, then she took out a compact and opened it upon a face in miniature sullen and discontented and sad. Beside her her father sat, his hands crossed on the head of his stick, the rigid bar of his moustache beaded with moisture like frosted silver. She closed the compact and from beneath her smart new hat she seemed to follow with her eyes the waves of music, to dissolve into the drying brasses, across the pool and the opposite semicircle of trees where at sombre intervals the dead tranquil queens in stained marble mused, and on into the sky lying prone and vanquished in the embrace of the season of rain and death. (N2, 398)

Faulkner's sixth novel, *Sanctuary* was published on February 9, 1931, at the height of the Great Depression, in an initial print run of 2,219 copies. Advertisements described it as a mosaic of exacerbated evil, of cold brutality, of human perversity, of human impotence. The reviews, longer and more numerous than for his previous novels, do not contradict the advertising, but the reception by the American press was generally favorable. Most critics, however, admitted their discomfiture with this novel, which they could not but admire while at the same time being horrified by it. "A Chamber of Horrors" is the title of the review published in the *New York Sun* on February 13, 1931, and its author, Edwin Seaver, called *Sanctuary* "one of the most terrifying books" but also "one of the most extraordinary" that he had ever read. Henry Seidel Canby, writing in the *Saturday Review of Literature* on March 21, found it both powerful and depressing. Even Hemingway, who was grudging in his admiration, read *Sanctuary* and acknowledged that when Faulkner was good, he was "damned good." In prudish England, on the other hand, the novel met with disapproval and revulsion, even after being bowdlerized. For the anonymous critic of the *Times Literary Supplement*, Faulkner's gifts were used only when he was describing terror and brutality, giving flesh to nightmarish doings perpetrated by creatures almost too sick or depraved to be called human. Rebecca West, a famous journalist and novelist of the time, was even more severe, panning *Sanctuary* in the *Daily Telegraph* on October 2, 1931.

Oxford, Mississippi, was even more scandalized by this new novel from this slanderer of Southern life than by his previous books, and at Mac Reed's drugstore it was practically sold under the counter. A professor from Ole Miss professed himself astonished that anyone could have written a book like *that*. Even Faulkner's friends, except Phil Stone, found *Sanctuary* repulsive, and, as expected, his family and in-laws were outraged, although this time Miss Maud defended her Billy.

Nonetheless, Faulkner was right: *Sanctuary* was his first commercial success. By early March, three weeks after publication, more than thirty-five hundred copies had already been sold, rising to over seven thousand in April. By July the novel was in its sixth edition. Although hardly a best seller, it was selling much better than his earlier novels. Two years later *Sanctuary* was translated into French by Maurice-Edgar Coindreau, with a preface by André Malraux, marking the start of Faulkner's fame in France.

MOURNING BECOMES THE BUNDRENS: *AS I LAY DYING*

In October 1929 the still penniless Faulkner, who was now the head of the family, started working nights at the University of Mississippi power plant. It was here on October 25—two days after the Wall Street crash—that he started to write his new novel, *As I Lay Dying*, in the cellar among the furnaces and boilers. He later told of the relatively unusual circumstances of its composition in his preface to *Sanctuary*:

I had invented a table out of a wheelbarrow in the coal bunker, just beyond a wall from where a dynamo ran. It made a deep, constant humming noise. There was no more work to do until about 4 AM, when we would have to clean the fires and get up steam again. On these nights, between 12 and 4, I wrote *As I Lay Dying* in six weeks, without changing a word. I sent it to Smith and wrote him that by it I would stand or fall. (*N2*, 1030)

As could be expected, Faulkner's telling of the story was not entirely accurate. In fact, he was not really a "coal porter" (*N1*, 1358), but was employed to supervise the work of two black men who fed the furnace with coal. It was not a very absorbing task. Between six in the evening and six in the morning, he had a lot of time to write.

At the bottom of the last page of the manuscript of *As I Lay Dying*, Faulkner wrote down the date of completion: December 11, 1929. If we are to believe the manuscript, the novel took barely six weeks to write. However, this does not take into account the months Faulkner spent typing up the manuscript, and, comparing both texts, it is clear that he did not just simply copy the manuscript but, as was his wont, revised it extensively. Nevertheless, there were far fewer changes made than to the earlier novels, and most of these were minor redrafts and stylistic alterations.

Even if it took Faulkner ten weeks to finish this novel, he did write it in a very short time. *As I Lay Dying* remains a breathtaking feat.

When asked about *As I Lay Dying*, Faulkner invariably answered that the novel was a "simple tour de force" (*SL*, 197). Tour de force, yes, but not the least bit simple for all that. *As I Lay Dying* has the seduction of a brilliant impromptu, the beauty of a perfectly executed high-wire act. Of all Faulkner's novels, it is perhaps the most unbound, the liveliest, the most insolently free while at the same time the most puzzling and elusive.

The puzzle starts with its title. "As I Lay Dying" is the announcement of a death, the narrator's death, which cannot be read without putting oneself in the place of the dying person. Faulkner borrowed the title from the lamentation of the shade of Agamemnon (assassinated by Clytemnestra, his unfaithful wife, and her lover, Aegisthus, upon his return from the Trojan War) overheard by Ulysses in the underworld in the eleventh book of *The Odyssey*: "As I lay dying the woman with the dog's eyes would not close my eyelids for me as I descended into Hades." This title quotation was borrowed from Homer, just as that of previous novel had been borrowed from Shakespeare. The title is uncertain in the tense of the verb ("lay," normally a past tense in English, is a present tense in the Mississippi hillbilly vernacular) and incomplete: the subordinate clause is left hanging, subordinate to nothing and hence calling for completion. Perhaps the completion comes simply from the text heralded by the title. Or perhaps the title is just the first of the monologues making up the novel.

The puzzle that is *As I Lay Dying* is compounded by the subject of the story: a death in a family, a family busying itself around a dead woman. Behind *The Sound and the Fury* there was the "mental image" of a group of children confronted with the death of their grandmother. In *As I Lay Dying* it is a mother who is dying, and her dying, her death, and her burial are the very heart of the novel. This book is also the first to have as its heroes the poor whites from the Mississippi hills, and the novelist treats them with as much respect as the more or less neurotic grandees who are still prisoners of their past and who up to then had played all the leading roles in fiction.

However, as French writer Valery Larbaud noted, *As I Lay Dying* is not in any way a "peasant novel." Nowhere in this book is there room for a generic definition, and the way the material is handled owes little to the realist tradition. Rather than representing the real, this novel aims to muddy any preconceived ideas. From the start, its title alone places it in the dual paradox of a dying life and an active death. Life and death are not opposed as being and nonbeing but are connected in a reciprocal relationship, cohabiting and communicating in the indistinct region that is their shared border. We are in a space of indecision, instability, interval, intermission and in the time of meantime, the suspended time of a journey, and the time, past due, of a burial scandalously delayed.

Not only does the novel tell us a new "story full of sound and fury," but even the stage on which the action takes place is presented as *another* stage, both familiar and fabulous. From the very first sections, everything is shown in an unusual, slightly disquieting light. In the Bundrens' house on the hill, voices emerge that sound close by, but we don't know where they are coming from: "As you enter the hall, they sound as though they were speaking out of the air about your head" (N2, 14). Inexplicably, the sounds linger, reverberating silently, close by even though no longer audible: "Cash labors about the trestles, moving back and forth, lifting and placing the planks with long clattering reverberations in the dead air as though he were lifting and dropping them at the bottom of an invisible well, the sounds ceasing without departing, as if any movement might dislodge them from the immediate air in reverberant expectation" (49). Few words recur as often in this novel as the word "fading"; nothing here is fully present or completely disappeared. The shadows also have this ability to persevere, and their continuous presence gives them an almost material consistency: "The air smells like sulphur. Upon the impalpable plane of it their shadows form as upon a wall, as though like sound they had not gone very far away in falling but had merely congealed for a moment, immediate and musing. [...] Below the sky sheet-lightning slumbers lightly; against it the trees, motionless, are ruffled out to the last twig, swollen, increased as though quick with young" (49).

Everything is threatened by both turbulence and inertia; everything is held in a "dynamic immobility" (N2, 49). The novel describes mobile figures in a space that is itself shifting: the Bundrens' wagon labors obstinately along poor roads; Jewel, on his horse, keeps doubling back around the funeral cortege; and the buzzards enticed by the already rotting corpse trace circles in the incandescent July sky. There is movement, but it is always suspended: watched by little Vardaman, the horses "wheeling in a long lunge, the buggy wheeling onto two wheels and motionless like it is nailed to the ground and the horses motionless like they are nailed by the hind feet to the center of a whirling plate" (37). There is immobility, but it is an immobility that is always like an infinite slowness, and in the secret of this slowness there is a buildup of energy that will eventually be discharged. Time, in Faulkner's work, is always pregnant with catastrophe. The Bundrens will not be spared. They have scarcely taken to the road when sinister omens start to pile up around them: "The sun, an hour above the horizon, is poised like a bloody egg upon a crest of thunderheads" (27). The atmosphere becomes electric, "the light has turned copper: in the eyes portentous, in the nose sulphurous, smelling of lightning" (27). And then a storm breaks, torrential rain pours down, the river bursts its banks, and the water surges, washing away everything in its path.

As I Lay Dying thrusts us into a world of violence, unstable and unpredictable, always being born, always dying, always on the point of appearing or disappearing. The center of this world in perpetual metamorphosis—and the heart of the book, dying and then dead, but a living dead, more alive than dead, running her family from beyond life—is Addie Bundren, whose family has undertaken to transport her body in a wagon drawn by two mules at the height of summer to the far-off Jefferson cemetery, where she wants to be buried. All the action of the novel gravitates around these mortal remains without a grave. The multiple adventures, dramatic or comical, of the Bundrens' mad escapade are recounted, all the difficulties they meet en route while trying to fulfill their mother's wish: under torrid sun and torrential rain, crossing a flooded river, and putting out a fire. And then, in the middle of it all, there is the incongruous, cumbersome corpse, starting to stink.

One of the family's first duties is to secure her grave. It is as if the corpse doesn't want to disappear—or can't. The time between Addie's death and her burial extends beyond what is tolerable. The Bundrens undertake their journey for pious reasons—to keep a promise, to fulfill their mother's wishes (Anse keeps telling everyone that he gave Addie his word)—but the funeral is put off for more than a week, and the community sees this delay as an insult to the dead woman. "I got as much respect for the dead as ere a man," says their neighbor Samson, "but you've got to respect the dead themselves, and a woman that's been dead in a box four days, the best way to respect her is to get her into the ground as quick as you can" (N2, 75). Rachel, his wife, is indignant: "It's a outrage," she says. "A outrage" (75). Lula Armstid thinks likewise: "It's a outrage [. . .]. He should be lawed for treating her so" (126).

There is more than scandal. On top of the indignation provoked by the corruption of the funeral comes the intimate distress of each mourner and the prodigious work of mourning, a response and retort to the loss, delivered to us little by little by their interior monologues. For each Bundren there is a death to be lived through, a dead woman to kill.

For Anse, the deceived husband, parasite and predator, the mourning is over quickly. No sooner is his wife dead than he exclaims: "God's will be done. [. . .] Now I can get them teeth" (N2, 35). Far from being a testing time of loss, Addie's death is for him a veritable godsend. Not only does he make the most of his time in Jefferson to get a new set of dentures, but he also wastes no time in replacing his late wife with a new Mrs. Bundren (she is called this even before Anse introduces her to the family). Anse only wants to put up a front. He doesn't live through his period of mourning; he acts it, mimes it, and turns it into a show for all to see. As Darl says, with his usual clear-sightedness: "It is as though upon a face carved by a savage caricaturist a monstrous burlesque of all bereavement flowed" (50).

For the five children, on the other hand, the bereavement is painful and difficult; Addie's death causes only torpor and anguish. However, at least three of them seem to accomplish the reappropriation and liquidation that is always the task of mourning.

To each his own grief, each child has to cope with the bereavement in his or her own way. The plaintiveness of Cash, the eldest, is initially in his sawing and hammering, in the panting of the craftsman working relentlessly. The work of mourning for the "good carpenter" (as Darl ironically calls him) is just that: work; the pernickety attention to detail, the methodical application and fierce energy put into making a handsome, solid coffin for Addie, under the window behind which she lies dying, within earshot of the regular back-and-forth movement of the saw. The coffin, a faultless object, will be the son's final offering to his mother. As for Jewel, the result of an affair with a preacher, he is even more Addie's son than Cash. A child of lust and of sin, he is her *jewel*, her "cross" and her "salvation" (N2, 113). What Darl and the last-born lacked, Jewel has in abundance, if not to excess; his mother's love for him is tough and jealous, and he loves her with the same dark passion. The violence of this love is pitted against the hate he feels for the other family members, whom he sees as intruders. Jewel wants to take his mother away, to shield her from the view of the others forever. He would kill both father and brothers in order to be alone with her: "It would just be me and her on a high hill and me rolling the rocks down the hill at their faces, picking them up and throwing them down the hill faces and teeth and all by God until she was quiet" (11). Nevertheless, when Addie dies, Jewel does not succumb to despair or madness. He even becomes the hero of the crazy funeral; it is thanks to his exploits and sacrifices that the enterprise is successful. Bereavement for him is a heroic ordeal, one from which he emerges the victor. He also transfers all the violence and ambivalence (all the "ambi-violence") of his love for Addie to his wild horse—a horse that he alternately beats and strokes, "cursing it with obscene ferocity" (9). As Darl says lucidly and repeatedly about his centaur brother: "Jewel's mother is a horse" (65). Jewel and his horse, Jewel and his mother: the same body, joint and several, indivisible, with his indomitable opacity, an existence all the more assured of its reality in that it has no self-awareness. Darl again: "Jewel knows he is, because he does not know that he does not know whether he is or not" (52).

The same cannot be said for little Vardaman, Dewey Dell, and Darl, who are the best examples of what Doctor Peabody calls "that abject nakedness which we bring here with us" (N2, 31), and Addie's death and the difficulty or impossibility of mourning precipitate all three into a veritable identity crisis. Through Vardaman, the youngest, it is childhood itself that is confronted once again with the scandal that is death. The loss of the mother revives in him the wound of initial separation and reopens a precarious infantile situation where relations to objects are not yet fully assured. This leads him into the most archaic regression: identifying his mother's body with that of a large fish, caught a few hours before her death, which he cuts into pieces, Vardaman lives Addie's death in orality and in fragmentation. "My mother is a fish" (54), he says. Eating fish therefore becomes a gesture of transubstantiation, like a totemic meal or Eucharistic celebration; it means reappropriating the lost flesh and reviving it, breathing life back into it: "And tomorrow it will be cooked and et and she will be him and pa and Cash and Dewey Dell and there wont be anything in the box and so she can breathe" (44).

On the other hand, mourning is impossible for Dewey Dell, the only daughter, barely out of adolescence and already pregnant. On the point of becoming a mother, Dewey Dell loses her own. She doesn't know what is happening to her, does not know what she feels, no longer knows who she is:

> The dead air shapes the dead earth in the dead darkness, further away than seeing shapes the dead earth. It lies dead and warm upon me, touching me naked through my clothes. I said You dont know what worry is. I dont know what it is. I dont know whether I am worrying or not. Whether I can or not. I dont know whether I can cry or not. I dont know whether I have tried to or not. I feel like a wet seed wild in the hot blind earth. (N2, 42)[23]

For Dewey Dell, the discovery of death is bound up with the stupor that takes hold of her when she feels life stirring inside her, a life she wants to get rid of. She has no time. Everything happens too soon, too quickly, taking her by surprise: "I heard that my mother is dead. I wish I had time to let her die. I wish I had time to wish I had. It is because in the wild and outraged earth too soon too soon too soon. It's not that I wouldn't and will not it's that it is too soon too soon too soon" (78).

Finally, Darl, the unwanted, unloved child, the excluded son, does not know how to mourn a mother who has never been there for him: "I cannot love my mother because I have no mother" (N2, 61). Already Quentin, in *The Sound and the Fury*, felt abandoned by his mother, but his sister had taken her place, at least for a while. Darl has nobody; Darl is nobody. Made entirely of absences, belonging to nothing, and with no family ties, he doubts not only his identity but his very existence as well: "In a strange room, you must empty yourself for sleep. And before you are emptied for sleep, what are you. And when you are emptied for sleep, you never were. When you are filled with sleep, you never were. I dont know what I am. I dont know if I am or not" (52). Darl is nothing but a vague, fluid being on the edge of oblivion. Nothing ties him to life and there is nothing to help him adapt to it. While his brothers eventually *replace* Addie—one with a horse, another with a fish, the third with a coffin—to him, his mother will always be *irreplaceable*. Neither coffin, horse, nor fish, she is the mother he cannot call Mother, the mother he cannot talk to. In the manuscript of the novel, Darl's first monologue contained a reference to "maw"; in the final version, "maw" is replaced by "Addie Bundren." For Darl, the death of his mother is only an agonizing reminder of the original emptiness. This absence of a relationship is also, however, a relationship *to* absence. Of all the Bundren children, Darl is, paradoxically, the most subjugated by his mother, precisely in that she has spurned him. He can join her only through destruction, and the reason he sets fire to the barn sheltering her coffin is both to wreak vengeance upon her and to appropriate her in a second death perpetrated by him.

His inability to mourn tips Darl over into madness. Darl is mad, raving mad, but his madness is not just irrationality. It is both a breakdown and a breakthrough. There is knowledge in his distress, wisdom in his loss of sanity: "It takes two people to make you, and one people to die. That's how the world is going to end" (N2, 27). Two, one, zero; sex, death, oblivion: this is how this great dreamer of apocalypses counts down.

From the wandering of his madness, Darl discovers the theatrical vanity of the world: "How do our lives ravel out into the no-wind, no-sound, the weary gestures wearily recapitulant: echoes of old compulsions with no-hand on no-strings: in sunset we fall into furious attitudes, dead gestures of dolls" (N2, 139). Darl, the all-seeing voyeur, sees beyond the visible, sees the reverse of death, is aware of its absent density, its double oblivion. He fore-sees events, senses thoughts, apprehends those close to him at their most intimate, knows all the family secrets. He knows that Jewel is not Anse's son and that he is Addie's favorite, he knows that Dewey Dell is pregnant (and Dewey Dell knows that he knows and hates him for it). He even knows when Addie dies, even before he is told, and gives a detailed account of it while he is on the road with Jewel, several miles away (31–35).

Just like his sister at family meals, Darl is nothing but bulging eyes, "his eyes gone further than the food and the lamp, full of the land dug out of his skull and the holes filled with distance beyond the land" (N2, 18). From being overfull, his eyes are empty; he is both blind and clairvoyant. Darl's madness comes from excessive, overly acute awareness, from too much thinking; the neighbors perceive him as thinking too much. For sensible Vernon Tull, the "brain it's like a piece of machinery" and "it's best when it runs along the same, doing the day's work and not no one part used no more than needful. I have said and I say again, that's ever living thing the matter with Darl: he just thinks by himself too much" (46–47). The Latin term for overthinking is *ultracogitare*, from which the French term *outrecuidance*, meaning presumption, is derived. Thinking too much is a presumption.

It is to this madman, both presumptuous and excessive, who sees too much, thinks too much, and knows too much, that Faulkner gives the monologues with the most poetic flourishes and one-third of the tale. Darl can be seen as the writer's fictional double, the character that incarnates the trouble of thinking and the ability to speak. He is, however, a negative double, an incomplete, ironic double. The character has no face, the poet no poems; he is a loose end.

As a character in a story, within his family and community, it is Darl himself who is de trop. Darl is in the way; he is bothersome and destruc-tive. He needs to be gotten rid of, at any cost. By the end of the novel the Bundrens have accomplished their task as undertakers, as Addie has finally been buried. Life can go back to normal. Anse has a new set of dentures; another Mrs. Bundren—"a kind of duck-shaped woman all dressed up, with them kind of hard-looking pop eyes" (N2, 177)—has already taken the place of the dead woman; Cash is going to get his "graphophone," and

Vardaman a small electric train. Everything is about to return to normal, but what normality requires is that the madman be locked up. Soon, Darl will be where he should be: behind bars, "foaming" (173), a madman among his own. As Cash, his carpenter brother and a man of order, measure, and reason, says: "It is better so for him. This world is not his world; this life his life" (178).

In his last monologue, talking to himself and talking about himself alternately in the third and first person, Darl tells us that two guards with mismatched clothes and shaven heads have come to get him to bring him to the asylum:

> Darl has gone to Jackson. They put him on the train, laughing, down the long car laughing, the heads turning like the heads of owls when he passed. "What are you laughing at?" I said.
> "Yes yes yes yes yes." (N2, 172)

Darl bursts out laughing, in the same way a truth might burst out, finally exposed after being long hidden. Or like a sob long held in. But where does the mad laugh come from? Darl himself at length puzzles over what makes him laugh. Is it, as he first presumes, the sight of the two guards and their revolvers? Is it that he has become a danger to the public, a target of police surveillance? Or does he laugh out of derision because he hates "the sound of laughing" (N2, 172)? Or, yet more obscurely, against a backdrop of fantasy, does he laugh to ward off the image that is both enigmatic and obscene—"a woman and a pig with two backs and no face" (172)[24]—a sort of "primitive scene" discovered through the little spy glass brought back from France? Or is he simply laughing at the ape-like spectacle of his family eating bananas? "'Is that why you are laughing, Darl?'" (172) The answers envisaged by Darl are questions in themselves. His only answer is the three salvoes of "yes" that punctuate his monologue and that, in turn, accost and question us because we no longer know what Darl is saying yes to and what he is laughing about.

Yes or no? Is this one final attempt to acquiesce to life or an ironic flat refusal? Possibly both. Possibly neither. Perhaps what makes his laugh incongruous and worrisome is not just the fact that it is mirthless but also that it is groundless and pointless. Darl cannot know what he is laughing at, because he is laughing at nothing. And therefore he is laughing at everything. Nothing and everything.

This novel of lost ways and madness, of death and mourning, *As I Lay Dying* can also be read as an ironic reflection on the power, the shortcomings, and the deceptiveness of words. During her first pregnancy Addie discovers that "living [is] terrible" and that "words are no good; that words dont ever fit even what they are trying to say" (*N2*, 115). As if lacking of itself, language completely fails to fulfill the function it is supposed to fulfill: words are just "the gaps in people's lacks" (117).

Emptiness also makes an appearance on the page, in the form of blank spaces. The text is twice punctuated by gaps, literally: the first time in the monologue of a neighbor of the Bundrens, where the white is surrounded by black, defining the shape of a coffin (*N2*, 56); the second time in the middle of Addie's monologue: "I would think: The shape of my body where I used to be a virgin is in the shape of a   and I couldn't think *Anse*" (117).

These blanks are not dumb: the first speaks of the absence and presence of death; the second the opening that is the female sex organs. The visible emptiness *between* the words in the text serves at a minimum to signal these absences. The emptiness *within* words is a buried emptiness, a hidden hole, filled in and undisclosed. Words delude us. Addie finds out that not only do words not match their referents, but they also mislead their world: "When [Cash] was born I knew that motherhood was invented by someone who had to have a word for it because the ones that had the children didn't care whether there was a word for it or not. I knew that fear was invented by someone that had never had the fear; pride, who never had the pride" (*N2*, 115). Although language cannot fully capture reality and offers only fraudulent supplements to experience, it still has its own reality, as attested by the insidious power of its effects. When she gets pregnant again, Addie realizes that words are all treacherous. All of her rage is due to the fact that she has been taken in by them: "It was as though [Anse] had tricked me, hidden within a word like within a paper screen and struck me in the back through it" (116). Addie at first resents Anse but soon realizes that he, like her, has also been had: "I realized that I had been tricked by words older than Anse or love, and that the same word had tricked Anse too" (116). Addie starts by noticing the deficiency of words and ends up acknowledging their insidious power. Men always think that they use language to act in the world and on the world, but language manipulates them, prompting them to do things they never intended. The order of language turns out to be as restrictive as the biological order or the social order, and everyone is taken in, from birth to death. Anyone looking for a place of truth will find only the disappointment of empty form. But this empty form has the effectiveness of an active force and no one eludes the tyranny of its law.

Her experience as a woman and mother has taught Addie to distrust words, and, in duty to "the alive, to the terrible blood, the red bitter flood boiling through the land" (*N2*, 117), in listening to "the dark land talking the voiceless speech" (118), she believes she has found a world of silence, a beat beneath words, a language outside language, cut into flesh, its roots tangled with the root of beings and things. In the urgency and failure of her desire to be, and in her acceptance of the ultimate silence that is death, Addie is one of Faulkner's earliest tragic heroines, although the portrait he sketches of her is not without irony. Addie's charge against language is conducted *within* language, through a rhetoric that glorifies words. The irony is doubled by the fact that her only monologue comes from beyond the grave and that no one—apart from us, the readers—hears her confession, no one reads her legacy. It would therefore be wrong to see her as the novelist's accredited spokesperson. Faulkner also came up against the limits of language. He knew that it was incapable of filling the gap separating reality from its representations, but he also knew its resources, its ruses, and continued to trust in its capacity to forge ties and weave meaning. His entire undertaking as a novelist was a gamble on language, with all the anxiety and uncertainties that entailed.

The gamble was risky, the undertaking pure madness. Writing means abandoning the reassurance of knowledge, exposing oneself to madness, venturing to its outer limits. It also means working the language (like Cash the carpenter works wood), carving out one's own language, escaping for a time from the mortal threat of madness by agreeing to undertake the project of writing.

Writing is a way of fending off, the written work a safeguard against madness. In *As I Lay Dying*, Faulkner—in contrast to his imaginary double Darl, the madman *in* the novel—again manages to save himself, again succeeds in and by failing. Again, he undoes with one hand what he creates with the other, weaving a text and then shredding it, building a story only to destroy its pretentions.

Like *The Sound and the Fury*, this novel can be defined as a Joycean polyphony, but instead of four monologues, we are given fifty-nine rather short monologues (the longest is seven pages, the shortest just five words),

distributed between fifteen narrators. These monologues crop up out of nowhere; they are impossible to locate in time. In contrast to *The Sound and
the Fury*, no dates are given—just a name, as in a play. In each section another voice is heard, the viewpoint moves constantly, the text twists and turns,
and these fragmented narratives are compounded by frequent ruptures in
tone and style. Against all likelihood, Faulkner puts words in his characters'
mouths that are beyond their linguistic capacities and cultural knowledge;
he jumps without notice within the same monologue from the roughest di-
alect to the refined audacity of ostentatiously poetic language.

   As I Lay Dying is a syncopated book: composed of breaks, interruptions,
fade-outs, silences, but also links and connections, producing rhythm and
music. It is also a dubious, ambiguous book. Through the rainbow of humor
(from innocent burlesque to insidious black), through the absurdity of situations and the buffoonery of some characters, the novel constantly skirts
the farcical. The Bundrens' stubbornness in performing their task is at
times reminiscent of the blind obstinacy of burying beetles, and at the end
of the funerary steeplechase, when they eventually arrive in Jefferson and
we see Anse "all hangdog and proud" introducing the new duck-like Mrs.
Bundren to his stunned children, the whole novel seems to collapse into
pure absurdity. A chronicle of a family adrift, a story of madness, death, and
mourning, *As I Lay Dying* is nonetheless an implacable tragedy. It is both
comedy and tragedy. For Faulkner, a great reader of Shakespeare, there was
no distinction between the two: "There's not too fine a distinction between
humor and tragedy, that even tragedy is in a way walking a tightrope between the ridiculous—between the bizarre and the terrible" (*FU*, 39). The
tragicomic is not incompatible with the epic. In its powerfully simple argument, *As I Lay Dying* is also, as Faulkner himself pointed out, a saga: "I took
this family and subjected them to the two greatest catastrophes which man
can suffer—flood and fire, that's all" (*FU*, 87).

   This balancing act of a novel offers us both comedy and its reverse, a
tragedy and its derision, a saga and its parody. It walks this fine line elegantly, to the end.

———

As I Lay Dying was published by Cape & Smith on October 6, 1930. The
print run was barely higher than that for *The Sound and the Fury*—2,522

copies—and in both the United States and the United Kingdom it was not well received. While acknowledging the novelist's talent, critics deplored his sensationalism and his taste for sordid and macabre stories. They were taken aback by the peculiarities of his narrative technique and were wholly repelled by his humor. This alternating praise and disapproval were to be ritually repeated in most reviews of his later novels. For decades American critics had little else to say on his work.

The novel was better received in France, where Maurice-Edgar Coindreau's translation was published in 1934, with a fine preface by Valery Larbaud. *As I Lay Dying* was first adapted for the theater in Paris by a young actor named Jean-Louis Barrault, who spent months rewriting it as a mime. He presented this piece, his first show, in June 1935 under the title *Autour d'une mère* (Around a Mother), at the Théâtre de l'Atelier, with sets by Félix Labisse.[25] The following month, Antonin Artaud wrote a review for *La Nouvelle Revue française*.

Alongside *Absalom, Absalom!*, *As I Lay Dying* is the Faulkner novel most often used as a model by other writers, in both Latin America and Europe. We know that Gabriel García Márquez, who greatly admired Faulkner, and who was attracted by both the rusticity of the setting and the audacity of the technique, provided his own version in *Leaf Storm* (*La Hojarasca*), his first novel, published in 1955. Carlos Fuentes did the same in *The Death of Artemio Cruz* (*La Muerte de Artemio Cruz*, 1962). This unclassifiable, incomparable novel continues to fascinate writers. On February 2, 1962, Julien Green wrote in his diary that he had read *As I Lay Dying*. He saw in it a sort of funereal delectation but with striking beauty on each page. According to Green, it was one of the very rare successes in a time when so many insignificant books were being hailed as masterpieces.[26]

VERSIONS OF THE SUN: *LIGHT IN AUGUST*

According to the dates written on the manuscript, *Light in August* was written in just six months, from August 17, 1931, to February 19, 1932. However, Faulkner had undoubtedly been thinking about it beforehand and even may have started work on it at an earlier time. In any case, it is unlikely that the date written on the last sheet of the manuscript marks the completion of the novel's final draft. Furthermore, while the manuscript dates are both followed by the words "Oxford, Mississippi," at least part of the novel was written in New York, where Faulkner stayed from November 4 to December 10, 1931. What's more, an interview published on November 28 in the *New Yorker* reported that Faulkner was spending most of his days alone, working on his next novel, which was to be called *Light in August*, and that it was about a quarter done. From August 1931 to February 1932, the drafting of this novel took up most of his time. The only other two texts dating from this period are "Turn About," a short story Faulkner sent to Ben Wasson on January 9, 1932, and published in the *Saturday Evening Post* on March 5 that year, and the provocative introduction to the Modern Library edition of *Sanctuary*, published in March.

Little is known about the sources and genesis of *Light in August*. If we are to believe the author, "that story begun with Lena Grove, the idea of the young girl with nothing, pregnant, determined to find her sweetheart" (*FU*, 74). As with *The Sound and the Fury*, Faulkner said that everything began with "a mental image." However, we now know that he hesitated between several openings and that in the first draft the novel started with the arrival in Jefferson of the young preacher, Gail Hightower (now related in chapter 3). We also know that for the story of Joe Christmas, Faulkner probably took inspiration from a news item in Oxford on September 8, 1908, when he was eleven: the lynching of a black man, Nelse Patton, who had killed a white woman by cutting her throat with a razor. After his arrest, a furious mob killed him in his cell before dragging his naked, emasculated, headless body outside the prison and hanging him from a tree. The next day, the local press congratulated the public for having done its duty.

Of the texts published prior to *Light in August*, only "Dry September," a short story published in *Scribner's* in January 1931, prefigures one of the novel's subplots. A number of characters already encountered in Faulkner's short stories make more or less discreet reappearances, in particular the suicidal Dr. Gavin Blount, a character from "The Big Shot," who comes back as Gail Hightower, and lawyer Gavin Stevens, who first appeared in "Hair," a short story published in May 1931, and who was to become a major character in five later novels.

This composite manuscript suggests that *Light in August* was more difficult to write than *The Sound and the Fury* and *As I Lay Dying*. And the multiple modifications in chapter and page numbering, the changes in ink color and paper quality, and the number of passages cut and pasted amply demonstrate that this novel was the fruit of work undertaken in several stages.

The typescript, itself full of redrafts, was sent to Ben Wasson and Hal Smith in March 1932. When correcting the galley proofs, Faulkner turned down most of the editor's suggested corrections. In September he wrote to Wasson: "I have just finished reading the galley of LIGHT IN AUGUST. I dont see anything wrong with it. I want it to stand as it is" (*SL*, 66). On October 6, 1932, the novel was published by Harrison Smith and Robert K. Haas, a newly founded publishing house.

⁓

At almost five hundred pages, the original version of *Light in August* is Faulkner's longest, and it is scarcely credible that a novel of this size could have been written in such a short time. *Light in August* is a panoramic novel, a *roman-fleuve*, in the manner of Faulkner's masters—Balzac, Dickens, James, and Conrad. In all likelihood it was originally designed as such. In late September 1932, after correcting the galleys, Faulkner wrote to Wasson: "This one is a novel: not an anecdote; that's why it seems topheavy, perhaps" (*SL*, 66). It has over sixty named characters—without counting the anonymous extras—several parallel and intersecting subplots, and fates are decided in a story full of ruptures and returns. Faulkner would never write a novel more teeming with life and yet more controlled in its proliferation.

This time there is no familial viper's nest. The main characters in *Light in August* are outsiders of the community of Jefferson. As outsiders they are therefore strange, other, potential troublemakers. Discomfiting and discommoding, they are more or less tolerated, more or less ostracized. Around Gail Hightower, the apostate preacher, the community has traced successive circles of scandal, disapproval, and rejection. Joanna Burden, the Yankee nigger-lover, is similarly ostracized, and both are condemned to live as recluses on the edge of town. Joe Christmas and Lena Grove are also strangers, two nomads, two characters of the road. For Lena, Jefferson is only a brief staging point, while for Joe it is a long halt after years of dreary wandering. Even secondary characters such as Lucas Burch, Doc Hines, and Percy Grimm are marginal, and nice guy Byron Bunch is not the only eccentric.

More than any of Faulkner's other novels, *Light in August* is a book of solitudes. Christmas is on his own against the world, alone from childhood to death, but solitude does not necessarily mean loneliness. Not all solitudes imply distress and desolation. *Light in August* opens and ends quietly on the pregnant figure of Lena, a fearless country girl, going about her way, looking for a husband and sure of finding one, whether the father of her child or another. She comes from a time without age, punctuated by "a long monotonous succession of peaceful and undeviating changes from day to dark and dark to day again, through which she advanced in identical and anonymous and deliberate wagons as though through a succession of creakwheeled and limpeared avatars, like something moving forever and without progress across an urn" (*N2*, 403–404). For Lena, time means becoming while returning, in an endless cycle of days, seasons, and years. She has time; she waits, serenely; and space holds her and wraps around her, enveloping her in its enfolding immensity, forming with her a living flesh of the same tissue. Life carries her and she carries life within her. She holds in her belly the child that she will shortly bear. Her surname speaks of fertile nature, her first name ("Lena," a shortened version of "Helen") means light. Lena travels in daylight and it is the light of late summer, peaceful, lusterless, hot on the body, and gentle on the eye. Her destiny is heralded in the happy conjunction of earth and sun. Lena is a woman of the sun, a woman without shadow, subdued by light, by its measure and its order—the Apollonian order of visible forces. As she is detailed in the novel's mischievous opening, Lena is both a very ordinary mortal walking barefoot in the dust and heat of summer and, like Eula Varner in *The Hamlet*, a Gaia, a Demeter, a Cybele, a Proserpine, a mother goddess of eternal fecundity. With the blue of her dress and palm-leaf fan, she is also a new Madonna, another Mary, soon to meet a gentle Joseph.

Luminous and earthy, Greek and Christian, Lena is the mother of the time before separation, before partition, prior to birth and death, before time itself. Unique because she is one and one because she is two, she lacks nothing and is lacking to us, forever. Fulfilled and intact, mother *and* virgin, Lena is at both ends of the book, and from one end to another her journey is drawn in a straight line, as sparing as a ray of light—a straight line that is also at the same time the most perfect circle.

Lena arrives in Jefferson on a Saturday in August. On the edge of town, smoke from a fire rises in thick columns. A house is on fire. The spell is broken, the pastoral idyll disappears. At this point another tale commences, the longest and most tragic in the novel, the story of the life and death of the "stranger," that singular man who had in him "something definitely rootless [. . .], as though no town nor city was his, no street, no walls, no square of earth his home" (*N2*, 421). This rootless stranger, this man without hearth or home is Joe Christmas, and the man who remembers his arrival in the planer shed another Friday, three years earlier, is Byron Bunch, a young laborer, who soon falls madly in love with Lena. However, this story has barely started when it is abruptly interrupted, switching to a long reminiscence of Byron's old friend Gail Hightower. The novel then returns to the present, when Byron tells Hightower that Christmas has black blood, that he was the secret lover of Joanna Burden, a white woman whose throat he has just slit, and that a manhunt has just begun.

From this point on, the tale is no more than the chronicle of a death foretold. "Is it certain, proved, that he has negro blood?" asks Hightower. "Think, Byron; what it will mean when the people—if they catch. . . . . . . Poor man. Poor mankind" (*N2*, 472). After this prophetic lamentation, Christmas's story takes over and a long series of flashbacks starts (from chapter 6 to chapter 12), forming the central plank of the book. First comes the story, from midnight to midnight, of the recent past, the breathless report of the twenty-four hours before the murder. Then comes the slow remembering of a life strangled by loneliness: Christmas's miserable childhood as a lost child, a foundling, in the orphanage; his unhappy and rebellious adolescence with his adoptive parents; his initial sexual experiences—his first adventure banal, sordid, and naive, with a waitress named Bobbie Allen; and, after fifteen years of wandering on the interminable and always deserted road, his mad and fatal liaison with Joanna Burden.

Lena Grove is far away at this point. Other women appear, women of the shadows, women who are *other*. As much as Lena belongs to the day, they belong to the shadows, to confusion, disorder, and savagery. It is no coincidence that most of the scenes in which Christmas is involved with women happen in twilight or at night. His first meeting with a black prostitute takes place at night. His secret rendezvous with Bobbie, his first mistress, take place at night. The scene when, having learned that she has started her period, he flees into the woods, into "the branchshadowed quiet, hardfeeling, hardsmelling, invisible," is nocturnal, and in this darkness, this violence, he seems to see "as though in a cave [. . .] a diminishing row of suavely shaped urns in moonlight, blanched. [...] Each one was cracked and from each crack there issued something liquid, deathcolored, and foul" (N2, 538). Overcome by nausea, Christmas leans against a tree and vomits.

Another scene of nausea is the first scene of his childhood to surface from his memory—a memory prior and subsequent to any remembering and perhaps to any remembering subject, a memory that "believes before knowing remembers" and "believes longer than recollects" (N2, 487). One day in the orphanage, he slid into the dietitian's bedroom, and, hidden behind a curtain, "squatted among the soft womansmelling garments and the shoes" (488), he stuffed himself with so much toothpaste that he made himself sick. At the same time, on the other side of the curtain, the young woman was making love with an intern. As he recollects this "primitive scene," the consumption of the sweet paste will always be associated with the romps of the nurturing mother and desire with revulsion and anxiety. Christmas will never recover. From the dietitian to Mrs. McEachern, the adoptive mother who brings him food behind her husband's back, and from Bobbie Allen, his first girlfriend, half waitress, half whore, to Joanna, into whose kitchen he steals at night, as if returning "to the allmother of obscurity and darkness" (568), all the women in his life are associated with maternity and nourishment. And all of his relations with them turn to disaster.

Of all Faulkner's novels, *Light in August* is the most haunted by the female body and female physiology, the novel that deals most with menstruation, pregnancy, and menopause. Terror before "the lightless hot wet primogenitive Female" (N2, 483), disgust, fear, and hatred of women ooze throughout. After his failed sexual initiation, related in chapter 7, the young Christmas fights with his friends: "There was no She at all now. They just fought; it was as if a wind had blown among them, hard and clean" (515). After his first sexual experience, Christmas runs to wash away the taint of menstrual blood in the blood of a sheep whose throat has been cut. And the day before the crime, he cuts off the buttons sewn by Joanna onto his undergarments, exposes his naked body to the lustral freshness of the night, and then goes to breathe in the smell of horses in an abandoned stable—"It's because they are not women. Even a mare horse is a kind of man" (479)—and to shave beside a stream.

It is only when the end is nigh that Christmas, exhausted by four days on the run, finally has a brief instant of the peace that has always eluded him and that he has ceaselessly sought:

> It is just dawn, daylight: that gray and lonely suspension filled with the peaceful and tentative waking of birds. The air, inbreathed, is like spring water. He breathes deep and slow, feeling with each breath himself diffuse in the neutral grayness, becoming one with loneliness and quiet that has never known fury or despair. "That was all I wanted," he thinks, in a quiet and slow amazement. "That was all, for thirty years. That didn't seem to be a whole lot to ask in thirty years." (*N2*, 643–44)

Peace in a rediscovered purity is also what Hightower was seeking. He became a preacher only for the asylum, the alibi of the seminary:

> It seemed to him that he could see his future, his life, intact and on all sides complete and inviolable, like a classic and serene vase, where the spirit could be born anew sheltered from the harsh gale of living and die so, peacefully, with only the far sound of the circumvented wind, with scarce even a handful of rotting dust to be disposed of. That was what the word seminary meant: quiet and safe walls within which the hampered and garmentworried spirit could learn anew serenity to contemplate without horror or alarm its own nakedness. (753)

Admittedly, the dreary reclusion of the stillborn, living dead Hightower, "a shadowy figure among shadows, paradoxical" (759), like that of Quentin Compson in *The Sound and the Fury*, has little in common with the tragic blundering of Christmas. One goes to earth; the other rears up. One withdraws from the world and from himself to hallucinate, night after night, about the return of the warrior ancestor and to relive the searing instant of his heroic death; the other, a rebellious pariah, claiming his solitude with fierce pride, plunges into it with the fury of despair. But in both, as in many other males in Faulkner's novels, there is a profound desire to escape from the anguish of living; both dream of a motionless peace, a peace wrested from life.

From life, from sex, from women and at their expense. Between the sexes there is no recognition; no reciprocity seems possible. And in *Light in August* as in *The Sound and the Fury*, man's blindness toward woman reduces her to nothing but the reflection of his fantasies, the instrument of his desires, or the target of his resentment. At least three women die as a result: Hightower's wife, spurned and immolated on the altar of his heroic "dream"; Milly, the unmarried mother bled dry by the fanaticism of old Doc Hines; and, finally, Joanna, whose throat is cut by Christmas to atone for an accursed passion.

But Joanna fervently colludes in her undoing. An angular, androgynous old maid, a woman stripped of her femininity, she is mannish even during the rape: "It was as if [Christmas] struggled physically with another man for an object of no actual value to either, and for which they struggled on principle alone" (N2, 572). No matter how much Christmas relaunches his attacks, the fortress remains impregnable. Joanna allows herself to be taken without giving anything away, inviolable even in rape. When she finally abandons herself, it is body and soul, with the "terrible and impersonal curiosity of a child about forbidden subjects and objects; that rapt and tireless and detached interest of a surgeon in the physical body and its possibilities" (589). The dual transgression of sexual and racial taboos, with the absolute certainty of being damned, is in fact the very object of her desire. For her, this leads to vocalization and dramatization: Joanna strikes "erotic attitudes and gestures as a Beardsley of the time of Petronius might have drawn" (590), murmurs obscenities into her lover's ear, and organizes their nightly rendezvous in a succession of "faultlessly played scenes" (593), indecent spectacles where she watches herself being watched, exhibitionist and voyeur at once.

The angel eventually becomes the beast, but only a beast in the eyes of an angel. And because it is an avenging angel, it will win. After the period of "the sewer" (N2, 588), their liaison enters its final phase; Christmas sees his mistress in a new light, "cold, remote and fanatic" (597). All femininity repressed, all sexuality recanted, she has now become again the daughter of her fathers and the docile executrix of their wishes. She orders Christmas to kneel and make his own act of surrender, but after begging him in vain to join her in prayer, she eventually admits that death is the only possible outcome:

> "Then there's just one other thing to do."
> "There's just one other thing to do," he said.

"So now it's all done, all finished," he thought quietly, sitting in the dense shadow of the shrubbery, hearing the last stroke of the far clock cease and die away. (606)

It is time to settle scores. Joanna dies at the hand of her lover, who cuts her throat; Christmas will die shortly later at the hand of Percy Grimm, who cuts off Joe's penis. Cutting, taking away. Death works with a razor, a knife, quickly, accurately, cleanly; it cuts neatly and tidily, as a surgeon's scalpel would cut off a gangrenous limb. The point now is to purify, to clean, to root out evil, to restore purity unflinchingly and without hesitation.

The fact that the deaths are of a white woman and a presumed black man is not fortuitous, and neither is the fact that their deaths are due to each other. Joe and Joanna were made to tear each other apart and to kill each other. They are victims not only of the eternal war between the sexes but also of a scourge that Faulkner tackles for the first time in *Light in August*—namely, racism. Already connected by their first names, Joe and Joanna are alike, mirror images of the other, as with so many other Faulknerian couples. Joanna, the last survivor of a line of abolitionist Calvinist preachers from New England, struggles under the burden of her family heritage while Joe has no mother or father, but they have racial obsession in common; their coming together is the murderous collision of two destinies afflicted with the same curse. For Joanna, Joe eventually becomes the shadow and cross revealed to her by her father. For Joe, Joanna ends up with the same intolerable look as old Doc Hines, his very first persecutor. When, remembering her father's words, she tries to bundle Joe up in his mythical black identity, Joe has no other recourse than to kill her.

But already, at the start of their affair, Joanna assails her lover with the cry, "Negro! Negro! Negro!" (N2, 590). Christmas's sexuality is forever linked to what he believes is his race, and it is important to him that this is known. He cannot make love without telling his partners that he has black blood, and it will take two police officers to stop him beating to death a white prostitute who is indifferent to the revelation of his (presumed) identity. Christmas feels black among whites, white among blacks. He is never the same color; he is always the other race. Therefore, all sexual intercourse is forbidden. Any couplings can only be unnatural, reciprocal rape ending in nausea or murderous fury.

Female and black identity, misogyny and racism are closely bound. The ultimate horror is summarized in the double, tightened "womanshenegro." More evidence of this is provided by the scene in Freedmen Town related at the end of chapter 5, where Christmas's nighttime visit to the black neighborhoods of Jefferson is described as a descent into hell: "As from the bottom of a thick black pit he saw himself enclosed by cabinshapes, vague, keroselit, so that the street lamps themselves seemed to be further spaced, as if the black life, the black breathing had compounded the substance of breath so that not only voices but moving bodies and light itself must become fluid and accrete slowly from particle to particle, of and with the now ponderable night inseparable and one" (*N2*, 483).

Darkness in August. From this darkness, full of "bodiless fecundmellow voices of negro women," rises the nightmare of "the lightless hot wet primogenitive Female" that threatens to swallow up Christmas's male identity. He then rushes away, up "out of the black hollow" to "the cold hard air of white people" (*N2*, 483). In this highly symbolic scene, Christmas, like most white men in Faulkner's work, flees the unpredictable and irrepressible ferment of the living. Hence the avoidance and repression strategies and the rites of exorcism. Hence the subjection of women to men, of blacks to whites. Hence the iniquitous order that imposes itself on society as a whole, on the individual, and on the integrated individual as much as on the marginal and the deviant. Woe to the recalcitrant, and woe to offenders. Sooner or later they will be broken, body and soul.

Sexism differentiates between gender to disjoin men and women; racism differentiates between skin color to separate white from black. Puritanism provides the endorsement of religion, consecrating these divisions by separating humanity into the chosen and the outcast. Every time sexist or racist prejudices are formulated in the novel, whether by the oddball fundamentalist Doc Hines, the Presbyterian bogeyman Simon McEachern, or Joanna's Calvinist father, the rhetoric takes off and immediately assumes the prophetic tone of the Old Testament, and the ultimate justification for all action is almost always defined in theological terms. Founded on the presumption of the innate depravity of man, puritanical morality affirms the necessity to discipline the body and mortify the flesh, condemning any search for happiness: "Pleasure, ecstasy, they cannot seem to bear: their escape from it is in violence, in drinking and fighting and praying;

catastrophe too, the violence identical and apparently inescapable *And so why should not their religion drive them to crucifixion of themselves and one another?* he thinks" (N2, 671).

With these thoughts Hightower denounces puritanism as generating distress and violence, and, far from being a reminder of a redemptive sacrifice, "crucifixion" here refers to the torture inflicted by men on each other. Life for the puritan can only be a life in death and for death. For Joanna, a martyr of Calvinism, and for Christmas, a puritan despite himself, it is assuredly nothing else.

One Sunday evening at dusk, sitting at his window as he does every evening, Hightower listens to the music from the church where he used to preach, before he was driven out by his parishioners:

> The organ strains come rich and resonant through the summer night, blended, sonorous, and with that quality of abjectness and sublimation, as if the freed voices themselves were assuming the shapes and attitudes of crucifixions, ecstatic, solemn, and profound in gathering volume. Yet even then the music has still a quality stern and implacable, deliberate and without passion so much as immolation, pleading, asking, for not love, not life, forbidding it to others, demanding in sonorous tones death as though death were the boon, like all Protestant music. (N2, 671)

This is the funereal music we hear in *Light in August*: an "abject" and "sublime" celebration of death, inspired by a religion of death.

Love is spurned, life is rebuffed, death is acclaimed and exalted. In this puritanical, racist society there can be no room for people like Christmas. His presence is a permanent scandal. It is impossible to know for sure if he has black blood or not. He himself believes—but doesn't know—that he does. In the orphanage a black worker tells him his fate: "You are worse than [a nigger]. You don't know what you are. And more than that, you wont never know. You'll live and you'll die and you wont never know" (N2, 683).

Christmas will never know where he comes from or who he is, which, according to Faulkner, "is the most tragic condition that an individual can have" (FU, 118). However, he is not just a stranger to himself (as are, in other ways and for different reasons, Quentin in *The Sound and the Fury* and Darl in *As I Lay Dying*); he is also a living challenge to communal classifications and norms: "He never acted like either a nigger or a white man. That was it. That was what made the folks so mad. For him to be a murderer and all dressed up and walking the town like he dared them to touch him, when he ought to have been skulking and hiding in the woods, muddy and dirty and running. It was like he never even knew he was a murderer, let alone a nigger too" (N2, 658). This is what the "town" has to say about Christmas's behavior, shortly before he is arrested. Christmas has unknowingly shaken the logic of identity of *either/or*; he has drawn attention to the extreme pre-carity of the social bond and pointed up the derisively tragic origin of all racism: in the heads, the eyes, the words, the madness, and the stupidity of men. The most revolting thing in the eyes of the Southern community is not that a white woman was raped and killed by a nigger; it is that the nigger is not like others, that he doesn't play according to the rules, that he doesn't even look or act like a nigger. What makes the presence of Christmas truly unbearable is less his mixed race than the erasure in him of all traces of mis-cegenation, the visible invisibility of his black blood: this black is white; the blackness in its whiteness cannot be verified.

In the manuscript of *Light in August* the narrator refers explicitly to Christmas's black blood. In the published text nothing proves that he has even the smallest drop of black blood: he became a "white nigger" in his own eyes and in that of others in his childhood, in the orphanage, with the baptismal curse hurled at him by the dietitian when she pulls him out from behind the curtain: "You little nigger bastard!" (N2, 489). And first of all under the baleful eye of Doc Hines, his grandfather, Faulkner conjectures that the little Christmas "might have thought": "*That is why I am different from the others: because he is watching me all the time*" (501). A man is a "nig-ger" if he seen as such; a man is a "nigger" if he is called a nigger. When he becomes an adult, Christmas continues naturally to disdain the disdain, to hate the hatred to which he has been subjected since his unfortunate arriv-al in the world. Christmas is both white racist and black victim in a single person; he is their battleground. Two identities beneath the same skin, like two cats in a bag.

The issue of miscegenation resurfaces in another manner in the tragic destiny of Charles Bon in *Absalom, Absalom!* and in the dense genealogy of the McCaslins in *Go Down, Moses*. This tenacious problem that haunts America, one of the main issues in the Civil War,[27] condenses the racist's most secret and shameful fear: that of the other who no longer bears the marks of his otherness, of the other who is now a lookalike, almost the same, practically a double—*another oneself.* Christmas is the incarnation of that fear. He must therefore be gotten rid of, immediately; he must be made to disappear forever.

But the story of his ignominious end, his castration and killing at the hand of Percy Grimm, the executioner dispatched by the lynch mob, is more reminiscent of a ritual murder than of a simple reprisal. The highly rhetorical detailing of the tortured man's last moments—"He just lay there, with his eyes open and empty of everything save consciousness" (*N2*, 742)—announces the posthumous transfiguration of the sacrificial victim by communal memory. A reversal has taken place: from the *agos*, a tainted figure, Christmas becomes a *pharmakos*, a scapegoat in whom the communal guilt is collected and whose death brings about purification and atonement. At the moment of death he seems to be reborn into the collective consciousness:

> [The blood] seemed to rush out of his pale body like the rush of sparks from a rising rocket; upon that black blast the man seemed to rise soaring into their memories forever and ever. They are not to lose it in whatever peaceful valleys, beside whatever placid and reassuring streams of old age, in the mirroring faces of whatever children they will contemplate old disasters and newer hopes. It will be there, musing, quiet, steadfast, not fading and not particularly threatful, but of itself alone serene, of itself alone triumphant. (743)

Once dead, Christmas will rise to mythical status. But the story does not end there. One last sentence, the last in the chapter, jeopardizes the triumphant serenity of this ascension: "Again, from the town, deadened a little by the walls, the scream of the siren mounted toward its unbelievable crescendo, passing out of the realm of hearing" (743). One final shrill note is heard, also ascending, but disappearing into inaudibility. This forces us to read the scene again, to try to open out all of its ambiguity. The fact that the community's memory has taken hold of Christmas does nothing to change any self-awareness that the community may have. The bloody ritual has not achieved its purpose, the sacrifice serves only to refuel the violence, the debts continue to accumulate, generation after generation. There will be other *bad people* to expel or sacrifice, other guilty and innocent people to crucify. Until the end of time.

In *Tristes Tropiques* Claude Lévi-Strauss differentiates between "anthropoemic" societies (from the Greek *émein*: to vomit) and "anthropophagic" societies (from *phagein*: to digest).[28] The former exclude deviants by "vomiting" them into prisons and asylums or by putting them to death, while the latter absorb them and "digest" them by assigning them a specific role within the community. The society described in *Light in August* obviously belongs to the former category, and the vomiting metaphor seems particularly appropriate here given the importance of the theme of nausea in the novelist's work. This society falls "sick" every time it is confronted with its "others" and eventually vomits out what it cannot digest: a case of intolerance, almost in the medical sense of the term.

In *Light in August*, Faulkner returns to his study of the South, which began in *Flags in the Dust* and continues up to *The Reivers*. Although it cannot be said to be a politically engaged novel, the book is without a doubt his most trenchant critique of Southern order, along with *Absalom, Absalom!* Critical thought is sharpened into a veritable indictment, impugning a closed and rigid patriarchal society based entirely on division, repression, and exclusion, a society that denies blacks and women their rights and that ultimately crushes anyone who contravenes its laws. The spectrum analysis of the South in the 1920s offered in *Light in August* is faultlessly lucid, and no other novel has denounced the combined ravages of puritanism, racism, and misogyny as forcefully or as intelligently.

Nevertheless, *Light in August* cannot be classified among the protest novels of the 1930s. Faulkner rejected any idea of political commitment; he believed that the novelist "will use the injustice of society, the inhumanity of people, as a—as any other tool in telling a story, which is about people, not about the injustice or inhumanity of people" (*FU*, 177). If we are to believe Faulkner (although we don't have to take him at his word when he is commenting on his books), the indictment of 1920s Southern society in *Light in August* was not designed as such and is in no way a call to reform it.

However, for this novel to be read properly, it must be read to the end. The killing of Christmas in chapter 19 is not the end; it is followed by two chapters in which Faulkner brings back Hightower and Lena one last time. Still on the road, but on another road (where she is no longer alone), Lena is continually astonished: "My, my. A body does get around. Here we aint been coming from Alabama but two months, and now it's already Tennessee!" (N2, 774). These words, the last in *Light in August*, are an almost literal repeat of the opening. Ending as it started, the novel closes like a circle.

More than any other of Faulkner's novels, *Light in August* is indeed circular. Of all the figures of speech in the text, the circle is undoubtedly the most frequently recurring, the most encompassing, and the most subtly restrictive. But the stakes are not just metaphorical, and the novel cannot be reduced to mere rhetorical flourish. The novel finds in the circle the matrix of its movement, and the thinking at work here is essentially circular, cyclical, endlessly returning to itself.

The circle moves. The circle moves, turns, stops and starts again, in the same direction or in the other direction. The sun is not the only thing that can turn bad. For Christmas, at the end of the line, time, the succession of days and nights, is disrupted, night follows night in an identical dusk, and day follows day, "as if the sun had not set but instead had turned in the sky before reaching the horizon and retraced its way" (N2, 645).

The circle multiplies. To each its own, to each circle its turns and returns. Lena is the luminous circle of the Virgin Mother, under the watchful eye of Father Sun; Joanna is the dark cycle of the Foolish Virgin cursed by dead Fathers. Christmas, at the end of his trajectory, realizes that the long "road" that he thought was straight also turned out to be a circle: "And yet I have been further in these seven days than in all the thirty years [. . .]. But I have never got outside that circle. I have never broken out of the ring of what I have already done and cannot ever undo" (N2, 650).

Another circle, the circle of circles, where previous circles are represented and come together is Hightower's "wheel," which appears in his final meditation in chapter 20, "the wheel of thinking" (N2, 760).

At the start of this penultimate chapter, Hightower sits at his window and waits once more for the galloping horsemen who come every day to visit him, with "the wild bugles and the clashing sabres and the dying thunder of hooves" (N2, 764). But tonight the scenario is disrupted. Hightower first sees the "ghosts" of his past. Then his thoughts, slow at first, gradually pick up in speed, rolling like a wheel:

> The wheel whirls on. It is going fast and smooth now, because it is freed now
> of burden, of vehicle axle, all. In the lambent suspension of August into which
> night is about to fully come, it seems to engender and surround itself with a

faint glow like a halo. The halo is full of faces. The faces are not shaped with suffering, not shaped with anything: not horror, pain, not even reproach. They are peaceful, as though they have escaped into an apotheosis; his own is among them. In fact, they all look a little alike, composite of all the faces which he has ever seen. But he can distinguish them one from another: his wife's; townspeople, members of that congregation which denied him, which had met him at the station that day with eagerness and hunger; Byron Bunch's; the woman with the child; and that of the man called Christmas. (762)

Up till now the destiny of each character seemed to be traced in isolation. Now they are all swept up in a gyratory movement, chained to one another and to the same "wheel." Hightower's ecstatic vision does not come from an individual perspective but from the absolute viewpoint of an all-seeing God, "cold, terrible because of Its omniscient detachment" (760). Everything is perceived at equal distance, in the same light, and there is now only one circle, one cycle forever starting again. The journeys of Christmas and Lena can be traced in adjoining curves, especially as the end of the cycle in the novel corresponds to the start of another. A child is born the day Christmas dies, in the cabin where he lived and not far from the house where Joanna has just been killed. A birth at dawn, a death in the afternoon. A life that is lost, a death that lives again: old Mrs. Hines persists in calling the as yet unnamed newborn "Joey," and Lena herself is troubled by this: "She keeps on talking about him like his pa was that—the one in jail, that Mr Christmas. She keeps on, and then I get mixed up and it's like sometimes I cant—like I am mixed up too and I think that his pa is that Mr—Mr Christmas too" (701). Christmas is thus reborn as Lena's husband and son, as the child and the father of the child. Indifferent to time, life regenerates at the crossroads of death. The wheel rolls; the wheel turns.

It turns but goes nowhere. What is was already and will be again. Everything is repeated, and the repetition does not take place in time, relative to a beginning and end; it is the essence of time itself. The revolving wheel stamps out singularity, evens out differences, cancels out opposition. Just as a clock marks midday and midnight at the same place on the dial, the same place is ultimately assigned to the faces of former enemies Christmas and Percy Grimm. Hightower sees them both on the wheel, "their faces which seem to strive ([. . .] not of themselves striving or desiring it [. . .] but because of the motion and desire of the wheel itself)" (N2, 763).

The circle is a zero, the roundness of oblivion. In the end, all that remains is the great game of the world, the game without end of birth, death, and metamorphosis, and it is also this game, constantly restarted, that the novel invites us to discover. It plunges us into tragedy without abandoning us there, evades tragedy by playing and interpreting it, transforms its terror into pleasure. This is how the "darkened house" becomes "light in August."

Pleasure is openly discussed in the comic and pastoral epilogue of the final chapter. A young furniture dealer, back home after a trip around Tennessee, tells his wife about "an experience which he had had on the road, which interested him at the time and which he considered amusing enough to repeat," and perhaps he found it interesting because "he and his wife are not old either, besides his having been away from home [. . .] for more than a week" (N2, 765). The story he tells is one that the novel has already told, that of another young couple, the amusing story of Byron Bunch and Lena. The woman listens to her husband, in bed, in the dark. The tale, peppered with coarse innuendo, is just for her. She is the only listener, and the furniture dealer, endeavoring to awaken a desire to hear the story and then simply to awaken desire itself, counts on getting some payback. This seductive tale, at the very end of the novel, is given in exchange for a body lusted over. This may be a way of reminding the reader—but this time with an ironic smile, miles away from the tragic scene—that there is no such thing as an innocent story.

⁓

When *Light in August* was published, Faulkner seems to have been pretty happy with it. In a letter he told Harrison Smith "the book looks fine" (*SL*, 66–67). The book also pleased some readers, but as with every time Faulkner published a novel, it was far from universally acclaimed. In the *Commercial Appeal* of October 9, 1932, George Marion O'Donnell claimed that *Light in August* was the best of Faulkner's published novels. J. Donald Adams and Margaret Cheney Dawson, two New York journalists, shared this opinion. Henry Seidel Canby, in the *Saturday Review of Literature* of October 8, hailed its extraordinary power, and in the *Commonweal* of November 30, Frederic Thompson, under the headline "American Decadence," referred to Faulkner's art as supreme in its extremity. However, overall, American critics continued to rehash the same grievances. When *As I Lay*

Dying was published, critics reproached Faulkner for paying homage to the cult of cruelty, for wallowing in horror, for unnecessarily complicating his stories, and for not having any positive values to offer his readers. James T. Farrell, a sturdy novelist in the naturalist tradition, was no more perceptive in his review for the *New York Sun*. He admired the virtuosity of Faulkner's technique and the force of his writing, but took offense, like many others, at his excessive propensity for violence and madness.

Opinions in England were also divided. While two-thirds of the reviews were full of praise, the austere Cambridge professor F. R. Leavis, writing in the magazine *Scrutiny*, denounced the abusive use of techniques à la Gertrude Stein. And in the *Daily Mail* of February 9, 1933, the novelist Compton Mackenzie, while admitting that *Light in August* was a good, perhaps maybe a great book, declared himself terrified by what he regarded as the decline of its author's imagination and forecast his imminent collapse, because to Mackenzie this type of writing was what happened when weakness simulated strength.

NOTES

1. [Translator's note: "El Orens' sheik" refers to T. E. Lawrence, also known as Lawrence of Arabia.]

2. William R. Ferris Jr., "William Faulkner and Phil Stone," *South Atlantic Quarterly* (Fall 1969): 540–41.

3. See Merle Wallace Keiser, *"Flags in the Dust"* and *"Sartoris,"* in *Fifty Years of Yoknapatawpha*, ed. Doreen Fowler and Ann J. Abadie, 44–70 (Jackson: University Press of Mississippi, 1980).

4. William Faulkner, quoted by Blotner from a manuscript held by Yale University Library. See (*B*, 531–32).

5. [Translator's note: a reference to the *Song of Roland*, a French medieval heroic poem.]

6. See Don H. Doyle, *Faulkner's County: The Historical Roots of Yoknapatawpha* (Chapel Hill: University of North Carolina Press, 2001), 24–25.

7. Preface to the French translation of *The Sound and the Fury*: *Le Bruit et la fureur* (Paris: Gallimard, 1938), 7.

8. *A Faulkner Miscellany*, ed. James B. Meriwether (Jackson: University Press of Mississippi, 1974), 158–59.

9. Ibid., 161.

10. Ibid., 158.

11. Ibid., 160.

12. In a letter to Ben Wasson in the early summer of 1929, Faulkner deplored the fact that it was not possible to use different inks to help readers distinguish between different temporal sequences. See *SL*, 44.

13. Marcel Proust, *A la recherche du temps perdu II* (Paris: Gallimard, Pléiade, 1954), 872, translation taken from *Proust's Imaginary Museum* by Gabrielle Townsend (Oxford: Peter Lang, 2008).

14. Jean-Paul Sartre, "A propos de *Le Bruit et la fureur*: la temporalité chez William Faulkner," *Situations I* (Paris: Gallimard, 1947), 72.

15. See Claude Romano, *Le Chant de la vie: phénoménologie de Faulkner* (Paris: Gallimard, 2005), 116–20.

16. The expression "reductio ad absurdum" appears incorrectly at the start of Quentin's monologue as "reducto absurdum" (*N1*, 935).

17. Herman Melville, *Moby-Dick*, edited by Hershel Parker and Harrison Hayford, Norton Critical Edition, 2nd ed. (New York: W. W. Norton, 2002), 526–27.

18. Samuel Beckett, *Proust and Three Dialogues with Georges Duthuit* (London: John Calder, 1965), 125.

19. Jean-Jacques Mayoux, *Vivants Piliers: le roman anglo-saxon et les symboles* (Paris: Julliard, 1960), 252.

20. In the published draft of the novel, Horace associates "the black thing" in turn with Popeye and Temple/Little Belle. In a highly oneiric scene in the first draft, he also associates it with the fantasized memory of the maternal body, reconstituted from a series of female figures (Narcissa, Ruby, and Belle), which transform the mother into the sister-wife whose flesh will open up to give birth to foulness.

21. The description is reminiscent of the famous portrait of the Mona Lisa by Walter Pater: "She is older than the rocks among which she sits; like the vampire, she has been dead many times, and learned the secrets of the grave." Walter Pater, *The Renaissance*, 2nd ed. (London: Macmillan, 1977), 135. Faulkner refers to Mona Lisa's smile in "Episode" (see *SNO*, 107).

22. In the original text the hallucination starts with a pronoun shift, in the same sentence, from masculine to feminine: "[He] leaned upon *his* braced arms while the shucks set up a terrific uproar beneath *her* thighs." William Faulkner, *Sanctuary* (1931; New York: Vintage Press, 1967), 234.

23. Note the alliteration and assonance in Dewey Dell's long, plaintive cry.

24. This Rabelaisian and Shakespearian image (*Othello* I.1.117) of "the beast with two backs" also surfaces in *The Sound and the Fury* at the end of Quentin's monologue, when he speaks of "swine untethered in pairs rushing coupled into the sea" (*N1*, 1012).

25. Jean-Louis Barrault, *Réflexion sur le théâtre* (Paris: Vautrain, 1949), 49.

26. Julien Green, *Œuvres complètes V* (Paris: Gallimard, Pléiade, 1977), 296.

27. The pejorative term "miscegenation" (from *miscere*, to mix, and *genus*, race) first appeared in the title of a pro-slavery pamphlet published in New York in 1863.

28. See Claude Lévi-Strauss, *Tristes Tropiques* (Paris: Plon, 1955), 418.

5
MIDWAY

SCENES FROM MARRIED LIFE

When *Light in August* was published, Faulkner had been married for over three years. In May 1929, when he had just finished *Sanctuary*, Estelle's sister, Dorothy, telephoned to tell him it was time he married Estelle. Separated from Cornell Franklin and in the process of divorce, Estelle and her two children, Victoria ("Cho-Cho") and Malcolm, had been living with her parents since 1927. It was said that she had been unfaithful to her first husband in revenge for his infidelities and that Malcolm was not his son. In fact, some even said that Malcolm was Faulkner's son. The truth will never be known. However, what is known is that Faulkner and Estelle had grown up together; they had a bond going back to Baudelaire's green paradise of childhood loves—or rather a nostalgic memory of that bond. For Faulkner, Estelle's marriage to Franklin in 1918 had been a barely forgivable betrayal, but nevertheless he continued to see her and court her each time she came back to Oxford. Courting mostly meant offering her poems he had written, and handwritten, illustrated and hand-bound books, and Estelle seemed to take no offense at the attentions of her indefatigable suitor.

Estelle and Franklin were divorced on April 29, 1929, leaving the way clear for Faulkner. On June 19, 1929, he asked her to marry him. But Estelle's father was no more enthusiastic than he had been eleven years earlier. The fact that Faulkner had published a number of novels in the meantime meant little to him. He still did not believe that Faulkner was a good match for his daughter. The Faulkners, for their part, detested the Oldhams and their grand airs. Miss Maud would never forgive them for having snubbed her eldest son, and she did not want Billy to marry a divorcee with two children, who, as everyone knew, had started to drink. Murry had his own reservations, believing that his eldest son should find stable employment before thinking of marriage. He told him he would be happy to help him find an administrative position, even if it provoked the indignation of those who remembered his son's scandalous tenure as a postmaster in 1922. Phil Stone was convinced that the marriage would be the end of his friend's literary career.

It is likely that the couple were already lovers at that stage. Estelle confided in Joseph Blotner that she had had an abortion, with Faulkner's help. Regardless of whether they were lovers or not, they were not really in love and both knew that their reconciliation had come too late. A few days before the wedding, Faulkner wrote a rather pompous letter to Harrison Smith telling him the news:

> I am going to be married. Both want to and have to. THIS PART IS CONFIDEN-
> TIAL, UTTERLY. For my honor and the sanity—I believe life—of a woman.
> This is not bunk; neither am I being sucked in. We grew up together and I dont
> think she could fool me in this way; that is, make me believe that her mental
> condition, her nerves, are this far gone. And no question of pregna[n]cy: that
> would hardly move me: no one can face his own bastard with more equanimity
> than I [. . .]. Neither is it a matter of a promise on my part; we have known one
> other long enough to pay no attention to our promises. It's a situation which I
> engendered and permitted to ripen which has become unbearable, and I am
> tired of running from devilment I bring about. This sounds a little insane.
> (B1, 240)[1]

Had the situation really become unbearable? It is difficult to see why it was so urgent that it needed to be ended. But Faulkner and Estelle were impatient to be married, not to make a previously secret relationship official but to obey an obscure need: "[We] have to." They were both convinced that marriage was in the order of things, that they were predestined to be married and condemned to live together, come what may and whatever the price. For Faulkner it was also an issue of honor; in marrying Estelle, he was settling a debt and was doing his duty as a gentleman.

On June 20 the couple went to the Oxford courthouse for their wedding license. The day was fine. In the little blue Chevrolet belonging to Faulkner's mother, they set off to look for a church. However, Faulkner's sense of ceremony required him to ask his future father-in-law to consent to the wedding—or at least that he be told. He therefore stopped at Lem

Oldham's house to tell him he intended to marry his daughter. Although Oldham did not give them his blessing, he acknowledged that Estelle and Bill were now adults and free to make their own decisions. He was no longer in a position to prevent their marrying and he wished them both well.

These formalities completed, all they needed to do was find a preacher. The Episcopalian rector, despite being a friend to both families, refused to marry them, because Estelle was divorced. They went to the old Presbyterian church of College Hill near Oxford, where the good Reverend Winn David Hedleston agreed to improvise a short wedding ceremony on the spot. After this, Faulkner borrowed his father's more comfortable car and brought Estelle and little Malcolm to Columbus, Mississippi. There, Malcolm was left in the care of his grandmother, the kind, generous Mrs. Hairston. The couple then spent their wedding night in a hotel in the neighboring town of Aberdeen. They returned to Columbus the next day to pick up Malcolm and drove to Pascagoula Beach, where Faulkner (using money borrowed from his friends) rented a dilapidated house surrounded by overgrown lawns.

The honeymoon quickly turned to disaster. Estelle arrived in Pascagoula with Mrs. Hairston's maid and some of her silverware. She also brought sumptuous silk and satin dresses bought in Hawaii and Shanghai, where her first husband worked for the State Department. She soon realized that there would be few opportunities to wear them and that she would now have to live frugally. In early July, a few days after their arrival on the coast, Faulkner received the proofs of *The Sound and the Fury*, which had been revised and corrected by Ben Wasson. Forced to revise the text and to deal with corrections by Wasson that he deemed unjustified, he was in very bad humor, and Estelle felt even more neglected. They were already having difficulties; the neighbors heard them squabbling, and both were drinking heavily. In late July, to take Estelle's mind off things, Faulkner took her to New Orleans. They stayed at the Monteleone, an elegant old hotel; dined with Faulkner's friends in the French Quarter; and spent their evenings in clubs and dance halls. But it was all to no avail. After their return to Pascagoula, Estelle started drinking again. Near the end of summer, on a moonlit night, after drinking a lot of whiskey she drove straight to the ocean dressed in one of the long silk dresses she had brought back from China and went in. Faulkner saw her from the house, called for help, and ran after her, dressed in a dinner jacket and pin-striped pants. A neighbor, hearing his cries for help, ran to the shore, managed to grab Estelle just as she was reaching deep water, and brought her home.

This attempted suicide was not the first—Estelle had already slit her wrists in Shanghai—nor would it be the last. Faulkner put her to bed and called a doctor, who gave her a sedative. A few days later they returned to Oxford and rented an apartment on the ground floor of a big white house at 803 University Avenue. The apartment was spacious; it had a sitting room, a dining room, two bedrooms, a kitchen, and a bathroom. In the sitting room there was an alcove that could be used as an office. This is where Faulkner set up the rickety oak table given to him by his mother, and at this table he typed the text of "A Rose for Emily," the first of his short stories to be published in a major national magazine.

Their married life lurched along. Faulkner worked (or exercised what he called his "talent for idleness") and Estelle was bored. Brought up like a princess, she was used to living in great style and to having all of her fancies indulged. She liked grooming herself, jewelry, large hats, worldly receptions, and dinners in town. She knew how to sew, how to cook exotic meals, and how to play the piano. She had started to paint while in China (a hobby she would return to after her husband's death). She was interested in literature and even wrote a novel herself, in 1926 or '27, called "White Beeches." Her husband endeavored in vain to have the book published and she eventually burned the manuscript. However, writing for Estelle was just a hobby, nothing more. She had no idea what work was and had no desire to find out. She was a Southern lady who had always had a multitude of servants at her beck and call and who had never been short of money, which meant, unfortunately, that she spent lavishly and left suppliers unpaid. She now had to cut her cloth to a much more modest lifestyle and learn to live with an eccentric, unpredictable man who didn't look after himself, was often unkempt, walked around barefoot, forgot to shave, and rarely had a bath. The only discipline he imposed upon himself, day after day, was his work as a writer. For Estelle, living in an old house that needed comprehensive refurbishment was not easy; neither was living with a husband who spent his mornings writing and his afternoons working on do-it-yourself projects. She would soon have no option but to turn to alcohol and psychopharmacology.

For almost forty years they made each other unhappy, relentlessly. Arguments occurred on almost a daily basis, and over the years, by dint of repetition, these rows became a kind of role play that terrified their daughter, Jill, from early childhood:

> Living with Ma-ma and Pappy was like living on a stage-set. Everybody was playing a role. You never knew who was being what today. They played roles to each other and, largely, I was left out of it. There was always lots of storming up and down the stairs and threats, on my mother's part, to slash her wrists. She really liked playing tragic parts. They really enjoyed it, and I even got to know it was not for real. But it was pretty exciting. [. . .] It would be hard for me to say that I could look at him [Faulkner] and say, "this is who he really is," because, almost always he was playing a part. When I was young, it gave me a feeling of unreality. I never knew whether I was real to them.[2]

For Jill, her parents "were just terribly unsuited for each other. Nothing about the marriage was right."[3] But although they were "unsuited," neither could live without the other and each needed to play off the other, like characters in a play condemned to act out the same role indefinitely. Ill-matched and discordant, these two ham actors were still a couple. When Faulkner was at Rowan Oak, he found Estelle unbearable. But when he was far from her, he missed her. The sincerity of his letters might be in doubt, but he always showed affection toward Estelle in them. The persistence of his attachment would seem undeniable. In October 1931, for example, he wrote to Estelle, who was ill at the time: "I dont think that I will need to tell you to give my love to the children, any more than to tell you that you already have about 1,000,000 tons of it yourself. But I do, nevertheless. Get well fast, darling, darling, darling."[4] There was tenderness there all the same, a strong relationship where affection and resentment were impossible to untangle.

Faulkner would later take mistresses, barely bothering to hide his liaisons, but he never really thought seriously about leaving Estelle. They stayed together to the end, and in the final years of their life together, tired of feuding, they even came to a sort of truce. Shortly after the wedding, Faulkner told a friend: "They don't think we're gonna stick, but it is gonna stick" (B, 626). It was a question of pride and honor. Faulkner kept his promise. But he paid the price.

THE MASTER OF ROWAN OAK

At the age of twenty, Faulkner saw himself as bound for a future as "a harmless possessionless vagabond" (*ESPL*, 21). But his vagabonding didn't last long. On April 12, 1930, less than a year after marrying Estelle, he bought a house on the outskirts of Oxford known as Shegog Place, after its first owner, Colonel Robert B. Shegog, an Irishman who had made his fortune in Tennessee and arrived in Mississippi in the mid-nineteenth century. After Shegog's death the house was bought by a family by the name of Bailey, after which it passed into the hands of Will Bryant, who rented it out. Bryant, who was a friend of the Oldhams, decided to help their daughter and son-in-law buy it. Turning down all other offers, he agreed to sell the house to Faulkner for six thousand dollars without a deposit, payable in monthly installments, at an interest rate of 6 percent. The agreement was favorable, but the debt was still substantial. For Faulkner it was a considerable burden, and it took him many years to pay it off.

Built in 1848 by an English architect who was unqualified but well respected in the area, Shegog Place was a colonial-style house typical of the South. It was an attractive house, featuring a portico with four white columns, a Georgian pediment, and an oak-lined drive, although by 1930, as many plantation houses in the county, it had become quite dilapidated. Faulkner, Estelle, and her two children moved into the house in June. Faulkner spent the whole summer working on badly needed restorations. The roof was leaking, there were mice and squirrels in the empty rooms, the wallpaper was blistered, the ceiling plaster was cracked, and the windows were difficult to open and close. Malcolm Franklin remembered it as being close to collapse in the next storm or high wind.[5] There was no electricity or running water, which was not unusual in Mississippi homes in the 1930s. The rooms were lit at night by oil lamps, water was drawn from an old well, and the toilets were outside. Faulkner, who was good with his hands, started with the parts of the house that had subsided, replacing rotten beams and broken windows; repairing the walls; painting fences, woodwork, and doors; replacing the planks on the veranda and mosquito screens on the windows; and installing plumbing in the kitchen and bathroom. He also started working on restoring the surrounding land.

The purchase of Shegog Place, quickly renamed Rowan Oak,[6] was highly symbolic for Faulkner. The family's possessions were a mark of the antiquity and continuity of the line and established a social identity that would have no foundation unless it was linked to permanence over time. Faulkner's great-grandfather had spent a lot of money building a showy pseudo-Italian villa, and his grandfather had done likewise with the Big Place. His parents, after moving several times, had been forced to set up home in a more modest abode. In becoming the owner of one of the old colonial houses in the region, Faulkner was taking his revenge. Thanks to him, the line had been reestablished; his family was restored to its rightful rank and came into its own once again.

In a small Mississippi town like Oxford, this "restoration" would have been incomplete without a large number of servants, and in an old plantation house these servants could only be blacks and, if possible, should be local folk. Ned Burnett, who had previously worked for Faulkner's grandfather and great-grandfather, became Faulkner's horse trainer, his manservant, his butler—in short, his factotum. Old Mammy Callie, ever devoted, acted as nursemaid to the two children and did the cooking part-time.

After Faulkner the dreamer, the delicate poet, the scruffy vagabond, the (fake) war hero came Faulkner the landowner, the county squire in his manor, on his land. For Faulkner, as for Thomas Sutpen and Flem Snopes, two of his least likable characters, buying or building a fine big house with white columns meant becoming somebody in the eyes of the community, being recognized and respected as a pillar of society, and Faulkner was proud of having become master of Rowan Oak. "I own a larger parcel of it than anybody else in town," he wrote to Robert Haas in June 1940, "and nobody gave me any of it or loaned me a nickel to buy any of it with and all my relations and fellow townsmen, including the borrowers and frank spongers, all prophesied I'd never be more than a bum" (SL, 128–29).

What was important for Faulkner, however, seems to have been the act of appropriation; taking ownership was more important than ownership itself. Once Rowan Oak was restored, he appears to have taken no further interest in its maintenance. When Saxe Commins, his literary agent who also became his friend, visited the Faulkners in the fall of 1952, he wrote to his wife that their house "left a strong and rather distasteful impression on me. It is a rambling Southern mansion, deteriorated like its owner, [. . .] The rooms are bare and what they do contain is rickety, tasteless, ordinary. There is none of the charm and orderliness and comfort that you give to a home."[7]

Faulkner could have contented himself with Rowan Oak. But Rowan Oak was not enough for him. In 1937, on the day of his fourth wedding anniversary, with the money he had earned in Hollywood, he bought Bailey's Woods behind the house. A year later he purchased a three-hundred-acre farm, Greenfield Farm, in the northeast of Lafayette County, which by happy coincidence had once belonged to the family of Joe Parks, the man from the hills who had ousted the Young Colonel as head of the bank and who had bought the house from Murry Falkner in Oxford. Revenge was sweet.

With Faulkner as owner, the farm grew over the years into a larger estate, incorporating a number of smallholdings rented out to black families, and a larger farm, where he raised livestock and which was managed by his brother John. In 1962, shortly before his death, Faulkner considered buying Red Acres, a fine property near the Blue Ridge Mountains, in Albemarle County, Virginia, which comprised a magnificent brick mansion, accommodations for the manager and stable hand, a large stable, a shed, a smokehouse, a silo, two barns, almost two hundred acres of woods and pastureland, and magnificent views. In one of his last letters, a few days before he died, he wrote to his rich friend Linton Massey: "I want to make an offer for Red Acres. I can make the offer as is. But if it is accepted, I will be broke. I will have to guarantee to write a book or books. I can earn about $10,000.00 or more any year from lectures etc. I will do this [. . .] to own Red Acres" (SL, 461).

Faulkner also imagined himself to be the owner of the fictional county he invented in his novels and short stories, even going so far as to proclaim himself "sole owner and proprietor" of the twenty-four hundred square miles of Yoknapatawpha County at the bottom of the map he drew after finishing Absalom, Absalom! (N3, 2–3). However, in this novel, as in others, he made a point of questioning private ownership, its origins, and its legitimacy and of denouncing its excesses. In Go Down, Moses, in particular, Ike McCaslin deplores at length the injustice that is the establishment of ownership rights (to the detriment of the Native Americans and to the sole benefit of the whites) to land in the New World, and in the Snopes trilogy, greed, not only Flem's but also shared by almost all the hamlet's farmers, is the prime target for his satire.

Faulkner the novelist always knew (as do the Native Americans) that land belongs to no one, that all possession is vanity, and in his novels he continually reminded his readers that the primary experience was that of dispossession. Faulkner the man was no dupe either. In December 1946 he wrote to Cowley:

> At 30 you become aware suddenly that you have become a slave of vast and growing mass of inanimate junk, possessions; you dont dare look at any of it too closely because you'll have to admit there is not one piece of it you really want. But you bear it for the next eighteen years because you still believe you will escape from it someday. Then one day you are almost 50 and you know you never will. (*SL*, 245)

At Rowan Oak, Faulkner's days were very full. He would rise before everyone, sometimes as early as five o'clock in the morning, starting his day with a huge breakfast that included fruit, eggs, porridge, bacon or grilled steak, toast with Dundee marmalade, and black Louisiana coffee. He would then withdraw to his study. His hours varied, but according to Estelle, he mostly wrote in the morning and never at night.[8] On days when inspiration ran high, he could work for over twelve hours, writing first by hand, with his neat, dense handwriting, and then typing up the manuscript on his typewriter. As there was neither a lock nor a bolt on the door to his study, he shut himself in by removing the doorknob. Writing requires solitude and silence. Doorbells, radios, and record players were banned, and it was only reluctantly that Faulkner allowed a telephone to be installed in the house. "He had a natural and sustained aversion to the telephone, anywhere, anytime, and under any conceivable circumstances" (*FOM*, 197).

At noon, in accordance with Southern tradition, he joined Estelle and the children in the dining room, presiding over luncheon, as his father had done before him. The afternoon was taken up by naps and walks, do-it-yourself projects, and gardening. From time to time, Faulkner went horse riding. At about five o'clock the couple met up under the veranda, sharing a bottle of whiskey or bourbon, after which dinner was served, with some ceremony, just as lunch. In the evening Faulkner read or reread Balzac, Dickens, Conrad, or *The Golden Bough* by James George Frazer.

In the early 1930s, Faulkner, the man of "violent sedentation," seems to have wanted to settle down, to live the quiet life, to become gentrified. He was now a head of household; he had a wife, two children (although not his), and devoted (albeit unpaid) servants. He owned a fine house that needed fixing up, a few acres of land, three horses, and several chickens. Eager to assert his respectability, he now regularly attended services at the Episcopalian church. His financial situation was assuredly not the best (and would not be for a long time), but a page had been turned and his bohemian decade seemed to have come to an end. Another phase was beginning, one that would be the most prolific of his career. But in his private life, his hopes were quickly disappointed.

THE FIRST SHADOWS

The year 1931 started badly. One January night, Estelle, who was then seven months pregnant, woke Faulkner complaining of pains. After notifying their doctor, Faulkner drove her to the hospital. On January 11, after a fourteen-hour labor, she gave birth to a daughter, named Alabama after Faulkner's paternal grand-aunt. A few days after Estelle returned to Rowan Oak, Mammy Callie came to tell Faulkner that the baby was having difficulty breathing. They feared the worst. By the time Faulkner went to Memphis to buy an incubator, it was already too late. On January 20, at just ten days old, Alabama died. Estelle's pregnancy had been difficult, and it is likely that her alcohol abuse had something to do with the infant's death. Faulkner was distraught. Estelle saw him cry for the first time. It was he who carried the tiny coffin to the cemetery where Alabama would be buried.

He later told Wasson that he had rung Doctor John C. Culley right away and that the doctor had refused to come, saying there was nothing that could be done. Mad with rage, Faulkner told Wasson that he raced to the doctor's and shot him with his revolver, wounding him in the shoulder. To others, he told different versions of this story, at least one of which resembled the equally violent stories from the lives of his father, his grandfather, and his great-grandfather. According to Phil Stone, none of these stories were true; they were, once again, pure fabrication.[9]

From the start of the 1930s, the Faulkners' marriage was a living hell, resembling a play by Strindberg or O'Neill. Estelle continued to drink, as did her husband. She attempted suicide again. One evening in New York, at a reception given by Bennett Cerf, the young cofounder of Random House, in a skyscraper looking out over Central Park, Cerf saw her standing at the window, looking out at the lights of the city. "When I see all this beauty, she said, "I feel just like throwing myself out of the window." Alarmed, Cerf drew her backward. "Oh now, Estelle, you don't mean that." She looked at him with her big blue eyes. "What do you mean? Of course I do" (*B1*, 295).

She was frequently hysterical. Dorothy Parker witnessed a tantrum at the Algonquin Hotel, when Estelle tore off her dress and tried to jump out the window. The screenwriter Marc Connelly remembered her as

> a very nervous girl who occasionally had some kind of slips of mental processes, of thinking. [. . .] I don't know what she did, but it was something with which Bill was obviously familiar. And quite objectively, without a bit of reproachment in it, he looked at his wife and reached out and slapped her face very hard. She went right back to completely normal conduct, and Bill, without any apologies or anything else, continued whatever he had been talking about. (*B1*, 295–96)

When she was troubled or enraged, Estelle was capable of anything. One day in March 1932, in a fit of rage, she threw the manuscript of *Light in August* out of the car window, and Faulkner had to pick up the sheets of paper scattered along the road.

However, there was a sunny interlude in 1933 after the birth in June of a little daughter, whom they called Jill. Faulkner was delighted to be a father at last. After bringing Estelle and the child home from the hospital, he convened the servants and invited them to toast the health of little Miss Jill. Harrison Smith, who came from New York for the baptism, found the parents happy in their parenthood. A tender, attentive father, Faulkner did not balk at warming up bottles and changing diapers. In mid-August he wrote to Wasson: "We are fine. Jill getting fatter and fatter. Estelle has never been so well" (*SL*, 74). Faulkner was now full of good resolutions; he even swore off drink for a year.

He lasted four months. And soon the marital discord was to resume in earnest. As he later confided to Meta Carpenter, the birth of Jill marked the end of his sexual relations with Estelle. Soon after giving birth (her fourth child, without counting the miscarriages), Estelle moved to the back room on the second floor and they stopped sleeping together. The couple started quarreling and getting drunk again; some of their arguments ended in slaps and scratches. One of the things they fought over was money. Both were spendthrifts—she by frivolity, he because he wanted to own things. Estelle spent money on grooming and fine clothes; Faulkner spent money on land, horses, airplanes, and yachts. Moreover, Estelle resented the fact that her husband had given money to Miss Maud and other members of his family, while Faulkner was outraged that as the legal guardian of Malcolm and Cho-Cho, his father-in-law held on to the child support paid by Cornell Franklin for his two children.

Professionally, the 1930s started out quite well, but the direction that Faulkner's career was taking was not at all what he wanted. He was first and foremost a novelist, and if it had been up to him, he would have written only novels. But because the market for short stories was more lucrative than that for novels, and because he had needed the cash, he turned increasingly to short stories. He wrote them at top speed, hastening to sell them to the major national magazines with the ink barely dry on the pages. In 1930 he sent out over twenty of them, as attested by a card on which he noted and dated his shipments from January 1930 to January 1932. He needed patience and doggedness. Most often his stories were turned down: "The Big Shot" was turned down by the *American Mercury*, and the four other magazines he sent it to didn't want it either. "All the Dead Pilots" and "Divorce in Naples" were each turned down five times, "Dry September" and "Rose of Lebanon" three times. Of the short stories sent out in 1930, however, four were published. On April 30 "A Rose for Emily" was published in *Forum*. This short story—a thrilling black fable, the most Gothic of Faulkner's fiction—was the first to be published in a major magazine (and also the first to be published in France, translated by Maurice-Edgar Coindreau, in *Commerce*, in 1932). That same year, in July, the *American Mercury* published "Honor." "Thrift" was published in September in the *Saturday Evening Post*, and in October that same magazine published "Red Leaves," one of his best stories about Native Americans. Two of the short stories published in 1930—"Thrift" and "Red Leaves"—earned him $750 each. None of his novels had made that much money.

Faulkner's reputation was growing. True, few critics were ready to acclaim him as a great writer. But when *Soldiers' Pay* was published in Great Britain, the English novelist Arnold Bennett stated: "Faulkner is the coming man. He has inexhaustible invention, powerful imagination, a wondrous gift of characterization, a finished skill in dialog; and he writes, generally, like an angel."[10] Two days later another reviewer in the same paper remarked that over the previous thirty years no first novel had achieved such perfection, ranking Faulkner above D. H. Lawrence and Hemingway.

American voices also began to sing the praises of the young writer. In his acceptance speech in Stockholm, Sinclair Lewis, the Nobel Prize laureate in 1930, congratulated Faulkner for having "freed the South from hoopskirts." And Sherwood Anderson, in "They Come Bearing Gifts," an essay published in the *American Mercury* in October 1930, hailed Hemingway and Faulkner as "the two most notable young writers who have come on in America since the war."

The truth was beginning to dawn on everyone: Faulkner was a young writer to be reckoned with. After the success of the scandalous *Sanctuary*, the major magazines, which had previously turned up their noses at his short stories, began taking more of an interest. *Harper's* accepted "Doctor Martino" and "Beyond," *Story* accepted "Artist at Home," and *Scribner's* brought out "Spotted Horses." Nineteen thirty-one was the year when the largest number of his short stories was published. In 1930 he had published four; in 1931 he published sixteen stories, if we include "Idyll in the Desert," which was published on December 10 by Random House in a limited edition of four hundred copies. That same year, on September 21, seven months after *Sanctuary*, his first collection of short stories, *These Thirteen*, was published.

At Ellen Glasgow's suggestion, Faulkner was invited to a gathering of Southern writers on October 23 and 24, 1931, in Charlottesville, at the fine neoclassical University of Virginia. Thirty-four writers took part. They included authors who were already known and respected, such as James Branch Cabell, Thomas Wolfe, Stark Young, Donald Davidson, Sherwood Anderson, Paul Green, and Allen Tate. Faulkner came to the conference wearing an aviator's cap—he had served in the Canadian Royal Air Force, he explained. During Ellen Glasgow's opening address, he sat on his chair with his elbows on his knees and his head in his hands—he was probably already drunk. He straightened up briefly from time to time to murmur his approval of what had just been said, which he had been more or less listening to. He made no further contribution to the discussions on Southern writers and their readers. The future of Southern literature was of no particular interest to him.

Harrison Smith had urged him to take part in this conference, and even paid his train ticket, but Faulkner didn't really know what he was doing there. Even at this early stage, he found literary chatter abhorrent. "I am not a literary man but only a writer," he later told Jean Stein. "I don't get any pleasure from talking shop" (*LG*, 252). Already, he was suspicious of journalists, and his relationships with them were highly ambiguous. To a reporter who managed to corner him in his hotel room, he told a story inspired by his supposed exploits during the Great War. To another journalist, he confided that his favorite writers were Melville, Conrad, and Alexandre Dumas and told him that Southern literature would produce nothing of value for the next twenty years.

Uncomfortable with the glare of curiosity, this shy man tended to keep his distances and, as always, used tall tales to protect himself. Nonetheless, he was thrilled with what was happening to him. He couldn't believe there was so much interest in him. In Charlottesville at first, and then in New York, where he spent seven weeks, he was caught in a whirl of cocktails, lunches, and dinners. Writers, publishers, journalists—everyone wanted to know what the author of the scandalous *Sanctuary* was like, and the object of this attention was really quite pleased by it all. On November 13, 1931, Faulkner wrote to Estelle:

> I have created quite a sensation. I have had luncheons in my honor by magazine editors every day for a week now, besides evening parties, or people who want to see what I look like. In fact, I have learned with astonishment that I am now the most important figure in American letters. That is, I have the best future. Even Sinclair Lewis and Theodore Dreiser made engagements to see me, and Mencken is coming all the way up from Baltimore to see me on Wednesday. I'm glad I'm level-headed, not very vain. But I dont think it has gone to my head. Anyway, I am writing. (*SL*, 53)

In the same letter, he told his wife that Hollywood had asked him to write a screenplay for Tallulah Bankhead (the daughter of an Alabama senator, the famous actress's eccentricities were making the headlines at the time) and that he stood to earn about ten thousand dollars for doing so. The contract was never signed, but Faulkner was soon in Hollywood. Publishers were also starting to court him. Alfred Knopf, Harold Guinzburg of Viking Press, and Bennett Cerf of Random House vied for his attention, offering him contracts. In February 1932, *Contempo*, a small literary magazine published in Chapel Hill, North Carolina, devoted an entire issue to him, comprising nine previously unpublished poems and a short story, also previously unpublished, titled "Once Aboard the Lugger." *Salmagundi*, a New Orleans magazine, also published a selection of his unpublished texts. Of course, Faulkner was not "the most important figure in American letters," but he intrigued many, and famous writers were eager to meet him. Nathanael West, who had just published his first novel, *The Dream Life of Balso Snell* (1931), invited him to lunch, and at a cocktail party he met Dashiell Hammett, the author of *The Maltese Falcon*, and his companion, Lillian Hellman. Both came, like him, from the South, and despite serious political disagreements, Faulkner became friends with them.

Hammett and Faulkner got on especially well, both being fond of drink. One day in November 1932 they were invited to a grand dinner hosted by Alfred Knopf, one of the major New York publishers. They had barely arrived when they started grabbing glasses from the trays nearby and soon got quite drunk. Hammett eventually slipped off a sofa onto the floor and passed out. Faulkner, after getting up to take leave of his host, fell over just as he was leaving. His friend Wasson had to help him get up and get back to his hotel.

By the early 1930s Faulkner's reputation as a drinker was well established. After the Charlottesville conference, Sherwood Anderson wrote to a friend: "Bill Faulkner had arrived and got drunk. From time to time, he appeared, got drunk again immediately, & disappeared. He kept asking everyone for a drink. If they didn't give him any, he drank his own."[11] Allen Tate remembered seeing him vomit on Mrs. Tate's brand-new dress. Faulkner drank morning and evening, day and night, quite openly. One day during the conference, two young admirers who came looking for him at his hotel found him sitting on the sidewalk like a bum, a bottle of whiskey beside him.

Many people attest to the fact that every time Faulkner went to a gathering, he ended the evening as drunk as a lord. He was born to it. Drinking, for the Faulkners, was a family thing. It was passed down like a tradition or a hereditary disease. All the men drank. The Old Colonel was a drinker, the Young Colonel was a drinker, Murry was a drinker. And perhaps even more than his forebears, William, Murry's eldest son, was also a drinker.

By the age of twenty Faulkner was well on the way to becoming an alcoholic, and he would remain one until his death. There was nothing classy about his drinking. Faulkner got drunk anywhere, in public or in private, but his intoxications were fundamentally solitary, cheerless, wholehearted, without conviviality, and sometimes had aggressive overtones. He could drink all day long and even for days on end, and—contrary to Francis Scott Fitzgerald, the Catholic Irishman—he seems to have abandoned himself to alcohol without the slightest remorse. By the end of the 1930s his drinking had become chronic. No day passed without its ration of bourbon, whiskey, gin, beer, wine, cognac, or martinis.

Unpredictable but generally heralded by an unusual excitability and silence, and by always identical signals (tapping his fingers, humming the same tune, reciting the same lines of Shakespeare), his benders could take place under any circumstances, anytime and anywhere—at home; at the homes of friends or strangers; in Oxford, New Orleans, New York, Hollywood, London, or Paris. In his biographical essay (vehemently repudiated by Faulkner), which first appeared in *Life* in September and October 1953, Robert Coughlan wrote:

> His alcoholic holidays from reality [. . .] became a necessary fixture of his life, and they produced violence; but generally they were as unobtrusive as his normal behavior. He would supply himself with whiskey and, after a period of elation, retire to his own bed, drinking until sleep or coma set in, drinking again when consciousness returned, until days and nights had passed and slowly he returned to the world. At such times, his friends and relatives would come and sit with him, taking turns so that he always had attention and care, as with a man suffering any other serious illness.[12]

His daughter, fifty years later, told a similar story:

> He went on binges. He would suddenly withdraw from the family and begin to drink. He could become quite violent during these binges, which could last anywhere from a few days to a few weeks. We had to keep away from him, and

there were a couple of men assigned to keep him from us, to protect us. He would drink until he collapsed again, and when he woke up he would drink again, till he collapsed again. There was no way of knowing when the whole thing would come to an end, but it would. He would go into the kitchen, pour himself a big bowl of Worcestershire sauce and raw egg. He'd drink that—a purgative. That would signal the end of the binge. After that, he would return to his normal drinking habits, just a drink or two before dinner, some wine with dinner, nothing more. When he wasn't on a binge, he could be quite disciplined about his drinking.[13]

When he was away from Rowan Oak, in New York or other cities, the scenario was a little different. At these times Faulkner was left completely to his own devices, and usually one of his friends had to step in to get him out of trouble. In late 1928 Jim Devine and Leon Scales, who had come to see him in his studio on Macdougal Street in Greenwich Village, found the door locked and ended up breaking it down. Faulkner was there, prostrate on the floor, surrounded by empty bottles, sleeping off the effects of whiskey. The same scene was repeated many times, and each time it was friends who, alarmed by his sudden disappearance, went looking for him and eventually found him blind drunk in his hotel room.

Why did Faulkner drink? For all the reasons people drink. To forget thwarted love affairs or professional setbacks. To relieve boredom, to wash away the blues, to feel a little less small or a little less lost, to feel different, to feel better. When Lauren Bacall plucked up the courage one day to ask him why he drank, he answered: "When I have a martini, I feel bigger, wiser, taller. When I have a second, I feel superlative. When I have more, there's no holding me" (*B1*, 582).

In 1916 he went on binges to get over Estelle's betrayal; in 1937 he got drunk the day Meta married Wolfgang Rebner; and in August 1954 he was drunk on his daughter's wedding day. Sometimes he also drank to banish the feeling of emptiness that took over him when, after many long months of work, he had finally finished a novel. In 1928 when Devine and Scales found him blind drunk in his studio, he had just finished correcting the galleys of *The Sound and the Fury*. Similarly, he stopped eating and started drinking in December 1935 after finishing the manuscript of *Absalom, Absalom!* Later, toward the end of his life, as the pain from his riding accidents grew, alcohol became a painkiller. But Faulkner didn't need any excuse.

Not everyone had his stamina. Dylan Thomas died at thirty-nine, Fitzgerald at forty-four, Lowry at forty-eight. Faulkner lived long enough to write almost twenty novels and many short stories. He drank heavily and his capacity for alcohol was scarcely believable. He could be seen at cocktail parties unceremoniously downing a quart of Scotch or more than a dozen martinis. One day Meta Carpenter saw him drink ten double bourbons one after the other. But his powers of recovery were no less stupendous. Like Samuel Beckett, he could hold his liquor, and his robust constitution meant a quick recovery from most of his phenomenal binges. Over the years, alcohol, imbibed so often and at such high doses, eventually took its toll, and increasingly, like his father and grandfather before him, he had to sign into clinics to dry out.

People have often wondered if Faulkner drank while he was writing. Bill Spratling, Maurice-Edgar Coindreau, and others were sure he did, and it seems likely that from *Absalom, Absalom!* on he sometimes did write while drunk. However, his work is not that of an alcoholic. As his brother John noted, nobody with his output could possibly drink as much as he claimed. Jill was categorical: "He did not drink while writing. [. . .] That was never the case. He always wrote when sober, and would drink afterwards."[14]

Further evidence is to be found in Faulkner's reply to his cousin Sallie after the publication of *Sanctuary*. To Sallie's question: "Do you think up that material when you're drunk?" Faulkner answered: "Sallie Murry, I get a lot of it when I'm drunk" (*B1*, 276).

———

In 1932 Faulkner wrote to Harrison Smith: "I am not young enough anymore to hell around and earn money at other things as I could once. I have got to make it by writing or quit writing" (*SL*, 60). Earn money writing what? Can a writer concern himself with selling his books without compromising his integrity as a writer? Very few American novelists have not had to face this nagging question. In a letter addressed to Robert Haas in 1940, Faulkner confessed his doubts: "But maybe a man worrying about money cant write anything worth buying" (*SL*, 121). He had quickly learned the implacable laws of the literary market and, not having a private income like Flaubert, James, Tolstoy, or Proust, he did not have the luxury of disdaining these laws. In order to make a living from his talents, he had to put on a show and attract customers. And yet in 1916, at the age of nineteen, while working as a bookkeeper at his grandfather's bank, he asserted that "money was a contemptible thing to work for" (*B1*, 52). But the carefree days were over. Since 1929 Faulkner had been a married man. He had become the head of the family, if not the head of the clan, just as his two paternal grandfathers had been. He felt obliged not only to provide for Estelle and her two children from her first marriage but also to help out his brothers and provide financial assistance to his mother, who had been widowed since 1932. "Dad left mother solvable for only about 1 year. Then its me" (*SL*, 65), he wrote to Wasson in September 1932. Already, the debts were mounting. He had not finished paying for his house, and the repairs needed to make it habitable were very costly. Finally, it was unthinkable in the South that a good white middle-class family should not have black servants, and while Faulkner did not pay his, he felt bound to provide them with room and board and to pay their bills.

He therefore needed money—a lot of it. Work was Faulkner's only means of making money. Unfortunately, he was not very good at managing it. His wife had expensive tastes and no head for figures. In 1930, as we have seen, he had taken on huge debts to buy Rowan Oak. In 1933, even though he was barely making ends meet, he bought an airplane. In 1937 he purchased a plot of forested land, followed by a farm a year later. He also had to have horses, and later, in 1948, he bought a yacht. He was also excessively generous. As his daughter remarked: "Pappy had no sense of money at all—never did. And he was the easiest touch. He always had several families completely dependent upon him. Anyone could come with a hard luck story, and he would accept it and put his hand in his pocket whether there was anything there or not and cheerfully give them whatever he had" (*LP*, 84).

Herman Melville, in a famous letter to Hawthorne, dated June 1, 1851, wrote: "Dollars damn me; and the malicious Devil is forever grinning in upon me, holding the door ajar."[15] Faulkner could have said as much and, in fact, did so incessantly in his letters. Moreover, most of the recipients of these letters were his agents and publishers, and although he spoke enthusiastically of his work and writing plans, his money problems were almost always mentioned: invoices, bills, insurance, or tax to pay and advance payments to ask for. For example, in a letter to Harrison Smith, dated January 31, 1934, he wrote:

As I explained to you before, I have my own taxes and my mother's, and the possibility that Estelle's people will call on me before Feb. 1, and also my mother's and Dean's support, and occasional demands from my other two brothers which I can never anticipate. Then in March I have $700.00 insurance and income tax of about $1500.00. So I seem right now to rush from pillar to post and return. (*SL*, 78)

BACK AND FORTH TO HOLLYWOOD

Not long after Faulkner's return to Oxford in December 1931, Leland Hayward, his New York agent, was contacted by Sam Marx, head of Metro Goldwyn Mayer (MGM), the most powerful and prestigious of the eight major Hollywood film studios at the time. Marx wanted to bring Faulkner to California and hire him as a screenwriter, but Faulkner had no desire to leave Rowan Oak, and, anyway, he wanted to finish *Light in August* first. He wrote to Wasson in January 1932: "I will be better off here until this novel is finished. Maybe I can try the movies later on" (*SL*, 82). But it was only a matter of time. Faulkner was in dire need of money and had no idea how to get it. Cape & Smith was bankrupt and could not pay him his royalties for *Sanctuary*. Magazines were tardy in buying his short stories. His attempts to publish *Light in August* as a serial foundered. So he went to Hollywood.

Since the advent of the "talkies," cinema could no longer do without writers. Others had gone to Hollywood already, and others would follow after him: Francis Scott Fitzgerald, Ben Hecht, Lillian Hellman, Dashiell Hammett, Raymond Chandler, Nathanael West, Dorothy Parker, and Anita Loos, along with a handful of English writers such as Aldous Huxley and P. G. Wodehouse. In truth, these authors were not hired for their writing talent but rather to enhance the prestige of the often uncultivated producers who hired them. Not that the latter held them in high esteem: Jack Warner never missed an opportunity to call writers "schmucks with Underwoods" (*B*, 1196–97). Irving Thalberg, the prince of Hollywood and head of MGM, who passed for a brilliant intellectual and was the source of inspiration for F. Scott Fitzgerald's *The Last Tycoon* (1941), was no less disparaging. He wondered why there was so much fuss about writers. After all, writing was simply putting words one after the other.[16]

In the Hollywood studio system of the 1930s and '40s, apart from the producers, directors, and stars, the other workers in the film industry were regarded as merely the hired help. The screenwriter was nothing more than a hired lackey, an employee with precarious status, most often paid by the week and sometimes by the day. Most scripts were written in collaboration or by two, three, or four screenwriters working in alternation, and producers, directors, and even actors felt entitled to change them, even at the last minute. There were no royalties and screenplays were not seen as literary works.

The first contract between Faulkner and MGM was signed on April 15, 1932. On May 7 Marx saw a man arriving in MGM's Culver City studios "short and shy, mild mannered and soft-spoken, exceedingly thin, with crew-cut iron grey hair, a wisp of a black moustache, entirely inconspicuous except for one noticeable attention-getter on his person. His head was bleeding from an open cut" (B, 772). Faulkner told him he had been hit by a cab and refused to go see a doctor. He fooled nobody.

For six weeks, for a weekly wage of five hundred dollars, Faulkner worked as a screenwriter, at first tentatively, without having much idea of what a screenplay should be. In fact, he was not very interested in filmmaking; he was unfamiliar with the medium and had everything to learn. At his first meeting with Sam Marx, he said he had an idea for a "screenplay for Mickey." Impervious to banter, Marx explained that Mickey Mouse belonged to the Walt Disney studios. Faulkner was then handed over to producer Harry Rapf, who set him to work on a film project called "Flesh," with Wallace Beery in the leading role. As Faulkner did not know who Beery was, Marx organized the projection of a film starring the actor. But Faulkner slipped away before the end of the film and disappeared for an entire week. When he came back to see Marx, the latter thought it wiser to ask him for original screenplays. Faulkner therefore started working on two synopses. The first, titled "Manservant," was taken from "Love," one of his short stories, written in 1921, which he had not managed to sell. The second was inspired by a conversation in New York with Tallulah Bankhead: "Night Bird," a three-page screenplay, rechristened "The College Widow," was the story of a loose young woman whose sordid, scandalous life was reminiscent of Temple Drake's in *Sanctuary*. Both synopses were shelved by MGM.

For his first stay in Hollywood, Faulkner rented a cottage at 4024 Jackson Street, not far from the studios. Most of the time he lived alone, worked alone, and rarely ate in the studio canteen. He was no more interested in his colleagues than in the actors for whom he was writing. However, he did meet James Boyd, a well-known author of historical novels eight years his senior, and also met up again with Laurence Stallings, whom he had already met in New York, the coauthor of the successful Broadway play *What Price Glory?* A veteran of World War I who had lost a leg in Belleau Wood, Stallings was the type of virile, self-confident man Faulkner admired and envied. Stallings took him under his wing and introduced him to his friends. Faulkner started to feel more at ease. In the evening he brought home piles of screenplays to study, with a bottle of whiskey at hand. After the first six weeks, on June 25 MGM decided not to renew his contract, but then reconsidered and offered him a one-year contract at a salary of $250 a week. Faulkner was able to turn down their offer because on June 16 Paramount paid $750 for a four-month option on *Sanctuary* to Leland Hayward, the American Play Company agent who had just taken Faulkner onto his books. The studio ultimately bought the adaptation rights for the novel for almost $7,000. Because the novel had caused a scandal, women's associations protested immediately and a number of newspapers demanded that the project be abandoned. Nevertheless, in 1933 Stephen Roberts, a filmmaker specializing in comedies, adapted the book under the title *The Story of Temple Drake*, from a screenplay written by Oliver Garrett (without the help of Faulkner), with Miriam Hopkins, one of Paramount's stars, as Temple and Jack La Rue as Popeye. The rape with a corncob was removed. The film could only be a watered-down version of the novel.

In July 1932 Faulkner met director Howard Hawks, who was already famous for *The Dawn Patrol* and *Scarface*. On the advice of his brother William, Hawks had just read "Turn About," a short story by Faulkner published on March 5 in the *Saturday Evening Post*. The brothers agreed that this war story, featuring a young American pilot and an English seaman, could make an excellent film. Hawks therefore had MGM buy the rights to the story and asked Faulkner to come and see him. At their first meeting, when Hawks introduced himself, Faulkner replied that he had seen his name on a check and then fell silent. Hawks started explaining the film he wanted to make from "Turn About." Faulkner still said nothing. After three-quarters of an hour, Hawks was starting to lose patience, but Faulkner promised to return in four or five days with the finished screenplay. According to legend, the two men then went on a bender that ended up in a motel in Culver City in the small hours. Hawks took Faulkner home blind drunk. There would be more meetings and more drinking sessions as Hawks and Faulkner became friends. Hawks was tall and Faulkner short, but they got along like a house on fire. Hawks, who, like Faulkner, had an appetite for danger, had driven racing cars, flown airplanes, and often went about on a spluttering motorbike. Apart from the fact that they both had bird names and were both pipe smokers, the two men had the same passion for flying, hunting, and fishing, and both loved alcohol, tobacco, and tweed. What's more, they were both great storytellers and inveterate liars.

When they first met, Faulkner promised to come back five days later with a script. He kept his word. After allegedly getting lost in Death Valley, he returned to Hawks with the draft. Hawks immediately brought it to his brother-in-law Irving Thalberg, vice president of MGM, then head of production. Thalberg read it immediately and encouraged Hawks to adapt it for the cinema without delay. He told Hawks to shoot it just as it was, saying that if he (Thalberg) touched it, he would ruin it. *Turn About* could have been a war movie as good as *Dawn Patrol*, but the star system changed the initial project: less than a week later, studio vice president Eddie Mannix asked Hawks to give up on the idea of an all-male cast and write in a part for Joan Crawford. Faulkner, never one to run out of ideas, immediately suggested getting the actress to play an ambulance nurse. He was rehired to work on the project, on a weekly salary of $250—just half of what he had earned under his first contract.

Faulkner's first stay in Hollywood was interrupted by the death, not wholly unexpected, of his father on August 7, 1932. He rushed back to Oxford for Murry's funeral and to help his mother settle his father's estate. Thanks to Hawks, he continued to be paid and to work for Hollywood. After reworking the screenplay for *Turn About* under the studio's direction, he sent a new version to Hawks in late August. A month later he finished reworking *Light in August*.

On October 3, 1932, after six weeks in Oxford, Faulkner went back to California with his mother and younger brother Dean. He stayed barely a month but continued to work for Hollywood, and after Hawks intervened on his behalf with MGM, he was paid six hundred dollars a week until May 1933. The shooting of *Turn About* began in December. Hawks did his best to salvage what he could, but the film—rechristened *Today We Live*—had very little in common with Faulkner's original screenplay. It premiered in Pasadena on March 16 and went on general release in New York on April 14, 1933.

Three of the main actors of *Today We Live*—Joan Crawford, Gary Cooper, and Franchot Tone—were major stars. Faulkner was rubbing shoulders with a number of celebrities at this time, forming friendships with some of them. But he was not in the least starstruck, as shown by this amusing anecdote, repeated many times by Hawks: At a hunting party in Imperial Valley, Clark Gable asked Faulkner what he should read and who he thought were the best living American writers. Faulkner replied: "Thomas Mann, Willa Cather, John Dos Passos, Ernest Hemingway and me." Surprised, Gable looked at him and said: "Oh. Do you write?" Faulkner replied: "Yes Mister Gable. What do you do?" (*B1*, 310).

Today We Live was not a resounding success. However, Hawks was determined to pursue his collaboration with Faulkner and persuaded Louis B. Mayer to let him work from home in Oxford, from November 28, 1932, to May 13, 1933, on a weekly salary of six hundred dollars. At the time, MGM was planning to adapt the diary of John McGavock Grider, which *Liberty* magazine had published in serial form in August 1926 under the title "War Birds." Faulkner was asked to write the screenplay. The diary of a young aviator shot down in full flight during World War I, who therefore had the heroic destiny the young Faulkner had dreamed of, caught his imagination. He had likely read it upon publication and had drawn from it when writing "Ad Astra" in 1930. When adapting it for the cinema, he drew on that short story and on "All the Dead Pilots," another war story featuring Bayard Sartoris, and on the story of John and Bayard as told in *Flags in the Dust*. But his script of "War Birds: A Ghost Story" (the subtitle is his), with a reassuringly happy ending, is a version that is very different from the story in the novel. The dialog, verbose and melodramatic, was that of an inexperienced screenwriter, but the script also contains many interesting suggestions for editing and camera movements. In mid-January 1933 Faulkner sent the script to Hawks, but Hawks never followed up on the project.

In 1930s Hollywood it was inconceivable that a screenwriter should work from home, far away from the studios. In May 1933 Faulkner was asked to go to New Orleans and meet Tod Browning, the outrageous director of *Dracula* (1931) and *Freaks* (1932), who was getting ready to shoot a film alternately called "Louisiana Lou" and "Bride of the Bayou." When Faulkner asked what the film was about, he was instructed to wait. For three weeks the crew traveled between New Orleans and the locations every day. Nothing happened. Faulkner later told Jean Stein the end of the story—although, as usual, his version is not wholly reliable. One evening after they returned home, he had just gone back to his room when the telephone rang. It was Browning. He asked Faulkner to come and see him right away, which he did. Browning showed Faulkner a telegram: *Faulkner is fired. MGM Studios*. Browning told Faulkner not to worry, saying that he would call somebody and that Faulkner would not only be reinstated but that he would be sent a letter of apology as well. There was a knock on the door. It was a bellboy with another telegram: *Browning is fired. MGM Studios*. Faulkner went home. He thought it likely that Browning did the same. As for the screenwriter, Faulkner imagined that he was still somewhere in a room, clutching his weekly check. The film was never made.

In June 1934 Hawks invited Faulkner back to Hollywood to work on "Sutter's Gold," a project to adapt *Gold*, the Blaise Cendrars novel published in 1925, on which Eisenstein had already done some work four years previously. From July 1 to 24, 1934, Faulkner stayed in Hollywood. On the seventh, he finished an initial synopsis; five days later he completed a second one; and three weeks later he had written a script 108 pages long. He continued to work on it after his return to Oxford. The hero and plot of Cendrars's novel may even have inspired his reworking of *Absalom, Absalom!*, which he started working on early the following year. However, the adaptation came to nothing. When Universal Studios, a company known for its stinginess, announced that the film should not cost more than $750,000, Hawks threw in the sponge.

Faulkner's financial situation again deteriorated. In July 1935 he wrote his agent, Morton Goldman, that he needed at least ten thousand dollars to live quietly for two years and go back to work on *Absalom, Absalom!* and that in the meantime he needed to find something to pay his taxes and settle his debts. In order to meet his debts, he was even prepared to sell some of his manuscripts:

> It's all written in long hand; besides the short stories, I have SOUND & FURY, AS I LAY DYING, SANCTUARY, LIGHT IN AUGUST, PYLON. Will there be any market for it? Will you inquire around, without committing yourself, and see? I hate like hell to sell it, but if I dont get some money somehow soon, I will be in danger of having some one put me in bankruptcy and I will then lose my house and insurance and all. (*SL*, 92)

But his publishers were unable to help him out. They were themselves in difficulty, and in early December they asked him to pay back immediately the loan they had given him.

Faulkner then turned to Hollywood again. On December 10, 1935, he met up with Hawks, who had just left MGM for Twentieth Century-Fox. Hawks managed to have Faulkner hired to work on the script for *The Road to Glory*. The starting point for this project was Raymond Bernard's film *Les Croix de bois* (*Wooden Crosses*), the first adaptation of Roland Dorgelès's famous war novel, produced by Pathé-Nathan, which premiered at the Geneva Disarmament Conference in 1932. Darryl F. Zanuck, who had formerly worked for Warner, bought the rights for Fox, not to distribute it in the United States but to shoot a Hollywood remake. The script was first entrusted to the writer Joel Sayre. When Zanuck decided to recruit someone else, Hawks suggested to Nunnally Johnson, an ex-journalist who was now an associate of Zanuck, that they hire Faulkner. Zanuck was reluctant, but Johnson agreed.

On December 16, 1935, Faulkner started working for Fox on a weekly salary of one thousand dollars. He took a room in a small, quiet hotel, the Beverly Hills, near the bars on Hollywood Boulevard. He would rise at five o'clock in the morning and work for three or four hours on *Absalom, Absalom!* before going to the studios with Sayre. A first draft of the script, 170 pages long, was ready by the end of December. In January 1936, having finished his work, Faulkner went home to put the final touches on his new novel. However, worn out by the work, he started drinking again and first needed to dry out. Estelle and Malcolm took him to Wright's Sanatorium, a private clinic in the small town of Byhalia in Marshall County, a few dozen miles north of Oxford.

After he had dried out, he set to work again. But before he was able to finish typing up his novel, he went back to Hollywood in late February 1936 because he needed the money. He rented a bungalow under the palm trees of Beverly Hills and stayed there until the end of May. As Faulkner was no longer needed on *The Road to Glory*, Nunnally Johnson suggested he work on the script for *Banjo on My Knee* (a title taken from the famous cowboy song "O Suzanna"), a tale about bargemen and lumberjacks. David Hempstead, Johnson's young assistant, who was shortly to become one of Faulkner's best friends, remembered: "Bill wrote magnificent things, practically blank verse, sometimes two or three pages long. They were beautiful speeches, but they were written for actors like Tony Martin, and I couldn't show them to Zanuck" (*B*, 367).

Indeed, Zanuck did not like Faulkner's work on *Banjo* and asked Johnson to rewrite the script. Faulkner's contract was not renewed, but when Goldman found him work at David Selznick's RKO Studios, he agreed to spend another five weeks in Hollywood on a thousand dollars a week. George Stevens was filming *Gunga Din*, a war and adventure movie based on a Kipling novel, with a cast that included Douglas Fairbanks Jr., Cary Grant, Joan Fontaine, Sam Jaffe, and Victor McLaglen. Asked to become co-screenwriter, Faulkner readily agreed; he knew Kipling's work well and believed that he understood the film's hero—a "colored man"—better than most. As his new job did not start until April 9, 1936, he had some time to revise and type up *Absalom, Absalom!* He does not seem to have made a decisive contribution to the script. The film credits list Ben Hecht, Charles MacArthur, Joel Sayre, and Fred Guiol, but not William Faulkner.

Faulkner was not bored in Hollywood. Although he was not very sociable, this does not mean that he lived like a recluse. In December 1935 he met Meta Carpenter, Hawks's pretty secretary, who was soon to become his mistress. But he also met actresses such as Claudette Colbert and ZaSu Pitts, joined up with Sayre and Hempstead again, and also met with friends from New York such as Marc Connelly, Dorothy Parker, and especially Nathanael West, with whom he went pigeon and pig hunting. He played poker from time to time and had the odd tennis match. But he still had a horror of society events and told the story of how one evening at a party he escaped through a third-floor window so as not to offend his host.

However, it is surprising that Faulkner remained so much on the margins of intellectual life in Hollywood. Many European artists, mostly Germans and Austrians, many of them Jews, had fled the Nazis and come to Hollywood. In his house at 165 Maberry Road, in Santa Monica, the Austrian screenwriter Salka Viertel used to hold a "salon" where Faulkner could have met Greta Garbo and Marlene Dietrich, Charlie Chaplin and Ernest Lubitsch, but also Thomas Mann (the German writer he seems to have admired most), Bertolt Brecht, Franz Werfel, Alma Mahler, Arnold Schoenberg, Hanns Eisler, Aldous Huxley, or Christopher Isherwood. Apparently, he had no desire to do so.

From 1936 on, the trips back and forth between Oxford and Hollywood became more frequent. In January, Faulkner went home to Mississippi. By late February he was back in Hollywood. In mid-May he returned to Oxford to celebrate Jill's third birthday. He didn't stay long. But on July 15, when he returned to California, he was not alone with Jack Oliver, his black driver, in his brand-new, all-blue Ford convertible. This time he brought Estelle with him, along with Jill and her nanny, Narcissus McEwen. He took a fine furnished house at an exorbitant rent in Pacific Palisades. The Faulkners did not have a very intense social life, but they had people over to dinner from time to time, with Estelle playing the piano to entertain the guests. Sometimes they went out with friends such as Ben Wasson, Joel Sayre, and the Hawks, and met up with actors such as Ronald Colman and Clark Gable.

On August first, two weeks after his arrival, Faulkner started to write dialogue for *The Last Slaver*, a film project designed for Wallace Beery. The script had already been drafted by Lillian Hellman and Gladys Lehmann, and the director was to be Tay Garnett. Faulkner also wrote dialogue for *Submarine Patrol*. According to Gene Markey, the producer of this war film: "It was good Faulknerian dialog, but it had nothing whatever to do with our story" (B1, 373). In the latter months of 1936 and up to the end of the summer of 1937, Faulkner switched abruptly from one project to another, but this did not seem to bother him too much. His work as a screenwriter was now very well paid: he earned almost twenty thousand dollars in 1936 and over twenty-one thousand dollars in the first eight months of 1937. His employers appreciated his ability to produce dialogue on demand. However, his dialogues were those of a novelist rather than a screenwriter and were deemed too wordy and "literary" to satisfy Hollywood's requirements, so most of the time there was little left when it came to filming.

Faulkner wrote scripts until the end of spring 1937. In March he worked on *Dance Hall* and from March to June on the adaptation of a popular novel by Walter D. Edmonds, *Drums Along the Mohawk*, John Ford's first color movie, starring Henry Fonda and Claudette Colbert. As always, he did his best, but he found scriptwriting more tedious than ever and work meetings with directors and producers increasingly burdensome. Nevertheless, he had to carry on, because he needed the money. "I just kept telling myself, 'They're gonna pay me Saturday, they're gonna pay me Saturday'" (*B*, 960).

He spent the whole summer in Hollywood, clocking in at the studio every morning, even though he had been given no particular task since June. And thanks to the thousand dollars Fox continued to pay him every week, he had all the time he needed to revise his collected short stories, which were to be published in *The Unvanquished*. He was now eager to go home. On July 28 he wrote to Estelle, who had returned home in May: "As far as I know, I will be through at studio Aug 15 and will start home sometime during that week, though according to my contract they can give me an assignment and hold me overtime until I finish it. [. . .] It's hot here and I dont feel very good, but I think it's mostly being tired of movies, worn out with them" (*SL*, 101). He came home to Rowan Oak on September 1, very happy to have finally left the "salt mines" (182) of Fox.

From 1932 to 1937 Faulkner had a dual career as writer and screenwriter. He was said to be a careless screenwriter. People also said that he didn't know how to write usable scripts. But as attested by Stephen Longstreet, with whom he had worked: "Bill worked very hard at being a screenwriter, and by the time he left Hollywood in September, 1945, he had become capable of writing with the best of his lot, the few real talents who were here then."[17] Nonetheless, Faulkner would only ever claim one single identity, one single vocation: "I'm a book-writin' man," he told Meta Carpenter, "not a scenarist" (*ALG*, 38). However, the fact that he spent almost four years in Hollywood in total and worked on over fifty films is not irrelevant. His work as a screenwriter had an impact on his literary work, as Faulkner was well aware. Writing to Harrison Smith in October 1933, he said: "I shall have to peg away at the novel slowly, since I am broke again with two families to support now, since my father died, and so I shall have to write a short story every so often or go back to Hollywood, which I dont want to do" (*SL*, 75).

Most Hollywood screenwriters, many of them talented writers, had nothing but scorn for their work and their employers. Ben Hecht, one of the best-known and best-paid screenwriters at the end of the 1930s, made no bones about it. "According to Hecht, there was no art in films and there never had been, no more than there was in the manufacture of toilet seats, pantyhose, or sausages. Film was an item of mass consumption . . . a bunch of platitudes bundled together, regurgitated plots."[18] Faulkner was no less severe: "Nobody would live in Hollywood," he told his brother Jack, "except to get what money they could out of it" (*B1*, 382). He advised Shelby Foote: "Always take the people seriously, but never take the work seriously. Hollywood is the only place on earth where you can get stabbed in the back while you're climbing a ladder" (447). He was even more vehement in this comment to a friend who denounced Hollywood as a dead place: "They worship death here. They don't worship money, they worship death" (456).

Faulkner didn't like California either. The climate, the landscape, the architecture, the people, their lifestyle, their ways of being—he disliked it all. "Golden Land," a short story with an ironic title written in 1935, is the only one inspired by his experience in California. Los Angeles, city of angels and factory of dreams, is portrayed here in sinister fashion:

> Had he looked, he could have seen the city in the bright soft vague hazy sunlight, random, scattered about the arid earth like so many gay scraps of paper blown without order, with its curious air of being rootless—of houses bright beautiful and gay, without basements or foundations, lightly attached to a few inches of light penetrable earth, lighter even than dust and laid lightly in turn upon the profound and primeval lava, which one good hard rain would wash forever from the sight and memory of man as a firehose flushes down a gutter—that city of almost incalculable wealth whose queerly appropriate fate it is to be erected upon a few spools of a substance whose value is computed in billions and which may be completely destroyed in that second's instant of a careless match between the moment of striking and the moment when the striker may have sprung and stamped it out. (*CS*, 719)

When Faulkner left California in 1937 with Ben Wasson, he stopped his old Ford on the state line, looked out over the desert in front of them, and said to his friend: "Maybe on the Arizona part they might put up a sign saying 'Science Fiction Country.' On the California side I'd suggest a sign to read: 'Abandon hope, all ye who enter here'" (*B1*, 382).

For Faulkner this artificial paradise was a place of exile, if not hell itself, and would remain so till the end. When, after his return to Hollywood in June 1945, the screenwriter Paul Wellman asked him how he was, he answered: "I'll be glad when I get back home. Nobody here does anything. There's nobody here with any roots. Even the houses are built out of mud and chicken wire. Nothing ever happens an' after a while a couple of leaves fall off a tree and then it'll be another year" (*B1*, 467). To his eyes, California was nothing but an extended Hollywood set. A desert land, a space without breadth or depth, neutral and abstract, a place outside the seasons, outside nature, where nobody lived and nothing happened. The negation of all that meant home. A lifeless non-place, a "futile land."

His time in Hollywood weighed heavily throughout Faulkner's life—too heavily—but it is not at all certain that it had much influence on his career as a writer. Critics have often wondered about the influence of cinematographic devices on novel-writing techniques. Certainly, the twentieth-century novel owes much to cinema, and in 1948 Claude-Edmonde Magny rightly highlighted the privileged relationship between the American novel and film.[19] True, novelists did not wait for the Lumière brothers to use ellipses, cutting techniques, diverse narrative viewpoints, and various shots. Storytelling technique had already become considerably more flexible and complicated during the nineteenth century—if you look carefully, you can find traveling and low-angled shots in Flaubert's *Sentimental Education*—but cinema obviously hastened this development, and we know that it had a decisive influence on many modern novelists. Passionate about the aesthetics of photography and cinema, John Dos Passos readily acknowledged that in *Manhattan Transfer* and *U.S.A.* he had taken inspiration from the editing principles of D. W. Griffith and Sergei Eisenstein as well as Dziga Vertov's "cine eye." However, cinema was not as important for Faulkner as it was for Dos Passos. While Faulkner's modernity is often close to the expressionist research into stage and cinema, his experience with filmmaking did not make him a film buff and he scarcely talked about it in interviews. And let's not forget that at least four of his most innovative novels—*The Sound and the Fury, As I Lay Dying, Sanctuary,* and *Light in August*—were written *before* his first trip to Hollywood.

Faulkner spent a great deal of time with the studios, but he was not a cinemagoer and does not seem to have been overly interested in the seventh art form. He may well have drawn on Eisenstein's parallel montages when designing the dual structure of *If I Forget Thee, Jerusalem* and the fact that *A Fable* was originally conceived as an idea for a film by a producer and director, from which Faulkner developed a script before writing his novel, is surely not insignificant. But nothing indicates that his experience as a screenwriter made any serious mark on his work as a novelist. Faulkner said it again and again: the time he spent in Hollywood was simply a waste of time in that he was writing texts from topics that he hadn't chosen and that he had no interest in. If he had been able to do without it, he probably would have produced even more literary work that would not have been all that different in inspiration or form.

Faulkner's own comments on his relationship with cinema do contain a number of contradictions. In 1935 he wrote Goldman: "The trouble about the movies is not so much the time I waste here but the time it takes me to recover and settle down again" (*SL*, 90). But in a letter to Robert Haas in 1947, he does not rule out the possibility that Hollywood might have damaged his work as a writer. "I have realised lately how much trash and junk writing for movies corrupted into my writing" (*SL*, 248), However, he categorically refuted this admission in the answer he gave Jean Stein in their 1956 interview when she asked him if he thought that writing for the cinema could damage one's personal work: nothing, he said, could damage someone's work if they were a first-class writer.

In any event, Faulkner would have happily stayed away from Hollywood, and he envied writers who had been spared monetary worries. "In some ways Proust was lucky," he told Ben Wasson. "He didn't ever have to contend with Hollywood for his bread and butter. I'd rather have spent my time in that corklined bedroom of his, asthma and all. Anytime" (*B1*, 370).

To put it plainly, Faulkner's work in film might never have happened. Six of his novels and two of his short stories were adapted for cinema—and not all were duds. However, to date, no great filmmaker has attempted to translate Faulkner into cinematographic language. One can only dream of the magnificent films (not necessarily "Faulknerian" but *inspired* by Faulkner) that Welles, Huston, Buñuel, Visconti, Bergman, Tarkovsky, Resnais, or Godard could have made from one of his novels, and it will always be a source of regret that neither Jean Renoir nor Carl Dreyer was able to bring their plans to adapt *Light in August* to fruition.

META

Faulkner hated Hollywood, but it was in Hollywood that he met the greatest love of his life. It all began in December 1935:

> He walked into the outer office at Twentieth Century-Fox Studios, a small, quick man in a tweed suit that had never fitted him, and looked at me for a long, surprised moment, as if he had forgotten a carefully rehearsed speech or had expected to see someone else behind the desk, before he said that he was William Faulkner and that Mr. Hawks was "kind of expecting me."
> "*The* William Faulkner?" (*ALG*, 15).

This is how Meta Carpenter (née Doherty) begins her memoir, in which she tells the story of their affair. What it lacks in talent the book makes up for in liveliness and detail. The question was flattering and Faulkner quickly answered: "I reckon I'm the one, ma'am. [. . .] Leastways, I don't know of any other" (16).

Yes, that "small, quick man" was him. At Hawks's invitation, Faulkner had returned to Hollywood to work for five weeks on the script of *The Road to Glory*. At the time, Meta Carpenter was Hawks's secretary. She was beautiful, blond, slim, and sweet. She had the smooth profile of Grace Kelly and the graceful body of Cyd Charisse, with long legs, a wasp waist, lovely brown eyes, impeccable teeth, and a complexion "with a suffusion of ivory and alabaster" (*ALG*, 83), a vision such that her dazzled lover had never before laid eyes on. "That I was pretty enough, with blond hair that fell in a straight sweep to my shoulders, with a ninety-two-pound body as lean and as lithe as a ballerina's, and with a waist that was a handspan around, I knew without undue vanity" (27). When Faulkner met her she was already divorced. They came from similar origins. Like him, Meta came from Mississippi, grew up in Memphis and on a plantation on the Delta, and was faithful to the values and traditions of the South. Each recognizing the other's accent, the pair hit it off immediately.

From this started a love story that was to last fifteen years, although they didn't yet know it. She was twenty-eight; he was ten years older. For her, he was not just the well-known novelist, the author of *Sanctuary*. Thirteen years earlier she had heard about an eccentric young man answering to the same name; it was in Oxford, at a dance at the University of Mississippi. That day in December 1935, when she finally met him, she was a little disappointed. Instead of the "darkly handsome" man (*ALG*, 16) she had expected, she saw a diminutive, thin man with a mustache. Likable, certainly, with his airs of a Southern gentleman, but not irresistibly attractive.

It was not love at first sight for Faulkner either, but he was charmed from the outset. Two days after they first met, he arrived at the studio: "Unsteady on his legs, maneuvering toward my desk with a rolling gait, he made a courtly bow in my direction. [. . .] He leaned dangerously forward, like a circus performer whose shoes are nailed to the floor" (*ALG*, 18–19), and asked her to dinner. Meta panicked, ran into Hawks's office, and begged him to tell his drunk friend that a respectable young Southern woman could not go out with a married man. Later, when they were working together and she was typing up his scripts, Faulkner behaved himself impeccably. Nevertheless, he kept asking her out to dinner and Meta eventually relented. He picked her up at studio reception and took her to the Musso & Frank Grill, a modest restaurant on Hollywood Boulevard, which was (and still is) very popular with cinema folk. That evening, Faulkner was chatty and charming. He wanted to know all about what she liked, what she hated, and what she hoped for. He talked at length about his own family, about his daughter Jill, and his dead brother, Dean. Afterward, they strolled along the boulevard looking at the storefronts. They stopped at a bookshop, where he bought and signed a copy of one of his books for her—*A Green Bough* (according to Meta) or *Sanctuary* (according to Blotner). The following evening he brought her to LaRue's, an elegant restaurant on Sunset Strip, where he ordered a bottle of Pontet-Canet and launched into an explanation of how he had come to work in Hollywood because he had had some bad harvests (even though he had no farm at the time) and rehashed the story about his past as a pilot and his war wounds.

From then on they went out together every evening. Clearly hoping for more, Faulkner continued to court Meta assiduously. Flattered and touched by so much attentiveness, she started to fall for him. They were happy to see each other and to talk. Sometimes they touched or held hands, but they had not yet kissed. And then one evening she went to his hotel room with him. Sometime later they drove to Santa Monica, on the Pacific Coast, booked in as Mr. and Mrs. Bowen at Hotel Miramar, and spent their first night together in a bungalow on the beach. Meta writes: "We made love with the windows open to the sea, curtains aflutter, and moonlight so brilliantly white that I could see my lover's face afterward peaceful and eased. It was the first time we had been together for a full night, no clock hands to send me hurrying back to the studio" (*ALG*, 79). Their first night of love: moonlit and right by the sea—a romantic setting par excellence. Faulkner was enthusiastic and insatiable in his lovemaking. Meta, taken aback, waxes lyrical: "In the act of love, Bill, the restrained, remote man by day, was seized with a consuming sexual urgency. Desire and sensation shook him as a storm wind buffets a stout tree" (62). Faulkner himself said that from their very first night together, he was full of lust: "'I've always been afraid of going out of control, I get so carried away. [. . .] I'm not myself anymore; I'm somebody else. There was a time I worried about myself with women a whole lot. I still do, in fact'" (62).

A fervent, bashful lover, he recited the poetry of Keats, Swinburne, and Housman to Meta and wrote some for her too—as he had done for Estelle and Helen. He could not conceive of intercourse without poetry. However, his lyricism became bolder: "'For Meta, my heart, my jasmine garden, my April and May cunt; my white one, my blond morning, winged, my sweetly dividing, my honey-cloyed, my sweet-assed gal. Bill'" (*ALG*, 75–76). He drew erotic sketches with India ink, portraying them before, during, and after sex. He gave her ribbons and scattered jasmine and gardenia petals on their hotel bed. Like Lady Chatterley's gamekeeper, he made up names for their genitals. Faulkner was a contented lover. In Meta he had found both an expert mistress who satisfied his adult desires and the woman-child of his adolescent fantasies.

At twenty-nine Meta looked nineteen. In her lover's eyes she looked even younger. He behaved toward her "as if I were just out of high school. I don't remember making an effort to play my assigned part at these times, for, if anything, I was confounded by his need to turn me into a sweet, tremulous girl" (*ALG*, 77). One day he gave her a ribbon for her hair: "The idealization of me as a girl far too young for him was to last for a number of years and to appear in some of his letters to me. I never protested, and my acceptance of his vision of me as a maiden nourished his fantasy" (78).

This fantasy was a long-held one; from his earliest poetry and fiction, Faulkner, under his poetic masks, affirmed his taste for beautiful, small-breasted virgins with flat stomachs, long legs, and a small butt. This man, who had always desired the young girl in the women he loved, was, at last, blissfully happy.

The faun had finally found his nymph, Pierrot his Colombine, Cyrano his Roxane. A possessive lover, Faulkner wanted Meta to have eyes only for him and found it difficult to accept that she should want to go out and see her friends. But Meta stood up to him. "If you had your way," she told him, "we would never see anyone. You'd let nothing intrude on us. We would live suspended in the world" (*ALG*, 59). For Faulkner, love meant the tender solitude of a couple, but Meta liked company and didn't like being penned up. "We were consuming each other in our self-isolation," she writes in her memoirs. "It wasn't natural. Bill had placed us in a bubble and we were using up air in it; one day we would not be able to breathe. I could not believe that I would always be fascinating to him, that he would never tire of my company. I was a woman, not a series of Chinese boxes within boxes. We needed others to impinge on us, others to relate to" (67). Faulkner made some concessions. He agreed to spend weekends with her at Hotel Miramar in the company of John Crown and Sally Richard, a young couple of pianists who had befriended Meta. From time to time he took her to Hollywood receptions, and she accompanied him on his weekly trips to Musso & Frank's, where he met up with the handful of writers who had become his friends. Meta, however, soon realized that his novel-writing would remain his main priority and that once he started work on his new novel, *If I Forget Thee, Jerusalem*, their evenings together would be much shorter (131). Even in intimacy Faulkner maintained a distance, was restrained, kept secrets. Meta soon realized that there were forbidden topics, questions that should not be asked. "I knew somehow that I had to be incurious. The insularity that he drew over himself like a second, tougher skin put him beyond common query" (50). Nonetheless, Faulkner was very much in love with Meta. "That is the girl I'm in love with," he told Ben Wasson after introducing them. "Can't get her out of my mind or system. And don't want to. You don't know what a wonderful person she is" (*CNC*, 143).

In Hollywood, Faulkner was answerable to nobody and he could see Meta whenever and wherever he wanted. In July 1936, six months after they first met, their affair had lost nothing of its ardor. His decision to bring Estelle and Jill to California may therefore seem surprising. A few weeks earlier, on June 22, he had published the following advertisement in the *Commercial Appeal*: "I will not be responsible for any debt incurred or bills made, or notes or checks signed by Mrs. William Faulkner or Mrs. Estelle Oldham Faulkner" (*B*, 372). Signed William Faulkner. This public slap in the face could have been the beginning of a separation, or a divorce, all the more so since his life with Estelle during his last two stays at Rowan Oak had been, in his own words, infernal. So why bring her to Hollywood? Most likely because of Jill. We know that he adored his little daughter and suffered when he was apart from her. But he could not bring Jill without bringing her mother and therefore had to resign himself to bringing them both.

Immediately after returning to Hollywood, Faulkner rushed to Meta, who had just moved into a bungalow on Crescent Heights Boulevard. As always attentive to detail, she relates their ardent reunion: "I felt the sudden tumescence of him against my body and heard the excitement in his softly whispered 'My love, my long-legged, big-mouf gal. I have been too long away from you.' We made love with half our clothes still on our bodies, then slept enwrapped for a time" (*ALG*, 164). Meta was nevertheless annoyed that her lover had come back to Hollywood with Estelle and Jill in tow. For the first time, she worried about the future of their relationship. "Bill, how are we going to see each other? You with a wife and child to go home to every night from the studio?" (166).

For Faulkner it was a double life on a daily basis. With Meta, he still had fire and passion. With Estelle, hostilities resumed. At the start of their stay in Hollywood, they tried to maintain at least a semblance of married respectability. But the truce did not last. Their relationship was as tense in Hollywood as it had been in Oxford. They both started drinking again— Estelle regularly, Faulkner in fits and starts. Their arguments became more and more frequent, more and more violent, generally starting with volleys of abuse and ending in blows. Bill and Estelle were like cat and dog, and everyone knew it. They made no attempt to hide their domestic disputes. Each started showing friends their scratches and bruises, as if to call on them to testify to the violence of the other. One evening at a reception at

Joel Sayre's house, Estelle was so tipsy that the host suggested that Faulkner take her home and then come back, which he did. However, when he returned, he had horrific scratches on his cheeks and neck. Another time he arrived at the studio with a large bump on his forehead, and when asked what had happened, he replied that Estelle had hit him with a croquet mallet while he was reading a magazine.

In Hollywood, where she knew nobody, Estelle felt neglected. Faulkner started to play with fire, to take more and more risks, as if he had nothing left to lose and didn't care what might happen. He slipped out to meet Meta for lunch or dinner and their relationship resumed as before. At first Estelle knew nothing about it. But apparently Faulkner, for once, found it hard to live a lie, or maybe—and more likely—he wanted to cause a scene. Whatever the reason, he asked Meta to dinner one day to meet his wife. Wasson, in his role as go-between, was to introduce Meta as his own girlfriend. Wasson thought it was a "terrible idea" and he felt "a sense of betrayal" (CNC, 145). Meta was also very reluctant. But both eventually agreed to play the game.

Meta was expecting to meet a formidable rival but found instead "a small, gray wren of a woman in a nondescript dress" (ALG, 173). Meta was astonished. How could Faulkner have married such a dull, provincial woman? How could he have stayed with her for so long? "If she had ever been pretty—and she must have possessed some beauty to have attracted her first husband—she showed little trace of it now. Of the first impressions swirling in my mind, the discovery that she was a pale, sad, wasted creature was the most startling" (173). The portrait Meta later traced of Estelle in her memoirs was of a rare ferocity: "In spite of the years she had spent in the Orient, the stamp of a small Mississippi town was upon her—dress lacking in distinction, hair stringy and uncontrollable, the splotch of rouge and layering of powder on her face giving her a pasty look" (178).

Faulkner's dinner went off without incident. "Bill, a far better actor than Ben or I, mixed drinks with steady hands, as if my presence were of no moment at all" (ALG, 174). Dinner was served, and the man of the house seasoned the salad and carved the roast. The conversation was "unflaggingly mundane" (173). Why did Faulkner insist on bringing his wife and mistress together for an entire evening at the same table? Many years later Meta still wondered why Faulkner had done it. "Was it to feed a morbidity in his nature that even he could not fully understand?—was it to compare the two women?—was it to experience a sexual thrill by playing a dangerous game?—I have never decided" (173). One could continue to speculate on the motives for this perverse staging. Perhaps, without admitting it, Faulkner wanted the clash between Meta and Estelle to provoke an irreparable scandal. Or maybe it was simply a way of saying that he didn't want to give up either, that he wanted both Rowan Oak *and* Hollywood, a respectable family in Oxford *and* a young, beautiful mistress with whom to spend his weekends on the beaches of California.

The day after that strange evening, Estelle telephoned Wasson: "You did not fool me for a second, you and Billy. I know that the person you brought to my house last night is Billy's girl out here and not your girl at all! I know about that movie actress you're so crazy about. I don't appreciate it one bit your flinging his mistress right in my face, and all these years you've been like a member of our family!" (*CNC*, 149). She hung up. Sometime later Faulkner called Wasson to apologize: "'If Estelle called you up, I'm sorry. Ain't there something you can do to get her off my back?' he asked. He paused. 'Get her a lover, anything, so she'll leave me alone'" (149).

Estelle was a burden; she drove him up the wall. He loved Meta and confided in Wasson that he intended to marry her, but it is unlikely that he ever seriously considered leaving Estelle. It is true that he did eventually broach the subject of divorce with her. But Estelle wouldn't hear of it: "'You may have Miss Carpenter, but I shall keep your name until the day I die'" (*ALG*, 185). Faulkner did not dare go against her wishes and ultimately resigned himself. "'I've told you I had hope," he told Meta. "Now it's gone. I can't get free, Meta. I know now, I can't get free. Not for a long, long time'" (186). The case was closed: Meta would never be his wife. It is also possible that he gave up on the idea of divorce because he was worried about losing his daughter, Jill, or because he saw himself as the guardian of a sick woman, or, more prosaically, because he was frightened of the scandal a divorce would cause in Oxford.

Because he would not leave his wife, it was Meta who left him. The morning after this conversation, she decided to finish with Bill. "As I drove to the studio, I beseeched all the angels of heaven to give me the strength to prevail against my love for him" (*ALG*, 188). Meta had already been courted for some time by Wolfgang Rebner, a talented German pianist from a rich Jewish family in Frankfurt, the son of an Austrian violinist, and a student of Arthur Schnabel and Paul Hindemith. In September 1936 Rebner asked her to marry him. In December, Meta wrote to him to tell him she accepted his proposal and then announced her engagement. But Faulkner, a bad loser, used delaying tactics and tried to persuade Meta to sleep with him again, arguing that she didn't really know the man she was marrying, and that he was "'off somewhere, a thousand miles or more away'" (191). But Meta, who was not without principles, turned him down flat. A week later he pestered her so vehemently that she had an aunt come to "protect" her until the wedding. All Faulkner could do was drown his sorrows in alcohol and fight with his nagging wife. Two days before the wedding, at midnight, he came to see Meta, "haggard in the weak light, livid gashes caked with blood disfiguring his face" (194). "'Estelle's signature,'" he said. In a violent argument, Estelle had lacerated his face with her nails. "'I think she wanted to kill me, if not herself,'" he told Meta (194).

Meta and Wolfgang were married on April 5, 1937. On the day of the wedding, Faulkner got blind drunk and had to be admitted to the emergency room in Los Angeles to dry out. In the six weeks it took him to recover, he lost weight and thus left the hospital looking like a ghost, his hands trembling, unrecognizable. Meta was on her honeymoon in Europe. On the first of the three hundred copies of the limited edition of *Absalom, Absalom!* he wrote: "for Meta Carpenter, wherever she may be."

In August 1937 Fox told Faulkner that they would not be renewing his contract. The writer returned to Oxford but then went to New York in September; met up with old friends; fell in with Bennett Cerf and Robert Haas; and met Saxe Commins, one of Random House's great editors, who had already worked with Theodore Dreiser, Gertrude Stein, Eugene O'Neill, and other major writers, and who was to become a devoted and loyal friend to Faulkner until his death in 1958. But what kept Faulkner in New York for three weeks was primarily Meta, who was living there with her pianist husband. One evening his friend Jim Devine went looking for him, as Faulkner was no longer answering his telephone, and, after forcing open the door to his room in the Algonquin Hotel, found him unconscious in the bathroom, in his underwear. Soon after, Meta and her husband arrived; Faulkner had invited them to dinner. After waiting for him in the foyer, they had come up to his room and found him "lying naked on the bed, genitals in full evidence" (*ALG*, 223). Having drunk himself yet again into a stupor, Faulkner had fallen against a hot-water pipe in the bathroom and had received third-degree burns on his lower back. He told Meta that he had been drinking because the idea of seeing her that evening knowing that she now belonged to someone else was unbearable. When asked by the doctor why he had done it, he said, "Because I like to" (*B1*, 387). The next day, as if nothing had happened, he again invited Meta and Wolfgang to dinner. That evening he received them in his hotel room, in white shorts, naked to the waist and served them a soup "with all the aplomb of a man entertaining in his home" (*ALG*, 225). But his burns were still hurting, and, seeing him wincing with pain, Meta and Wolfgang decided to leave.

Their married life had not gotten off to a great start. In 1938 and 1939 all went badly for Wolfgang. After the *Anschluss* of Austria and the invasion of Czechoslovakia by the German army, several of his friends and family committed suicide in Vienna and he did everything he could to save his parents. His career as a concert pianist seemed in danger. He was sometimes asked to accompany great soloists such as Isaac Stern, Nathan Milstein, Ezio Pinz, or Emmanuel Feuermann. But in order to earn a living he was reduced to giving lessons. The couple's resources were dwindling, and their bank accounts were depleted; they had to rent a smaller apartment and sell Wolfgang's Steinway. This embittered him and he sometimes took it out on Meta. Their relationship was increasingly stormy and their domestic disputes were increasingly frequent. Meta confided in Faulkner. He sympathized moderately and reacted harshly when he saw her cry. "'Buck up, Carpenter,'" he said harshly. "'I've never seen you like this'" (*ALG*, 237). As she moved away from Wolfgang, Meta drew closer to Bill. They started seeing each other again every day, met for drinks at Faulkner's hotel, and he thought there would be nothing to stop Meta from becoming his mistress again if he so wanted.

He saw her again in New York in September 1938, when he was correcting the final galley proofs of *The Wild Palms*. After returning to Oxford, he received a panic-stricken note from Meta telling him that her marriage was over and that she needed money to go back to her parents in Arizona. The money—five hundred dollars, more than she needed—arrived the next day via Western Union, along with a message from Faulkner asking her to pass by Mississippi and arranging a date on the Louisiana state line. They decided to spend a few days together in New Orleans and went to a hotel in the French Quarter. But their reunion was brief. Faulkner was soon home in Oxford, and Meta, after resting for a while at her parents' home, went back to her husband in New York in April 1939.

Wolfgang and Meta tried to patch things up. In early 1940 they left for Hollywood. Wolfgang was to play piano in bars, and Meta found a job as a producer's assistant. But their marriage started to fall apart again. Meta wanted a divorce. Wolfgang left. They divorced in 1942. In July, Faulkner joined her in Hollywood. She writes in her memoirs: "One Saturday at dusk, I pulled my car up in front of my apartment and there was Bill sitting cross-legged in front of my door, his luggage stacked neatly on the steps" (*ALG*, 276). She had already been sending him tender, passionate letters for some time, and Meta herself, as she became more distant from Wolfgang, started pining for her former lover, feeling the need "to see Bill again, to feel the warmth of his skin under his shirt, to meet the heated gaze of the great brown eyes, to hear the voice that could be haunting only to another Southerner" (260). He had told her that he was coming back to Hollywood, but she hadn't believed him. Next thing, they were back at their favorite table at Musso & Frank's, celebrating their reunion. Five years had passed since they had first met. Faulkner was not entirely the same; Meta found that he had aged: "his hair, now almost completely gray, his moustache bristly and full, his eyes pouched. The last traces of the young man that I had seen in his face when I first looked at him long and searchingly had vanished; I could see lineaments now of middle age; that old guarded eagle look that would become more pronounced was already visible in the sharpness of his nose and the furrowing brows" (277). Although they were happy to see each other again, their love was not as ardent as before. As Meta wrote:

> We had resumed our relationship as though no time at all had passed, as though we were both unchanged by the passage of years, but almost at once we realized that it was not the same and could never again be as it was. Too much time had passed. Neither of us was what we had been. I was now my own woman, making my own way in the world, solving my problems; no longer credulous, untutored, capitulatory, I had outgrown gifts of puppy dogs and hair ribbons and rubber ducks for my bath. When I fell in love with Faulkner, I had the reasonable, if simple-hearted, expectation that we would eventually be married.

> Now I looked for nothing at all, asked for nothing at all, except his love and his emotional support. He was my lover, my rock; it was not enough, but I made it enough. (283)

It was the end of illusion. Meta had perhaps not entirely lost hers: since Jill was almost a teenager now, she hoped that Faulkner would no longer have any scruples about getting a divorce. However, he explained that it would be a serious mistake and showed no hesitation in bringing Estelle and Jill to Hollywood again in June 1944. When he told her they were coming, she was very upset:

> For the first time in our long relationship, I felt myself put upon cruelly, my most personal feelings wholly overlooked. No wonder Faulkner had delayed telling me of his decision. The inequity of it angered me. I wanted to shout at Bill, he to whom I had never raised my voice, that it was unfair, thoughtless, hurtful. Hollywood was my province with him! Estelle and Jill belonged to his life in Oxford! Why was Bill doing this to me—to us? I had the short end of the stick, the sweepings, the leavings. His wife and daughter had everything. Why did they have to intrude on my poor little piece of earth with Bill? (*ALG*, 301)

Meta felt betrayed, and so angry that she decided to break with him. "You just go your way from now on and let me go mine," she told him (303). But at the end of the summer, after Estelle and Jill had returned to Oxford, having learned that Faulkner had started drinking again and knowing that he was unhappy, she came to him and they met from time to time on the set where Hawks was filming *The Big Sleep*. But nothing was the same as before. Faulkner found Hollywood harder and harder to bear, and Meta knew he wouldn't stay for long. And, in fact, he returned to Oxford in 1945. They split up for a third time. Meta remarried Wolfgang three months later but divorced him again almost immediately.

From 1946 on Bill and Meta met less and less and their relationship started to fade, although Faulkner wrote to her in October 1948 that he still loved her and that she still haunted his nights. In his letter some of his thoughts about love echo *The Wild Palms*: "'I know grief is the inevitable part of it, the thing that makes it cohere; that grief is the only thing you are capable of sustaining, keeping; that what is valuable is what you have lost, since then you never had the chance to wear out and so lose it shabbily'" (*ALG*, 317). As with Quentin in *The Sound and the Fury* and Harry in *If I*

Forget Thee, Jerusalem, Faulkner was an incurable romantic who idealized and valued what was lost over what was real. The most important thing was to avoid sliding into the mediocrity of the day-to-day. And again in his letter, Faulkner quotes a phrase that Meta already knew by heart: "Between grief and nothing I will take grief" (*B1*, 509).

On his return from Stockholm, he wrote to Meta saying that he wanted to see her. On January 29, 1951, a letter came announcing his imminent arrival in Hollywood. Meta was impatient to see him again. She went to his room in the luxurious Beverly Carlton, and after five years apart they rekindled their affair, but only for a few snatched nights and weekends. On March 4, the day he left, Meta went with Faulkner to the airport. Before leaving her, he gave her a copy of *Notes on a Horsethief*, which had just been published, with the inscription: "This is for my beloved." They promised to meet again before the end of the year, but the promise was not kept: other women had already come into his life, and when he left Meta, it was to see Joan Williams, a Memphis student he had met in 1949 and with whom he had fallen in love. And Else Jonsson, his new Swedish girlfriend, was waiting for him in Paris.

They would continue to write each other, often. Meta would remain one of his confidantes until the end. In 1952, when he was very ill, he wrote to her: "'I could spend about two weeks with you, lying on my face with the sun on my back. That would do more good than anything'" (*ALG*, 323). But they never saw each other again.

NOTES

1. This letter is not included in the 1974 edition of the Blotner biography or in *Selected Letters*, published in 1977.

2. Jill Faulkner Summers in an interview with Judith L. Sensibar, quoted in *Faulkner and the Craft of Fiction*, ed. Doreen Fowler and Ann J. Abadie (Jackson: University Press of Mississippi, 1989), 139.

3. Jill Faulkner Summers in an interview with Jay Parini in 2003. See Parini, *One Matchless Time: A Life of William Faulkner* (New York: Harper Collins, 2004), 130.

4. Letter from William Faulkner to Estelle Faulkner, October 1931, Faulkner Collection, Alderman Library, University of Virginia. Letter cited by Stephen B. Oates in *William Faulkner*, 140.

5. Malcolm A. Franklin, *Bitterweeds: Life with William Faulkner at Rowan Oak* (Irving, TX: Society for the Study of Traditional Culture, 1977), 21.

6. The rowan oak or mountain ash was alleged to banish evil spirits and provide safety. James Frazer's *The Golden Bough* probably gave him the idea for the house's name.

7. Letter from Saxe Commins to his wife, Fall 1952, *Faulkner: A Comprehensive Guide to the Brodsky Collection*, 90.

8. See Estelle's interview dated November 30, 1931, in *LG*, 26.

9. Letter from Phil Stone to Robert Coughlan, dated October 10, 1952, *Guide to the Brodsky Collection*, ed. Louis Daniel Brodsky and Robert W. Hamblin. Vol. 2: *The Letters* (Jackson: University Press of Mississippi, 1984), 92.

10. Arnold Bennett, "American Authors 'made' in England," *Evening Standard*, June 26, 1930.

11. *Letters of Sherwood Anderson*, edited by Howard M. Jones and Walter B. Rideout (Boston: Little, Brown, 1953), 252.

12. Robert Coughlan, *The Private Life of William Faulkner* (1954; New York: Cooper Square, 1972), 104–105.

13. Interview with Jill Faulkner Summers quoted by Jay Parini in *One Matchless Time*, 251.

14. Jill Faulkner Summers in an interview quoted in Parini, *One Matchless Time*, 217.

15. Herman Melville, *The Writings of Herman Melville: Correspondence*, edited by Lynn Horth (Evanston, IL: Northwestern University Press, 1993), 191.

16. See Edward Jay Epstein, *The Big Picture: Money and Power in Hollywood* (New York: Random House, 2006), 278.

17. "Interview with Stephen Longstreet," by Louis Daniel Brodsky, in *Stallion Road* (Jackson: University Press of Mississippi, 1989), xxvi.

18. Interview with Ben Hecht, Columbia University Oral History Collection, 713.

19. See "Roman américain et cinéma," in *L'Age du roman américain* (Paris: Editions du Seuil, 1948), 11–113.

6
FROM *PYLON* TO
GO DOWN, MOSES

THE HELL OF FASCINATION: *PYLON*

Throughout his Hollywood years Faulkner continued to write with a rare perseverance. Between 1935 and 1942 he published more than twenty short stories and six novels: *Pylon, Absalom, Absalom!, The Unvanquished, The Wild Palms, The Hamlet,* and *Go Down, Moses.*

In *Pylon*, his eighth, he returns to one of his great passions—flight, aviation, and airmen—which had fascinated him since adolescence as the noble conquerors of the sky and the last adventurers of the modern world, and which had stimulated his writerly imagination since "Landing in Luck," his very first short story to be published. Fighter pilots had already featured in *Soldiers' Pay* and *Flags in the Dust*, "Honor" (1930), "All the Dead Pilots" (1931), "Ad Astra" (1932), "Death Race" (1932), "Turn About" (1932), and in two of his short stories written in the 1930s—"Honor" and "Death Race"—the protagonists were those acrobats of the air known as barnstormers.

Finally fulfilling a dream he had cherished for over fifteen years, Faulkner took some flying lessons in Memphis in February 1933 with Captain Vernon Omlie, a veteran of World War I, and even before getting his pilot's license he bought a single-seater Waco 210 with the money from the film rights for *Sanctuary*. One of the few photographs in which Faulkner looks happy shows him in a white linen shirt and pants, his necktie nonchalantly tucked between two buttons on his shirt, smiling radiantly in front of his Waco.[1] On April 20, 1933, he made his first solo flight, even though he still didn't have a license. In the following months he would make many more, and as he gained in experience and assurance, he often took family members up with him   including little Jill, who was just three months old, to the vexation of Estelle's doctor, who was worried about the baby's eardrums. These flights were risky, all the more so because Faulkner was not, and never would be, a decent pilot. In late September 1933 he had his first accident, overturning after a failed landing. Nonetheless, on December 14, 1933, he obtained his pilot's license.

By January 1934 he had accumulated six and a half hours of flying time. In February he flew with Omlie to New Orleans to take part in the events, races, and air displays being held to celebrate the inauguration of an airport named after Colonel A. L. Shushan, which had just been built on the shores of Lake Pontchartrain. On the fourteenth, the day before they arrived, an airplane crash-landed, killing its pilot; other fatal accidents occurred over the following days as well. In the fall of 1934 Faulkner himself, along with his brother Dean and Omlie, sponsored an air show in Markette Field, a few miles south of Oxford.

In April 1934 he wrote "This Kind of Courage," a short story inspired by what he had seen a few weeks earlier in New Orleans, but no magazine wanted to publish it. He therefore decided to turn it into a novel. On October 18, 1934, he asked his agent, Morton Goldman, to send him back the text of the short story right away (*SL*, 85).

This novel would become *Pylon*. He wrote it quickly in the fall of 1934, in less than two months, between mid-October and mid-December. Only *As I Lay Dying*, his first "tour de force," had been written at a similar pace. Contrary to his usual practice, Faulkner barely reviewed the typescript, replacing only a few dirty words with ellipses, and sent the seven chapters of his new novel to Harrison Smith between November 11 and December 11, as and when he had completed them. The first galley proofs were ready by early January. *Pylon* was published on March 25, 1935.

What attracted and intrigued Faulkner in the barnstormers was their fragile, feverish marginality:

> They were ephemera and phenomena on the face of a contemporary scene. That is there was really no place for them in the culture, in the economy, yet they were there, at that time, and everyone knew that they wouldn't last very long, which they didn't. That time of those frantic little aeroplanes which dashed

around the country and people wanted just enough money to live, to get to the next place to race again. Something frenetic and in a way almost immoral about it. That they were outside the range of God, not only of respectability, of love, but of God too. That they had escaped the compulsion of accepting a past and a future, that they were—they had no past. They were as ephemeral as the butterfly that's born this morning with no stomach and will be gone tomorrow. (*FU*, 36)

Pylon is obviously the fictional transposition of his experience of that world. He may have changed the place-names, but it is easy to recognize New Orleans in the narrow streets, paved courtyards, and wrought-iron balconies of New Valois, Lake Pontchartrain in Lake Rambaud, and Louisiana in Franciana. The story of the inauguration of the fictional Feinman Airport clearly draws on his memories of the inauguration of Shushan Airport; the air show described by Faulkner differs little from what he had seen in New Orleans; and the incidents and accidents related in the novel, including the accidental death of the pilot Shumann, whose airplane plunges into a lake, correspond to actual events relayed by the local press. Similarly, the streets invaded by crowds of onlookers and revelers celebrating Mardi Gras, the carnival floats, masks, streamers, and confetti littering the sidewalks—all of these are taken from remembrances that were still quite fresh.

From his memories, Faulkner could have written a documentary novel in the realist tradition. *Pylon* describes and deconstructs a merchant society, with its exploiters, its exploited, and its excluded, and Faulkner does not fail to check off the implacable economic forces that operated even into show business. The air acrobats survive only by ceaselessly risking their lives. They have no choice. As Jiggs so eloquently puts it: "Burn to death on Thursday night or starve to death on Friday morning" (*N2*, 813). Along with *If I Forget Thee, Jerusalem*, *Pylon* is the novel that deals the most with money and where lack of money most often turns to obsession. The story starts with a haggling over a pair of boots, ends with a note from a reporter to his boss asking him for "some jack" (992), and contains in all more than sixty financial transactions.

However, *Pylon* is not a realistic novel, as is evident from any page. The writing is frustrated baroque. Unwieldy and overly wordy in both dialogue and description, saturated with unusual comparisons and metaphors, it resolutely proclaims itself as a rhetoric of excess and, right up to its chapter titles, flaunts its links with Shakespeare, Joyce, and T. S. Eliot. Nowhere else (except perhaps in Rosa Coldfield's extravagant monologue in chapter 5 of *Absalom, Absalom!* and certain pages of *The Hamlet*) does Faulkner's prose crumble so much under the weight of rare terms and polysyllabic words, often produced by joining words together and sometimes compressed into Joycean portmanteau words. One also cannot help but be struck by the singularity of the layout, by the variations in typography; the profusion of texts within the texts; and their highlighting by capital letters, use of italic and bold type, and varying spacing distances. These texts—photograph captions; mimeographed poster programs of the airport's inauguration day; notes to pilots and parachutists taking part in the air displays; newspaper headlines; and, toward the end, two articles and a handwritten post-scriptum by a journalist—could have been used to reinforce the referential illusion, but in *Pylon* they rarely fulfill this function, particularly because they are most often truncated or reduced to jumbles of barely intelligible words. Rather than authenticate the text, they prevent the narration from running straight, point to the arbitrariness of its crafting, and reflect the text back on its textuality.

Despite all of this, this text more or less shapes the story into quite a simple narrative taking place over the course of four days. Roger Shumann, the daredevil airman; Jack Holmes, the parachutist; Laverne, the girl with whom both are romantically involved; Jack, the little boy who could be either Shumann's or Holmes's; and a mechanic named Jiggs, have all just arrived in New Valois, where Shumann and Holmes are to take part in an air show to celebrate the opening of a new airport. Because he needs the money, Shumann is going to fly an old crate that everyone knows is extremely dangerous. And, of course, the dreaded catastrophe happens: the airplane crashes into a lake, killing Shumann. Widowed now and pregnant again, Laverne leaves with her lover, Jack, after leaving her son with Shumann's father in a small town in Ohio.

Pylon tells a story, but the narrative is one of confusion rather than order. As often in Faulkner's fiction, time stands still on its head, cancels itself out as succession. From the start, the reader is struck by the use of time shifts and derealization. References to the world of show business (pantomime, comedy, music hall, circus, and cinema) and of imagery (photographs, caricatures, lithographs, postcards, and comic strips) abound. When we see the reporter and Jiggs together, they remind us of "the tall and the short man of the orthodox and unfailing comic team" (N2, 812) or of "a tableau reminiscent [...] of the cartoon pictures of city anarchists" (829). The scene of the action is converted into theater sets, spaces for performance and illusion, starting with the town carnival, the earthbound festival of Mardi Gras taking place alongside the air show where the airmen perform their feats and risk their lives. A world of show business, of ghosts, that ends in phantasmagoria, New Valois is a labyrinthine town with underground and underwater depths, an "unreal city" such as depicted by T. S. Eliot in *The Waste Land*—duplicated and canceled out by its inverted image, just like the French pilot's upturned airplane during the show: "Perhaps it was the bilious aspect of an inverted world seen through a hooded lens or emerging in grimacing and attitudinal miniature from stinking trays in a celibate and stygian cell lighted by a red lamp" (933).

The characters, apparently, are taking off from reality. They have no separate identity, barely a "psychology"; they are first and foremost roles that are being played. They are almost like actors in a 1930s Hollywood production, with Holmes, the handsome parachutist with the thin mustache and effeminate features, playing the role of the young lead, and Laverne, the woman with maize-colored hair, that of a Jean Harlow–like vamp. There is hardly any character who is not subjected to this almost caricatural typecasting: Jiggs the mechanic is a "cartoon comedy centaur" (N2, 961); the capitalist Feinman comes complete with double-breasted suit, rings, and cigar (927); and the assured elegance of the airport speaker is reminiscent of Hollywood Avenue (795). The characters wear themselves out and disappear into their roles. Their masks serve as faces. These are indeed Faulkner characters in that nothing can dispel the enigma of their impenetrability.

The world in *Pylon* is a world of performance. From the opening words, the novel sets the scene as Jiggs stares covetously at a handsome pair of boots on display in a store window. Other scenes are built on the same model, such as the one at the end of the novel, after Shumann's fatal accident, when Laverne is targeted by reporters: "the faces pressed to the glass and looking in at her where she sat on one of the backless stools at the counter between a policeman and one of the mechanics" (N2, 946). From fetish to female and from female to fetish, this beating of desire arouses *fascination*, which is perhaps the main impulse and deep subject of this novel.

Jiggs, the drunken mechanic, is the first victim of this fascination, soon followed by the reporter tasked by his newspaper to report on the air show. The first time that this plainly unbelievable character appears in the novel, he is portrayed not as a person, but rather as "something which had apparently crept from a doctor's cupboard and, in the snatched garments of an etherized patient in a charity ward, escaped into the living world" (*N2*, 788). His appearances throughout the novel give rise to macabre comparisons, likening him to a corpse, a skeleton, a scarecrow, a bat, a ghost, a shadow, or Lazarus risen from the dead. He seems scarcely to even have a face, skin, or a body, and he does not seem to have any civil status: "a creature who apparently never had any parents either and who will not be old and never was a child, who apparently sprang full-grown and irrevocably mature out of some violent and instantaneous transition like the stories of dead steamboatmen and mules" (802). Moreover, the reader never finds out his name (in an interview, Faulkner even declared that he didn't know it himself, and we learn only that the mere mention of it provokes incredulous laughter). The son of nobody, the man from nowhere, without future or origin, the reporter is only a restless shadow of a man. However, he is the indispensable *witness*. As Jean Pouillon has remarked: "Nothing happens to him, everything happens to others."[2] If he didn't get mixed up in things that were none of his business, there would be no tale to tell, no story to write.

The reporter's eyes are in turn compared to "holes burned with a poker in a parchment diploma" (*N2*, 866) and "two spots of dying daylight caught by water at the bottom of abandoned wells" (867). The reporter has dead eyes. More precisely, he is nothing more than a look. This look is funny at first, with its "amazed quiet immobility" (788); then "a curious glazed expression" (828); and, finally, the empty stare of one who is comatose or dying: "sprawled in the door with his eyes open and quiet and profoundly empty—that vision without contact yet with mind or thought, like two dead electric light bulbs set into his skull" (858). It is the story of a look, therefore, and its extinguishings and surprises, its mistakes and miscalculations; the story of an eye hole that nothing can fill, that does not see what it looks at, that does not look at what it sees. Reality comes to him like a hallucination, dazzles him like a mirage.

Everything in *Pylon* is played, won or lost in the increasingly tense and ambiguous relationship between the reporter and the quartet of aviators.

And yet the reporter initially denies them any humanity: "Because they aint human like us; they couldn't turn those pylons like they do if they had human blood and senses and they wouldn't want to or dare to if they just had human brains. Burn them like this one tonight and they dont even holler in the fire; crash one and it aint even blood when you haul him out: it's cylinder oil the same as in the crankcase" (N2, 804). The reporter reiterates this denial of humanity almost word for word at the end of the fifth chapter: "They aint human. It aint adultery; you cant anymore imagine two of them making love than you can two of them aeroplanes back in the corner of the hangar, coupled. [. . .] Yair; cut him and it's cylinder oil; dissect him and it aint bones: it's little rockerarms and connecting rods" (933). The reporter is mistaken. The novelist, at least, has no trouble imagining them making love. Proof of this can be seen in the long scene, both sublime and grotesque, that describes in close-up Shumann and Laverne having sex midair before she makes a parachute jump above a small Kansas town, where, as soon as she touches the ground, her dress in tatters, almost naked, she is pursued by a yelling mob of overexcited men (908–909). The fact that the reporter repeats the same thoughts is all the more astonishing because since his first meeting with Shumann and his comrades he has had the time to discover their vulnerable humanity. Far from rejecting them, he approaches them, becomes attached to them, tries to help them, and eventually brings them back to his room, moved, it seems, "put in motion [. . .] by the sheer solid weight of their patient and homeless passivity" (828). He also falls hopelessly in love with the inaccessible Laverne. Is it because she does not want him, because she looks at him "with pale blank complete unrecognition" (816) that he persists in seeing them as merely robots?

The lack of humanity comes from the reporter and his voyeuristic readers rather than the aviators. His role in this affair is more than seedy, his generosity more than suspect. It is the reporter who provides Shumann with the airplane in which he is going to die—he is the one who signs Shumann's death warrant. Shumann's tragic death is the coup de théâtre without which the performance would lose its power to stun and seduce. It is the end and the climax of the show; it does not transcend it. For the reporter and for the crowd, it is in itself a show and nothing but a show, although he was the primary agent of its staging and will be its most attentive spectator. The space of the air race around the pylon then becomes, in a singular short-circuit of reality and imagination, a giant screen where his fantasies are projected, the theater where the apotheosis of his heroic dream of flight is accomplished by proxy at the same time his envied rival is ritually killed. In *Pylon* death is what is at stake at the beginning of the show, and it also becomes its final truth.

The reporter, a spectral figure, symbolizes this, and it is he who writes the hero's funerary oration. At first, Shumann's death seems to inspire him: "He could not feel his fingers on the keys either: he just watched the letters materialize out of thin air, black sharp and fast, along the creeping yellow" (*N2*, 982). But the outpouring of letters and words is deceptive; what inspires the reporter is not the stuff of inspiration. In the evening a young copyboy finds an "astonishing amount of savagely defaced and torn copy" strewn about the floor and the reporter's desk (990–91). He gathers them up, sorts them, and salvages "the sentences and paragraphs which he believed to be not only news but the beginning of literature" (991). Then, in the newspaper editor's office, he finds another text, more in line with the norms of obituary writing, the version that will be published. Two texts ("reproduced" in the novel): one "literary," the other journalistic. Both are mediocre. Poor literature, lifeless journalism. Once again, words fail to convey the violence of reality. But never mind! As the paper's editor, Hagood, has already explained, journalism has nothing to do with literature: "The people who own this paper or who direct its policies or anyway who pay the salaries [. . .] have no Lewises or Hemingways or even Tchekovs on the staff: one very good reason doubtless being that they do not want them, since what they want is not fiction, not even Nobel Prize fiction, but news" (808). Biased, misleading news, perhaps, but the demands of both owners and readers will have been satisfied.

After all of his misadventures and mishaps, the reporter has not learned how to live or write. A ghost adrift, he has not finished wandering in the badlands of the imagination. In the enraged postscript that ends the novel, he announces that he is going to a brothel to get drunk—returning to alcohol and to the maternal home, the madam's house, where a bevy of Lavernes wait to keep him company for a fistful of dollars. As for Horace Benbow at the end of *Sanctuary*, the journey through hell ends for him in a quest for oblivion and the derision of impotence.

Yet another "story full of sound and fury told by an idiot," *Pylon* is a novel where signs are both inflated and broken down. The urban space is marked out, saturated with inscriptions and instructions, and a space where an entire public discourse is disgorged, relayed, and amplified by the press and advertising—tentacular media ceaselessly referenced by repeated allusions to newspaper headlines, posters, and billboards announcing the air show. Signs and signals of the modern town, stereotyped, standardized, and so easy to decipher in their banality that they become insignificant. They are printed everywhere, crisscrossing the entire space, but it is as if their very proliferation has deprived them of all meaning. This novel contains an over-abundance of adjectives with negative prefixes or suffixes: "incomprehensible," "impenetrable," "inscrutable," "illegible." Through their hammered repetitions, a world is drawn that is both opaque and absurd.

With its fictional detours and rhetorical devices, *Pylon* offers us a commentary on the threefold failure of seeing, writing, and speaking. What is shown here is not so much that they coincide but that they are defective in that looking cannot appropriate the visible any more than reading can appropriate the legible, and writing itself is a merely a tenuous net stretched over an abyss of illegibility. In this feverish, disordered novel the same movement blinds the signs and opens them out, ready for deciphering.

The reaction to *Pylon* held little surprise, as reviewers' complaints resembled closely those about Faulkner's previous books. In the *New Republic* Malcolm Cowley deplored its gratuitous horror and violence. In *New Masses*, the great Marxist magazine of the 1930s, as was to be expected, Granville Hicks attacked the sensationalism of a "bourgeois" author, which he had also criticized in *Sanctuary*. The Irish novelist Seán Ó Faoláin, on the other hand, writing in the *Spectator*, hailed Faulkner as one of the best American writers of the day, and William Troy, in the *Nation*, deemed *Pylon* to be his best novel. Finally, Hemingway, who had already praised *Sanctuary* highly, said in the June issue of *Esquire* that he had read and admired the new novel.

Faulkner himself did not think highly of *Pylon*. For him, this novel was a diversion and a detour: "I wrote that book because I'd got in trouble with *Absalom, Absalom!* and I had to get away from it for a while so I thought a good way to get away from it was to write another book, so I wrote *Pylon*" (*FU*, 36). A shadow of a book under way, a book yet to appear, *Pylon* is not the most daring or innovative of Faulkner's novels, but it is the most extravagant. It could be said that in his career *Pylon* was the first setback, the first failure, but failures, as we know, like Freudian slips, rarely happen by chance and are sometimes much more telling than the most dazzling successes.

Pylon is one of the rare Faulkner novels to have been made into a film. In 1957–1958, over twenty years after it was published, the novel was adapted under the title *The Tarnished Angels* by Douglas Sirk, a Hollywood filmmaker who was admired by Truffaut and Fassbinder. It starred Rock Hudson, Robert Stack, Dorothy Malone, and Jack Carson and is a fine film noir such as those still being made in Hollywood at the end of the 1950s, scarcely spoiled by its barely believable happy ending.

———

Strangely, *Pylon* was also an ill omen, a prophet of doom, in Faulkner's life. Scarcely eight months after it was published, on Sunday, November 10, 1935, in the Waco 210 that Faulkner had sold him (for a derisory sum), Dean, his youngest brother, the one to whom he was closest, crashed near Thaxton, Mississippi, with three passengers on board. There were no survivors. As soon as he heard about the accident, Faulkner went straight to the crash site, accompanied by his mother and Dean's young wife, Louise. The wreckage was still smoldering in the field, but the mutilated bodies of Dean and his passengers—young farmers whom he had taken up to give them an aerial view of their properties—had already been brought to a funeral parlor in Pontotoc.

After sending his mother and sister-in-law back to Oxford, Faulkner went to the funeral home to help a mortuary makeup artist reconstruct his brother's mutilated body and face (using a photo of Dean), to make the corpse more presentable before the funeral. This macabre task haunted his nights for many long months. According to Louise, Dean's widow:

> Oh, I think it was the worst thing that ever happened in his [Faulkner's] life. [...] I remember one morning we were eating breakfast, just the two of us, and I said, "Oh, I didn't sleep last night, I had such horrible dreams." And he said, "Did you dream about the accident?" I said, "Yes, I did, I dreamed it all over." And he said, "Love, I have done it every night since it happened." (*LP*, 82)

The funeral took place on November 11, the day of the armistice of World War I. Dean was buried in St. Peter's Cemetery in Oxford. On his gravestone Faulkner had the following inscription engraved: "I bare him on eagles' wings, and brought him unto myself," an epitaph borrowed from Exodus 19:4,[3] which he had already used for John Sartoris in *Flags in the Dust*.

For Faulkner, Dean's death was more than the loss of a beloved younger brother. Added to the distress of grief felt by all the family, he was tormented by a guilt that was his alone. It was he who had encouraged Dean to become a pilot, he who had paid for his flying lessons, and it was because of him that Dean had ended up an air acrobat like Roger Shumann in *Pylon*. It was as if Faulkner had wanted to realize his own dreams as a young man, belatedly and by proxy. And Dean, not yet thirty, had died in his stead.

THE NOVEL AS RESEARCH: *ABSALOM, ABSALOM!*

In February 1934 Faulkner wrote to Harrison Smith that he had set aside the two books he had been working on—the Snopes novel and *Requiem for a Nun*—in order to start on a historical novel:

> It is the more or less violent breakup of a household or family from 1860 to about 1910. It is not as heavy as it sounds. The story is an anecdote which occurred during and right after the civil war; the climax is another anecdote which happened about 1910 and which explains the story. Roughly, the theme is a man who outraged the land, and the land then turned and destroyed the man's family. Quentin Compson, of *The Sound and the Fury*, tells it, or ties it together; he is the protagonist so that it is not complete apocrypha. I use him because it is just before he is to commit suicide because of his sister, and I use his bitterness which he has projected on the South in the form of hatred of it and its people to get more out of the story itself than a historical novel. To keep the hoop skirts and plug hats out, you might say. (*SL*, 78–79)

On February 11, 1934, he did indeed start work on a new novel, which he initially called "Dark House," a title he had previously considered for *Light in August*. But as we know, beginnings, with Faulkner, are always *fresh* beginnings, and none of his texts is without antecedents. The "primitive scene" of the novel—the scene of the door barred to the child messenger—had already been sketched out in "The Big Shot," a short story written around 1926, and in "Dull Tale," another version of the same story. Two other short stories—"Evangeline," probably written in July 1931, which he reworked in 1934 and remained unpublished until 1979, and "Wash," written in the fall of 1933 and published in *Harper's* in February 1934—had already featured the Sutpen family. "Evangeline" was the first to tell the tragic story of Colonel Thomas Sutpen's three children; "Wash" related the colonel's murder by his most faithful servant.

It took Faulkner two years to write *Absalom, Absalom!*, longer than his previous novels. He first put it aside in the spring of 1934 to write short stories as a writer for hire on the Civil War and Reconstruction, stories he later reused in *The Unvanquished*. In August he wrote to Harrison Smith:

> I believe that the book is not quite ripe yet; that I have not gone my nine months, you might say. I do have to put it aside and make a nickel every so often, but I think there must be more than that. I have a mass of stuff, but only one chapter that suits me; I am considering putting it aside and going back to REQUIEM FOR A NUN, which will be a short one, like AS I LAY DYING, while the present one will probably be longer than LIGHT IN AUGUST. I have a title for it which I like, by the way: ABSALOM, ABSALOM; the story is of a man who wanted a son through pride, and got too many of them and they destroyed him. (*SL*, 83–84)

But instead of returning to *Requiem*, Faulkner wrote *Pylon*. As soon as the novel was published, in March 1935, armed with his new title, borrowed from the Bible's book of Kings,[4] he went back to work on what was to become the final manuscript of *Absalom, Absalom!* The pages mounted up, but everything had to be rewritten. "I almost rewrote the whole thing," Faulkner remembered in 1957. "I think that what I put down were inchoate fragments that wouldn't coalesce and then when I took it up again, as I remember, I rewrote it" (*FU*, 76). In November, after Dean's death, he redoubled his efforts, writing at night by candlelight at the dining room table, while his mother and Louise, Dean's widow, slept in their rooms. It was as if hard work could ease the pain of grief. On December 4 he wrote to Goldman: "I am working like hell now. The novel is pretty good and I think another month will see it done. Needless to say, I have written no short stories nor contemplated such nor [will I] do so until after the novel" (*SL*, 93). However, he would not have the leisure to finish it at home. On the tenth he had to go back to California. He spent five weeks in Hollywood, continuing to work on his novel early in the morning before going to the studio. On January 13, 1936, when he left Hollywood, the manuscript was more or less finished. But the text had still not found its definitive form. After returning to Oxford, Faulkner took it up again but wasn't able to finish the task, as another drinking binge forced him to sign into a clinic to dry out. After his return to Rowan Oak, he went back to work on it, and on January 31, 1936, the manuscript was finally completed.

But the novel was not quite ready for publication. Between late February and early June, Faulkner, back in Hollywood, typed up the text and, as was his wont, made copious changes in the process. In May he wrote the chronology and genealogy sections, placed at the end of the novel. Back in Rowan Oak, he drew his fine map of Yoknapatawpha, which would be inserted in the form of a foldout in all copies of the first edition.

In July, again in Hollywood, he read and corrected the galley proofs. *Absalom, Absalom!* came out three months later, on October 26, 1936. It was published by Random House, which would remain his publisher until the end.

———

With *Absalom, Absalom!* Faulkner was again reaching for the heights. His writing is reinvigorated and expansive; with it he achieved the height of his inventiveness. The novel retraces the rise and fall of Thomas Sutpen, a rich Southern planter and slave owner before the Civil War. The story is of a cursed lineage, similar to that of the Labacides or the Atrides. It is the story of a dynasty, or rather a dynastic dream barely born and already dead. It is the cautionary tale "of a man who outraged the land, and the land then turned and destroyed his family," or again in the author's words, "of a man who wanted a son through pride, and got too many of them and they destroyed him" (*SL*, 84). Dominating the novel, the haughty, enigmatic Sutpen is portrayed as an adventurer from a race of conquerors and empire builders. However, his ambition is primarily a humiliated child's dream of revenge. The son of poor whites from the mountains of West Virginia, he had been prevented by a "monkey nigger" in livery from crossing the threshold of a planter's house to whom his father had sent him to convey a message: "he never even remembered what the nigger said, how it was the nigger told him, even before he had had time to say what he came for, never to come to that front door again but to go around the back" (*N3*, 192). This was his first experience, simple but startling, of *power* and the conditions under which it is exercised: how one man must do what another tells him. The experience is all the harsher because the other is only telling him what another told him to say. As he later tells Quentin's grandfather, Sutpen could not leave it at that: "He knew that something would have to be done about it; he would have to do something about it in order to live with himself for the rest of his life" (193). So, after much thinking, he comes up with his grand design: he will not avenge the offense by punishing the offender but will instead become as like him as possible, become a planter himself, build a big house, found a dynasty, leave behind descendants who look like him, in a purely masculine line where the father indefinitely re-engenders himself in his sons, where the other is the endless replica of oneself.

Sutpen starts by going to Haiti, where he marries the daughter of a French planter and has a son, repudiating them both when he finds out (or thinks he does; nothing is certain) that his wife is of mixed race. Years later, on a Sunday in June 1833, he shows up in Jefferson, coming from God knows where, accompanied by a band of wild blacks. He sets up camp on some wasteland and little by little acquires what is to become his estate, "Sutpen's Hundred"; builds a house; and marries Ellen Coldfield, daughter of Goodhue Coldfield, a respectable small merchant from Jefferson, who bears him a son, Henry, and a daughter, Judith. When the Civil War breaks out, he replaces Colonel Sartoris at the head of his regiment and fights valiantly. After the defeat of the Confederate Army, he returns to find his plantation in ruins. Henry has fled, Judith has been widowed before becoming a bride, and his wife is dead. Sutpen's dream is shattered, but he is not yet ready to give up. He proposes to Rosa, his young sister-in-law, but stipulates that she must first bear him a son. When Rosa refuses the abhorrent deal, he impregnates Milly, granddaughter of the loyal Wash Jones. Milly has a daughter. "Well Milly, too bad you're not a mare too. Then I could give you a decent stall in the stable" (N3, 236), he tells her. Upon this final insult, Wash kills Sutpen with a scythe and then cuts the throat of the mother and infant before setting the cabin on fire, after which he is killed by the sheriff.

The story of Thomas Sutpen is that of a man driven to his own downfall by willful blindness, by what the Greeks called *hubris* or *hamartia* and which Quentin's father and grandfather ironically call his indestructible "innocence." It is a tragedy, if you will, in which—through biblical curse or Greek fatality—the sequence of events follows an inexorable course, but it is also one where the main protagonist is no tragic hero. While Sutpen is the author of his own misfortune, he ascribes his failures to a simple error of calculation, entrenched to the end in his paranoid delusion and inflexible will to dominate, equally blind to others and to himself until the final defeat.

But *Absalom, Absalom!* is perhaps even more the tragic story of his offspring: his white children, Henry and Judith, legitimate and acknowledged; Charles, the child (possibly mixed race; his black lineage is as hypothetical as that of Christmas) of his first marriage, whom Sutpen refused to acknowledge as his son; and Clytie (short for "Clytemnestra" one of the great heroines of *The Oresteia*, already discreetly alluded to in the title of *As I Lay Dying*), his illegitimate "black" daughter. Henry, Judith, and Charles are actors in a mad, monstrous, and murderous love triangle. Henry loves Judith narcissistically, as Quentin loves Caddy in *The Sound and the Fury*: "the two of them, brother and sister, curiously alike as if the difference in sex had merely sharpened the common blood to a terrific, an almost unbearable, similarity" (*N3*, 142–43). To complete their union, to consummate their incest, he needs a double, an intercessor: the attractive Charles Bon. Henry meets him at college, unaware that he is his half brother, and is so enthralled by his new friend that he imitates him in everything and wants to make him his brother-in-law by giving him Judith. It would be "pure and perfect incest: the brother realizing that the sister's virginity must be destroyed in order to have existed at all, taking that virginity in the person of the brother-in-law, the man whom he would be if he could become, metamorphose into, the lover, the husband; by whom he would be despoiled, choose for despoiler, if he could become, metamorphose into the sister, the mistress, the bride" (80). Because of the incestuous fantasy of Henry, who is the legitimate son, Charles, the disowned son, enters the forbidden house of his father.

To prevent the planned marriage between Charles and Judith, all Sutpen would have to do is admit that Charles is his elder son, but acknowledging him would compromise his grand "design." Therefore, he opposes the marriage without being able to reveal the reasons for his opposition. However, he eventually reveals to Henry, first, that Charles is his half brother and then, in a final meeting, that he has black blood. Henry can willingly accommodate an incestuous relationship, but he cannot allow his sister to marry someone of mixed race. When Charles challenges him—"I'm the nigger that's going to sleep with your sister. Unless you stop me, Henry"

(*N3*, 294)—he prefers fratricide to the sullying of the bloodline and kills Charles on the edge of the estate. From then on, tragedy follows its inexorable course to the fall of the House of Sutpen. The ultimate irony is that Sutpen's will shall be done, his wishes fulfilled, as Theseus's prayers are met in *Phaedra*. Charles has had a son with an octoroon, whom Judith takes in at the age of twelve. This son, Charles Etienne Saint-Valery Bon, who, like Christmas in *Light in August*, could easily pass for a white man, proclaims himself a negro, constantly provokes and causes scandal, and ends up impregnating a negress as black as coal and as ugly as sin, who bears him a retarded son named Jim. In September 1909, on the night when Miss Rosa and Quentin visit Thomas Sutpen's dilapidated house, they find there Jim, Clytie, and Henry, sick and in hiding. Three months later Clytie sets fire to the house. In the final scene, the only survivor, Sutpen's last descendant, forty years after his death, is Jim Bond, Charles Bon's grandson, an "idiot negro" prowling around the ashes of the burned-out house and screaming, like Benjy at the end of *The Sound and the Fury*.

This is, in a nutshell (and hence unduly simplified), the story of the Sutpens. To summarize it is to misrepresent it. Not only is it impossible to summarize, but the entire novel seems to have been written to prove that it is riddled with so many uncertainties that it cannot even be told. It is, quite simply, untellable. Faulkner could have tried to tell a linear, conventionally crafted story. Instead, he opted for confusion and did everything to preserve the enigma.

The narrative thread in *Absalom, Absalom!* is so bewilderingly complex that Faulkner saw fit to balance his novel with a chronology, a genealogy, and a map. The tale is as tangled as they come. Rather than trace a line to be followed, rather than begin at the beginning and wend its way to a conclusion, it goes around in circles, wraps around itself, tangles its threads, comes undone, and slips away indefinitely. Ellipses, redundancies, and anachronisms abound. In the initial pages of the novel, the tale Rosa tells Quentin has not yet started when the entire history of the Sutpens is given a brief summary (*N3*, 6–14). Similarly, the meeting arranged by Rosa between Quentin and Henry in the secret room in the Sutpen house, related in the final pages of the novel, is signaled at the end of chapter V, with Rosa revealing to Quentin: "There's something in that house [. . .]. Something living in it. Hidden in it. It has been out there for four years, living hidden in that house" (143). As well as signals and signs, the tale also makes frequent use of flashbacks, the longest being the telling of Thomas Sutpen's childhood and youth by Quentin in chapter VII.

Another singularity of the story, already evident in *Sanctuary* and *Light in August*, is the deliberate retention of information, the almost systematic recourse to deferral. The narrative economy of *Absalom, Absalom!* resembles that of a crime novel in that effects are related before causes are explained, and the information that is essential to understanding the story is released sparingly, in dribs and drabs, and sometimes withheld until the end. In the first six chapters, the story of the Sutpens is told from Thomas Sutpen's arrival in Jefferson in 1833 to the collapse of his grand "design" after the Civil War. But the genesis and nature of this design is only revealed in chapter VII. The murder of Charles Bon, first mentioned at the very end of chapter IV, remains an enigma for a long time: the reader has to wait until chapter VI to find out that Charles is Sutpen's elder son and chapter VIII to find out that he (probably) has black blood. Finally, the key to Rosa Coldfield and Quentin's visit to Sutpen's Hundred in September 1909 and Quentin's meeting with Henry, is deferred to the end of the last chapter, whereas chronologically it should have followed chapter V.

The complexity of the story also derives from the plethora of narrative voices. *Absalom, Absalom!* involves an external narrator who ensures that the story is whole, but far from monopolizing the narrative, this narrator acts as more of a stage manager and happily hands over the job to narrators who are also characters in the story being told, often letting them speak at length. Thus the first five chapters relate Quentin's conversations with Rosa and then with his father, Mr. Compson, in Jefferson, in the afternoon and evening of a hot day in September 1909. Chapters VI–IX follow the laborious attempts by Quentin Compson and Shreve McCannon, his Harvard roommate, to reconstruct the Sutpens' story.

Some stories seem to write themselves. This is not the case with Faulkner's stories: the tale takes hold of them without hiding the fact that they are narratives; what is said never eclipses the act of speaking. In *Absalom, Absalom!* the reader cannot forget that the story is carried and miscarried by voices that never stop calling, answering, contradicting, and mingling with one another. There are four narrators inside the novel: In chapter I and even more so in chapter V, the dominant voice, overexcited, declamatory, and incantatory, of Rosa; in chapters II–IV we hear the reasonable, reasoning, often sardonic voice of Mr. Compson. Chapters VI–IX are mostly made up of dialogs between Quentin and Shreve, a "happy marriage of speaking and hearing" (N3, 261).

But the dialog has always already begun, before any word is spoken between them, in a silent symposium between two selves. In the first chapter, "two separate Quentins [are] talking to one another in the long silence of notpeople in notlanguage" (N3, 6). In contrast to these internal split personalities, the initially complementary voices of Quentin and Shreve eventually become one and the same. Better still, in chapter VIII, in one of the most daring and astonishing scenes in the novel, speech is interrupted and narrator and narrated disappear, drawn into each other, engulfed in each other in the play of identifications, each becoming, at once, both Henry Sutpen and Charles Bon:

> He ceased again. It was just as well, since he had no listener. Perhaps he was aware of it. Then suddenly he had no talker either, though possibly he was not aware of this. Because now neither of them was there. They were both in Carolina and the time was forty-six years ago, and it was not even four now but compounded still further, since now both of them were Henry Sutpen and both of them were Bon, each of both yet either neither. (289)

It could be said that *Absalom, Absalom!* is a polyphony, but it is not merely an orchestration of individual voices. As often with Faulkner, and in this novel more so than elsewhere, the inner voices, the throaty voices of the characters are run through by a voice from somewhere else, of no identifiable origin, and this voice sometimes breaks free from any speaker and any narrative device, the voice of nobody, erupting enigmatically within a sentence. Who is speaking here? People, speaking to each other, at each other, through each other, within each other. It is impossible to know which subject is responsible for what is said, impossible to know who is *speaking*.

Consider, for example, Rosa's long monologue that takes up most of chapter V. From the very first words, Rosa addresses Quentin, but what she says is not presented as speech signaled by quotation marks, and the entire passage is italicized. Nothing is less like the transcription of a living word. It is indeed Rosa talking, at length, with frenetic eloquence. And yet her eloquence is that of a speech from which all probability has been removed.

Nobody has ever talked for this long, this *flumen orationis* is highly improbable coming from her mouth. The voice heard in her speech is exalted, both recognizable and unrecognizable, hers and yet not hers. Of course, one could say the same of the voices of Benjy and Quentin in *The Sound and the Fury*, or Addie and Darl in *As I Lay Dying*, which are also as if stolen from silence. Faulkner rarely stuck to the probable in his characters' speech. But the rhapsodic extravagance of Rosa's monologue brings us, with perhaps even more temerity, to the brink of what can be said. That which is not said, which cannot be said, can yet be written. Not always, but every now and then. Whose voice is it here? Perhaps merely the silent, written voice of a text. As Pierre Michon comments, in *Absalom, Absalom!* "it is literature itself that speaks."[5]

This novel offers us both a braiding of voices and a plurality of viewpoints. Just like the voices, the viewpoints split and disperse. Four perspectives, four viewpoints dominate the novel, however. The reader is first invited to share Rosa's fevered, hallucinated vision—a "Gothic" vision where Thomas Sutpen, the first object of her resentment, becomes a demon, an ogre, and his estate a new Castle of Otranto. It is relayed by the more distanced, more historical, more speculative viewpoint of Mr. Compson, who undertakes to raise the fate of the Sutpens to the level of myth, turning its protagonists into a tragedy worthy of the ancients. After this comes Quentin's somber, tormented, and romantic vision in the final chapters, (re)reading the story of his own family through that of the Sutpens and deciphering his own fate as a culpable son and incestuous brother through Henry's story. Added to these is Shreve's view, the "stranger's" view, more peripheral, more objective, more demystifying—or so it seems at first—later becoming loaded in turn, as if by contagion, by powerful affects, and less and less discernible from Quentin's.

All of these complications in the tale are disconcerting; they frustrate expectations and thwart the desire to read a story that stands up. Everything happens both too slowly and too quickly, and the reader is often tempted to tell the novelist, as Shreve does Quentin: "Wait. For Christ's sake wait" (*N3*, 238). At times Shreve can no longer follow Quentin; sometimes Quentin himself loses the thread. Notwithstanding this, Quentin and Shreve are the master craftsmen of this hazardous enterprise, applying themselves to unwinding the obscure entangled story of a family going back over forty years. The documented information amounts to just a handful of inscriptions: the five epitaphs found on the gravestones in the cemetery under the cedars and a few letters, "letters without salutation or signature, in which men and women who once lived and breathed are now merely initials or nicknames out of some now incomprehensible affection which sound to us like Sanskrit or Chocktaw" (83). On top of this comes incomplete, hypothetical information: Rosa's evidently suspect *pro domo* testimony, half speech for the prosecution, half speech for the defense; the voluble version of facts offered by Mr. Compson on the faith of "a few old mouth-to-mouth tales" (83); and Sutpen's revelation to Henry that Bon is "black," which Henry relates to Quentin when they meet at the end of the novel but may be mere conjecture.

These are the pieces of the puzzle, the meager, fragile materials from which the tale must be reconstructed. For Mr. Compson the enterprise is doomed to failure: "It's just incredible. It just does not explain. Or perhaps that's it: they dont explain and we are not supposed to know" (*N3*, 83). No matter how hard they try, the essential evades reason and the mystery persists. What are left are "just the words, the symbols, the shapes themselves, shadowy inscrutable and serene, against that turgid background of a horrible and bloody mischancing of human affairs" (84). All that remains is words, talk—and nothing but talk—no silent truths hidden, waiting to be told, nor a final subject apparent to validate and authenticate what is being said.

This does not stop Quentin and Shreve, the two young historian-detectives, from persevering in rebuilding this story, from trying to grasp the how and the why and if possible apprehending its meaning; where necessary, the imagination will fill in what is lacking in sound information. Thus, in chapter VIII the decisive conversation between "Colonel" Sutpen and his son Henry at the end of the Civil War, when the wind of defeat is already blowing, is wholly invented by Quentin and Shreve. Unbeknownst to the two historians, their voices mingle and they become novelists. The true story they wanted to tell turns into fiction, "the two of them creating between them, out of the rag-tag and bob-ends of old tales and talking, people who perhaps had never existed at all anywhere, who, shadows, were shadows in turn of what were (to one of them at least, to Shreve) shades too quiet as the visible murmur of their vaporising breath" (*N3*, 250).

"Something happened" (a phrase repeated several times in the text), events took place, but facts, as Nietzsche says, are always *facta ficta*: "A historian has to do, not with what actually happened, but only with events supposed to have happened: for only the latter have *produced an effect*. Likewise only with supposed heroes. [. . .] All historians speak of things which have never existed except in imagination."[6] Neither Quentin nor Shreve see it this way; they are not resigned to merely revealing the shadows, and they have no intention of releasing their prey. They are conducting an investigation, which takes place under our eyes, right now, an investigation that is halting, hesitant, spiraling in a circular movement whose orbits never quite overlap, endlessly returning to the same enclosed spaces and the same uncrossable thresholds, coming back tirelessly to the same events, the same scenes, the same characters and the same acts, multiplying parallels and echoes ad infinitum. Most of the high points of the action—the humiliation of little Sutpen by a planter's black servant, the spurning of the first wife, Sutpen's sudden arrival in Jefferson, his refusal to acknowledge Charles as his son, Henry's break with his father, Charles's murder by Henry, the clash between Sutpen and Rosa—are told and retold several times. The story continually comes back on itself, bumping up against tableaux where time stands still for a brief eternity. One example is the virginal, widowed Judith holding up her poor unfinished wedding dress when her bedroom door bursts open upon "her brother, the wild murderer whom she had not seen in four years and who she believed to be [. . .] a thousand miles away" (N3, 112; see also 142). Another is Judith again, standing in front of the same closed door, behind which lies Charles's bloody body (136–42), or Clytie stopping Rosa at the bottom of the staircase, holding her back by force and preventing her from entering Judith's room (113–14).

Finding the past as it was when it was present, as it was when it happened, and faithfully retracing its passage cannot be done. Human memory is unreliable; Rosa even says that it does not exist: "The brain recalls just what the muscles grope for: no more, no less: and its resultant sum is usually incorrect and false and worthy only of the name of a dream" (N3, 118–19). In *Absalom, Absalom!* everything comes down to guesswork that is more or less plausible but unverifiable, such as Shreve's guess about Eulalia Bon and her lawyer in chapter VIII. And no history can be enclosed forever in a story, no event can be definitively contained inside time, any one time is always preceded and followed by other times: "*Maybe nothing ever happens once and is finished. Maybe happen is never once but like ripples maybe on water after the pebble sinks, the ripples moving on, spreading, the pool attached by a narrow umbilical water-cord to the next pool which the first pool feeds, has fed, did feed*" (216).

Absalom, Absalom! is the story of the search for a story, or more accurately the telling (by an anonymous and remarkably discreet narrator) of the unfinishable narration (by four intradiegetic narrators) of an "incredible" history. One of the striking features of this novel is that, throughout, it follows the "present" movement of an *enunciation*, of immediate speech, which is not guaranteed and which seems to hide and improvise itself from one page to the next. The novel thus becomes the risky retracing of its own creation. Faulkner retraces the steps of a historian but does it backward, going back to the time when the history was not yet written, not yet fixed in the letter of a text that is authoritative. From the text he goes back to the fabric, from the fabric to the weaving, from the built structure to the disorder of the building site.

For the novel's narrators the issue is to find out what happened and, if possible, to draw events out into the open, to understand the logic of their sequencing. Other questions arise for us readers, more general and more properly epistemological: how, under what conditions, and through what processes does a history—any history and all of history—become a story, and from what does a story, about anything and by anybody, draw its legitimacy?

None of these questions are answered in the novel, no worthwhile truth is revealed at the end of this long unfurling of words, as is so elegantly suggested by the conversation-palindrome at Sutpen's Hundred between Quentin and the dying Henry, related at the end of the novel:

> *And you are—?*
> *Henry Sutpen.*
> *And you have been here—?*
> *Four years.*
> *And you came home—?*
> *To die. Yes.*
> *To die?*
> *Yes. To die.*

And you have been here—?
Four years.
And you are—?
Henry Sutpen (N3, 306)

Quentin and Henry finally meet, but they do not truly get to know each other. One asks questions, the other responds, briefly, and the little that is said over the course of this strange interrogation is said twice, as if to ensure through repetition that what has been said has been heard. Of the dialogues in this novel, this is the pithiest and most troubling in its extreme constriction—a play of questions and answers in the form of a chiasmus that closes in upon itself and teaches us nothing except the imminence of a death foretold.

However, speaking and listening rarely happen without effect in *Absalom, Absalom!* Despite it all, something *happens* in the words exchanged, in the conversations, and in the letter sent by Charles Bon to Judith, which she entrusts to Quentin's grandmother, leaving it up to her to read it or not, to keep it or destroy it:

> Because you make so little impression, you see. You get born and you try this and you dont know why only you keep on trying it and you are born at the same time with a lot of other people, all mixed up with them, like trying to, having to, move your arms and legs with strings only the same strings are hitched to all the other arms and legs and the others all trying and they dont know why either except that the strings are all in one another's way like five or six people all trying to make a rug on the same loom only each one wants to weave his own pattern into the rug; and it cant matter, you know that, or the Ones that set up the loom would have arranged things a little better, and yet it must matter because you keep on trying or having to keep on trying and then all of a sudden it's all over and all you have left is a block of stone with scratches on it provided there was someone to remember to have the marble scratched and set up or had time to, and it rains on it and the sun shines on it and after a while they dont even remember the name and what the scratches were trying to tell, and it doesn't matter. And so maybe if you could go to someone, the stranger the better, and give them something—a scrap of paper—something, anything, it not to mean anything in itself and them not even to read it or keep it, not even bother to throw it away or destroy it, at least it would be something just because it would have happened, be remembered even if only from passing from one hand to another, one mind to another, and it would be at least a scratch,

something, something that might make a mark on something that *was* once for the reason that it can die someday, while the block of stone cant be *is* because it never can become *was* because it cant ever die or perish. (N3, 105)

Each wants his own destiny, his own destiny marked by the seal of one's own will and one's own identity, whereas one is only a puppet among other puppets. And yet one can leave a trace—not on inert stone like marble or granite but in the memory of a man or woman, in quivering, living flesh. The most important thing is not that the trace is legible but that it is visible, recognized as a trace, and that it can be retraced, reproduced, and reactivated through its reproduction and transmission, passing "from one hand to another, one mind to another." This is the case of the letter "without date or salutation or signature" (107) that passes from Bon to Judith, from Judith to Quentin's grandmother, from the grandmother to the grandfather, and from the grandfather to Quentin himself. In *Absalom, Absalom!* the ultimate person to recover the trace and retrace it is no other than the reader. It is the reader who, in reading it, will give it shape and, if possible, meaning. It is the reader who will take over from the writer, rewriting the book by reading it. It is the reader who will follow the quest of the story, knowing that it cannot be ended. Rosa speaks of the "quiet in the raging and incredulous recounting" and sees the telling as that "which enables man to bear with living" (133). If language is impotent to recount what happens and what has happened in the heart of the truth, it nonetheless hosts and links events in the weaving of its tales, thus saving it temporarily from disorder and oblivion. Truth, as Quentin's grandfather reminds us, is "that meagre and fragile thread [. . .] by which the little surface corners and edges of men's secret and solitary lives may be joined for an instant now and then before sinking back into the darkness where the spirit cried for the first time and was not heard and will cry for the last time and will not be heard then either" (208).

Traces left by the dead: calling, recalling, reference points for the living. Traces and networks of traces, traceries of signs without which the world would no longer be habitable.

The staggeringly baroque construction and torrential, tormenting rhetoric of *Absalom, Absalom!* obviously follows in the footsteps of Melville, James, Dostoevsky, and especially Conrad, but in pushing the boundaries back even further, in taking even more risks, Faulkner opened up new avenues for the novel. *Absalom, Absalom!* is one of those texts, admittedly relatively rare in the history of the genre, where the novel ventures outside itself, roves beyond itself, to resurface and reappear elsewhere, other.

Absalom, Absalom! has been called a cubist novel. In the same way as Picasso and Braque destroyed the monofocal perspective inherited from the *Quattrocento* by pluralizing viewpoints and linking them in a purely formal fashion, Faulkner, in this novel, as he had already done in *The Sound and the Fury* and *As I Lay Dying*, broke the unity of the story by multiplying the voices and narrative focuses without even leaving any hope that they will eventually come into harmony. As in cubist painting, the figurative is not at an end, but it is in crisis, disfigurement is under way.

With *Absalom, Absalom!* the novel well and truly heralds the "age of suspicion." This book is not only a key landmark in Faulkner's oeuvre; it is also a major milestone in the great adventure of the Western novel. Faulkner, incidentally, was well aware of this. Before leaving Hollywood, he told David Hempstead, the young man to whom he had temporarily entrusted the novel: "I think it's the best novel yet written by an American" (*B1*, 364).

The book's initial reviewers, with three or four exceptions, did not share these sentiments. Outdoing each other once again in terms of incompetence and incomprehension, most repeated the charges already laid against his previous novels. Clifton Fadiman, writing in the *New Yorker* on October 31, 1936, called it "the most consistently boring novel by a reputable writer to come my way during the last decade." Philip Rahv, in *New Masses* (November 24, 1936) agreed, deploring the fact that despite his talent, Faulkner "seems quite unable to realize himself in a truly significant work." Bernard De Voto, in the *Saturday Review of Literature* (October 31, 1936) noted merely "the brilliant technique that promises us everything and gives us nothing." Similarly, Malcolm Cowley, in the *New Republic* (November 4, 1936), expressed his disappointment; in his eyes, *Absalom, Absalom!* was a barely updated Gothic novel in the tradition of Poe. Describing the book as "the strangest, longest, least readable, most infuriating and yet in some respects the most impressive novel that William Faulkner has written," the anonymous reviewer in *Time* (November 2, 1936) summed up the general perplexity. William Troy, in the *Nation* (October 31, 1936), was practically the only reviewer who attempted to understand the novel's originality in comparison with the realist tradition and the only one to hail it as Faulkner's best book.

In Great Britain, where *Absalom, Absalom!* was published a year later, the reception was no less ambivalent. The anonymous review in the *Times Literary Supplement* (February 20, 1937) ended with the observation: "The book has almost everything against it—a tiring prose, an exasperating method, a distasteful subject matter dubiously attaining the dignity of the tragedy it hints at," but conceded that "the author's very passion, that conflicting love and hate finding no rest or resting-place, gives to its pages indubitable vitality." In contrast, Howard Spring, writing in the *Evening Standard* on February 18, 1937, recognized its prodigious prowess: "Hampering himself with every disability, Mr. Faulkner nevertheless achieves a triumph such as few novelists can reach. You have the sense of watching a blindfold man, with his hands tied behind his back, crossing Niagara on a tight-rope."

The initial print run of *Absalom, Absalom!* in the United States was six thousand copies, plus three hundred copies in a limited edition. It did not sell well. Margaret Mitchell's *Gone with the Wind*, published in June that same year, was to become one of the best-selling novels of the twentieth century. It sold over one million copies in six months, including fifty thousand in a single day. Mitchell's novel also won the Pulitzer Prize in 1937 and was adapted for the screen by Victor Fleming with an all-star cast. Alongside it, *Absalom, Absalom!* cut a sorry figure.

SOUTHERN TALES: *THE UNVANQUISHED*

In the spring of 1934, Faulkner temporarily put aside *Absalom, Absalom!* to write some short stories, hoping to sell them to the *Saturday Evening Post*. From the outset, he planned to write a sequence of stories about the Civil War and Reconstruction, and when "Ambuscade" was published in the *Post* on September 29, 1934, the editor's note announced it as "the first in a series of stories by Mr. Faulkner in which these same two boys will appear." The next two stories, "Retreat" and "Raid," were published on October 13 and November 5 of the same year. However, the last three stories proved more difficult to write than Faulkner had expected. In the late spring or early summer of 1934, he complained to Morty Goldman:

I have been stewing for about three weeks now on the Post stories. I have been trying to cook up three more with a single thread of continuity, like the other three, with the scene during Reconstruction time. I cannot get started, I seem to have more material than I can compress. I have now decided that the trouble is this:

The Reconstruction stories do not come next. In order to write them, I shall have to postulate a background with the characters which they embrace. Therefore, there must be one or two stories still between the War-Silver-Mule business ["Riposte in Tertio"] and the Reconstruction; I am just starting one which will be a direct continuation of the return home with the mules, which should be included in the series of three which are done; perhaps it will bring to an end that phase, and I can get into the Reconstruction ones which for some reason will not start themselves. Please pass this on to the Post; I will send in this fourth story as soon as possible. (*SL*, 80–81)

Because the *Post* did not pay him as much as he wanted for the series, Faulkner agreed to return to Hollywood to adapt *Gold* by Blaise Cendrars but resumed work on his short stories again as soon he got home to Oxford. The story "The Unvanquished," retitled "Riposte in Tertio" in the novel, and "Vendée" were sent to the *Post* in September, and by mid-October he had also finished "Drusilla," published under the title "Skirmish at Sartoris" in *Scribner's* in April 1935.

Since Faulkner had no immediate plans for another novel after *Absalom, Absalom!*, he suggested that Bennett Cerf bring the stories together in the same volume: "I have a series of six stories about a white boy and a negro boy during the civil war. [. . .] What do you think about getting them out as a book?" (*SL*, 97–98). The timing seemed perfect for a book about the Old South and the Civil War. In July 1934 Stark Young had published the best seller *So Red the Rose*, the story of two Southern families during the Civil War, made into a film the following year by King Vidor. *Gone with the Wind* was published two years later, to immediate acclaim. It is easy to see why Faulkner wanted to take advantage of this craze for the South. However, during this difficult period—with America still in the Great Depression—what the public wanted was a romantic South, the South of dreams. Faulkner's dark novels could not compete with Margaret Mitchell's magnolias and crinolines. But a collection of skillfully written good old Southern stories might have a chance of success.

Should *The Unvanquished* be read as a novel or as a collection of short stories? Faulkner himself pondered this question, even many years after it was published (see *FU*, 257), and the same question arises for other works. Of the ten previously published novels, five were compiled in the same manner, constructed from short stories that had already been written and often already published: *The Hamlet*; *Go Down, Moses*; *Knight's Gambit*; *The Town*; and *The Mansion*. But apart from *Knight's Gambit*, a very minor text, none of these books duplicated texts already published. Each time, Faulkner revised and reworked them to turn them into novels. The plots may have been lax, the stories episodic, but structure was provided by other means. Nonetheless, of the novels written from preexisting material, *The Unvanquished* is one of those that Faulkner reworked the least.

The Unvanquished is a wartime chronicle. It is not about the horrors and miseries of war, or rather, yes, it is, but held at a distance, defused by humor or ennobled by legend. In these stories, ruse and temerity usually prevail over the brute force of weapons. Because the enemy cannot be openly engaged in battle, it is harassed through incessant guerrilla warfare; the invader's blunders are taken advantage of to make a fool of it. *The Unvanquished* is the Civil War seen from *below*—not by the politicians or soldiers waging it, but by the civilians who either undergo it passively or take part in it intermittently and marginally, meaning the elderly, women, and children.

Seven stories are assembled here. Although not forming a continuous whole, a single voice carries them and relates them—that of Bayard Sartoris. The narrator's name alone speaks of adventure. Bayard is the elder son of John, the "Colonel," founder of the Sartoris line and heroic commander of the first regiment of Jefferson. This character, directly inspired by Faulkner's great-grandfather, the "Old Colonel," had already featured in *Flags in the Dust*, to which *The Unvanquished* is a sort of sequel. In chronological terms, however, the book predates the 1929 novel. In the Southern tradition of the plantation novel, it is one of Faulkner's rare novels where the action takes place in the nineteenth century. And in contrast to *Absalom, Absalom!* and *Go Down, Moses*, it evokes an enclosed past. The contemporary South is absent, unless one looks for clues in the narrative present tense and the presence of the narrator.

In most of the stories told in *The Unvanquished*, Bayard Sartoris features both as narrator and as character or witness. A man of indeterminate age, but who can be presumed to have reached maturity, he looks back over his childhood and adolescence. Similar to the later *Go Down, Moses*; *Intruder in the Dust*; and *The Reivers*, *The Unvanquished* tells a coming-of-age story in the tradition of the bildungsroman. At the start of the novel, Bayard is twelve; at the end, now a law student, he is twenty-four. The time for growing, changing, maturing. The time for "education."

In the beginning is childhood, the freshness of innocence, the pleasure of play. Two children are playing soldiers: Bayard, a little white boy, and Ringo, a little black boy, born the same month, both nourished from the same breast, who have lived so long together that they are no longer black or white, "not even people anymore: the two supreme undefeated like two moths, two feathers riding above a hurricane" (*N3*, 323–24). The first two "unvanquished" in the novel are these two foster brothers, Bayard and Ringo—unvanquished and invincible as long as the paradise of childhood friendship endures, where there is no need to have a separate identity or to belong to a race. And as long as the battlefield is only the "living map [. . .] scraped into the packed earth."

"Ambuscade," the first story, opens on a description of this "map" representing Vicksburg, a fortified town on the Mississippi that the Confederates were trying to defend against the Yankee army. Under the description of this map comes a meditation on the permanence of Earth and the implacable law of Time, both of which reduce "the most brilliant of victories and the most tragic of defeats" to nothing but "the loud noises of a moment" (*N3*, 321). For Bayard and Ringo the setting of their little stage has been an almost Sisyphean task. The sunbaked earth is not easy to mold, and they have already had to combine forces against "a common enemy, time" to create "the pattern of recapitulant mimic furious victory like a cloth, a shield between ourselves and reality, between use and fact and doom" (321). They are getting ready to do battle again when Loosh appears; the only rebellious black on the plantation, he sweeps away their fortress of chips with the back of his hand. He knows that the battle has already taken place, that the Confederates have lost, and that they are about to lose the war. Vicksburg and Corinth have fallen; Sherman's troops are invading Mississippi. But Bayard and Ringo continue to play soldiers while they keep watch over the road, expecting blue-uniformed riders, even shooting one with an old rifle. Their game is less innocent now. The grown-ups' war has caught up with their *Kriegsspiel*. Bayard kills a horse and almost kills a man. But there are no reprisals. When the Yankees come to search the house, Rosa Millard, Bayard's grandmother, hides the two boys under her ample skirts. Even though Colonel Dick is not fooled by the trick, Bayard and Ringo are left alone.

In "Retreat" Bayard's battle-hardening continues with an initial departure. On John Sartoris's instructions, Rosa and her family take the road to Memphis. They are intercepted by Northerners, who steal their mules. Bayard and Ringo "borrow" a horse from an abandoned stable and set off in pursuit of the thieves. John finds them the next morning, and in a daring bluff, the trio manage to capture a detachment of sixty Yankees. In this mock-heroic episode, the trick played on the enemy again masks the cruelty of war, but it also sees Bayard earn his first stripes: "And I was still a child at that moment when Father's and my horses came over the hill" (*N3*, 364). A few minutes later, his father calls him "Lieutenant."

The war games continue when, after returning to the plantation, John, pretending to be crazy, manages to fool the Yankees who come to find him and, with the help of his black servant Louvinia, escapes from under their noses. Almost incidentally, the reader learns that the Yankees have set fire to the house and taken the chest of silver, the location of which is revealed to them by Loosh.

However, as one story moves into another, the atmosphere darkens. In "Raid" the war is right here, at home. The Sartorises are now living in their servants' quarters. They soon leave Jefferson for Hawkhurst, Alabama, where Rosa's sister lives. The tale of their turbulent trip gives rise to the most poignant pages in the novel: the detailing of the human tide of blacks looking for the promised land, on the road to "Jordan." With Drusilla Hawk, Bayard's fiery cousin, the Sartorises attempt to prevent the blacks from crossing the river on a bridge that the Northerners are about to blow up. Their horses drown but they are saved by the Northerners. Rosa demands to be brought to see Colonel Dick, who compensates her for her losses by giving her ten chests of silver, some mules, and a large number of blacks along with a signed order authorizing her to make further requisitions.

This gift will be her undoing. In "Riposte in Tertio" Rosa trades hundreds of mules extorted from the Yankees using fake requisition orders. Egged on by the sinister Ab Snopes, she gets involved in increasingly dubious and risky deals but believes that she is fighting a good cause by distributing her gains to the county poor. The end of this story marks a dramatic turn. Rosa, who thought that nobody would "harm a woman" (N3, 421), is killed by Grumby, an ex-Confederate outlaw.

In "Vendée"—its title probably inspired by Balzac's *The Chouans*—the novel takes an even more ominous turn. After a manhunt lasting over two months, Bayard and Ringo kill Grumby, peg his corpse to a door "like a coon hide" (N3, 445), and lay his severed hand on the grandmother's grave. An eye for an eye, savage justice has been done. Bayard has killed for the first time. Having missed the Yankee, he would not miss Grumby and thus becomes "a Sartoris," equaling his father in the sovereign exercise of violence. But when he must avenge the murder of his father, the memory of that first act of vengeance prevents him from accomplishing a second.

"Skirmish at Sartoris" takes place in the postwar period. After defeat, reconstruction starts in the South. But for Colonel Sartoris, returned home from the battlefield, peace is war pursued by other means. Assisted by Drusilla and his former regiment colleagues, he uses all his authority and energy to restore order to the Old South, even if it means killing a few troublemakers to win the elections. The first skirmish sees him fighting a couple of carpetbaggers, the Bundrens, whom he shoots down unceremoniously. The second, handled in the lighter register of a comedy of manners, features Drusilla, who, having run away from home to fight like a boy alongside John Sartoris, is beset by a pack of matriarchs. Aunt Louisa, her mother, supported by a veritable delegation of unbending zealots of Southern respectability, forces her daughter to dress like a woman and demands that she marry the colonel. The colonel, however, converts his house into a polling station, not a wedding chapel, and instead of celebrating a wedding, the mob acclaims the murderer.

"An Odor of Verbena" was written almost three years after the last of the other stories and a year after the publication of *Absalom, Absalom!* The story happens nine years after the events recounted in "Skirmish at Sartoris." This seventh story, the only one previously unpublished, is not just an adjunct to the others; it breaks with them, forces us to read them again from a different angle, inverting the eminently nostalgic or mock-heroic view used up till then.

At twenty-four, Bayard, a law student at Oxford, now known as "Sartoris" (N3, 487), learns that his father has been murdered by his former associate Redmond. The Southern code of honor requires him to avenge his father's death by carrying out another murder. Drusilla, Sartoris's former comrade in arms, and the entire community of Jefferson expect nothing less. But instead of repeating the cycle of violence, Bayard refuses the two loaded pistols Drusilla offers him. Under the implacable midday sun, he goes, unarmed, to Redmond's office. Redmond shoots twice but misses him and then goes away, leaving Jefferson forever.

This final story makes Bayard Sartoris Faulkner's first "positive" young hero, and his tale could be read as a veritable bildungsroman. His education is nothing less than sentimental. Bayard does his apprenticeship in the school of violence. Three times he is confronted by the possibility of a homicide: the first time, in "Ambuscade," he wants to but can't; the second time, in "Vendée," he wants to, can, and does; the third time, in "An Odor of Verbena," he could but no longer wants to. Violence desired, violence accomplished, violence refused. From the morality of the tribe, Bayard turns to the more complex demands of an ethics of responsibility; the honor of the clan is replaced by honor according to individual conscience. However, Bayard's morality remains the morality of a master in that he refuses to shoot but does not evade the risk of being killed. Initiation remains an ordeal. It matters little that his unusual behavior initially scandalizes everyone, even his nearest and dearest; his courage during the showdown with Redmond is eventually acknowledged and admired by all. Bayard succeeds where Quentin Compson and the "Young Bayard" in *Flags in the Dust* fail: in deviating from tradition, he nonetheless remains faithful to it. The point for him is not to betray the values of his class, even less to disown his father. Like Faulkner's other young heroes, Bayard is subject to the dual paternal constraint: "be like me and don't be like me." But for the first time, the oedipal conflict is resolved without tragedy. By refusing to take on the avenging role assigned to him by tradition, Bayard seems to be rejecting his ancestral heritage. But he rebels against his father by identifying with him, modeling himself not on the predatory father but on the dying father who renounces violence.

Ultimately, his most formidable opponent in this test is neither the dead father nor the murderer to be killed but his cousin Drusilla, who has become his father's widow, "the woman of thirty, the symbol of the ancient and eternal Snake" (*N*3, 474). Before he even reaches the house where the corpse of John Sartoris lies, Bayard imagines her waiting for him "beneath all the festive glitter of the chandeliers, in the yellow ball gown and the sprig of verbena in her hair, holding the two loaded pistols" (468). The colonel's former comrade in arms cannot conceive that her husband's murder should go unavenged. It is she who now incarnates the virile code of honor; it is she who calls for vengeance in accordance with ancient law. But this fanatical high priestess of the Old South is still a woman, a new Eve, or rather a new Lilith, a seductive demon who serves death, whose emblem is verbena, flower of Venus and Mars. Absent from the first six stories, sexuality returns in the last. As always with Faulkner, it goes hand in hand with transgression. Drusilla, his father's widow, offers Bayard her body in payment for avenging his death. The scent of verbena is also an incestuous promise and it follows Bayard wherever he goes, just as the scent of honeysuckle follows Quentin in *The Sound and the Fury*. And, like Quentin again or the Bayard of *Flags in the Dust*, he is breathless and choking. The atmosphere is heavy and troubled, as in all great Faulknerian scenes. But Bayard holds out. Nothing will divert him from his intent.

The *Unvanquished* is the first account in Faulkner's writing of a successful apprenticeship. Up until then his novels related only failed or impossible apprenticeships. Despite all that separates them, Quentin in *The Sound and the Fury*, Temple in *Sanctuary*, and Christmas in *Light in August* are nonetheless alike in their common inability to learn anything from what they experience. In contrast, in *The Unvanquished* individual time is open to the possibility of learning from experience. Bayard, like Chick Mallison after him, manages to free himself from the prestige of the past and the fatality of its echoes. He carries within him the hope of another, new South, more peaceful, more civilized, if not more fraternal.

However, the break with the past sustained by this hope does not exclude nostalgia for that same past. While *Absalom, Absalom!* is a radical critique of the old order, this is tempered by indulgence in *The Unvanquished*. Is this because John Sartoris, unlike Sutpen, is not a vulgar upstart but an authentic patrician? John Sartoris sees himself as a providential savior. Although unscrupulous about liquidating his adversaries, he believes that this is because his decisions must all be motivated by the superior interest of the Southern community of which he is the natural leader. Similarly, Rosa Millard, a highborn lady aware of her responsibilities, takes care of "her" poor, black and white, by redistributing to them the money from her swindling and plundering. And the manner in which the McCaslin brothers free their slaves seems to point to a similar sense of responsibility—noblesse oblige. The corollary to of the assertion of aristocratic rights is a keen awareness of one's duties toward those whom providence has entrusted to one's care. Of course, in this novel Faulkner is not justifying the quasi-feudal order of the Old South. Rosa Millard is not irreproachable; she severely punishes the smallest lie within her family and yet allows herself to be led into lying, cheating, and stealing. Her unshakable Episcopalian good conscience hides so much bad faith that it would be terrifying if it weren't so funny: "I did not sin for gain or for greed [...] I did not sin for vengeance [...] I sinned first for justice" (*N3*, 419). In her blind pride, Rosa is truly a member of the Sartoris clan. As for the colonel, "Skirmish at Sartoris" and "An Odor of Verbena" tarnish somewhat the ideal image offered to us in the earlier stories. Beneath the well-mannered patrician, Bayard eventually recognizes the wild animal: his "intolerant eyes [...] had acquired that transparent film which the eyes of carnivorous animals have and from behind which they look at a world which no ruminant ever sees, perhaps dares to see, which I have seen before on the eyes of men who have killed too much, who have killed so much that never again as long as they live will they ever be alone" (476).

Pride leads John Sartoris and Rosa Millard to fatal hubris. And yet they remain tragic characters. Rosa is above all the valiant Southern grandmother defending her mules from the Yankees by hitting them with her parasol. John Sartoris is first and foremost the hero idolized by two little boys who dream of "powder and glory" (*N3*, 325), and the final pages of the novel imply that the prestigious image of "Father" remains intact in the son's mind.

Those who reproach Faulkner for having sacrificed to Southern mythology are therefore not wholly wrong. While Bayard, his narrator, does not hide the weaknesses of Rosa Millard and John Sartoris, he never questions the legitimacy of the "lost cause," and the way his story idealizes relations between whites and blacks bears little resemblance to reality. At the Sartoris plantation there are only happy slaves, unfailingly faithful to their white masters, with the exception of young Loosh, the only one who betrays them. As in *Flags in the Dust*, stereotypes triumph: Louvinia is the perfect mammy, Joby is the model of the loyal and devoted servant, and Loosh also plays the role of the uppity nigger. Ringo, Bayard's funny, clever foster brother is the alibi negro par excellence, even though the boys' friendship does not survive their adolescence.

The Unvanquished is most certainly not an apology of slavery, but the desperate march of the freed slaves toward the "Jordan" as described in "Raid" implicitly denounces their emancipation as decreed by the Yankees: they march toward chaos and death, not freedom. As for the pages on the spontaneous reformism of the McCaslin brothers, why insert these into the novel unless to hint at what emancipation decided and promoted by the South itself would have been like? Here are the first traces of the prudent paternalism that Faulkner was later to defend publicly when the blacks started to campaign against segregation and fight for their rights: freedom and equality, yes, but let the South solve its problems itself; give the whites time to come around and let the blacks first get educated.

Set alongside the passionate questioning of the South and its heritage of guilt in *Light in August, Absalom, Absalom!,* and *Go Down, Moses, The Unvanquished* may seem somewhat bland. Faulkner himself thought little of it. This is what he wrote to Goldman in August 1934: "As far as I am concerned, while I have to write trash, I dont care who buys it, as long as they pay the best price I can get. Doubtless the Post feels the same way about it; anytime that I sacrifice a high price to a lower one it will not be to refrain from antagonising the Post; it will be to write something better than a pulp series like this" (*SL*, 84). Nevertheless, when asked one day which of his books he would recommend reading first, he suggested *The Unvanquished,* "because it's easy to read. Compared to the others, I mean" (*FU*, 2). But his easiest novels are not the most exciting. It is not certain that the best way to tackle the Faulkner continent is by the most accessible routes. Rather, the best way is to start with the steeper slopes. Those who have consented to be there and are happy to lose themselves in it will enjoy this book.

When *The Unvanquished* was published in February 1938, the domestic reviews were mixed, as always, but for the first time the favorable reviews outnumbered the unfavorable. Even in Mississippi the novel was quite well received, while up until then Faulkner had been almost unanimously despised and hated. Here, finally, was a book, according to the *Oxford Eagle,* that Oxonians "can understand, can enjoy, can leave lying on their living room tables" (quoted in *B1*, 392).

The day after its publication, the film rights to *The Unvanquished* were sold to MGM for twenty-five thousand dollars. After paying his agent's and other fees, the author's share was nineteen thousand dollars. Faulkner could finally pay off his many debts. Better still, he consolidated his status as a landowner by buying a wood and a farm. He could now claim, more or less truthfully, to be "a farmer who tells stories." And, he thought, he could take his time writing them. On February 19, 1938, he wrote to Goldman: "I'm in fair shape now. Will finish a novel this spring, and for a year or so now I can write in leisure, when and what I want to write, as I have always someday fondly dreamed" (*B1*, 132).

FAULT LINES, FLUX, AND FLOODS: *IF I FORGET THEE, JERUSALEM*

In two letters sent to Morton Goldman in December 1936 and January 1937, Faulkner announced that he had a novel in mind.[7] The novel was to become *If I Forget Thee, Jerusalem*, first published under the title *The Wild Palms*. According to Meta Carpenter, Faulkner was already working on it in Hollywood, telling her in the spring of 1936: "I'm excited about *The Wild Palms*. I think I have something fine going" (*ALG*, 140). However, it is more likely that the text to which Meta Carpenter refers was a six-page unpublished short story, the manuscript of which is held by the University of Mississippi under the title "The Wild Palms." The setting is reminiscent of Pascagoula, and the story is about a doctor in his forties summoned by a young painter to help his girlfriend, who is losing blood. When Faulkner was typing up the manuscript, he divided it into three numbered sections. The first two are similar to the first chapter of the story; the third focuses on the doctor as the central conscience of the novel, but the characters of Harry and Charlotte are sketchy.

When did Faulkner start work on the novel as we know it today? The start of the first chapter of the manuscript bears the date September 15, 1937. Other chapters are also dated throughout the book, and the last page bears the words "Rowan Oak / Mississippi / June 15, 1938."

The novel took almost eight months to write. It was not easy. When Faulkner started it, he was not yet over the loss of Meta and was not in good physical shape. He had such constant back pain that he couldn't sleep, which explains why, as with *As I Lay Dying*, this novel was mostly written at night. The beginning was slow. On November 29, 1937, he wrote to Robert Haas: "I have got into the novel. It has not begun to move very fast yet, but I imagine it will soon and that I will be able to send it in by May first, though I cant give my word as to this, not having any great degree of peace in which to write" (*SL*, 102). But three weeks later he seemed to have regained confidence: "The novel is coming pretty well," he wrote Haas. "I found less trouble than I anticipated in getting back into the habit of writing, though I find that at forty I dont write quite as fast as I used to. It should be done by May first, though" (102).

If I Forget Thee, Jerusalem was not finished in May 1938, as he had told Haas, but it was only two or three weeks late. On June 17 Random House received a telegram from Faulkner in capital letters: "NOVEL FINISHED, SOME REWRITING DUE TO BACK COMPLICATIONS; SENDING IT ON IN A FEW DAYS" (*SL*, 105). In late June he sent Haas the typescript of the novel, with the title "If I Forget Thee, Jerusalem." In late September he went to New York to read through the final galley proofs. The novel was published on January 19, 1939.

For once, Faulkner was not sure that his book was any good. When he first finished it, he did not know quite what to make of it. In July 1938, he wrote to Haas: "I have lived for the last six months in such a peculiar state of family complications and back complications that I still am not able to tell if the novel is all right or absolute drivel" (*SL*, 106).

Writing *If I Forget Thee, Jerusalem* did not bring Faulkner the same happiness as *The Sound and the Fury*, but the two novels are quite similar in that they are both profoundly autobiographical. *If I Forget Thee, Jerusalem* is confessional in nature. It contains the discernible, still acute, trace of a cruel wound. Faulkner later admitted to Joan Williams that he had come up with the idea "in order to try to stave off what I thought was heart-break" (*SL*, 338). In *Mosquitoes* he had put the following cynical observation in the mouth of one of his characters: "Lucky he who believes that his heart is broken: he can immediately write a book and so take revenge [. . .] on him or her who damaged his or her ventricles. [. . .] No, no, you don't commit suicide when you are disappointed in love. You write a book" (*NI*, 442).

If I Forget Thee, Jerusalem is a text full of heartache, a text to avoid dying of grief, suicide deferred, deflected, foiled by the power of fiction. After losing Meta, Faulkner first tried to drown his sorrows with alcohol. Writing was another way of skirting around death, of mourning, another attempt to fill the unbearable absence.

If I Forget Thee, Jerusalem was also the renewed experience of a sudden shock, of divestment, a hazardous journey through the dark. If we are to believe a letter Faulkner sent to Haas shortly before publication, the novel was written in the feverishness of an altered state, similar although less euphoric than the writing of *The Sound and the Fury*: "To me it was written just as if I had sat on the one side of a wall and the paper was on the other and my hand with the pen thrust through the wall and writing not only on invisible paper but in pitch darkness too, so that I could not even know if the pen still wrote on paper or not" (*SL*,106).

—

The biblical title chosen by Faulkner for this novel, which he vainly attempted to retain, comes from Psalm 137: 4–6:

> How shall we sing the Lord's song in a strange land?
> If I forget thee, Jerusalem, let my right hand forget her cunning.
> If I do not remember thee, let my tongue cleave to the roof of my mouth; if I
>   prefer not Jerusalem above my chief joy.

The title echoes the steadfastness of the Hebrews to their spiritual faithfulness during their exile by the rivers of Babylon. It was the perfect fit for this fine novel against oblivion, but the publisher disliked it, favoring "The Wild Palms" instead, and fifty years were to pass before it would be published under its initial title.

The action takes place this time outside Yoknapatawpha County, farther south, in the low-lying Mississippi valley, in New Orleans (like *Mosquitoes* and *Pylon*), but also in Chicago, Wisconsin, and even as far as the mountains of Utah. Two distinct stories—"The Wild Palms" and "Old Man" (the Mississippi's nickname)—alternate systematically in ten chapters. The first is tragic, the story of the love until death of Harry Wilbourne and Charlotte Rittenmeyer (a character inspired by Helen Baird and Meta Carpenter, both of whom Faulkner had loved and lost). The other is mock-heroic, relating the incredible tribulations of two young convicts and an anonymous woman on the Mississippi, ten years earlier, during the great flood of 1927. The necessity of this counterpoint appeared so unclear to the publisher that he quickly published the two stories separately, even though Faulkner, when talking about this novel, always insisted that it had been written spontaneously and deliberately in the order it appeared:

> That was one story—the story of Charlotte Rittenmeyer and Harry Wilbourne, who sacrificed everything for love and then lost that. I did not know it would be two separate stories until after I had started the book. When I had reached the end of what now is the first section of the "The Wild Palms," I realized suddenly that something was missing, it needed emphasis, something to lift it like counterpoint in music. So I wrote on the "Old Man" story until "The Wild Palms" story rose back to pitch. Then I stopped the "Old Man" story at what is now its first section, and took up "The Wild Palms" story until it began to sag. Then I raised it to pitch again with another section of its antithesis, which is the story of a man who got his love and spent the rest of the book fleeing from it, even to the extent of voluntarily going back to jail where he would be safe. They are only two stories by chance, perhaps necessity. The story is that of Charlotte and Wilbourne. (LG, 247–48)

Two stories in one, two stories because one is not enough. Everything here happens in twos: there is a couple in both stories, a man and a pregnant woman; two doctors in the first; two convicts in the second. But in both of these stories, which leapfrog over each other without coming into contact, in these two stories with no visible link between them, couples form only to become undone. Two, it seems, do not a pair make; two do not add up. Two is the start of division and the figure of misfortune, and the arrival of the three, the *terzo incommodo*, can only complicate things even more.

At the beginning of the book, the first story is already almost over; its end is imminent: "The knocking sounded again, at once discreet and peremptory, while the doctor was descending the stairs, the flashlight's beam lancing on before him down the brown-stained stairwell and into the brown-stained tongue-and-groove box of the lower hall" (N3, 495). It is Harry Wilbourne, come to wake up the doctor in the middle of the night to ask for his help. A conversation ensues between the two men. What do they speak about? A woman who is bleeding. Harry, her lover, knows she is fatally wounded, but the old doctor does not want to see or know anything. Hemoptysis? "Lungs. And why in the world I didn't—[. . .] She's just coughing a little blood then?" (503–504) Then, confused, casting around for a diagnosis: "You say she is bleeding. Where is she bleeding?" To which an exasperated Harry answers with another question: "Where do women bleed?" (504). It is *the* question.

The woman they are talking about, the woman who is bleeding, suffering, and dying, is Charlotte, the adulteress, Harry's mistress, who has been bled dry by her clumsy lover, delivered unto death by a failed abortion. Blood takes the place of the child to be born; death comes from the very source of childbirth, that lacuna in the female body that opens onto "the precipice, the dark precipice" (*N3*, 588), that which Harry, during his conversation with McCord, calls "the pervading immemorial blind receptive matrix, the hot fluid blind foundation—grave-womb or womb-grave, it's all one" (589). Everything comes back to this fleshy, bloody hole, this red slit that in *As I Lay Dying* was masked by a blank space in the text. The entire novel, as we will discover, is about gaps and flows, staunching and overflowing. Everything refers back to the female, the body always already failing, always on the verge of expressing loss, represented here, at the outset of the novel, by "the secret irreparable seeping of blood" (496) of the dying Charlotte.

"The Wild Palms" is a love story that ends badly, a story that like all true love stories is faithful to its mythical destiny, that could only end badly, and that from its searing birth contains the premonition of disaster. As required by romantic tradition, it starts with love at first sight. The lovers are first stunned and distraught:

> [She] stopped, facing him. "What to—Do they call you Harry? What to do about it, Harry?"
> "I dont know. I never was in love before." (*N3*, 523)

Even before their affair has started, their break with the world is consummated. The well-to-do Charlotte abandons husband and children; the intern Harry gives up his career as a doctor. Another life starts for them, a marginal, rootless, difficult life, a long fleeing, frantic and exhausting, across America. Their love needs to be accomplished within the solitude of a couple, far from the madding crowd and from all established order; it can only affirm itself *against* this order, this crowd.

The story line has been a familiar one ever since the tales of courtly romance: to burn itself out, passion must be illicit and preferably adulterous. It needs obstacles to overcome, taboos to break. But Harry and Charlotte's love is not just a revolt against the society in which they live. Rejecting all social bonds, refusing all compromises with reality, it cannot in truth either unfold over time or settle in the one place: "Love [. . .] cant last. There is no place for it in the world today, not even in Utah" (*N3*, 587). Harry thinks that modern society, with its capitalist economy and bourgeois values, is contrary to love, but what he and Charlotte fear above all is the socialization, in any form, of their love affair; they fear it being trivialized by respectability, dulled by habit, eroded by time. The alternative is "to conform or die" (590). To conform, for them, means losing their love; loving means agreeing to lose one's life. Charlotte is a devotee of Eros: she devotes herself to love as one devotes oneself to a task, a cause, or, even better, a vocation. For her, love is an absolute outside time, which occurs briefly inside time only to withdraw from it immediately. Nothing is ever established: "They say love dies between two people. That's wrong. It doesn't die. It just leaves you, goes away, if you are not good enough, worthy enough. It doesn't die; you're the one that dies" (551). Love is Charlotte's religion; the lover is but an instrument of worship, at best an altar. Harry is well aware of this, saying: "So it's not me you believe in, put trust in, it's love" (551). Charlotte is ready to sacrifice everything and even die for her faith, if need be.

Love is a divine gift that must be earned. Charlotte and Harry work hard at love, diligently toiling to be worthy of their love, but they will never know the grace of loving. Their love is sad, narrow, and tense. Nothing in their story suggests the jubilant, overwhelming reciprocity of a great passion or even the warmth of tender intimacy. One would look in vain for a moment of shared happiness. This folie à deux is the opposite of crazy love.

For Harry, loving means regressing back to a childish dependency, or even a prenatal calm. Before he meets Charlotte, his life is nothing but torpor: "On the morning of his twenty-seventh birthday, he waked and looked down his body toward his foreshortened feet and it seemed to him that he saw the twenty-seven irrevocable years diminished and foreshortened [. . .] as if his life were to lie passively on his back as though he floated effortless and without volition upon an unreturning stream" (*N3*, 516–17). Later, he is often portrayed lying on his back, "merely existing in a drowsy and foetuslike state, passive and almost unsentient in the womb of solitude and peace" (570).

He is a child still enclosed in his mother's womb, at best a child enfolded in his mother's arms. Harry himself defines his relationship with Charlotte as a mother-son relationship: "There is something in me she is not mistress to but mother" (*N3*, 591). Thus we have a masculinized mother, a feminized son. As often with Faulkner, the traditional gender roles are inverted: "She's a better man than I am" (586) acknowledges Harry. Charlotte *takes*. Think of Caddy Compson, who, in her games with her brothers, "was always a king or a giant or a general" (*NI*, 1010); and that other rebel, Addie Bundren, "taking" Anse as her husband and then Pastor Whitfield for her lover; or Emma Bovary, as Baudelaire saw her: a bizarre androgyne, an "almost male" being who gives herself, "in a completely masculine way, to wretches who are not her equals."[8]

Charlotte is energetic, resolute, dominant; it is she who takes the initiative, finds boarding and work, chooses itineraries; it is she in the couple who has the monopoly of action and verb. For Charlotte, being means *doing* things with her body: "I like bitching, and making things with my hands" (*N3*, 555). Harry prefers to be bossed around. His life has never belonged to him; it now belongs to his mistress. A man-child, he clings to Charlotte like an infant to its mother. He is aware of this, although he keeps this awareness to himself: "*Maybe I'm not embracing her but clinging to her because there is something in me that wont admit it cant swim or cant believe it can*" (552). At the same time, he discovers that Charlotte's love is a love of nobody, a love of nothing: "*There's a part of her that doesn't love anybody, anything*" (551). He wonders if "there was a part of her which [. . .] did not even love love" (556).

Charlotte knows something that Harry does not yet know and perhaps never will: she knows that no love can take the place of love. She is convinced that love can only be an interminable asceticism, that it can only be approached through renunciation and suffering. Charlotte goes so far as to say that "love and suffering are the same thing and that the value of love is the sum of what you have to pay for it and anytime you get it cheap you have cheated yourself" (*N3*, 526). Love, for her, is not a gift or a favor. It must be earned through the trial of suffering, and all that is gained from this trial is yet more suffering. Therefore, to avoid taking the easy way out, the lovers take a vow of poverty from the outset. Charlotte would never have run away with Harry if he hadn't been penniless. "Listen. Tell me again you haven't got any money. Say it. So I can have something my ears can listen to as making sense even if I cant understand it. Some reason why I—that I can accept as the strong reason we cant beat even if I cant believe or understand that it could be just that" (527). At the start, the couple has just twenty dollars. Once in Chicago, Charlotte has to work as a window dresser in a large store. Harry, a shameful pornographer, writes "sexual gumdrop[s]" (578) for magazines. Later he accepts a position as a doctor in a mining camp in remote Utah, in the winter cold, and that is where they live, outside time, outside the society they loathe and that has condemned them. They experience penury and destitution, shame and despair.

"The Wild Palms" is part of the long tradition of the *antiromantic* novel. Running after "real life," the lovers want to live a beautiful love story, a romance that escapes the monotony of daily life and the mediocrity of routine. At the very start of their affair, Charlotte tells Harry that her ideas of love all come from books (see N3, 526), and she is determined to live out these ideas with him. One thinks of Francesca and Paolo in Dante's *Divine Comedy*, of Don Quixote and of Emma Bovary; reading novels was fatal to these heroes, as it will be for Charlotte.

The imagination wants everything. It does not recognize nuance, cannot bear half measures. "Listen: it's got to be all honeymoon, always," Charlotte tells Harry. "Forever and ever, until one of us dies. It cant be anything else. Either heaven or hell" (N3, 551). There will be no purgatory, no in-between. It will therefore be hell.

The Wild Palms is a novel about the illusions and dead ends of passionate love and about the dead ends of romanticism. It is a reflection on the impossible merging of souls and the impossible consubstantiality of the flesh. Two will never become one. Everyone remains for himself, apart, alone: Harry's madness is not desire for her; Charlotte's madness is not desire for him. Neither one for the other nor one through the other. Just one with the other, and not for long. Their love, full of mistakes and misunderstandings, leads them inevitably toward death, but Harry and Charlotte are no Tristan and Isolde. Fate has not destined them to die together.

Their illicit love subjugates them to the harshest of laws. But another law manifests itself when Charlotte becomes pregnant. Giving life would mean betraying love by bringing it back into the natural order of reproduction. Thus Harry, at her request, tries to induce an abortion. She dies as a result and her lover ends up in jail.

There will be no *Liebestod*. Harry will not join Charlotte in death. When he finds himself alone in his cell overlooking the bay, with a solitary palm tree standing like a monument to her memory, anguish gives way to despair: "Without realising it he had assumed the immemorial attitude of all misery, crouching, hovering not in grief but in complete guttish concentration above a scrap" (*N3*, 704). But his despair seems to rouse Harry from stupor, bringing him close to an obscure knowledge: "That was the first time when he almost touched it. But not yet; and that was all right too" (706); "That was the second time he almost got it. But it escaped him again" (709); "And now he was about to get it, think it into words, so it was all right now" (714).

And for the first time in Faulkner's writing, the loss of the loved one does not lead to the extremes of death or madness or to the usual coming to terms with mourning. After Charlotte's death, Harry, in his cell, refuses to take the poison offered to him by her husband. As his last monologue points out, Harry will continue to live; he will survive Charlotte's death in his faithfulness to memory, which is only a memory because it is rooted in the carnal:

> So it wasn't just memory. Memory was just half of it, it wasn't enough. *But it must be somewhere*, he thought [. . .]. *So it is the old meat after all, no matter how old. Because if memory exists outside of the flesh it wont be memory because it wont know what it remembers so when she became not then half of memory became not and if I become not then all of remembering will cease to be.—Yes* he thought *Between grief and nothing I will take grief.* (*N3*, 715)

"Grief": the etymology of the word underscores the heaviness of mourning. Harry prefers prison to suicide, the almost nothing of mourning to absolute nothingness. What he wants—and this is the first time he wants, the first time he is capable of wanting—is a mourning period that is indefinitely prolonged, transfigured by his stubbornness, mourning that no longer means withdrawal and disconnecting, but reconnecting and perpetuating, in suffering and through the flesh, the link with the object hosted, gathered, and sheltered in a body still alive, in *"the old meat, the old frail eradicable meat"* (*N3*, 709).

In Harry we find the fantastical capacity to deny loss, to keep what has been lost alive as an object lost, a capacity that is, as we know, peculiar to melancholia and that has already manifested itself in other Faulknerian characters such as Quentin Compson and Darl Bundren. But this time the refusal to mourn as an enterprise of liquidation is described as the triumph of life over death, of carnal memory over oblivion: Harry in his imprisonment has become what Shakespeare in his thirty-first sonnet called "the grave where buried love doth live."

An ironic if not derisory triumph to be sure: at the end of "The Wild Palms" we see Harry in his prison cell: "It would stand to his hand when the moment came" (N3, 714), and then "now it did stand to his hand, incontrovertible and plain, serene" (715). These sentences are incomprehensible unless they contain a masked reference to Harry's erect penis when he remembers the heat of "the body, the broad thighs and the hands that liked bitching and making things" (715). Harry can no longer make love to Charlotte, but he can go on masturbating, as he did before he met her. He goes back to his solitary pleasure, which is now a sort of commemorative onanism. Harry is still regressing.

—

"Old Man," the second story, is simultaneously a mischievously spun metaphor and an ironic inversion of the first story. The tone is different, as is the register. It starts with a fable or tale: "Once [. . .] there were two convicts" (N3, 509). What we are told is, first, the story of these convicts, one tall and thin, sentenced to fifteen years' hard labor for the attempted armed robbery of a train; the other, short and fat, sentenced to ninety-nine years for an unknown crime. When the story opens the Mississippi has already burst its banks. Parchman, the penitentiary, has been evacuated and the convicts' shackles have been removed so that they can help shore up the levees and save lives. Freed from their chains, they set off to rescue a woman in a bayou. Some time later the short convict sees "the skiff begin to spin and his companion vanish violently upward like in a translation out of Isaiah" (592). The tall convict has apparently drowned only to resurface a few chapters later, clutching his paddle. Alone in the skiff, he was carried off into the bayous by the current, spinning in the water, which "at one time had held him in iron-like and shifting convolutions like an anaconda" (593).

Exhausted and bleeding copiously from the nose, he continues to be propelled by "a final measure of endurance, will to endure which adumbrated mere muscle and nerves" (594).

Through sheer force of will, the tall convict manages to overcome all obstacles. He is one of those people who endure in Faulkner's writings, who last because they endure, survive because they accept life as it comes, sometimes surprised by the blows of fate but never complaining or fighting back, as if they want to show that they are worthy of what happens to them, without even asking any questions, as if they have always known that the disorder of life is part of the order of things.

They are inhabited by an obscure knowing that is in a way the other side of knowledge. The convict understands nothing and does not even seek to understand. Like Anse Bundren, the great halfwit in *As I Lay Dying*, he is always amazed as well as amazed that he continues to be amazed. This type of amazement is not quite astonishment. It is an amazement that has already started, almost ironic, almost mocking, and from which no questions emerge. Nothing could really surprise the convict. When he accidentally finds a woman perched in a tree who calls out to him: "It taken you a while" (*N3*, 595), he doesn't think to justify himself but calmly starts looking after her as if he had indeed been expected. The improbable couple set off, dragged off by the water, the man, "bloody as a hog," and the visibly pregnant woman he can't wait to get rid of: "He wanted nothing for himself. He just wanted to get rid of the woman, the belly, and he was trying to do that in the right way, not for himself, but for her" (604). In contrast to Harry the doctor, who kills the woman he loves by performing an abortion on her, the convict calmly helps the woman to give birth in the worst of circumstances, cutting the umbilical cord with the cutting edge of a can lid on a snake-infested Indian burial mound with the waters raging all around.

If "The Wild Palms" is the tragic story of a failed escape from social order, "Old Man" is the comical story of a forced embarkation. Harry and Charlotte, like the two convicts, go from the comfort (reassuring but suffocating) of order to the uncertainty and risk of disorder. Or again, from immobility to movement, from steadiness to flux.

In "Old Man" the river rises, speeds up, wears itself out. Flow becomes fury; the flood is unleashed. All boundaries are rubbed out, landscapes fade and dissolve, and nothing withstands the confusion and turbulence of chaos. The world has lost its foundation and its bearings, the convicts' skiff is carried off in violent eddies, as if projected into another dimension: "now instead of space the skiff became abruptly surrounded by a welter of fleeing debris—planks, small buildings, the bodies of drowned yet antic animals, entire trees leaping and diving like porpoises above which the skiff seemed to hover in weightless and airy indecision like a bird above a fleeing countryside, undecided where to light or whether to light at all" (N3, 601).

The most powerful and arresting metaphor of disorder in this novel is this great liquid unfurling, the devastating Mississippi flood, described at length and admirably in "Old Man" (nobody describes the indescribable better than Faulkner). But there are other flood tides, other runoffs, more carnal and more intimate. In "The Wild Palms" as in "Old Man" there is a plethora of body flows: menstrual cycles and Charlotte's fatal hemorrhage, the convict's hemophilia, the thread of blood running from the lips of the woman about to give birth, the bleeding of the alligators, digestive flows and respiratory flows. All of these flows contribute to the unstoppable passing of time, intensified in the text by the fluidity of the writing, which corrupts the codes and disorientates the reader through its interminably stretching and swirling sentences.

"The Wild Palms" and "Old Man" are similar and dissimilar to each other. In both stories, man is struggling with elementary forces, the powers of vertigo and disorder that threaten to destroy him. Both stories deal with gestation and decline, with childbirth and death throes. Its cosmic orchestration raises these two lamentable and tragic stories above themselves. All the elements are summoned: dry and damp earth; a burning, all-consuming fire; the air stirred by the wind—"the black wind [. . .] risible, jeering, constant, inattentive" (N3, 692), which shakes the palm trees and twists around the houses; and above all water, in all its forms, the running water of the streams, the dormant water of the lakes, the muddy water of the bayous, and finally the raging floodwaters of the Mississippi, devastating everything in their path.

It is the mirroring of "The Wild Palms" and "Old Man" that gives the novel its density and its volume, from which it derives its multiple sources of irony, and that succeeds in making servitude desirable. The convict has left the penitentiary against his will and is anxious to return there, to "surrender his charge [. . .] and turn his back on her forever, on all pregnant and female life forever and return to that monastic existence of shotguns and shackles where he would be secure from it" (*N3*, 599). True, when the short convict later asks him if he didn't try to sleep with "the woman" (we never find out her name), he remembers that "at first when if it had not been for the baby he might have, might have tried. But they were just seconds because in the next instant his whole being would seem to flee the very idea in a kind of savage and horrified revulsion" (722). In fact, he is constantly seeking to be rid of her. When after his return the prison warden asks him, almost apologetically, "'You had bad luck, didn't you? [...] They are going to have to add ten years to your time,'" he says nothing. "'All right,' [he] said. 'If that's the rule'" (720). The prospect of remaining "'ten more years to do without a woman, no woman at all that a fellow wants,'" does not frighten him in the least. He almost celebrates. Good riddance. It is he, the misogynist convict, who has the last word: "Women, shit" (726).[9]

The convict unreservedly agrees to the extension of what people no longer dare to call his "sentence." After all this uproar, he is back home and at peace again. Paradoxically, at the end of his adventure, which has now become a story, this taciturn man starts to speak: "Suddenly and quietly, something—the inarticulateness, the innate and inherited reluctance for speech, dissolved and he found himself, listened to himself, telling it quietly, the words coming not fast but easily to the tongue as he required them" (*N3*, 721).

Similarly, Harry, ripped away from his dreary bachelor life by an all-consuming passion, finds a final refuge in prison after Charlotte's death and in this refuge a new peace. Far from being a place of penitence, the penitentiary is, for him as for the tall convict, a protected and protective environment, a maternal haven, the prenatal paradise almost regained. When the convict looks at the woman who has just given birth, he thinks: "*And this is all. This is what severed me violently from all I ever knew and did not wish to leave and cast me upon a medium I was born to fear, to fetch up at last in a place I never saw before and where I do not even know where I am*" (*N3*, 651).

Being born does not mean coming into the world; it means being thrown into it. No one will ever be at home here. What people want is to be able to come home, to return to the blissful warmth of the first enclosure. It is no coincidence that the title initially chosen by Faulkner for this novel was taken from a psalm about the captivity of the Hebrews in Babylon. *If I*

Forget Thee, Jerusalem is an ironic elegy to captivity. For Harry and the convict, imprisonment is the only effective recourse against the disorderliness and excess of life. Everything rather than desire. Everything rather than freedom. Better not to have been born.

———

The Wild Palms was not a critical success. Many critics saw in it the arbitrary juxtaposition of two stories. Clifton Fadiman, writing for the *New Yorker*, again showed his ignorance, stating that the two stories alternated "like an endless sandwich" (January 21, 1939). In the *New York Herald Tribune* (January 22, 1939), Alfred Kazin found it strange and violently uneven, and even Malcolm Cowley, in the *New Republic* (January 25, 1939), turned up his nose. But in *New Masses* (February 7, 1939), Edwin Burgum detected a complex if not organic relationship between the two stories and hailed *The Wild Palms* as Faulkner's best novel. Similarly, Conrad Aiken in the *Atlantic* (November 1939) thought this novel one of the finest. On January 23, 1939, *Time* magazine put Faulkner on the cover, dressed as a farmer (in open shirt and suspenders), and made him its cover story. *The Wild Palms* was a clear commercial success, selling a thousand copies a week, more than *Sanctuary* and *The Unvanquished*.

The *Wild Palms*, or *If I Forget Thee, Jerusalem* as it is now known, is today unanimously acknowledged to be one of Faulkner's best novels. It was also hailed as such in France when the translation by Maurice-Edgar Coindreau was published in 1952. Yet it must be remembered that by 1952 Faulkner had already been awarded the Novel Prize two years previously and that few now doubted his genius as a novelist.

A COMICAL PASTORAL: *THE HAMLET*

After *If I Forget Thee, Jerusalem*, set outside Yoknapatawpha, Faulkner returns to his county. The first volume in the Snopes trilogy, *The Hamlet* was published on April 1, 1940; the second, *The Town*, was published seventeen years later, in 1957; and the third, *The Mansion*, in 1959, three years before his death. In Faulkner's career the genesis of this trilogy was a complicated story extending over thirty years. It started with a series of sketches, of which the first and most developed was "Father Abraham," a good twenty pages long and probably written in the winter of 1926–1927. At the end of the 1920s and into the 1930s, Faulkner reworked this text several times, tinkering with other titles—"Abraham's Children," "The Peasants," "As I Lay Dying" (bearing little or no relation to the novel of the same name), and finally "Aria Con Amore." From the 1930s he started to capitalize on the Snopes material, converting it into a sequence of short stories, all located at Frenchman's Bend, the hamlet that was to serve as the backdrop to the novel. Most of the stories were first published in magazines.

He formed a clear conception of the Snopes trilogy only in late 1938 as he was putting the final touches to the first volume. On December 11, in a long letter to Haas, he summarized the contents and indicated the titles as follows: "The Peasants" for the first volume, "Rus in Urbe" for the second, and "Ilium Falling" for the third, adding that he had already written half of the first volume. At the time, he believed he would be able to write the first volume of the trilogy in three months and then move right on to the second. On January 19, 1939, he told Bennett Cerf that the novel would be finished in April, but in fact "The Peasants" was to take a whole year to write.

In "The Peasants" Faulkner reworked and revised six of his short stories: "Spotted Horses" (1931), "The Hound" (1931), "Lizards in Jamshyd's Courtyard" (1932), "Fool about a Horse" (1935), "Barn Burning" (1939), and "Afternoon of a Cow," a lighthearted spoof written in 1937, elements of which were to be reused in book III. In addition to the six short stories, at least a quarter of the final manuscript of the novel seems to have been put together from older fragments cut and pasted. Although *The Hamlet* was "incepted as a novel" (*SL*, 197), its composition was makeshift. As successive versions of the text show, from the manuscript to the final typescript, Faulkner hesitated between a number of openings (the novel almost started with "Barn Burning"), reworked it several times, and added multiple grafts and layerings.

In late 1939, when he sent the final part of the typescript to Saxe Commins, he changed the titles. The three novels were now to be called *The Hamlet*, *The Town*, and *The Mansion*.

—

"Snopes." Sibilant and grubby, the name is worthy of Dickens, evoking snail and snake, snot and snout, sniff, snoop, and snarl. Who are the Snopeses?

Where do they come from? What do they want? Where are they going? Here is how Faulkner described them in 1926 in "Father Abraham":

> The Snopes sprang untarnished from a long line of shiftless tenant farmers—a race that is of the land and yet rootless, like mistletoe; owing nothing to the soil, giving nothing to it and getting nothing of it in return; using the land as a harlot instead of an imperious yet abundant mistress, passing on to another farm. Cunning and dull and clannish, they move and halt and move and multiply and marry and multiply like rabbits: magnify them and you have political hangerson and professional officeholders and prohibition officers; reduce the perspective and you have mold on cheese, steadfast and gradual and implacable. (*FA*, 19–20)

The Snopeses seem to belong to a different sort of humanity than the higher orders. To be a Sartoris, a Compson, or a McCaslin means being part of a family, fitting in with the continuity of kinship, having forefathers and usually descendants, being subject to vertical time, having one's place in a family tree. Being a Snopes, on the other hand, means being part of a prolific and proliferating tribe, claiming no ancestry, no heritage, advancing over a slack period of time that has no memory. With the Sartorises, the Compsons, and the McCaslins, the name refers to the permanence of a lineage, and the same first names are passed down from generation to generation. The Snopeses, for their part, are called Mink, Oreste, Elmo, Virgil, Lancelot, Byron, Colonel Sartoris, Bilbo, Vardaman, Admiral Dewey, Wallstreet Panic, and Montgomery Ward. The names veer from the heroes of Greek tragedy and courtly romance to mail-order catalogs—anything will do. The act of naming seems random, identity counts for little, the animal rivals with the human. The Snopeses, above all, are a bestiary: rats, raccoons, rattlesnakes, vipers, termites.

These rapacious parasites appear very early in Faulkner's writing and are never far away. From *Flags in the Dust* to *Sanctuary*, not one of his novels fails to mention them, and "Spotted Horses," the first short story fully devoted to them, was published in June 1931. However, *The Hamlet* was the first to portray them center stage.

The Hamlet traces the start of Flem's career, the most ambitious and crafty of them all. The novel is spun from a multitude of stories and can be read in various ways, first and foremost as a mocking version of a Horatio

Alger–type rags-to-riches story. It is true to say that through Flem's rise, Faulkner describes the ineluctable ascent of a hitherto dispossessed social class—the "po' whites"—at the expense of the class that had been dominant up till then, and shows us how this rise breaks traditions and upsets the rules of the game in a small village community in Mississippi. It is true that the satirical treatment of the Snopeses attests to the contempt of one class for another. But one should be wary of oversimplification, as did the very conservative Phil Stone when explaining that the "core of the Snopes legend was that the real revolution in the South was not the race situation but the rise of the redneck, who did not have any of the scruples of the old aristocracy."[10] In the Snopes trilogy the "race situation" in the South is certainly remarkably absent (although there are many references to blacks), but class warfare—an expression studiously avoided by the Agrarians when speaking about the South—is not reduced to antagonism between the amoral, greedy hoi polloi and virtuous aristocrats on the defensive.

The fact that the novel's title (and those of the other two volumes of the trilogy) refers to an inhabited place and that the novel starts with a description of that place is not insignificant. The hamlet in question is Frenchman's Bend, "a section of rich river-bottom country lying twenty miles southeast of Jefferson" (*N*3, 731), haunted by the remote, hazy memory of the "foreigner," presumably a Frenchman, who founded the plantation, whose story and even name have been forgotten.[11] In *The Hamlet* a shared destiny is asserted from the start; it could even be said that it imposes itself at the expense of the individual. But to define this novel as the chronicle of a community or to read it simply as a sociological novel, a study of provincial mores à la Balzac, would be equally reductive. This book cannot be boxed into preset categories; its strength comes precisely from its capacity to evade and overrun these.

Another novelty is the text layout. In its final version the novel is made up of four books divided into numbered chapters, some of which are in turn divided into numbered sections. The first two books focus on one character ("Flem," "Eula"), the third on a season ("The Long Summer"), the fourth on a social class (with the title taken from Balzac: "The Peasants"). Each of these four books is a tale, or rather a bunch of tales, but they do not follow the usual order of plot. *The Hamlet* seems to take place in space rather than over time, rolled out like a carpet or a tapestry rather than advancing over a period of time. The technique is like collage, which assembles different types of fragments and plays on this difference. Everywhere is speckled, shimmering, mottled. The novel is like its piebald horses.

But at the same time, it is overtly in the Romantic tradition. The start could have featured in a nineteenth-century novel. Balzac and Dickens are not far away. After briefly skirting over the history of Frenchman's Bend, book one introduces us to a number of characters: landholder Will Varner, lazy, jovial, and cunning, who over the years has risen to become "the chief man of the county" (*N3*, 733); his son, Jody, "a prime bulging man, slightly thyroidic" (734); and then "a man smaller than common, in a wide hat and a frock coat too large for him, standing with a curious planted stiffness," whose face is characterized by "a pair of eyes of a cold opaque gray between shaggy graying irascible brows and a short scrabble of iron-gray beard as tight and knotted as a sheep's coat" (735–36). This man is none other than Ab Snopes, the sharecropper with a Luciferian name and a clubfoot, who not without reason is suspected of having set fire to his bosses' barns. First glimpsed behind a window by Jody, then emerging with the arresting, almost supernatural suddenness of a Popeye or a Sutpen, comes Flem, son of Abner:

> He saw suddenly, leaning against a tree beside the road, the man whose face he had seen in the window of the house. One moment the road had been empty, the next moment the man stood there beside it, at the edge of a small copse— the same cloth cap, the same rhythmically chewing jaw materialised apparently out of nothing and almost abreast of the horse, with an air of the complete and purely accidental which Varner was to remember and speculate about only later. (749)

From the very first chapter of book one, the figure of Flem intrigues by his enigmatic allure and his physique, so inexpressive that it becomes worrying: a "broad flat face [. . .] as blank as a pan of uncooked dough," and eyes "the color of stagnant water" (*N3*, 749). He remains impenetrable to the end, until death, as does Popeye in *Sanctuary*, and as do, to varying degrees, most of the other characters in *The Hamlet*. It is true that the narrative viewpoint is sometimes taken over by Labove, Houston, and Mink, but most often the story has an external focus. Here, we are far from the streams of consciousness of *The Sound and the Fury* and *As I Lay Dying*.

At the start of the second chapter we learn that the Varners have hired Flem as a sales clerk in their store as a precautionary measure, to guard against fire risk. Flem is not a sales clerk like the others. While before his arrival customers served themselves and placed money in a box, they now have to deal with him for the most minor transaction. A meticulously accurate bookkeeper, he charges five cents for each wad of tobacco, refuses to give an old customer credit, and, contrary to Jody, never gets it wrong when giving change, even if this is to his advantage. Flem is primarily a behavior, a habitus, a physiognomy, and an outfit, and his upward mobility can easily be traced through his sartorial changes. The white shirt and minuscule bow tie he favors once he takes up his clerk's duties are visible marks of distinction: before him, the Varners were the only ones in the community to wear these. Flem increasingly extends and diversifies his field of activity, eventually setting up as landowner, lender, speculator, and entrepreneur. He quickly understands that there is "no benefit in farming" (*N3*, 750). Before long, he is monitoring the cotton gin, helping Will Varner to settle his yearly accounts with his debtors, lending money to the locals (787), and engaging in a series of transactions that are highly profitable for him: he fires the old smith and replaces him with two of his cousins; builds a new blacksmith shop; buys new equipment; hires an old apprentice; sells Varner the new forge in return for the tools from the old shop, which he sells on to a junk man; moves the new equipment to the old workshop; and sells the new building to a farmer to turn it into a cowshed (see *N3*, 791–92). A calculating cynic and impassive manipulator, a foreigner to both the community and himself, this monomaniac is one of Faulkner's most peculiar and sinister characters. Flem is nothing, but in his environment he can do anything. He is one of those Faulknerian characters whose maleficence goes hand in hand with a vertiginous vacuity.

Some have seen him as representing urban corruption taking over the traditional Southern agrarian, but the Snopeses do not come from elsewhere. Flem is also a man of the South, a poor white from Mississippi, born like Thomas Sutpen into poverty and prepared to do anything to get out. Flem is a cold monster, but he is a monster of his society and of his time, and his upward mobility is made easier by the fact that he is living in a community where "men established the foundations of their existence on the currency of coin" (*N3*, 916).

They also founded it on the currency of the word. Frenchman's Bend is first and foremost a small backward community, where oral culture is perpetuated through men's conversations, through the stories they constantly tell one another. But "the currency of coin" is on the verge of supplanting barter, in transactions that are increasingly distorted by inequality. The togetherness of old is thus reduced to a precarious cohabitation that recognizes neither the solidarity of sharing nor the reciprocity of giving. *The Hamlet* was for many years read as the nostalgic celebration of a traditional agrarian community. But what the novel describes is in fact a community that has been plundered, that no longer raises anything above it, and that can in no way be held up as a model of sociability. Market values are the only values its members still have in common, and, far from forming a fabric of solidarity, the relations they have with one another are reduced to rivalry, manipulation, and domination.

Undoubtedly, Flem embodies the new socioeconomic order more brutally, in a way that is more "successful" and more "modern" than that of old Varner, and the novel underlines the contrast between the latter's almost good-natured craftiness and the former's dirty tricks, but, all things considered, they differ merely in degree and method. In *The Hamlet*, everyone, from the most disadvantaged to the most privileged, is greedy: a poor farmer like Henry Armstid does not hesitate to steal his wife's savings and waste all her money buying a wild horse. Even more absurdly, Ab Snopes's wife sells her one and only cow to buy a milking machine! To achieve their ends, everyone tries to cheat his neighbor: Jody Varner uses Ab Snopes's bad reputation to rob his harvest. I. O. Snopes manages to persuade nice-guy Eck to pay 90 percent of the price of Ike's cow. The vile Lump Snopes incites Mink to rob Houston's corpse. In fact, Flem differs from the others only in the methodical and formidably efficient intelligence with which he promotes his interests at the expense of others.

His main rival in *The Hamlet* is V. K. Ratliff,[12] a raconteur invariably described as "courteous," "affable," and "chatty," with whom Faulkner declared that he had fallen in love. A mobile, rootless figure who is both central and peripheral, Ratliff is a sewing-machine agent, but he is above all a Yankee peddler:

> He sold perhaps three machines a year, the rest of the time trading in land and
> livestock and second hand farming tools and musical instruments or anything

else which the owner did not want badly enough, retailing from house to house the news of his four counties with the ubiquity of a newspaper and carrying personal messages from mouth to mouth about weddings and funerals and the preserving of vegetables and fruit with the reliability of a postal service. (N3, 741)

Hawking goods and gossip: in the community of Frenchman's Bend, V. K. Ratliff provides both services. A collector and transmitter of information, a facilitator of trade, he somewhat resembles Hermes, the cunning god of paths and crossroads, traders and robbers. A traveler among settled people, it is he who circulates goods and yarns. He has skill and knows "how good a man's voice feels running betwixt his teeth" (N3, 804). In the first book he tells three good stories to the farmers gathered on the veranda of Varner's store. The first is about Ab Snopes and his troubling past as a horse thief and arsonist (already mentioned in *The Unvanquished* and "Barn Burning"). The second tells how Ab was swindled by Pat Stamper, a legendary horse dealer. The third relates obscure transactions between Ratliff and Flem. But Ratliff is not just a storyteller. Through the years this old bachelor has become the itinerant conscience and the memory of the county, more aware than others of the grave threat posed by the Snopeses to the community and resolved to resist them with all his might: "I never made them Snopeses," he says, "and I never made the folks that cant wait to bare their backsides to them" (1031).

In book two, however, the novel abandons the Snopeses for a time and radically changes register to evoke the grand dream of carnal opulence called Eula. Here the novelist's prose becomes heated and elated. After Ratliff's vernacular idiom comes the splendor of a furiously "literary" rhetoric. An excess of words responds to an excess of flesh.

Who is Eula? She is Varner's daughter, but described from the beginning as a precocious Helen of Troy, whose "entire appearance suggested some symbology out of the old Dionysic times—honey in sunlight and bursting grapes, the writhen bleeding of the crushed fecundated vine beneath the hard rapacious trampling goat-hoof" (N3, 817). Even more than Lena Grove in *Light in August*, Eula comes to us from a luminous, pagan Greece predating both modesty and sin. For Labove, the young schoolmaster, who knows his classics, she represents "the ungirdled quality of the very goddesses in his Homer and Thucydides [. . .] at once corrupt and im-

maculate, at once virgins and the mothers of warriors and of grown men"
(834). Beyond these contradictions, Eula is everything "at once." She defies
all knowledge, circumvents all laws: "serene and intact and apparently even
oblivious, tranquilly abrogating the whole long sum of human thinking and
suffering which is called knowledge, education, wisdom, at once supremely
unchaste and inviolable: the queen, the matrix" (836–37).

"All fabulation is the fabrication of giants," observes Gilles Deleuze,
writing about Balzac, Melville, Proust, Kafka, and Faulkner.[13] In his fab-
ulations Faulkner continuously produces giants. In his Virginia interviews
he says that Eula "was larger than life" and "the little hamlet couldn't have
held her" (FU, 31). Indeed, as she is portrayed in *The Hamlet*, as she is seen
there (by men, always; forever imprisoned by their watchful eyes), she is
not a character on a human scale. She is not just female; she is excessively, monstrously, divinely female: "too much of leg, too much of breast, too
much of buttock; too much of mammalian female meat" (N3, 822). Provocative, on display, impossible to clothe, more naked than naked, of a nudity
more unchaste than nudity itself: he "saw the incredible length of outra-
geously curved dangling leg and the bare section of thigh between dress
and stocking-top looking as gigantically and profoundly naked as the dome
of an observatory" (823). Eula is reminiscent of Baudelaire's giantesses; of
the women painted by Rubens, Courbet, and Picasso in "Siesta"; and of the
disproportionately full contours of archaic statues depicting fertility. Eula
is fertile matter, *natura naturans*, radiating plenitude.

For many years she leads a purely vegetative life and dreams only of
eating sweet potatoes. Once she becomes a woman, she exacerbates men's
desire while at the same time inspiring in them a sort of panicked terror.
The mere presence, the mere passage, the mere lingering scent of her body
instantly causes acute turmoil. As her brother crudely puts it, with his male
vulgarity: "She's just like a dog! Soon as she passes anything in long pants
she begins to give off something. You can smell it. You can smell it ten feet
away!" (N3, 821). A few pages later the narrator observes, more delicately:
"By merely walking down the aisle between them she would transform the
very wooden desks and benches themselves into a grove of Venus" (836).
Both animal and divine, Eula is wholly within her body and her whole body
is within her sexuality. *Tota mulier in utero*. Opposite her there is another
body, stiff, rough, male—that of Labove, the young schoolmaster, another
excessive character, encapsulated as follows:

[He was] a man who was not thin so much as actually gaunt, with straight black hair coarse as a horse's tail and high Indian cheekbones and quiet pale hard eyes and the long nose of thought but with the slightly curved nostrils of pride and the thin lips of secret and ruthless ambition. It was a forensic face, the face of invincible conviction in the power of words as a principle worth dying for if necessary. A thousand years ago it would have been a monk's, a militant fanatic who would have turned his uncompromising back upon the world with actual joy and gone to a desert and passed the rest of his days and nights calmly and without an instant's self-doubt battling, not to save humanity about which he he would have cared nothing, for whose sufferings he would have had nothing but contempt, but with his own fierce and unappeasable natural appetites. (827)

Soon, this ascetic, this fanatically chaste anchorite would learn all the torments of the flesh: "Then one morning he turned from the crude blackboard and saw a face eight years old and a body of fourteen with the female shape of twenty, which on the instant of crossing the threshold brought into the bleak, ill-lighted, poorly-heated room dedicated to the harsh functioning of Protestant primary education a moist blast of spring's liquorish corruption, a pagan triumphal prostration before the supreme primal uterus" (835). For three years Eula becomes his daily obsession. For three years he lusts after her with the furious hatred of impotence, "sweating in the iron winter nights, naked, rigid, his teeth clenched in his scholar's face and his legs haired-over like those of a faun" (839). Once, just once, he wanted her "as a man with a gangrened hand or foot thirsts after the axe-stroke which will leave him comparatively whole again" (839). He knows he cannot marry her, but after he finishes his law studies, this parochial social climber will remain the schoolmaster at Frenchman's Bend "for the privilege of waiting until the final class was dismissed and the room was empty so that he could rise and walk with his calm damned face to the bench and lay his hand on the wooden plank still warm from the impact of her sitting or even kneel and lay his face to the plank, wallowing his face against it, embracing the hard unsentient wood, until the heat was gone" (840). When he finally dares to touch her, Eula vigorously knocks him down, tells him curtly to stop pawing her, and, the ultimate insult, does not even bother to tell her brother. That night, Labove leaves Frenchman's Bend for good.

And still the young men of the county continue to swarm around Eula "like wasps about the ripe peach which her full damp mouth resembled"

(*N3*, 848). Along comes Hoake McCarron, a stranger, who courts, seduces, and deflowers her. Three months later he finds out she is pregnant and disappears. Her brother wants vengeance; her father looks for a solution, which he finds in his clerk. Flem is to be the "crippled Vulcan to that Venus" (840); it is he who will marry Eula, and on their wedding day he will receive from old Varner a check for three hundred dollars and a property deed for the old Frenchman's estate. Eula and Flem spend their honeymoon in Texas until Eula gives birth. But Eula is no longer the same. She has learned in the meantime that she was nothing but an instrument of fate: "It was as if she really knew what instant, moment, she was reserved for, even if not his name and face, and was waiting for that moment rather than merely for the time for the eating to start, as she seemed to be" (849). Eula is now one of Faulkner's damned women. Later we see her, furtively, like an apparition, at the window of the Varners' house:

> She was in a white garment; the heavy braided club of her hair looked almost black against it. She did not lean out, she merely stood there, full in the moon, apparently blank-eyed or certainly not looking downward at them—the heavy gold hair, the mask not tragic and perhaps not even doomed: just damned, the strong faint lift of breasts beneath the marblelike fall of the garment; to those below what Brunhilde, what Rhinemaiden on what spurious riverrock of papier maché, what Helen returned to what topless and shoddy Acropolis, waiting for no one. (1016–17)

Around Eula, a white goddess with golden hair, everything is false, like an opera set. At the end of the novel, just as she is leaving the hamlet for Jefferson, she is nothing more than an effigy, a petrified body with a "face calm and beautiful and by its expression carven or even corpse-like" (1072).

While book two is animated and dominated by the great mythical figure of Eula, she disappears in book three, and Flem is also absent throughout the "long summer." This time the major characters are new arrivals: Ike Snopes, Jack Houston, and Mink Snopes.

Like Benjy in *The Sound and the Fury*, Ike is an idiot, and the most extravagant pages in *The Hamlet* tell us the story of his love for a cow. Bewildering and shocking, the story echoes and mocks the other love stories told in the book. It starts with a feat: Ike saves a cow from a prairie fire, an episode already related as farce in "Afternoon of a Cow," the spoof where

Faulkner mischievously portrays himself as a farmer, handing the narrative over to his secretary, Ernest V. Trueblood, alias Ernest B. Toogood. But in *The Hamlet* the farce is no longer treated as such; the reader is no longer expected to laugh. The idyll of the idiot and the cow gives rise to a prose adorned with all the rhetorical ornaments of ancient courtship. The entire pastoral tradition, the whole history of courtly romance and chivalry is summoned up by this astonishing oration. Here is a poor cow transformed into an object of desire and devotion—like Eula, who is in a way its double (in "Afternoon of a Cow" the cow is named Beulah)—the placid incarnation of the immemorial matrix.

The next two chapters are also about sexuality, about men and women. They deal in large part with the pathetic and pitiable amorous adventures of the farmer Jack Houston and the sharecropper Mink Snopes. After this, in more sober prose, comes the story of Houston's violent death and the meticulous tale, told from the viewpoint of Mink, the killer, of three long, exhausting nights during which he tries to get rid of not just Houston's corpse but also of his victim's howling dog, who keeps following and attacking him while all the time, just like in *As I Lay Dying*, buzzards start circling above the decomposing corpse. Mink, in these pages, is nothing more than prodigious tenacity, a crazy will to endure. The tale is told without compassion or complacency, but with an overwhelming understanding, just as Faulkner does every time he writes of men or women confronted with extreme situations.

In book four, "The Peasants," the story brings the reader back to Frenchman's Bend, where Flem, home from Texas with his sidekick Buck Hipps, organizes an auction of horses "gaudy, motionless and alert, wild as deer, deadly as rattlesnakes, quiet as doves" (*N3*, 983). The auction soon becomes a circus and a rodeo, and the wild horses eventually rush out of the enclosure "to crash through the gate [. . .] carrying all of the gate save the upright to which the hinges were nailed with them, and so among the teams and wagons which choked the lane, the teams springing and lunging too, snapping hitch-reins and tongues" (1013), before scattering throughout the village. Armstid is carried into Mrs. Littlejohn's hotel with a broken leg. The horse given to Eck Snopes by Hipps breaks through the gate of Mrs. Littlejohn's yard, goes up the front steps, vanishes through the front door, and crashes into Ratliff's room. Later it rushes into Vernon Tull's wagon as he and his family are passing over a bridge. Tull is thrown out of the wagon by his two "frantic mules," falls headfirst onto the bridge, and is carried, unconscious, into Mrs. Littlejohn's backyard (1015).

Tull lodges a complaint against Eck Snopes, Armstid against Flem Snopes. Both cases are dismissed. Mink, sentenced to life with hard labor for Houston's murder, waits till the last moment for his cousin to come to his rescue: "Flem Snopes! Is Flem Snopes in this room? Tell that son of a bitch—" (N3, 1043). But Flem never replies; Flem is never there for anyone, and he eventually pulls a fast one on everyone, including—who would have believed it?—Ratliff, convincing him that treasure has been hidden on his land since the Civil War. Ratliff, Bookwright, and Armstid buy the land off him at a high price. Honest, wise, and cunning, Ratliff succumbs to greed just like the others. The novel ends in his defeat and the victory of Flem, now in possession of a tidy sum in the bank, a beautiful wife, and a half share in a Jefferson restaurant. We see him heading to the town, passing in front of stalled wagons and farmers who have come from all around to watch the poor, foolish Armstid in the sun digging up the land for which he gave up all he had to buy, and which—although he obstinately refuses to admit it—contains no treasure: "Snopes turned his head and spat over the wagon wheel. He jerked the reins slightly. 'Come up,' he said" (1075).

For Faulkner, *The Hamlet* was primarily a comical book: "It's a humorous book—Ah mean it's a tribe of rascals who live by skullduggery and practice it twenty-foh hours a day" (*LG*, 40). The comic treatment of the crazy horse auction is reminiscent of the slapstick devices of tall tales and comic strip gags. Some scenes in the novel are pure vaudeville, such as the one where Mrs. Varner tells Jody that Eula is pregnant, and where Jody rages against his father because he seems indifferent to the news. In this rural chronicle, Faulkner engages with and stunningly revitalizes the tradition of southwestern humorists such as Augustus Baldwin Longstreet, Joel Chandler Harris, and Mark Twain.

The Hamlet is a comic novel but it is not just that. It is a novel and more than a novel, belonging as of right to this genre without laws or limits, which sustains itself only through its inexhaustible capacity to disown and reinvent itself. It could be called realistic, in its asserted determination to portray a rural community known firsthand to the author, a rustic realism, thick and meticulous, Bruegel-like, but also magical and fairy-like, almost

Chagall-like, never hesitating to upset the codes of mimetic realism. It is also assuredly a Southern novel but in no way regionalist. *The Hamlet* does not just happily perpetuate the local tradition of slapstick; it also casually appropriates almost the entire Western literary tradition. Its teeming intertext is woven through with nods to the Bible (the *Song of Songs*), Homer (*The Odyssey*), and discernible shades of Balzac (*The Peasants*), Flaubert (*Madame Bovary, The Temptation of Saint Anthony*), Zola (*Nana*), Thomas Hardy (*The Return of the Native*), Washington Irving (*The Legend of Sleepy Hollow*), and John M. Synge (*Playboy of the Western World*). Within the novel is an entire library.

Of all of Faulkner's books, *The Hamlet* is the most saturated with literature and mythology and, along with *Absalom, Absalom!*, the most rhetorical and lyrical, with astonishing points of preciosity from time to time (in the style of the "metaphysical" seventeenth-century English poets). Eula's first outings evoke a "bizarre and chaperoned Sabine rape" (*N3*, 818). When her brother drives her to school, he sees himself "transporting not only across the village's horizon but across the embracing proscenium of the entire inhabited world like the sun itself, a kaleidoscopic convolution of mammalian ellipses" (822). And here is Ike the idiot, lying down in the damp early morning grass, waiting for his beloved cow to arrive:

> He would not move. He would lie amid the waking instant of earth's teeming minute life, the motionless fronds of water-heavy grasses stooping into the mist before his face in black, fixed curves, along each parabola of which the marching drops held in minute magnification the dawn's rosy miniatures, smelling and even tasting the rich, slow, warm barn-reek milk-reek, the flowing immemorial female, hearing the slow panting and the plopping suck of each deliberate cloven mud-spreading hoof, invisible still in the mist loud with its hymeneal choristers. (883)

The tale of Ike's love for a cow opens onto a dawn dripping with mist and dew. The earth wakes up in a liquid swarming, as if emerging again from the primeval waters. With each new dawn it becomes porous again, an immense, water-laden sponge. The mist is its steaming emanation. It rises from the stream, seeps out of the meadows, erodes contours and boundaries, reestablishes between things and creatures the freshness of unhindered communication, caressing and shaping Ike and the cow "somewhere in immediate time, already married" (883). The nuptials are a reunion. The mist bathes Ike in elementary happiness, both liquid and vegetal, recalling the bliss of the child in the womb, about to be born. It is no coincidence that he smells a "milk-reek, the flowing immemorial female" (883).

Borne along by a vast aquatic fantasy that would have enchanted Gaston Bachelard, Faulkner's writing advances here without haste, itself "rich, slow, warm," through a flow of nonrestrictive and relative clauses, adjectives, adverbs, alliterations, and assonances. The succulence of this prose could repel; its excessiveness could be seen as extreme. The sublime, as we know, is only a stone's throw from the grotesque, and in *The Hamlet* Faulkner continually plays on this proximity. In the following paragraph, the cow, emerging from the mist, finally visible, leaves mythology and becomes a real cow again, "standing in the parted water of the ford, blowing into the water the thick, warm, heavy, milk-laden breath," and Ike the transfixed lover becomes Ike the idiot again, wallowing "from thigh to thigh, making a faint, thick, hoarse moaning sound" (N3, 883). Further on, after falling into a ditch with the cow, he receives "the violent relaxing of her fear-constricted bowels" (891).

The Rabelaisian humor of this scene introduces a brutal dissonance into the poetic recitation of the idyll. In fact, the recitation is preceded, at the end of the first section of the first chapter of "The Long Summer," by the announcement of the mysterious show that the men seated on the veranda are preparing to see, and is followed, in the third section of the same chapter, by the revelation that the show is a peep show where Lump Snopes charges the voyeurs to witness Ike frolicking with the cow in Mrs. Littlejohn's stable (N3, 912–15).

Ike Snopes is alternately a practicing zoophile and the perfect lover. One cannot escape the suspicion that this sumptuous orchestration of the love of an idiot for a cow is just a distorted pastoral or a parody of the topos of the nymph surprised while bathing—in brief, the mock-heroic treatment of a vulgar, even frankly obscene subject. Similarly, alternating between bitch in heat and Aphrodite, Eula is a character of uncertain and fragmented status; the celebration of her prodigious sensual aura seems at times to mock itself, and here again the lyrical juxtaposes buffoonery.

In any case, the writing in *The Hamlet* is wonderfully extravagant and of a rare virtuosity. All the stylistic registers are mixed and blended here. As in

As I Lay Dying, but with perhaps even more abandon, the story moves from (apparently) the most uncouth orality to the most refined rhetoric. The vernacular vigor of Ratliff's tales meets the extreme mannerism of its poetic flights of fancy. Faulkner, now fully matured as a writer, seems enchanted with his own magical powers. More than ever master of his resources, his writing in *The Hamlet* is like a painter painting, posing the words on the page as a painter applies touches of color to the canvas, like Cézanne's flecks of blue, white, and brown. His writing loses itself in itself and, as a result, reveals itself as never before. One could almost say that the fiction on display here is nothing more than an alibi or a pretext. Look at Eula, for example. In the story, as a character, she is portrayed as a desirable woman, as an object of desire for the entire male population of the county, but doubtless she was primarily the object of the writer's desire to write, the woman to be laid on paper.

The enchantments of *The Hamlet* defy all realism. And like a true writer, Faulkner invents his own language here, a brand-new language rustling through the undergrowth of common language. As Proust remarked, "Fine books are written in a kind of foreign language."[14] *The Hamlet* is a fine book.

⌒

The Hamlet, dedicated to Phil Stone, was published in late March 1940. The first reviews appeared in late April. Ralph Thompson, in the *New York Herald Tribune* of April 1, hailed *The Hamlet* as "nothing short of superb—subtle and yet direct, humorous, homely, brilliantly evocative of a decaying South in the generation after the Civil War. [. . .] In this book, Faulkner is unsurpassable." Malcolm Cowley, in the *New Republic*, called *The Hamlet* Faulkner's best novel since *Sanctuary. Newsweek* saw it as a "bucolic idyll of insanity, avarice, cruelty, rape, and murder," with pages "that would make Dostoevsky weak with envy." Frederick W. Dupee, in the *New York Sun*, declared Faulkner to be the most brilliant, most fertile novelist in America at that time. But this praise came with the usual reservations, and once again Faulkner was criticized for the obscurity of his prose. For Burton Rascoe, in the *American Mercury*, "It is his misfortune—and his fortune perhaps—to be ecstatically praised by people who haven't the vaguest notion what he is writing about," and the *Times Literary Supplement* was equally harsh, finding Faulkner "more nearly unreadable in this new novel than in any previous one." The originality of the novel's structure was also unrecognized, and for many *The Hamlet* was nothing but a hodgepodge of short stories. Even Robert Penn Warren, in a review published in the spring 1941 issue of *Kenyon Review*, found the framework of the book too loose, lamenting the rigorous novelist of *Light in August*.

Faulkner himself does not seem to have doubted the excellence of his new novel. On April 24, 1939, he wrote to Robert Haas to tell him about the latest changes to his manuscript. At the end of the letter, he added, in ink: "I am the best in America, by God" (*SL*, 112).

LEGACIES: *GO DOWN, MOSES*

Like *The Unvanquished* and *The Hamlet*, *Go Down, Moses* was compiled from short stories that had been already written and for the most part already published. However, Faulkner revised them all with a view to strengthening the ties between them and, if necessary, creating new ones. In his eyes, *Go Down, Moses* was a novel. He wrote to Haas: "Moses is indeed a novel. [. . .] Indeed, if you will permit me to say so at this late date, nobody but Random House seemed to labor under the permission that GO DOWN MO-SES should be titled 'and other stories.' 'I remember the shock (mild) I got when I saw the printed title page. I say, reprint it, call it simply GO DOWN MOSES, which was the way I sent it in to you 8 years ago'" (SL, 284–85). But it was only in the second reprint of the first edition and in the Modern Library edition of 1955 that "and other stories" was removed from the title.

The genesis of *Go Down, Moses* dates back to the 1930s, when Faulkner was writing his first stories about Native Americans and his first hunting tales. In "Red Leaves" and "A Justice," he created characters such as Issetibbeha and Ikkemotubbe, Mississippi Indians who had become land dealers and slave owners, and the McCaslins had already made appearances in *Absalom, Absalom!* and several short stories from the 1930s. But the first kernel of *Go Down, Moses* was a collection of short stories about Southern blacks. The first time Faulkner talked about the book to Haas, toward the end of April 1940, the project was part of an emergency plan to settle his debts: "Ober has four stories about niggers," he wrote on May 22. "I can build onto them, write some more, make a book like THE UNVANQUISHED, could get it together in six months, perhaps" (SL, 124). A year later, on May 1, 1941, he explained to Haas the plan for his new book, and his letters show that in December he was working on what was to become "The Bear," the fourth part of *Go Down, Moses*. More difficult than he had expected, the work advanced slowly and Faulkner was not able to meet his deadlines. On December 2 he wrote to Haas: "My promise re mss. Dec 1 is already broken. There is more meat in it than I thought, a section now that I am going to be proud of and which requires careful writing and rewriting to get it exactly right. I am at it steadily, and have been" (*SL*, 146). It took him two more weeks, but in mid-December Saxe Commins received 121 typed pages: the completely new text of the fourth section of "The Bear."

A new turning point in Faulkner's career, *Go Down, Moses* is both a culmination and a recap, a meditative and elegiac palimpsest, where almost all of his previous work is rewritten and recast in a new light. The title and dedication indicate the stakes from the outset. "Go Down, Moses" is the first phrase from the chorus of a famous negro spiritual: "Go down, Moses / Way down into Egypt land / Tell old Pharaoh / 'Let my people go.'" Thus, from the very title, by recalling the subjugation and liberation of the Jewish people as told in the book of Exodus, which prefigure the destiny of the black people in the spiritual, the novel fits into both the continuity of the Scriptures and the tragic context of the African American experience. The dedication to Caroline Barr, the black "Mammy" "born into slavery," whose funeral oration was delivered by Faulkner in 1940, attests from the outset to the author's personal involvement in his fiction.

Go Down, Moses, Faulkner's third genealogical novel, like *Absalom, Absalom!* deals with the destinies of a Southern planter family, following them from the mid-nineteenth century through 1941, the year before the novel was published. Through the tangled threads of the white, mixed-race, patrilineal and matrilineal, legitimate and illegitimate descendants of Lucius Quintus Carothers McCaslin, the founding ancestor, Faulkner resumes his questioning of the "curse" of the South. The constitutive illegitimacy of Southern order;, the perpetuation of violence and injustice; the transmission of shame, guilt, and resentment within families; the burden of legacy (for whites) and the bitterness of dispossession (for Native Americans, blacks, and mixed-race people) are the major themes. Even more than

Absalom, Absalom!, which *Go Down, Moses* rereads and rewrites in more
ways than one, Faulkner undertakes to untangle the web of interracial relations. None of his other novels have as many African American characters or show the ravages of racism through so many generations. And in *Go
Down, Moses*, as in *Absalom, Absalom!*, these themes are approached in the
context of both family and region and dealt with in a historical perspective,
except this time the history of the South is told as a chapter of the history of
the United States, and the unresolved question of the relationship between
white and black is closely linked to that, no less fundamental, of the relationship between the white man and the wild spaces of the New World and
its first inhabitants, the Native Americans. Close to the concerns already
formulated in the nineteenth century by James Fenimore Cooper and Na-
thaniel Hawthorne, Faulkner gives unprecedented attention in this novel
to the conditions under which the American continent was colonized. *Go
Down, Moses* is his most expansive meditation on beginnings and, after *Absalom, Absalom!*, his most ambitious study of original sin: the brutal establishment by whites of a socioeconomic system founded on both the despo-
liation of Native Americans and the subjugation of imported Africans.

Whites, blacks, Native Americans—three distinct cultures—rub
shoulders, are interwoven, confront one another. In *Go Down, Moses*,
Faulkner becomes an anthropologist.

———

"Isaac McCaslin, Uncle Ike, past seventy and nearer eighty than he ever
corroborated anymore, a widower now and uncle to half a county and father
to no one" (N4, 5); thus begins "Was," the short story that opens *Go Down,
Moses*. The story that follows was "not something participated in or even
seen" by Ike (5). It is 1859, "the old time, the old days" (6), when the Mississippi was still "border" country, on the plantation owned by Theophilus
and Amodeus McCaslin, alias "Uncle Buck" and "Uncle Buddy," Carothers
McCaslin's twin sons. It all starts and ends with the hilarious spectacle of
Buddy and a pack of hounds chasing after a trained fox. Next comes the
story of another hunt, the ritualistic manhunt of the slave Tomey's Turl,
who, twice a year, escapes to court a girl in the neighboring plantation, inhabited by Hubert Beauchamp and his sister, the ugly Miss Sophonsiba, an
old maid in search of a husband, more resolved to catch Buck than he is de-

termined to recapture his slave, and who he ends up marrying. A fox hunt, a manhunt, a hunt for a husband—these are hunts where the hunter or huntress disguise themselves as prey, innocent and perverse games, as are the mad poker games at which the McCaslin brothers coldly gamble away Miss Sophonsiba's and Turl's fates. These are games where the rules and roles are reversed and where the loser wins. "Was" is at the same time a tall tale, a comedy of "moods" in the picaresque tradition of Smollett, and the beginning of a dual genealogy, the mischievous chronicle of the forming of two couples: Tennie Beauchamp and Tomey's Turl, two young blacks whose marriage is decided by the end of the chapter, and a white couple, still virtual—Sophonsiba and Uncle Buck, the future parents of Isaac McCaslin.

Adopting the naive point of view of a nine-year-old boy, Cass McCaslin Edmonds, the narrator of "Was" does not tell everything he knows and pretends not to understand what he is saying. This is the false candor and the feigned blindness of a humorist. But as Faulkner himself underlined in an interview, the manhunt related in this short story tackles "more of a deadlier purpose than simple pleasure" (*FU*, 40), and already there are issues of gifts and debts, miscegenation and incest; everything is about circulation and trade—in goods, women, and money. This comical prologue is nothing less than anodyne. But one needs to read further to find this out.

In "The Fire and the Hearth," the second and longest of the short stories after "The Bear," Faulkner recycles three short stories, two of which—"A Point of Law" and "Gold Is Not Always"—had already been published. This story describes the relationship between blacks and whites on a Mississippi plantation, but it is set in 1941, and the plantation now belongs to Carothers Roth Edmonds, the great-great-grandson of old Carothers's daughter. The hero of this story is not Roth, however, but one of his "black" sharecroppers, who is also one of his relatives. Lucas Quintus Carothers McCaslin Beauchamp is the younger son of Tennie Beauchamp and of Tomey's Turl, who is the son of old Carothers and his own daughter, conceived with a black slave, making Lucas both the grandson and the great-grandson of the founder of the McCaslin dynasty, of which he is, with Isaac, the last male descendant. A crafty liar, a cheat, and even a thief from time to time, as blacks were often depicted in the negro stories told in the South by whites, Lucas does not fully escape stereotype and somewhat resembles the cunning Brer Rabbit, the trickster in black animal folklore. But as portrayed in the novel, the character is much more complex than his namesake in the three short stories from which he is sourced. In terms of social status, he is a black man in the rural South in the first half of the twentieth century, subject to the laws of white men and the implacable tenancy system in force in Mississippi. But he proves, at risk to his life, that he is the match of his white masters when, as a young husband whose male pride is wounded, he challenges one of his white cousins, whom he suspects of sleeping with his wife, and fights him sportingly, as an equal. As we will later see in *Intruder in the Dust*, in all circumstances Lucas not only affirms his dignity as a man but, proud of being a descendant of old Carothers, also claims a nobility that places him above the common man.

"Pantaloon in Black" tells the tragic story of Rider, a veritable black Hercules, strong and muscular, who works as a foreman in a small industrial business. Rider has just lost his wife; he is mad with grief, and he will die of it. This magnificent short story is primarily a blues song, a wail of lost love and impossible mourning, but it can also be read as the story of a black man rebelling against his condition as a slave, almost a hundred years after the Civil War. After his wife's death, Rider has nothing more to lose, but once he quits the game, there is nothing to stop him from breaking the rules. When he kills Birdsong, the white night watchman he catches cheating at a card game, he countersigns his own death warrant, but also, before disappearing, settles his score with his oppressors. Rider, the inconsolable widower, is portrayed in his sharpest, most violent humanity. Thus the reader is not fooled when, in the second section of the story, the narrative perspective suddenly switches to the white deputy sheriff in charge of the case: "Them damn niggers [. . .] they aint human. They look like a man and they walk on their legs like a man, and they can talk and you can understand them and you think they are understanding you, at least now and then. But when it comes to the normal human feelings and sentiments of human beings, they might just as well be a damn herd of wild buffaloes" (*N4*, 116–17). The irony is pure Swift. The inhumanity, in this case, is not that of "them damn niggers" but that of the white man who flatters himself by thinking of himself as "normal" and, to an even greater extent, that of Rider's lynch mob.

Another story starts in "The Old People," which tells of Isaac Mc-Caslin's initiation into the rituals of hunting and the brotherhood of hunters. His initiator is an old Indian, Sam Fathers, the natural son of Ikkemotubbe, nicknamed "Doom,"[15] chief of the Chickasaw tribe, and a quadroon slave woman descended from an African chief, whom Ikkemotubbe subsequently married off to a black slave. If Sam Fathers has two fathers, as his Indian name (Had-Two-Fathers) indicates, Isaac has three: Uncle Buck, his progenitor; Carothers McCaslin Edmonds, his adoptive father; and Sam Fathers, his spiritual father.

It is Fathers, the solitary old man, the hermit-priest of the forest, who will teach the twelve-year-old boy "to hunt, when to shoot and when not to shoot, when to kill and when not to kill, and better, what to do with it afterward" (*N4*, 126). But the lesson does not end there. It is no coincidence that the story begins and ends with the almost supernatural apparition of a buck:

> At first, there was nothing. There was the faint, cold, steady rain, the gray and constant light of the late November dawn, with the voices of the hounds converging somewhere in it and toward them. [. . .] Then the buck was there. He did not come into sight; he was just there, looking not like a ghost but as if all of light were condensed in him and he were the source of it, not only moving in it but disseminating it, already running, seen first as you always see the deer, in that split second after he has already seen you, already slanting away in that first soaring sound, the antlers even in that dim light looking like a small rocking-chair balanced on his head. (121)

This buck, appearing out of nowhere, whose fleeting beauty is offered up to the dazzled gaze of the hunters, will be killed by the young Ike. He crosses this sacred threshold by carrying out a bloody sacrifice under the orders of Sam Fathers. By smearing his face with the still-hot steaming blood from the beast's throat, the old Indian transforms the death into a baptism, thus putting the finishing touches to the brotherhood linking him to his initiator.

Another meeting occurs that same November afternoon. While the hunters prepare to break camp, another buck appears:

> It was coming down the ridge, as if it were walking out of the very sound of the horn which related its death. It was not running, it was walking, tremendous, unhurried, slanting and tilting its head to pass the antlers through the undergrowth, and the boy standing with Sam beside him now instead of behind him as Sam always stood, and the gun still partly aimed and one of the hammers still cocked. (*N4*, 136)

This buck is not a buck like the others, like the one they have just killed, but the totem animal, as the Bear will also be. Sam Fathers recognizes it as such when he raises his arm and says: "Oleh, Chief [. . .] Grandfather" (137). Many years before, after Ike's cousin Carothers McCaslin had killed his first buck, Sam Fathers had brought him to the same place and he had seen the same buck. Thus Ike's initiation is identical in all ways to the prescriptions of an ancient ritual, a tradition incumbent on all.

"The Old People" is the nostalgic evocation of an undivided community where the existence of men was wholly determined by the intangible symbolic order that bound them together. A long story divided into five sections, "The Bear" tells of the disappearance of that order and that community. Like "Old Man" in *If I Forget Thee, Jerusalem*, the story begins like a tale: "There was a man and a dog too this time" (*N4*, 140). As the hunting story continues, it takes on the status of an epic poem. And soon the great woods will metamorphose into a forest of dreams, secret and wild, a forest out of time and out of register: a wilderness. From his very first visit, Ike the child marvels at this closed world that fills the entire horizon with its mass: "the tall and endless wall of dense November woods under the dissolving afternoon and the year's death, sombre, impenetrable" (142). It is a space without boundaries, a time without linearity. Everything that happens in this forest has happened before, has been foretold, before all memory, by the same premonitory dream: "the bear which had run in his listening and loomed in his dreams since before he could remember and which therefore must have existed in the listening and the dreams of his cousin and Major de Spain and even old General Compson before they began to remember in their turn" (147). Here what has happened before has primacy; repetition rules endlessly.

Reserve of dreams and matrix of myths, the wilderness calls for ritual celebration. Every year, the hunters come back to the same woods to hunt the same bear. Ike's initiation will be accomplished in the immutable setting of this seasonal rite. On Sam Fathers's advice, he will little by little divest himself of the old man whose vice, child as he is, he carries within him. Knowing that a weapon will be no use to him, he sets off after the animal without gun, watch, or compass. Unless he agrees to lose himself in the forest, to lose all trace of himself, he cannot track the beast. It is only at the very end of this dangerous but plotted tracking through the mysteries of the forest that he will meet the bear: "It did not emerge, appear: it was just there, immobile, fixed in the green and windless noon's hot dappling, not as big as he had dreamed it but as big as he had expected, bigger, dimensionless against the dappled obscurity, looking at him" (*N4*, 153). Old Ben lets himself be approached only by this boy whose primordial innocence has been returned to him by his initiation. And the bear will be beaten only by the pure forces incarnated by Lion the dog.

However, the bear's death is not a replica of the buck's. The buck's ritual murder is one of those symbolic transactions that govern the economy of the sacred and attests to man's involvement in the natural order. The same is not true of the bear. Ben is not an animal destined for sacrifice; it is not simply a bear among bears—it is the "Great Bear," the totemic animal par excellence, the living soul of the forest. He thus inspires only veneration, and his killing is simply sacrilege. In the relationship between man and nature, it marks the passing from a pious, passive position of belonging to an active position of confrontation and domination. The end of Ben is both the ultimate affirmation of the sacred and its negation, the apotheosis of the myth and its irreversible decline. Yet another ceremonial, already an assassination.

It is because Lion is already part of the wilderness that it manages to bring down Ben. But this wilderness has been diverted from its natural destination to serve the predatory designs of white men; Lion betrays the forest. Between bear and dog the relationship is of the same nature as that between the old Indian Sam Fathers and Boon Hogganbeck, Lion's trainer. Just as both men inherit the same soil and the same blood, both beasts are bound by a shared belonging. But while Sam Fathers, the "natural" aristocrat according to Faulkner, acts as a watchful guardian over the original order, Boon the plebeian is an accomplice to the intruders by whom this order will be destroyed. Similarly, while the bear is the "epitome and apotheosis of the old wild life" (*N4*, 142), the dog will be the instrument of its annihilation. Each has his animal double: Ben is to Sam Fathers what Lion is to Boon. And their opposition is that of the bear and the dog. Sam Fathers is to Boon what Ben is to Lion. This play of dual personalities and oppositions illustrates the paradoxical manner in which the natural law of the native Indians switches to the new, unnatural law of the white invaders. To make their work of destruction possible, an initial corruption had to happen within the very heart of this mythical universe. Boon and Lion are the blind agents of a disaster foretold. Sam Fathers, who is well aware of this, does nothing to prevent the bear's death. Similarly, Ike is nothing but a fascinated spectator: "he should have hated and feared Lion. Yet he did not. It seemed to him that there was a fatality in it. It seemed to him that something he didn't know what, was beginning; had already begun. It was like the last act on a set stage. It was the beginning of the end of something" (166). The final bloody act, both scandalous and inevitable, is the death of Old Ben, the death of Lion, and then the death of Sam Fathers, whom Boon buries right beside the Bear's maimed paw. Thus, one last time, beyond life, the ancient alliance between man and beast is affirmed, united in the same destiny.

Section 3 ends with the recounting of these three, almost simultaneous, deaths. Written retrospectively, section 4 has no direct narrative link with either those coming before it or the one coming after. Faulkner took care to mark it out from the other sections, even down to its layout. In contrast to the latter, section 4 starts in lowercase, and as if to liberate the flow of Faulkner's fluvial prose, each paragraph starts without a capital letter and ends without a period. As much as the hunting tale of the Bear belongs to the universe of myth, the fourth section is alien to it. The earth is now domesticated instead of wild; the farmer has replaced the hunter; the tribal fraternity of Indians has been replaced by the white patriarchal family; the symbolic trading of archaic societies has been replaced by a semi-feudal, semi-capitalist economy, iconically located in the plantation commissary. Initially dreamed up as legend, the past is now consulted like a chronicle, scrutinized like a civil register, deciphered like a secret. The time of no return, of history, has returned. The long sentence with which this section starts, meandering over more than two pages, is like an initial dive into the mysteries of memory—a memory that is no longer arranged around a few essential gestures, but that becomes entangled in the uncertain search for that which once was.

Section 4, written while Faulkner was already well advanced in his revisions, relates two visits by Ike McCaslin to the commissary: the first during the winter of 1883–1884, when he was sixteen, after the death of Old Ben and Sam Fathers; the second in October 1888, on the day of his twenty-first birthday. Reading the ledgers reveals to Ike that

the whole plantation in its mazed and intricate entirety—the land, the fields
and what they represented in terms of cotton ginned and sold, the men and
women whom they fed and clothed and even paid a little cash money at Christ-
mas-time in return for the labor which planted and raised and picked and
ginned the cotton, the machinery and mules and gear with which they raised
it and their cost and upkeep and replacement—that whole edifice intricate
and complex and founded upon injustice and erected by ruthless rapacity.
(*N4*, 221)

Behind this "edifice" is the untrammeled desire, energy, and unshakable
determination of Lucius Quintus Carothers McCaslin, the scandalous ancestor, the founding-fornicating Father, guilty not only of greed but of a
double crime combining incest, the culmination of endogamy, and miscegenation, the culmination of exogamy.

Ike thus discovers the accursed share of his heritage. On the day of his
majority he seems resolved to reject adulthood. His decision to renounce
his inheritance is the starting point of his long discussion with his cousin
Cass: a meditation with two voices on the way of the world and the detours
of evil, an inquiry into the origins of the South, its past, present, and future.
Here inquiry becomes exegesis, involving the deciphering and interpretation of three texts: the ledgers of the plantation commissary, the Bible, and
John Keats's "Ode on a Grecian Urn," subjected to a mise en abyme as it had
already been in *Light in August*. Family archives, a sacred text, and poetic
expression—three distinct ways of using writing, each time the question of
whether it is possible to re-apprehend the truth that has been lost.

The entries in the ledgers are merely crude fragments of a prototext:
figures, names, dates of birth and death, already half worn by oblivion.
In these yellowing, dusty pages, the poor words inscribed by the clumsy
hand of almost illiterate scribes, Ike finds nothing but a crumbling chronicle. As in *Absalom, Absalom!* for Quentin and Shreve the information is
incomplete and terse; the entire story needs to be resurrected. However,
shrillness arises from these dumb letters; tragedies sleep beneath the ash of
words: "*Eunice Bought by Father in New Orleans 1807 $650. dolars. Marrid to
Thucydus 1809 Drownd in Crick Cristmas Day 1832*" (*N4*, 197). Eunice was
old Carothers's black mistress; her drowning was a suicide, and Ike imagines her entering the frozen creek, six months before her daughter Tomasina (Tomey) gives birth to a baby conceived with her white lover.

Reading the ledgers, Ike discovers not only the story of his family but the entire history of the South, whose chaotic course also needs to be clarified. Hence the recourse to the Bible, the recourse to "the Book," read simultaneously as the story of Creation, Fall, and Redemption, as "the tedious and shabby chronicle of His chosen" (*N4*, 190) and as a sacred text bearing revealed truths. To justify giving up his inheritance, Ike needs a finalized vision of history, and the most difficult thing for him is to reconcile Sam Fathers's teachings with Christian eschatology. In his curious and confused theodicy, all the events of history are involved in an economy of salvation, God having drawn up a plan to regenerate fallen humanity by transforming the initial damnation into a felix culpa, through which good comes from evil. But this second chance offered to man is in turn wasted, and ultimately a deadly war, with all its legacy of suffering, will be needed to rouse the men of "this land which He still intended to save" (211).

The third text within the text is the ode by Keats. It emerges in the middle of the discussion, when Ike suddenly remembers Cass reading it seven years earlier. For Cass the point was to use the poem to understand Ike's suspended gesture, his refusal to kill the bear. The scene depicted on the Grecian urn and described in the ode is the pursuit of the beloved, it too suspended, immobilized, forever engraved in marble. Equally far from the prosaic wording in the ledgers and from the sacred word of the Book, opposed to both the constraints of reality and the constructions of myth, Keats's poem reestablishes the indistinction of truth and beauty. But the truth of the poem is not the truth of the world; its fixed time is not the time of living men. Ike mulishly mixes everything up, forgetting that old Carothers's incestuous rape did indeed happen and that the victim bore no relation to the "still unravish'd bride of quietness" in Keats's poem.

In the wilderness the meaning of the world was revealed to all in the intact evidence of myth and rite. Born of uncertainty, the *disputatio* between Ike and Cass feeds on the confrontation of opposing viewpoints. Although it is true that both recognize the injustice of the plantation system, for Cass, the presumed realist, private property is a necessary evil, while Ike the idealist assimilates it with original sin and convinces himself that refusing his heritage will guarantee his freedom.

A somber epilogue to "The Bear," "Delta Autumn" brings us up to the start of the 1940s—that is, the present day. Now over seventy, Ike, the last white male descendant of the McCaslin dynasty, has become "Uncle Ike" in the community. The short story relates his last hunt. Everything has changed: the hunt no longer takes place in the lowlands, which have long been paved and settled, but hundreds of miles away, in the Delta region. Besieged, surrounded, carved up, given over to men's avarice, the primeval forest is constantly receding and is condemned to vanish completely. In just two generations the country has been "*deswamped and denuded and derivered* [. . .]. No wonder the ruined woods I used to know dont cry for retribution [. . .]. The people who have destroyed it will accomplish its revenge" (*N4*, 269).

Ike acts as devastated witness to this destruction but is not really disturbed. "Born old" as we already learned in "The Fire and Hearth," he has become "steadily younger and younger until, past seventy himself and at least that many years nearer eighty than he ever admitted anymore, he had acquired something of a young boy's high and selfless innocence" (*N4*, 82). Like most Faulknerian idealists, Ike is doomed to regress. Clinging to his juvenile—and very American—dream of Adamic innocence, forever entrenched in the enchanted, sanitized kingdom of his adolescence, he believes himself "set free" (222), but his freedom is just a delusion, his innocence is simply a refusal to confront reality in any way.

The unexpected recounting of his meeting with a young woman and her child in the hunters' encampment cruelly tarnishes the portrait of the old dreamer. This young woman with almost white skin is the granddaughter of Tennie's Jim, another son of Tomey's Turl and Tennie Beauchamp. Unaware that they are related, Roth Edmonds, son of Zack Edmonds and grandson of Carothers McCaslin Edmonds, has made her his mistress but refuses to marry her and acknowledge his son. Thinking, like old Carothers, that he can buy a good conscience through monetary compensation, he asks Ike to give the young woman an envelope containing a sheaf of banknotes. Initially at a loss, Ike eventually realizes that she is also part of Old Carothers's "black" posterity and "not loud, in a voice of amazement, pity, and outrage" says to her: "You're a nigger!" (*N4*, 266). He is ready to recognize his kinship with her, and in a gesture that is both generous and derisory, he offers her son the hunting horn left to him by General Compson. We even see him touching the woman's hand, "the gnarled, bloodless, bone-light bone-dry old man's fingers touching for a second the smooth young flesh where the strong old blood ran after its long journey back to home" (267). For a brief instant, all distance is eliminated; the body of the old man has communicated with the body of a young woman, and their consanguinity is finally recognized. This does not stop Ike from refusing to envisage the virtual promise of reconciliation offered by the child in whom, for the first time, both branches of the McCaslins have been joined. Miscegenation horrifies him to such an extent that he indefinitely postpones this reconciliation: *Maybe in a thousand or two thousand years in America*, he thought. *But not now! Not now!*" (266). He therefore urges the young woman to return to the North and marry "'a man in [her] own race'" (268).

"'Then,'" he tells her, "'you will forget all this, forget it ever happened, that he ever existed.'" To which she calmly responds: "'Old man [. . .] have you lived so long and forgotten so much that you dont remember anything you ever knew or felt or even heard about love?'" (N4, 268). The question is its own response. Outside the wilderness, Ike has in fact loved no one, and while he did manage to renounce the family heritage, he has not been able to rid himself of the prejudices of his race. Ike, the good soul above suspicion, the intransigent idealist who sees himself as the most righteous of the righteous, has failed miserably. After the young woman leaves, he lies back on his narrow cot "trembling, panting, the blanket huddled to his chin and his hands crossed on his breast" (268), almost like a corpse wrapped in its shroud. For Ike, fall is the season, not of wisdom and serenity, but of defeat and death. Like Old Ben and Sam Fathers, this childless man will die alone.

Like "Delta Autumn," "Go Down, Moses," the text that ends the novel, is the story of an ending. The hero of this story is Butch, alias Samuel Worsham Beauchamp, grandson of Lucas and Mollie. Like thousands of blacks during the "Great Migration" of the early twentieth century, he has left the South to try his chances in the industrial cities of the North; the young delinquent of Jefferson is now a small-time hoodlum in Chicago. His pitiful fate seems to confirm Ike's prejudices about Old Carothers's mixed-race descendants. In his way, he also wanted to disavow his heritage and wipe out his origins, but the family "curse" has caught up with him. Condemned to death for killing a policeman in Chicago, he is portrayed, like Popeye at the end of *Sanctuary*, lying on his bed in his prison cell, smoking his last few cigarettes, about to be executed.

"Go Down, Moses" is both epilogue and epitaph. It is a kind of "*tombeau*." It could also be read as an apologue, an ironic version of the return of the prodigal son. Butch has never known his mother or father; his return is posthumous, as only his remains will be returned to his native, ancestral homeland. His funeral is organized by two old women, one white, one black—Mollie Beauchamp and Miss Worsham—and a white gentleman, Gavin Stevens. With the help of a journalist, Stevens manages to collect the two hundred dollars needed for a suitable send-off for Butch, but when he finds the grief-stricken family in Miss Worsham's house, gathered around the brick hearth where "the ancient symbol of human coherence and solidarity smoldered" (*N4*, 278), everything in him refuses to take part in the ritual lamentation for the dead man and, panicked and nauseous, he eventually runs away.

For Stevens, Butch is just a bad boy and the "bad son of a bad father" (*N4*, 274); for Mollie, who knows her Bible, he is a new Benjamin,[16] the last of the brothers betrayed and sold, the last of the disinherited heirs, the last black to pay for the faults of his white ancestor. She not only wants Butch to have a decent burial; she also wants the whole truth to come out in the open and be known. "'I wants hit all in de paper. All of hit'" (280). All—not just as a brief news item, not just Butch's miserable life, but the entire story of the McCaslins, the Edmonds, and the Beauchamps, white and black, the entire history of violence, injustice, and suffering that we have just read.

On the occasion of this mourning, a community of the living, made up of blacks and whites, could have stood up to the community of the dead. But the time for mutual recognition and sharing is not yet nigh. Moses is taking his time going down.

———

Go Down, Moses was published on May 11, 1942. When the first copies arrived at Rowan Oak, Faulkner found that they looked "very well" (*SL*, 149) but readily acknowledged that it was not the best time to publish a collection of short stories in the United States. Nevertheless, the reviews were almost all favorable. Never had there been such a chorus of praise for a work by Faulkner. In the *New York Times Book Review* of May 10, 1942, Horace Gregory recommended *Go Down, Moses* to his readers as a carefully written book, not just simply a simple selection of short stories, and placed Faulkner as one of the contemporary writers "who deserves increasing respect and admiration." However, Faulkner still frustrated some. Lionel Trilling, a renowned essay writer, complained in the *Nation* (May 30, 1942) that he had had to read the new novel twice to understand it. *Time* renewed its chorus that Faulkner was the greatest living novelist—unfortunately. People were now ready to acknowledge him as the most talented living American writer and even to rank him on a par with Hawthorne, Melville, Twain, or Joyce, but there seemed to be nothing yet to guarantee his permanence. The anonymous reviewer writing in the *Times Literary Supplement* of October 10 put it more bluntly. The review, titled "Faulkneresque," starts as follows: "It needs to be said every time a new book of his appears: Mr. William Faulkner is an exasperating writer."

NOTES

1. See "Faulkner with Waco," *B1*, chapter 36.

2. Jean Pouillon, *Temps et roman*, new exp. ed. (1946; Paris: Gallimard, collection "Tel," 1993), 297.

3. In Exodus, God addresses Moses: "I bare you on eagle's wings, and brought you unto myself."

4. The title refers to the cry of King David when he learns of the death of his rebellious son: "O my son Absalom, my son, my son Absalom! would God I had died for thee, O Absalom, my son, my son!" (II Samuel 19:4). In contrast to King David, Henry Sutpen does not weep for his lost son. Faulkner's novel contains many parallels and contrasts with the story of David and his son. Thus, Absalom kills his brother Amnon for raping their sister Tamar, just as Henry kills Charles to stop him from marrying Judith.

5. Pierre Michon, "Le Père du texte," in *Trois auteurs* (Paris: Verdier, 1997), 81.

6. Friedrich Nietzsche, *Daybreak*, trans. R. J. Hollingdale (Cambridge: Cambridge University Press, 1997), 156; emphasis in original.

7. See William Faulkner, *Selected Letters*, 97 and 99.

8. Baudelaire, "*Madame Bovary*," in *Œuvres complètes*, ed. Y. G. Le Dantec (Paris: Gallimard, Pléiade, 1954), 1008–1009.

9. The convict's final words were removed in the first eight editions, and it was not until 1990 that they were finally printed in the new edition published by Library of America.

10. Phil Stone in a 1957 letter quoted by James B. Meriwether in his introduction to *Father Abraham* (see *FA*, 4).

11. In the other two volumes of the trilogy, as in *Intruder in the Dust, Knight's Gambit, Requiem for a Nun*, and *The Reivers*, the Frenchman is named Louis Grenier.

12. The character V. K. Ratliff already appears under the name of Suratt in *Father Abraham, Sartoris*, and *As I Lay Dying* and in a number of short stories. The Russian names to which the initials refer—Vladimir Kyrilytch—are only revealed in *The Town*.

13. Gilles Deleuze, *What is Philosophy?*, trans. Graham Burchell and Hugh Tomlinson (London, Verso, 1994), 171.

14. Proust, *Contre Sainte-Beuve*, 297.

15. "Doom" is a contraction of "Du Homme," which is what Ikkemottubbe is named by a French companion calling himself Chevalier Soeur-Blonde de Vitry (see N3, 123). "Doom" is one of Faulkner's fetish words.

16. Mollie—or rather Faulkner—confuses Benjamin (which in Hebrew means "son of my right [hand]"), the last-born son of Jacob, with Joseph, the son sold into Egypt by his brothers. The same confusion arises with regard to Benjy in *The Sound and the Fury* (see N1, 1008).

7
THE DARK YEARS

DIRE STRAITS

From the end of the 1930s on, Faulkner's life became increasingly overcast. The 1940s were to be, to use the expression of one of his biographers, the "dark years."[1] In 1940 his financial situation was more catastrophic than ever. He had rashly spent all the money he had earned in Hollywood during the good years, including the $25,000 paid in February 1938 by MGM for the film rights to *The Unvanquished*. While his income fell to no more than $4,000 a year, he remained crippled with debts and the Internal Revenue Service was demanding arrears of $450 on his 1937 income tax.

Harold Ober, his literary agent since 1938, did what he could to help. In January 1940 he managed to sell "Point of Law" to *Collier's* for a thousand dollars. The short story was published in June, and between September and November another four stories were published: "The Old People," "Pantaloon in Black," "Gold is Not Always," and "Tomorrow." But Faulkner's accounts were still in the red and his letters were exclusively about money. In April he complained bitterly to Robert Haas about the deadlock he found himself in.

> By the time I have paid the income tax assessment and a note at the bank here, that will be gone. And I will still have to keep trying to write trash stories which so far are not selling even fifty percent, because I am now like the gambler who simply has to double and pyramid, the poker player who can neither call nor throw in his hand but has got to raise. (*SL*, 122)

Faulkner was also upset that the sales of *The Hamlet* were not as high as he had hoped. On April 30 he learned from Haas that 6,780 copies had been sold but that he should not expect to make more than $3,000 per book.

Haas offered the writer a plan covering three books, with an immediate advance of $1,000, a second payment of $2,000 in 1941, and $250 per month for the next two years. On May 3 Faulkner responded: "Your promptness was kind, your response comforting, your suggestion generous" (*SL*, 122), but his letter seethes with anger: he was enraged that his time as a writer was not free.

In June, Haas paid him another advance of $2,400 for the forthcoming collection of short stories. But Faulkner wanted more. On June 7 he sent Haas a long letter outlining his difficult situation: "I need $9,000.00 more to give me economic freedom for two years, in which to write, or $5,000.00 more for one year. Otherwise I will have to liquidate myself, sell some of my property for what I can get for it, in order to preserve what I might. I wont hesitate to do this when I come to believe that I have no other course" (*SL*, 127). Haas answered that sales were too low to warrant another advance. Faulkner then contacted Harold Guinzburg of Viking Press, who had previously offered his services. Guinzburg offered him $6,000, which he transferred to Random House, while indicating that from then on he was going to publish through Viking. But Bennett Cerf was not ready to let him go. The negotiations with Guinzburg hit a snag over the repayment of typesetting costs and the twenty-five hundred unsold copies of *The Hamlet*. In July, Guinzburg informed Faulkner that Random House's demands were too high and that Viking would have to retract its proposal and give up on the project.

Cerf then tried to reassure Faulkner: "I beg you to put aside all thoughts of going to another publisher," he wrote in August. "I promise you that we will do everything in our power to make things as easy for you as we can. In my own opinion, you and Eugene O'Neill are the two keystone authors on the whole Random House list and we simply cannot afford to lose you" (*B*, 1056). Faulkner therefore remained with Random House. His money troubles were more overwhelming than ever. Since his marriage, he had family obligations, and over the years, after the accidental death of his brother Dean and his father's death, these obligations had become a crushing burden. He had had enough of providing for the whole clan and complained of this in his letters to Haas, such as this one, dated May 3, 1940:

> Every so often, in spite of judgment and all else, I take these fits of sort of raging and impotent exasperation at this really quite alarming paradox which my

life reveals: Beginning at the age of thirty I, an artist, a sincere one and of the first class, who should be free even of his own economic responsibilities and with no moral conscience at all, began to become the sole, principal and partial support—food, shelter, heat, clothes, medicine, kotex, school fees, toilet paper and picture shows—of my mother . . . [a] brother's widow and child, a wife of my own and two step children, my own child; I inherited my father's debts and his dependents, white and black, without inheriting yet from anyone one inch of land or one stick of furniture or one cent of money; the only thing I ever got for nothing, after the first pair of long pants I received (cost: $7.50) was the $300.00 O. Henry prize last year. I bought without help from anyone the house I live in and all the furniture; I bought my farm the same way. I am 42 years old and I have already paid for four funerals and will certainly pay for one more and in all likelihood two more beside that, provided none of the people in mine or my wife's family my superior in age outlive me, before I ever come to my own. (SL, 122–23)

There is bitterness and pride in this letter, but also blindness. Faulkner does not seem to have realized that in spending his money rashly, he only made his troubles worse. The weight of his "economic responsibilities" was to become heavier and heavier, and the need to constantly earn more was not without effect on his life and his work as a writer. The renewed creativity that marked the winter and early spring of 1940, which produced a good part of Go Down, Moses, was followed by a state of lethargy and black mood that was to last until the end of summer. As always, alcohol was his sole recourse.

The telegrams sent by Faulkner to Ober in early 1941 are cries for help that are uncannily similar to those sent by Scott Fitzgerald to the self-same Ober a few years earlier. On January 16 Faulkner told him that he urgently needed a hundred dollars. Ober immediately sent him a thousand dollars, for which Faulkner was very grateful: "Thank you for the money. I did not intend the wire to ask for a loan, but I used the money and thank you for it. [. . .] When I wired you I did not have $15.00 to pay electricity bill with, keep my lights burning" (SL, 138). To settle his taxes, pay his bills, repay his debts, and keep his large family, he continued to write short stories and was ready to make any number of concessions and comply with all requests. On February 21, 1942, he wrote to Ober: "If there is a chance yet to place it ["Knight's Gambit"], return it to me and I will rewrite it. [. . .] If you have anything else of mine which any editor ever intimated he might buy if it were simplified, send that back too. As usual, I am not quite a boat's length ahead of the sheriff" (199). On June 23 he wrote to Bennett Cerf:

> Right now, I cant move at all. I have 60¢ in my pocket, and that is literally all. I finished a story and sent it in yesterday, but with no real hope it will sell. My local creditors bother me, but so far none has taken an action because I began last year to give them notes for debts. But the notes will come due soon and should I be sued, my whole house here will collapse: farm, property, everything. (154)

In 1941 Faulkner made only thirty-eight hundred dollars from all of his writing combined—books, tales, and short stories. In 1942 the sum total of all his royalties earned him just three hundred dollars. Once again he was unable to live decently from his occupation as a writer. In the early summer of 1942, he wrote to Bennett Cerf: "I have reached the point where I had better go to Cal. with just r. r. [railroad] fare if I can do no better" (*SL*, 155). It was obvious that he needed a new contract with Hollywood.

Meanwhile, World War II had broken out. After the Japanese attack on Pearl Harbor in December 1941, the United States entered the war. The country was mobilized. Affected by conscription, the young men of Oxford left one after the other. At Rowan Oak, Faulkner read the press. As in 1917, when he tried to join the RAF, he wanted to take part in the war effort. It was his last chance, but what army would want him at the age of forty-two? "I got my uniform out the other day," he wrote to Haas in May 1940. "I can button it, even after twenty-two years; the wings look as brave as they ever did. I swore then when I took it off in '19, that I would never wear another, no how, nowhere, for no one. But now I dont know. Of course I could do no good, would last about two minutes in combat" (*SL*, 125). He did not become demoralized, however. His brother Jack was assigned to counterespionage and was preparing to leave for England; Haas was squadron leader in the National Guard; Malcolm, his adopted son, and Jimmy, his brother John's son, were heading off to a marine commando training camp. So why not him? He had not given up on the idea of being taken on by Naval Aviation and still hoped that he would be commissioned as a lieutenant to a combat position. In March 1942 he wrote to Haas:

I am going before a Navy board and Medical for a commission, N.R. I will go to the Bureau of Aeronautics, Washington, for a job. I am to get full Lieut. and 3200.00 per year, and I hope a pilot's rating to wear the wings. I dont like this desk job particularly, but I think it better to get the commission first and then try to get a little nearer the gunfire, which I intend to try to do. (149)

Faulkner was not recalled by the RAF and eventually enlisted in the Civil Defense to teach radio-aerial navigation to young volunteers from Mississippi, but with no illusions about his usefulness. In truth, he no longer had any clear idea what his purpose was and where his life was going. Even writing seemed to have abandoned him. But he knew it would come back. On May 27, 1940, he wrote to Haas: "Maybe the watching of all this coming to a head for the last year is why I cant write, dont seem to want to write, that is. But I can still write. That is, I haven't said at 42 all that is in the cards for me to say" (*SL*, 125).

HOLLYWOOD AGAIN

Interviewed by the *Commercial Appeal* on November 17, 1937, Faulkner admitted: "I dont like scenario writing, because I don't know enough about it. I feel as though I cant do myself justice in that type of work." At the time, he didn't think he would return to Hollywood, and, in fact, he did not go back for four and a half years. But in 1942, as we have seen, he was again deeply in debt. Magazines did not seem eager to publish his short stories and he was in favor only in Hollywood. In the spring he sent numerous letters to Ober, urging him either to sell his short stories or to find him work in Hollywood. People hesitated to rehire him because of his reputation as a drinker, and the negotiations for the new contract were to give rise to an unprecedented imbroglio in his Hollywood career.

On July 11, 1942, Ober informed him that Hollywood was ready to use his services again and asked him to make contact immediately with H. N. Swanson, his agent on the West Coast. But in the meantime, another agent, young William Herndon, had been working on Faulkner's behalf, garnering the support of James Geller, head of Warner Brothers's story department, and of the producer Robert Buckner. He had aroused Jack Warner's interest by showing him "Turn About," Faulkner's wartime short story that had been made into a film a few years earlier. Herndon set up a contract with Warner Bros. for three hundred dollars a week. This was when Swanson came on the scene. Faulkner authorized him to represent him in Hollywood and now tried to get rid of Herndon. But Herndon, who had also been appointed to defend Faulkner's interests, accused him of lacking "integrity" and threatened to sue. Faulkner took offense but ended up giving in. On July 22 he telegrammed Geller that he was accepting the contract negotiated by Herndon.

Two days later he was back in Los Angeles, and on the twenty-seventh he went to the Warner Bros. offices in Burbank. The new contract was very one-sided. Faulkner did not want to work in Hollywood for more than a year, but his contract gave Warner Bros. the option to extend it at the end of each contractual period for the same term, thus allowing them to retain Faulkner's services on an exclusive basis for seven years. He was paid three hundred dollars a week; five years earlier he had been paid a thousand. Faulkner was now one of the worst-paid scriptwriters in Hollywood—a bargain for Jack Warner, who publicly boasted about it: "I've got America's best writer for $300 a week."

Faulkner's final exile in California started in the summer of 1942 and ended in the fall of 1945. This time he took a room with a balcony on the top floor of the Highland Hotel, a stone's throw from Hollywood Boulevard. He worked Monday through Friday from nine thirty in the morning to five forty in the evening in a corner office on the second floor of the Writers' Building in Burbank, known as "the Ward," where, along with six other scriptwriters, he churned out scripts for the megalomaniac who saw himself as the "Ford" of the film industry.

Faulkner's slight, stiff figure, along with his mustache and pipe, was now familiar to all. Anthony Quinn remembered him as follows: "Faulkner could be seen in the clubs and bars, a walking stick in his hand, wearing a Harris tweed jacket with elbow patches. Nobody dressed like that in Hollywood except Faulkner."[2] He now had his rituals and habits. On Friday evenings he went to Musso & Frank's, where he would order fish soup and Irish whiskey; on Saturday afternoons he could be seen at the bar of the same restaurant, with the full cohort of scriptwriters, including Dalton Trumbo, Lillian Hellman, James M. Cain, Raymond Chandler, Dashiell Hammett, Horace McCoy, Clifford Odets, Stephen Longstreet, and John Fante. He was often seen at LaRue's in the company of Jo Pagano, who published short stories in the same magazines as him, and Albert I. Bezzerides ("Buzz"), another young writer turned scriptwriter, who was one of his most loyal friends. On the weekends he went hunting or fishing with Clark Gable and Howard Hawks. He also visited his old friend Dorothy Parker, who had set up home on the West Coast.

After the United States entered the war in 1941, Hollywood mobilized on a scale that was even more massive than during World War I. Film output in the early 1940s was dominated by patriotic propaganda, and all the studios were converted into "a sort of war industry."[3] At President Roosevelt's instigation Warner Bros. decided to make a film about the career of Charles de Gaulle, head of the Free French Forces. Faulkner was put to work on the script and given ten weeks to help put the movie into shape. Successively called "Journey Toward Dawn," "Journey Toward Hope," "Free France," and then "The De Gaulle Story," the project inspired Faulkner, the great-grandson of a valiant Civil War officer, who had always been attracted by rebellious heroes and their exploits.

Faulkner set to work on the same day he arrived in Burbank, and the next day he typed up an initial nine-page synopsis. He worked on the project from July to November 1942 and then again in early 1943. His extravagant script contrasts the general's career with a fictional story about two brothers: one a member of the Resistance from the very start, the other a collaborator who ends up rallying to the Free French cause. Faulkner used his memories and worldview as a Southerner and a novelist to conjure up a critical moment of twentieth-century history. De Gaulle is portrayed as a great spiritual leader, an almost Christlike figure; Brittany resembles Mississippi; the invasion and occupation of France by the German army resemble the invasion and occupation of the South, after its defeat, by Northerners.

In September 1942 Faulkner had written approximately one-quarter of the final script, but his work was interrupted by the intervention of Adrien Tixier, the Free French representative in Washington, who identified major factual errors, was indignant at the liberties Faulkner dared to take with events, and demanded that a greater role be given to the French Resistance.

Faulkner wrote up another twenty-eight-page treatment, taking account of Tixier's objections, and then went back to work on the script, which he finished on October 30. However, in November another Free French representative, Henri Diamant-Berger, criticized the script. He was astounded by what he had read, finding the opposition drawn between Brittany and France "inadmissible and even insulting" (*DGS*, 376), adding that "the details around which the story evolves are so insignificant that they cannot be part of a story whose magnitude is the first condition" (408). He pointed out that General de Gaulle and the Free French were absent from the script after the first third. Again, Faulkner initially agreed to revise his text without protest. And then he fought back. Why encumber the project with French experts? Indeed, why bother with a French general at all? Faulkner, without compunction, proposed to write de Gaulle out of "The De Gaulle Story." In a note dated November 19, 1942, he wrote to writer/producer Buckner: "Let's dispense with General de Gaulle as a living character in the story." He argued that by doing so the studio could "gain the freedom to produce an entertaining movie for an American audience," one that paying spectators would understand and find credible and interesting. He went on to suggest relating what de Gaulle "has done by means of [its] poetic implications, in terms of some little human people, with their human relationships which an audience can understand, whose lives and destinies were affected, not by him but by the same beliefs that made him de Gaulle" (xxix–xxx).

Faulkner is believed to have written over a thousand pages in all on this project—for nothing. The film on de Gaulle would never see the light of day. Was it because his screenplay was impossible to film? Or because there was nobody capable of playing de Gaulle on screen? The political explanation is the most likely, as in the meantime, Winston Churchill had told President Roosevelt about a serious confrontation he had had with de Gaulle. In response, Roosevelt, who had initially encouraged his friend Jack Warner to make the movie, let him know that there was no longer any need to laud the troublesome general. Warner immediately abandoned the project to focus on another of the president's ideas: a "Mission to Moscow" celebrating his new ally, Joseph Stalin.

The text of this screenplay does not really form part of Faulkner's oeuvre, and the France that is portrayed there is not only the conventional Hollywood version, complete with berets a little too large, kepis a little too high, and Gallic mustaches a little overwaxed; it is also a France reinvented by someone not familiar with the country, a France where Breton countrywomen have modern stoves and where villages are policed by constables.

However, the screenplay holds a considerable place in his literary career and often resurfaces unexpectedly in later texts. For example, its echo can be perceived in the Compson Appendix, written in 1945 for Malcolm Cowley's *The Portable Faulkner*, where we see Caddy, after divorcing from her second husband, "a minor movingpicture magnate" "vanished in Paris with the German occupation" (*NI*, 1133), and then reappearing in a photo published in a luxury magazine, beside "a handsome lean man of middle age in the ribbons and tabs of a German staffgeneral" (1134). Similarly, "They endured," Faulkner's laconic commentary on the fate reserved for Dilsey and her family that ends the Compson Appendix returns to a major motif in "The De Gaulle Story."

"The De Gaulle Story" also heralds the humanist message of Faulkner's Nobel Prize speech, even down to its vocabulary and the rhythm of its rhetoric. For example, these musings attributed to a priest in the original treatment were substantially changed in the final screenplay:

> The land is constant. It will remain. Earthquake and flood and drought come and pass as this man [Hitler] will pass, and there is still the land. Oppression and suffering come upon mankind and even destroy him as individuals. But they cannot destroy his immutable spirit. That endures. It is more than the simple will to freedom and contentment. It is his immortality, his hope and belief that out of his suffering his children and all the children of man to follow him will be free. In his suffering and his resistance to tyranny and evil and oppression he finds himself. (*DGS*, 31)

The similarities are even more numerous in *A Fable*, the book that Faulkner started on after "The De Gaulle Story." As a Christlike figure, the famous general without a doubt foreshadows the obscure corporal of *A Fable*.

The scripts entrusted to Faulkner after the abandonment of the de Gaulle project also form part of the texts he wrote to support the Allied war effort. He was first set to work on "Liberator Story." Three or four days later he was asked to adapt a thriller by Eric Ambler, one of the founding fathers of modern spy novels. The star was George Raft, the director Raoul Walsh. A screenplay had already been prepared by W. R. Burnett, and Daniel Fuchs, one of the most brilliant Jewish novelists of his generation, was marked down as co-scriptwriter. But Fuchs, paralyzed by his profound admiration for Faulkner, barely dared to speak to him, and their collaboration proved even more delicate because he suspected Faulkner of being an anti-Semite and because Faulkner knew of his suspicions. They eventually had it out, and Faulkner extirpated himself with a pirouette: "Well, it's troo-oo," he confessed to Fuchs, "I don't like Jews—but I don't like Gentiles neither" (*B*, 1133).

After two weeks Faulkner withdrew, even though, according to producer Jerry Wald, "He did a really magnificent job" (*B*, 1133). He was then put to work on the script of "Liberator Story," which he was allowed to write at Rowan Oak—a concession by Jack Warner to a writer who cost him little. The script suited Faulkner, because it was about airplanes and the production of the film was directly linked to the war effort.

In September 1942 Hawks asked Faulkner to rewrite two scenes in *Air Force*, a propaganda film glorifying democracy, from a script by Dudley Nichols telling of the odyssey of a bomber in the Pacific at the time of the Pearl Harbor attacks. Hawks was not happy with the tragic end to the story. He counted on Faulkner to find another one. "With a script that didn't work," he told another scriptwriter, "he would take a key scene and make it go . . . What Bill did was to make the whole picture better" (*B1*, 444). The cast included John Garfield, Harry Carey, Gig Young, and Arthur Kennedy. The world premiere took place in New York on February 3, 1943. *Air Force* was a considerable commercial success and remains one of the best films inspired by World War II.

After spending Christmas at Rowan Oak, Faulkner returned to Warner Bros. on January 16, 1943, at $350 a week. He initially worked on *Northern Pursuit*, the screenplay for an adventure movie written for Errol Flynn, and then on *Deep Valley*, a film by Jean Negulesco, with a screenplay of thirty-eight pages, including a scene in a penitentiary that is reminiscent of the convicts' story in *The Wild Palms*. But the screenplay was rewritten and Faulkner's name was removed from the credits. He next worked, after five other scriptwriters, on *Country Lawyer*, a film project inspired by the memoirs of Bellamy Partridge, telling the story of two rival families over four generations and two wars. Faulkner worked on this project from March 20 to April 6, 1943. Attracted by the topic but with little concern for faithfulness, he appropriated the story, transferred the plot from New York State to Yoknapatawpha County, and took inspiration from episodes and characters from his short stories, culminating in a typical Faulknerian story. For once, the scriptwriter remembered the novelist, but Faulkner's fifty pages remained in a drawer; the film was never made.

In 1942 Charles Feldman had come up with an ambitious project that, if it had been realized, would have been a kind of summary or fresco in film of World War II, covering all the fronts, from Asia to Africa and Europe. Feldman wanted the film to be co-produced, with a budget of four million dollars, and wanted all profits to go to a charitable foundation. As was to be expected, the film industry was hostile to the project, but Feldman was able to garner the support of the best Hollywood scriptwriters, including Clifford Odets, Lillian Hellman, Dalton Trumbo, and Ben Hecht, and many of his actor friends, including Marlene Dietrich and Randolph Scott, offered to help. In early 1943 Feldman publicly announced his project and asked Hawks to direct it. Hawks agreed and immediately asked Faulkner to write two episodes of the film, which was now called "Battle Cry." Hawks set up his friend in his own office at Warner Bros. Faulkner set to work right away, wrote 140 pages, and rewrote them in two weeks at Hawks' request. On May 16, 1943, Faulkner wrote to his daughter: "It is to be a big one. It will last about 3 hours, and the studio has allowed Mr. Hawks 3 and ½ million dollars to make it, with 3 or 4 directors and about all the big stars" (SL, 174). But on August 4, Warner Bros., panicked by the film's escalating budget, decided to shut down production. For Hawks himself, who knew how to watch his back, it was not a disaster, as he was paid the $100,000 due under his contract. Faulkner received $17,340 for his trouble.

After "Battle Cry" was dropped, Faulkner agreed to work off contract with producer William Bacher and director Henry Hathaway on a film project about World War I. With an advance of one thousand dollars paid by Bacher, he returned to Oxford in mid-August 1943 to write a synopsis, "a fable, an indictment of war perhaps" (SL, 178). A variation on the dual theme of the reincarnation of Christ and the "unknown soldier," this synopsis was the first outline of A Fable, published eleven years later.

Hawks, for his part, was ready to move on to other projects. Warner Bros. offered him two movies, ready to shoot right away: an adaptation of Hemingway's 1937 novel To Have and Have Not and Dark Eyes, a Broadway comedy created in 1943. Hawks had been thinking about a filmed version of To Have and Have Not since 1939, but Hemingway was not interested.

Hawks then challenged him: "I can make a picture out of your worst book." Hemingway responded: "What is my worst book?" "That goddamned piece of junk called *To Have and Have Not*." "You can't make a picture out of that," said Hemingway. Hawks replied: "OK, I'll get Faulkner to do it. He can write better than you can anyway."[4]

Once Humphrey Bogart, the unflappable tenderhearted tough guy from *Casablanca* (1942), had agreed to play the lead role in *To Have and Have Not*, the studio immediately gave it the green light. With such a popular actor topping the bill, Jack Warner hoped to pack the theaters and make a huge profit. Hawks started by asking for the help of Jules Furthman, an experienced scriptwriter, along with two of his friends, crime writers Cleve F. Adams and Whitman Chambers. Furthman handed in his version in mid-January. But difficulties began to surface and censorship was a threat. Joseph Breen, the enforcer of public morality, condemned the sordid atmosphere of the story and its taint of pimping, and demanded numerous changes. Another problem was that the Office of the Coordinator of Inter-American Affairs thought that the story went against the interests of neighborliness between the United States and Central American countries. Hawks therefore decided to shift the story from Cuba to Martinique and called on his "script doctor," who was always ready to carry out emergency surgery.

Faulkner returned to Hollywood in February 1944. He was put up there for six months by his generous young friend Bezzerides. He hoped he would find time to write. He did not. But after reducing his alcohol consumption, he managed, in the space of a week, to solve some of the problems posed by the adaptation of Hemingway's novel. Already familiar with opposition to the Vichy regime from his work on the de Gaulle and Free French screenplay, he immediately converted the Cuban revolutionaries in Hemingway's novel into Gaullist *résistants* and their enemies into Vichy collaborators. He also upped the tempo of the story by reducing the action to just three days. By May, the screenplay, sufficiently distanced from Hemingway's novel, was almost finished. Hawks started shooting the film on February 29 with Humphrey Bogart playing opposite a nineteen-year-old model whose photograph Hawks had noticed on the cover of *Harper's Bazaar*: Lauren Bacall. Every morning, Faulkner arrived at the studio and typed up the pages that were to be shot the next day. He imposed iron discipline upon himself to remain a day ahead of Hawks. But he still tended to be long-winded. One day Lauren Bacall saw him on the set with a new scene, including a six-page monologue for Bogart. After reading it, an incredulous Bogart asked: "I'm supposed to say all that?" (*B1*, 455).

Faulkner's final screenplay was 118 pages long. The film came out on October 11, 1944. Under the terms of their contracts, Hawks was paid a hundred thousand dollars, Furthman almost fifty thousand, and Faulkner barely five thousand—less than Chambers and Adams had earned for their modest contribution. A victim of his disastrous contract with Warner Bros., Faulkner was scandalously underpaid, but for the first time in eight years he was credited for a film, which boosted his standing in Hollywood.

To Have and Have Not became an overnight classic and Bogart and Bacall one of Hollywood's legendary couples. For Faulkner this film marked the climax of his scriptwriting career. Not that he attached much importance to it. He had hoped to work on *A Fable* while he was in Hollywood. He was considered for a number of film projects of little interest, such as *The Damned Don't Cry*, based on a Harry C. Hervey novel. From late 1941 to early 1942 he agreed to do about six film treatments, hoping to get a studio contract, but none of these projects really interested him.

The only other important film on which he worked in the 1940s was *The Southerner*, shot by Jean Renoir in Hollywood and adapted from a novel by the Texan George Sessions Perry titled *Hold Autumn in Your Hand*, the story of a young farm laborer who sets up on his own and manages to grow a handsome cotton harvest that is then destroyed by a storm. Nunnally Johnson had worked on the screenplay but was not available when Renoir wanted to make changes. Zachary Scott, the film's star, then recalled that Faulkner had told him how much he admired the French filmmaker. The two men met and Faulkner ended up bringing the screenplay home with him. Later, in his autobiography, Renoir remembered Faulkner's judicious advice, adding that the influence was certainly a major factor in the success of the film, which was shot in 1945 and was still being shown all around the world.[5] *The Southerner* came out on April 30, 1945, to immediate acclaim. It was boycotted by the Ku Klux Klan (like John Ford's 1940 adaptation of *The Grapes of Wrath*) and won the Grand Prize at the 1946 Venice Biennale. The extent of Faulkner's contribution to the making of this film is uncertain, but at least two scenes bear his imprint. Faulkner told Malcolm Cowley that he thought *The Southerner* was his best film. But to what extent was it his? As often happened, his name was not listed on the credits.

For *The Big Sleep*, an adaptation of the novel by Raymond Chandler (who was very popular at the time and whose *Double Indemnity*, cowritten with Billy Wilder, was a resounding success), Hawks called on Faulkner and Leigh Brackett, a young novelist who had just published a remarkable detective novel. Above all, Hawks wanted to make another film with Humphrey Bogart and Lauren Bacall, and his aesthetic ambitions were modest: "It's not supposed to be a great work of art, just keep it going" (*B1*, 460). Shooting started on October 10, 1944, with Bogart playing Philip Marlowe and Bacall as the venomous Vivian Sternwood. During the first half of the shoot, Hawks pushed Faulkner to condense the screenplay, but the latter started to lose interest in the work. About halfway through shooting, he thought only of returning to Mississippi and getting back to writing. He told Meta: "A new novel? I'll never get it written in this town. Sometimes I think if I do one more treatment or screenplay, I'll lose whatever power I have as a writer" (*ALG*, 309). He asked the studio for six months' leave without pay, starting December 13, but as a favor to Hawks he promised to write twelve pages of revision on the train, free of charge. The screenplay was completed on December 15, 1944. The film came out on August 23, 1946. Faulkner was credited, alongside Leigh Brackett and Jules Furthman, who had been hired subsequently.

At Rowan Oak for Christmas 1944, he went back to work on *A Fable*, but again he had to face facts: his work as a writer did not bring in enough money to sustain his lifestyle. On March 19, 1945, he wrote to Ober: "I had my usual vague foundationless dream of getting enough money to live on out of it while I wrote and finished it. But I ought to know now I dont sell and never will earn enough outside of pictures to stay out of debt" (*SL*, 191).

In early June 1945, accompanied for the second time by Estelle and Jill, Faulkner went back to work for Warner Bros. in Hollywood, for five hundred dollars a week (what he had been making at the start, thirteen years earlier), remaining there until September 19, 1945. His most significant scriptwriting work in the summer of 1945 was the treatment followed by the screenplay adaptation of *Stallion Road*, a Stephen Longstreet novel. He worked diligently on the project and also continued to work on *A Fable*, his "work in progress." On June 16 he handed in a 17-page treatment; by July 26 he had written 145 pages; and on September 1 he delivered the final section of the revised screenplay, which now totaled 151 pages. This screenplay, his last for Warner Bros., is undoubtedly one of his finest. Longstreet admired it: "I thought it was a magnificent thing, wild, wonderful, mad. Utterly impossible to be made into the trite movie of the period. Bill had kept little but the names and some of the situations of my novel and had gone off on a Faulknerian tour of his own despairs, passions and storytelling. Today it could be made as a New Wave film."[6] The studio rejected Faulkner's screenplay and asked Longstreet to rewrite it. It was this version that was made into a film, starring Ronald Reagan, Alexis Smith, Zachary Scott, and Peggy Knudsen. Faulkner was not listed on the credits.

Faulkner had long thought that he could reconcile his duties as a scriptwriter and his work as a writer. But in Hollywood he lost a lot of time and now realized that he had not completed any of his own projects in three years. On August 20, 1945, he wrote to Ober about his dismay:

> I think I have had about all of Hollywood that I can stand. I feel bad, depressed, dreadful sense of wasting time, I imagine most of the symptoms of some kind of blow-up or collapse. I may be able to come back later, but I think I will finish this present job and return home. Feeling as I do, I am actually becoming afraid to stay here much longer. For some time, I have expected, at a certain age, to reach that period (in the early fifties) which most artists seem to reach where they admit at last that there is no solution to life and it is not, and perhaps never was, worth the living. (*SL*, 199)

He was no longer able to write screenplays and just wanted to go home and get back to work on *A Fable*. In September he resolved to leave Hollywood come what may. Faulkner first tried to rid himself of Herndon, his burdensome agent, who continued to claim substantial fees, and on October 15 he asked Jack Warner to free him from his contract, pleading incompetence:

> I feel that I have made a bust of moving picture writing and therefore have misspent and will continue to mis-spend time which at my age I cannot afford [...]. I have spent three years doing work (trying to do it) which was not my forte and which I was not equipped to do, and therefore I have mis-spent time which as a 47 year old novelist I could not afford to spend. And I dont dare mis-spend any more of it. (*SL*, 204)

Warner would not be moved, and Faulkner's request was turned down. Some time later, after renewed negotiations, he was offered six months' unpaid leave, but according to the terms of the new contract, Warner Bros. retained the film rights for any novel that Faulkner wrote after he left. However, because Faulkner had already sold the film rights for *A Fable* to the producer Bacher, he could not accept this arrangement.

He felt trapped. He complained to Haas: "Warner seems to insist he owns everything I write, and so Faulkner wont do any writing until he finds out just how much of his soul he no longer owns" (*SL*, 210). By September 1945 he had left the studio, apparently with no thought about the legal consequences of his move. On the twenty-first he got into his large Cadillac. Attached to the car was a trailer containing Lady Go-Lightly, the gentle mare that Jill rode during her stay in California. The horse was heavily pregnant, and for Faulkner it was out of the question that she foal in Hollywood.

He arrived in Oxford on the night of September 23, the day of his forty-eighth birthday.

LUCAS'S LESSON: *INTRUDER IN THE DUST*

Originally, *Intruder in the Dust* was to be a short detective novel. According to Faulkner, it all started from a twofold idea: "And I thought of an idea for one would be a man in jail just about to be hung would have to be his own detective, he couldn't get anybody to help him. Then the next thought was, the man for that would be a negro. Then the character of Lucius—Lucas Beauchamp came along. And the book came out of that" (*FU*, 142). Conceived in 1940 as a short story, Faulkner went back to work on *Intruder in the Dust* in January 1948 after putting aside the large manuscript of *A Fable*. On February 1 he told Ober about his new project:

> The story is a mystery-murder though the theme is more relationship between Negro and white, specifically or rather the premise being that the white people in the south, before the North or the govt. or anyone else, owe and must pay a responsibility to the Negro. But it's a story; nobody preaches in it. I may have told you the idea, which I have had for some time—a Negro in jail accused of murder and waiting for the white folks to drag him out and pour gasoline over him and set him on fire, is the detective, solves the crime because he goddam has to keep from being lynched, by asking people to go somewhere and look at something and then come back and tell him what they found. (*SL*, 262)

This commentary, like the novel itself, underlines the extent to which, as far back as the 1940s, Faulkner was preoccupied by the growing tensions between whites and blacks. The issue of civil rights was at the heart of political debate in the United States at the time; Congress was preparing to legislate, and the entire white South was mobilizing in order to maintain the status quo. Faulkner was fully aware of the urgent need to repair injustices and implement reforms.

Returning to the fictional Yoknapatawpha, the novelist found his kingdom and its familiar characters again, and he was soon working on his novel with renewed self-assurance. The work progressed swiftly. By the end of February he had completed the manuscript but was still unsure about the title. On April 20 he told Haas he was sending him the text and asked his opinion: "Let me know what you think of the book. It started out to be a simple quick 150 page whodunit but jumped the traces, strikes me as being a pretty good study of a 16 year old boy who overnight became a man" (*SL*, 266). Faulkner wanted to delay publication of the novel so that he could sell excerpts to magazines. His wish was not granted; Random House was eager to finalize it. *Intruder in the Dust*, his first novel since *Go Down, Moses*, was published on September 27, 1948. It had been six years in the making.

Intruder in the Dust is more of a detective novel than *Sanctuary*, but, as in that novel, appearances are deceptive. The plot essentially hinges on a whodunit, and Faulkner uses all the devices of the genre—starting with a red herring, where an innocent person comes under suspicion—and conventional formulas, such as the search for a vanished corpse. However, the truth is discovered not through Poe-like rational deduction, but by the fact that the novel's three "detectives," whom nobody, apart perhaps from the presumed murderer, had asked to investigate, are ready "to put all thought ratiocination contemplation forever behind them" (*N4*, 354).

The first paragraph of the first chapter tells us that "the whole town (the whole country too for that matter) had known since the night before that Lucas had killed a white man" (*N4*, 285). Already a major character in *Go Down, Moses*, Lucas Beauchamp, now in his sixties, is the central figure in this novel. It is he, the grandson of Old Carothers McCaslin and his slave daughter Tomasina, who is the intruder, the intolerable killjoy. Without ever overtly revolting against the Southern order, he continues to disturb and provoke it by refusing, as he had already done in *Go Down, Moses*, to be a "nigger," by adamantly asserting and defining himself in this refusal, through which he finds his dignity and freedom as a man. However, it must be noted that his refusal to be a "nigger" coincides with a refusal of black identity itself. In *Intruder in the Dust* no more than in *Go Down Moses*, Lucas does not claim his African roots and never shows any solidarity with the black community. As in *Go Down, Moses*, he defines himself solely in relation to his white ancestry: "I aint a Edmonds. I dont belong to these new folks. I belongs to the old lot. I'm a McCaslin'" (*N4*, 297). However, for the whites in the county, an individual is defined first and foremost by his ethnicity. Before being part of a family, before even being human, he is black or white and the recognition of his humanity is subordinate to his race: "*We got to make him be a nigger first. He's got to admit he's a nigger. Then maybe we will accept him as he seems to intend to be accepted*" (296).

Lucas Beauchamp is tracked by the brothers of Vinson Gowrie, the murder victim. The Gowries are a clan of nasty, coarse, white hillbillies. Once captured, Lucas is to be lynched immediately, according to custom. Too proud to protest his innocence, he takes refuge in haughty silence. Naturally, the murderer is not the one suspected by the white community, and in the end we find out that the real culprit is one of the victim's brothers. All the novel's suspense comes from the expected lynching and from the macabre twists and turns of the investigation conducted by Chick Mallison, a young white man; Aleck Sander, his black friend; and Miss Eunice Habersham, who was raised with Molly, Lucas's wife—two teenagers and an old spinster from Jefferson whose courage and cunning save Lucas from an ignominious death. The fact that this trio, reminiscent of the trio formed by Miss Rosa Millard, Bayard, and Ringo in *The Unvanquished*, contains two members of Oxford's white middle class, is obviously no coincidence. Neither is the fact that those getting ready to lynch Lucas are poor white trash.

The story seems complicated but in fact it is not. When Chick and Aleck open the dead man's grave they discover that it is not Vinson Gowrie, and when they come back the grave is empty. The corpse is eventually found in quicksand under a nearby bridge. The real murderer is finally identified and Lucas definitively exonerated.

In a flashback at the beginning of the novel, we see Lucas, four years earlier, saving Chick from drowning. He pulls him out of a frozen creek, takes him home, dries his clothes, and feeds him, but when Chick tries to give him the four nickels he has in his pocket to thank him for his hospitality, Lucas not only refuses to take them but also gets two little black children to pick them up after Chick throws them on the ground. This unexpected refusal means that the white boy remains in debt to the black man. This troubling reversal is a crushing experience for Chick, and for a long time he remembers "that old once-frantic shame and anguish and need not for revenge, vengeance but simply for re-equalization, reaffirmation of his masculinity and his white blood" (N4, 303). In the following years, he tries several times to repay his debt to Lucas—first with cigars and snuff, later with a dress for his wife Molly—but each time Lucas gives him a gift in return. The debt of gratitude remains unpaid.

Aghast, Chick discovers that behind Lucas the "nigger" there is a man like other men, vulnerable and capable of feeling just like any other: *"He was grieving. You dont have to not be a nigger in order to grieve"* (N4, 302). He therefore decides to attempt the impossible and take all kinds of risks to save his rescuer. In taking these risks, Chick puts himself to the test, and in doing so the child becomes an adult. Like *The Unvanquished* and "The Bear," *Intruder in the Dust* is a coming-of-age story, and, like those two stories, it is the story of a successful coming of age.

However, becoming an adult also means becoming aware of one's heritage and learning to manage it. Like all young men in Faulkner's writing, Chick has inherited the history of the South, a history that, for Southerners, does not yet belong to the history of historians. As his uncle reminds him, for a Southerner the die has not yet been cast; the Civil War has not yet been lost:

> It's all *now* you see. Yesterday wont be over until tomorrow and tomorrow began ten thousand years ago. For every Southern boy fourteen years old, not once but whenever he wants it, there is the instant when it's still not yet two oclock on that July afternoon in 1863, the brigades are in position behind the rail fence, the guns are laid and ready in the woods and the furled flags are already loosened to break out and Pickette himself with his long oiled ringlets and his hat in one hand probably and his sword in the other looking up the hill waiting for Longstreet to give the word and it's all in the balance, it hasn't

happened yet, it hasn't even begun yet, it not only hasn't begun yet but there is still time for it not to begin. (N4, 430–31)[7]

Gavin Stevens is one of those who has not yet given up on the Old South, and he wants to teach Chick how to become a gentleman according to tradition. But in truth what Chick learns over the course of the few dramatic days during which he endeavors to uncover the truth of a murder is nothing like what he learns from his uncle or at school. His moral education does not involve transmission or instruction; it is acquired outside the schoolroom, even in opposition to it, and is derived from an individual test and choices rather than social conditioning. From his first meeting with Lucas and the progressive discovery of his humanity to the risky commitment to establish his innocence and shield him from the lynch mob, Chick Mallison, in his capacity to break the rules of the prevailing social code whenever is necessary, continually matures and asserts himself as a free, responsible individual. This profoundly changes his relationship with the white community, and his discovery that Lucas is innocent coincides with his discovery of collective culpability. Something comes to light: "something shocking and shameful out of the whole white foundation of the county which he himself must partake of too since he too was bred of it, which otherwise might have flared and blazed merely out of Beat Four and then vanished back into its darkness or at least invisibility with the fading embers of Lucas' crucifixion" (388).

In just a few days, Chick learns more than his uncle has ever known. In another ironic twist, he receives his real lesson in dignity not from Gavin Stevens, but from Lucas—a lesson that is all the more forceful for being silent. Lucas is to Chick a little like what Sam Fathers was to the young Ike McCaslin in *Go Down, Moses*: a paternal figure from somewhere else, outside the family, outside kinship, outside institutions, solitary and sovereign, and whose intervention allows Chick to become a man. On the other hand, Stevens, who wants to make Chick his spiritual son, merely bores him with his long-windedness. Confronted with the complexities of reality, this "liberal" intellectual, ardent champion of truth and justice, and indefatigable righter of wrongs again displays pitiful blindness. Lucas hires him as his lawyer, but far from believing his client innocent, Stevens is just as ready as the most racist redneck to assume he is a murderer and coldly advises him to plead guilty of second-degree murder. And once Stevens realizes his mistake, he is incapable of taking any action to save Lucas. In the novel's final scene, Lucas comes to see his lawyer to pay his fees and Stevens takes Lucas's two dollars, even though—as he himself agrees—he did nothing to clear his name. Lucas asks for a receipt, determined as always not to owe anything to the condescending generosity of his white "benefactors."

The scene is superb, and *Intruder in the Dust* contains a number of scenes of equal force, but overall the novel is disappointing in that the issue of "relations between White and Black," its stated theme, is cleverly evaded, despite appearances. Lucas is no longer the same man as in *Go Down, Moses*: he has not only aged; he has withered. Rooted in the position of the solitary uncompromising old patriarch, he barely moves, scarcely speaks, and we never know what he thinks or feels. He is less an agent in a story than an object of description, and the reader mostly retains a physical portrait of him: "always in the worn brushed obviously once-expensive black broadcloth suit [. . .] and the raked fine hat and the boiled white shirt of his own grandfather's time and the tieless collar and the heavy watch-chain and the gold toothpick like the one his own grandfather had carried in his upper vest pocket" (*N4*, 301). This inventory, with its strong connotations, is repeated several times throughout the novel. Like Flem in *The Hamlet*, Lucas sometimes seems to be little more than the sum of his picturesque clothes. He is less a fictional character than a dumb effigy, resembling a totem or an icon. For Chick, his meeting with Lucas is certainly a decisive moment in his coming of age. The problem is that in this novel, Lucas exists only for Chick and through the effect he has on him. In contrast to the Lucas in *Go Down, Moses*, the Lucas in *Intruder in the Dust* is one of those blacks who, in Faulkner's fiction, are nothing outside the views and discourse of whites. For the novelist, Lucas is this time little more than a pawn on a chessboard.

Stevens also does not play an active role in the plot, but while Lucas is taciturn, Stevens never tires of speaking. How should his monologues be read? Stevens is again inconvenient, because while the reader may find hollow the confused rhetoric of his lectures on morality, his noble exhortations to his nephew often foreshadow Faulkner's public speeches: "Some things you must always be unable to bear. Some things you must never stop refusing to bear. Injustice and outrage and dishonor and shame. No matter how young you are or how old you have got. Not for kudos and not for cash: your picture in the paper nor money in the bank either. Just to refuse to bear them" (N4, 439). We are not far from what Faulkner was to say two years later in Stockholm, extoling "the old universal truths: [. . .] love and honor and pity and pride and compassion and sacrifice" (*ESPL*, 120). But Stevens is not only a garrulous lecturer on humanism; he also holds very firm views on Southern society. Instead of leaving this story of buried and dug-up corpses to speak for itself, Faulkner thought best to entrust its interpretation to Stevens. Stevens, in fact, is the first commentator of the plot in this novel. From the seventh chapter, the actual story is increasingly interspersed by his sententious diatribes about "Sambo" and how he can be liberated. *Intruder in the Dust* is certainly not Faulkner's first novel to tackle these questions, but up to then none had allocated so much space to the role of commentator, none had yielded to such an extent to the dual temptation of didacticism and grandiloquence.

Stevens is a Southern "liberal"—that is, an extremely timid reformist, whose goodwill and good intentions barely mask the tenacious prejudices of class and race. He asserts that the population of the South is "a homogenous people" (N4, 400); in other words, they all come from the same stock, with the same values and culture, and "only from homogeneity comes anything of a people or for a people of durable and lasting value—the literature, the art, the science, that minimum of government and police which is the meaning of freedom and liberty, and perhaps most valuable of all a national character worth anything in a crisis" (400). This homogeneity (a fetish concept among the Agrarians) is so dear to him that he intends to preserve it at all costs and to defend it against any intrusion by "foreigners."

Concern for homogeneity is portrayed as an attachment to the values of a culture. In fact, it relays the fear of interbreeding, the phobia of miscegenation. What Stevens says amounts to nothing more than the age-old puritanical and racist obsession with purity. What's more, as soon as blacks are mentioned, his arguments founder in mushy rhetoric. "'That's why we must resist the North,'" he tells Chick:

"not just to preserve ourselves nor even the two of us as one to remain one nation because that will be the inescapable by-product of what we will preserve: which is the very thing that three generations ago we lost a bloody war in our back yards so that it remain intact: the postulate that Sambo is a human being living in a free country and hence must be free. That's what we are really defending: the privilege of setting him free ourselves" (N4, 400–401)

What is this "thing" that has to be kept "intact"? Who decreed that the black man must be free in "a free country"? Stevens's words are so confused that the casual reader could be led into thinking that the South fought not to perpetuate the slavery of blacks but to safeguard their freedom. Stevens's "that's why" and "because" provide no explanations. One must make of it what one can.

It is clear, on the other hand, that Stevens believes he has a vocation to defend "Sambo from the North and East and West—the outlanders who will fling him decades back not merely into injustice but into grief and agony and violence too by forcing on us laws based on the idea that man's injustice to man can be abolished overnight by the police" (N4, 437–38). But under the pretext of defending the blacks, he is actually defending the status quo—that is, maintaining the traditional prerogatives of the white Southerner. He wants everything to continue to depend on the latter's goodwill, nothing to be imposed by the authority of common law, and any necessary changes to be made without disruption and as slowly as possible. To the objection that since the Civil War the white Southern elite, instead of trying to improve the condition of the blacks, has consistently endeavored to perpetuate inequality and injustice, he responds, rewriting history in total disregard for the facts, that things would not be where they were now if the Northerners had not meddled in matters that did not concern them, going so far as to claim, without explanation, that if they had left the South to the Southerners, the slaves to slave owners, Lucas would today be a free man (see N4, 446–47).

Not only are Stevens's assertions appallingly ignorant and in bad faith, but the assumptions on which they are based are refuted by the novel itself. Thus, regardless of what Stevens thinks, Lucas is everything but a "Sambo." A marginal member of a society that is nothing less than homogenous, the exemplary and astonishingly positive epitome of interbreeding, he has the distinction of those "natural aristocrats" against whom Faulkner always contrasted the vulgarity of the hoi polloi. Is there ironic intent behind this contradiction? Certainly, in *Intruder in the Dust*, as in all Faulkner novels where he plays the busybody, Stevens is a ridiculous character (and would be even more so in *The Town*), and in his conversations with Malcolm Cowley, the novelist took care to distance himself: "Stevens [. . .] was not speaking for the author, but for the best type of liberal Southerners; that is how they feel about the Negroes" (*FCF*, 110–11). But was Faulkner not himself part of this minority of "liberal Southerners"? In truth, what the latter thought of blacks was not very far from his own thinking. Faulkner was certainly right to ask his readers not to confuse the opinions of one of his characters with his own. "I'm writing about people, not trying to express my own opinion" (*LG*, 160–61). Nevertheless, Stevens's sanctimoniously paternalistic thoughts about "Sambo," his distrust of the North, his rejection of swift integration imposed by the federal government, and his fear of generalized interbreeding are not only reminiscent of the stance already defended by Ike McCaslin in "Delta Autumn" but also herald the tempered racism and temporizing reformism that the novelist would defend a few years later in his interviews and public statements.

Edmund Wilson was no doubt wrong to reduce this novel to "William Faulkner's Reply to the Civil Rights Program."[8] But, as later in *Requiem for a Nun* and *A Fable*, it does testify to the author's newfound wish to deliver a "message" to his readers, as unambiguously as possible. Fiction is increasingly subject to demonstrative and didactic aims. The South is no longer primarily a matter of fiction; it has patently become the object and purpose of sociopolitical reflection. Of course, *Intruder in the Dust* is not the first time this reflection occurs, but this is the first novel where it surfaces in generalizations. No longer presented as a series of ongoing questioning, it is portrayed as a fixed set of reassuring certitudes.

Stevens's effusive arguments in favor of the South and his bitter diatribes against the North can no longer be read today without some discomfort. As a *roman à thèse*, *Intruder in the Dust* is a failure (if a *roman à thèse* can indeed be successful), if only because both plot and characters contradict the ideology Stevens advocates and that they are meant to illustrate. And it is not certain that Faulkner was aware of the contradiction.

In the famous letter to his brothers of December 21, 1817, Keats referred to "Negative Capability, that is when man is capable of being in uncertainties, Mysteries, doubts, without any irritable reaching after fact & reason."[9] Faulkner's greatest novels, from *The Sound and the Fury* to *Absalom, Absalom!*, and from *The Hamlet* to *Go Down, Moses*, draw their strength from this unsurpassable irresolution. Faulkner was too good a writer to ever wholly forget that the writer's job is to ask readers questions, not answer them, to give them food for thought, not think for them. But it cannot be denied that from *Intruder in the Dust* on, he started to yield to the evils of didacticism. Up until then he had been wary of the weight of ideas (always received and ready-made) and the gregarious stupidity of opinions. His thinking was that of a novelist; he saw himself and felt himself to be outside the realm of concept (outside frozen metaphors). His thinking was open, free, and always active, forming as he wrote, without any guarantee, stubbornly faithful to the astonishment from which it sprang. In fact, this thinking was not so much that of the novelist as of his novels, which always knew more than their author and said more than he wanted to say.

From *Intruder in the Dust* on, ideas are expressed and thinking withers. This does not mean that Faulkner lost the upper hand as a novelist. *Intruder in the Dust* is not one of his major books, but the hallmark of a great writer is never completely eclipsed, and whenever it frees itself from didacticism (in other words, whenever Gavin Stevens shuts up), Faulkner's writing regains all of its power to surprise and shock. Here, for example, is Faulkner describing hogs being stuck and hung on a winter's morning in the backyards of Yoknapatawpha farmsteads: "By nightfall the whole land would be hung with their spectral intact tallowcolored empty carcasses immobilised by the heels in attitudes of frantic running as though full tilt at the center of the earth. (*N4*, 286)

Intruder in the Dust was not a turning point in Faulkner's literary career, but the topicality of racial issues meant that this minor novel became an instant best seller. Over fifteen thousand copies of the book were sold in the first year; none of Faulkner's novels since *Sanctuary* had sold so well. Moreover, Bennett Cerf sold the rights to MGM for fifty thousand dollars, as much as David Selznick had paid ten years earlier for *Gone with the Wind*. Faulkner was very pleased. A visitor who came to congratulate him found him barefoot. "Anybody who can sell a book to the movies for $50,000 has a right to get drunk and to dance in his bare feet," he said (*B*, 1257).

Up to that point Faulkner had been held in contempt by his fellow townspeople. According to Shelby Foote, at the end of the 1930s, if anyone from Oxford was asked where William Faulkner lived, "he would be apt to turn his head and spit." The town had not forgiven him for *Sanctuary*; he was known as "the corn cob man and they thought he was sullying the atmosphere" (*LP*, 34). *Intruder in the Dust* was no better received on its publication. When Judge John Wesley Thompson Falkner Jr., the uncle who had publicly called the young Faulkner a good-for-nothing, was asked if he had served as the model for Gavin Stevens, he exclaimed that he did not recognize himself in the negrophile Stevens, adding that he didn't read Bill's books, that Billy could write what he wanted, and that he probably made money writing nasty stuff for the Yankees.[10]

However, the filming of *Intruder in the Dust* would bring about Faulkner's reconciliation with Oxford. Admittedly, not everyone was happy to see a movie about a lynching being filmed in the town itself, and as a black man was at the time being held in jail on suspicion of raping a white woman, MGM's public relations department was worried that the mob scene might provoke an actual lynching. But director Clarence Brown, himself a native of neighboring Tennessee, was confident, declaring to the *Oxford Eagle*: "We can make this film the most eloquent statement of the true Southern viewpoint of racial relations and racial problems sent out over the nation" (*B1*, 502). Moreover, since money was at stake this time, the shoot was of interest to the local chamber of commerce. The *Oxford Eagle* brought out a full-page advertisement, paid for by the town's shopkeepers, stating that they were proud that Oxford was to be the setting for "Mr. William Faulkner's Great Story, *Intruder in the Dust*."

Brown, a Hollywood veteran, filmed *Intruder in the Dust* in Oxford in the first few months of 1949. In February he arrived with four assistants in tow to scout locations and find accommodations for the crew. In this heavily segregated town, whites could stay where they wanted, but blacks would be fed and housed by black families.

Faulkner went out scouting locations with Brown and made some minor modifications to the script, but that was where his collaboration ended. The film made from his novel had nothing to do with him. Once shooting had ended, the Faulkners threw a wrap party at Rowan Oak. However, Juano Hernández, the excellent Puerto Rican actor who played the part of Lucas Beauchamp, was not invited. Faulkner had yielded to local pressure. In Oxford one still did not associate with blacks. There was no question of inviting them into one's house. The exquisite courtesy of the white Southern upper class had its rules and its limits. Faulkner felt bound to respect them that day. A pity.

A preview screening of *Intruder in the Dust* was held in Memphis, and the world premiere took place amid great fanfare in Oxford on October 9. Faulkner received a standing ovation. At the end he slipped away with his family and friends. The unexpected success of both the book and the film version of *Intruder in the Dust* brought his money worries to an end. He would no longer have to take on tedious work to feed his family or spend his days in the "salt mines." He now had enough to buy himself a yacht, fix up the house, and live comfortably. The fifty thousand dollars was quickly spent. But there would soon be other large checks.

A CONVENTIONAL DETECTIVE STORY: *KNIGHT'S GAMBIT*

On November 24, 1948, Faulkner wrote to Saxe Commins:

> I am thinking of a "Gavin Stevens" volume, more or less detective stories. I have four or five short pieces, averaging 20 pages, in which Stevens solves or prevents crime to protect the weak, right injustice, or punish evil. There is one more which no one has bought. The reason is, it is a novel which I tried to compress into short story length. It is a love story, in which Stevens prevents a crime (murder) not for justice but to gain (he is now fifty plus) the childhood sweetheart which he lost 20 years ago. It will probably run about 150 pages, which should make a volume as big as *INTRUDER*. (*SL*, 280)

Knight's Gambit was published a year later, on November 27, 1949, by Random House. The volume is made up of six texts: the first five are short stories published in magazines between 1932 and 1946; the last is not a condensed novel but rather a revised and considerably expanded version of an unpublished short story written in 1941—what Faulkner in his correspondence called a "novella" (*SL*, 285), meaning a long short story or short novel. The texts collected are all police procedurals in the tradition of Edgar Allan Poe and Arthur Conan Doyle. Faulkner's interest in detective stories was not new; he read voraciously and had written "The Big Shot" as far back as the end of the 1920s. But his contribution to the genre was slim. Faulkner was neither a new Poe nor another Conan Doyle, and he was no writer of thrillers or hard-boiled novels like Hammett or Chandler, even though *Sanctuary* and *Intruder in the Dust* both have elements of the crime novel. His portraits of killers are admirable, but his detective stories are second-rate.

Faulkner himself was under no illusions. As with many of his short stories and, as he himself admits, the first version of *Sanctuary*, they were written above all to "make money." On October 5, 1940, after receiving a check for a thousand dollars from the *Saturday Evening Post*, he confided in Haas: "I am doing no writing save pot-boilers. Ober sells just enough of them to keep my head above water, which is all right." The first five short stories of *Knight's Gambit* were all written hastily and under pressure for a quick buck and were aimed at the middlebrow readership of the large magazines. As he had already done many times before, Faulkner was only meeting demand.

Knight's Gambit adds nothing to his reputation. It is Faulkner, just not great Faulkner. Poor hillbillies, an idiot abandoned to his own innocence, a crazy old maid, a solitary and irascible old man, a brother madly jealous of his sister's suitor, and even an indomitable stallion—this is familiar territory. But Monk is not Benjy, Max is not Quentin, Fentry is not Mink. The difference is one of density, of texture. The characters move by quickly; they have no time to take shape and leave no lasting impression. The language is not disappointing as long as it remains rooted in the story, but the tics and mannerisms of Stevens's eloquence are so predictable and his posturing so inevitable that at times it becomes nothing but verbal gesticulation. This small condensate of Faulknerian rhetoric reads in effect like a self-parody, as can be seen here: "The lowly and invincible of the earth—to endure and endure and then endure, tomorrow and tomorrow and tomorrow" (*KG*, 104). Of all of Faulkner's books, *Knight's Gambit* is assuredly the least inspired and the most dull. However, despite this, it still bears his mark.

"Smoke," the first short story in the book, is the oldest. Published in *Harper's* in 1932, it was written two years earlier between the two versions of *Sanctuary*, as suggested by the furtive presence of a character whose description strongly resembles Popeye: a hit man from town, "with a face like a shaved wax doll, and eyes with a still way of looking and a voice with a still way of talking" (*KG*, 27). The short story starts, conventionally enough, with the discovery of a corpse: that of Anselm Holland, dragged along by his horse, his foot caught in the stirrup. Nobody mourns this brutal bully of an old farmer, who married the richest woman in the county but didn't love her; who had no respect for his wife or her land; and who had driven away his twin sons, Anselm Junior and Virginius. The sons therefore come under suspicion, but the attorney Gavin Stevens easily shows, through his investigation and following a line of reasoning worthy of Poe's Auguste Dupin, that the murderer is a cousin of the twins, who not only killed old Anse to grab the Hollands' property, but hired a hit man from Memphis to get rid of a judge whose suspicions he feared. Manufactured according to the tried and tested recipes of the genre, "Smoke" is the most disappointing of the five stories, but a question that Faulkner asks in all of his short stories and novels, particularly *Go Down, Moses*, is also raised here: that of the relationship of man to land, of the "indomitable undefeat of a soil" (*KG*, 46) he inherits, which he has to work and make bear fruit, which he in turn will hand down from generation to generation, to his descendants, and which he cannot leave without going astray and getting lost.

This question is posed directly or obliquely in all of his short stories. The same antagonism is everywhere, forcefully underlined from the very first story, between "us" and "them"; between country and town; between a homogenous rural community faithful to its traditions, and outlanders, rootless men who come to steal the farmers' daughters and their land, threatening the very foundations of communal order. Faulkner tackles the contradictions and internal divisions of the South in many of his novels and short stories. But in *Knight's Gambit* this questioning is eclipsed by a simplistic and demagogical postulate: the South is no longer portrayed in conflict with itself, but with external forces. History is rewritten according to one of the favorite scenarios of Southern paranoia: evil comes from outside; the disruptive force either comes from elsewhere—Anse Holland, the usurper from God knows where in "Smoke"; Joel Flint, the Yankee stranger (*KG*, 93) in "An Error of Chemistry"; Harriss, the millionaire bootlegger from New Orleans in "Knight's Gambit"—or returns to the country after a long absence, like Monk's father, "where gone none knew for ten years, when one day he returned, with a woman—a woman with hard, bright, metallic, city hair and a hard blonde city face seen about the place from a distance [. . .] looking out upon the green solitude with an expression of cold and sullen and unseeing inscrutability" (41). The comparison says it all: the city, the woman, the city woman, is the snake in the chicken coop.

That *Knight's Gambit*, Faulkner's most commercial novel, is the most inspired by the puerile mythology of the Agrarians is doubtless no coincidence. The agrarian fable is shattered in Faulkner's great novels. Here, it seems self-evident. The community evoked in *Knight's Gambit* is to be sure a society with brutal values and elemental passions, but it is not reprehensible in its foundations. What's more, *Knight's Gambit* conveys a resolutely optimistic message: the border between good and evil is clearly traced here, and good unfailingly triumphs over evil in the end. Too many nuances and ambiguities would not have appealed to the busy but lazy readers of the *Saturday Evening Post.*

In the middle of this community, but standing apart and away from it and above it, is Gavin Stevens. A minor character in *Light in August* and *Go Down, Moses,* he had a major role in *Intruder in the Dust.* In *Knight's Gambit* he takes center stage and will also play an important role in *Requiem for a Nun* and the last two volumes of the Snopes trilogy. Gavin is Gawain, one of the Knights of the Round Table. He is the knight of the title, the fearless champion of justice and righteousness. In the above-mentioned letter to Saxe Commins, Faulkner describes Gavin as a sort of secular saint whose aim is "to protect the weak, right injustice, or punish evil." But in his short stories, he makes sure not to make him an entirely admirable character. This white-maned man in his fifties is often mocked, particularly by Chick Mallison, his young nephew, who laughs at his sententious speechifying and his set bachelor ways. Faulkner also develops Gavin from one story to another, from one case to the next. In the short stories, he always arrives too late: while he carries out his investigations capably and succeeds in unmasking the culprit, he cannot prevent crime or always ensure that justice prevails. In "Monk," for example, he is unable to prevent the hanging of a simpleton, initially imprisoned for a murder he didn't commit and then induced by a cellmate to commit another for which he should not be held responsible. In "Knight's Gambit," on the other hand, which is not only the last and longest story in the collection but also the most dense and the most engaging, Gavin is both investigator and avenger; he is also embroiled in a plot in which he has his own stake and, in preventing a murder, he manages to give this story—a story that, after all, is also his own—a happy ending. Gavin has changed and he knows it. "They made me older," he says at the end. "I have improved" (*KG*, 246). He has moved from simply detecting crime to preventing it and has therefore taken responsibility, the beginning of an undertaking, also attested to by his upcoming marriage to Melisandre, his childhood sweetheart. As in *The Unvanquished, Go Down, Moses,* and *Intruder in the Dust,* what Faulkner is offering us here is the tale of an "education." Besides, although *Knight's Gambit* was published after *Intruder in the Dust*, the short stories comprised in it were written (except the last one) before the novel, so that the latter should be seen as an extension of the former, as the tale of another challenge.

In *Knight's Gambit*, as in *Intruder in the Dust* and to a lesser extent *Light in August*, and later in *Requiem for a Nun*, the question is to what extent the always forthcoming Gavin Stevens is the writer's mouthpiece. In "An Error of Chemistry" he tells the sheriff that he is "more interested in justice and in human beings" (*KG*, 111) than in truth, and it is again as "champion not so much of truth as of justice" (*N4*, 505–506) that he is defined in the first scene of *Requiem for a Nun*. In other words (as always with Faulkner), the truths he holds most dear are the "the old verities and truths of the heart" that are the mainstay of his Nobel Prize acceptance speech a year later. Stevens again speaks for the writer when, in the same story, the sheriff asks him, the man of culture, the well-versed man of letters, what book the truths are in, to which he responds that they all speak the same truth: "It's in all of them [. . .]. The good ones, I mean. It's said in a lot of different ways, but it's there" (*KG*, 131).

The publication of *Knight's Gambit* was not hailed by the press. Although there were many reviews, they were rarely enthusiastic. It is perhaps Edmund Wilson, writing in the *New Yorker* on December 24, 1949, who delivered the fairest judgment, stating that regardless of what could be said against the book, which assuredly was not the best Faulkner, each of his short stories, even the most far-fetched, managed to arouse an anguished expectation of what was to be exposed, inducing discomfort in the face of human aberrations, that made his best fiction so powerful.

JOAN

In December 1946 Faulkner was in Oxford, bored to death. "It's a dull life here," he wrote to Cowley. "I need some new people, above all probably a new young woman" (*SL*, 245). That young woman could have been Ruth Ford, a beautiful actress and, like him, a native of Mississippi, whom he had met through his brother Dean in 1933, and whom he met again ten years later in Hollywood when she was under contract with Warner Bros. He met her again in New York in 1947 and gave her the exclusive rights to *Requiem for a Nun.* Was this another way of wooing, another attempt to convert his texts into the currency of love, as he had done so many years ago when he offered Estelle or Helen collections of poetry—handwritten, illustrated, and hand-bound? If it was, it failed as miserably as the previous attempts. Shortly afterward, Ruth Ford married again, to actor Zachary Scott.

The "new young woman" entered his life two years later, at the end of the summer of 1949. She came from Memphis and was named Joan Williams. She was twenty-one years old; he was almost fifty-two. Joan was pretty, with hazel eyes, freckles, and a beautiful smile. She was fresh, fragile, smart, ambitious, and had all the audacity of a shy person. A student at Bard College in the state of New York, she wrote short stories and had already won a competition organized by *Mademoiselle* magazine. But she had not yet fully embarked on a career as a writer. Uncertain in her vocation, with no family support, she was looking for a father figure, a mentor who would read her work and give her advice, someone who could make her believe in herself. It all began with a young writer starting out admiring a famous writer.

Their first meeting did not bode well. One morning in August, Faulkner received a telephone call from John Reed Holley, a friend of Malcolm Franklin. Holley told him that one of his cousins, who was passing through Oxford, would like to meet him. Faulkner, mistrustful, said he was busy. Instead of giving up, Holley drove Joan over to Rowan Oak. By coincidence, Faulkner was there, in a meadow with his horses. Holley stopped, went up to him, and told him how much his cousin, who was sitting in the back of the car, wanted to meet him. Caught off guard, Faulkner didn't say no but was somewhat intrigued: "Well, what does she want to see? Why does she want to see me? Does she want to see if I have two heads?" (*WFO*, 88). He came toward the car, exchanged a few pleasantries with Holley and his wife, and then walked away. Mortified, Joan barely looked at him, and Faulkner only caught a glimpse of her face, but we can imagine that he had time to notice she was pretty.

Joan sent him a long letter upon her return to Memphis. This letter forms part of the Faulkner–Joan Williams correspondence held by the University of Virginia's Alderman Library, which for many years was accessible for consultation and quotation solely to Joseph Blotner, Faulkner's official biographer, but in *The Wintering*, her third, clearly autobiographical novel, published in 1971, Joan Williams provides a version that can be assumed to be very close to the original. Here is the text:

> I know you have a secretary and probably you will never see this but I have to write it anyway, as I am the girl who came there today when you told us not to, and I wanted you to know it was not for the reason you thought, to stare at you, but because I like your work so much. I am unhappy and I know you are unhappy too. I wanted to tell you you shouldn't be so unhappy and lonely when you have done so much for the world. There were so many things I had wanted to ask you because I know you have thought and felt and suffered everything I ever have and I wanted to ask you the reason for suffering. Why some people have to and others don't? In the end do you gain something from it? I knew after reading your books I could ask you everything and you would answer and I could tell you everything about myself, that my dog just got run over, and you would understand. Could I come again by myself? You don't have to worry as I know all about your drinking and that doesn't make any difference to me. My father drinks too. So don't worry or be embarrassed. I hope I have not bothered you again by writing. But I couldn't go on thinking that you thought I came there to stare when I so much did not come for that reason, at all.[11]

Faulkner responded cautiously that he didn't know if it would be a good idea for her to come back, as they didn't know each other and that this would likely remain the case. However, Joan's letter touched him, a fact he did not conceal, telling her he did not want rid of her, because her letter deserved more: "Something charming came out of it, like something remembered out of youth: smell, scent, a flower, not in a garden but in the woods maybe, stumbled on by chance, with no past and no particular odor and already doomed for the first frost: until 30 years later a soiled battered bloke aged 50 years smells or remembers it, and at once he is 21 again and brave and clean and durable" (*B*, 507).[12]

Back at Bard College, Joan plucked up the courage to send Faulkner a list of questions. He replied on October 14: "These are the wrong questions. A woman must ask these of a man while they are lying in bed together . . . when they are lying at peace or at least quiet or maybe on the edge of sleep so you'll have to wait, even to ask them" (*B*, 507). In the same letter, he tells her that in his dreams he associates her with the very academic paintings of William Bouguereau, a painter of predatory satyrs and nymphs with "curved pink female flesh," already referred to in *Elmer* (*ELM*, 432).

It may seem surprising that in writing to a barely glimpsed young stranger, Faulkner refers so directly to the carnal intimacy of a couple. But the "message" is clear: he wants to answer Joan's questions but on his conditions. In this initial exchange of letters, she has already become an object of desire and nostalgia. His own youth resurfaces through Joan's, and as their epistolary flirtation continues, he becomes more and more insistent.

Joan, for her part, was doubtless shocked by this strange letter. But she was also flattered. She finally felt she was living for somebody, and being desired by a man she admired deeply bolstered her self-confidence: "I was not to him the oddity my parents thought me. To pass through childhood I'd invented at an early age the belief I would go someday to a place where people would love me, and I would not be hurt anymore. I could not keep myself from believing I was not worthless, as I was told at home" (B, 508).

But the relationship that would develop was founded on a misunderstanding: Joan, daughter to an alcoholic father who understood nothing and a mother who thought only of marrying her off, was looking for a mentor, a writing teacher, perhaps also a big brother or protective father figure; Faulkner simply wanted a new mistress, and if she also wanted to be his little daughter and his little sister, so much the better. The misunderstanding was soon cleared up. Joan could not mistake her correspondent's intentions for long.

In December 1949 they met for lunch with Estelle. They as yet had nothing to hide. A week later, on December 29, he wrote to her that one October day, realizing he wanted to see her very badly, he had almost gone to the East Coast that fall for that very reason.[13] A few days after Christmas 1949, he wrote that he wanted to see her—but not at his house. He said that would not be enough, that it would be nothing at all, and therefore proposed that they meet elsewhere.

On the morning of January 3, 1950, however, he received Joan at Rowan Oak. Estelle was unperturbed; she even prepared a picnic, and all three spent a pleasant day on the *Minmagary*, Faulkner's houseboat on Sardis Reservoir, the large lake about twenty miles northwest of Oxford where he sometimes went sailing. Joan brought a few manuscripts she wanted to read to Faulkner. Overcoming her timidity, she started talking to him about her plans and difficulties. Faulkner listened to her, promised to help her as best he could, advised her to read and reread the Bible and Shakespeare, and lent her his copy of Malraux's *La Condition humaine*.

On January 7, after Joan had returned to Bard College, Faulkner wrote to her about his difficulty in speaking about literature, explaining that as soon as he saw the white page, he just wanted to write her a love letter.[14] From then on he courted her assiduously. A few days later they met again, secretly this time, at the Memphis bus station. The start of the date was deeply uneasy, as for hours they drove around in Joan's car, embarrassed, barely looking at each other, not knowing what to say, driving aimlessly for miles. Joan eventually stopped the car on a cliff overlooking the Mississippi River. A conversation finally began, but when Faulkner put his hand on her arm, Joan tensed in surprise. He withdrew it immediately. She suggested they go have lunch. They went to a deserted drive-in, where a Mills Brothers song was playing on the jukebox: "You Always Hurt the One You Love." Faulkner told Joan the song could have been written for her. At the end of the meal, they drove off. Joan was so tired she brought him home to meet her mother.

Joan admired Faulkner but she wasn't in love with him. Or, more accurately, she loved the writer but not the man. She therefore resisted his advances, pushing him away each time he touched her or tried to kiss her, and the more she resisted, the more he projected himself into the role of Pygmalion, "creating not a cold and beautiful statue, in order to fall in love with it, but [. . .] taking his love and creating a poet out of her—something like that. Will you risk it?" (*B1*, 512). He encouraged her to take up a career as writer, complimented her, and started giving her advice. Thus, on January 13, 1950, discussing "Rain Later," a short story by Joan he had read in *Mademoiselle*, he wrote to her: "It's all right. You remember? 'to make something passionate and moving and true'? It is, moving and true, made me want to cry a little for all the sad frustration of solitude, isolation, aloneness in which every human being lives, who for all the blood kinship and everything else, cant really communicate, touch" (*SL*, 297).

On February 2 Faulkner arrived in New York for ten days. Joan met him at the bar in the Biltmore Hotel. Over a drink, he told her about a play he wanted to write, which he intended to give the title of an unfinished short story he had started in 1933: "Requiem for a Nun." He suggested that she collaborate with him on this project. A four-handed composition, the fantasy of a writer in love? His proposal was likely not devoid of ulterior motives, but this did not make it any less sincere and earnest. As soon as he returned to Oxford, he sent her pages of notes written on the train. Almost all the letters he sent her thereafter contain thoughts and suggestions about their joint enterprise. And he kept telling her how dear their collaboration was to him. "I tell you again, the play is yours too," he wrote to her on March 2.

> If you refuse to accept it, I will throw it away too. I would not have thought of writing one if I hadn't known you . . . I have the notes you sent: they are all right, so all right there is no need to comment on them. The thing now is to get *everything* down on paper, even, written of course, to be cleaned and made right later, which it will be or neither of us will be content with it. (*SL*, 300)

At Easter they had dinner at a drive-in in Memphis and were spotted by an acquaintance of Estelle's. A few days later, Joan received a letter from Estelle asking to meet her at the Peabody Hotel in Memphis. When they met, Joan was struck, as Meta had been a few years earlier, by Estelle's fragility. The meeting was courteous but Estelle's questions were direct. She asked Joan if she wanted to marry her husband, to which Joan replied that she did not, which may or may not have reassured Estelle. But Estelle could not understand why Billy and Joan should continue to see each other.

From now on, Estelle was on her guard. She started intercepting Joan's letters, began drinking again, and subjected her husband to spectacular fits of jealousy, sometimes even in front of Jill and the servants. She called Joan's parents to tell them about their daughter's behavior, and Faulkner had great difficulty preventing his wife from going to see them in Memphis. He tried to recover Joan's letters and asked her to send all future mail care of the post office—addressed to Quentin Compson!

That summer, they saw each other only rarely but continued to correspond. In late August, Faulkner told Joan how work was going on *Requiem*. Joan wrote him in September about her own projects. He replied on September 29, 1950:

> I have an idea for you. . . . A young woman, senior at school, a man of fifty, famous—could be artist, soldier, whatever seems best. He has come up to spend the day with her. She does not know why, until after he has gone. They talk, about everything, anything, whatever you like. She is more than just flattered that a man of fame has come up to see her; she likes him, feels drawn to an understanding, make it wisdom, of her, of people, man, a sympathy for her in particular; maybe he will of a sudden talk of love to her. But she will know that

is still not it, not what he came for; she is puzzled a little; when he gets on the train, she is sad, probably worried; she does not know why, is uncomfortable because she is troubled. There is something inconclusive, yet she cannot imagine what conclusion there could be between the two of them. But she knows that he came for some reason, and she failed to get it, whether he thought she would or not or is disappointed that she didn't. Then she finds why he came, what he wanted, and that he got it. She knows it the next day; she receives a telegram that he is dead, heart; she realises that he knew it was going to happen, and that what he wanted was to walk in April again for a day, an hour. (*SL*, 307)

The letter ends with professional recommendations: "Write that one, fairly short, objectively, from the outside, 3rd person, but of course from the girl's point of view. You can do it" (*SL*, 307). The mature writer's intention was to impart his knowledge and experience to a young novelist still finding her way and to boost her confidence in her future as a writer. He wrote to her again on January 28, 1951: "You will write, some day. Maybe now you haven't anything to say. You have to have something burning your very entrails to be said; you dont have that yet but dont worry about it; it is not important whether you write or not; writing is important only when you want to do it, and nothing nothing else but writing will suffice, give you peace" (312). Faulkner took his role as mentor very seriously but never forgot to remind Joan of his tender feelings. The night before leaving for Stockholm, he wrote that he did not know when he would see her again but that she was the one he thought about ceaselessly, that she was the young woman alongside whom he lay before falling asleep, that he knew every red hair and every sweet curve of her body.[15]

However, as far as we know, they were not lovers at that time and would not be for many months yet. When Faulkner invited Joan to join him in Hollywood in February 1951, she declined. But when his return flight from Europe landed in Memphis in the late afternoon of June 17, 1952, she was there to meet him. They spent the evening together; he got back to Rowan Oak at two thirty in the morning. That night was probably the first time they made love. When he wrote to her two days later, he compared himself to old Goethe, over seventy and madly in love with the very young Ulrike von Levetzow, and was overjoyed and proud as punch at "having conquered (I mean half-conquered anyway) a young and pretty woman." But with happiness came worry: "Only, in this case, there is a rather terrible amount of no-peace too. If we could meet whenever we liked, it might be different with me, though probably not. [. . .] Maybe I can even do more for you then, after there is no more barrier, no more mystery, nothing to remain between" (*B1*, 557).

In the heat of late June and early July 1952, Faulkner continued to provide Joan with advice and encouragement. The previous winter he had sent her critical observations on a short story she was writing:

> The trouble with the short story is, it doesn't move. It's static. You can write about a lazy, inner character, but the character must be told in motion. Why not start the story when she is sent to pick up Ben, instead buys the dress, lets Ben get wet because she deviated to buy the dress, show all this in action, dialogue which carries action, tell the story from the OUTSIDE instead of INSIDE. This is not an essay, remember. (*SL*, 323)

In a letter written in mid-August 1952 he closely examined the manuscript of another short story written by her that had just been rejected by *Harper's*. The hero was a forty-year-old simpleton not unlike Benjy Compson. As always, Faulkner knew how to measure out compliments, criticisms, and technical advice. He thought it very good and would not recommend taking anything out of it. He suggested that if she cut the idiot section into shorter paragraphs or even reduced a paragraph to a single sentence, it would have more effect, would better translate the simplicity of the psychic processes and innocent mental fumblings.[16] On August 20 he sent the revised manuscript to Harold Ober; on September 29 he warmly recommended the author: "She has been my pupil 3 years now, when nobody else, her people, believed in her. I am happy to know my judgment was right. She is shy and independent, will ask no help. But for my sake, do whatever you can for her" (341). Bearing the title "The Morning and the Evening," suggested by Faulkner, the short story was published in the *Atlantic* in January 1953.

Between "student" and master, relations seemed excellent. Between the twenty-year-old woman and the lovesick man in his fifties, they were much more ambiguous and difficult. After three years they no longer knew where they stood, if they ever had known. On August 7, 1952, Faulkner wrote to Joan. He had been examining his conscience and worrying, trying to understand their relationship, to understand her and her unconscious reasons for her actions. He could not or would not believe that she had ever deliberately wanted or intended to confuse him, bewilder him, or make him unhappy, and sick with astonishment, frustration, and deferred hope, he took full responsibility for that.[17]

In August the following year, Faulkner joined Joan in Holly Springs, Mississippi, midway between Oxford and Memphis. They found a pretty wood near a lake where they could be alone, but Joan was still reticent. The day after his return to Oxford, Faulkner sent a letter to Joan to tell her how much this failed meeting had disappointed and bothered him. His disappointment and pique were this time expressed with a rare boorishness. He told her that, after all, it was her mouth and her ass and that she had the right to say no, and anyone who didn't like it should just go home and stay there.[18]

In the fall of 1952 Joan went back to New York, where she worked as an editor for *Look* magazine. Faulkner submerged her with entreating letters that became more and more erotic. He was very unwell, and in October he had to be hospitalized. Joan rushed to his beside and at that time was the woman closest to him. In November he went to Princeton, New Jersey, and took up lodgings in the elegant Princeton Inn, where he intended to work. Joan visited him from time to time. Against all expectations, he asked Saxe Commins to give Joan the manuscript of *The Sound and the Fury*. They made love again, but there was no true carnal intimacy between them; they were not truly lovers. The unease persisted. Faulkner started to drink again and ended up in the hospital. When he went back to Oxford for Christmas, he longed for Joan, but she was less and less inclined to tie herself to a man thirty-three years her senior.

They finally broke up in 1953. They saw each other from time to time in Memphis or Holly Springs, but when Faulkner asked Joan to go to Paris, Mexico, or New England with him that summer, so that they could work together, she went to Florida on her own instead. She returned to Memphis in early September but seemed in no rush to see him again. Faulkner was very bitter, all the more so since he had been alone at Rowan Oak since August 25. He wrote to Joan: "One of the nicest conveniences a woman can have is someone she can pick up when she needs or wants him; then when she doesn't, she can drop him and know that he will still be right there when she does want him again" (*B1*, 573).

They met one last time in mid-October 1953. Joan picked Faulkner up at the Memphis airport and they headed north in her car. He was so weak that she had to keep driving the entire first day and part of the second.

Upon his arrival in New York, he rented a suite at 1 Fifth Avenue, right by Washington Square, and Joan sometimes came to work there in the mornings. They met less and less often. One of their last outings was a night at the theater. He took her to see *Cyrano de Bergerac*, with José Ferrer in the role of Cyrano (who played the same role in the 1951 film version and who had also put in a remarkable performance as Toulouse-Lautrec in John Huston's *Moulin Rouge*).

The choice of *Cyrano de Bergerac* was no coincidence. Faulkner was long familiar with Edmond Rostand's play; he knew it very well, particularly these three lines at the end of the third act:

> Your name in my heart goes dring-a-ling-ling
> Like a tiny brass bell, and I shake all the time;
> All the time the bell shakes and your name gives a ring.

In Faulkner's novel *Mosquitoes*, Mark Gordon, when thinking of Patricia Robin, says to himself: "Your name is like a little golden bell hung in my heart" (*M*, 267–68), citing Cyrano, who falls in love with her over the course of a conversation (270). A variant of the same phrase—"thy name like muted silver bells / Breathed over me" (*FM/GB*, 46)—appears in poem 24 of the collection *A Green Bough*. We know that Faulkner recited verses from *Cyrano* to Estelle, Meta, and Joan when he was courting them, and the *Mosquitoes* quotation is contained in a draft letter addressed to Helen Baird. In *The Wintering*, Joan Williams's third novel, aging novelist Jeffrey Almoner (Faulkner's fictional double) recites the same passage to his young friend Amy Howard (Joan's fictional double), at first in an approximate version of the original, and then in his own translation, explaining to an enchanted Amy: "That's why one of the great lovers said it to his love, long before I. Cyrano to Roxane."[19]

Comparing Faulkner to Cyrano may seem somewhat surprising. But the fact that Faulkner identified with Rostand's comic romantic hero, with the great lover, ill-favored and spurned, with this gallant poet more lucky with words than with women, is easy to understand.

With Joan about to leave him, Faulkner was once again thrust into the role of the spurned lover. Although reluctant to hurt his feelings, Joan made no secret of her belief that the age difference between them was too much for a long-term relationship. Moreover, since September she had been dating a young man, Ezra Bowen, son of the biographer Catherine Drinker

Bowen and himself a writer, with whom she had fallen in love and went on to marry the following year. Before long, she announced this to Faulkner in a letter. For him, a scenario familiar since Estelle and Helen was repeating itself: once again the woman he loved was leaving him for another. They broke up in November. Their relationship, often tender, rarely happy, had lasted five years.

For Faulkner it was a hard blow. His feelings had been hurt and he had great difficulty rising above it. In a letter full of bitter recriminations sent to Joan a few days later, he reproached her: "You take too much, and are willing to give too little." He lectured and reprimanded her, rejecting the accusation that he was annoyed only because she didn't sleep with him every time they were together: "People have attributes like animals; you are a mixture of cat and mule and possum—the cat's secretiveness and self-centeredness, the mule's stubbornness to get what it wants no matter who or what suffers, the possum's nature of playing dead—running into sleep or its pretence—whenever it is faced with a situation which it thinks it is not going to like" (*B1*, 578–79). Faulkner was angry with Joan for wanting to play her own game, to live her own life, without him and far away from him, and scolded her for keeping bad company. In New York she was dating men her own age. Faulkner badmouthed them without knowing them and warned Joan about those irresponsible parasites who "go through the motions of art—talking about what they are going to do over drinks, even defacing paper and canvas when necessary, in order to escape the responsibility of living" (see *B1*, 579).

This time, however, Faulkner was not as distraught and despairing as he had been when Meta left him. He was a famous writer with female admirers, among whom a number were on the lookout for love. Other women would soon distract and console him. In late 1953, at Saint-Moritz, he met the ravishing Jean Stein, who fell madly in love with him. He also spent some time in Stockholm with Else Jonsson, his Swedish girlfriend. This did not mean that all links with Joan were broken. As with Meta, Joan would remain a friend and confidante. They continued to write to each other. In December 1953, while in Switzerland, he wrote:

> I am very happy to know that you are working, and that you know that nothing basic has changed between us. It never will, no matter what course your life might take. I believe you know that until I die, I will be the best friend you ever had [. . .]. I think I was—am—the father which you never had—the one who

never raised his hand against you, who desired, tried, to put always first your hopes and dreams and happiness.[20]

In Faulkner's life as in his novels, nothing ever ends, nothing ever fully disappears, something remains, even in loss. Joan was gone; she had left him like others before her, but he needed to believe that "nothing basic has changed." They were no longer lovers, but their love did not die. It survived them, eluding the vagaries of time, more beautiful in memory than in actuality, now become an immutable souvenir of love. Faulkner continued to see himself in the position of the benevolent, protective father and wanted Joan to be his appreciative "daughter": "I know I am better for it, and I know that someday you will know that you are too" (B, 1484). What he feared above all was that Joan, after spurning him to marry another, would become ashamed of what had passed between them: "You did something fine and brave and generous, and the gods will love you for it. You'll see in time. Dont regret and grieve" (578).

In 1959 they again exchanged letters. Although they had not seen each other for six years, Faulkner wrote love letters intimating that he was still not over her: "I'm not going to see you again," he wrote, "at least now. It's too painful. . . . I love you but I can do it with less pain from a distance" (B1, 675). She wrote back that she had just finished a novel based on her short story "The Morning and the Evening" but that she was worried, fearing that reviewers would see her as a pale imitator. Faulkner chided and reassured her:

> Never give one goddam about what anybody says about the work if you KNOW you have done it as honestly and bravely and truly as you could. [. . .] Every writer is influenced by everything. Whatever touches him, from the telephone directory to God. I was in your life at an age which I think you will find was a very important experience, and of course it will show on you. But dont be afraid. There are worse people and experiences than me and ours to have influenced you. Dont be afraid. Do the work." (666)

In 1962, when Joan published *The Morning and the Evening*, Faulkner sent her a letter of congratulations: "Splendid news. . . . That not only justifies us but maybe absolves me of what harm and hurt I might have done you; maybe annoyance and exasperation are better words" (B1, 689).

They missed their penultimate meeting. On May 24, 1962, the awards ceremony for the Gold Medal for Fiction, awarded each year by the National Institute of Arts and Letters, took place in New York. Joan had won an award for her first novel. Faulkner was also there to receive a medal. When Joan mounted the podium to accept her award, she received no sign of recognition from Faulkner. He had fallen asleep.

But on June 26, a few days before his death, she came to visit him at Rowan Oak one last time. As he walked her back to her car, she found him pale.

NOTES

1. David Minter, *William Faulkner: His Life and Work* (Baltimore: Johns Hopkins University Press, 1980), 192.

2. Anthony Quinn, quoted by Jay Parini in *One Matchless Time: A Life of William Faulkner* (New York: Harper Collins, 2004), 272.

3. Jack Warner, *My First Hundred Years in Hollywood* (New York: Random House, 1965), 282.

4. Bruce F. Kawin, *Faulkner and Film* (New York: Frederick Ungar, 1977), 109.

5. Jean Renoir, *Ma vie et mes films* (Paris: Flammarion, 2005), 217.

6. Stephen Longstreet, quoted in William Faulkner with Louis Daniel Brodsky and Robert W. Hamblin, *Stallion Road* (screenplay) (Jackson: University Press of Mississippi, 1989), 16.

7. Gavin Stevens is referring to "Pickett's Charge," an assault by the Confederates on the Yankee army on July 3, 1863, the last day of the deadly Battle of Gettysburg, which was the major turning point in the Civil War.

8. Edmund Wilson, *Classics and Commercials: A Literary Chronicle of the Forties* (New York: Farrar, Straus & Giroux, 1950), 460.

9. *Letters of John Keats*, ed. Robert Gittings (Oxford: Oxford University Press, 1970), 43.

10. James Dahl, "A Faulkner Reminiscence: Conversations with Mrs. Maud Faulkner," *Journal of Modern Literature* (April 1974): 1029.

11. Joan Williams, *The Wintering* (New York: Harcourt Brace Jovanvich, 1971), 57–58.

12. Faulkner Collection, Alderman Library, University of Virginia.

13. Ibid.

14. Blotner Papers, Louis Daniel Brodsky Collection, Kent Library, Southeastern Missouri State University.

15. Letter dated December 5, 1950, Blotner Papers.

16. *Faulkner: A Comprehensive Guide to the Brodsky Collection*, ed. Louis Daniel Brodsky and Robert W. Hamblin. Vol. 2: *The Letters* (Jackson: University Press of Mississippi, 1984), 80.

17. Faulkner Collection, Alderman Library, University of Virginia.

18. *Guide to the Brodsky Collection*, 81.

19. Williams, *Wintering*, 229.

20. Letter quoted in Stephen B. Oates, *William Faulkner: The Man and the Artist* (New York: Harper & Row, 1989), 273.

8
FAME—AT LAST

THE NOBEL PRIZE

After World War II, Faulkner's stock in the United States was at its lowest point: the New York Public Library held just two books by him—*A Green Bough* and *The Hamlet*—and *Sanctuary* was his only book still available in the bookshops. However, it would be an overstatement to say that his compatriots were forgetting him. In January 1939 Faulkner had been elected to the National Institute of Arts and Letters, alongside John Steinbeck and Marjorie Kinnan Rawlings. A few days later, when *The Wild Palms* was published, he was on the cover of *Time* magazine, which featured a major piece on "the most talented but least predictable southern writer," and in November of that same year, the renowned poet, novelist, and critic Conrad Aiken—whom Faulkner had read in his youth and whom he had highly praised in a 1921 article—published a handsome essay in the *Atlantic* titled "William Faulkner: The Novel as Form." Faulkner had also been rehabilitated by George Marion O'Donnell, a second-generation Agrarian, in a clearly biased essay published in 1939 in the *Kenyon Review*, clearing him of all suspicion of nihilism and hailing him as a traditional moralist in the best sense of the word,[1] thus paving the way to prosaically humanistic and insidiously conservative interpretations that were to dominate American academic criticism for many years.

Faulkner was still not a popular author but he had become more socially acceptable. The time for rediscovery was ripe. Malcolm Cowley was to be the prime mover in this rehabilitation. A respected literary critic, advisor to Viking Press, Cowley had edited and provided the preface to the 1944 anthology *The Portable Hemingway*. Convinced that a similar anthology of Faulkner's works would be a revelation to many readers, he started corresponding with Faulkner beginning in February 1944. He first told him that he was preparing to write a long essay on Faulkner's career and work and asked if he could interview him to "ask questions about his life and his aims" (*FCF*, 6). Faulkner responded three months later: "I would like the piece, except the biography part" (*SL*, 182). Cowley went on to publish three articles: the first in the *New York Times Book Review* on October 29, 1944; the second in the *Saturday Review* on April 14, 1945; and the third in the *Southern Review* in the summer of 1945. Faulkner was wholly in favor of an anthology of his works. In August 1945, when Cowley told him that Viking had agreed to publish a *Portable Faulkner*, his reaction was enthusiastic: "By all means let us make a Golden Book of my apocryphal county. I have thought of spending my old age doing something of that nature: an alphabetical, rambling genealogy of the people, father to son to son" (*SL*, 197).

The collaboration between Cowley and Faulkner had not always been easy while the anthology was being prepared, but when *The Portable Faulkner* was published in April 1946, Faulkner generously congratulated Cowley: "The job is splendid. Damn you to hell anyway. But even if I had beat you to the idea, mine wouldn't have been this good" (*SL*, 233).

Nothing could have predicted the role Cowley was to play in Faulkner's career. Between 1935 and 1942, Cowley published five reviews of Faulkner's novels in the *New Republic* that were not shining examples of discernment, and his subsequent overall interpretation of Faulkner's work was also lacking in this regard. It was Cowley who, when planning *The Portable Faulkner*, put forward the highly contentious argument that Faulkner's work constituted a vast saga and should be read as a *comédie humaine* in the tradition of Balzac. While he failed to grasp Faulkner's modernity, Cowley nonetheless realized that he was a great writer who needed to be recognized in his own country. His anthology made a decisive contribution to bringing Faulkner out of the wilderness. Two years after *The Portable Faulkner*, Random House published *Intruder in the Dust*, which, as we have seen, sold very well and would soon be adapted for the screen. In 1948 Faulkner was back on the national stage.

There was no comeback in Europe, however, for the simple reason that Faulkner had never been forgotten there. He had been brought to the attention of the French public by Maurice-Edgar Coindreau's translations in the early 1930s, and in France Faulkner's reputation had never stopped growing. In June 1931 Coindreau wrote an essay about him in the *Nouvelle Revue Française*, where he portrayed him as "one of the most interesting figures of young American literature."[2] Two short stories, "A Rose for Emily" and "Dry September," were reviewed in 1932, followed in August 1933 by "There Was a Queen." The translation of *Sanctuary*, with a preface by André Malraux, was published by Éditions Gallimard in 1933; Coindreau's translation of *As I Lay Dying*, with a preface by Valery Larbaud, in 1934; and *The Sound and the Fury*, also translated by Coindreau, in 1938. A year later, in a brilliant review of this last novel in the *Nouvelle Revue Française*, Jean-Paul Sartre hailed Faulkner's fiction writing as among the most innovative of the twentieth century.

After the Liberation, American novelists from the interwar period—Faulkner, Hemingway, Dos Passos, Steinbeck, and even Caldwell—enjoyed enormous prestige. Cowley noted that according to Sartre, Faulkner was a god for young people in France (*FCF*, 35). The situation was very different in the United States, even though the publication of *The Portable Faulkner* in 1946 pointed to renewed interest. That same year, Faulkner was awarded second prize—$250—for a short story he had entered into a competition run by *Ellery Queen's Mystery Magazine*. "What a commentary," he wrote to Ober. "In France, I am the father of a literary movement. In Europe I am considered the best modern American and among the first of all writers. In America, I eke out a hack's motion picture wages by winning second prize in a manufactured mystery story contest" (*SL*, 217–18).

In France, at the same time, after Sartre, Malraux, and Valery Larbaud had acknowledged Faulkner as one of the major figures of the modern novel, French critics started reading him more closely, identifying his singularity, as attested by two critical works of a rare clear-sightedness, published in 1946 and 1948 respectively: *Temps et roman* by Jean Pouillon and *L'Age du roman américain* by Claude-Edmonde Magny. It was the beginning of international recognition, which, in the first half of the twentieth century, had to involve Paris, then the still-uncontested capital of world literature and the arts. Faulkner's recognition in France was a factor in his rediscovery by America, and it clearly hastened his achievement of global status.

In the spring of 1950, Mark Van Doren told Faulkner that he was to be awarded the Howells Medal of the American Academy of Arts and Letters and invited him to come and receive it at a ceremony on May 25. Faulkner replied that he was honored by the award but declined to come to New York to receive the medal under a pretext that nobody could have taken seriously: "I am a farmer this time of year; up until he sells crops, no Mississippi farmer has time or money either to travel anywhere on" (*SL*, 302). But above all, 1950 was the year he received the supreme accolade: the Nobel Prize in Literature. On the morning of November 10 the telephone rang at Rowan Oak. It was Swen Ahman, the New York correspondent of Stockholm daily *Dagens Nyheter*, calling to tell Faulkner that the Swedish Academy had just awarded him the 1949 prize. Rumors had been circulating for three years, but Faulkner had apparently paid little notice to them. Earlier that year, he wrote to Joan Williams: "It's not the sort of thing to decline; a gratuitous insult to do so but I dont want it. I had rather be in the same pigeon hole with Dreiser and Sherwood Anderson, than with Sinclair Lewis and Mrs. Chinahand Buck" (*SL*, 299). Faulkner may have been sniffy, but he was not as detached as he wanted to appear, and when his old friend Mac Reed, the Oxford drugstore owner, came to congratulate him, he shook his hand and said: "Mac, I still can't believe it" (*WFO*, 186). And then, as he wrote to Joan, a Southern gentleman could never be discourteous. Thus, he accepted the prize, albeit not without fuss, as he did almost every time he had to travel to receive a prize or medal. Again citing his farming obligations and distance, he indicated that he would not be able to travel to Stockholm. The next day, he left Oxford to spend a week in a hunters' encampment in the Delta near Cypress Lake, as he did every year. He told his hunting companions nothing about the prize, but they had heard about it and insisted on celebrating with him. On the morning of November 27 he was back at Rowan Oak with a heavy cold.

It took the concerted efforts of the Department of State, Erik Boheman, the Swedish ambassador to the United States, and Faulkner's own family to change his mind about going. On November 27 he finally telegraphed Boheman: "WILL BE PLEASED TO JOURNEY STOCKHOLM. APPRECIATE VERY MUCH YOUR UNDERSTANDING. WILLIAM FAULKNER" (*SL*, 309). After this he withdrew to his room with a good supply of bourbon. "I will take my last drink at six o'clock Monday night," he told Estelle and his adopted daughter, Victoria. "Then I'll be ready to go to Memphis on Tuesday and on Wednesday we'll fly to New York" (*B1*, 528). In the meantime, Jill looked after the passports, and after taking her husband's measurements,

Estelle asked Saxe Commins to rent him a suit. Anxious to get him back on his feet in time, his family tried to convince him that Monday had already arrived. Faulkner was not fooled. But he kept his promise and by Wednesday he was sufficiently sober to travel. Friends came to see him off on the morning of his departure to Stockholm. "Now, Bill, you do right," said Phil Stone, to which Faulkner replied: "I'm so damn sick and tired of hearin' that. Everybody from the Swedish ambassador to my damn nigger houseboy has been tellin' me to do right!" (*B1*, 529).

On Thursday, December 7, after being more or less put back into shape by his family, Faulkner took off from Memphis with Jill by his side. In New York, Robert Haas and his wife were waiting at LaGuardia Airport, with numerous reporters and photographers on the lookout. "What do you consider the decadent aspect of American life today?" asked a journalist. "It's what you're doing now" (*B1*, 529), retorted Faulkner.

His publishers held a dinner in his honor, which was attended by his friends Malcolm Cowley and Maurice-Edgar Coindreau. Faulkner drank. On Friday, December 8, he flew to Sweden with his daughter and started writing his acceptance speech. Upon his arrival in a snowy Stockholm, he was assailed by journalists' questions and photographers' flashes. On the tenth, the day of the awards ceremony, he arrived at the concert hall dressed in black suit and white tie. He had refused to shave, but Jill thought he looked very well and declared herself very proud of her Pappy when they made their entrance into the main hall. Faulkner sat beside Bertrand Russell, who had also won an award and who tried in vain to engage him in conversation. He was so intimidated and so nervous that he forgot to come down off the podium to accept the prize, and King Gustavus Adolphus had to come to him to hand it to him. An official banquet was then held at the Stockholm city hall, after which the award winners made their acceptance speeches. When Faulkner rose to deliver his, he looked well. But this "small elegant figure, very far away"—as later described by Else Jonsson, the beautiful widow of his Swedish translator, who had grown close to him (*B1*, 533)—was a poor speaker. He stood too far away from the microphone and spoke too fast in his high-pitched voice and unreconstructed Southern drawl. When he sat down, there was stunned silence in the hall. Nobody had understood his speech. People had to wait until the next day to read it in the press.

"I believe that man will not merely endure: he will prevail. He is immortal, not because he alone among creatures has an inexhaustible voice but because he has a soul, a spirit capable of compassion and sacrifice and endurance" (*ESPL*, 120): this was Faulkner's profession of faith in his Nobel Prize acceptance speech. In this speech, as in others made to high school graduates in Oxford in 1951 and in Pine Manor, Massachusetts, in 1953, the vigor with which Faulkner asserted his humanism was surprising. However, the sincerity of this rhetoric may be questioned. In his private correspondence Faulkner's humanism was much less assertive. For example, a letter written to Malcolm Cowley in early November 1944 reads: "Life is a phenomenon but not a novelty, the same frantic steeplechase toward nothing everywhere and man stinks the same stink no matter where in time" (*SL*, 185). And ten years later, when Mississippi was booming, he wrote to Else Jonsson: "But human beings are terrible. One must believe well in man to endure him, wait out his folly and savagery and inhumanity" (382). Faulkner's humanism was not self-evident.

Faulkner left Sweden with a check for over thirty thousand dollars in his pocket. According to the American embassy's report, he had made a very good impression: "Critics who met him were enthusiastic over his personality, and the press in general was pleased with his simplicity and modesty and apparently surprised by his courtly and gracious manners" (*B*, 1369). On December 12 he arrived with Jill at Le Bourget Airport near Paris, leaving for London on the fifteenth, and taking off almost immediately for New York. On the eighteenth he was back in Oxford, where he was welcomed by the high school brass band. On January 1, 1951, he went back to work.

Faulkner had finally obtained the public recognition that he had been deprived of for so long. Flattered that a Southerner had won the Nobel Prize, the local press, starting with the *Oxford Eagle*, congratulated him, but the *Jackson Daily News*, an extreme right-wing daily, continued to denounce this "propagandist of degradation," who belonged in the "privy school of literature." And while the national press was more respectful, it rued the fact that such a prestigious prize had been awarded to an American writer who was so unrepresentative and so unsuitable. The *New York Times* ironically noted that incest and rape were perhaps common distractions in Faulkner's

Jefferson, Mississippi, but not elsewhere in the United States. The *New York Herald Tribune* did not hold back either, asserting that nothing would justify a quarrel about the prize, although a more smiling winner who did not live in a world that was constantly darkening would have been preferable. These lukewarm and frankly poisonous reactions outraged Coindreau— and rightly so: "I must confess that one of the reasons prompting me to talk about the author of *Sanctuary* is the extreme reservation—to say the least—with which the American press seems to have welcomed the news that William Faulkner had been awarded the Nobel Prize."[3]

After the Nobel Prize, however, the accolades and honors flowed. In 1951 French president Vincent Auriol awarded Faulkner the Légion d'honneur on October 26 at the French consulate in New Orleans. Invited in late May 1952 to a festival in Paris to celebrate twentieth-century works, he received a standing ovation. On January 25, 1955, he received the National Book Award and the Pulitzer Prize for *A Fable*. In March 1957 he received the Silver Medal of the Greek Academy of Letters. And on May 24, 1962, a few weeks before his death, Eudora Welty presented him with the Gold Medal for Fiction from the American Academy of Arts and Letters, an award he himself had presented to Dos Passos in 1957.

All the baubles of glory; a veritable avalanche of medals and ribbons— Faulkner did not hide his disdain for these from Cowley: "Of course I give no fart for glory" (*SL*, 182). Does this mean that he had never sought it, that it had sought him out, in his hidey-hole in Oxford, that he was indifferent to the acclaim? In truth, while he showed contempt for honors, there is no evidence that he declined them, and although it took a long time to convince him, he did eventually go to Stockholm. In New Orleans, at a time when he had published virtually nothing, he claimed he could write *Hamlet* in prose. In 1936, after finishing *Absalom, Absalom!* he asserted that it was the best novel ever written in America. In 1939, after completing *The Hamlet*, he reminded Haas that he was "the best [writer] in America" (*SL*, 113). Was this bragging on a par with that of Hemingway? Faulkner must at times have felt the need to reassure himself, but nothing suggests that he underestimated himself, and a close friend said of him that he demanded absolute adulation.[4] Later, when his daughter, to whom he was very attached, asked him in a moment of distress not to forget her, he replied loftily: "Nobody remembers Shakespeare's children" (*B1*, 473). It is hard to believe such a man was without vanity.

THE PUBLIC MAN

Fame and success always come at a price. After the awarding of the Nobel Prize, tourists began arriving at Rowan Oak to see the great writer in his home, tormenting him with their cameras. He could no longer go incognito. Up until then, Faulkner had ferociously defended his private life against any intrusion by the press, in both his correspondence and his public statements. On September 15, 1948, when Hamilton Basso asked for permission to profile him in the *New Yorker*, he replied: "Oh hell no. Come down and visit whenever you can, but no piece in any paper about me as I am working tooth and nail at my lifetime ambition to be the last private individual on earth" (*B1*, 496). In October that same year, while he was staying with the Cowleys in Connecticut, Malcolm told him that *Life* magazine, which had already done a profile of Hemingway in Cuba, was planning to do another on Faulkner. On January 5, 1949, he wrote to Cowley:

> About 10 years ago I had no little difficulty in convincing Life (or somebody) that I didn't want a piece about me in their mag. and two years ago it took six months and a considerable correspondence and telegrams to convince Vogue that I would have no part of their same project. I still dont want it, I mean, me as a private individual, my past, my family, my house. I would prefer nothing about the books, but they are in the public domain and I was paid for that right. The only plan I can accept is one giving me the privilege of editing the result. Which means I will want to blue pencil everything which even intimates that something breathing and moving sat behind the typewriter which produced the books. (*SL*, 315–16)

He made the same plea for privacy in a letter to Haas dated August 3, 1951:

> My point of view re publicity piece has not changed. I still contend that my printed works are in the printed domain and anyone can bat them around. But my private life and my photographed face are my own and I will defend them as such to the end. I have deliberately buried myself in this little lost almost illiterate town, to keep out of the way so that news people wont notice and remember me. (319)

That same month, journalist Robert Coughlan arrived in Oxford to interview Faulkner. Faulkner at first slammed the door in his face but then relented and allowed him in. On September 28, 1953, against the novelist's wishes, *Life* published "The Private World of William Faulkner," the first

part of Coughlan's biographical essay. On October 5, the second part, titled
"The Man Behind the Faulkner Myth," was published. Faulkner was outraged and he made no bones about it:

> It's too bad the individual in this country has no protection from journalism,
> I suppose they call it. But apparently he hasn't. There seems to be in this the
> same spirit which permits strangers to drive into my yard and pick up books or
> pipes I left in the chair where I had been sitting, as souvenirs.
>
>   What a commentary. Sweden gave me the Nobel Prize. France gave me the
> Legion d'Honneur. All my native land did for me was to invade my privacy
> over my protest and my plea. No wonder people in the rest of the world dont
> like us, since we seem to have neither taste nor courtesy, and know and believe
> in nothing but money and it doesn't much matter how you get it. (SL, 354)

This is what Faulkner wrote on October 7 to Philip Mullen, chief editor
of the *Oxford Eagle*. Appalled by the two *Life* articles, he responded forcefully in "On Privacy," published by *Harper's* in July 1955 (*ESPL*, 62–75).
Coughlan's biographical essay was to his eyes an unacceptable intrusion
into his privacy, and he deplored the manner in which the much-vaunted
American freedom had been betrayed and replaced by pure impunity. His
personal indignation was converted into an indictment of the commercialism of America at that time: "America has not yet found any place for him
who deals only in things of the human spirit except to use his notoriety
to sell soap or cigarettes or fountain pens or to advertise automobiles and
cruises and resort hotels, or (if he can be taught to contort fast enough to
meet the standards) in radio or moving pictures" (75).

While working as a scriptwriter in Hollywood, Faulkner had been a
victim of the commercialism of American culture, and his public recognition as a writer was a long time coming. But in 1955, after so many prizes
and official awards, his complaints rang hollow. And for anyone familiar
with his public attitudes, his vehement denunciation of attacks on his privacy is questionable. Faulkner was no Salinger or Pynchon. "I will protest to
the last: no photographs, no recorded documents," he wrote to Cowley in
February 1949 (SL, 285). But he did not refuse to pose for photographers or
painters and passed on to posterity hundreds of personal portraits, enough
to fill many albums. He was never indifferent to his image at any time in his
life. From youth, as we have seen, he took extreme care with his appearance.

At Ole Miss people found him arrogant and affected. And while he had had a difficult relationship with journalists since the start of his career, it could not be said that he avoided them: his first interview dates from 1926, and there were at least a dozen before 1950. It is therefore hardly surprising that in the 1950s, after the Nobel Prize, the self-proclaimed recluse from Oxford consented to become an official persona and to tread the boards of celebrity.

His fame now followed him wherever he went. He could no longer pass unnoticed. At social functions all eyes and ears were now riveted on him. The *New Yorker* reporter noted that at the cocktail party after the National Book Award Ceremony on February 7, 1953, "the lion of the afternoon was . . . William Faulkner, who, very small and very handsome, with a voice that never rose above a whisper, stood with his back to the wall and gamely took on all comers." According to another observer, "It was hard to get a word with him, so closely packed around him were his admirers. His famed reticence and dislike of publicity were much in evidence, as were his dignity, poise and shy friendliness" (*B1*, 567). This shy, quiet man now started sending "open letters" to the press, giving lectures all over the place, publishing essays on societal issues and granting long interviews, patiently answering the most embarrassing and ludicrous questions. In November 1952 he even agreed to be filmed at Rowan Oak, in the streets of Oxford, and in Phil Stone's office by a television crew financed by the Ford Foundation.

In awarding him the Nobel Prize the Stockholm jury had not just recognized his work; it had turned him into an international star, giving him the authority of a scholar whose every pronouncement was seized upon with reverence.

⌒

Faulkner had no head for politics. Prior to the 1950s he had had little interest in the ways of the world or in the affairs of his country and his region. In contrast to Dos Passos, Hemingway, and Steinbeck, he was anything but a politically conscious writer. True, he was not indifferent to the rise of fascism and Nazism in Europe between the wars, and in 1938, in a letter to the president of the League of American Writers, he openly took a stance against Francoism: "I most sincerely wish to go on record as being unalterably opposed to Franco and fascism, to all violations of the legal government and outrages against the people of Republican Spain" (*ESPL*, 198). Unlike Hemingway, Malraux, and Orwell, he did not go to war alongside the Republicans, but he did show solidarity with a handsome symbolic gesture, offering to donate the manuscript of *Absalom, Absalom!* to raise money for them.

That said, his antifascism was not that of a left-wing intellectual. On the rare occasions when he discussed politics, he did not hide his aversion to the idea of progress, and he deplored Steinbeck's yielding to the illusions of sentimental liberalism in *The Grapes of Wrath* (see *B*, 1470). In domestic politics his sympathies lay with the most conventional form of right-wing conservatism. A Democrat, as all Southerners had been since the end of Reconstruction, he distrusted federal power, defended the rights of states, and condemned all the social and economic reforms of the 1930s. He disliked Franklin Delano Roosevelt, whom 96 percent of Mississippi voters had favored in the 1932 presidential election, and detested his lively, influential, and very "liberal" wife, who was detested by all right-wing Americans. At Greenfield Farm one of his mules was called Jim Farley, the other Eleanor Roosevelt (*B1*, 412).

However, Faulkner voted for Adlai Stevenson against Dwight Eisenhower in the 1952 presidential election. Two years later, at a reception in Virginia, he told a *Washington Evening Star* reporter that he was proud to be a Democrat and deplored the harm being done by Senator Joe McCarthy. Nevertheless, he remained a Southern conservative to the end. On May 15, 1952, addressing the Delta Council in Cleveland, Mississippi, he repeated the legend of the founding fathers, extoling the great principles that inspired them, reminding the audience that it was "the duty of a man, the individual, each individual, every individual, to be responsible for the consequences of his own acts, to pay his own score, owing nothing to any man" (*ESPL*, 129). The reverse of this duty is the right of every man to freely enjoy the fruit of his work and the ownership of the soil he cultivates.

A vehement individualist in the tradition of the South and West, Faulkner distrusted all government intervention and called for a new era where "the welfare, the relief, the compensation, instead of being nationally sponsored cash prizes for idleness and ineptitude, could go where the old independent uncompromising fathers themselves would have intended it and blessed it: to those who still cannot, until the day when even the last of them except the sick and the old, would also be among them who not only can, but will" (*ESPL*, 133). In the same way as he disapproved of the New Deal aid and compensation programs, Faulkner now condemned farming subsidies as measures aimed at returning order to the markets. His ideological preconceptions prevented him from admitting that the time of the self-sufficient farmer in Jefferson was definitively over and from acknowledging the need for a national agricultural policy.

This liberal talk, inherited from Locke and the Enlightenment, suited the Southern aristocrats at whom it was aimed. This same antipathy to statism and interventionism were apparent in "The Tall Men," a short story published in 1941 that celebrated the patriotism of a family of small farmers, the McCallums, and their valiant resistance to government officials who have come to organize an assistance program under the New Deal. Faulkner's hostility to the federal government would never falter. It remained equally resolute under Harry Truman's administration.

———

Faulkner's thinking about blacks had evolved substantially. As a child, he had gone to a public school reserved for young white children, and his teacher, Miss Annie Chandler, had inculcated in him the basics of "white supremacy." *The Clansman: An Historical Romance of the Ku Klux Klan*, the vehemently racist Thomas Dixon novel published in 1905, which sold over a million copies and was made into the most expensive and popular silent movie ever, D. W. Griffith's *The Birth of a Nation*, glorified the Ku Klux Klan. Faulkner had spent his formative years in an environment where white racism was self-evident, where segregation was law, and the ideology of this environment had not changed much since then. In fact, it could be said that at the end of the nineteenth century, racism in Mississippi, as among the vast majority of Southern whites, had intensified. Since being freed, the black had become a foul beast in the white imagination, a lewd monster that had to be kept on a leash at all costs and slain if necessary, and it was not until the 1920s that the image of the ape-like, violent, rapist black started to fade.

Racism went further underground, but throughout the twentieth century, white Mississippians remained staunch supporters of segregation. Faulkner's family was openly racist, a tradition passed on from father to son. The "Old Colonel" had been a strong advocate of white supremacy; the

"Young Colonel" had been attracted by the militant negrophobia of Vardaman and Bilbo. Faulkner himself adhered to family tradition for many
years. That blacks and whites could live together with equal rights in a free
society was inconceivable to him. In 1921 he wrote to his father from New
Haven, Connecticut, after seeing free blacks for the first time:

> Well, sir, I could live in this country a hundred years and never get used to
> the niggers. The whites and niggers are always antagonistic, hate each other,
> and yet go to the same shows and smaller restaurants, and call each other by
> first names [. . .]. You cant tell me these niggers are as happy and contented as
> ours are, all this freedom does is to make them miserable because they are not
> white, so that they hate the white people more than ever, and the whites are
> afraid of them. There's only one sensible way to treat them, like we treat Brad
> Farmer, Calvin and Uncle George. (*LMF*, 154)

Ten years later his ideas on the issue were no less primitive, his disdain
for blacks no less evident, and he sometimes reverted to the most churlish
populism. In a letter titled "Mob Sometimes Right," published on February
15, 1931, by the *Commercial Appeal* in response to a letter from a black man
thanking the Association of Southern Women for the Prevention of Lynching for its endeavors in seeking to end this abominable practice, Faulkner,
without going so far as to justify lynching, found numerous attenuating circumstances for Southern lynch mobs and even suggested that most blacks
who were lynched deserved their fate. The idea that Southern blacks could
one day have the same rights as whites had not even occurred to him. In October of that same year, in an interview with the *New York Herald Tribune*,
he said that blacks would have everything to gain from a "benevolent au-
tocracy" and that "they'd be better off because they'd have someone to look
after them," adding: "I don't think it would be as good for the white peoples
as for the Negro to have slavery come back—theoretically, anyhow" (*LG*,
20). It has been said that the interview went badly and that Faulkner may
have been drunk, as he was during the infamous 1956 interview with Russell Warren Howe. Provocation or no, to treat blacks with so much disdain,
one had to be a Southern white.

But Faulkner did eventually become aware of the injustice and absurdity of Southern segregation. In 1945, when the town of Oxford was planning
to erect a commemorative plaque for its young men who had died at the

front, and the question arose as to whether the names of blacks and whites should be placed alongside each other, he told the chief editor of the *Oxford Eagle* that the plaque should include names from both races, adding that he was no doubt the only one in the community who dared to think and say that the only time when they're not niggers is when they're dead.[5]

In March 1950, in a letter to the editor of the *Commercial Appeal*, he protested against the scandalously lenient sentence pronounced against three whites convicted of the murder of three black children, expressing astonishment that the crime was not punished as severely "as robbing three banks or stealing three automobiles" (*ESPL*, 204). A year later Willie Mc-Gee, a black man accused of raping a white woman, was tried and sentenced to death three times. Before his execution, white women fighting for civil rights came to see Faulkner to ask for his support. Believing that his words had been misinterpreted, he sent a clarification to the newspapers, stating his opposition to the execution, not because he was convinced that McGee was innocent, but "because it will make him a martyr and create a long last-ing stink in my native state" (*ESPL*, 211). This immediately sparked a flurry of protests, including a letter from a preacher accusing Faulkner of flouting Mississippi law and showing contempt for the Supreme Court, and a judge who denounced Faulkner as a communist fellow traveler. McGee was exe-cuted in Laurel, Mississippi, in May 1951, four months after the Supreme Court rejected a third appeal.

Four years later the same Supreme Court declared that school segre-gation was unconstitutional. The South was stunned. Like most Southern whites, Faulkner disapproved of this federal ruling and feared that its im-plementation would lead to renewed violence. This did not mean that he was in favor of the status quo. On March 20, 1955, in a letter to the *Commer-cial Appeal*, he readily acknowledged that "we Mississippians already know that our present schools are not good enough" (*ESPL*, 215), and contest-ed the utility of two separate school systems that, due to lack of resources, were equally mediocre.

His stand earned Faulkner a deluge of indignant, insulting letters, in-cluding one from his brother John, an active member of the White Citizens Council, who was prepared to take up arms against school integration. Even his close friends and family disavowed him, and most Mississippi whites held him in contempt. John later remembered that as soon as Bill started speaking about integration, he began receiving anonymous telephone calls at unusual times. Mysterious voices cursed him, and his mailbox was full of anonymous, insulting letters. As none of these callers and letter writers shared Bill's views, they thought it served him right and that he should have known what would happen (*MBB*, 264). Phil Stone, his lifelong friend, disloyally suggested that Faulkner was simply looking for publicity.

But Faulkner—"Weeping Willie," as one indignant letter writer to the *Commercial Appeal* called him—did not bow to pressure and continued to say what he thought in public. In June 1955, while he was in Memphis to promote *Land of the Pharaohs*, reporters asked him about interracial relations. In the *Commercial Appeal* of June 14 he responded that opposing desegregation was in his view "like living in Alaska and saying you don't like snow" (*B1*, 599), a comparison he repeated in a speech delivered in November that year (*ESPL*, 146) and in his essay "On Fear," published in *Harper's* in June 1956.

As the clouds gathered, he became increasingly worried. On June 12, 1955, he wrote to Else Jonsson:

> We have much tragic trouble in Mississippi now about Negroes. The Supreme Court has said that there shall be no segregation, difference in schools, voting, etc. between the two races, and there are many people in Mississippi who will go to any length, even violence, to prevent that, I am afraid. I am doing what I can. I can see the possible time when I shall have to leave my native state, something as the Jew had to flee from Germany during Hitler. (*SL*, 381–82)

In the meantime he traveled far away. In July he left for Japan, on a trip sponsored by the State Department. On August 1 he arrived at Tokyo airport, so drunk that he needed emergency treatment before he could meet his hosts. "I'll keep faith with you," he promised an embassy official. "I won't let you down. The U.S. government commissioned me to do a job and I'll do it" (*B1*, 602). He kept his word. For three weeks he fulfilled his duties most conscientiously. He met Japanese writers, gave interviews, took part in a seminar in Nagano, and answered all questions with good grace, including those on relations in the South between whites and blacks.

Then he was back on the airplane, with a short stopover in the Philippines, before flying to Italy, where Jean Stein was waiting for him. It was while he was in Rome in September 1955 that the Emmett Till case broke out. A fourteen-year-old black boy from Chicago, who had come to visit his great-uncle in Money, Mississippi, near Greenwood, Till foolishly wolf-whistled at a white woman. His beaten, tortured, mutilated body was found attached to an iron wheel at the bottom of the Tallahatchie River. In accordance with the Southern tradition of impunity for race crimes committed by white people, his two killers were acquitted. The jury took just one hour and seven minutes to reach its verdict. The killers were photographed with their wives outside the courthouse. The case caused a sensation, however, when a photograph of Till's bloated face appeared in all the newspapers. When journalists asked Faulkner to comment on the case, he published a four-hundred-word press release qualifying the jury's decision as a "sorry and tragic error" (*ESPL*, 223). "Because if we in America have reached that point in our desperate culture when we must murder children, no matter for what reason or what color, we don't deserve to survive, and probably won't," he concluded (223).

By October 1955 Faulkner was back in America. James Silver, a history professor at the University of Mississippi, invited him to take part in a round table on the race issue at the twenty-first convention of the Southern Historical Association in Memphis. Faulkner accepted. In his address on November 10, 1955, he declared, "It is our white man's shame that in our present southern economy, the Negro must not have economic equality; our double shame that we fear that giving him more social equality will jeopardize his present economic status; our triple shame that even then, to justify ourselves, we must becloud the issue with the purity of white blood" (*ESPL*, 150). He intervened to ensure that blacks were allowed into the Peabody Hotel for this meeting, which explains the title under which his speech was published the next day in the *Commercial Appeal*: "A Mixed Audience Hears Faulkner Condemn the 'Shame' of Segregation." Again the newspaper's readers protested. One of them wrote that white Southern parents would not agree to see their race die out by sending their children to integrated schools. Faulkner's boyhood friend and hunting companion John Cullen, along with most of his neighbors, thought it was "a poor speech, poorly timed" (*B1*, 615).

In February 1956, while Faulkner was in New York with Jean Stein, tensions in Alabama mounted again. In Montgomery a young, elegant black preacher, Martin Luther King Jr., had just organized an effective boycott of public transportation. In Tuscaloosa there were riots when Authorine Lucy, a black student, tried to enroll in the university. Ruling on a Supreme Court injunction, a federal judge had ordered that she be allowed to enroll by March 5 at the latest. When she arrived on campus, white demonstrators lit burning crosses, threw stones at her car, and threatened to kill her. After university officials suspended Lucy under false pretenses, NAACP lawyers filed suit. Faulkner became more and more worried. In his interview with Russell Warren Howe, he said he was convinced that "Miss Lucy" would be killed as soon as she came on campus, that the federal government would again send in troops, and that this policy of confrontation would ignite the entire South. He noted that in Oxford one could no longer even buy shot for hunting guns and that people who up to then had never owned a gun were now starting to stock up. A new civil war no longer seemed improbable to him. Disaster, he believed, could be avoided only if supporters of integration agreed to wait and give white Southerners the time to adapt. To broadcast this message, he needed national coverage. Ober managed to sell one of his texts, "A Letter to the North," to *Life* magazine, which published it on March 5, 1956. In it, Faulkner warned the North and argued for moderation, restating his opposition to compulsory segregation and forced integration alike and urging the NAACP and other civil rights activists to give Southern whites room to breathe: "Go slow now. Stop now for a time, a moment. You have the power now; you can afford to withhold for a moment the use of it as a force" (*ESPL*, 87).

There was no question of discussing these problems with representatives of the black community. When, as reported by the *New York Times*, W.E.B. Du Bois, one of the founding members of the NAACP, then eighty, proposed a debate on integration on the steps of the courthouse in Sumner, Mississippi, where the Emmett Till case had been tried, Faulkner evaded the issue, declaring the debate pointless. On April 17, 1956, he sent a telegram to Du Bois, reproduced in the *Times*, worded as follows: "I DO NOT BELIEVE THERE IS A DEBATABLE POINT BETWEEN US: WE BOTH AGREE IN ADVANCE THAT THE POSITION YOU WILL TAKE IS RIGHT MORALLY LEGALLY AND ETHICALLY. IF IT IS NOT EVIDENT TO YOU THAT THE POSITION I TAKE IN ASKING FOR MODERATION AND PATIENCE IS RIGHT PRACTICALLY THEN WE WILL BOTH WASTE OUR BREATH IN DEBATE" (*SL*, 398).

The race issue broke out again in September 1957 when the federal government sent troops to Little Rock, Arkansas, to enforce integration at Central High School. Faulkner reacted to the event in a letter to the *New York Times*, published on October 13, 1957. In his eyes the tragedy of Little Rock revealed what everyone knew already but nobody had as yet dared to admit: "the fact that white people and Negroes do not like and trust each other, and perhaps never can" (*ESPL*, 230). Yet whites and blacks urgently needed to "federate together, show a common unified front not for dull peace and amity, but for survival as a people and a nation" (230). Faulkner did not specify what measures should be taken to achieve this federation but once again displayed his distrust of any solution imposed by the federal government.

This was to be his final declaration to the press on the race issue, but at the University of Virginia, in February 1958, he returned to it one last time during a conversation at the English Club that was later titled "A Word to Virginians." Using his position as writer-in-residence, he endeavored to persuade the oldest of the Southern states to take the first step in implementing reasonable reform. Noting that a society "can no more get along in peace with ten percent of its population arbitrarily unassimilated than a town of five thousand people can get along in peace with five hundred unbridled horses loose in the streets" (*FU*, 209), he called on the wisdom of Virginians: "So we alone can teach the Negro the responsibility of personal morality and rectitude—either by taking him into our white schools, or giving him white teachers in his own schools until we have taught the teachers of his own race to teach and train him in these hard and unpleasant habits" (211). As always, Faulkner recommended a pedagogy of freedom and responsibility. But he had his doubts: "Perhaps the Negro is not yet capable of more than second class citizenship. His tragedy may be that so far he is competent for equality only in the ratio of his white blood" (210). So does the issue, then, boil down to a problem of blood, of genes? This would be merely racism by the back door. What's more, the ensuing discussion confirmed that Faulkner had retreated to a distinctly more conservative standpoint.

Faulkner never really stopped being conservative, no more than he ever wholly overcame his racism. It must be remembered, however, that for the majority of white Mississippians, he had become a traitor to the Southern cause. His fellow citizens had long held him in contempt; now they detested him. His neighbors, his brothers, his oldest and closest friends, including Phil Stone and even Estelle, all vehemently disapproved of his position. Even Hooding Carter, a liberal journalist from Greenville who had known him for a long time, thought that he had ventured beyond the extreme limits of the Southern experience.[6] And yet, far from being a dissident, Faulkner had never dissociated himself from the white community and had always professed his loyalty to the South. In October 1948, when *Intruder in the Dust* was published, he told the *New York Herald Tribune*: "I'd be a Dixiecrat myself if they had not hollered 'nigger.' I'm a States' Rights man" (*LG*, 60). Six years later his opinion had not changed. On February 21, 1956, in an interview in Saxe Commins's office with Russell Warren Howe, then New York correspondent of the *Sunday Times* of London, he clearly asserted his ultimate priorities: "I will go on saying that the Southerners are wrong and that their position is untenable, but if I have to make the same choice Robert E. Lee made then I'll make it" (*LG*, 262). If there was to be a new civil war, he was ready to take up arms: "But if it came to fighting. I'd fight for Mississippi against the United States even if it meant going out into the street and shooting Negroes" (261). These words, reprinted in *Time* and *Newsweek* and then, in a slightly different form, in *The Reporter*, caused a sensation and earned him the immediate disapproval of New York progressives. Faulkner himself hastened to disown them in a letter to the editor of the *Reporter*:

> If I had seen it before it went to print, these statements, which are not correct, could never have been imputed to me. They are statements which no sober man would make, nor, it seems to me, any sane man believe [. . .]. The statement that I or anyone else would choose any one state against the whole remaining Union of States, down to the ultimate price of shooting other beings in the streets, is not only foolish but dangerous. (*ESPL*, 225)

But this denial came with a barely disguised confession: when he had made these statements, Faulkner was probably not sober. Once again he had been drinking. Howe had probably trapped him, but he wasn't lying when he said that he had faithfully transcribed Faulkner's words. And Saxe Commins, who had been present at the interview, did not deny this either.

Whether sober or not, Faulkner was sincere. As James Baldwin judiciously noted, "Faulkner means everything he says, means them all at once, and with very nearly the same intensity."[7] But his thinking as a citizen was full of contradictions; the duty of justice and the interests of fairness were constantly in conflict with tribal allegiance. In contrast to most contemporary white Southerners, Faulkner had long been aware of the imperious necessity of repairing the colossal injustices that had been perpetrated on the blacks. Equal rights between whites and blacks seemed desirable to him and in fact were much more important to him than integration, as he stated several times in interviews, particularly in his 1958 "A Word to Virginians": "I think that the only thing that will solve that problem is not integration but equality, for [the] Negro to know that he has just as much and just as valid rights in this country as anybody else has" (FU, 227). Integration seemed unlikely to him because he thought nobody really wanted it: "I myself think that integration as they mean it now will never occur, that the Negro doesn't want it either [...] the Negro himself as a race doesn't want to mix with white people, he don't like white people that well" (215).

Transforming the conditions of blacks was, in Faulkner's view, a historical duty that was incumbent on the South, and he was convinced that given enough time—fifty years—it could be accomplished, especially if the federal government stayed out of it. As mentioned above, in his "A Letter to the North," published in Life in May 1956, he pleaded for patience: "Go slow now. Stop now for a time, a moment" (ESPL, 87). Nothing should be rushed; the time for equality had not yet come, the blacks were not ready for it, and the most urgent thing to do was educate them.

Faulkner was a moderate Southern reformer, a liberal supporter "in the middle" (ESPL, 87). But his condescending paternalism could only exasperate civil rights activists, and it should also be noted that in his public stances, political considerations seem to have been at least as important as concern for justice, if not more so. Although he was opposed to the execution of Willie McGee, we have already seen that this was only to prevent him becoming a martyr. There was also some unfortunate backtracking in his views on race. For example, during the Emmett Till case in 1955, after challenging the jury's decision, Faulkner retracted somewhat by suggesting on local radio that even though the killing of children was unjustifiable, Till in some way deserved what had happened to him.[8]

While Faulkner acknowledged the need to improve the conditions of blacks, there was for him no question of relinquishing white hegemony. In 1956, in a letter addressed to a student at the University of Alabama, he advocated desegregation using curious arguments: "I vote that we ourselves choose to abolish it [segregation], if for no other reason than, by voluntarily giving the Negro the chance for whatever equality he is capable of, we will stay on top; he will owe us gratitude" (*SL*, 395). Finally, we know that in both his private conversations and his correspondence, blacks were unfailingly "niggers" and that he at times used racist language frankly and crudely when speaking about them. In 1958, at a reception held in his honor at Princeton University, Robert Oppenheimer, to start a conversation, asked him his opinion on television. "Television is for niggers," answered Faulkner (*B1*, 656).

But even though he *called* them "niggers," even though he sometimes reverted to the obtuse and odious racism of his environment, it must be remembered that this man—the same man, another version of himself, *wrote* texts that are among the most clear-sighted and the most unrelenting ever written *against* racism: *Light in August*, *Absalom, Absalom!*, *Go Down, Moses*, "Dry September," and "Pantaloon in Black." And it is difficult to believe that his staggering letter to the *Commercial Appeal* and "Dry September" were written at the same time and by the same hand. It is perhaps in this intractable contradiction that the gap between the man and the writer is most evident. It would be naive to dwell on it, but it must be acknowledged that during these difficult years, Faulkner the citizen never quite managed to unequivocally shed the traditional prejudices of his family, his class, his race, and his region and that in the great turbulence of the blacks' fight for their rights, he rarely found the right words.

His stances could only anger everybody, and as nobody listened to him anyway, he finally shut up. By the time he died in 1962, Southern segregation had barely been dented.

On the other hand, in the ideological confrontation with the Soviet empire that had held sway since the start of the Cold War, Faulkner's position betrayed no discomfiture. An avowed anticommunist and patriot who wished to serve his country, he readily agreed to act as roving ambassador for American culture and willingly traveled the world with the blessing of the State Department. In 1955 he undertook a world tour lasting almost three months, which brought him to Japan (August 1–23), the Philippines (August 24–27), Italy (August 28–September 16), France (September 16–

October 7), and England (October 7–12). He was amazed and enchanted to be traveling so much: "I move about a great deal lately," he told Else Jonsson (*SL*, 381).

These were official visits. There seemed to be little else to them for Faulkner, and it is unclear what satisfaction he derived from them. In any case, he had little interest in meeting other writers. In Rome the ambassador Clare Boothe Luce introduced him to Alberto Moravia and Ignazio Silone, but Faulkner had nothing to say to them. In Paris, at a cocktail party organized in his honor by the Gallimard publishing house in their garden on rue Sébastien-Bottin, attended by over four hundred guests, he gave monosyllabic answers to questions and eventually hid at the bottom of the garden, under a tree, his back against a wrought-iron gate. When he was introduced to Albert Camus, the meeting was reduced to a handshake. "It's appalling!" said one of the guests returning from the garden. "I can't watch it; it's like seeing someone being tortured" (*B*, 1578).

Faulkner had become a public man against his will, but up till the end of the 1950s he continued to take on official duties. Thus, in September 1956, out of duty more than conviction, he went to Washington to take part in a three-day conference sponsored by the Eisenhower administration, on the implementation of the People-to-People Program, aimed at promoting cultural exchanges between America and communist countries. The aim was to invite artists, writers, musicians but also doctors and religious representatives, and to send them behind the Iron Curtain so that they could help spread Western democratic values.

On September 13 Faulkner wrote to Harvey Breit, a journalist at the *New York Times Book Review*, that he wanted him to clear the way. Advocating that an executive committee comprising around a dozen persons be set up, he enclosed with his letter to Breit a mimeographed letter bearing his signature and asked Breit to send a copy to all the writers he knew. He started by explaining that President Eisenhower wanted to bring American writers together "to see what we can do to give a true picture of our country to other people." This was followed by some amusing suggestions of his own:

1. Anesthetize, for one year, American vocal chords.
2. Abolish, for one year, American passports.
3. Commandeer every American automobile. Secrete Johnson grass seed

in the cushions and every other available place. Fill the tanks with gasoline. Leave the switch key in the switch and push the car across the iron curtain.

4. Ask the government to establish a fund. Choose 10,000 between 18 and 30, preferably communists. Bring them to this country and let them see America as it is. Let them buy an automobile on the installment plan, if that's what they want. Find them jobs in labor as we run our labor unions. Let them enjoy the right to say whatever they wish about anyone they wish, to go to the corner drug store for ice cream and all the other privileges of this country which we take for granted. At the end of the year they must go home [. . .]. This is to be done each year at the rate of 10,000 new people. (*SL*, 404)

The circular letter was sent to a few dozen writers in late September. The responses were mixed. Robert Lowell, John Steinbeck, and Robert Hillyer were in favor of the plan; Archibald MacLeish, Lionel Trilling, Conrad Aiken, and William Carlos Williams did not see the value in it; and Edmund Wilson wondered why Faulkner was getting involved. Wilson wrote that he didn't hold with national propaganda plans and had always refused to participate. He was surprised that Faulkner had let himself been dragged into it. He had just returned from Europe, where he had seen Faulkner's books on sale in London, Paris, and Munich and suggested that the best propaganda that he and any other writer could make was through translations of their books, because they had something to say to people in other countries.[9]

On November 29, at Harvey Breit's home in Manhattan, Faulkner chaired a meeting of fourteen writers who had agreed to take part and who had come to discuss the project. He chaired another meeting in New York in February 1957. It would be the last. Faulkner pulled out. "I don't go along with that stuff," he told Breit. "We don't need any foreign writers here, and our writers don't have to go anywhere. Writers all over the world understand each other. What we need is an exchange of plumbers and carpenters and businessmen" (*B*, 1629).

After this disappointing experience, Faulkner was even more reluctant to cooperate with other writers. But from the outbreak of World War II to the end of the 1950s, he was extremely interested in public affairs, motivated by the desire that came upon him after he turned fifty to speak to the coming generations, a desire that the Nobel Prize comprehensively confirmed. In a long letter written at the height of the war to his adopted son, Malcolm, applauding him for wanting to fight for freedom and democracy, he says that after the time of young people on the battlefield, "perhaps the time of the older men will come, the ones like me who are articulate in the national voice, who are too old to be soldiers, but are old enough and have been vocal long enough to be listened to" (*SL*, 166). For a long time, Faulkner had simply wanted to be left alone to write what he wanted to write. But the time had come when it was no longer enough for him to write and be read. He now wanted to be *listened to* by the nation.

Writing novels was no longer a priority. His work was no longer before him; it was already being cut up into select pieces. During the years after the war, a plethora of collections and anthologies had been brought out: in 1950 there was *Collected Stories*, comprising forty-two of his short stories written over almost twenty-five years and carefully divided into six sections by Faulkner; in 1954 there was *The Faulkner Reader*, an anthology combining the text of *The Sound and the Fury*, short stories, his Nobel Prize speech, and an author's preface; and in 1955 his hunting stories were collated in *Big Woods*. This period also saw an increase in his output of nonfiction prose. Faulkner's collected essays edited by James B. Meriwether and published in 1965 were all written after 1950, and they are all ad hoc texts, written to order or on the occasion of some public or private event. It is unlikely that Faulkner was deeply engaged with them as a writer and, truth be told, they add nothing to his reputation.

Faulkner was neither a great poet nor a brilliant essayist. Only the power of his fiction gives us the full measure of his genius, and it is no coincidence that his best essays are about fiction, such as "A Note on Sherwood Anderson" (*ESPL*, 3–11), or grow out of his novels, such as "Mississippi" (11–43), a long, superb meditation on fiction, history, geography, and autobiography in which Lafayette County and Yoknapatawpha County ultimately occupy the same territory, doubly imaginary, doubly real. On the other hand, the nonliterary essays, in which Faulkner shares his thoughts on serious issues such as desegregation in the South, the Cold War, or the future of humanity after the explosion of the first atomic bombs, have not aged well. In these a senior Southern gentleman talks about his concerns, his convictions, and his opinions. The concerns are sincere, the convictions respectable, the opinions contentious. As Faulkner's voice became more public, it also became more trivial, spouting commonplaces and defending common values that were shared by his tribe and ensured its cohesion. It often sounds like a mocking echo in that it is full of familiar words and rhythms, Faulknerian in its rhetoric to the point of self-parody. But Faulkner is no longer entirely Faulkner when he does Faulkner.

In his essays, as in his Stockholm speech, Faulkner argued for man, painting himself as the guardian of man's legacy and the prophet of his future, apparently without much thought for national or racial differences. His generous humanism had not made him immune to ethnocentric prejudices, however. At various occasions, while praising blacks for their sound virtues and great successes, and applauding them for producing men as remarkable as Ralph Bunche, George Washington Carver, and Booker T. Washington, he noted that these people "only three hundred years ago lived beside one of the largest bodies of inland water on earth and never thought of sail" (*ESPL*, 104), "yearly had to move [. . .] without thinking of wheel" (104), and "were eating rotten elephant and hippo meat in African rain-forests" (149). In other words, Faulkner thought fit to point out that they were so backward, they would have remained savages if they had not been brought to America by force. This is racism barely tempered by paternalism and even, sotto voce, justification after the fact of the "peculiar institution" of the Old South: because slavery wrenched blacks from their savagery and taught them some white virtues, it was no longer wholly reprehensible.

It must also be noted that the humanism professed by Faulkner is an American take on universalism. While aspiring to freedom, democracy, and progress is common to all men, for Faulkner and many of his compatriots, only one country, one nation on earth, had started to accomplish that dream and could guarantee its realization in the future, and that country was the United States of America. It is astonishing how quickly Faulkner belatedly rallied to the nationalist and imperialist myth of America's singularity and excellence. This does not mean that he stopped criticizing his country—far from it. But as with his quarrel with the South, his quarrel with America was a lovers' quarrel. "On Privacy" rails against contemporary mores, but it is above all a rhetorical celebration of the American myth, another rant in the Puritan tradition, both deploring decline and extolling a collective dream. The past is now rich with promise; the fathers of the tribe are no longer denounced as greedy adventurers but revered as heroic founders of a new order. And just as the Puritans of New England believed themselves to be the new chosen people, standing against the profane nations of the earth, Faulkner saw Americans "as the last people unified nationally for liberty in an inimical world which already outnumbers us." And he saw America as "the rallying point for all men, no matter what color they are or what tongue they speak, willing to federate into a community dedicated to the proposition that a community of individual free men not merely must endure, but can endure" (*ESPL*, 230).

America, land of asylum, citadel of liberty, haven of democracy, model of civilization for the whole world—this was the vision that citizen Faulkner had of America in the 1950s. It was the vision the American people needed in times of crisis, when all the nation's energies were mobilized in the fight for the "free world," against Soviet totalitarianism. The Eisenhower years were years of political conservatism, cultural lethargy, and ideological consensus. It must be acknowledged that, far from overturning received ideas, Faulkner's official statements sat easily with the chauvinistic and conformist mood of the nation.

Does this mean that he naively allowed himself to be used? In any case, it is regrettable that his public voice was not more strident, that it was merely the voice of the 1950s, with a strong Southern accent. It was difficult to reconcile the freedom needed by a writer with the responsibilities of the public figure. Faulkner could not but compromise his share of wildness, even if it meant he ended up being sidetracked. For many years he had done things his own way. Conceived in the secrecy of solitude, his novels were imperiously dictated by what he called his voices. "I listen to the voices," he told Cowley, "and when I put down what the voices say, it's right. Sometimes I don't like what they say, but I don't change it" (*FCF*, 114). Another voice could now be heard in his novels—less plural, less secret, more sonorous; concerned, as it had never been before, to be heard by the largest number and thus less troubling, more seemly; a voice that was difficult to distinguish from that of the lecturer, the essay writer, the interviewee.

However, the break was far from sudden. In the three prologues for *Requiem for a Nun* and in *A Fable*, both published at the start of the decade,

Faulkner was a thousand miles from the complacent mythology celebrated in his essays; his vision of history was as ironic as always. But it was no longer tragic. Without disowning himself, the writer had indeed changed. For years his mood had been less somber and his ink less black. He no longer frequented the abyss. *The Unvanquished* had marked an initial turnaround, a preliminary softening in that for the first time, the novel's hero was a pleasant, virtuous young man and the curse of the South was starting to recede. In *Go Down, Moses* the confrontation between Ike McCaslin and Cass Edmonds in the fourth section of "The Bear" attested to a new need to express ideas and define values. Finally, Gavin Stevens's pompous speechifying in *Intruder in the Dust* heralded the novelist's public stances in the 1950s.

After receiving the Nobel Prize, Faulkner had no more serious financial difficulties. But he had not yet quite finished with Hollywood. In the 1950s he again worked as a scriptwriter for brief periods. From February to March 1951 he spent five weeks in Hollywood reworking the script of *The Left Hand of God*, adapted from William E. Barrett's best seller. His old friend Howard Hawks offered him two thousand dollars a week and a substantial bonus if he finished his work quickly. Within a month he had finished the script. It was to be his last sojourn in Hollywood, and the best paid, for a film that Hawks eventually decided not to shoot. However, the film was made four years later from a script by Alfred Hayes, directed by Edward Dmytryk, with Humphrey Bogart and Gene Tierney in the leading roles.

In late November 1953, after sending the final chapters of *A Fable* to his publisher, Faulkner left for Paris to meet Hawks, who offered him fifteen thousand dollars plus all expenses to work on a blockbuster he was planning to make in Egypt called *Land of the Pharaohs*. Hawks had already hired scriptwriter Harry Kurnitz and then Harold Jack Bloom, a young New Yorker. On December 1, 1953, Faulkner arrived at Geneva Airport, while Hawks, photographer Robert Capa, and Kurnitz waited for him at Orly Airport in Paris. Realizing his mistake, Faulkner took the train for Paris, but it was another twenty-four hours before a couple of gendarmes delivered him to Hawks. He had got lost in Montmartre, where he was found in a very drunken state, bleeding from a nasty cut on his head, and if it hadn't been for the Légion d'honneur medal fastened in his buttonhole, he likely would have spent the night in the drunk tank.

Soon afterward, Hawks and Faulkner left Paris for the lakes and mountains of Switzerland, where Bloom soon joined them. Faulkner, for once, did not seem to be taking his work seriously, and Bloom later judged him harshly, saying that Faulkner didn't like the cinema and refused to read the news. When Bloom asked what he had read recently, Faulkner replied that he didn't read new books, he only reread the classics.[10] According to Bloom, Faulkner was a grumpy old man, locked up in himself, indifferent to others, and racist into the bargain. He laughed only at his own jokes, and he was unflattering in his depictions of blacks, to say the least, even though publicly he affected a paternalist attitude toward them.[11]

It was Christmas 1953. Hawks, Kurnitz, and Faulkner were preparing the filming of *Land of the Pharaohs*. In Saint-Moritz, Switzerland, productivity slowed considerably in the afternoons, after the lunchtime libations. Faulkner had gotten into the habit of fortifying himself at lunch with a couple of martinis and a half bottle of Chassagne-Montrachet. He accepted an invitation from friends of Hawks on Christmas Eve, and it was there that he met a young nineteen-year-old woman, Jean Stein, the ravishing daughter of Jules Stein, founder of the MCA (Music Corporation of America). A student at the Sorbonne and a fervent admirer of Faulkner, she fell in love with him immediately. He accompanied her to midnight mass in a Catholic church and walked her back to her hotel afterward. It was the start of another affair, probably his last.

Oddly, on January 11, 1954, Faulkner felt compelled to tell Joan Williams all about it:

> A curious thing has happened, almost repetition, her name is even Jean. She is 19. At a Xmas party of people nearer my age, the hostess told me that she had asked to be invited, the only young person there. It was a dull stuffy party, so I invited her to go with me to a midnight mass at a Catholic church, which she did. I fetched her back home and left her, thought no more about it. Then when I got back here last Monday, she had sent me a Xmas gift, a leather carved travelling clock, much too expensive, also a letter, and by now a telephone call. I think an infatuation partly with my reputation and partly with the fact that I try to be gentle and serious with young people. It will run its course.[12]

Three months later, while in Egypt, he sent Saxe Commins a letter that started in the same way, but said a little more about his new mistress:

> Incidentally, a queer thing has happened to me, almost a repetition; this one is even named Jean [. . .]. She came to me in St. Moritz almost exactly as Joan did in Oxford. But she has none of the emotional conventional confusion which poor Joan had. This one is so uninhibited that she frightens me a little [. . .]. She is charming, delightful, completely transparent, completely trustful. I will not hurt her for any price. She doesnt want anything of me—only to love me, be in love.[13]

Jean was not a Southern belle like Estelle, Meta, and Joan. She was a Jewish upper middle-class New Yorker. Faulkner had never met a young woman like her. Lively, liberated, and cultivated, she had the almost exotic attraction of the beautiful foreigner. And when he met her, she was not even twenty years old. Born in 1935, she was two years younger than his daughter. But there was no question of playing mentor with her. Faulkner didn't even have time to court her; it was she who seduced him, almost brusquely, and Faulkner, delightfully shocked by her audacity, was easily led and joined in enthusiastically.

The day after Christmas he left for Stockholm, saw Else Jonsson, passed through London, and on January 6, 1954, returned to Saint-Moritz, where Jean was waiting for him. He spent a few days with her in Paris, where he met Monique Salomon (née Lange), the Gallimard press attachée, and her husband, with whom he had become friendly during previous stays in Paris. On January 19 he arrived in Rome and checked in at the Palazzo e Ambasciatori, a four-star hotel on the elegant Via Veneto. He met up again with Hawks, Humphrey Bogart, and Lauren Bacall, and Jean joined him there some time later. Rome fascinated him as much as Paris; he loved its architecture and atmosphere, "full of the sound of water, fountains everywhere, amazing and beautiful—things full of marble figures—gods and animals, naked girls wrestling with horses and swans with tons of water cascading over them."[14]

On February 10, 1954, Hawks and his entourage took off for Egypt to start filming *Land of the Pharaohs*, and Faulkner spent a few days in Paris with Jean Stein, who had just turned twenty. On the fifteenth he arrived at Cairo Airport in the early hours of the morning. During the flight he had emptied almost two bottles of cognac and was in such a pitiful state that he had to be brought by ambulance to the Anglo-American hospital. He took some time to recover and caught a bad cold after his release from the hospital. He was indifferent to Egypt and had other things on his mind; thus he wrote unconvincingly, handing in mediocre work to Kurnitz, who had to rewrite it (Kurnitz later claimed that only one of Faulkner's lines remained unchanged in the final movie, a question from the pharaoh to his architect: "So . . . how is the job getting along?"). Hawks let him go after five weeks, just before they started shooting. This time Faulkner had finished with the film industry.

SETBACKS, DISTRESS, AND OTHER MISERIES

Faulkner is a small man (5 ft. 5, I should judge), very neatly put together. Small, beautifully proportioned hands. His face has an expression like Poe's in photographs, crooked and melancholy. But his forehead is low, his nose Roman, and his gray hair forms a low wreath around his forehead, so that he also looks like a Roman emperor. Bushy eyebrows; eyes deeply set and with a droop at the outer corners; a bristly mustache. He stands or walks with an air of great dignity and talks—tells stories—with a strong Mississippi accent. (*FCF*, 103–104)

This is how Malcolm Cowley described Faulkner in his notebook on Sunday, October 23, 1948. Now that he was over fifty, Faulkner, although short, still had presence and the difficult years seemed finally behind him. The publication of *Intruder in the Dust* and its film adaptation had solved his chronic debt problems. Since the international accolade of the Nobel Prize, he was recognized, welcomed, and celebrated everywhere as a great writer. His novels finally began to make money. By the end of the 1950s more than one hundred thousand copies of his books had been sold in the Modern Library edition, almost two and a half million in paperback.

But success did not suit him, honors did not bring him serenity, and age had made him neither prudent nor sociable. In public he continued to behave in the same strange manner, sometimes the distant but courteous Southern gentleman, sometimes the sullen lout or the staggering drunk. Uneasy at social functions, he usually stayed in a corner, expressionless, taciturn, absent, *elsewhere*. His silence disconcerted and intimidated others. Cowley recalled that "trying to enlist Faulkner in a small talk across

the big round table merely resulted in silences, for any threat of social involvement made him retire into himself" (*FCF*, 148). Similarly, Robert N.
Linscott, one of Faulkner's editors at Random House, claimed that "he'd sit
beside you for an hour without speaking. If you asked him a direct question,
he'd answer in a word or two, and again be silent [. . .]. It was just his natural
way. He didn't believe in chitchat, or in talking unless he had something to
say."[15] French essayist and critic Gaëtan Picon recalled that when Faulkner
was to make a speech at the end of a festival to celebrate twentieth-century works organized by the Congress for Cultural Freedom in Paris in May
1952, "At the last minute, when the organizers had almost given up hope of
him appearing, he suddenly appeared, as if out of a box, shook hands with
a strange, mechanical movement, looked between the faces, behind them,
said a few words and disappeared."[16] French Romanian poet and artist
Isidore Isou is also said to have thrown a handful of Lettrist tracts printed
on red paper from a balcony, and Faulkner, upon seeing the color, jumped
onto the rostrum to deliver an anticommunist diatribe.[17]

As related in a letter by W. H. Auden, during the same festival Faulkner
was "shut up in his hotel room throwing furniture out of the windows and
bottles at the ladies and saying the most dreadful things about coons."[18] But
it must also be said that when he hadn't drunk too much, he could be posi-
tively charming. In Nagano, Japan, and in the Philippines, he had everyone
eating out of his hand. In Manila in 1955, journalists had been expecting
the worst, but he surprised them with his vivaciousness and kindness. The
internal US State Department report, which had sponsored the visit, described him as "sincere, kind, humble and unfailingly patient" (*B2*, 609).

Faulkner's private life was as unpredictable and chaotic in the 1950s
as it had been in the 1940s. In New York on October 20, 1948, when Ruth
Ford called him at the Algonquin Hotel to invite him to a party, he turned
her down. His voice on the telephone seemed strange to her. Three days
later he could not be reached. Now other friends were starting to get worried. When Ruth Ford and Harvey Breit managed to enter the room, they
found him in a semi-comatose state. Bob Haas and Malcolm Cowley were
already there. After Cowley helped him get dressed, Breit helped him down
the stairs and into a waiting ambulance, which brought them to Fieldstone
Sanatorium. The next morning, when Ruth and Breit came back, Faulkner begged them to get him out of there, but the doctor believed he would

need at least four days to recuperate. In the end the Cowleys brought him to their house in Connecticut, where they gave him vegetable soup and watered-down drinks. A few days later, according to Cowley, he seemed to have recovered somewhat: "He showed extreme self-control, pacing up and down the living room with beads of cold sweat on his forehead and not asking for a drink except at long intervals of perhaps three hours, and then only politely: 'Do you think I could have a beer, ma'am?'" (B1, 498). And after returning to Oxford, he went back to work, "though not too hard," he told Haas, "as our deer hunting camp opens next week and due to the deaths this past year of the two senior members, most of the work—getting the dogs and horses sent up, cook, tents, feed etc., has fallen to my lot" (SL, 280).

There were to be many more episodes like this. Faulkner eventually wore himself out. True, he was still attractive, but he was exhausted and knew that time was running out for him. Even so, he continued to push himself and to drink excessively. Blackouts, hallucinations, and memory loss were becoming frequent and he was hospitalized more and more often. Increasingly worried about his health, his friends did everything they could to limit the damage. He knew he could count on them. This loner had always surrounded himself with people who were willing to look after him when he was ill. But his friends were not able to save him from himself.

To take his mind off his troubles, he decided to travel to Europe. On May 19, 1952, he landed at Le Bourget Airport, where the Salomons were waiting to meet him. He had a good time with them in Paris and with Else Jonsson, who had come from Stockholm to join him. However, after a few days he became unwell, and after his triumphal reception at the festival organized by the Congress for Cultural Freedom, he spent a few days at a Paris clinic to treat a recurrence of back pain due to an old horse-riding injury. X-rays revealed that he had several vertebral fractures and the doctors recommended surgery, but Faulkner categorically refused to be operated on. He left Paris in late May and stopped off in London, where he met up again with Harold Raymonds of Chatto & Windus, his English publisher. As his back pain was unrelenting, he decided not to return to Paris but to go to Oslo to see Else Jonsson. She found him a masseur who did wonders for his back. Feeling much better, he took the plane for New York on June 14. But his morale was very low. Back in Oxford in July, he complained to Commins:

For the first time in my life, I am completely bored, fed up, my days are being wasted. It is just possible that I shall do something quite drastic about the matter before long [. . .]. I am really sick, I think. Cant sleep too well, nervous, idle, have to make an effort not to let the farm go to pot, look forward only with boredom to the next sunrise. I dont like it. Maybe I will have to get away, for at least a year, almost vanish. Then maybe I will get to work again, and get well again.[19]

And on August 19 he wrote to Else Jonsson:

Back not much better; probably impossible with my nature and occupation—natural nervousness, inability to be still, inactive, and the farmwork, to take care of, though I am off horses, not been on one since I got home. Though probably the great trouble is unhappiness here, have lost heart for everything, farming and all, have not worked in a year now, stupid existence seeing what remains of life going to support parasites who do not even have the grace to be sycophants. Am tired, I suppose. Should either command myself to feel better, or change life itself, which I may do. (SL, 339)

Faulkner dreamed sadly of another life, one less overwhelming, more free, far away from "parasites." But nothing seemed to work anymore. In August, Estelle had to be hospitalized after a bender, and her husband, again suffering from lumbar pain and knocked out by the massive intake of beer and sedatives, was in turn admitted to the hospital in Memphis from September 18 through 26. He was no better when he got out. His nights were sleepless and he again self-medicated with beer and sedatives. In early October he fell down the stairs at Rowan Oak. Estelle called Commins to come and help, and this is how he found him:

I found Bill completely deteriorated in mind and body. He mumbles incoherently and is totally incapable of controlling his bodily functions. He pleads piteously for beer all the time and mumbles deliriously. Every twenty minutes or so through the night I had to carry him virtually to the bathroom. His body is bloated and bruised from his many falls and bears even worse marks.

Of course I do what I can but this is a case for commitment and professional care. The disintegration of a man is tragic to witness.[20]

The next day, Commins brought him back to the hospital, where he stayed until October 21. The doctors discovered that five vertebrae in his lower back were fractured. He was given sleeping pills and medicine to treat his delirium tremens. Because he refused to undergo surgery, he now had to wear a back brace, as he had done when he was thirteen.

Faulkner was more miserable than ever. His life with Estelle was hell, he could no longer work, and he was suffocating. On October 25 he wrote Commins that he was in a "terrible situation" and that as far as he remembered, he had never been "so unhappy and downhearted and despaired."[21] In November, at the Westhill Sanatorium, a private clinic in New York, on the initiative of a psychoanalyst and without the prior consent of either the patient or his family, he underwent a course of electric shock treatment (which was then all the rage), which rendered him sweet as a lamb after each session.

The year 1953 was punctuated by more hospital admissions. On January 31 Faulkner went to New York. He spent a week alone in Harrison Smith's Manhattan apartment. His back pain returned. He started drinking heavily again. There were more binges, more blackouts, more memory losses. His health deteriorated, and his friends worried. He did not, however, stop writing. In February, after a stay at Charles B. Townes Hospital, a private clinic near Central Park, he went every day to Commins's smoke-filled little office on the third floor of Random House to work on *A Fable*.

He collapsed again in early March. Commins, who had learned how to look after alcoholic writers with Sinclair Lewis and Eugene O'Neill, took him to his house in Princeton and put him to bed with some lemonade and a pack of aspirin. A day or two later Faulkner felt able to return to New York and get back to work. But he started drinking again and almost immediately there was another binge. He was again hospitalized and underwent more tests, including cranial X-rays and an encephalogram. On March 31 he went to see a renowned psychiatrist, Professor S. Bernard Wortis, clinical director at Doctors Hospital in Manhattan. That same day, he wrote to Else Jonsson:

> I have had a great deal of doctor, medical expense. [. . .] I would wake up in a hospital, and have just finished a series of examinations for a possible skull injury when I fell off the horse. There is no skull injury. According to the doctor, the tests show that a lobe or part of my brain is hypersensitive to intoxication. I said "Alcohol?" He said, "Alcohol is one of them." The others are worry, unhappiness, any form of mental unease, which produces less resistance to the

alcohol. He did not tell me to stop drinking completely, though he said that if the report had been on him, he would stop for 3 or 4 months and then have another test. He said that my brain is still normal, but it is near the borderline of abnormality. Which I knew myself; this behavior is not like me. (*SL*, 347)

Professor Wortis started asking him about his childhood and his relationship with his mother. Faulkner had no desire to answer. After a few sessions he pulled the plug. The professor's bill was huge: $450. Faulkner was outraged. He never went to see a psychiatrist again.

He knew that he was neurotic but was not the type to lie on a couch and unburden his heart. Writing was not therapy for him, but it had always fed off his malaise, and his malaise remained bearable for as long as writing served as an intermediary. It is impossible to imagine Faulkner well and happy. He had always known that he had no talent for happiness and paid it no heed: "Only vegetables are happy" (*SL*, 308), he wrote to Joan Williams in November 1950, claiming the right to despair, the right to live in despair and not die from it. This despair was visible to the naked eye; it was chronic desolation under the black sun of melancholy. Meta Carpenter, during their first meetings, had found that he had the "immurement of a troubled animal" (*ALG*, 33), and Cowley thought that he had the same sad, tense face as Poe. Tennessee Williams recounted an evening spent with Faulkner and Jean Stein in a Paris restaurant in the fall of 1955: "He looked slowly up, and his eyes were so incredibly sad that I, being a somewhat emotional person, began to cry uncontrollably. I have never seen such sad eyes on a human face."[22]

This extreme sadness, so profound but also so fecund that it is better classed as melancholy, can be seen in almost all the photographs we have of the man. It is evident in his eyes, his mouth, his face, and his writing; it is part of his life and of his books. Like Poe, Baudelaire, and Nerval, like Melville, Flaubert, and Dostoyevsky, Faulkner was a writer born under the sign of Saturn, that slow planet of delays and detours and the god of voracious time, also known as Kronos/Chronos.

Melancholy had been his intimate companion since adolescence. It had worsened over the years, becoming increasingly laden with bitterness and nostalgia as he aged. And now, near the end of his tormented life, he was mourning his genius. Writing suddenly no longer seemed self-evident; his inspiration started to run dry and he became tired more quickly. But Faulkner had long known that his creative energy would decline one day. As early as his forties, he was already regretting the vigor and daring of his thirties. In 1940, when a visitor asked him if his writing had improved over the years, he answered with a smile: "Ten years ago I was much better, used to take more chances. Maybe I'm tired. I've had insomnia lately" (*B*, 1054). Four years later, in April 1944, he wrote to Ober: "I have a considerable talent, perhaps as good as any coeval. But I am 46 now. So what I will mean soon by 'have' is 'had'" (*SL*, 181). Nine years later the feeling that his resources were dwindling had grown even more. On April 29, 1953, he confided in Joan Williams: "I know now that I am getting toward the end, the bottom of the barrel. The stuff is still good, but I know there is not very much more of it, a little trash comes up constantly now, which must be sifted out" (*SL*, 348). On October 20, 1955, in a letter to Else Jonsson, he wrote: "I know I wont live long enough to write all I need to write about my imaginary country and county, so I must not waste what I have left" (*SL*, 387).

A fabulous adventure in writing was coming to an end. In an astonishing letter to Joan Williams dated April 29, 1953, Faulkner marveled at what he had accomplished as if they were the miraculous exploits of another:

> And now I realise for the first time what an amazing gift I had: uneducated in every formal sense, without even very literate, let alone literary, companions, yet to have made the things I made. I dont know where it came from. I dont know why God or gods or whoever it was, selected me to be the vessel. Believe me, this is not humility, false modesty: it is simply amazement. (*SL*, 348)

The same retrospective amazement was already manifest in a letter from Faulkner to Cowley of April 1946, after he had received the first copies of *The Portable Faulkner*: "By God I didn't know myself what I had tried to do, and how much I had succeeded" (*FCF*, 91). And it resurfaced again in early August 1953, in a letter to Saxe Commins: "Damn it, I did have genius, Saxe. It just took me 55 years to find it out. I suppose I was too busy working to notice it before" (*SL*, 352).

REQUIEM FOR A NUN: THE EDUCATION OF TEMPLE DRAKE

In October 1933 Faulkner wrote to Harrison Smith: "I have been at the Snopes book, but I have another idea now, and a good title, I think: REQUIEM FOR A NUN. It will be about a nigger woman. It will be a little on the esoteric side, like AS I LAY DYING" (*SL*, 75). That year, he started work on a short story—or a novel?—with this title, but the plot had nothing to do with the novel and Faulkner rapidly abandoned it.[23] In February 1934 he wrote to Smith: "I have put both the Snopes and the Nun one aside. The one I am writing will be called DARK HOUSE or something of that nature" (*SL*, 78). Meanwhile, he had started work on what was to become *Absalom, Absalom!* In a letter to Smith dated August 1934 he spoke of his plans to go back to *Requiem* (*SL*, 84). But it took him sixteen years to get back to it; the work known to us today under this title was written between 1948 and 1951.

Why was this book put off for so long, and why was it finally finished? If we are to believe Faulkner himself, he had not finished with Temple Drake, the scandalous heroine of the scandalous *Sanctuary*, and wanted to find out, and therefore imagine, what she had become or might have become, twenty years after that first novel: "I began to think what would be the future of that girl? and then I thought, What could a marriage come to which was founded on the vanity of a weak man? What would be the outcome of that? And suddenly that seemed to me dramatic and worthwhile, but that was—you're quite right—I hadn't thought of that when I wrote Sanctuary" (*FU*, 96). In *Requiem*, Faulkner brings back two characters from *Sanctuary*: Temple Drake and the pathetic Gowan Stevens, now her husband. He also brings back the lawyer Gavin Stevens, a major character in a number of previous novels. The black woman, Nancy Mannigoe, the "nun" of the title, is also not unknown, having made her first appearance in "That Evening Sun"—a poignant short story initially published in the *American Mercury* in March 1931—where she was an occasional cook for the Compsons and a sometime prostitute.

Two women played a decisive role in the genesis of *Requiem*. One of these was Ruth Ford, an actress Faulkner first met at Ole Miss who became friendly with him in the early 1940s in Hollywood. One day she told him: "The one thing I want most in the world is for you to write me a play" (*B1*, 515). Faulkner promised nothing but did not forget her wish, and it may have been at that time that he had the idea of turning Temple Drake into the heroine of a play and giving the lead role to his friend.

The other woman associated with *Requiem* is Joan Williams. On February 2, 1950, Faulkner arrived in New York for ten days. When Joan met him there he immediately told her about an idea for a play about Temple, which he intended to call *Requiem for a Nun*. He invited her to help him write the play and started writing it on the train home on February 12. The next day he sent a letter with three pages of notes written on Algonquin Hotel stationery. These contained a first draft of act 1:

> You can begin to work here. This act begins to tell who Nancy is, and what she has done. She is a "nigger" woman, a known drunkard and dope user, a whore with a jail record in the little town, always in trouble. Some time back she seemed to have reformed, got a job as nurse to a child in the home of a prominent young couple. Then one day suddenly and for no reason, she murdered the child. And now she doesn't even seem sorry. She seems to be making it almost impossible for the lawyer to save her.
>
> So at the end of this act, everybody, sympathy is against her. She deserves to hang, a sentiment which reflects even on the lawyer defending her. (*SL*, 298)

As attested by Faulkner's correspondence with Joan Williams, *Requiem for a Nun* was initially designed as a play, and Faulkner was no doubt wholly sincere when he asked her to work with him on it. A few days after his letter of February 12, he sent another, urging her to play an active part in writing the play: "Rewrite this first scene if you want to, write any of the rest of it; this is just first draft; all we want is to get something on paper to pull apart and save what is good and right" (*SL*, 299). On February 22 he told Joan he had just "got the first act laid out, rough draft of about twelve pages" (300); on March 22 he told her "2nd act going slow but it moves" (301).

Like Balzac and James, Faulkner was one of those novelists who would have liked to be a good playwright as well, and we know that he had been drawn to the theater at the start of his literary career; after all, *The Marionettes*, his short symbolist play, was written in 1920. When he started *Requiem* he again yielded to the pull of the theater, but he had barely started on the second act when he began to have serious doubts about his talents as a playwright. On May 15 he wrote to Haas: "I realise more than ever that I cant write a play, this may have to be rewritten by someone who can. It may be a novel as it is" (*SL*, 302–303). And to Joan on May 19, 1950: "It is not a play, will have to be rewritten as a play. It is now some kind of novel, can be printed as such rewritten into a play" (304). It was a play that had become a novel, or rather was becoming one, but Faulkner persisted in thinking that it could be converted into a play. He explained his thinking at more length in a letter written to Haas three days later:

I have finished the first draft of the play. I will rewrite it. That is, my version or complete job will be a story told in seven play-scenes, inside a novel; it will run about 200 typed double-spaced pages. This summer, I will set Joan at it, see if she can lift the play scenes and condense the long speeches into a workable play script. Then get advice from some playwright who knows how to do it. Mine will print as a book, will be—to me—an interesting experiment in form. I think it's all right. (305)

The experiment continued into 1951. Faulkner struggled to finish it. On January 1, 1951, he wrote to Haas:

I want to finish the Requiem for a Nun mss. So I wont divert to the other one until this is done. I have about a month's farm work, building new pasture, etc; that and mss. will keep me busy until March probably. As soon as I finish the mss. I would like to bring it up, ask Bob Sherwood maybe to look at the play part of it and tell me whether it is a play or whether I can write a play or not. (SL, 311)[24]

He wanted it over and done with but was delayed by one final trip to Hollywood, at Hawks's bidding, from February to March 1951.

At the end of March 1951, after returning from Hollywood and before taking off for Europe, he sent Commins the first act, titled "The Golden Dome" and preceded by a long prologue. Three months later he seemed to have finished. On June 4 he wrote to Else Jonsson: "The mss. is about finished. I'll be glad; I am tired of ink and paper; I have been at it steadily now since New Year's, look forward to spending the summer planting dirt, raising crops and cattle and training horses" (SL, 315). Five days later he told her that the manuscript was finally finished (315). But was it really? The galley proofs were printed on May 25 and July 13, but on July 19, 1951, he wrote to Else saying that he had just spent two weeks in New York "working very hard on the script, I am still at it here" (319). This was confirmed by his letter to Haas on August 3, 1951: "Am now swotting away at the play, am close to having another draft done" (320).

In mid-September Joan Williams received a copy of the final typescript. Requiem for a Nun was published on September 27, 1951.

~

Although Requiem for a Nun is not a play, it is divided up, like a play, into three "acts," each of which is made up of two sections, one narrated, the other in dialogue. In this novel—as Faulkner insisted on calling it—as in *If I Forget Thee, Jerusalem*, the text is doubled, and to justify this doubling, Faulkner used the same musical analogy: "The longer—I don't know what you would call those interludes, the prefaces, preambles, whatever they are—was necessary to give it the contrapuntal effect which comes in orchestration" (*FU*, 122). Another commonality between *Requiem* and *If I Forget Thee, Jerusalem* is that both tell two separate, alternating stories with very few points of contact—they are told in counterpoint, as Faulkner termed it.

In the three narrated sections (which Faulkner hesitated to call prologues and numbered them like acts in a play), the novelist, or more precisely, the narrator, is a historian or at least a chronicler. But as if to remind us once again of the artifice and arbitrariness of any segmentation of time, whether collective or individual, Faulkner designed these three sections as inseparable chunks of narrative. Each paragraph ends in a semicolon; each section is made up of a single, long sentence. The first section, "The Courthouse," tells the story of the imaginary county of Yoknapatawpha, from the arrival of the first settlers at the very beginning of the nineteenth century and the founding of the town of Jefferson around the courthouse and prison, to the Civil War and Reconstruction and beyond, through the days after World War II. "The Golden Dome," the second section (the subtitle is from the Gospel of John: "In the beginning was the Word"), retraces both the genesis of the earth, the formation of the Mississippi Valley, and the history of the state of Mississippi, from the founding of its capital, Jackson, up to the 1950s. "The Jail," the final section, returns to the history of Jefferson and goes right back to the beginning, but the story takes a new turn when the narrator, mid-sentence, starts speaking directly to the narratee: "—until suddenly you, a stranger, an outlander say from the East or the North or the Far West, passing through the little town by simple accident" (*N4*, 642).

This interpellation, maintained right up to the end through repeated use of the second person, lends the text renewed orientation and urgency. In truth, the narrator never restricts himself to simply relating the facts; he continually questions them, stages them, raises them to the level of myth, or balances them out with irony, and his rhetoric postulates a listening audience. The tale is, however, more of a chronicle, a saga, or a parody of a saga than the reasoned history of historians, and this time we are far from the stultifying studies of Southern history offered in *Absalom, Absalom!* and

Go Down, Moses. Nevertheless, some constants are marked out in the text, motifs are sketched out, obsessive fears are confessed, such as the nostalgia of origins and the dread of impermanence.

In the beginning, at the dawn of the world, is chaos, "untimed unseasoned winterless miasma not any one of water or earth or life yet all of each, inextricable and indivisible; that one seethe one spawn one mother-womb, one furious tumescence, father-mother-one, one vast incubant ejaculation already fissionating in one boiling moil of litter from the celestial experimental Work Bench" (N4, 540). Then comes the ice age, "the blind and tongueless earth spinning on, looping the long recordless astral orbit, frozen, tideless" (540). Then, once the ice has melted, life starts to spread and the wilderness begins to emerge: "one jungle one brake one impassible density of brier and cane and vine interlocking the soar of gum and cypress and hickory and pinoak and ash" (541).

In the time of the wilderness, the earth was still an undivided space, one and multiple, with no paths or tracks, as already detailed in *Go Down, Moses*. After this immutable order comes the growing disorder of historical time, destined for perpetual change. The South as recounted in the three prologues to *Requiem* is a South undergoing constant metamorphosis. Everything—economy, institutions, mores, mankind—quickly becomes null and void; everything is doomed to obsolescence. First come the Native Americans, the wilderness, its bears and stags, "anachronism out of an old dead time and a dead age" (N4, 499). Then come the white pioneers, the first settlers, the first destroyers of the primeval forest. Time has its revenge, history its irony: those who dispossess the Native Americans will be dispossessed in turn, the adventurers of the heroic frontier age will be ousted by stolid farmers and respectable townspeople. There is no security, no stability in this increasingly mercantile society, caught up in the irresistible advance of "progress": land is appropriated and exploited, plantations are born, King Cotton accedes, and then, after the Civil War, comes true capitalism, industrialization, and urbanization—these are the major milestones in the history of the South retraced by Faulkner in his prologues. History becomes more and more turbulent, increasingly frenetic. Things change faster and faster the closer we come to the present, and time starts to race, "that fast, that rapid" (625).

The three prologues evoke a history of unforeseeable turmoil, and the narrator never misses an opportunity to note the blind workings of fate. The founding of Jefferson, for example, is recounted in the first prologue as a contingency: the courthouse has "come into existence [. . .] by chance and accident" (N4, 475); nothing is less expected, less anticipated than the fantastical episodes that led to the town being built. Afterward, of course, what was nothing but a coincidental sequence of unforeseen circumstances always seemed marked by the seal of determinacy, as if what had happened could not possibly have happened otherwise. But what if determinacy is merely fate seen from behind? How can we be sure that the destiny of communities, of nations is not decided by a throw of the dice?

Fate, destiny, and doom recur unceasingly in the text, like a reminder of the inevitable and the irreversible. Even though the town's transformation into a small colony of settlers is ascribed to chance, the founding of Jefferson and even the building of the courthouse are described as the necessary stages of a historical process. Every place has a destiny; every public place becomes a place of memory. The fate of the courthouse "is to stand in the hinterland of America, its doom is its longevity" (N4, 505). The discovery and settlement of America by whites is similarly presented as the accomplishment of manifest destiny as decreed from the outset: "This was a white man's land; that was its fate, or not even fate but destiny, its high destiny in the roster of the earth" (499). In other words, men—Pettigrew, Ratcliffe, and Compson, but also Caesar, Napoleon, and Jefferson—do not *make* history; they are not actors in history, but merely its docile performers. As stated at the end of the first prologue, everything started with the "the first loud dingdong of time and doom" (505), and at the beginning of the second prologue, when the story starts to celebrate the epic of origins, we learn of the capitol dome in Jackson, which "in the beginning was already decreed this rounded knob, this gilded pustule" (RN, 113).

If the end is already in the beginning, a preestablished cosmic plan must be postulated. On the other hand, if history is nothing but a succession of chance events, it would be futile to look for any pattern in its weave. *Requiem* envisages both hypotheses but retains neither. Faulkner does not take sides. Search as we may, there is no master story in *Requiem*, no more than in *Absalom, Absalom!*, *Go Down, Moses*, or *A Fable*.

History as detailed in *Requiem* seems to be reduced to a carnival-like spectacle, a kaleidoscopic parade of scenes and tableaux, "a furious beating of hollow drums toward nowhere" (*N4*, 476). History, as the narrator unceasingly reminds us, is theater. Mohataha, the old Chickasaw matriarch driven out of her realm, disappears on her wagon "like a float or a piece of stage property dragged rapidly into the wings across the very backdrop and amid the very bustle of the property-men setting up for the next scene and act before the curtain had even had time to fall" (622).

The spectacle is fascinating, but nobody can tell if there is a scriptwriter, or even a script. History was assuredly a constant obsession for Faulkner, but for him there is no reference to a "sense of history." There is no evidence in his work that history is a pathway leading to salvation or that it is guided by progress, that there is any overarching totality, a promised land in sight. There is no brighter future. The only thing we can be sure of is that this collective, increasingly frenetic race we call history is leading mankind to disaster: "The land, the nation, the American earth, whirled faster and faster toward the plunging precipice of its destiny" (*N4*, 625). Things will end badly: this was not what Faulkner said in his Stockholm speech, but it is what his novels imply.

Against the senseless torrent of history, against the inexorable passage of time, for Faulkner there is no resistance, no recourse other than memory—man's capacity to if not stop or suspend time, at least to slow down the work of erosion by keeping track of the past. From Indian burial mounds to the tombstones of the cemeteries and the graffiti on the jail walls, the same impulse to leave behind a trace has been repeated since prehistoric times in defiance of oblivion and death. In *Requiem* nothing speaks more eloquently of the urge to endure than the signature and date scratched on a window-pane in April 1861 by the "frail and workless hand" (*N4*, 627) of Cecilia Farmer, the jailer's daughter. The final prologue ends with a mention of this very modest message to posterity:

> You know again now that there is no time: no space: no distance: a fragile and workless scratching almost depthless in a sheet of old barely transparent glass, and [. . .] there is the clear undistanced voice as though out of the delicate antenna-skeins of radio, further than empress's throne, than splendid insatiation, even than matriarch's peaceful rocking chair, from the long long time ago: "*Listen, stranger; this was myself; this was I.*" (648–49)

According to the metaphorical template that had dominated Western thinking since the pre-Socratics, memory in Faulkner's work is portrayed as *typography*, as that which is written, printed. Keeping memory alive means making nicks, notches, and other cuts; leaving marks on stone or wood, on wax tablets, papyrus, parchment, or paper, or, as in *Requiem*, on windowpanes. Collective memory is perpetuated by surfaces covered in inscriptions, palimpsests. It holds time in space, fixes it in matter; transforms objects into relics, totems, or monuments, and places into temples and sanctuaries that endure long after the individual and defy the centuries.

Requiem is organized around three places of memory. And the history of Jefferson, as told by Faulkner, started with another place: a counter, the first communications hub, the first meeting place for trade between the Native Americans and the white settlers, but also—as underlined by the text—the first repository of *archives*. As already in *Go Down, Moses*, history here is about registers and is read as a vast and interminable enterprise in writing.

It started thousands of years ago, with the "the broad blank mid-continental page for the first scratch of orderly recording" (*N4*, 541). Similarly for the writer, everything starts with the blank page defended by its whiteness. Pages must be filled, written in. The writer's primary concern is to keep trace, to retain memory. His work is to produce signs; to collate and bequeath them is his ultimate purpose. The voice, both near and distant, fragile and stubborn, that is raised at the end of the final prologue in *Requiem* is also and perhaps first and foremost Faulkner's, and it has an addressee; it wants to be heard, and, switching to the vocative, it addresses us, his unknown readers: *"Listen, stranger; this was myself; this was I."*

At the University of Virginia in March 1957, a student asked Faulkner why he wrote. This was his answer: "Really the writer doesn't want success, [. . .] he knows he has a short span of life, that the day will come when he must pass through the wall of oblivion, and he wants to leave a scratch on that wall—Kilroy was here—[25] that somebody a hundred, a thousand years later will see" (*FU*, 61).

The part in *Requiem* that is meant to be acted out on a stage is, at first glimpse, another story. For all that, the dialogues are more suited to a novel

than a play, dialogues designed to be read rather than heard and are immediately taken over by a narrator-director whose stage directions, going far
beyond simple acting instructions, provide a copious narrative, descriptive,
and even interpretative context such as one would expect to find in a novel.
Moreover, these dialogues are often juxtaposed monologues; the characters
speak more to themselves than to each other. Gavin Stevens and Temple,
in particular, inflict long tirades on the reader, and it is easy to understand
why Albert Camus, in adapting *Requiem* for the stage, felt the need to cut
and rewrite Faulkner's text.

The links between the dramatic sections and the historical sections are
also problematic. Although there are plenty of correspondences, these are
less obvious than they are in *If I Forget Thee, Jerusalem*. Nonetheless, the
three "prologues" are indeed introductory texts. The individual fates staged
through the dialogues are part of a collective history, a past that coexists
with the present, and, as always in Faulkner, the present is always hostage
to the past.

The plot of the tragedy follows on from *Sanctuary*. This does not mean
that *Requiem* is merely a sequel to *Sanctuary*. It would be more judicious to
say that it is a form of *repentance*. As in all of Faulkner's late novels, *Requiem*
harks back to the earlier novels, rereading and revising them, but also perhaps responding to an obscure desire to make amends, as if the Temple of
Sanctuary needed not redemption but one last chance to explain herself—
to the readers as well as herself.

Temple is back, now married to Gowan Stevens and mother to two
children. Nancy Mannigoe, a black prostitute who had been her confidante
and her accomplice, but who has repented, looks after the couple's children. Temple is pursued by Pete, younger brother of Red, the man she had
loved before in a Memphis brothel and who was killed by the jealous, impotent Popeye. Pete, who holds compromising letters she sent to her lover,
is blackmailing her. She has agreed to run away with him not just because
of the blackmail but also out of nostalgia for her troubled past. To stop her
from leaving, Nancy strangles Temple's six-month-old daughter. She is sentenced to death by hanging. Gavin Stevens, Temple's uncle by marriage and
Nancy's lawyer, pushes Temple to go to the state governor in the middle
of the night to plead for mercy, knowing full well that the request has no
chance of success. In fact, what Stevens wants is for Temple to publicly con-

fess her misconduct: "What we came here and waked you up at two oclock in the morning for is just to give Temple Drake a good fair honest chance to suffer—you know: just anguish for the sake of anguish, like that Russian or somebody who wrote a whole book about suffering, not suffering for or about anything, just suffering" (N4, 562). Stevens then forces Temple to visit Nancy in prison the day before the execution and to forgive her crime by way of atonement for her own past baseness.

In *Requiem for a Nun* everything is played out between two killings, one of which, in the eyes of the law, commands and leads to the other: the savagery of infanticide results in the lawful punishment of the murderer. A death for a death, one death avenged and erased by the other. This is how the justice of the courthouse settles its accounts. Once Nancy has been hanged, everything will return to normal—except for Temple. Caught in the crossfire between the two deaths, Temple, the runaway, the tramp, is finally on the ropes, on her knees, with nowhere to run or hide, far from all "sanctuary."

Her daughter has been killed, strangled in her cradle, an act of criminal madness in the eyes of the world. Or holy madness in the eyes of God? Is this sacrifice necessary to prevent even more dreadful straying? Could this be a homeopathic murder? In his comments on Nancy, the "nun" of the play, Faulkner did not question the disinterested nature of her motivation: "She was just doomed and damned by circumstances to that life. And despite that, she was capable within her poor dim lights and reasons of an act which whether it was right or wrong was of complete almost religious abnegation of the world for the sake of an innocent child" (FU, 196). Nancy, the pure-hearted murderer, is absolutely convinced that her murderous act was an act of love, that she did evil to outsmart it—to save a marriage in peril and souls on their way to perdition. If she strangled the child and in doing so sacrificed her own life, it was with the sole intent of returning Temple to her senses, her husband, her home, and returning her, in shame and sadness, through her dead daughter, to her still living son, to become for him the mother she had not been to either child.

Gavin Stevens, the pontificating do-gooder, is absolutely convinced that good can come out of evil and it is he, in this singular economy of sacrifice and salvation, who takes over from Nancy in a way, endeavoring to continue the work of redemption that she started. Nancy struck the first blow on Temple, opened the first wound, made the first dent. Temple will henceforth live in suffering, in the shadow of two deaths, but the delicate task of managing the stock of pain now falls on Stevens. Stevens is there to ensure that the pain is maintained and put to good use. For Temple's suffering to become fertile, it must first be humbly accepted, in the spirit of submission and contrition without which there can be no forgiveness. Therefore the most important thing is to get Temple to talk, to compel her to go back into herself, to confess. Only then will Temple get to know her pain; only then, believes Stevens, can she be saved.

This is the standard reading of *Requiem*: the edifying supplement to *Sanctuary*. After *Sanctuary*, a novel where evil triumphs, comes *Requiem*, a novel of just punishment and promised redemption. It is true that the question of faith—belief or nonbelief in the immortality of the soul, in the existence of God the Savior, and in the redemption of sins through suffering—seems to be at the heart of it. But faith remains a question; it is not an answer, or, if it becomes an answer, as it does for Nancy, it can only be unfounded—blind submission to an indeterminate imperative rather than adherence to a belief system.

NANCY (MOVING ON AFTER THE JAILOR): Believe.

TEMPLE: Believe what, Nancy? Tell me.

NANCY: Believe.

(*N4*, 662–63)

For Nancy, as for the black preacher in *The Sound and the Fury* and in *A Fable*, "believe" is an intransitive verb.

The question is asked through the encounter between two women, "two sisters in sin" (*N4*, 580), Nancy and Temple, the woman who believes and the woman who does not. One, armed with her candor and confident in her faith, facing death with the fearless humility that is the secret pride of saints and martyrs; the other lost, helpless, distraught, deprived of all certainty except that of knowing that she will now live with the tormenting memory of her abjectness and guilt: "Tomorrow, and tomorrow, and tomorrow," she murmurs, quoting *Macbeth*, and Gavin Stevens, with a kind of sadistic jubilation, goes on, taking up the tale, in the future tense, of the fatal *accident* caused by Gowan that started Temple's nightmare all those years ago: "—he will wreck the car again against the wrong tree, in the wrong place, and you will have to forgive him again, for the next eight years until he can wreck the car again in the wrong place, against the wrong tree" (611).

Eight years after the horror at the Old Frenchman place and Memphis, Temple is no longer the same woman, even though her experience of abjectness continues to fascinate her. Temple is trapped; for her, everything is starting all over again, the same and different. In the closed session of the interrogation, Popeye's captive becomes Stevens's detainee. The brutality of the rape with a corncob is followed by the blank violence of the inquisitor. There is no accessory this time, but Temple is again assaulted and forced, except this time the attack is not physical. Stevens wants only to make her talk, to extract a confession, if possible authenticated by tears of shame and repentance. With delicate farsightedness, he goes so far as to offer his handkerchief in advance, to mop her eyes.

Stevens is the technician of confession who asks the right questions, corrects the answers, interrupts the confession each time it veers beyond protocol, and has no scruples about getting what he wants. He pushes Temple to the very edge and harangues her until he receives a full confession. This way he thinks he can get at the truth by which she judges and condemns herself and, in condemning herself, redeems herself. But Stevens fails. Although he manages to get Temple to speak, he cannot make her cry. Temple's eyes remain dry to the end; her sins are not washed away. She goes so far as to confess the unconfessable, but she has not entirely given of herself and therefore cannot be saved.

Time, for Temple, does not bring hope. During her interview with the governor, she already knows that the die is cast. Unlike Nancy, Temple will not die, but her tomorrows are without a future. Time for her is virtually reduced to what it was for Quentin in *The Sound and the Fury* and for Christmas in *Light in August*: a past that cannot be overcome, where the same act is played out again and again ad nauseam and where there is no atonement. Temple is a prisoner of an irremediable and irreparable past she is told is hers and in which she no longer recognizes herself. The first Temple, the dirty little bitch of *Sanctuary*, remains an enigma for the second Temple, who will never know why she did what she did.

In the end, each will be judged (by men, of course, the only ones authorized to do justice)—one by public trial, in accordance with the procedures laid down by law, the other more discreetly, in the courthouse confessional designed by Gavin Stevens. But neither woman can hear the other: "I dont know. I believes" (*N4*, 661), Nancy keeps saying, and she urges Temple to make a leap of faith like her, to believe without understanding and trust in the infinite benevolence of God. Yet Temple cannot help but doubt; she is not even sure that she has a soul, and the desperate vehemence of her questioning calls out to the reader at least as strongly as Nancy's unreasoned faith. Of the two women, Nancy, the black woman, is perhaps the more admirable in her madness, but Temple, the white woman, is by far the more pathetic in her extreme distress.

As for Faulkner, he neither judges Temple nor canonizes Nancy. Whatever his intentions, *Requiem for a Nun* is not at all the Christian tragedy it was taken to be. Nancy is the only one who believes that her sacrifice will be fruitful, the only one who thinks that she is the instrument of divine grace. *Requiem* is indeed a tragedy, but it does not end in catharsis. Contrary to what its title promises, peace is not restored. Faulkner wrote his requiem, but for Temple there will be no peace.

"Doomed. Damned," says Temple as she leaves prison after her last meeting with Nancy. It is the final scene in the play, and these would have been the final words in the book if Faulkner had not added two words to the final proofs: Gowan, offstage, calls, "Temple," and Temple answers, "Coming." Does this mean that Gowan and Temple will find each other again? Did Faulkner want to give his tragedy a less despairing end? Whatever the answer, this final addition adds nothing.[26]

The fact that *Requiem for a Nun* came out just ten months after Faulkner's Nobel Prize speech had an impact on its reception by the American press. There were more reviews than for *Intruder in the Dust*, but most of them were no warmer than they had been for his previous novels. Irving Howe, in the *Nation* (September 29, 1951), saw it as nothing more than "an ambitious failure" (the same would be said of *A Fable*), and many critics agreed. But the novelist was no longer regarded in quite the same way. Now that he had won the Nobel Prize, Faulkner was no longer a writer like any other; after his noble Stockholm speech, his "humanism" could no longer be held in doubt. Malcolm Cowley, in his review for the *New York Herald Tribune* (September 30, 1951), wrote:

Once, there was an unregenerate Faulkner, careless of his readers but not unwilling to shock them; the author of novels about incest, rape, arson, and miscegenation. Now there is a reformed Faulkner, conscious of his public duties, who has become the spokesman for the human spirit in its painful aspirations toward "love and honor and pity and pride and compassion and sacrifice," to quote from his Nobel Prize address.

But *Requiem* was also turned into a viable play. In 1951 Faulkner was already working on a stage adaptation, and in mid-June, even before the book came out, Ruth Ford, the New York actress to whom he had probably sent a set of proofs, called him to tell him she had talked to a young producer, Lemuel Ayers, and a young director, Albert Marre, who were both interested in staging the play. On June 18 a very excited Faulkner wrote to both Joan and Ruth to tell them he was coming to New York to talk about the project. To the actress, he said: "The play, part, was written for you, so no contract is needed." But he did not hide the fact that his play was not yet playable: "I realise the whole second act should be rewritten [. . .] maybe the third." He went on: "I may not be playwright enough to do so. But I would like to try [. . .]. I have already thought of how to get the husband into the second act, and so break up the long speeches." Without minimizing the difficulties, he remained confident: "It will be pretty fine if we can make a good vehicle for you. I would like to see that title in light, myself. It's one of my best, I think: Requiem for a Nun" (*SL*, 318).

He arrived in New York in early July, took a room at the Algonquin, and returned to Oxford on July 19. He knew that his text needed to be reworked for the stage and was ready to collaborate on the reworking. Over the course of the fortnight spent in New York, he wrote synopses of each act and endeavored to make the text more compatible with the demands of the stage but came up against Ayers, who had very different ideas. Was Ayers thinking of entrusting the role of Temple to another actress? For Faulkner it was out of the question. On December 29, 1951, he wrote to Ayers: "This play is for Ruth, the part, character-part, is hers until she herself refuses it," and demanded "that whatever mutations and shifts of design and control and ownership the rights to it as a play might pass through, Ruth will be protected in her first claim to this part, or an equity in the play" (*SL*, 324). A few days later he sent a copy of his letter to Harold Ober and asked him to do whatever was necessary to legally protect his friend's rights. "I have known Miss Ford a long time," he added, "admire her rather terrifying determination to be an actress, and wrote this play for her to abet it" (324).

Ayers eventually gave up, and as no other director was prepared to take over, the first performances of *Requiem for a Nun* (in a version drafted by Faulkner, Ruth Ford, Ayers, and Marre) were in Europe. The worldwide premiere was in the Zurich Schauspielhaus on October 9, 1955, directed by Leopold Lindtberg; on November 10 the same year, Erwin Piscator, one of the greatest German directors of the interwar period, presented his version of the play at the Schlosspark Theater in Berlin. Albert Camus, with Faulkner's permission, put on his own adaptation (in two acts and seven scenes), opening in Paris at the Théâtre des Mathurins on September 20, 1956. The set designer was Leonor Fini.

Suddenly, everyone wanted to stage *Requiem*—even Broadway, which had stubbornly turned down a Ruth Ford production. It is true that the Ruth Ford version premiered in the United States in 1951 at the Brattle Street Theater in Cambridge, Massachusetts. But the New York premiere did not take place until January 28, 1959, at the John Golden Theatre. Directed by the English filmmaker Tony Richardson, the play featured Ruth Ford as Temple; her husband, Zachary Scott, as Gavin Stevens; and Bertice Reading as Nancy Mannigoe. Faulkner did not attend the premiere but asked several family members to go in his place. The press reviews were lukewarm. *Requiem for a Nun* was withdrawn at the end of February, after just forty-three performances.

In France, on the other hand, Camus's adaptation drew the crowds and the run lasted until January 12, 1958. Between 1955 and 1958, adaptations were staged in a number of European cities. The play was also staged in South America, Argentina, and Mexico. Outside the United States, *Requiem for a Nun* did very well.

THE GOSPEL ACCORDING TO FAULKNER: *A FABLE*

Published in 1954, *A Fable* was the belated realization of a project dating back to 1943, when Faulkner was in Hollywood, and on which he worked sporadically for almost eleven years. The idea for this book originally came from an idea for a script. As Faulkner acknowledged in his dedication, the idea was not his but that of director Henry Hathaway and producer William Bacher. It was about a mysterious reincarnation of Christ, with his sacrificial image ultimately merging with the "unknown soldier." According to Hathaway, Faulkner was the only writer capable of handling such a difficult subject. It was agreed that Hawks, Hathaway, and Faulkner would produce the film independently, far from the nit-picking tyranny of the Hollywood studios. After getting leave from Warner Bros., Faulkner went home to start work on the project.

On October 30, 1943, he wrote to Ober: "I am working on a thing now. It will be about 10–15 thousand words. It is a fable, an indictment of war perhaps, and for that reason may not be acceptable now" (*SL*, 178). In November he sent Ober a fifty-page synopsis and was already planning "to rewrite it as a story [. . .] as a magazine and book piece" (179) or a play. With this in mind, he was preparing to "smooth it out, give the characters names, remove the primer-like biblical references and explanations, and let the story reveal its Christ-analogy through understatement" (179). In early 1944, in a letter to Haas, he clarified his intentions: "In the middle of that war, Christ [. . .] reappeared and was crucified again. We are repeating, we are in the midst of war again. Suppose Christ gives us one more chance, will we crucify him again, perhaps for the last time" (180).

On January 8, 1944, Faulkner completed an initial draft of *A Fable*. But after returning to Hollywood in February, he had to put the book on hold and wait until January 1945 to get back to work properly. He did so with some apprehension. He wanted to make *A Fable* the masterpiece of his maturity but was not at all sure that he could pull it off. On January 10, 1945, he wrote to Cerf and Haas:

> I am doing a thing which I think is pretty good. Unless I am wrong about it, have reached that time of an artist's increasing years when he no longer can judge what he is doing, I have grown up at last. All my writing life I have been a poet without education, who possessed only instinct and a fierce conviction and belief in the worth and truth of what he was doing, and an illimitable courage for rhetoric (personal pleasure in it too: I admit it) and who knew and cared for little else.
>
> Well, I'm doing something different now, so different that I am writing and rewriting, weighing every word, which I never did before; I used to bang it on like an apprentice paper hanger and never look back. (*LC*, 222–23)

He now knew that the incubation period for the project would be long. On March 19, 1945, he wrote to Ober: "It will take some time yet to finish the mss. It may be my epic poem. Good story: the crucifixion and the resurrection. I had about 100,000 words, rewrote them down to about 15,000 now" (*SL*, 191). On May 25 he told Ober he was "rewriting the fable," adding: "It's a novel now and not just a lot of rhetoric as when I sent it to Bob" (192). But once again the deplorable state of his finances forced him to interrupt his writing and return to Hollywood, on June 7, 1945. While writing scripts, he continued to work on his new novel and for several weeks imposed strict discipline upon himself. In the mornings, he got up at four o'clock and wrote until eight, then went to the studio in Burbank to work as a scriptwriter. And for the first time in a long time, he stopped drinking.

His sobriety did not last, but Faulkner wanted to get ahead with *A Fable* at all costs, even though he wasn't sure he would be able to complete the book. "It may not be any good and I may be wrong about it. But I'll have to keep at it a while yet to know" (*SL*, 189). By the end of the year he had sixty-five pages, which he had rewritten and edited three times over. "I think it's all right," he wrote to Haas, adding that it "may be good enough for me to quit writing books on, though I probably wont quit yet" (213).

The turning point came in 1946. On March 26 Ober sent sixty-four pages of *A Fable*—still titled "Who?"—to Jacob Wilk, Warner Bros.' New York agent: "I think this will give you a good idea of what the novel is to be. I hope that you can tell Mr. Warner about it while he is here and get his permission to let Faulkner finish the novel" (*B1*, 474). On the twenty-eighth Wilk told him that Warner had agreed to free him from his obligations. Moreover, Cerf told him that Random House wanted to publish *A Fable* as quickly as possible and that it was offering him a one-thousand-dollar advance and undertook to pay him five hundred dollars a month until the novel was finished. Faulkner could scarcely believe his luck: "I feel fine, am happy now, thanks to Harold and you" (*SL*, 232).

By early 1947 the manuscript was about 150 pages long, but Faulkner was not happy with it. By July he had 400 pages and was contemplating 1,000 pages in all. In August he told Haas that he was "now in the middle of a hundred page new chapter which itself is a good story, a complete novelette, about a white man and an old Negro preacher and the preacher's 14 year old grandson who stole a crippled racehorse and healed its broken leg"

(*SL*, 253) and who spent a year running away from the police. In October he informed Haas that the "horse story section [was] fairly complete" (256) and asked if Ober could place it in a magazine or review. *Partisan Review* turned it down. It was published in 1951 by a small publisher in a limited edition of 975 signed copies, under the title "Notes on a Horsethief," and, after some reworking, this wholly fable-like story, with no visible link to the meat of the novel, was later reinserted into the manuscript of *A Fable*.

Faulkner had finally hit his stride. He wrote to Ober in early 1947: "The conviction is growing on me that this book is going to be a book" (*SL*, 246). But none of his other novels had given him so much trouble for so long. In August 1953, when he thought the end was in sight, he was still tormented by doubt, as attested by the letter he wrote Commins that month: "Am so near the end of the big one that I am frightened, that lightning might strike me before I can finish it. It is either nothing and I am blind in my dotage, or it is the best of my time" (352). The same awareness of the extent of the challenge and the same uncertainty surface in a letter to Haas written on October 18, 1947: "I believe it is a tremendous idea; some of the trouble I seem to have getting it written to suit me is because of its size and (myself) being so close to it all the time. It's like standing close to an elephant; after a while you cant see the elephant anymore at all" (258).

Faulkner had taken on a task that he wasn't sure he could fully finish. In 1947 he thought his troubles were over, but in fact his project would not be completed for many long years to come. In January 1948 he abandoned his work on *A Fable* to write *Intruder in the Dust*. In November 1949 he published *Knight's Gambit*. In August 1950 his final collection of short stories came out, followed by *Requiem for a Nun* in September 1951. The hiatus lasted four years.

A Fable was completed during the difficult years of 1952 and 1953 but not without difficulty. He was no longer riding a wave of inspiration; he had to knuckle down. On January 2, 1953, he wrote to Joan Williams: "The work, the mss. is going again. Not as it should, in a fine ecstatic rush like the orgasm. [. . .] This is done by simple will power; I doubt if I can keep it up too long. But it's nice to know that I still can do that" (*SL*, 344). Three days later he wrote to Commins: "Am working at the mss. daily. The initial momentum ran out, and it is getting more and more difficult, a matter of deliberate will power, concentration, which can be deadly after a while" (345). In April

1953 he told Joan Williams that the book "may be the last major, ambitious work" (348). Back at Rowan Oak in June, he decided to finish it. On the wall of his study he inscribed a chronology of the major events told in his new book, laid out in columns reading from top to bottom. He worked on it all summer long. By late September the manuscript was almost finished. There was only one chapter left to write and then the whole book had to be closely edited. In early November, Faulkner went back to Princeton, where he stayed, as usual, with the Comminses. Soon after his arrival he spread the manuscript over the long mahogany table in the dining room. Saxe Commins stood beside him, suggesting modifications and corrections. Faulkner sometimes rewrote entire passages in pencil or circled paragraphs to be cut and pasted elsewhere in the story. The day after his arrival in Princeton, Joan Williams came to visit him and helped him sort and number the pages. In three days the manuscript was finally completed. On November 5, 1953, Commins wrote to Donald Klopfer telling him that "the script is as near perfection as we can make it."[27] The last page of the manuscript reads: "December 1944 Oxford, New York Princeton November 1953."

Commins spent many long days correcting the manuscript and taking notes, and after going over it three or four times he conceded that he was still a little perplexed by some of the rhetorical extravagances and by the contorted advances and flashbacks in the unfurling of a story that was irresistible and simple, full of disputable coincidences, and with a narrative infrastructure that prevented the entire edifice from collapsing.[28] He was not entirely convinced by *A Fable*.

⁓

Of all his work, *A Fable* is the least like a Faulkner book. Not only does it take place outside Yoknapatawpha, but it also has little to do with the South, or even the United States (except for the stolen horse episode), and most of its characters are French or English. In this novel Faulkner was venturing into a world he did not know, to speak about events he had access to only through testimony and reading. The project was quite a challenge. His lack of familiarity with his material assuredly added to the difficulty.

The action takes place five months before the end of World War I, during Easter week 1918. A French regiment is refusing to go over the top of the trenches to attack. Instead of taking advantage of the situation, the German regiment facing them also digs in its heels. From the Alps to Boulogne, the butchery stops for twenty-four hours, to the despair of the commanding officers on both sides, and we do not know whose orders the mutineers are obeying. When the novel opens, the mutiny has already been quashed. The ringleaders—French infantrymen, a corporal and twelve men—have been disarmed and arrested and the three thousand men from the mutinous regiment are being brought by truck to Allied Forces Headquarters in Chaulnesmont. As required by the rules of warfare, the corporal will be condemned to death and shot, the war will continue, and everything will return to normal—except that after many adventures, the corporal's remains will be buried in Paris, under the Arc de Triomphe, in the Tomb of the Unknown Soldier.

In writing *A Fable* Faulkner drew on a number of mutinies that took place in the early summer of 1917, after the bloody defeat of the offensive ordered by General Robert Nivelle at Chemin des Dames. Faulkner also recalled Humphrey Cobb's 1935 successful novel, *Paths of Glory* (better known today in its film adaptation by Stanley Kubrick), the story of a regiment court-martialed for "cowardice" where three men are selected at random and executed. *A Fable* is not, however, a war novel, such as those written by Henri Barbusse, Roland Dorgelès, Ernst Jünger, or Erich Maria Remarque. Neither is it fiction drawn on personal experience of war like *Three Soldiers* by Dos Passos, *A Farewell to Arms* by Hemingway, *Journey to the End of the Night* by Louis Ferdinand Céline, or *The Flanders Road* by Claude Simon. Faulkner, as we now know, twice missed out on the opportunity to go to war: he was too young for the first and too old for the second. But war had long haunted this son of the South, who had grown up in a society still scarred by the Civil War, a war that had barely been lost when it started being mythologized and celebrated by that society, despite its defeat, as a glorious epic. His paternal grandfather, his black nurse, and many others had told him the story. For a man of the South like Faulkner, World War I was a reminder and a replay of the Civil War, on another stage and with other heroes, and it is no coincidence that on his first stay in France in 1925, he went to visit the trenches and battlefields of the Great War.

From the start of his career, war had fired Faulkner's imagination as a novelist and short-story writer. But *Soldiers' Pay*, his first novel, and *Flags in the Dust*, his third, dealt more with the confusion of the postwar period than the chaos of war itself. *A Fable* tells the story of a war as it happens—or so it may seem. It does not contain any descriptions of battles. One of the surprises of this novel is that it speaks about an unprecedented wartime event: a moment when, against all expectations, war is suspended and everything comes to a halt. War is certainly omnipresent, it is always there, but it is not, strictly speaking, the focus of the plot. Perhaps for Faulkner war was nothing but an overarching metaphor for this novel.

The title is the only one in Faulkner's work to designate a genre. It has nothing to do with Aesop, Phaedrus, or La Fontaine except that from the outset it suggests there may be a moral. Similarly, *Parabole*, the French title, and *Legende*, the German title, also suggest a cautionary tale. The three titles suggest that the text should not be gauged against realism, that it is close to the medieval debate, where allegorical figures discuss the past, present, and future of mankind. The author himself was well aware of this. In his letter to Ober dated April 18, 1946, he remarked that the book he was working on was "something new for me, really not a novel" (*SL*, 233). And he did not deny that he was using allegory. In his interview with Jean Stein, he said: "In *A Fable* the Christian allegory was the right allegory to use in that particular story, like an oblong square corner is the right corner with which to build an oblong rectangular house" (*LG*, 246).

A Fable is undeniably the most pensive, the most meditative of Faulkner's novels. A handful of events in a particular war evolves into a more general reflection on the origin, function, and purpose of all war; on the interests it brings into play and the passions it engenders; and on what, each time, focuses and unleashes the ordinary violence of an established order in this collective human sacrifice that is periodically revisited. Up to *A Fable*, Faulkner's novels dealt with the destiny of individuals taken in their own individuality as well as in their social existence. *A Fable*, for the first time, looks at the conditions men are placed in and at what happens to them during wartime. The general is more important than the particular, the collective more important than the individual. This slightly changes the status of the characters, who are often portrayed nameless or faceless (like the young woman "thin and poorly dressed" (*N4*, 672) and the "sergeant" reduced to his functions in the first chapter). They are defined less by their "psychology" than by their social or military ranking or their role in the allegory underlying the story. This means there is a tendency to stylize and simplify, and at times characters are crudely sketched, reduced to mere caricatures. Thus, the German general in the seventh chapter is pure stereotype: his intransigence, monocle, brandy swigging, and heel clicking all inevitably call to mind Erich von Stroheim playing a German general. True, not everyone is so schematically drawn, so summarily handled, and the main characters are all given a backstory. But they lack depth and are dull, and in contrast to Quentin Compson, Addie Bundren, or Joe Christmas, the reader has little interest in their fate.

Is this because the leading character in the novel is the crowd? In any event, the seething masses, moving crowds—fluid, amorphous, and mostly uncontrollable and unpredictable—are described at length. *A Fable* opens on a "vast tongueless brotherhood of dread and anxiety" (*N4*, 669), a portrayal of a crowd gathered on the Place de l'Hôtel de Ville of the old medieval town of Chaulnesmont. Four other chapters also start with collective scenes, and the novel ends with a crowd scene in Paris, near the Arc de Triomphe.

But what perhaps truly marks *A Fable* out in Faulkner's oeuvre is the presence of a text within the text. *A Fable* is obviously a novel with a secondary layer, where the *hypertext* barely hides the *hypotext*.[29] Like Joyce's *Ulysses*, it is a rereading and a rewriting of one of the great mythical tales of the West. However, while with Joyce the *Odyssey* is transposed in a fashion that is both methodical and subtly masked, with Faulkner the references to the Gospel (fairly evident and sometimes even explicit) do not saturate the entire novel but are easily recognizable as such. At least any reader with a Judeo-Christian background, alerted from the start by the presence of a great cross on the cover and by the proliferation of little crosses used as asterisks (as per the author's instructions), cannot help but notice the many analogies between the story and the Gospel. A story both distant and familiar is retold, with the same figures incarnated in other characters, and the same situations and events transposed to another time and space. It is not necessary to read the whole novel in order to note that Stephan, the corporal with a martyr's name, is a Christlike figure. The fact that he was conceived in the Balkans and born on Christmas night, on straw, in a stable, is no coincidence; nor is the fact that he has twelve disciples, with whom he has one last supper, like Christ and his apostles. One of his disciples, Polchek, betrays him and then, like Judas, hangs himself; another, Pierre Bouc, denies him and then joins him; a third represents him in his absence, like Paul the Apostle. The three women who follow him—his two half sisters, Marthe and Marya, and the ex-prostitute from Marseille who has become his companion—are obvious replicas of Martha, Mary, and Mary Magdalene, the holy women of the Gospel. When the corporal is brought before the old general, he is tempted, as Jesus was tempted by Satan for forty days in the desert. He dies on a Friday, tied to a post, between a murdering pimp and a simpleton, and his head becomes covered with a crown of thorns when it gets caught in barbed wire. Finally, like the body of Christ, his body is buried on a Saturday by three women and ultimately disappears.

The mutinous corporal is the presumed hero of the story. He is not the hero of the novel. While he is mentioned in the first chapter, thereafter he is only rarely center stage and is given very little to say. The dominant figure is incontestably the old commander in chief of the Allied armies. If this book has a character out of the ordinary, it is this marshal, a great war chief, highborn, from one of the wealthiest, most aristocratic, and most powerful French families, a man with a murky past but who has been marked out by fate since birth. Endowed with almost superhuman capacities and exceptional stature, the marshal is portrayed more as a mythical or epic figure than a character in a novel. But he lacks the compact singularity of the mythical or epic hero. As an allegorical figure, he fulfills at least three distinct, even contradictory roles. While he is obviously God the Father, certain episodes in his youth recall the life of Jesus, and when he tries to tempt the corporal by promising him all the power in the world, he takes on the role of Satan. As Faulkner pointed out in an interview, the marshal is also a "dark, splendid, fallen angel [. . .] Satan who had been cast out of heaven—and because God himself feared him" (FU, 62).

We can see here to what extent Faulkner blurs the biblical tale and how much he corrupts biblical typology. The marshal is and is not God the Father; the corporal is and is not Jesus Christ. The description of him at the end of the first chapter, at that stage just another anonymous figure, merely suggests a man of cold intelligence, bearing no resemblance to Christ: "a face merely interested, attentive, and calm, with something else in it which none of the others had: a comprehension, understanding, utterly free of compassion" (N4, 682). There is certainly something of the saint in this illiterate mountain dweller and he will end up a martyr. His simplicity, patience, goodness, tolerance, and serenity are admirable. He has a talent for brotherhood and must be credited with effective charisma because he succeeds in leading an entire regiment into mutiny. And we soon learn that this plebeian is the natural son of the marshal, meaning the man who is about to order his execution is his father.

In the New Testament, the Son, through his freely given sacrifice, accomplishes the will of the Father. In *A Fable*, a son refuses to submit to his father and a father tries to save his rebellious son. "I was primarily telling what to me was the tragic story, of the father who had to choose between the sacrifice or the saving of his son" (*LG*, 179). The marshal and the corporal are God the Father and Jesus Christ, but also Abraham and Isaac. The question, primordial for Faulkner, of generation, paternity, and kinship resurfaces in *A Fable*, and once again the father has a hold over the son. But this is no ordinary oedipal rivalry; there is no question of eliminating the father to take his place. To escape his condition as son and emerge as a subject, the son, paradoxically, needs to be recognized as such by the father. In *A Fable*, as in *Absalom, Absalom!*, (non)recognition is the primary issue of their relationship. But while in *Absalom, Absalom!* the father refuses to acknowledge the son and recognize himself in him, in *A Fable* he wants to make him his heir, and it is the son who refuses to defer to the rules of inheritance and transmission. Moreover, in this novel, as in *Go Down, Moses*, the confrontation between father and son is played down and depersonalized in that it is less a conflict between people than a confrontation of ideas—or at least it is presented as such.

The key scene in *A Fable* is the face-off between the corporal and the marshal related in chapter 8—a replay of the encounter between father and son that started with the fevered dialogue between Quentin and Mr. Compson in *The Sound and the Fury* and continued in *Go Down, Moses* with the impassioned debate between Ike McCaslin and his cousin Cass. In *A Fable* Faulkner may be remembering the scene opposing Christ to the Grand Inquisitor in *The Brothers Karamazov*. As in Dostoyevsky's novel, the cynical realism of the powerful opposes the eternal and impotent protest of idealism. While the Machiavellian marshal defines himself as the "champion of this mundane earth" (*N4*, 988), the corporal is described as the "champion of an esoteric realm of man's baseless hopes and his infinite capacity—no: passion—for unfact" (988). But their encounter is not really the confrontation between two lines of thought, between two ethical codes. The debate does not take place; the dialogue is short-lived. Instead, an interminable monologue unwinds, a speech whose declamatory rhetoric has the sole aim of charming and persuading its addressee. Faulkner himself called this scene in the novel the "scene of temptation." The marshal employs all the resources of his eloquence to tempt his son, as Satan tempted Christ on the mountain, offering him not only freedom but also, in the words of the Gospel, "all the kingdoms of the world and their glory."

If their opposition seems intractable, it does not appear so to the marshal. Their positions, he contends, "are not inimical really; [. . .] they can even exist side by side" (N4, 988), and as he describes them, they do in fact emerge as complementary and come together in a shared faith in mankind. The marshal's speech ends in an fervent profession of faith:

> "Oh yes, he will survive it because he has that in him which will endure even beyond the ultimate worthless tideless rock freezing slowly in the last red and heatless sunset, because already the next star in the blue immensity of space will be already clamorous with the uproar of his debarkation, his puny and inexhaustible and immortal voice still talking, still planning; and there too after the last ding dong of doom has rung and died there will still be one sound more: his voice, planning still to build something higher and faster and louder [. . .]. I dont fear man. I do better: I respect and admire him. And pride: I am ten times prouder of that immortality which he does possess than ever he of that heavenly one of his delusion. Because man and his folly—"
>
> "Will endure," the corporal said.
>
> "They will do more," the old general said proudly. "They will prevail." (994)

The marshal has the first and last word; the corporal says little or nothing. The only words he says—"will endure"—finish off the marshal's sentence. True, the corporal will not be won over by the other's arguments and is therefore quickly put to death. It doesn't matter: the executioner and his victim agree in their wager on mankind.

However, this humanist profession of faith is at times almost literally taken from Faulkner's Nobel Prize acceptance speech in Stockholm and is therefore as much a profession of the writer's faith as it is that of one of his characters. So what credence should it be given? Demanding our approval, the assertion that man "will endure" and "prevail" is based on the certainty that "his puny inexhaustible voice" (*ESPL*, 120) will never cease to be heard. But in the Stockholm speech as in the novel, these proclamations are like incantations. Prevail over whom? Prevail over what? These questions are not answered: like "believe," "prevail" is for Faulkner an intransitive verb.

It is indeed a profession of *faith*, extending beyond or falling short of all reason, perhaps even of all beliefs, comparable to that of Nancy in *Requiem*. However, in contrast to Tertullian's *credo quia absurdum*, Faulkner's credo is purely secular. In this story saturated with references to the New Testament, Christianity is nothing more than a reserve of analogies, a mythical backdrop, and the Passion that is described here bears no resemblance to the Scriptures. Faulkner's new Christ has not come to deliver mankind from original sin; he has not surfaced in the story of mankind to change the course of its history and bring salvation. He is not a man-God who has entered time to save it from itself by attaching it to eternity. He embodies nothing other than the spirit of revolt against the world order, an order that is unjust but unshakable. There will always be the poor and the powerful; there will always be corporals to rebel, generals to have them shot, and women to mourn them. The challenge to order is itself part of the order, the challenge to order guarantees its endurance, the heroic illusion of revolt consolidates the reality of power.

As in *Light in August*, nothing can break the cycle of time. In rewriting the Christian myth of God incarnate, slain and redeemed, Faulkner retains the tragic canvas but severs it from all transcendence and historicity. The Christ who is reborn as the corporal in *A Fable* is only the Christ of atrocity, the crucified Christ. Deconsecrated, the Passion, in Faulkner, is no longer the unique, overwhelming event it is to all Christians, and there is no evidence that anything is redeemed. The crucifixion takes place over and over again. In his way, in a way that is different from that of Blaise Pascal, Faulkner is telling us that the agony of Christ will continue to the end of time. In the novel's final scene another Christ is already there, in the huge crowd that has come to pay their last respects to the marshal, to respond to his challenge. "'That's right,' he said: 'Tremble. I'm not going to die. Never'" (*N4*, 1072). But Faulkner's Christ is not immortal as the son of God; he is immortal only insofar as his successive avatars will ensure the permanence of the fraternal values he represents.

This is the Gospel according to Faulkner. It is always being rewritten, but it assuredly does not bring "good tidings." Neither does it bring bad tidings, but rather asserts the impossibility of any news, any novelty—of the impossibility, fundamentally, of any event—in a world that is continually at "war," where the same battles are replayed over and over, the same massacres are repeated indefinitely, and where, ultimately, there are no winners or losers. Quentin Compson's sententious father already said as much in *The Sound and the Fury*: "No battle is ever won [. . .]. They are not even fought. The field only reveals to man his own folly and despair, and victory is an illusion of philosophers and fools" (*N1*, 935).

"Tomorrow," the title of the final chapter, will therefore be no better and no worse than today or yesterday. Instead of the history of the people of God, organizing themselves according to the design of providence and wending their way, via tumult and heartbreak, toward Parousia, the Final Judgment, and the end of days—that is, moving toward the ultimate accomplishment of a shared destiny—*A Fable* proposes a story without *kairos* or *telos*, ossified in the unsurmountable conjunction of opposites and the immutable return of the same. Sainthood is no longer possible, and heroism is reduced to the fleeting brilliance of a fine gesture. All that exists is a frugal wisdom, a kind of stoicism, perhaps, that is not very distant from Nietzsche's *amor fati*, whose cardinal virtue seems to be endurance. To endure means to undergo, suffer, bear, withstand, last, stand firm, persevere. In *A Fable* both noun and verb occur perhaps even more frequently than in Faulkner's other novels. The ability to endure is the daily heroism of the humble, the hidden strength of the weak, the inalienable freedom of slaves, a way of coping by lying low: Dilsey and her family in *The Sound and the Fury*; the Bundrens, except for Darl, in *As I Lay Dying*; Lena Grove in *Light in August*; the two convicts in *If I Forget Thee, Jerusalem*; Lucas Beauchamp in *Intruder in the Dust*; Mink in *The Mansion*. Poor people, women, and blacks.

Enduring, for Faulkner, does not mean accepting suffering to atone for one's sins or fatalistically resigning oneself to suffering. It means taking suffering into oneself and onto oneself; it means knowing how to suffer "learning through suffering" as the chorus says in Aeschylus's *Agamemnon*. Or as a Prophet puts it: "He who has not suffered, what does he know?"

The wisdom of endurance, according to Faulkner, comes from an acquiescence that in fact is a backward refusal. It does not deliver us from tragedy; it is formed and confirmed in tragedy without resolving it. In *A Fable* this wisdom, this active patience is heroically embodied by the corporal until death. Three major characters in the novel are defined by endurance. In an interview Faulkner declared:

> What I was writing about was the trilogy of man's conscience represented by the young British Pilot Officer, the Runner, and the Quartermaster General. The one that said, This is dreadful, terrible, and I won't face it even at the cost of my life—that was the British aviator. The Old General who said, This is terrible but we can bear it. The third one, the battalion Runner who said, This is dreadful, I won't stand it, I'll do something about it. (*FU*, 62)

Faulkner refers to three iconic figures, like Flask, Stubb, and Starbuck in *Moby-Dick*: David Levine, the young tormented idealist who, like Quentin Compson in *The Sound and the Fury*, cannot bear the spectacle of evil and, unable to either endure or combat it, escapes from it by committing suicide; the major general, who puts up with it while deploring it; and the runner, the reckless disciple of the mutinous corporal, who not only resists but risks his life in exposing himself and in fighting an iniquitous order.

A Fable was to have been Faulkner's magnum opus, the crowning of his literary career. He wanted it to be a summation, a book of knowledge and wisdom from a fully matured writer, fulfilling "the desire of the artist before he dies to say all he possibly can of what he knows of truth in the most moving way" (*LG*, 113). But in attempting to say everything, *A Fable* says much less than *The Sound and the Fury* or *Absalom, Absalom!* and it does not say what it has to say "in the most moving way." Ideas in a novel are not necessarily toxic; a philosophical novel is not necessarily boring. But to succeed, ideas must be more than abstractions shackled inside statements; they must free themselves of all tutelage and incandesce in fiction. There are plenty of great novels where philosophical speculation becomes part of the fictional experience, including *Moby-Dick*, *The Brothers Karamazov, Doctor Faustus, The Death of Virgil*, and *The Man without Qualities*. But Faulkner is no Melville or Dostoyevsky, no Thomas Mann, Hermann Broch, or Robert Musil. His genius is elsewhere. His thought, when it moves, takes other paths, follows other routes, and it is never stronger than when it brings clarity to the darkest places, waives its privileges and its powers, and ventures to the limit of language, to the threshold of the irrational, as it does, for example, with outstanding chutzpah, in the monologue of the idiot Benjy or the pre-Socratic witticisms of Darl.

In *A Fable* this thought loses both its shading and its flourish. It must be acknowledged that this novel, Faulkner's most ambitious book, the one in which he placed his highest hopes, does not live up to his awesome ambition. Weighed down with long and confusing commentaries and similarly interminable descriptions (there is page upon page about uniforms), his prose becomes bloated and winded, the rhetoric so rehashed and jaded that it no longer touches us.

Grandiloquence—that linguistic one-upmanship favored by Southern rhetoricians since the nineteenth century and which formed part of Faulkner's heritage—had been one of his greatest temptations from the start of his literary career. He first began to yield to this temptation in the fourth section of "The Bear" in *Go Down, Moses,* and in Stevens's wordy tirades in *Intruder in the Dust.* In *A Fable* redundancies abound, sentences stretch on and on, overlap, dovetail, and become mangled, at times with no regard for syntax. Language is inflated to the maximum; its evocative power is extremely low. The narrative does not have any urgency and the tale continually gets bogged down. As in other Faulkner novels, scenes tend to be staged in tableaux, but here these tableaux are not *tableaux vivants;* they have ceased to thrill, and the events related do not really take place, because they have no space in which to happen. In most of Faulkner's novels the landscape is closely bound up with the action and the characters. This is not the case in *A Fable,* where, as in "The De Gaulle Story," France becomes an allegory of the universal values of the "free world." While a realistic description was not expected, fewer clichés would have improved the text. But the Paris described in this novel is the long-gone Paris of Hugo and Balzac, a Paris mythologized by literature, more *read about* than experienced. All the action takes place against the pasteboard backdrop of a fantasized and stereotypical France that the reader does not believe in for a second (especially if he himself is French).

Faulkner of course remains faithful to his obsessions. *A Fable,* like his other novels, deals with distress and suffering, and the novel's narrative material is rich in tragic events. Death—murders, suicides, executions, massacres—is omnipresent. But it is generally abstract and distant; the reader is rarely moved. Of all of Faulkner's novels, *A Fable* is the coldest, the one where affections are held the furthest at bay. While there are still many signs to decipher, nuggets of joy are few—except in the pages where the novelist comes home to the South, as he does in the breathtaking episode of the horse thieves, a fable within a fable. On first reading, this episode might seem monumentally incongruous, but it may well be the novelist mocking himself and can also be read as an ironic mise en abyme, where the corporal's idealism resurfaces sardonically in the passion of a white and a black groom for an improbable three-legged race horse.

Other admirable scenes include these where derision defuses the solemnity, such as the comical and macabre scene echoing *Sanctuary* at the end of chapter 8, where General Gragnon is executed by a curious trio of American soldiers (a white farmer from Iowa, a black man from Mississippi, and a gangster from Brooklyn), or the episode, crammed with irony and black humor, at the end of the last chapter, where thirteen (mostly drunk) soldiers charged with bringing a corpse from the ossuary of Vallaumont (alias Douaumont) to Paris barter it along the way with a crazy peasant woman in exchange for alcohol and buy another from a farmer who found it in his field. The second corpse is that of the corporal, but nobody knows—and nobody ever will know—that the Tomb of the Unknown Soldier, intended to commemorate all the soldiers who died in battle, now hosts a mutineer.

The best moments of this serious novel are, paradoxically, its moments of slapstick. It starts brilliantly with a masterful crowd scene and ends beautifully with the recounting of the old marshal's grandiose funeral on the Champs-Elysées. But this handful of bravura flourishes are not enough to make it a great book. *A Fable* is not Faulkner's "most splendid failure," but it is undoubtedly the most monumental and the most mesmerizing.

⁓

A Fable was published on August 2, 1954. That same day, Faulkner's photograph was on the cover of *Newsweek*. In thirty years none of his novels had won any prize in America. Things could not be left there; something had to be done. *A Fable* was therefore awarded the Pulitzer Prize. And on January 25, 1955, at the Commodore Hotel in New York, Faulkner was given the National Book Award by Clifton Fadiman, the *New Yorker* critic who since *The Sound and the Fury* had been the most relentless and the least well-informed of his detractors. A journalist reported that Faulkner looked despondent throughout the ceremony.[30]

The critical reception to *A Fable* was mixed. Poet Delmore Schwartz, in the winter 1955 issue of *Perspective*, saw this novel as the "unique fulfillment of Faulkner's genius." Maxwell Geismar, in the *Saturday Review* of July 31, 1954, deemed it "the best novel Faulkner has published in the last decade," and Carvel Collins, in the *New York Times* of August 1, thought it was one of the most important works of a major novelist. Most reviews, however, were extremely reserved. In the *New York Herald Tribune* of August 1, Malcolm Cowley, manifestly embarrassed, took a metaphor from Proust's *Time Regained*, comparing the novel to "a cathedral, if an imperfect and unfinished one, above a group of well built cottages." For Charles Rolo, in the September issue of the *Atlantic*, it was a heroically ambitious failure, while Brendan Gill, in the *New Yorker* of August 28, called it a pure calamity. But the most severe and virulent panning appeared in the September issue of *Commentary*. It was written by Norman Podhoretz (future godfather to the neoconservatives), who found *A Fable* the most pretentious, the most inept, and the most dull of Faulkner's books (revealing his own foolishness when he deplores the fact that Faulkner's work has not been visited by the spirit of tolerance and moderation of the Enlightenment).[31] Hemingway did not mince his words either, but was both more impetuous and coarse. "His latest book, *A Fable*," he wrote a friend, "is not pure shit, it is impure, diluted shit."[32]

What did Faulkner himself think of *A Fable*? He had had doubts the whole time he was writing it, and these doubts did not dissipate once it was finished. As if to reassure himself, he wrote to his mother in October 1953: "I believe the book is a good one. All the people here like what they have seen of it" (*SL*, 355). He was less confident in a letter he sent to Saxe Commins in February 1954, six months before the novel's publication: "I love the book, gave ten good years of my life to it: if any part of it should taste like dust on the tongue, I had better never have done it" (361–62). And in August 1954, after *A Fable* came out, he told a *Time* journalist: "It does not please me."[33] Jill thought that her father was "dissatisfied with it when it was finished [. . .]. The theme is religious, so this was to be a great work. But it wasn't. I think he knew it all along. He knew that he was out of his element" (*B1*, 588–89).

A Fable did not lack admirers, however. Among them was one of the major names in political philosophy in the twentieth century, Hannah Arendt. Her praise would have gratified Faulkner. In her eyes *A Fable* was a great war novel, one of those exceptional books that manages to portray "the inner truth of the event" such that we can say: "Yes, this is how it was."[34]

NOTES

1. George Marion O'Donnell, "Faulkner's Mythology," *Kenyon Review* (Summer 1939): 286.

2. Maurice-Edgar Coindreau, "William Faulkner," *La Nouvelle Revue Française* (June 1931): 926.

3. Maurice-Edgar Coindreau, "L'art de Faulkner," *France-Amérique*, December 3, 1950.

4. Quoted by Robert Coughlan in *The Private Life World of William Faulkner*, 132.

5. William Faulkner, quoted in Frederick R. Karl, *William Faulkner: American Writer* (New York: Weidenfeld & Nicolson, 1989), 724.

6. See Hooding Carter, "Faulkner and His Folk," *Princeton University Library Chronicle* (Spring 1957): 102.

7. James Baldwin, "Faulkner and Desegregation," *Partisan Review* (Fall 1956): 56.

8. A. Nicholas Fargnoli and Michael Golay, eds., *William Faulkner A to Z* (New York: Checkmark Books, 2002), 234.

9. Letter from Wilson to Faulkner dated September 25, 1956, in *Edmund Wilson: Letters on Literature and Politics, 1912–1972* (New York: Farrar, Straus & Giroux, 1977), 540.

10. Quoted in Todd McCarthy, *Howard Hawks: The Grey Fox of Hollywood* (New York: Grove Press, 1997, 1984), 657.

11. Ibid.

12. Faulkner Collection, Alderman Library, University of Virginia. Letter quoted in Jay Parini, *One Matchless Time: A Life of William Faulkner* (New York: Harper Collins, 2004), 359.

13. *Faulkner: A Comprehensive Guide to the Brodsky Collection*, ed. Louis Daniel Brodsky and Robert W. Hamblin. Vol. 2: *The Letters* (Jackson: University Press of Mississippi, 1984), 138.

14. Letter from William Faulkner to Joan Williams, January 24, 1954, Faulkner Collection, Alderman Library, Library of Virginia.

15. Robert N. Linscott, "Faulkner without Fanfare," *Esquire*, July 1963, 3.

16. Gaëtan Picon, "L'angoisse et le désordre," *Les Nouvelles littéraires*, July 12, 1962, 3. See also Guy Dumur, "Faulkner ou le dernier tragique," *France Observateur*, July

12, 1962, 24. Founded in Berlin in 1950, the Congress for Cultural Freedom was one of the spearheads of American cultural diplomacy during the Cold War.

17. This incident is related by Otto Hahn in "Le second Faulkner," *Les Temps Modernes*, August 1962, 351. It is not mentioned by any of Faulkner's five biographers.

18. Letter from W. H. Auden to Tania and James Stern, February 6, 1952. Quoted in Parini, *One Matchless Time*, 347.

19. *Guide to the Brodsky Collection*, 80.

20. Ibid., 89.

21. Ibid., 80.

22. Tennessee Williams, quoted in A. I. Bezzerides, *William Faulkner: A Life on Paper* (Jackson: University Press of Mississippi, 1980), 102. See also Tennessee Williams, *Memoirs* (New York: Bantam Books, 1976), 215.

23. Three handwritten pages of this first draft of *Requiem* were found at Rowan Oak. They are transcribed in Noel Polk, *Faulkner's Requiem for a Nun: A Critical Study* (Bloomington: Indiana University Press, 1981), 238–39, 240–41.

24. Faulkner had met Sherwood in New York in 1931.

25. Faulkner used the same expression in the same manner in his interview with Jean Stein (*LG*, 252).

26. In Albert Camus's adaptation, the end is even more promising: we see Temple going home to her husband and son.

27. *Guide to the Brodsky Collection*, 126.

28. Dorothy Commins, *What Is an Editor? Saxe Commins at Work* (Chicago: University of Chicago Press, 1978), 202.

29. Terms borrowed from Gérard Genette, *Palimpsestes* (Paris: Editions du Seuil, 1982).

30. See Paul Flowers, *Memphis Commercial Appeal*, January 30, 1955, 3.

31. See "William Faulkner and the Problem of War: His Fable of Faith," reproduced in *Faulkner: A Collection of Critical Essays*, ed. Robert Penn Warren (Englewood Cliffs, NJ: Prentice-Hall, 1966), 243–50.

32. Letter from Ernest Hemingway to Mr. Rider dated July 29, 1956.

33. "Books: Faulkner Speaking," *Time*, August 23, 1954, 76.

34. Hannah Arendt, *Men in Dark Times* (New York: Harcourt Brace and World, 1968), 20. *A Fable* was prescribed reading for Hannah Arendt's undergraduate students at the University of California, Berkeley, in 1955.

9
THE END

THE VIRGINIA YEARS

From 1956 on, Faulkner started spending more and more time in Virginia, where Jill lived with her husband, Paul Summers. In order to be close to their daughter, son-in-law, and first grandson, Paul, born on April 15, William and Estelle set up home in the handsome Georgian-style red-brick house that Jill found for them at 917 Rugby Road in Charlottesville. They bought the house three years later.

From February to June 1957 and from February to May 1958, Faulkner was writer in residence at the University of Virginia, funded from the estate of Emily Clark Balch, which provided him with "a house to live in and someone to clean it." His duties were not overly onerous. Although he had no teaching duties, he willingly made himself available to answer students' questions. As a member of the teaching body, he received students and occasionally colleagues in the Department of English in Cabell Hall twice a week. Faulkner performed his duties conscientiously, but when he started his second semester, Colgate W. Darden, the president of the university, refused to grant him a permanent position because of his moderate views on desegregation. However, everything worked out in the end.

Faulkner liked Virginia. At the press conference he gave on February 15, 1957, he declared his love for the state: "I like Virginia and I like Virginians. Because Virginians are all snobs, and I like snobs. A snob has to spend so much time being a snob that he has little left to meddle with you, and so it's very pleasant here" (*FU*, 12). Virginia is not Mississippi; Charlottesville is not Oxford. Faulkner was not sorry about this change of air and company. In Oxford he was under constant suspicion, whereas in Charlottesville he was respected. Nobody dared to call him "Billy," and nobody reproached him for disparaging the South. Faulkner liked Virginians because they were snobs, just as he was in his own way. This is where he put on his last costume, took on his last role—that of gentleman rider. And again he went even further, inventing an entire family history of noble highlanders. This time he had company, as from now on he mixed only with the good citizens of Albemarle County, one of the richest counties in Virginia. The county folk, as they liked to call themselves, lived mostly on large estates with smart names such as Hunting Ridge or Eden Farm. They were rich—sometimes very rich—landowners, snug in their wealth, unshakably certain of their entitlement to be who they were and to have what they had. Apparently Faulkner was quite at home in this privileged environment. The fact that they were ultraconservative, racist, anti-desegregation, and supported the White Citizens Councils does not seem to have bothered him.

In Virginia Faulkner was able to pursue two of his interests—namely, horse riding and hunting. Albemarle County is a paradise for horsemen, and fox hunting has been practiced there since the time of Lord Fairfax. However, for Faulkner, horse riding was not just another sport among others; it was perhaps first and foremost a way of playing chicken with oneself: "'I'm scared to death of horses,' he said, speaking rapidly, 'that's why I can't leave them alone'" (B1, 658). Earlier in life, when his mother asked him not to go horse riding anymore after one of his falls, he had answered: "No, Mother, [. . .] I love the thrill of the danger" (658).

Faulkner was the size and weight of a jockey, but he was a terrible horseman and his poor physical condition was a severe handicap. However, he took jumping lessons at the Dixie Flying Field riding school, and this is when his falls and injuries began. During these exercises he soon broke a rib, as revealed by an X-ray taken sometime later. He fell at a horse show on March 14, 1959, and broke his right collarbone. That afternoon he was back in the saddle with his shoulder bandaged and his right arm in a cast. Finally suffering real injuries, the martyred horse rider was atoning for the lies of the fake fighter pilot.

His collarbone eventually mended, but over the following weeks he suffered from almost unbearable back pain. Returning to Oxford in April, he wrote to Albert Erskine, his editor since the death of Saxe Commins: "I am at home again, still sore but sober and think I can ride again soon" (SL, 427). Although his doctor asked him to wait a little longer, he was back riding horses again from mid-May until the day his horse bolted and threw him to the ground. He suffered from internal bleeding and X-rays revealed that he had broken several vertebrae. He needed crutches for a number of weeks.

It would have been sensible to stop, but the doctors' warnings went unheeded. Nothing seems to have been able to divert Faulkner from his follies, and he put as much energy into fox hunting as he had done twenty years previously flying airplanes or hunting deer. He still had a taste for physical danger: "There is something about jumping a horse over a fence, something that makes you feel good. Perhaps it's the risk, the gamble. In any event, it's a thing I need."[1] To continue to feel alive, he was ready to put his life in danger. In a letter to Joan Williams in November 1959 he wrote: "It is very fine, very exciting. Even at 62, I can still go harder and further and longer than some of the others. That is, I seem to have reached the point where all I have to risk is just my bones" (*SL*, 439). There were to be a few more falls, up until 1962, the year of his death. His last fall would be fatal.

Faulkner was now spending most of his time in Virginia, but he was not yet done with Mississippi. On January 3, 1960, he took the train for Oxford to visit his sick mother in the hospital. "She keeps getting smaller and smaller and smaller," he told a friend.[2] He returned to Virginia in February, resumed his activities at the university in March, and in early June he returned to Oxford. Faulkner kept himself busy, riding in the morning, doing a little hunting with his nephew Jimmy and some sailing on Sardis Lake. Faulkner stayed busy but wrote little. In early October, as he was getting ready to return to Charlottesville, he learned that his mother had just had a brain hemorrhage. Miss Maud knew the end was near and had let her last wishes be known. She made Sallie Murry promise that there would be no overly aggressive treatment. She wished to be buried in a simple wooden coffin, telling Jimmy: "I want to get back to earth as fast as I can" (*B1*, 680). Watched over for six days by her friends and family, she finally slipped into a coma and died on October 16, 1960, at the age of eighty-eight.

Maud's death would precipitate Faulkner's break with Oxford and Mississippi. As he already owned a house in Charlottesville, he decided to set up home for good there with Estelle. The University of Virginia had just appointed him lecturer with tenure, at an annual honorarium of $250. However, what delighted and pleased him most was when Farmington Hunt, a highly exclusive hunting club that strove to perpetuate the English tradition of riding to hounds, invited him to join their ranks.

In January 1961 Faulkner went to the studio of Jack R. Cofield, his photographer in Oxford since the early 1930s, to have another portrait taken. In his elegant hunting costume—complete with top hat, red jacket with blue collar, white jodhpurs, white scarf, black boots, leather gloves, and whip—he posed for a series of color photographs, where he is seen sitting or standing, with or without the top hat. He seems so impeccably aristocratic as to be almost a fake. Of the roles that Faulkner played during his lifetime, this last one suited him neither more nor less than the others—in other words, it did not suit him *exactly*. When the "Old Colonel" ordered his own statue of Carrara marble in Italy, he fully identified with this idealized image of himself. It is unlikely that Faulkner was so taken in. His horse-rider portrait is anything but natural: it evokes a fancy-dress ball and hints to us that Faulkner is acting, that we are once again at a show. However, his head is indeed the one bestowed on him by time or that he acquired over time—that of a handsome, sad patrician.

Here again, Faulkner seemed to thumb his nose at fate. Behind the handsome mask and outfit, this was a man living on borrowed time, worn out and sick, who would soon be dead. Since receiving the Nobel Prize, his health had continued inexorably to decline. On March 18, 1956, he fell into a coma and spent ten days at the Baptist Hospital in Memphis. On the twenty-fourth he wrote to Jean Stein: "Last Sunday I suddenly began to vomit blood. I passed completely out and they brought me here, had some oxygen and a transfusion Monday, and Friday they began tests, stomach and back too. Xray shows nothing, no ulcer. The Dr thinks an ulcer may be there but is closed up with stomach shrinkage. Next test will be Monday. That should tell the tale" (*SL*, 397). In the same letter, he announced that over the next three months he was going to "cut out alcohol and coffee, etc., live on baby food" (397). These were the promises of a drunkard. He was neither able nor willing to stop drinking; alcoholism would not loosen its grip and his falls from the saddle would do the rest.

He persisted in surviving, without grumbling, as if indifferent to the advent of death. He refused to look after himself, acting as if nothing had happened. He continued to kill himself slowly. When Hemingway shot himself in the head in July 1961, Faulkner was disapproving: "I don't like a man that takes the short way home" (*B1*, 690). He was in no hurry himself. He took his time, waiting for death to come for him, not because he liked to suffer but because waiting for death was another way of holding out, of standing up to oblivion, of refusing to give up before the game was lost. The watchword was always the same: endurance. Between death and pain, Faulkner chose pain.

And although he drew closer to his family, he did not withdraw completely, continuing to fulfill what he considered to be his duties as a public person and giving interviews to journalists. The year 1956 saw both his worst and best interviews: to Russell Howe he said terrible things, while with Jean Stein he spoke with tact and intelligence about his occupation. Between March and September he published seven open letters: two in *Life* in March; one letter to the *Reporter* on April 19; a letter to *Time* on April 23; a "Letter to the Leaders of the Negro Race" in the September issue of the black review *Ebony*; and in December, in *Time* and the *New York Times*, two letters approving of the intervention of France, England, and Israel in the Suez Canal.

From 1956 Faulkner's positions on the black question became fixed and hardened. In the letter published in *Ebony* in September 1956, he hypothetically put himself in the place of a black person to appeal to his "brothers" for moderation and caution. He acknowledged that if he were black he would be a member of the NAACP, "since nothing else in our U.S. culture has yet held out to my race that much of hope" (*ESPL*, 109). However, on February 24, 1960, in a rather terse letter to Paul Pollard, a former servant of the Faulkners in Charlottesville, who had written to ask him to join the NAACP, he stated that he completely disagreed with the politics of that organization and once again rehearsed his arguments in favor of accommodation:

> As I see it, if the people of your race are to have equality and justice as human beings in our culture, the majority of them have got to be changed completely from the way they now act. Since they are a minority, they must behave better than white people. They must be more responsible, more honest, more moral, more industrious, more literate and educated. They, not the law, have got to compel the white people to say, Please come and be equal with us. If the in-

dividual Negro does not do this by getting himself educated and trained in responsibility and morality, there will be more and more trouble between the two races. (*SL*, 444)

At the end of the 1950s, blacks became increasingly rare in his work and seem to disappear from his concerns. As nobody paid any attention to his stances on civil rights, he eventually lost interest in the issue. The blacks disappointed him because of their impatience and intransigence, although he laid the blame for racial violence fully at the door of poor whites. He saw the election of Ross Barnett as governor of Mississippi as the triumph of an awful Snopes supported by the rednecks, willfully ignoring the fact that in the Meredith affair the white middle class, including his own family, had been just as enraged as the poor white farmers.

His romantic career was coming to an end. He never saw Meta again after 1951. His relationship with Joan ended in November 1953. In early February 1957 he was due to meet Jean Stein while in New York, but she called to cancel. She too married a man of her own age. Once again, for the last time, Faulkner had been spurned. He had no further liaisons; the time had come to give up young women. After Joan and Jean had both married, Faulkner saw them one last time, in 1962 in New York, shortly before he died. However, after the missed opportunity with Jean Stein, he no longer thought about leaving Estelle, even though they continued to quarrel. Although Estelle eventually gave up alcohol, it had already done its worst. She had aged badly. However, it was Estelle who was now contemplating divorce. She had indeed been thinking about it for some years. On February 11, 1954, she wrote to Saxe Commins: "Bill has been at home very little the past four years, and a good bit of that time spent here has been a nightmare of drunkenness—He must be very unhappy—so the only cure I know of is to help him get free—legally—Heaven only knows he has been free in every other sense."[3] Three years later, on February 18, 1957, she expressed the same wish in another letter to Commins:

> I would like to be free, not from Bill, for once I love it's forever—but from the utterly false undignified position I have occupied the past six years—I am tired of being the poor deceived wife in the background—to his loves, that is—Ac-

tually Bill has told me, in his cups, about his affairs, and I've tried very hard to rationalize my reactions and see *his* way as a *necessity*—and forget it all—.[4]

However, Commins advised her against divorce. For his part, Faulkner, the fickle husband who had often thought of divorce but could never quite bring himself to ask for one, wanted to hear no more about it. With age, tensions ease. They were to grow old together in Charlottesville. The marriage did not fall apart, although this did not mean that Faulkner had settled down.

While he would no longer travel around the world as he had done in 1955, he spent two weeks in Greece in April 1957, where he visited the islands and stayed some time at Mycenae. A few weeks after his return, during an interview in Virginia, he described his trip to Greece as "a strange experience" that had revealed "the Hellenic light" to him and "Homer's wine-dark sea" (*FU*, 129). In Greece, Faulkner discovered another way of being in the world, of being of the world, another relationship with time, and a different relationship, both closer and happier, with the divine. Although they could be considered alien to his puritanical nature, the inception of these relationships doubtless dates back to his reading as a young man. In the same interview, he said that Greece was

> the only place I was in where there was a sense of a very distant past but there was nothing inimical in it. In the other parts of the Old World there is a sense of the past but there is something Gothic and in a sense a little terrifying . . . The people seem to function against that past that for all its remoteness in time it was still inherent in the light, the resurgence of spring, you didn't expect to see the ghosts of the old Greeks, or expect to see the actual figures of the gods, but you had a sense that they were near and they were still powerful, not inimical, just powerful. (*FU*, 129–30)

In March and November 1958 he stayed briefly at Princeton University. In October 1959 he delivered an address to the seventh national conference of the US National Commission for UNESCO. In April 1961 he spent two weeks in Caracas at the invitation of the State Department, where he was warmly welcomed, despite the anti-American stance of the Venezuelan intelligentsia.

He continued to write, albeit less often, less copiously, and with less passion. As he wrote in a letter to Else Jonsson in October 1955, he was concerned not to waste whatever time and talent he had left. For a time there was a suggestion that his inspiration would reach beyond his native land. He told one of his Charlottesville hunting companions that he intended to write an allegorical novel about fox hunting, but this novel was never written.

Although Faulkner had left Oxford in Lafayette County, the novelist remained in Jefferson, Yoknapatawpha. By the 1950s the best of his work was behind him and his imaginary landscape no longer needed its demiurge, but Faulkner was unable to break away from it. The farewell ceremony was not yet over.

Saying farewell means saying good-bye forever, but as long as the ceremony went on, the separation was not fully achieved; there was still time to go back and recapitulate. The three books that Faulkner wrote between 1955 and 1962, the year of his death—*The Town*, *The Mansion*, and *The Reivers*—are part and parcel of this leave-taking. The work of Faulkner could be said to be completed with *A Fable*. The work that came afterward involved a rereading and a rethinking of his previous work—almost like those panoramic visions ascribed to the dying whose entire lives flash before them—and a celebration of what it had achieved. The point of this postscript was not to repair an oversight but to point the way to the work already done.

THE SNOPES, SECOND AND FINAL INSTALLMENT: *THE TOWN* AND *THE MANSION*

The Hamlet was published in 1940, more than thirteen years after "Father Abraham." Over fifteen years went by before Faulkner wrote *The Town* and *The Mansion*, the last two volumes of his trilogy.

When he started *The Town* in November 1955, his heart was no longer fully in it: "Doing a little work on the next Snopes book," he wrote Commins. "Have not taken fire in the old way yet, so it goes slow, but unless I'm burnt out, I will heat up soon and go right on with it" (*SL*, 390). In this difficult period of his life, when both his family and his community disapproved of his alleged "negrophilia," returning to writing was always a welcome diversion: "Miss. such an unhappy state to live in now, that I need something like a book to get lost in" (390).

In early January 1956 he sent a part of his manuscript to Jean Stein, his new muse. Her response was enthusiastic. Reassured but lucid, he wrote to her on January 13: "I feel pretty good over your reaction to the new Snopes stuff. I still feel, as I did last year, that perhaps I have written myself out and all that remains now is the empty craftsmanship—no fire, force, passion anymore in the words and sentences. But as long as it pleases you, I will have to go on" (SL, 391). In the spring of 1956, despite being again in poor health, he was working regularly at Rowan Oak. In June he was preparing to send a substantial part of his new novel to Commins. He felt better in the summer, drank less, slept better, spent more time on the farm, and started to enjoy writing again. "Book is going splendidly, too easy," he wrote to Jean Stein in August (402). In mid-October he sent 436 typed pages to Commins. In December he corrected the proofs. Dedicated, as *The Hamlet* had been, to Phil Stone, who "did half of the laughing for thirty years," *The Town* was published on May 1, 1957.

Like *The Unvanquished*, *The Hamlet*, and *Go Down, Moses*, *The Town* is a collection of connected, previously published short stories. Once again, Faulkner shies away from plot. Telling not a story but a multitude of stories, *The Town* is by far his most diverse novel.

There is no one dominant tone. On August 22, 1956, as he was finishing the novel, Faulkner wrote to Jean Stein: "I thought it was just a funny book but I was wrong" (SL, 402). Like *The Hamlet*, *The Town* was first conceived as a comic novel, but once finished, this was no longer quite true, although the stories in it are all comical. The first chapter starts with a story first published in 1932, "Centaur in Brass." The sixth chapter incorporates "Mule in the Yard," a short story reminiscent of Twain, first published in 1934. And in the last twelve pages of the final chapter, immediately after the story of Eula's death, Faulkner gives us one ultimate farce, hilarious and terrifying: the arrival in Jefferson of Byron Snopes's four dreadful children and his Apache wife, whom Flem tries to send back to Texas before they wreak havoc on the town. However, these excesses are a surprising rarity in this novel of manners, which is much more prosaic than *The Hamlet*. The novelist has calmed down. While *The Hamlet* contains a degree of madness, magic, and fable, *The Town* rarely diverges from the plausibility of the realist novel.

The narrative technique is also different. There is no longer one master narrator to the story who provides all the narration. Instead, the stories are told in turn by three narrators already known to the reader—V. K. Ratliff, Gavin Stevens, and Charles Mallison—but these three do not share equal billing. Ratliff, the wonderful storyteller of *The Hamlet*, has just six short chapters out of the novel's total of twenty-four. Eight are given over to Gavin and ten to his nephew Charles, who both already featured in *Intruder in the Dust* and *Knight's Gambit*. Curiously, more than half of the narration is provided by this fourteen-year-old boy, even though many of the tales he tells predate his birth and almost all his information is secondhand. No matter. Charles is still defined from the outset as the voice of the community: "When I say 'we' and 'we thought' what I mean is Jefferson and what Jefferson thought" (*N5*, 3). However, what Jefferson thinks is open to doubt and the collective voice has no more authority than any of the narrators. This community has limited knowledge, transmitted by hearsay and giving rise to multiple interpretations. As in *The Hamlet*, what is said is often what someone else has said or what has been heard, rumors of uncertain origin and veracity. Gossip is never very far away.

In *The Town* the community is omnipresent, as it was in *The Hamlet* and would be again in *The Mansion*. Everything happens between 1909 and 1927, in Yoknapatawpha County, in Jefferson and its environs, and all roads inevitably lead back to the Snopes family. The novel moves from village to small town, but the same tale continues, with the same actors and a handful of newcomers. The novel also goes back over events previously told in the first volume of the trilogy—the episode of the spotted horses, the story of Eula and McCarron, the murder of Houston by Mink—and there are slight variations from one account to another in the narrative order, point of view, or the story itself.

The Town starts where *The Hamlet* leaves off. Flem, his wife, and his daughter have left the hamlet for the town. Flem is now the owner of a greasy spoon in Jefferson, where he manages the till while Eula grills steaks and hamburgers. Thanks to Major Manfred de Spain, the young mayor of Jefferson, who is sleeping with Flem's wife, Flem becomes the president of the town's power plant, and, when Bayard Sartoris, the manager of one of the local banks, is killed in a car accident and replaced by de Spain, Flem is elected its vice president. He buys a little house, fixes it up, and furnishes it as befits a man of his position, and becomes a member of the Baptist church. It is not long before being rich and powerful is no longer enough for him. As Ratliff remarks to the young Mallison: "'When it's jest money and power a man wants, there is usually some place where he will stop; there's always one thing at least that ever—every man wont do for jest money. But when it's respectability he finds out he wants and has got to have, there aint nothing he wont do to get it and then keep it'" (*N5*, 227–28). At the end of the novel, after much blackmail and manipulation, he gets everything he wants: not only does he take Manfred de Spain's place at the head of the bank, but he also buys his rival's beautiful mansion, to which he adds large white columns so that it looks just like a planter's house. Most ironically of all, to reinforce his respectability he energetically starts to distinguish himself from his compromising cousins, sending sex-shop pioneer Montgomery Ward Snopes to the penitentiary on a trumped-up charge of bootlegging, and paying off I. O. Snopes, an insurance swindler who specializes in arranging for mules to wander onto the railroad and then suing when they are killed. Some Snopeses arrive; others leave—they are no longer an invading force. Flem is getting old. Seeing himself now as the guardian of community values and "civic virtue," he resolves to defend Jefferson against any form of disorder and to punish any offenses against public decency. In the last episode of the novel, it is he who sends the terrifying progeny of Byron Snopes back to Texas. In another ironic twist, the newly gentrified Flem becomes a cumbersome ally to Ratliff and Gavin Stevens in their fight against Snopesism.

The Town can be read after *The Hamlet* as a new, American, Southern version of the peasant made good, but this novel about ambition is also, in its own way, a new variation on love and adultery, another traditional fictional theme. On August 22, 1956, Faulkner wrote to Jean Stein: "Just finishing the book. It breaks my heart, I wrote one scene and almost cried" (*SL*, 402). The scene was the suicide of Eula, whose tragic fate gives the novel its gravity and emotional charge. Eula, the prodigious Eula of *The Hamlet*, returns in *The Town*, but it is another Eula, even though the description given by Charles Mallison in the first chapter echoes the descriptions in *The Hamlet*: "'It was that there was just too much of what she was for any one human female package to contain and hold: too much of white, too much of female, too much of maybe just glory, I dont know'" (*N5*, 5). For the people of Oxford she has remained the beautiful scandalous woman, in the blinding brightness of her relentless nudity. The first time he sees her crossing the main square, Charles has the impression that "'her flesh itself would burn her garments off, leaving not even a veil of ashes between her and the light of day'" (13). In Faulkner's novels women scarcely exist away from the eyes and words of men, and this is also true of Eula. However, like Caddy in *The Sound and the Fury*, Eula is more than these eyes and words would reduce her to. In *The Town* she becomes an individual and her description is more detailed. A new Eula gradually emerges, no longer simply incandescent flesh, no longer simply some luscious goddess descended from Mount Olympus to throw men into a panic. She remains a giant among gnomes, is always "too much," but now the dwarfs will have the better of her.

Eula is one of those women, commonly seen in Faulkner (as women in most of the great nineteenth-century novels, including Emma Bovary, Effi Briest, Anna Karenina, and Tess of the d'Urbervilles), that the order of men dispossesses of their life. While still almost a child, she is already the object of lechery. Barely nubile, she is already traded like an object. In the market economy of her community, she immediately becomes a tradable female body in the circuit of commercial transactions, starting with the bartering between her father, old Varner, and Flem. The latter is paid to marry her, and once she becomes Manfred de Spain's mistress, he cynically exploits her adulterous affair to oust her lover from the presidency of the bank.

In Jefferson only honest women have an acknowledged place. Eula the sinner finds hers in the cemetery. Death returns her virtue and honor to her, magnified by the epitaph engraved on the white marble tombstone that Flem buys to commemorate her:

EULA VARNER SNOPES
1889–1927
A virtuous Wife is a Crown to her Husband
Her Children rise and call Her Blessed (N5, 312)[5]

In Faulkner's work, monuments are often lies set in stone. Like the corporal in *A Fable* under the Arc de Triomphe, Eula is buried in a tomb that abolishes forever the memory of what she actually was.

She did, however, have the time to love and be loved: her liaison with Manfred lasted eighteen years, "a kind of outrageous morality of adultery [...] based on an unimpugnable fidelity" (N5, 237). In the novel this liaison is not narrated in a sustained manner, but everything suggests that it was a passionate, happy affair that was not just tolerated but tacitly approved by the community of Jefferson as long as it remained clandestine. Better still, Mallison sees the carnal love of Eula and Manfred as "the wild glory of blood" and seems to consider Eros as the only force that can oppose "the cold stability of currency" (270). Of all the couples in Faulkner's fiction, this one is perhaps the happiest and the most "divine." Eula and Manfred are Venus and Mars: Eula is the most feminine of women; Manfred is the most masculine of men, an almost perfect incarnation of the heroic model of virility, according to Faulkner. The son of a Confederate cavalry officer, a former West Point student, this dashing aristocrat served in Cuba as a second lieutenant in the Spanish-American War, returning with a glorious war wound, "a long scar running from his hair through his left ear and down his jaw" (9).

But their love does not survive the scandal. Eula kills herself and Manfred leaves town the day after her funeral. A weeping Gavin Stevens delivers her eulogy: "She loved, had a capacity to love, for love, to give and accept love. Only she tried twice and failed twice to find somebody not just strong enough to deserve it, earn it, match it, but even brave enough to accept it" (*N5*, 315). Eula had to die before Gavin could find out who she was and what kind of fate she could have had if the world had been a different place. Although he was in love with her, he did not know how to love her. He rejected her when she came to him in a moment of compassion. Later he refuses to marry her daughter Linda to save her from Flem. Gavin, Temple's sadistic confessor in *Requiem for a Nun*, is not just a misogynist but also a woman hater. Women always scare him because, as he says himself, social order has little hold over them. As with most of Faulkner's male characters, a woman "shapes, fits herself to no environment, scorns the fixitude of environment and all the behavior patterns which had been mutually agreed on as being best for the great number; but on the contrary just by breathing, just by the mere presence of that fragile and delicate flesh, warps and wrenches milieu itself to those soft unangled rounds and curves and planes" (249). Thus he can love women only from afar, untouchable idols forever forbidden. His romantic strategy can only be a strategy of avoidance and flight: he wants to avoid meeting the woman he desires: "That was me: not to encounter; continuously just to miss her yet never be caught at it" (84). When Eula comes to his office to offer herself to him, he panics. Twice he tells her, "Dont touch me!" (82, 83), as if there can be no physical contact between man and woman without mortal contagion. Gavin does feel desire, but his desire is deaf and blind and knows nothing of its object. Ratliff and Eula point this out to him: "You dont know very much about women, do you?" (199).

Gavin can do nothing for Eula, he can do nothing for Linda, and he can do nothing against Snopes. He has good intentions and even tries to put them into practice, but he's all talk. He is first categorized as a ridiculous, comical character, seen as an aging romantic adolescent, an eternal lover doomed to remain celibate, a Don Quixote without a Dulcinea. After all, this unrepentant idealist challenges his rival to a duel solely on the grounds of "the principle that chastity and virtue in women shall be defended whether they exist or not" (N5, 67). Constantly referring to his noble principles and to "poets' dreams" (199), Gavin refuses to understand what is happening around him. "Because he missed it. He missed it completely" (135), his friend Ratliff's laconic reflection, which constitutes the entire eleventh chapter, sums up his incurable blindness for once and for all.

This young man of means is a graduate of Harvard and Heidelberg, a law graduate of the University of Mississippi, a member of the prestigious Phi Beta Kappa fraternity, a well-read lover of poetry who spends his free time retranslating the Old Testament into ancient Greek, and a county lawyer to boot who commands unanimous respect. He is the intellectual par excellence in Faulkner's work, and the novelist is obviously attached to him, making him a major character in five of his novels. To what extent is he Faulkner's double? Truthfully, there is no other character in all of Faulkner's writing with a more problematic status. As an agent of fantasy, Gavin Stevens—like Quentin Compson, Horace Benbow, Harry Wilbourne, and the reporter in *Pylon* before him—is obviously an autobiographical projection where irony and self-derision play their part. However, the way the character is perceived becomes murkier each time it becomes apparent how closely Gavin's pronouncements resemble the novelist's public pronouncements. While the reader is not required to agree with these, they raise the question of how much authority Faulkner gives Gavin when he makes him the commentator of what is happening, the interpreter of events, a sort of untrained sociologist. In *The Town* it is Gavin who, in chapter 17, feels compelled to explain Flem's behavior and motives, but it must be acknowledged that his extended ramblings are more confusing than revealing. Here, as elsewhere,

Gavin's rhetoric bores us to tears. However, at times—albeit rarely—Gavin *speaks* with a poignant eloquence, just as Faulkner the novelist *writes* in a state of grace. One example is this superb rendition (echoing the metaphysical ruminations of Quentin in *The Sound and the Fury* and Darl in *As I Lay Dying*) of the moment when Eula, after their last meeting and shortly before her suicide, moves away from him into the night to go home:

> I watched her, through the gate and up the walk, losing dimension now, onto or rather into the shadow of the little gallery and losing even substance now. And then I heard the door and it was as if she had not been. No, not that; not *not been*, but rather no more *is*, since *was* remains always and forever, inexplicable and immune, which is its grief. That's what I mean: a dimension less, then a substance less, then the sound of a door and then, not *never been* but simply *no more is* since always and forever that *was* remains, as if what is going to happen to one tomorrow already gleams faintly visible now if the watcher were only wise enough to discern it or maybe just brave enough. (*N5*, 293)

Gavin is also the one Faulkner chooses to represent him within the novel in the role and position of the creator contemplating his creation. Toward the end of *The Town*, in chapter 20, we see Gavin at dusk—a time that is pure Faulkner—withdrawing to Seminary Hill overlooking the town. The landscape is unveiled before his eyes, and he holds it in his gaze. Seen from the ridge, from far away and high up, everything seems to be in just the right place:

> And now, looking back and down, you see all Yoknapatawpha in the dying last of day beneath you [. . .] And you stand suzerain and solitary above the whole sum of your life [. . .] First is Jefferson, the center, radiating weakly its puny glow into space; beyond it, enclosing it, spreads the County, tied by the diverging roads to that center as is the rim to the hub by its spokes, yourself detached as God Himself for this moment above the cradle of your nativity and of the men and women who made you, the record and chronicle of your native land proffered for your perusal in ring by concentric ring like the ripples on living water above the dreamless slumber of your past; you to preside unanguished and immune above this miniature of man's passions and hopes and disasters— ambition and fear and lust and courage and abnegation and pity and honor and sin and pride—all bound, precarious and ramshackle, held together by the web, the iron-thin warp and woof of his rapacity but withal yet dedicated to his dreams. (*N5*, 277)

This meditation on the hilltop is reminiscent of "The Hill," one of Faulkner's earliest prose texts, and of the final scene of *Soldiers' Pay*, his first novel. However, Gavin's speech quickly moves from realistic description to rhetorical incantation, and, even more remarkably, it is given in the second person (as in the last pages of "The Prison" in *Requiem for a Nun*), marked by a reflectiveness laden with memory and resonant with irony. Gavin is again portraying a character, playing a role, acting the part of the "old man" even though he is not yet forty (interestingly, Faulkner was sixty when he wrote this). He is already taking stock of his meager life, realizing that he has been nothing but a spectator to it: "And you stand there—you, the old man [. . .] standing there while there rises to you, about you, suffocating you, the spring dark peopled and myriad, two and two seeking never at all solitude but simply privacy, the privacy decreed and created for them by the spring darkness" (278).

On December 13, 1956, Faulkner wrote to Else Jonsson: "I am now working on the third volume, which will finish it, and maybe then my talent will have burnt out and I can break the pencil and throw away the paper and the rest, for I feel very tired" (*SL*, 407). He had just started *The Mansion*, nine months after the publication of *The Town*. The reception by the press to the second part of the trilogy had disappointed him. A number of journalists implied that he was beginning to run out of steam. Alfred Kazin, in the *New York Times Book Review* of May 5, 1957, found his new novel "tired, drummed up, boring and often merely frivolous," and in the *New Republic* even his friend Cowley asked if the time had not come to bring the chronicle of Yoknapatawpha to an end. When asked about it in 1957, Faulkner acknowledged that "you shouldn't put off too long writing something which you think is worth writing," and talking about his books about the Snopeses, he said that he had had them "in mind for thirty years now" and that there "may have been a staleness" (*FU*, 107).

His work was progressing slowly. On April 14, 1958, he wrote to Else telling her he had almost finished the first third. At the end of May he started "Linda," the second part. On January 23, 1959, he telegraphed Estelle that he had just finished the novel. On March 9 he finished the final type-up and sent "Flem," the third and final part, to Albert Erskine. Erskine, who had already noted a number of contradictions between *The Hamlet* and *The Town*, found new ones when reading the type-up of *The Mansion* and was eager to make the whole trilogy consistent, but Faulkner had no wish to undertake the rewriting this would require. Therefore, rather than correcting the "contradictions" in his novel, he explained himself in an introductory note, warning readers that "the author has already found more discrepancies and contradictions than he hopes the reader will—contradictions and discrepancies due to the fact that the author has learned, he believes, more about the human heart and its dilemma than he knew thirty-four years ago; and is sure that, having lived with them that long time, he knows the characters in this chronicle better than he did then" (N5, 331).

Presented in the author's foreword as "the final chapter of, and the summation of, a work conceived and begun in 1925," *The Mansion* was published on November 13, 1961, more than three years after *The Town*. Its publication had been postponed to allow the author to pocket the twenty-five hundred dollars offered by *Esquire* for the publication of the first chapter.

⌣

Divided into three sections and eighteen chapters, the story of *The Mansion* is shared by four narrators who are characters (Ratliff, Charles Mallison, Gavin Stevens, and Montgomery Ward Snopes) and an anonymous third-person narrator. As in the first two parts of the trilogy, the narrators, regardless of their status, are both circumspect and voluble and are happy to relate their stories down to the smallest detail, without any attempt to establish the why and wherefore of anything with certainty. We are rarely allowed to forget that every tale is hypothetical, and Ratliff, far from seeking to impose his version of events, contents himself with justifying the validity of his assumptions: "My conjecture is as good as yourn, maybe better since I'm an interested party, being as I got what the fellow calls a theorem to prove" (N5, 441). The narrator does not tell the truth but rather what he considers to be the most likely: "And that's when I believe it happened. I dont even insist or argue that it happened that way. I jest simply decline to have it any other way except that one because there aint no acceptable degrees between what has got to be right and what jest can possibly be" (442).

As always with Faulkner, there are frequent flashbacks, but the story mainly takes place in the 1930s and 1940s and in chronological order. As it goes on, the tale expands, moving beyond Yoknapatawpha County. While *The Mansion* is neither political nor historical, it is the novel with the most references to great events, such as the Spanish Civil War and World War II, and to major political figures in America, such as Roosevelt, Truman, and Huey Long, and in Europe (Hitler, Mussolini, Franco, and Stalin) in the first half of the twentieth century. Although *The Mansion* moves away from Yoknapatawpha only briefly—to Memphis, Parchman, and Pascagoula—and for a short trip to New York, and the county continues to hang on to its Southernness and to resist change, of all Faulkner's novels it is the most open to the world and the one where the sound of the outside world is heard most clearly.

"The Jury said 'Guilty' and the Judge said 'Life'" (*N5*, 333): the opening sentence of the first chapter is repeated almost word for word in the second chapter. *The Mansion* starts by recalling Mink Snopes's life sentence with hard labor for the murder of Jack Houston in 1908 and retraces the trial scenes already related at the end of *The Hamlet* and in the fourth chapter of *The Town*, but this time the narrative is provided indirectly, from Mink's viewpoint (at least in the first two and fifth chapters), even taking his voice at times. The story retraces at length the conflict between Mink and Jack Houston, his richer neighbor, culminating in the ambush and Mink's killing of Houston before returning briefly to the trial and then relating his first three years in Parchman prison. A model prisoner, Mink hopes to get out of prison one day. He is obsessed by one thing, clearly stated at the end of the second chapter: "It looks like I done had to come all the way to Parchman jest to turn right around and go back home and kill Flem" (377). However, the execution of this planned fratricide is delayed by Flem, who, fearing that Mink will be pardoned and will come back to Jefferson to kill him, bribes his nephew Montgomery to allow himself to be sentenced to prison for two years and to incite Mink to escape. The prison guards are alerted, the escape ends in failure, and, just as Flem wanted, Mink is sentenced to another twenty years. In 1946, when he is eventually freed—secured by Gavin and Linda two years before his sentence is up—he is sixty-three.

Faulkner's titles can sometimes be misleading. In "Mink," the first section of *The Mansion*, Mink often appears, but of these five chapters only the first two and the last are wholly devoted to him, and in the second part he disappears completely. As with "Eula" and "The Long Summer" in *The*

Hamlet, "Linda," the middle section of *The Mansion*, breaks the thread of the story in order to start another. The first part of the novel ends with Mink setting out on his journey home; the second opens on the return to Jefferson of Linda, Eula's daughter, after a ten-year absence. A long flashback tells of her departure from New York; her passionate affair with Barton Kohl, a young Jewish sculptor from Greenwich Village; her membership of the Communist Party; and her participation in the Spanish Civil War as an ambulance driver alongside the Republicans. Barton is killed in the war, while Linda herself, permanently deafened by an exploding shell, returns with a "duck's voice: dry, lifeless, dead" (*N5*, 333). Here she is, at age thirty, back in her hometown. She does not deny her commitments, is still a communist, allies herself with two Finns, Jefferson's only socialists, and comes up with extravagant plans to promote black education. Phrases in chalk soon appear on the sidewalks: first "Nigger Lover," then "Communist Jew Kohl." An FBI agent comes to Oxford to make inquiries about her, but this is before the McCarthy witch hunts, and during World War II Linda goes to work as a riveter in an armaments factory in Pascagoula.

Linda is unlike any other of Faulkner's heroines. Her portrayal as a liberal, left-wing intellectual is hackneyed and therefore unconvincing. Linda the activist is no more convincing than Linda the lover. Her character is even less convincing given that in *The Mansion*, Faulkner portrayed her as deaf, depriving her of any dialogue. Gavin can communicate with her only by means of a writing pad. He writes and listens; Linda speaks and reads. Having become Keats's "inviolate bride of silence, inviolable in maidenhead, fixed, forever safe from change and alteration" (*N5*, 514), Linda is now the ideal object of Gavin's desire. But their relationship, already mentioned in *The Town*, when Linda was still an innocent, is more fluid than troubled, where motives and stakes remain uncertain. *The Mansion* tells us a love story that is not a love story. The time has passed when Gavin (attracted, like his creator, to women much younger than him) used to buy the young schoolgirl banana splits in an Oxford drugstore and read her the poems of John Donne and Robert Herrick. Meanwhile, Linda has had a passionate love affair with Barton and is apparently still in mourning, although this does not stop her from repeatedly telling Gavin that she loves him, asking him to marry her, and offering bluntly to sleep with him, as her mother had done before. But Gavin once again is evasive: "We were the 2 in all the world who can love each other without having to" (547), he writes to Linda, and when she kisses him, all he can say is: "Your mouth is a mess" (711). There is no intensity between them during their laborious conversations via the writing pad. Gavin, the white knight whose hands are too white, acts the role of platonic lover to the hilt, and a highly tedious role it is too.

Although the title of the third section indicates a refocusing on Flem, this character has become ever more distant since *The Hamlet* and will return to center stage only to be killed by Mink. Instead, what we get is the Snopeses in a new series of farcical episodes similar to those in *The Hamlet* and *The Town*. Truly Rabelaisian in its earthiness, the second chapter of "Flem" is wholly devoted to relating the brutal political downfall of Clarence Egglestone Snopes, engineered by Ratliff, while the third chapter tells the attempts by Orestes Snopes to get hold of a plot of land belonging to a cantankerous neighbor. Again the story breaks up into juxtaposed scenes, some of which have already been visited and which do not have a clear function in the economy of the novel. Nevertheless, this third section has one incontestable hero, Mink, who at last has been released from the penitentiary and has resolved to wreak immediate revenge on his cousin, whom he sees as guilty of not coming to his aid.

Mink is just as unlikable as the other Snopeses. Of all of Faulkner's characters, no other is as uncouth or nasty as this stubborn little brute. He does, however, have the distinction of having powerfully stimulated his creator's imagination. Every time the novel comes back to Mink, the writing gets tighter and more muscular. And it is never as lively, dense, or suggestive as when it describes how Mink *moves.* In *The Hamlet* the story of the three days of madness when he tries to get rid of Houston's body is extraordinarily powerful. In *The Mansion* the most forceful pages are those that relate his eventful return to Jefferson and, at the end of the novel, his peaceful return to the earth.

At the end of the 1950s, when Faulkner was working on this novel, his writing had lost the abrupt, forceful cruelty that animates his great tragic novels. Although it is true that *Go Down, Moses* had its elegiac moments, elegy is the dominant tone almost throughout this late novel. Nostalgia for a lost world runs through *The Mansion*, and it is no coincidence that Mink's return starts with an awakening. Like Rip Van Winkle, the eponymous hero of Washington Irving's famous story, Mink has been out of the world for a long time. After his many long years in prison, he no longer recognizes this world; he has lost his bearings. When he realizes that Mink hasn't even heard about World War II, the young man who gives him a lift asks him: "Where you been the last five years, dad? Asleep?" (*N5*, 427). To which Mink answers: "I been away" (427). Nothing will stop him now. He first heads for Memphis, where he plans to buy a gun. Before he can do this, he hitchhikes; buys food in a shop along the road; is put up for a few days by Goodyhay, a former marine sergeant turned itinerant preacher; arrives in Memphis; buys a rusty old pistol and three bullets for $12.10; goes back on the road; stops off to help a black farmer harvest his cotton; and the next day sets off for Jefferson. Like a picaresque hero, Mink travels the road alone, meeting people and encountering obstacles along the way—while all the time his wandering is set to culminate in the impending, inevitable moment of the murder.

Just like a target at the end of an arrow's path, Flem's death is at the end of the road, foretold, expected, and unavoidable. This time the old rogue is waiting calmly for his killer in his sitting room, sitting in his rocking chair, wearing his black planters hat. Although warned by Gavin that Mink's return was imminent, he apparently has no desire to defend himself. When the pistol fails to fire, he leaves his cousin time to aim again and it is the final cartridge that kills him. Like Popeye in *Sanctuary*, Flem faces death with dignity, almost as if it is a deliverance, beaten not by a champion of the old order but by another Snopes. In an irony worthy of Greek tragedy, evil finally destroys evil.

Mink is not forgotten; we grow attached to him. Although he is "as deadly as a small viper—a half-grown asp or cobra" (*N5*, 368), although he has killed two men in cold blood, the more we learn about him, the more we are inclined to forgive him. Mink is no vulgar predator like Flem. Gavin sees him as "looking as small and frail and harmless as a dirty child" (368) and so distraught that at first he inspires only pity. Without dwelling excessively on the dark side, Faulkner shows us that this poor white Mississippi sharecropper is one of the wretched of the earth, and if he weren't such a tragic figure, Mink could have featured in a novel by Erskine Caldwell.

He is wretched but not despicable. As Ratliff notes: "He was the only out-and-out mean Snopes we ever experienced. [. . .] But we never had run into one before that was just mean without no profit consideration or hope atall" (*N5*, 69–70). In fact, he is a stranger to greediness. A landless farmer who does backbreaking work, he knows he is dispossessed and almost has an inkling of class consciousness: "All you rich folks has got to stick together or else maybe some day the ones that aint rich might take a notion to raise up and take hit away from you" (366). However, this does not mean that he is politically aware, as he seems to accept the rules of the social game without a murmur: there is him and "them—they—it, whichever and whatever you want to call it, who represented a simple fundamental justice and equity in human affairs, or else a man might just as well quit" (335). He knows that this collective power is testing him "to see if he was a man or not" (336), and, like the big convict in *If I Forget Thee, Jerusalem*, he knows how to take the blows and suffer in silence: "He had learned that the hard way; himself taught that to himself through simple necessity: that a man can bear anything by simply and calmly refusing to accept it, be reconciled to it, give up to it" (350). This passive resistance to fate is what Faulkner calls "endurance."

Mink also has a sense of honor that is lacking in the other Snopeses. He claims the right to fight back and the right to kill if the rules have been disregarded. He kills Houston and Flem to settle his accounts, to regain his dignity and integrity. Once this task has been accomplished and he has found vengeance, his honor is safe and all debts have been paid. Ratliff and Gavin come to see Mink, who is hiding out in the cellar below the ruins of the Old Frenchman place, not to bring him to justice but to help him escape. The hour of forgiveness has arrived and, paradoxically, it is Gavin the fair-minded lawman, the dour moralist, who gives the final absolution: "There aren't any morals. [. . .] People just do the best they can" (*N5*, 715). To which Ratliff adds: "The pore sons of bitches" (715).

As Mink prepares to leave again, he knows where he is going and what will happen to him: "In fact, the ground itself never let a man forget it was there waiting, pulling gently and without no hurry at him between every step, saying, Come on, lay down; I ain't going to hurt you. Jest lay down. He thought I'm free now. I can walk any way I want to. So he would walk west now, since that was the direction people always went: west" (*N5*, 720).

Mink heads west, toward the setting sun. We are not told if he is going to die. In any case, it seems that it is time for him to reconcile himself with the earth, to give himself up to its call, to lie down on it without fear and let it softly take him back. It is time to let go, to go back to the beginning. As he falls asleep, "he could feel the Mink Snopes that had had to spend so much of his life just having unnecessary bother and trouble, beginning to creep, seep, flow easy as sleeping; he could almost watch it, following all the little grass blades and tiny roots, the little holes the worms made, down and down into the ground" (*N5*, 720).

The big sleep is now, for Mink, a promise of peace. He is ready to go back to the kingdom or rather the great democracy of the departed, the indistinct crowd of the nameless, the faceless (the *nônumnoii* of the *Odyssey*), the powerful and the scruffy, all gathered in the cold fraternity of death:

> leaving the folks themselves easy now, all mixed and jumbled up comfortable and easy so wouldn't nobody even know or even care who was which anymore, himself among them, equal to any, good as any, brave as any, being inextricable from, anonymous with all of them: the beautiful, the splendid, the proud and the brave, right on up to the very top itself among the shining phantoms and dreams which are the milestones of the long human recording—Helen and the bishops, the kings and the unhomed angels, the scornful and graceless seraphim. (*N5*, 721)[6]

—

The Mansion ends magnificently, but it must be acknowledged that the Snopes trilogy is very uneven. While *The Hamlet* is one of the high points of Faulkner's work, the same cannot be said of *The Town* or *The Mansion*, both of which are composite, summarizing novels where skill too often outdoes inspiration, where Faulkner's rhetoric, in its excesses and redundancies, has a self-mocking tone—even more so than in *The Hamlet*, albeit less maliciously—and where the novelist's writing finds it increasingly difficult to catch its breath. As in *Requiem for a Nun* and *A Fable*, the spark of Faulkner's genius is caught only in glimpses.

With its scenes reminiscent of Flemish peasant paintings; its cohort of earthy, unsettling or pathetic characters; its incessant murmuring of village rumor, gossip, and tittle-tattle; its humor by turn good-natured and savage; and its grand poetic flights of fancy, this trilogy is nevertheless a pastoral, comical fresco unequaled in American literature.

THE FAREWELL SMILE: *THE REIVERS*

As with all of Faulkner's late books, *The Reivers* was the culmination of a project of many years' standing. In 1940 a letter to Haas announced:

> a sort of Huck Finn—a normal boy of about twelve or thirteen, a big, warm-hearted, courageous, honest, utterly unreliable white man with the mentality of a child, an old negro family servant, opinionated, querulous, selfish, fairly unscrupulous, and in his second childhood, and a prostitute not very young anymore and with a great deal of character and generosity and common sense, and a stolen race horse which none of them actually intended to steal. (SL, 123)

Although they do not exactly match the brief description given in the letter to Haas, these characters do feature in *The Reivers*, and the plot summary that follows the character listing in the letter gives the broad outline of the novel written twenty years later.

At the beginning of the 1960s it seemed unlikely that this long-standing project would come to fruition. *The Mansion* was published in November 1959, and in 1960 Faulkner was no longer working, instead enjoying himself in Charlottesville and Oxford. "It's been two years now since I've done anything much but ride and hunt foxes," he wrote in February 1961 (SL, 451). A month later he seemed to have definitively given up on writing: "Since I ran dry three years ago, I am not even interested in writing anymore: only in reading for pleasure in the old books I discovered when I was 18 years old" (452). Yet against all expectations, he was again bitten by the writing bug; the well of his inspiration had not yet run dry. Before he died, he wrote *The Reivers*, apparently without difficulty and in a state of high euphoria, for his own pleasure as much as for that of his readers.

This time everything happened very quickly. It was all done in a matter of weeks. Faulkner started writing in June. In early July he finished typing the first three chapters and gave them to Joseph Blotner, his future biographer, to read. A few days later, he gave him the rest, telling him cheerfully: "This book gets funnier and funnier all the time" (B1, 692). On August 2 he wrote to Erskine "the new job going well" (SL, 455) and told him he had finished almost a third of the book. Always the joker, he asked him to insert the following: "An extremely important message . . . eminently qualified to become the Western World's bible of free will and private enterprise," signed "Ernest V. Trueblood. Literary & Dramatic Critic, Oxford, (Miss.)

Eagle" (455). On August 28 he told Erskine he had just finished the "the first draft of this work" (455). On September 19 he told him he was just about to send the finished manuscript. *The Reivers* was published in June 1962.

He initially titled this novel "The Horse Stealers" and then "The Stealers," before settling on *The Reivers*, an old Scottish word for thieves or cattle raiders.

—

The Reivers surprises and delights. This final book, which Faulkner dedicated to his grandchildren, is the most relaxed, the most joyous, and the most serene of all his novels. Everything ends in a smile, on a note both dreamy and nostalgic. The novel opens with the sentence "Grandfather said" (*N5*, 725). A grandfather talks—and to whom else would he be talking but his grandchildren? The tale is presented as the oral retelling, by an old man answering to the luminous, sacerdotal name of Lucius Priest, of an episode from his distant childhood. Speaking in 1961, Priest remembers Jefferson in 1905, during a happy time when a simple livery stable saw storytellers gather every day. He tells what happened to him when he was eleven, recalling his own grandfather, in a tale that covers almost a century of Jefferson's history. Later his grandson will in turn tell his own grandchildren what his grandfather had told him. The story has a binding and connecting power and an immutable magic: time is overcome every time a child is there to listen to his grandfather.

Lucius Priest relates the madcap adventure he went on fifty years earlier in a car stolen from his paternal grandfather. Boss Priest, president of one of Jefferson's two banks, had just bought the automobile, a Winton Flyer, less out of personal taste than to defy a ban on driving through the center of town on a motorized vehicle that had been pushed through by his nemesis, Colonel Sartoris, the town mayor and director of the rival bank. While the rest of the family is away at a funeral, young Lucius and Boon Hogganbeck take the car and set off for Memphis. On the way they discover a stowaway in the trunk, the crafty Ned McCaslin, a stable hand working for the Priests, who is the illegitimate son of old Lucius Quintus Carothers McCaslin and a black slave and the cousin of the no less crafty Lucas Beauchamp from *Go Down, Moses* and *Intruder in the Dust*. A character of masks and mischief in the tradition of the African American trickster, Ned is a magical Prospero and practical joker in this joyous *Tempest*.

The trip is fraught with pitfalls and full of twists and turns. After crossing, not without difficulty, the potholes of Hurricane Creek and the muddy flatlands of Hell Creek (recalling the Bundrens' crossing of the swollen river in *As I Lay Dying*), and spending the night at Ballenbaugh's, an inn with a colorful past, the three reivers arrive in Memphis. Boon goes straight to a special kind of "boardinghouse" for single ladies, Miss Reba's brothel (already visited at length in *The Mansion*), where Miss Corrie, a woman of easy virtue with a heart of gold, is waiting for him. She will eventually marry him. Ned happens across his young cousin Bobo Beauchamp, who tells him about his money problems. To help Bobo pay off his debts, Ned comes up with an ingenious plan that he immediately sets about implementing. He connives with Bobo in trading Priest's car for a horse called Coppermine—later renamed Lightning—belonging to Mr. Van Tosch, his cousin's boss, convinced that he can get him to win a race (by giving him a taste for sardines, a ruse that had worked for him several years earlier in a mule race) and use his winnings to pay off his cousin's debts and buy back the automobile.

With the help of Boon, Lucius, and Miss Reba's girls, Ned organizes for Lightning to be transported to the neighboring town of Parsham, Tennessee, where a race is to be held on the property of Colonel Linscomb, a local landowner. The horse is driven through the streets of Memphis in the middle of the night and put on board the train that is to bring him to the racecourse, giving rise to dizzying tales where all of Faulkner's storytelling talent is on display. It is Ned, the deus ex machina of the story, who does all the scheming, but, because of his weight and size, it is Lucius who will ride Lightning. In the first race, Lucius, following Ned's instructions, does not try to beat Linscomb's horse, Acheron (formerly known as Cerberus, another reference to hell).

The trouble begins when the brutish, lewd deputy sheriff, who answers to the almost oxymoronic name of Butch Lovemaiden, seeks to dispute the ownership of Lightning, fights with Boon, and has Boon and Ned arrested. They are set free the following morning thanks to a self-sacrificing Corrie, who (despite her promise to Lucius to abandon vice in favor of virtue) gives herself to Butch to secure their release. Barely out of prison, Boon corrects Corrie and gives Butch what for. Mr. Poleymus, the old constable, then puts everyone in prison. Ned and Lucius nevertheless manage to run Lightning in the second race. However, the results are suspended because Acheron leaves the track and finishes on the wrong side of the rail.

It is decided that the winner of the third race will be deemed the overall winner. Against all expectations, Ned the magician manages to make Lightning win. Meanwhile, we learn that old Priest has arrived and that the business of the horse and the car is finally to be settled once and for all. Otis is forced to return the gold tooth he stole from Minnie, Miss Reba's black maid. The last race takes place, with Van Tosch setting the stakes: if Lightning wins, the horse will be returned to Priest and Van Tosch will learn Ned's secret to making him run. If Lightning loses, his owner keeps him and Priest will have to pay him $496. As Ned and his miracle sardines are not there, it is Acheron who wins, but because Ned has bet on the latter, he wins handsomely and is able to pay off the bond and get his cousin released from jail. Priest recovers his car in return for $500. Boon marries Corrie, the reformed prostitute, who reverts to her name Everbe Corinthia, and returns with her to Jefferson, where she gives birth to a son whom she names Lucius Priest Hogganbeck, after Lucius.

Faulkner adored stories involving horses traded, stolen, and resold and put so much eloquence and humor into them that they remain as entertaining as they are enduring. However, in *The Reivers*, the real story is elsewhere. The telling of this farcical odyssey is first and foremost a tale of initiation. Like Bayard Sartoris in *The Unvanquished*, Ike McCaslin in "The Bear," and Chick Mallison in *Intruder in the Dust*, Lucius has moved from childhood to manhood, from innocence to experience. *The Reivers* is another bildungsroman, but again "education" for Faulkner is not so much a process of socialization and integration as an adventurous apprenticeship in individual autonomy through the risky exploration of unknown and forbidden lands and the initiator is always a proponent of liberty. In *Go Down, Moses* this role was played by Sam Fathers; in *The Reivers* it is played by Ned, who, like Sam Fathers, has an ironic wit and is full of vivacity and cunning.

In the four days he spends in Memphis, in a brothel and on a racecourse, young Lucius at first feels lost: "I was having to learn too much too fast, unassisted" (*N5*, 850). He doesn't understand what is happening to him; he doesn't yet understand what he is learning. This is not to say that he is oblivious to the concept of good and evil. At age eleven he already knows that there are things that should not be said and things that should not be done. When Corrie asks him if he promised his mother never to steal, he answers: "'You dont have to promise anybody that,' I said. 'You dont take things'" (900). When Otis scoffs at the tacit rules of honor, Lucius fights him with his bare fists and is even prepared to brave a knife attack. But it is Memphis that Lucius discovers lust, lying, theft, gambling, and violence, and he is so astounded and sickened by this discovery of human depravity that he ends up hating "having to hear about it, learn about it, know about it" (866) and "hating that such not only was, but must be, had to be if living was to continue and mankind be a part of it" (866). He dreams of going straight home, "back to Jefferson, in reverse if necessary, travelling backward to unwind, ravel back into No-being, Never-being, that whole course of dirt roads, mudholes" (866) as if everything he has just lived through had never happened. However, he suddenly changes his mind: "It was too late. Maybe yesterday, while I was still a child, but not now; innocence and childhood were forever lost, forever gone from me" (866).

When he eventually comes home to Jefferson Lucius is astonished to find that nothing has changed, that his loss of innocence has not, apparently, shattered his relationship with the world. The experience he has just lived through is meaningful for him only if it is meaningful for others. It is important for him that this experience is acknowledged and validated:

> If those four days—the lying and deceiving and tricking and decisions and undecisions, and the things I had done and seen and heard and learned that Mother and Father wouldn't have let me do and see and hear and learn—the things I had had to learn that I wasn't even ready for yet [. . .] if all that had changed nothing, was the same as if it had never been [. . .] then something had been wasted, thrown away, spent for nothing" (N5, 967).

This acknowledgment comes in the form of punishment, which Lucius awaits like a deliverance. However, when his father brings him down into the cellar to give him a hiding, he realizes that it does not meet his expectations, because "if after all the lying and deceiving and conniving I had done, all he could do about it was to whip me, then Father was not good enough for me. And if all that I had done was balanced by no more than that shaving strop, then both of us were debased" (N5, 968). Maury's father, Boss, then intervenes to persuade Maury not to hit his son. When Maury points out that Boss would have done the same twenty years earlier, his father answers: "Maybe I have more sense now" (968). The father clings to the tradition of fathers, whereas the grandfather paradoxically has more authority now that he has finally freed himself of this authority. The important thing for him is not to judge in order to punish or forgive but to make the child understand that he has to come to terms with everything he has done and learned. When Lucius asks how he will "live with it," the grandfather answers: "A gentleman can live through anything. He faces anything. A gentleman accepts the responsibility of his actions and bears the burden of their consequences, even when he did not himself instigate them but only acquiesced to them, didn't say No though he knew he should" (969). Lucius then starts to weep hot tears, kneeling between his grandfather's knees, "holding my face down against his stiff collar and shirt" until his grandfather asks him to stop sobbing: "That should have emptied the cistern. Now go wash your face. A gentleman cries too, but he always washes his face" (969).

It is no accident that in this novel the relationship between grandfather and grandson is more important than the one between father and son and that the father's father takes over from the father in exercising paternity. The relationship between father and son ends in failure while the relationship between grandfather and grandson is sealed by transmission. Of all the dialogues between a paternal figure and a son that punctuate Faulkner's work, the dialogue between old Lucius and young Lucius is the first—and last—to contain a touching scene. Here, finally, is the ideal father (or the idealized father, as psychoanalysts would have it), who exercises his authority advisedly, without violence or weakness, to teach the son a moral lesson that is also a lesson in living. Thus, the initiation of Lucius is almost a happy one. The experience of evil has toughened him up without sullying him; he has not been wounded by his adventures and now knows his duties as a gentleman.

The Reivers has a happy ending with a general amnesty. As in *The Town* and *The Mansion*, in his last novel Faulkner calls back many characters who are already familiar to his readers, brings them back center stage one last time, like actors taking their curtain call. While it is true that the Priests, the "younger branch" of the McCaslin clan, and the Edmonds are new arrivals, we again encounter Boon Hogganbeck, the giant with the mind of a child, who was already a prominent character in *Go Down, Moses*. Here is Miss Reba, still young and not yet widowed, "a kind hard handsome face and hair that was too red" (*N5*, 804), easily recognizable as the brothel keeper in *Sanctuary*. Here is Minnie, her maid; and Miss Corrie, one of her girls; and Miss Corrie's depraved nephew Otis, a thief, voyeur, and bird killer, age fifteen but looking only ten, whose villainy is reminiscent of Popeye's. A number of ghosts also furtively pass by in the distant background: Colonel Sartoris, General Compson, Thomas Sutpen, Ike McCaslin, and Flem Snopes. But in the comedy that is *The Reivers* there is no room for them. This novel has its share of rascals, its petty thieves, its hussies, and even its brutish, wicked characters. Although Faulkner takes care not to portray this little world as a perfect paradise, his characters are shown in the soft light of peaceful memory. Jefferson is a small, quiet town, and the inhabitants of Yoknapatawpha, white and black, form a real community with shared values. This is now an undivided society with no major conflict, a welcoming, tolerant society where everything can be fixed. This is a puppet theater where Punch always manages to beat the nasty constable. *The Reivers* has nothing of the murky atmosphere of *Sanctuary*, and it is no accident that in Faulkner's last story, the Snopeses, so invasive in his late novels, no longer have any role to play. Although it is true that the fight between light and darkness (portrayed through the race between Lightning/Lucius and Acheron, which takes its name from the dark river of Hades) is not over and that evil has not vanished, this time it is held at arm's length and somewhat disarmed by the comedy. All's well that ends well.

The *Reivers* is also a final homage to the writer's ancestors. The great-grandfather returns once more in the form of Colonel Sartoris, "soldier, statesman, politician, duelist," who built "his railroad in the mid-seventies" (*N5*, 784) and is the narrator's grandfather. He also returns in the form of Lucius Priest, the Boss, president of Jefferson's oldest bank, rival of John Sartoris, and owner of the town's first automobile, who is modeled on Faulkner's grandfather, the "Young Colonel." Even more surprising is the reconciliatory, almost affectionate nod to Murry, Faulkner's long-despised father, through the character of Maury Priest, father of young Lucius and his three brothers, who also runs a livery stable, although the portrayal is not the most flattering. Alison, the mother in the novel, is a woman too soft and tolerant to have any connection to the imperious Maud, but Mammy Callie, the black nurse, is there, renamed as Aunt Callie, and the crafty

Ned McCaslin resembles Ned Barnett, the retainer for three generations of Faulkners.

The original edition of the novel bore the subtitle "A Reminiscence." *The Reivers* can be leafed through like an album of happy memories and read like a joyous legacy. Behind the mask of a wise old grandfather, Faulkner remembers the freshness of his lost childhood while looking back over the work accomplished, the fictional universe that he thought of as "a kind of keystone in the universe," which, "if it were ever taken away, the universe itself would collapse" (*LG*, 255). In *The Reivers* he summons his creation one last time and courteously takes his leave in a dual farewell: to life and to what made it bearable.

⌒

Faulkner's last novel was received as coldly as his others. Granville Hicks, in the *Saturday Review* of June 3, 1962, and Irving Howe, in the *New York Times Book Review* of June 2, 1962, were quick to rank *The Reivers* among his lesser works. For George Plimpton of the *New York Herald Tribune* (May 27, 1962) and Stanley Edgar Hyman of the *New Leader* (July 9, 1962), it was a more or less successful novel of adventures for adolescents in the tradition of *Huckleberry Finn* and *Tom Sawyer*. Very few critics saw the novel as anything other than an anodyne entertainment from a novelist on his way out, and Leslie Fiedler, in the *Manchester Guardian* of September 28, 1962, deplored what he saw as its sententious banality. Rereading today the reviews of his books published from the late 1920s to the early 1960s in the American and British press, one is struck by the incapacity of most critics to read Faulkner without prejudice and without accompanying their eulogies with serious reservations.

It is true that the list of great artists ignored or unknown during their lifetime is a long one. Nevertheless, the opinionated resistance of journalistic criticism to Faulkner in the United States and Great Britain is astounding.

THE RIDER UNSEATED

Faulkner spent the summer of 1961 in Oxford writing *The Reivers*, returning to Charlottesville in October. As usual, he rose at dawn every morning.

He continued to ride and was now hunting four days a week. The writer was finally taking a break. On November 3, 1961, he wrote to Bennett Cerf: "I am not working on anything at all now, busy with horses, fox hunting, I wont work until I get hot on something; too many writing blokes think they have got to show something on book stalls. I will wait until the stuff is ready, until I can follow instead of trying to drive it" (*SL*, 458). At the end of November Faulkner was in New York to settle some business and put the final touches to *The Reivers*. In December he returned to Charlottesville. He caught a cold and had a backache, and on the eighteenth he was diagnosed with a respiratory tract infection combined with acute alcohol intoxication. His doctor decided to send him to the University of Virginia Hospital for treatment.

A few days later he returned home to spend Christmas with his family, but on Christmas Eve he was admitted to the hospital again, this time to the Tucker Neurological and Psychiatric Hospital in Richmond. Apart from the usual backache, he was found to be in relatively good condition. The treatment prescribed was none too taxing: a little dieting, sedatives, and rest. On the twenty-ninth he was allowed to return home. On January 3, 1962, believing he had recovered, he got back in the saddle and rode through the snowy countryside around Charlottesville. His horse, Fenceman, stumbled and fell, throwing him to the ground. When he came to, he was in great pain. He had bruising everywhere, a black eye, a large bump on his forehead, broken teeth, and chest pain, followed soon afterward by terrible coughing fits and the onset of sudden bouts of fever. He was given sedatives and self-medicated with bourbon—but to no avail. On January 8 he was back in a Richmond hospital. Fearing pneumonia or pleurisy, the doctors carried out a lung examination and ordered an electrocardiogram. Although the worst had been feared, everything appeared normal. On the fifteenth, after his third discharge in less than a month, Faulkner returned to Rowan Oak, where he rested for a few days waiting for the weather and his health to improve.

His hectic lifestyle barely slowed down. By late January he was already back in the saddle and hunting quail. In early April he went to Caracas, Venezuela, for two weeks at the invitation of the State Department. On his return to Charlottesville he accepted an invitation from General William C. Westmoreland (the future commander in chief of US forces in Vietnam) to spend a couple of days at West Point. He was welcomed with full honors. An air force DC3 picked him up in Georgia with his wife, daughter, and son-in-law.[7] They were put up in the presidential suite of a grand hotel. On April 19 Faulkner read passages from his just-finished *The Reivers* to an audience of over a thousand people and was warmly applauded. The following morning he spoke to the cadets. Henri Cartier-Bresson was there to take photographs. Before returning home Faulkner spent a few days in New York. When he arrived back in Charlottesville at the end of the month, however, he turned down an invitation from President Kennedy to dine at the White House with fifty other American Nobel Prize–winners. When asked why, he answered: "Why, that's a hundred miles away. That's a long way to go just to eat" (*FCF*, 148). However, West Point was just as far and Faulkner had been quick to accept General Westmoreland's invitation. Perhaps he would have gone to Washington if there had been a different White House incumbent. Kennedy was unpopular in the South, and many white Mississippians saw him as an enemy of the United States or even a communist sympathizer.

Faulkner and Estelle were now considering leaving their house on Rugby Road for "Red Acres," a large beautiful property in Albemarle County in the Blue Ridge Mountains. The owner's asking price was high but Faulkner could afford it. In January 1959 his account with Random House had forty-five thousand dollars in it; the royalties for his books now provided him with a regular income, and the film adaptations of three of his novels in the 1950s—*Pylon* in 1957, *The Hamlet* in 1958, and *The Sound and the Fury* in 1959—had netted him over a hundred thousand dollars.

Ten days before the publication of *The Reivers* on May 24, 1962, Eudora Welty presented Faulkner with the Gold Medal for Fiction from the American Academy of Arts and Letters. The next day he had lunch with Jean Stein, now Jean Van den Heuvel. After his return to Rowan Oak, life carried on as usual, with excursions on foot or horseback in the morning, a trip to Oxford to pick up his mail and buy tobacco and a newspaper, and sometimes dropping in on a friend. He had been spending long hours trying to train a horse bought in Oklahoma, which answered to the imposing and evocative name of Stonewall,[8] and which he admired for its intractability. He rode out on the morning of June 17. As he was leaving the property, Stonewall suddenly shied and unseated him, throwing him to the ground.

After first running away, the horse turned around and came back to the man lying on the edge of the road, nuzzling him as if telling him to get up. But Faulkner was unable to grab hold of the reins. He limped back to Rowan Oak, got back in the saddle, and galloped Stonewall around the paddock, taking jumps. When his doctor remonstrated with him, he answered: "You don't think I'd let that damned horse conquer me, do you? [. . .] I had to conquer him" (B1, 708).

As so often before, once again he picked himself up, dusted himself off, and hobbled away, but this time he would not recover from his fall. Two days later his back was so painful that he took to his bed. He felt death nearby and was fearful. "Felix, I don't want to die," he said to a doctor neighbor (B1, 709). However, over the last days of June, he seemed to have recovered somewhat. On the morning of July 3 he went to the Oxford post office to pick up his mail, and then, as was his habit, he dropped by the drugstore of his old friend Mac Reed to buy a newspaper and some tobacco. As he had forgotten his glasses, he asked Mac to write the address of his friend Else Jonsson on an envelope so that he could send her a copy of *The Reivers*. That evening, he ate out in town with Estelle. As usual, he ordered a filet mignon but had little appetite. He told Estelle he didn't feel very well, adding "the meat and the bread taste alike" (711). His back was still giving him enormous amounts of pain, and before he went to bed, he took some painkillers and a stronger measure of alcohol than usual.

By July 4 he was in a very bad way. The pain had become unbearable and nothing seemed to alleviate it. His speech became muddled and incoherent. By the next day he was in agony. Estelle and his nephew suggested taking him to hospital, and this time, to their amazement, he readily agreed. At 6 pm he was admitted to Wright's Sanatorium in Byhalia, where he had first been admitted in January 1936, and to which he had already been readmitted several times. Estelle and Jimmy left him in the care of a nurse and promised to come back and see him the next day. A doctor came to examine him in his room but found no cause for alarm. The nurse gave him sedatives and he fell asleep. In the middle of the night, he suddenly sat up, cried out, and fell to the floor. The doctor on duty rushed to help him but it was too late. His heart had given up. Not even forty-five minutes of heart massage could revive him.

At about half past one on the morning of July 6—the birth date of the "Old Colonel"—according to his death certificate, Faulkner died of "coronary occlusion" with the probable cause listed as "thrombosis." His body was initially transferred to his house in Rowan Oak, where his family was in mourning. They watched over him through the night. Faulkner would have wanted a simple coffin like his mother's, but Dot Oldham, Estelle's sister, ensured that it was made of cypress, with silver-plated handles and lined with felt.

The funeral took place on Saturday, July 7, attended by about eighty people, according to the local press. Telegrams of condolence poured in from everywhere, including one from President Kennedy. However, for the people of Oxford the event barely registered. Stores displayed the following notice on their closed shutters: "In memory of William Faulkner, this business will be CLOSED, from 2:00 to 2:15 pm today"—a quarter of an hour, not a minute more. Under the scorching sun of the Mississippi summer, the funeral procession made its way slowly through the town, skirted around Courthouse Square and the statue of the Confederate soldier, and then slowly headed for the new cemetery, Saint Peter's. According to a report in the *New York Times* on July 9, only the rare passerby stopped to watch the cortege. The good people of Oxford neither respected nor admired Faulkner during his lifetime. They didn't like his books—most of them had not taken the trouble to read even one or two—and his death, therefore, did not greatly affect them.

At the cemetery William Faulkner's coffin was lowered into a grave dug into a gentle slope, between two enormous oak trees.

While still a child, Faulkner had told his teacher that he wanted to become a writer like his great-grandfather, and after he had finished his first book, *The Marble Faun*, he knew that writing would be a major feature in his life: "It was 1923 and I wrote a book and discovered that my doom, fate, was to keep on writing books: not for any exterior or ulterior purpose: just writing the books for the sake of writing the books" (*ESPL*, 180). Writing was his vocation and he considered it both the finest and most thankless of vocations. Like Beckett, he might have said that he was "good at nothing else."

But because literature was not seen as a manly profession by his provincial community in the deep South, it took some time before he acknowledged this vocation.

For Flaubert, literature had been an absolute from his earliest school days. For Faulkner, by contrast, it was simply one of a range of options. His overlong adolescence was a time of confusion and indecisiveness. In the elation of his twenties he dreamed of being an action hero and would have liked nothing better than to die nobly, shot down in full flight over France. His wish for death and immortality was not fulfilled: he did not go out in a blaze of glory, and for this orphan of history, the decision to write was perhaps at first the choice of a lesser evil.

In *The Unvanquished* Bayard Sartoris speaks of "the immitigable chasm between all life and all print—that those who can, do, those who cannot and suffer enough because they cant, write about it" (N3, 474). For Faulkner the distinction between the man of action and the writer seems to have been primordial. Heir to a patriarchal culture in which a man could find fulfillment only through public deeds in the town or on the battlefield, he would have liked to match the prowess and panache of his great-grandfather, the "Old Colonel," and, like him, achieve heroic status. However, he never had the opportunity. Nor did he have the temperament. Having realized, like Baudelaire before him, that "action was not the sister of dreams," he withdrew into solitude and pursued his writerly quest. But writing, for Faulkner, was more than a substitute. Writing did not mean surrendering; it meant pursuing the heroic ideal in other, less direct, longer, and slower ways, exposing himself to other risks and living a different kind of adventure. It also meant *doing*, making use of memory and imagination, carving out an oeuvre with words and thus bargaining for a sort of immortality.

He was often distracted by the tedious business of feeding himself and fumed at not being able to devote his entire life to novel-writing. In order to write, Flaubert had shut himself off in his *gueuloir* in Croisset, Henry James in Lamb House, and Proust in his cork-lined bedroom. These three men lived to write—and lived like hermits so they could write without being disturbed. They didn't need to make a living out of writing. Faulkner did not have the luxury of being able to listen only to his "demons." His fate as a novelist is closer to that of Balzac, also eternally in debt, and it was only toward the end of his life that a jaded Faulkner was able to escape from the constraints of the marketplace.

It has been said that the life of Tolstoy was a Dostoevsky novel and the same could be said of Dostoevsky himself. William Faulkner's life was not like something out of a novel. It was not a life of adventure, where he was inventing his own legacy in the Byronic tradition, like his contemporaries Hemingway, Malraux, Jünger, or Malaparte. Neither was it, despite the gradual ravages of alcoholism, which eventually became suicidal, a race toward disaster like the life of Scott Fitzgerald or Malcolm Lowry. Faulkner was tough. He had an energy for life and a will to write that for a long time allowed him to withstand what was wearing him out and would eventually destroy him. His life had highs and lows, most certainly more lows than highs. It was chaotic, shambolic, and often unhappy, but it was also often full of bounce, recovery, and new beginnings. It was a life that gave the work time to arrive at fulfillment and thus shape his destiny.

NOTES

1. William Faulkner, quoted in Elliot Chaze, "Visit to a Two-Finger Typist," *Life*, July 14, 1961, 11–12.

2. William Faulkner, quoted in Joel Williamson, *William Faulkner and Southern History* (New York: Oxford University Press, 1993), 324.

3. *Faulkner: A Comprehensive Guide to the Brodsky Collection*, ed. Louis Daniel Brodsky and Robert W. Hamblin. Vol. 2: *The Letters* (Jackson: University Press of Mississippi, 1984), 134.

4. Ibid., 206.

5. The text of the epitaph is repeated word for word in *The Mansion*. See *N5*, 513. [Translator's note: The epitaph cuts and pastes two excerpts from Proverbs: 12:4 and 31:28.]

6. The allusion to Helen of Troy, to the bishops and kings, which had already appeared in the third book of *The Hamlet* (see *N3*, 898), comes from John M. Synge, *The Playboy of the Western World* (Barre, MA: Imprint Society, 1970).

7. A few days later Estelle gave James Silver a short account of the visit. It would be interesting to know why she felt the need to tell him that the crewmembers were Jewish (*FCF*, 300).

8. The horse was named after Thomas Jonathan Jackson, nicknamed Stonewall, one of the finest Confederate generals.

CHRONOLOGY

1897

SEPTEMBER 25 William Cuthbert Falkner born in New Albany, Mississippi, first of four sons to Murry Cuthbert Falkner and Maud Butler

1898

Family moves to Ripley, Mississippi

1899

JUNE 26 Murry Charles Jr. ("Jack") is born, second son of Murry and Maud Falkner

1901

SEPTEMBER 24 John Wesley Thompson III ("Johncy") is born, third son of Murry and Maud Falkner

1902

SEPTEMBER 22 Family moves to Oxford, Mississippi

1903

Meets Estelle Oldham, one year his senior

1905

SEPTEMBER 25 Starts school

1906

DECEMBER 21 Paternal grandmother, Sallie Murry Falkner, dies

1907

JUNE 1 Maternal grandmother, Lelia Dean Swift Butler ("Damuddy"), dies
AUGUST 15 Third brother, Dean Falkner, is born

1909

JUNE Starts work in father's stable

1914

Leaves school
Meets Phil Stone, a student at Yale, four years his senior

1916

JANUARY Works as clerk at paternal grandfather's bank

1917

APRIL Publishes his first drawing in *Ole Miss*, University of Mississippi yearbook

1918

APRIL 4 Joins Phil Stone in New Haven, Connecticut, and finds work as clerk in an
 arms factory
JULY 9 Arrives in Toronto to start ground training as cadet; enters the military
 aeronautical school at University of Toronto (RAF cadet), registration number
 173 799
DECEMBER Discharged, returns to Oxford

1919

SPRING Begins writing poems that will make up *The Marble Faun*
AUGUST 6 Publishes "L'Après-Midi d'un Faune," his first poem, in the *New Republic*
SEPTEMBER 19 Enrolls as a special student at University of Mississippi

1920

JANUARY 1 Dates and signs "William Faulkner" in a collection of hand-lettered poems titled "The Lilacs"

JANUARY–APRIL Publishes four adaptations of Verlaine poems in student journal *The Mississippian*

SUMMER Works as house painter

NOVEMBER 5 Leaves University of Mississippi

1921

FALL First visit to New York, at invitation of Stark Young

DECEMBER Returns to Oxford and takes examination to become postmaster at university

1922

MARCH 10 Publishes "The Hill" in *The Mississippian*

MARCH 13 Grandfather John W. T. Falkner dies

DECEMBER 15 Publishes review of three novels by Joseph Hergesheimer

1923

JUNE Submits "Orpheus and Other Poems" for publication to Four Seas Company

1924

MAY Four Seas Company agrees to publish *The Marble Faun*, his first collection of poems

SUMMER Works as scout camp leader

OCTOBER 31 Resigns from position as postmaster

NOVEMBER First trip to New Orleans, where he meets Sherwood Anderson

DECEMBER 15 *The Marble Faun* published

1925

JANUARY 4 Returns to New Orleans; meets Helen Baird

FEBRUARY 8 *Times-Picayune* publishes the first of sixteen short texts, the last of which is published in September

MARCH 3 Returns to New Orleans after brief trip to Oxford

JULY 7 Sets sail for Europe on the *West Ivis*, a mixed cargo/passenger ship with friend, painter William Spratling

AUGUST 2 Arrives in Genoa

AUGUST Visits northern Italy (Rapallo, Pavia, Milan, Stresa, and little village of Sommariva, near Lake Maggiore)

AUGUST 12 Arrives in Paris, where he stays for four months

AUGUST 18 Takes room at 26 rue Servandoni in the Latin Quarter

OCTOBER 11–15 Visits England

DECEMBER 25 Returns to Oxford

1926

JANUARY 27 Finishes manuscript of *Mayday*, dedicated to Helen Baird

FEBRUARY 25 *Soldiers' Pay* published

SEPTEMBER Finishes typescript of *Mosquitoes* in Pascagoula

DECEMBER Publication of *Sherwood Anderson and Other Famous Creoles*, a collection of caricatures by William Spratling, with foreword by Faulkner

WINTER 1926–1927 Writes "Father Abraham," first sketch of Snopes trilogy

1927

FEBRUARY Gives *The Wishing Tree* to Estelle's daughter Victoria

APRIL 30 *Mosquitoes* published

1928

APRIL Starts *The Sound and the Fury*

SEPTEMBER Ben Wasson offers *Flags in the Dust* to Harrison Smith

OCTOBER Revises and types up manuscript of *The Sound and the Fury* in New York

DECEMBER 12 Returns to Oxford

1929

JANUARY 31 *Sartoris* published by Harcourt Brace & Company

APRIL 29 Estelle Oldham and Cornell Franklin divorce

JUNE 20 Marries Estelle Oldham Franklin

JUNE 21 Faulkner and Estelle arrive in Pascagoula for their honeymoon

EARLY JULY Receives proofs of *The Sound and the Fury*

OCTOBER 7 *The Sound and the Fury* published by Jonathan Cape and Harrison Smith

OCTOBER 25–DECEMBER 11 Writes *As I Lay Dying*

1930

JANUARY 23 Starts to keep a record of short stories submitted to national magazines

APRIL 12 Buys Rowan Oak, a rundown old Oxford house

APRIL 30   "A Rose for Emily" published in *Forum*

JUNE   Moves in to Rowan Oak with Estelle and her two children

OCTOBER 6   *As I Lay Dying* published

1931

JANUARY 11   Daughter Alabama is born prematurely and dies after a week

FEBRUARY 9   *Sanctuary* published

JULY 10   Memphis *Press-Scimitar* publishes a second interview with Faulkner

SUMMER   Works on *Light in August*

SEPTEMBER 21   Publication of *These Thirteen*, his first collection of short stories

OCTOBER 23–24   Attends Southern Writers' Conference in Charlottesville, Virginia

1932

FEBRUARY 19   Finishes manuscript of *Light in August*

MAY 7–JUNE 26   First works as scriptwriter in Culver City, California

JULY   Meets Howard Hawks

AUGUST 7   His father dies

OCTOBER 3   Returns to Hollywood

OCTOBER 6   *Light in August* published

1933

FEBRUARY   Takes flying lessons

APRIL 20   Publication of *A Green Bough*, his second and last collection of poems

APRIL 28   Publication of *Today We Live* (based on Faulkner's short story "Turn About")

MAY 12   Publication of *The Story of Temple Drake*, adapted from *Sanctuary* by Stephen Roberts

JUNE 24   Birth of Jill, the writer's only daughter

DECEMBER 14   Gains pilot's license

1934

FEBRUARY 15   Participates in inauguration of Shushan Airport, New Orleans

SPRING   Starts a series of short stories that will be reused later in *The Unvanquished*

APRIL 16   *Doctor Martino and Other Stories* published

JULY 1–24   Works at Universal Studios, Hollywood

JULY 24   Returns to Oxford

MID-OCTOBER–MID-DECEMBER   Writes *Pylon*

1935

MARCH 25 *Pylon* published

NOVEMBER 10 Brother Dean killed in airplane accident

DECEMBER 10 Returns to Hollywood, where he meets Meta Carpenter, Hawks's script girl and secretary

1936

JANUARY 31 Finishes the manuscript of *Absalom, Absalom!*; checks into Wright's Sanatorium in Byhalia, Marshall County, Mississippi

APRIL 9 Starts work on the script of *Gunga Din* at RKO studios in Hollywood

LATE MAY Returns to Oxford

JULY 15 Takes Estelle and Jill to Hollywood

SEPTEMBER 4 Release of Hawks's *The Road to Glory*, adapted from the French novel *Les Croix de bois* by Roland Dorgelès; Faulkner listed on the credits

OCTOBER 26 *Absalom, Absalom!* published by Random House

DECEMBER 25 Family celebrates Christmas in Pacific Palisades, California

1937

LATE MAY Estelle and Jill return to Oxford

JUNE 20–26 Maurice-Edgar Coindreau stays with Faulkner, who offers him the typescript of "Afternoon of a Cow"

JULY 2 Release of *Slave Ship* by Tay Garnett; Faulkner listed on the credits

SEPTEMBER 1 Returns to Oxford

SEPTEMBER 15 Starts *The Wild Palms*

SEPTEMBER 25 Buys Bailey's Woods

MID-OCTOBER Spends three and a half weeks in New York; meets Saxe Commins in New York; sees Meta Carpenter again; drinks heavily; suffers third-degree burns after falling on a radiator in his hotel room

1938

FEBRUARY 15 *The Unvanquished* published

FEBRUARY 16 Film rights to *The Unvanquished* sold to Metro Goldwyn Mayer for $25,000

SEPTEMBER–OCTOBER In New York to read proofs for *The Wild Palms*

NOVEMBER 7 Starts *The Hamlet*

1939

JANUARY 18 Elected to National Institute of Arts and Letters
JANUARY 19 *The Wild Palms* published
OCTOBER Sends last chapter of *The Hamlet* to Saxe Commins

1940

JANUARY 31 Death of Caroline Barr ("Mammy Callie"), the black nurse
APRIL 1 *The Hamlet* published

1942

MAY 11 *Go Down, Moses* published
JULY 22 Agrees to long-term contract with Warner Bros.
JULY 26 Returns to Hollywood
JULY–NOVEMBER Works on script of "The De Gaulle Story"
DECEMBER 14 Leaves Hollywood for Oxford

1943

JANUARY 16 Returns to Warner Bros. studios for seven months at $350 a week

1944

FEBRUARY 14 Returns to Hollywood after a trip to Oxford
MAY Starts correspondence with Malcolm Cowley; finishes screenplay adaptation of
Hemingway's *To Have and Have Not*
JUNE 1 Joined by Estelle and Jill
AUGUST 28 Starts work on adapting Chandler's *The Big Sleep* for Hawks
SEPTEMBER Estelle and Jill return to Oxford
OCTOBER 11 *To Have and Have Not* released; Faulkner listed on the credits
DECEMBER 15 Returns to Oxford

1945

SPRING Works on *A Fable*
JUNE 7 Returns to Hollywood for the last time; writes screenplays and works with Jean
Renoir on *The Southerner* while also working on *A Fable*
SEPTEMBER 24 Returns to Oxford

1946

MARCH Random House manages to release him from his commitments to Warner Bros.

APRIL 29 *The Portable Faulkner* published

AUGUST 23 *The Big Sleep* by Hawks released; Faulkner listed on the credits

1947

APRIL Meets students at University of Mississippi

Works on *A Fable*

1948

JANUARY 15 Sets *A Fable* aside to write *Intruder in the Dust*

JULY 11 MGM buys films rights to *Intruder in the Dust* for $50,000

SEPTEMBER 27 *Intruder in the Dust* published

NOVEMBER 23 Elected to American Academy of Arts and Letters

1949

MARCH Clarence Brown starts filming *Intruder in the Dust* in Oxford

AUGUST Meets Joan Williams

OCTOBER 11 *Intruder in the Dust* premieres in Oxford

NOVEMBER 27 *Knight's Gambit* published

1950

FEBRUARY 2–12 Meets Joan Williams and Ruth Ford again in New York

MARCH 26 Writes letter to the editor of *Commercial Appeal* on the murder of three black children

MAY Receives Howells Medal for Fiction from American Academy of Arts and Letters

AUGUST 21 Publication of *Collected Stories,* his final collection of short stories

NOVEMBER 10 Awarded the 1949 Nobel Prize in Literature

DECEMBER 8 Flies to Stockholm

DECEMBER 10 Attends Nobel Prize Award Ceremony in Stockholm; meets Else Jonsson

DECEMBER 12–15 In Paris

DECEMBER 18 Returns to Oxford

1951

FEBRUARY 1 Returns to Hollywood to work as scriptwriter

FEBRUARY 10 *Notes on a Horsethief* published

MARCH 4 End of affair with Meta

MARCH 27 Releases statement on the sentencing to death of W. McGee

APRIL 12–29 Stays in Paris; visits Verdun

SEPTEMBER Stays in New York

SEPTEMBER 25 Returns to Oxford

SEPTEMBER 27 *Requiem for a Nun* published

OCTOBER 26 Receives the Légion d'honneur in New Orleans

NOVEMBER 17–23 Goes hunting

1952

MAY 19 Arrives in Paris

MAY 30 Attends festival to celebrate twentieth-century works in Paris

JUNE 14 Flies back to New York

JUNE 17 Meets Joan Williams in Memphis and then returns to Oxford

SEPTEMBER–OCTOBER Hospitalized several times in Memphis

NOVEMBER Features in short television biopic

DECEMBER Admitted several times to private clinic

1953

JANUARY 31 Arrives in New York

MARCH Readmitted to hospital for more medical examinations

APRIL 18 Returns to Rowan Oak to be near Estelle, who has suffered a hemorrhage

MAY 9 Returns to New York

JUNE 8 Gives commencement address at Jill's graduation from Pine Manor Junior College

SEPTEMBER 8 Re-hospitalized in Memphis

SEPTEMBER 28 AND OCTOBER 5 *Life* publishes a two-part article on Faulkner by Robert Coughlan

NOVEMBER Finishes the manuscript of *A Fable*; Joan Williams ends their liaison

DECEMBER 1 Arrives in Geneva then goes to Paris to meet Hawks

DECEMBER 25 Meets Jean Stein in Saint-Moritz

1954

JANUARY 1 Arrives in London

JANUARY 6 Returns to Saint-Moritz to see Jean Stein

JANUARY 19 Leaves Paris for Rome, where he meets up with Hawks

FEBRUARY 11–14 Weekend in Paris with Jean Stein

FEBRUARY 15 Travels to Cairo to join up with Hawks for the filming of *Land of the Pharaohs*

MARCH 6 Joan Williams marries Ezra Bowen

MARCH 29 Leaves Egypt to spend three weeks in France

APRIL 1 *The Faulkner Reader* published

APRIL 19 Leaves Paris for New York

APRIL "Mississippi" published in *Holiday*

AUGUST 2 *A Fable* published

AUGUST 6 Flies from Memphis to Latin America

AUGUST 7 Spends a day in Lima, Peru

AUGUST 11–14 Attends an International Writers' Conference in Saõ Paulo

AUGUST 16 Returns to Oxford

AUGUST 21 Jill marries Paul D. Summers

SEPTEMBER 10 Arrives in New York

DECEMBER 25 Spends Christmas at the Comminses' house in Princeton with Jean Stein

1955

JANUARY 25 Awarded the National Book Award for Fiction for *A Fable*

LATE FEBRUARY Signs an agreement authorizing Albert Camus to adapt *Requiem for a Nun*

MARCH 20 First of four open letters to the *Commercial Appeal* of Memphis opposing school segregation

JULY 2 Premiere of Hawks's film *Land of the Pharaohs*; Faulkner listed on the credits

JULY 29 Goes on a trip to Japan for three weeks under the auspices of the cultural service of the State Department

AUGUST 1 Arrives in Tokyo

AUGUST 5 Leaves Tokyo for Nagano

AUGUST 16 Returns to Tokyo

AUGUST 23–25 Spends three days in Manila

AUGUST 28 Arrives in Italy

SEPTEMBER 6 While in Rome, releases a statement on the murder of a young black boy from Chicago, Emmet Till, in Mississippi

SEPTEMBER 16 Leaves Rome for Munich, where *Requiem for a Nun* is being screened

SEPTEMBER 17 Leaves Munich for Paris, where he stays fifteen days

SEPTEMBER 29 Cocktail party thrown in his honor in garden of French publishing house Gallimard

OCTOBER 7 Leaves Paris for London

OCTOBER 12–17 Stops over in Iceland

OCTOBER 14 *Big Woods* published
NOVEMBER Starts *The Town*
DECEMBER Takes Jean Stein to New York and Pascagoula

1956

MARCH 4 First publication of Faulkner's interview with Russell W. Howe in the *Sunday Times*
SPRING Publication of interview with Jean Stein in the *Paris Review*
APRIL 15 Birth of Paul D. Summers III, Jill's first son
SEPTEMBER 11–14 In Washington, DC, to attend People-to-People Program, launched by the Eisenhower administration
SEPTEMBER 20 Albert Camus's adaptation of *Requiem for a Nun* premieres

1957

FEBRUARY–JUNE Writer in residence at University of Virginia, Charlottesville
MARCH 17–31 Travels to Greece
MAY 1 *The Town* published
MAY 22 Presents John Dos Passos with Gold Medal of the American Academy of Arts and Letters
JUNE 26 Leaves Charlottesville for Oxford
SEPTEMBER 11 Publishes a new open letter in the *Commercial Appeal* on school integration
NOVEMBER 13 Returns to Charlottesville

1958

JANUARY 30 Start of second semester in University of Virginia
JANUARY Release of *The Tarnished Angels*, Douglas Sirk's adaptation of *Pylon*
MARCH 1 Arrives in Princeton to spend two weeks at the university

1959

Works on *The Mansion*
JANUARY 28 *Requiem for a Nun* opens in New York
MARCH 14 Falls from horse and fractures right collarbone
AUGUST 21 Buys a house in Charlottesville
OCTOBER 2 Delivers a speech to the US National Commission for UNESCO, in Denver, Colorado
NOVEMBER 13 *The Mansion* published

1960

Divides his time between Charlottesville and Oxford; hospitalized briefly at Byhalia

OCTOBER 16   Maud Faulkner, his mother, dies

1961

JANUARY   Bequeaths all his manuscripts to the William Faulkner Foundation of the University of Virginia

APRIL 2–10   In Venezuela for two weeks; gives two press conferences in Caracas

JUNE–SEPTEMBER   Writes *The Reivers*

OCTOBER 21   Returns to Charlottesville

NOVEMBER 27   Revises *The Reivers* in New York, with the help of Albert Erskine

1962

JANUARY 3   Injures himself falling from a horse

APRIL 19–20   Visits West Point with Estelle, Jill, and son-in-law

APRIL 29   Turns down an invitation from President Kennedy to the White House

MAY 24   Presented with the Gold Medal of the American Academy of Arts and Letters by Eudora Welty

JUNE 4   *The Reivers* published

JUNE 17   Falls from horse again

JULY 5   Admitted to Byhalia

JULY 6   Dies suddenly of coronary occlusion

SELECTED BIBLIOGRAPHY

REFERENCE EDITIONS

William Faulkner, ed. Joseph Blotner and Noel Polk. New York: Library of America, 1985–2006.

Vol. 1. *Novels 1926–1929: Soldiers' Pay, Mosquitoes, Flags in the Dust, The Sound and the Fury*, 2006;

Vol. 2. *Novels 1930–1935: As I Lay Dying, Sanctuary, Light in August, Pylon*, 1985;

Vol. 3. *Novels 1936–1940: Absalom, Absalom!, The Unvanquished, If I Forget Thee, Jerusalem [The Wild Palms], The Hamlet*, 1990;

Vol. 4. *Novels 1942–1954: Go Down, Moses, Intruder in the Dust, Requiem for a Nun, A Fable*, 1994;

Vol. 5. *Novels 1957–1962: The Town, The Mansion, The Reivers*, 1999.

[As volume 1 had not yet been published when André Bleikasten was writing Faulkner's biography, works from this period are listed according to the first American editions of Faulkner's works.]

FAULKNER, MISCELLANEOUS

Conversations with William Faulkner, ed. M. Thomas Inge. Jackson: University Press of Mississippi, 1999.

Faulkner: A Comprehensive Guide to the Brodsky Collection, ed. Louis Daniel Brodsky and Robert W. Hamblin. Vol. 2: *The Letters*. Jackson: University Press of Mississippi, 1984.

Faulkner's MGM Screen Plays, ed. Bruce F. Kawin. Knoxville: University of Tennessee Press, 1982.

Lion in the Garden: Interviews with William Faulkner, 1926–1962, ed. James B. Meriwether and Michael Millgate. New York: Random House, 1968.

Vision in Spring, introduction by Judith L. Sensibar. Austin: University of Texas Press, 1984.

BIOGRAPHIES

Bleikasten, André. *William Faulkner: une vie en romans*. Paris: Editions Aden, 2007.

Blotner, Joseph. *Faulkner: A Biography*. 2 volumes. New York: Random House, 1974. One-volume edition, edited and abridged, in 1984.

Gray, Richard. *The Life of William Faulkner: A Critical Biography*. Oxford: Blackwell, 1994.

Gresset, Michel. *A Faulkner Chronology*. Jackson: University Press of Mississippi, 1985.

Karl, Frederick R. *William Faulkner: American Writer*. New York: Weidenfeld & Nicolson, 1989. Translation: *William Faulkner*. Paris: Gallimard, 1994.

Minter, David. *Faulkner: His Life and Work*. Baltimore: Johns Hopkins University Press, 1980. Translation: *William Faulkner*. Paris: Balland, 1984.

Oates, Stephen B. *William Faulkner: The Man and the Artist*. New York: Harper & Row, 1989. Translation: *William Faulkner: une biographie*. Paris: Hachette, 1989.

Parini, Jay. *One Matchless Time: A Life of William Faulkner*. New York: Harper Collins, 2004.

Saporta, Marc. *Les Erres du faucon: une psychobiographie de William Faulkner*. Paris: Seghers, 1989.

Weinstein, Philip. *Becoming Faulkner: The Art and Life of William Faulkner*. Oxford: Oxford University Press, 2010.

COLLECTIONS

Louis Daniel Brodsky Collection, Kent Library, Southeastern Missouri State University. Includes the Blotner Papers, notes, and other materials assembled by Joseph Blotner when writing his biography of Faulkner.

William Faulkner Foundation Collection, Special Collections, Alderman Library, University of Virginia, Charlottesville.

REMINISCENCES

Bezzerides, A. I. *William Faulkner: A Life on Paper*. Jackson: University Press of Mississippi, 1980 (transcription of a documentary film produced by the Mississippi Center for Educational Television).

Carpenter, Meta, and Orin Borstin. *A Loving Gentleman: The Love Story of William Faulkner and Meta Carpenter*. New York: Simon & Schuster, 1977.

Coindreau, Maurice-Edgar. *Mémoires d'un traducteur*. Paris: Gallimard, 1974.

Coughlan, Robert. *The Private World of William Faulkner*. New York: Harper & Brothers, 1954.

Cullen, John B. *Old Times in the Faulkner Country*. Chapel Hill: University of North Carolina Press, 1961.

Falkner, Murry C. *The Falkners of Mississippi*. Baton Rouge: Louisiana State University Press, 1967.

Faulkner, Jim. *Across the Creek: Faulkner Family Stories*. Jackson: University Press of Mississippi, 1986.

Faulkner, John. *My Brother Bill: An Affectionate Reminiscence*. New York: Trident Press, 1963.

Franklin, Malcolm A. *Bitterweeds: Life with William Faulkner at Rowan Oak*. Irving, TX: Society for the Study of Traditional Culture, 1977.

Spratling, William. "Chronicle of a Friendship: Faulkner in New Orleans." *Texas Quarterly* (Spring 1966): 34–39. Reprinted in William Spratling and William Faulkner, *Sherwood Anderson and Other Famous Creoles*. New Orleans: Pelican Bookshop Press, 1926; reprt. Austin: University of Texas Press, 1967.

Wasson, Ben. *Count No 'Count: Flashbacks to Faulkner*. Jackson: University Press of Mississippi, 1983.

Webb, James W., and A. Wigfall Green, eds. *William Faulkner of Oxford*. Baton Rouge: Louisiana State University Press, 1965.

Wolff, Sally, with Floyd C. Watkins. *Talking about William Faulkner: Interviews with Jimmy Faulkner and Others*. Baton Rouge: Louisiana State University Press, 1996.

ICONOGRAPHIC DOCUMENTATION

Cofield, Jack. *William Faulkner: The Cofield Collection*. Oxford, MS: Yoknapatawpha Press, 1978.

Dain, Martin J. *Faulkner's World: The Photographs of Martin J. Dain*. Jackson: University Press of Mississippi, 1997.

Durand, Régis. *Yoknapatawpha: The Land of William Faulkner*. Text by Régis Durand, photographs by Alain Desvergnes. Paris: Marval, 1990.

Mohrt, Michel. *Album Faulkner*. Iconographie choisie et commentée par Michel Mohrt. Paris: Gallimard, 1995.

Morris, Willie. *Faulkner's Mississippi*. Text by Willie Morris, photographs by William Eggleston. Birmingham, AL: Oxmoor House, 1990.

Wilson, Jack Case. *Faulkners, Fortunes and Flames*. Photographs and text by Jack Case Wilson. Nashville: Annandale Press, 1984.

ENGLISH-LANGUAGE CRITICISM

Adams, Richard P. *Faulkner: Myth and Motion*. Princeton, NJ: Princeton University Press, 1968.

Backman, Melvin. *Faulkner: The Major Years*. Bloomington: Indiana University Press, 1966.

Beck, Warren. *Faulkner: Essays*. Madison: University of Wisconsin Press, 1976.

————. *Man in Motion: Faulkner's Trilogy.* Madison: University of Wisconsin Press, 1961.

Bleikasten, André. *Faulkner's As I Lay Dying.* Bloomington, IN: Indiana University Press, 1973.

————. *The Ink of Melancholy: Faulkner's Novels from* The Sound and the Fury *to* Light in August. Bloomington, IN: Indiana University Press, 1990.

————. *The Most Splendid Failure: Faulkner's* The Sound and the Fury. Bloomington, IN: Indiana University Press, 1976.

Bockting, Ineke. *Character and Personality in the Novels of William Faulkner: A Study in Psycholinguistics.* Lanham, MD: University Press of America, 1995.

Brooks, Cleanth. *William Faulkner: The Yoknapatawpha Country.* New Haven, CT: Yale University Press, 1963.

————. *William Faulkner: Toward Yoknapatawpha and Beyond*, New Haven, CT: Yale University Press, 1978.

Clarke, Deborah. *Robbing the Mother: Women in Faulkner.* Jackson: University Press of Mississippi, 1994.

Dabney, Lewis M. *The Indians of Yoknapatawpha.* Baton Rouge: Louisiana State University Press, 1974.

Davis, Thadious M. *Faulkner's "Negro": Art and the Southern Context.* Baton Rouge: Louisiana State University Press, 1983.

Doyle, Don H. *Faulkner's County: The Historical Roots of Yoknapatawpha.* Chapel Hill: University of North Carolina Press, 2001.

Fargnoli, A. Nicholas, and Michael Golay, eds. *William Faulkner A to Z.* New York: Checkmark Books, 2002.

Godden, Richard. *Fictions of Labor: William Faulkner and the South's Long Revolution.* Cambridge: Cambridge University Press, 1997.

Grimwood, Michael. *Heart in Conflict: Faulkner's Struggles with Vocation.* Athens: University of Georgia Press, 1987.

Hannon, Charles. *Faulkner and the Discourses of Culture.* Baton Rouge: Louisiana State University Press, 2005.

Hlavsa, Virginia V. James. *Faulkner and the Thoroughly Modern Novel.* Charlottesville: University Press of Virginia, 1991.

Hönnighausen, Lothar. *Faulkner: Masks and Metaphors.* Jackson: University Press of Mississippi, 1997.

————. *William Faulkner: The Art of Stylization in His Early Graphic and Literary Work.* Cambridge: Cambridge University Press, 1987.

————. Inge, M. Thomas. *William Faulkner: Contemporary Reviews.* Cambridge: Cambridge University Press, 1995.

Irwin, John T. *Doubling and Incest / Repetition and Revenge.* Baltimore: Johns Hopkins University Press, 1975.

Jehlen, Myra. *Class and Character in Faulkner's South.* New York: Columbia University Press, 1976.

Kartiganer, Donald M. *The Fragile Thread: The Meaning of Form in Faulkner's Novels.* Amherst: University of Massachusetts Press, 1979.

Kawin, Bruce F. *Faulkner and Film*. New York: Frederick Ungar, 1977.

Kinney, Arthur F. *Faulkner's Narrative Poetics*. Amherst: University of Massachusetts Press, 1978.

Kreiswirth, Martin. *Faulkner: The Making of a Novelist*. Athens: University of Georgia Press, 1983.

Labatt, Blair. *Faulkner the Storyteller*. Tuscaloosa: University of Alabama Press, 2005.

Lockyer, Judith. *Ordered by Words: Language and Narration in the Novels of William Faulkner*. Carbondale: Southern Illinois University Press, 1991.

Lurie, Peter. *Vision's Immanence: Faulkner, Film, and the Popular Imagination*. Baltimore: Johns Hopkins University Press, 2004.

Matthews, John T. *The Play of Faulkner's Language*. Ithaca, NY: Cornell University Press, 1982.

Millgate, Michael. *The Achievement of William Faulkner*. New York: Random House, 1966.

Minter, David. *Faulkner's Questioning Narratives: Fiction of His Major Phase, 1929–42*. Urbana: University of Illinois Press, 2003.

Moreland, Richard C. *Faulkner and Modernism: Rereading and Rewriting*. Madison: University of Wisconsin Press, 1990.

Morris, Wesley, and Barbara Alverson. *Reading Faulkner*. Madison: University of Wisconsin Press, 1989.

Mortimer, Gail L. *Faulkner's Rhetoric of Loss: A Study in Perception and Meaning*. Austin: University of Texas Press, 1983.

Parker, Robert D. *Faulkner and the Novelistic Imagination*. Urbana: University of Illinois Press, 1985.

Peavy, Charles D. *Go Slow Now: Faulkner and the Race Question*. Eugene: University of Oregon Press, 1971.

Polk, Noel. *Children of the Dark House: Text and Context in Faulkner*. Jackson: University Press of Mississippi, 1996.

Railey, Kevin. *Natural Aristocracy: History, Ideology, and the Production of William Faulkner*. Tuscaloosa: University of Alabama Press, 1999.

Roberts, Diane. *Faulkner and Southern Womanhood*. Athens: University of Georgia Press, 1994.

Ross, Stephen M. *Fiction's Inexhaustible Voice*. Athens: University of Georgia Press, 1989.

Schwartz, Lawrence. *Creating Faulkner's Reputation*. Knoxville: University of Tennessee Press, 1990.

Sensibar, Judith L. *The Origins of Faulkner's Art*. Austin: University of Texas Press, 1984.

Singal, Daniel J. *William Faulkner: The Making of a Modernist*. Chapel Hill: University of North Carolina Press, 1997.

Snead, James A. *Figures of Division: William Faulkner's Major Novels*. New York: Methuen, 1986.

Stonum, Gary L. *Faulkner's Career: An Internal Literary History*. Ithaca, NY: Cornell University Press, 1979.

Sundquist, Eric J. *Faulkner: The House Divided*. Baltimore: Johns Hopkins University Press, 1983.

Taylor, Walter. *Faulkner's Search for a South*. Urbana: University of Illinois Press, 1983.

Vickery, Olga W. *The Novels of William Faulkner*. Baton Rouge: Louisiana State University Press, 1959. Revised edition, 1964.

Volpe, Edmund L. *A Reader's Guide to William Faulkner*. New York: Farrar, Strauss & Giroux, 1964.

Watson, James G. *William Faulkner: Self-Presentation and Performance*. Austin: University of Texas Press, 2000.

Watson, Jay. *Forensic Fictions: The Lawyer Figure in Faulkner*. Athens: University of Georgia Press, 1993.

Weinstein, Philip M. *The Cambridge Companion to William Faulkner*. Cambridge: Cambridge University Press, 1995.

———. *Faulkner's Subject: A Cosmos No One Owns*. Cambridge: Cambridge University Press, 1992.

Welty, Eudora. *On William Faulkner*. Jackson: University Press of Mississippi, 2003.

Williamson, Joel. *William Faulkner and Southern History*. New York: Oxford University Press, 1993.

Wittenberg, Judith Bryant. *Faulkner: The Transfiguration of Biography*. Lincoln: University of Nebraska Press, 1979.

Zender, Karl F. *The Crossing of the Ways*. New Brunswick, NJ: Rutgers University Press, 1989.

———. *Faulkner and the Politics of Reading*. Baton Rouge: Louisiana State University Press, 2002.

FRENCH CRITICISM

Bleikasten, André. *Parcours de Faulkner*. Paris: Ophrys, 1982.

———. *William Faulkner: Sanctuaire*. Paris: Gallimard, collection, "Foliothèque," 1993.

Geoffroy, Alain. *Le Ressac de l'enfance chez William Faulkner*. Paris: Didier, 1991.

Glissant, Edouard. *Faulkner, Mississippi*. Paris: Stock, 1996.

Gresset, Michel. *Faulkner ou la fascination: poétique du regard*. Paris: Klincksieck, 1982.

Guillain, Aurélie. *Faulkner: le roman de la détresse*. Rennes: Presses Universitaires de Rennes, 2003.

Nathan, Monique. *Faulkner par lui-même*. Paris: Seuil, 1963.

Pitavy, François. *Oublier Jérusalem: The Wild Palms de William Faulkner*. Paris: Didier, 1988.

———. *William Faulkner: le Bruit et la fureur*. Paris: Gallimard, collection "Foliothèque," 2001.

Pothier, Jacques. *William Faulkner*. Paris: Belin, 2003.

Romano, Claude. *Le Chant de la vie: phénoménologie de Faulkner*. Paris: Gallimard, 2005.

Rouberol, Jean. *L'Esprit du Sud dans l'œuvre de Faulkner*. Paris: Didier, 1982.

BIBLIOGRAPHIES

Bassett, John E. *Faulkner: A Checklist of Recent Criticism.* Kent, OH: Kent State University Press, 1983.

———. *Faulkner in the Eighties: An Annotated Critical Bibliography.* Metuchen, NJ: Scarecrow Press, 1991.

———. *William Faulkner: An Annotated Checklist of Criticism.* New York: David Lewis, 1972.

Massey, Linton R. *"Man Working," 1919–1962: William Faulkner: A Catalogue of the William Faulkner Collections of Virginia.* Charlottesville: University Press of Virginia, 1968.

McHaney, Thomas. *William Faulkner: A Reference Guide.* Boston: G. K. Hall, 1976.

Meriwether, James B. *The Literary Career of William Faulkner: A Bibliographical Study.* Princeton, NJ: Princeton University Library, 1961.

INDEX OF NAMES

NOTE: Initials WF refer to William Faulkner.

INDEX OF WORKS

André Bleikasten (1933–2009) was Professor of American Literature at the University of Strasbourg, France, and a prominent Faulkner scholar, internationally acclaimed for his study of Faulkner's early works in *The Ink of Melancholy* (IUP). He is also known for his studies of Philip Roth, Eudora Welty, and Flannery O'Conner.

Miriam Watchorn, MA, MITIA, MCIL is a graduate of Université Charles de Gaulle, Lille, France and Dublin City University, Ireland. She also holds the Diploma in Translation awarded by the Chartered Institute of Linguists, UK. She has over twenty years' experience in translation and has a broad and diverse range of translation experience and interests. She teaches as a university lecturer in translation studies at Dublin City University, Ireland.

A friend of André and Aimée Bleikasten since 1963, **Roger Little** translated André's book on *As I Lay Dying* (IUP) and early or partial versions of his subsequent books on *Faulkner: The Most Splendid Failure* and *The Ink of Melancholy* (both IUP). His own research centers on French poetry since Rimbaud and on the representation of blacks in Francographic literature. As author, editor, or translator, he has published some 350 books. As general editor, he launched *Research Bibliographies and Checklists* and Critical Guides to French Texts and now directs *Autrement Mêmes*. He retired from the 1776 Chair of French at Trinity College, Dublin, the oldest in the world, in 1998.